RAY'S ARRAY

Raymond D Fogelson's

Selected Works

Contents

CHEROKEES

1 The Life and Scholarship of Raymond D Fogelson
8 Nabokov
10 Southeast American Indians
19 Cherokee Economic Cooperatives: The Gadugi
44 Change, Persistence, and Accommodation in Cherokee Medico-Magical Beliefs
52 The Cherokee Ballgame Cycle: An Ethnographer's View
60 An Analysis of Cherokee Sorcery and Witchcraft
71 Cherokee Notions of Power
78 Poses Gearing
82 On the Varieties of Indian History: Sequoyah and Traveller Bird
88 Cherokee Booger Mask Tradition
106 Stoneclad 80
120 Who Were the Aní-Kutánî?
127 The Ethnohistory of Events and Nonevents
137 The Keetoowah Movement in Indian Territory

TRIBUTES

146 George Stocking
148 Alfonso Alex Ortiz
152 Bob Thomas
161 Mary Haas
165 Raymond DeMallie
169 Namings

COGITATIONS

176 Music sex
184 C&P 61
195 Self 82
217 Psyche 85
235 Nite Thawts 85
244 Gassy 87
248 Ray 89 + sum 259
264 Red City 91
275 St Louis 93
279 Recog 93
286 Perspectives 98
300 Nationalism 99
306 Totemism 02 523
318 Advanced Social Sciences:
   Religious Movements In Native North America 318

THE LIFE AND SCHOLARSHIP OF RAYMOND DAVID FOGELSON

Born in Red Bank, New Jersey, on August 23, 1933, Raymond David Fogelson describes himself as "an anti-intellectual child who did not read much and wanted to become a professional ping-pong or baseball player. As a young teenager Ray liked to read sports books. A biography of John McGraw of the New York Giants was one of his favorites.

Ray has had a lifelong interest in music. He had an aunt who was a concert pianist and taught at the Julliard School, while his older sister, who graduated from Julliard, was a soloist with the Robert Shaw Chorale. As a teenager Ray would make pilgrimages to New York City to hear Charlie Parker, Dizzy Gillespie, and other revolutionaries of American jazz.

Ray's father had high ambitions for his son: he wanted Ray to become a physician. After studying at a "mediocre local high school" for a while, Ray was sent for three years to a private school in eastern Pennsylvania, partially on a football scholarship. There he improved his grades, and in 1951 he was admitted as a premed student at Wesleyan University. Ray found chemistry and other required disciplines "boring," however, and finally decided that medical school was not for him. He did become interested in psychology, and ended up majoring in that discipline.

Wesleyan had an excellent psychology department at the time, with [xxii] such prominent scholars on the faculty as Joseph Greenbaum who later became a dean at the New School for Social Research), David McClelland (who later served as the head of the Department of Social Relations at Harvard), Michael Wertheimer, David Beardslee, and others. Ray began to work particularly closely with Beardslee, writing a bachelor's paper for him on sexual arousal in music. The paper compared differential sexual arousal in female and male college students, using projective essays written by students in response to music. A published essay based on this project (Beardslee and Fogelson 1958, p176 herein) was assigned as required reading for years at several universities to exemplify an interesting experimental design in psychology.

Despite this scholarly accomplishment, Ray began to question whether he wanted to become a psychologist. As he put it, "I had this image of psychology controlling and predicting human behavior, which I didn't want to do, since I was very idealistic. I thought psychology was going to take over the world." Gradually he became interested in anthropology (which only seemed to aim at describing and explaining human behavior), even though his grade in his first anthropology course was rather low. David McAllester, a well-known specialist in Navajo ethnology and ethnomusicology, taught this course. Despite his poor performance Fogelson and McAllester became good friends, with McAllester supporting Ray's experimental study of music and writing recommendations for his graduate school applications,

Even after his shift to anthropology, Ray retained a strong interest in psychology and psychoanalysis. The latter interest developed when he took a course in classical mythology from Wesleyan's prominent classicist, Norman O. Brown, for whom he wrote a number of Freudian interpretations of Homeric hymns. It was in Brown's course that Ray first read such anthropological classics as James Frazer's *The Golden Bough* and Bronislaw Malinowski's *Magic, Science, and Religion*.

In 1955 Ray arrived at the University of Pennsylvania to begin his graduate work in anthropology, which led to an MA in 1958 and a PhD in 7962. Penn's primary attraction for him was the University Museum and the presence of psychological anthropologist A.I. Hallowell. At the time the anthropology department at Penn was rather small, and although it included a number of leading anthropologists representing the discipline's four subfields, physical anthropology and archaeology were dominant. That situation began to change soon after Ray arrived, with the hiring of two young professors, Ruben Reina and Robbins Burling, who were later followed by Paul Friedrich. A.F.C Wallace, who had completed his PhD under Hallowell in 1950, began teaching courses in the anthropology [xxiii] department in 1957. Among the department's older and more established members were Hallowell, Carleton Coon, Loren

Eiseley, Ward Goodenough, Alfred Kidder II, Wilton Krogman, and Linton Satterthwaite. Ray did very well in his graduate anthropology courses, although he received a C- in Goodenough's introductory freshman course! A number of fellow graduate students at Penn – particularly Igor Kopytoff, Paul Kutsche, and Ben Saler – became Ray's lifelong friends.

Ray learned a great deal from most of his teachers in graduate school, but he attributes his abiding interest in psychological anthropology, religion, and ethnohistory to Pete Hallowell and Tony Wallace. Because Wallace was younger than Hallowell, Ray developed, as he put it, a "somewhat closer relationship with him than with Hallowell." During his second year at Penn, Ray enrolled in Wallace's course on the anthropology of religion, which focused on religious experience and revitalization movements. Ray recalls being "very impressed with both the course and the instructor," who at the time had an adjunct affiliation with the anthropology department. Inspired by Wallace's research on what are now known as "culture-bound syndromes," Ray conducted research on the Windigo disorder, which led to an article published in Hallowell's festschrift (Fogelson 1965; see also 1980c). At the same time, because Wallace had himself been Hallowell's student, Ray was indirectly absorbing many of the senior psychological anthropologist's ideas.[1]11

Ray's decision to focus his doctoral research on a Native American culture was fortuitous. While taking a course on culture change, he, like all the other students, had to pick a geographic area of specialization. Initially he chose the Caribbean "because of the nice beaches there," but since another student had already done field research in Trinidad, Ray was assigned the American Indians instead. His interest the Eastern Cherokee developed due to a special field project run by John Gulick, an anthropologist at the University of North Carolina, Chapel Hill. Funded by the Ford Foundation, the Cross-Cultural Laboratory of the Institute for Research in Social Science initiated in 1956 a summer field project focusing on the Cherokee Indian Reservation in western North Carolina. For three summers a group of graduate students (mainly from the University of North Carolina) conducted field research on various aspects of contemporary Cherokee culture and society under the direction of a few professional anthropologists (see Gulick 1960). Ray's participation in the project began in the summer of 1957 and continued in December of that year and again during the summer of 1958. Two years later he returned to the area on his own to conduct additional research for his doctoral dissertation. [xxiv]

Although the stipend given to each graduate student participating in the project was minimal, it did cover some of Ray's basic living expenses. Most importantly, participation in the Cherokee project provided the young anthropologist with a group of colleagues with whom he could discuss his findings, try out various ideas and interpretations, and so forth. Ray names four older colleagues – John Witthoft, William C Sturtevant, William N Fenton, and the Cherokee scholar Robert K Thomas – as his most important informal mentors.[2]12 Among the participating graduate students, Paul Kutsche was Ray's closest associate. The two of them worked together on traditional Cherokee work cooperatives (*gadugi*), eventually publishing an important paper on the subject (Fogelson and Kutsche 1961). Another graduate student taking part in the project, whom Ray credits with "teaching him more about field methods than anyone else," was Charles Holzinger, an older PhD candidate at Harvard who was already a professor at Franklin and Marshall College.

Ray recalls the Eastern Cherokee reservation of the late 1950S and early i960s as being a rather isolated and poor community where "life was hard and the dogs were skinny." However, he found the

---

1 Editors Sergei Kan and Pauline Turner Strong gratefully acknowledge the support of their families and institutions during the years this volume was in preparation. We thank Gary Dunham and the staff at the University of Nebraska Press for their interest, the contributors for their dedication and patience, and the generous financial support of Dartmouth College and the University of Texas at Austin.

On Wallace's career and ideas, See Grumet 1998; Jennings 1990; and Wallace 1978. Fortuitously, in the original introduction, these notes are 11-15, so here they have dropped a decade.

2 See Fogelson 1998 (honoring Thomas); Fogelson and Brightman 2002 (honoring Sturtevant).

people generally friendly toward anthropologists. Although Gulick and most of his associates focused on the contemporary sociocultural life of the Cherokee and issues of acculturation, Ray became much more interested in traditional Cherokee culture, aspects of which could still be found on the reservation, particularly among the members of the older generation. Although Ray's initial assignment was to administer Rorschach tests to the more acculturated Cherokees, neither he nor the Cherokees were comfortable with this. By this time he had clearly made the transition from experimental and clinical psychology to more humanistic psychological anthropology and to cultural anthropology more generally.

A number of factors seem to have influenced Ray's turn from acculturation studies to more ethnohistorically inspired studies of those aspects of Cherokee culture that could still be traced directly to their eighteenth-and nineteenth-century antecedents. On the one hand, there was a lot of social disorganization in the Cherokee community at the time, including alcoholism and fighting. Ray felt that he "did not have to go to an isolated Indian village to study anomie." On the other hand, he felt inspired by the research of such prominent ethnologists and ethnohistorians of the past as James Mooney and Frank Speck as well as by that of one of his contemporaries, John Witthoft. Mooney's work (e.g., Mooney 1890, 1891, 1900; Mooney and Olbrechts 1932) was particularly influential on the young anthropologist. It was exciting for Ray to return to a society Mooney had studied fifty years earlier and to find aspects of the old Cherokee [xv] medicine and religion still alive. As Ray put it in his interview, "I used to read Mooney every day. I love to just kind of read the myths and think of new interpretations and so forth. [Mooney] is one of my bibles. So he was very important as an indirect kind of teacher."

Ray describes his approach to the study of the traditional Cherokee culture as "iceberging," contrasting it with William Fenton's (1955) "up-streaming." While Fenton would take a present-day institution and work his way backward to uncover its earlier version, Fogelson's method was to look for institutions that the Cherokees themselves considered to be traditional or old. In his words, by searching through those institutions "you kind of get to the deeper and deeper levels of the culture, which would expand, so that the tip of the iceberg would lead you down into the deeper cultural structure." One of the institutions that Ray's Cherokee consultants clearly identified as traditional was the free-labor association known as *gadugi*. Though the outer forms of the *gadugi* as well as some of the tasks it accomplished had changed since the eighteenth and the nineteenth centuries, it still remained "a kind of native social security," as Ray put it. Moreover, the members of the *gadugi* kept rosters of their officials and took minutes, so as Ray continued to study this institution he was able to uncover vestiges of the old Cherokee town system and gain a better understanding of its nature.

Ray also became interested in the Cherokee stickball game. By the late 1950s the game was played mainly as a tourist attraction, but the players still took it seriously, purifying themselves in the traditional manner by "going to the water" and performing other rituals. A number of Ray's Cherokee teachers were willing to talk to him about this. Fascinated by the game, Ray began working his way from its contemporary version back to its earlier manifestations, as documented by Mooney (1890) and others. This research led Ray to insights into patterns of political organization and warfare, and eventually the traditional Cherokee ball game became the subject of his PhD thesis (Fogelson 1962; also 1971).

Similarly, Ray's work on what he called the local "medico-magical beliefs" – the subject of his 1958 master's thesis (Fogelson 1958) and several subsequent articles (Fogelson 1961, 1975, 1980a) – led him to interesting discoveries about the relationship between past and present. The medicine man with whom Ray worked most closely was Lloyd Runningwolf Sequoyah, who was well regarded in North Carolina and served as the conjuror for the stickball team of the Big Cove community. One of Ray's favorite methods of working with Lloyd Sequoyah, which established a relationship of openness and reciprocity, was to bring him copies of the old magical formulas contained in Mooney's field notes at [xxvi] the Smithsonian Institution. Important moments in the relationship between the medicine man and the young anthropology student were trips the two of them took to Oklahoma in the summers of 1958 and 1960, when they attended several stomp dances and contacted the more traditional Cherokees affiliated with the Redbird Smith movement, including Redbird's youngest son, Stokes Smith. This political and religious revitalization movement, rooted in the older "Keetowah movement," was initiated by traditional ("full-blood") Cherokees in the Indian Territory in the late 1890s and early 1900s in response to the Allotment Act and the dissolution of the Cherokee Nation. It has continued to attract followers to this very day (Thomas 1961; Fogelson 1993a).

The trip to Oklahoma was important for Ray's growth as a student of the Cherokees, since it gave him a comparative view and allowed him to see firsthand the continuing exchange of ideas between the Eastern Cherokees and the Oklahoma Cherokees. He watched Lloyd Sequoyah reacquaint his Oklahoma relatives with social and ceremonial dances that the Eastern Cherokees had retained but that were no longer being performed in the west (see Jackson and Levine 2002). Sequoyah also shared with the Western Cherokees some medicinal plants from the original Cherokee homeland. As Ray put it, "this was the beginning of a kind of a cultural exchange."

When asked why Lloyd Sequoyah might have been willing to share his knowledge with an anthropologist, Ray pointed out that in the 1950s few local younger people "took the elders seriously". The medicine men might have been feared for their spiritual power, but the idea of "progress" was still strong among most of the people, and the traditionalists were seen as being "in its way." In Ray's words, "at that time, not too many community members or even other anthropologists were interested in what Lloyd and the other medicine men had to teach, except for this white guy from Philadelphia." Sequoyah even entrusted Ray with the books in which he recorded his sacred formulae in syllabary. By comparing these texts with the ones recorded earlier by Mooney, Ray was able to get a much better sense of continuities in the Cherokee magico-religious worldview. For his part, Sequoyah came to appreciate Mooney's work in preserving the ancient formulae, which led him to see the value of Ray's own ethnographic research. A kind of mentoring relationship developed between the two of them, somewhat similar to that between a medicine man and a younger Cherokee interested in his knowledge.[3]13

In addition to working closely with a small group of medicine men and other traditionalists. Ray participated fairly regularly in various community social activities, such as "pie socials" and church meetings. One of the [xxvii] highlights of those activities was participating in the stick ball game (which proved to be utterly exhausting) and going over the mountains through Smokey Mountain National Park to Cosby, Tennessee, for moonshine. On the whole, Ray enjoyed his doctoral fieldwork and, in his words, "learned a lot there about culture and society in operation."

While writing his dissertation Ray received some advice from Hallowell and Wallace, but he says that he was "on his own" for much of the time. During that period (1960-61) Ray was a research fellow at the Eastern Pennsylvania Psychiatric Institute, where Wallace was the director of clinical research. Ray's research at the institute – which involved an ethnography of an open ward of schizophrenic women with good prognoses – strengthened his interest in psychological anthropology. The research resulted in two joint publications with Wallace, including a major paper on identity struggles arising in family therapy sessions (Wallace and Fogelson 1961, 1965).

Ray's work at the Eastern Pennsylvania Psychiatric Institute was interesting but time consuming, and the dissertation progressed rather slowly. Luckily, a job offer from the University of Washington's anthropology department in 1961 made him work very hard to complete the PhD. It was then that Pete Hallowell was particularly helpful – even coming to his student's apartment to read sections of the dissertation as they were being written!

Ray found the prospect of teaching large undergraduate classes at the University of Washington a bit daunting, since he had not gained much teaching experience at Penn. Among the courses he taught at UW were "Introduction to Anthropology," "Anthropology of Religion," "Psychological Anthropology," "Theories of Race," and a course on "The History of Anthropology" with Simon Ottenberg. The course on race was a particularly memorable experience, since it was offered at 7:30 a.m. during the winter

---

3 For a 1959 photograph of young Ray Fogelson with Lloyd Sequoyah, see Jackson, Fogelson, and Sturtevant 2004a: 40.

quarter, when it was still pitch dark. Only by the end of the lecture would the sun finally come up. Because courses at UW were more or less permanently assigned to particular faculty members, Ray never had the opportunity to reach Native American ethnology. This was the domain of senior colleagues such as Viola Garfield, Erna Gunther, Melville Jacobs, and Verne Ray. Nevertheless, Ray learned a great deal from them about Boasian anthropology as well as the indigenous cultures of the Plateau and the Northwest Coast. Mel Jacobs was a particularly important source of stories about Boas.

While in Seattle Ray initiated a new research site by conducting some preliminary psychological and ethno-ecological research among the Shuswap Indians of interior British Columbia. His teaching and research [xx] experience at UW contributed to a broad, comparative view of American Indian cultures, which served Ray well in his subsequent research and teaching. Ray has always insisted that his graduate students specializing in Native North America develop a similar comparative view, familiarizing themselves with ethnographic works (especially the classics) that deal with topics and geographic areas far beyond the immediate focus of their dissertation research.

The presence of colleagues such as Ottenberg, Edward Harper, Kenneth Read, Mel Spiro, and James Watson added to the attractiveness of the position at the University of Washington. Ottenberg and Spiro, both of whom shared Ray's interest in psychological anthropology, became his lifelong friends, as did Gananath Obeyesekere, who had just completed his PhD and was temporarily holding a postdoctoral teaching position. Spiro and Fogelson had another common bond, as both had been graduate students of Hallowell. The two of them coauthored the introduction to the Hallowell festschrift edited by Spiro (Fogelson and Spiro 1965). Eleven years later, when Fogelson edited a major posthumous edition of Hallowell's papers (Hallowell 1976), Spiro wrote the introduction to one of the book's sections (the others were authored by Wallace, Fred Eggan, George Stocking, and Wilcomb Washburn).

Being at the University of Washington was a good learning experience, but the position had its drawbacks. Ray began to dread the thought of having to teach the same courses year after year. (He had to teach the anthropology of religion course six times in three years!) In addition, the UW administration was not delivering on its earlier promise to help fund the department's expansion. So when the University of Chicago made him an offer in 1965, he reluctantly left the Northwest for the Midwest, where he joined his former associates Paul Friedrich, Mel Spiro, and Manning Nash (who had taught briefly at the University of Washington). Ray has remained at Chicago ever since, except for occasional visiting appointments at Princeton, the University of California at San Diego, the University of California at Santa Cruz, and the University of Texas at Austin.

Ray's appointment was the first of a new type of appointment at Chicago: he was an assistant professor in both the anthropology department and the social science division of the (undergraduate) college. Later he also accepted appointments in the Committee on Human Development and the Department of Psychology. After having been at Washington for three years, he appreciated Chicago's approach to teaching, in which faculty could choose what they taught. Over the three and a half decades of his tenure at Chicago, Ray has taught an impressive variety of courses, from his standard psychological anthropology and North American [xxix] Indian ethnology lecture courses to seminars on such topics as primitivism, shamanism, and "The Culture of Nature," which was developed in response to Marshall Sahlins's popular course "The Nature of Culture." In reminiscing about the teaching he has done at Chicago, especially in the late 1960s and 1970s, Ray uses such words as "fresh," "exciting," and "experimental." He also recalls fondly his experiences team-teaching with such colleagues as Bob Adams, Jim Fernandez, Les Freeman, Bill Hanks, Tanya Luhrman, Marshall Sahlins, George Stocking, and two former students, Sharon Stephens and Anne (Terry) Straus.

When the editors of this volume look back at the highlights of our own graduate education at Chicago in the late 1970s and early 1980s, Ray's North American Indian ethnology course stands out. The course not only inspired many of the contributors to this volume to specialize in this particular area but also introduced them to each other and encouraged them to collaborate and exchange ideas. Among Ray's effective pedagogical methods was his use of guest lectures by the department's more senior North

Americanists (Sol Tax and Fred Eggan, who were professors emeritus at the time). A recent PhD, Terry Straus, was also a guest lecturer, and she gave the class a sense of the excitement and challenges of doing ethnographic research in contemporary Native American communities. Another way of helping his students find common intellectual ground was an assignment that required each student to write a research paper on a single aspect of American Indian culture. In 1977-78, when this book's editors took the class, the topic was Native American architecture, and several of the research papers were incorporated into theses and publications.[4]14

Ray played an instrumental role in developing a popular undergraduate program in anthropology at the University of Chicago, both by teaching a variety of undergraduate courses and encouraging his departmental colleagues to do likewise. He points out that reading classical works in anthropology and the social sciences more generally with bright undergraduates has been a rewarding reaching experience and helped to broaden his own theoretical outlook. It is well known that at a research university such as Chicago not every faculty member takes undergraduate teaching seriously, but Ray always has. He attributes his attitude, at least in part, to his own undergraduate experience at Wesleyan, where "teaching was where it was at." He also notes that he was exposed to some fine teachers at Penn. Thanks to Ray's dedication to undergraduate teaching, an innovative undergraduate concentration in anthropology was established at Chicago, and many alumni of the undergraduate program have gone on [xxx] to do successful graduate work in anthropology and other social sciences (Fogelson 1999).

At Chicago Ray developed a strong interest in Levi-Straussian structuralism and symbolic anthropology, which he has retained to this day. In the 1960s and 1970s Chicago was a major center of symbolic anthropology, with such prominent scholars as Clifford Geertz, Nancy Munn, Marshall Sahlins, David Schneider, Terry Turner, and Victor Turner on its faculty (see Fogelson 2001b; Handler 1995; Stocking 1979). In the area of American Indian ethnology, Ray benefited greatly from having two senior colleagues who worked in the area, Fred Eggan and Sol Tax (DeMallie 1994; Eggan 1974; Fogelson 1980b; Foley 1999; Hinshaw 1979; Stocking 2000). Ray found Eggan (who had been a close friend of Hallowell) particularly supportive as a colleague. Other Chicago colleagues with whom Ray has been particularly close over the years include Friedrich, Nash, Stocking, Jim Fernandez, Les Freeman, and Raymond Smith.

Although Chicago's anthropology department has had its share of fine lecturers and effective mentors, Ray Fogelson is well known as one of the most "student-friendly" professors. As Ray stated in the remarks he delivered at the close of the last of the AAA sessions held in his honor, he has always found himself learning as much from his graduate students as from reading or talking to colleagues. Ray's office door is always open, and his graduate students have benefited greatly from conversing with him in his cluttered office, borrowing books from his vast library, and interacting with him, his friends, and each other at the famous parties at his North Side home. Known to some of his students' children as "Uncle Ray," he has always shown an interest in his students' lives and families as well as their scholarship. Ray has successfully created a true community of scholars, and many of his students, including a significant number of the contributors to this volume, have become lifelong friends as well as colleagues.

Ray's commitment to mentoring graduate students is further illustrated by his longstanding support for the Central States Anthropological Association, which he served as president in 1983-84. He has faithfully participated in its annual meetings, and encourages his students to present their first scholarly papers at these small and supportive meetings. Ray has also been deeply involved in the American Society for Ethnohistory, whose presidency he assumed in 1987-88 and whose membership he helped increase (particularly by encouraging his graduate students and recent doctorates to join and attend meetings). Ray's talent for composing thought-provoking and humorous comments on his colleagues'

---

4 See Art 1979; Kan 1978, 1989; Strong 1979. As Nabokov notes in the afterword and elsewhere (Nabokov and Easton 1989: 413), these and other seminar papers were sources for his book Native American Architecture.

papers at scholarly meetings is legendary. His talent in this area is particularly [xxxi] worthy of admiration because quite often this work is done the night before the session, if not at the session itself. Not all of these comments find their way onto the printed page, but when they do we are treated to wonderful ethnological essays in their own right (see Fogelson 1981, 2001a).

Ray has also been a strong supporter of the D'Arcy McNickle Center for the History of the American Indian at the Newberry Library. He served on the center's advisory board from 1971 to 1985 and again from 1989 to 1992, and contributed some of his most provocative papers to its curriculum series (Fogelson 19850, 1986, 19890). Ray's involvement with the American Society for Ethnohistory and the D'Arcy McNickle Center coincided with the further development of his interest in exploring Cherokee culture through a combination of ethnographic and ethnohistorical research. During the Chicago years Ray has continued publishing articles on the Cherokees, while also exploring other areas of interest such as psychological anthropology (Fogelson 1982b, 1994a), the anthropology of power (Fogelson 1977; Fogelson and Adams 1977), ethnohistory (Fogelson 1984, 1985c, 1989b), the anthropology of religion (Fogelson 1987b; Fogelson and Brightman 2002), the history of anthropology (Fogelson 1985b, 1987a, 1987b, 1997, 1999a), and the history of representations of American Indians in Europe and the United States (Fogelson 1991b).

Since the mid-1960s Ray has carried on ethnographic research among the Oklahoma Cherokees and Creeks (Muskogees), a natural development after his trips with Lloyd Sequoyah. One of his major contacts in Oklahoma was his old friend and colleague Bob Thomas (see Fogelson 1998a). An important new development in Ray's involvement with southeastern Indian people occurred in 1986 when he and a group of Newberry Library Fellows (Jay Miller, C.B Clark, Robert McKinley, and Richard Sattler) participated in the stomp dances of the Oklahoma Creeks. Since being welcomed into the stomp dance community, he has been going there almost every summer (see Fogelson 20013; Miller 2001). Ray has not published any works based on this experience and emphasizes that he does not view it as fieldwork in the strict sense of the term. But the experience of fasting and following other prohibitions, taking medicinal teas, getting initiated into the ritual system, and being given a Creek name has informed his teaching and helped him better understand many aspects of Southeastern Indian culture and history. He has also been invited to present papers at scholarly conferences organized by the Oklahoma Cherokees (e.g., Fogelson 1993a). When discussing his experience in Oklahoma, Ray talks about "a new kind of fieldwork" that he calls "observant participation." Always keeping an eye on the most recent political and cultural [xxxii] developments in Indian Country, Ray continues to publish thoughtful and provocative essays on such topics as Native American identity, past and present (Fogelson 1998b). An important but relatively unknown dimension of Ray's involvement with Native American people and issues has been his congressional testimony on federal recognition criteria and on specific recognition cases, such as that of the Lumbees (Fogelson 1988b, 1989c). Congressional testimony has also given him a chance to do informal ethnographic research on the Branch of Acknowledgment and Recognition (a subdivision of the Bureau of Indian Affairs). At the 1993 Mashantucket Pequot History Conference and the 1998 meetings of the American Anthropological Association he gave papers exploring the cultural and political biases entailed in recognition criteria (Fogelson 1988a, 1993b). Ray also became involved in the Dickson Mound controversy in the state of Illinois – a controversy that eventually ended public visits to a large complex of exposed prehistoric graves (Fogelson 1991c). He has been an early and consistent supporter of the Native American Graves Protection and Repatriation Act (NAGPRA), which has caused some disagreements between him and some of his friends and colleagues at the Smithsonian. He has spoken out on the Indian mascot issue on a number of occasions, and maintains a keen interest in the vibrant cultural and artistic life of Chicago's diverse Native American community.[5]15

Ray recently completed one of his most significant scholarly projects: editing the monumental

---

5 The Chicago Indian community is described in two volumes edited by Ray's student and colleague Anne "Terry" Straus (1990; Straus and Arndt 1998).

Southeast volume of the Smithsonian Institution's *Handbook of North American Indians* (Fogelson 2004b). One of twenty projected *Handbook* volumes, the *Southeast* contains Fogelson's latest articles on the history of anthropology (Jackson, Fogelson, and Sturtevant 2004) and Eastern Cherokees (Fogelson 2004a), while the introduction (Jackson and Fogelson 2004) offers a valuable discussion of the principles that have organized scholarly knowledge about Native North America. The latest in a series of important general works he has published on the cultures of the Southeast (Fogelson 1974, 1979a, 1994b), the Handbook volume is among the most impressive accomplishments of the great scholar, mentor, and friend this volume honors.

Ray's Office and Desk

Peter Nabokov

My initiation [490] into Ray's Kula Ring began back in the 1970s after Tim Buckley told me over the phone about this unusual professor I just had to meet. And, yes, Ray proved to be, in the jazz argot of a slightly outmoded era that strangely suited him, quite the cat – as well as a hip prof who Lord Buckley might have riffed. Ray thereafter graciously served as my adoptive paternal clan uncle, one of those guides who among the Crow Indians function as quasi-guardian figures with special rights to cast their shadows over your inner life, to impose their benevolence over you on key occasions – namings, feast days (dissertation defenses), special turns in life's road – but always in such an intrusive yet mysterious manner that you never forgot that these oversize familiars were imbued with what the Crows called *Maxpe* – "power."

What was disconcerting, however, was that this analyst of power never waited only for those special occasions. Any wee hour would do, whether at the drag end of those intense all-night Sedgewick Street shindigs or, as Greg Urban remembers, just when you were recognizing the onslaught of a massive hangover only a few hours before your Triple-A paper was to be delivered.

During the daytime things generally went ok. I know: one of my glorious stretches under Ray's peerless hospitality was over my predoctoral McNickle fellowship in Chicago, when John Aubrey and Helen Tanner joked that we were Newberry Library's odd couple (my Lemmon to his Matthau?). Before the sun went down Ray could be so charming – pawing through his apartment's archaeological site of newspapers and magazines like the third Collier brother, emerging with a review of some exhibit he absolutely commanded that I see or book that I must memorize by morning, meditatively watering and feeding bugs to the utterly hateful jungle that steamed up his sitting room, or staring up at me with an expression bordering on adoration when he discovered that I knew how to steam broccoli.

But come the nightfall, dishes piling to the ceiling, things changed, and one fell under his assault. Now, I don't think of the scholars at that AAA gathering in San Francisco as shrinking violets, and perhaps some of them also shared my genetic allergy to advice. Yet we still refrained from committing prof-icide when, in the deep dark a.m, we felt as though we had been set upon by some monstrous amalgam of John Belushi, Franz Boas, and the Ayatollah Khomeni.

Here was both Greg Urban's "power as authority" and Rob Brightman's "anti-power as subversion" thundering at you like – dare I say it – a force of nature, telling you before you hit the books or the field to look for, listen for, stay attuned to all those multiple souls, covert categories, [491] epitomizing events, architectural cosmograms, indigenous critiques, structural "persons," binary oppositions, and the rest of those undersize, oversize, left-handed, handcrafted, and inverted beings that could be found in those glancing moments and under-appreciated representations that just might become clues to the stories behind the stories we read about in this volume from Ray's victims. And as E.O Wilson has said, we do love our monsters, we are transfixed by them, and I remain under my beloved uncle's spell to this day.

Ray's many long journeys into night had the same gradual effect on him as the four bounces-in-place he takes prior to his class lectures – popping him into that shamanic zone where all ambivalences and foreign forms of self-consciousness are rendered accessible, readable, inhabitable, communicable, cross-reference-able. It was his inspired art of play.

And in this volume we encounter some of those attempts at the deeper stories inspired by Ray's teachings and writings, contributions that I briefly rearrayed in San Francisco to my liking. Prefacing my remarks to the session's papers by Tim Buckley and Barrik Van Winkle on narrative expressions of a self-and-other consciousness, I proposed that Ray's much pillaged neologism – "ethno-ethnohistory" – basically asked that we overlook the missteps of Levi-Bruhl for the moment and give "*mentalité*" another shot, or, as activist-comedian Dick Gregory used to say, let's just stop the insults – to anybody's intelligence. That posture of granting our informants and their societies an intellectual and self-reflective life on and through their own terms could open up all sorts of real work, as these scholars exemplified. Nor long ago Ray was my guide through an essay I was writing on Indian concepts of history, so I can fully appreciate the interpretive twists and turns as Van Winkle and Buckley unveiled the ethno-agendas that underlay both spoken and written accounts of the past. I even wound up dedicating a book on that topic to my Chicago uncle.

Van Winkle's marvelous case of the Washo Indians aghast at the sight of starving pioneers eating each other at Donner Pass seemed to validate Ray's long fascination with diversities of the monstrous, and put the "Big" on the other "Foot" so to speak. Van Winkle's account seemed the very reverse of folklorist Jarold Ramsay's view of Indian prophecy as retroactive composition. It became a delicious example of life anticipating art and replicating cosmology, since in terms of the dark history of Washo-white relations that ensued, after this moment in time it would only be more monsters all the way.

SOUTHEAST AMERICAN INDIANS [218]

The Southeastern American culture area is bounded on the east and south by the Atlantic Ocean and the Gulf of Mexico (though some scholars would place the southern portion of aboriginal Florida within the orbit of the circum-Caribbean culture area). To the west, the Southeastern area merges with the southern Plains and the extreme easternmost part of the Southwestern culture area. To the north, the Southeast blends into the northeastern woodlands area with no discernible break in cultural tradition (see NORTH AMERICAN PLAINS INDIANS, EASTERN WOODLANDS INDIANS).

GENERAL CHARACTERISTICS OF THE SOUTHEAST CULTURE AREA

Physiographically, the Southeast is characterized first by a coastal lowland belt broadly encompassing the subtropical zone of southern Florida; the scrub forest, sandy soil, and savannah grassland of the Atlantic and Gulf coastal plains; and the alluvial floodplains of the Mississippi drainage. Second, there is the piedmont of the midland interior, where the landscape changes to rolling hills, crisscrossed by several major river systems and covered predominantly with oak-hickory forest. Third, there is the southern Appalachian Mountains area of eastern Tennessee and the western Carolinas, a land of high peaks and deeply etched valleys, containing hardwood forests and, at high elevations, flora and fauna typical of more northerly regions.

Populations. The Southeast was one of the more densely populated areas of native North America, having an aboriginal population conservatively estimated at 120,000. The bulk of this population resided inland, where advantage could be taken of extensive game resources, wild plant foods, and an abundance of arable land. Only the non-horticultural peoples of south Florida appear to have satisfactorily adjusted to a basically maritime way of life.

Population was distributed among a large number of separate groups – independent villages, autonomous village clusters, and "tribelets." Most of those tribelets disappeared soon after white contact and left only faint traces in recorded history. They perished through the lethal combination of newly introduced diseases, removal into slavery, and direct warfare with white invaders or intertribal conflicts generated by white pressure. The survivors, if any, were assimilated into such larger, more powerful tribes as the Choctaw and Cherokee and various member tribes of the Creek Confederacy. These latter tribes persist to the present as distinctive peoples possessing a rich history and viable cultural heritage. Other intermediate-sized groups, such as the Houma, Catawba, and Chickasaw, survive as marginal enclaves but have lost much of their historic Indian identity. Such groups as the Seminoles (a branch of the Creek that migrated to Florida in the 18th century) and the Lumbee (a large group of Indians in Robeson County, North Carolina, whose precise Indian ancestry is unknown) appear to be entering an active phase of retribalization in which their Indian identification is being reasserted.

Muskogean-speaking peoples constituted the major linguistic family in the aboriginal Southeast. The Muskogean family included the following five main subdivisions: (1) Choctaw and Chickasaw, two different dialects of the of a single language, found in Mississippi and western Southeast Tennessee; (2) Apalachee, a long extinct language of northwestern Florida; (3) Alabama and Koasati, two closely related languages spoken in the central Southeast; (4) Hitchiti and Mikasuki, two related dialects, formerly spoken in Georgia; and (5) Creek and Seminole, also closely related dialects, spoken in eastern Georgia and later in Florida.

Four Lower Mississippi Valley languages, namely Natchez, Tunica, Chitimacha, and Atakapa, are thought to have distant affinity to Muskogean, but they show sufficient divergence both from the main Muskogean languages and from each other to warrant semi-independent status as linguistic isolates. Timucua, the major language of aboriginal north Florida, was once thought to be related to Muskogean, but its present status is problematic. One linguist believes it may be related to a language spoken in Venezuela, while others feel it may bear ultimate relationship to Siouan.

There are four definite representatives of the Siouan family in the Southeast: Tutelo, Biloxi, Ofo (Mosopelea), and Catawba. These tribes were widely scattered and, with the exception of Biloxi and Ofo, show little relationship to one another and probably represent different prehistoric penetrations of Siouan speakers into the Southeast. Yuchi, the language of a major tribal group once residing in eastern Tennessee and later in Georgia, also demonstrates distant affinities to Siouan but is sufficiently distinctive to be classified as an isolate. Many small piedmont tribes were probably Siouan speaking, but surviving data are insufficient to make definite identifications.

The Cherokee represent the sole member of the Iroquoian family in the presently demarcated Southeast, though the Iroquoian-speaking Tuscarora, Nottaway, and Meherrin, residing on the margin of the area, are included in the Southeast in some culture area maps. The Caddoan speakers on the western boundary of the Southeast belong to a distinctive language family that shows distant relationships to the Siouan and Iroquoian families. The affiliations of many of the smaller coastal and piedmont tribes are unknown. Mention should also be made of Mobilian, an important trade language containing many Choctaw components, which served as a lingua franca in the Mississippi Valley.

TRADITIONAL CULTURE PATTERNS

It is difficult to describe the Southeast in terms of a total cultural pattern or dominant ethos. The environment provided possibilities for such different ecological adaptations as the dependence on maritime resources and the wild zamia root by the Calusa of south Florida and the seasonal buffalo hunts of the horticultural Caddoan tribes. Besides the internal diversity, the external relations of the Southeast are also complex. The lack of geographic barriers to the north and west allowed significant cultural interchange between the Southeast and adjacent areas. There is evidence of overseas' cultural connections with the Antilles; however, the dominant thrust of this diffusion seems to have been from the mainland to the islands. Such individual culture traits as the cane blowgun, double-weave basketry, fibre-tempered pottery, and miscellaneous musical, ritual, and mythological details suggest at least limited contact with northern South America. More definite is prehistoric cultural contact with Meso-America. Not only did such basic cultivated plants as maize, beans, and squash ultimately derive from Meso-America, but numerous symbolic motifs in Southeast religious art have close analogues in ancient Mexico.

The picture of the Southeast that emerges at the time of first European contact is one of intensive cultural change. One senses a period of cultural leveling marked by considerable population movement, warfare, and the formation of confederacies, all of which was accompanied by [219] large-scale technological and ideological diffusion. A distinctive Southeastern cultural tradition or style was in the process of being forged, but this fusion was far from complete on the eve of European contact.

Social organization. Settlement patterns. The basic political unit for most Southeastern tribes was the local village or town. This basic unit varied in size and configuration depending on differences in local ecological potential and cultural preference. Some towns attained populations of over 1,000 individuals, but the more typical Southeastern village numbered less than 500 people. Settlement patterns conformed to two basic types: (1) dispersed hamlets, with households strung out for several miles, usually following valley bottoms or streams, and (2) tightly nucleated settlements often surrounded with protective timber palisades. The heart of the local town was a ceremonial centre consisting of a central council house or temple, which in the interior region might be semisubterranean or located on a pre-existing mound; a central plaza or square, which, among the Muskogean-speakers, was usually surrounded by three or four benches or arbors oriented in the cardinal directions; a ball pole or scalp post sometimes culminating in a carved animal emblem; the residences of the chief and other important local dignitaries; and sometimes storage structures for communal produce.

Considerable variation in house types existed. In much of the area, the Indians constructed circular, conical-roofed winter "hot houses," sealed tight, except for an entryway and smoke hole. Summer dwellings tended to be rectangular, gabled structures made from a framework of upright poles, lashed together and covered with lath, grass, cane matting, or bark and plastered with clay. To the south, housing tended to be more flimsy, with raised floors, palmetto thatched roofs, and, often, open sides. To the west, the Caddoans lived in domed "grass houses." A homestead might contain auxiliary storage buildings and a special cookhouse.

Each town or village was fairly autonomous. Superordinate control at the tribal level tended to be weakly developed, although pressure for tribal consolidation and even the formation of intertribal confederacies was greatly increased with the coming of Europeans. A village [219b] might be linked to other villages in the same area by ties of kinship, language, and shared cultural traditions; nevertheless, each village claimed sovereignty over its local area and was governed by its own chiefs and war leaders.

Stratification. Over most of the Southeast, chieftain- Chiefs ship tended to be hereditary within certain lineages. The and degree of chiefly power and authority varied, however, other from the almost divine kingship of the Great Sun among leaders the theocratic Natchez to the self-effacing status of the peace-making, consensus-seeking *micos* and *ukus* among the more egalitarian Choctaws, Creeks, and Cherokees. War leaders normally achieved their positions on the basis of past accomplishment. War chiefs tended to be active, assertive, and younger, by about a generation, than the peace chiefs.

The alternation between peace and war or the occurrence of such competitive activities between alien groups as ball games, communal hunts, and trading expeditions helped to imbue much of Southeastern social structure with a characteristic dualism. The peace chief held sway in the domestic village, whereas the war chief was ascendant in areas external to the village, except when the village was under threat of imminent attack. Young men in the village alternately adjusted to roles appropriate to war and peace, often symbolically represented as red and white activities, and these transformations were usually effected through extensive ritual. This dualistic emphasis was also frequently expressed in the organization of clans, subtribes, and villages into complementary social divisions.

Social stratification was highly developed in some parts of the Southeast, while its significance in other subareas was minimal. Although much has been written about the supposed caste systems among the tribes of the Lower Mississippi, the Chitimacha appear to have been the only society to have possessed true castes in the sense of ranked groups that practiced strict endogamy (marriage within the group).

Social ranking among the Natchez. The elaborate rank system of the Natchez consisted of four groups: three upper classes, composed hierarchically of the suns, the nobles, and the honored people, and a lower class of commoners (or stinkards, as they are referred to in the early French sources). Upper class individuals [220a] were required to marry into the lower class of commoners, and many commoners also married other commoners. Offspring of males in the upper classes would assume a rank one step below that of their fathers (thus, the child of a sun father and commoner mother would become a member of the noble class). The progeny of upper class females, however, would retain the rank of their mothers rather than descend to a lower station. The system, as described, would be unstable, since the supply of available commoner women would soon be depleted after several generations. Many explanations have been advanced to explain this so-called "Natchez paradox," but the difficulties probably reside in the inaccuracies or incompleteness of the original French sources.

Social stratification also was highly elaborated among the aboriginal inhabitants of Florida. Among the Timucua, for instance, the "king" enjoyed an elevated status considerably above that of his followers and was sometimes carried about in a litter. In many other Southeastern societies there was a trend toward the ranking of towns or clans. Member towns of the Creek Confederacy were sometimes ranked in terms of their tribal affiliations or on the basis of outcomes of inter-town ballgames. The Caddo were said to have ranked their clans on the basis of the reputed strength of the totemic animal ancestor in a kind of natural "pecking order." In other tribes, such as the Cherokee, stratification was only weakly developed, though certain clans might possess special ceremonial prerogatives and recruitment to certain offices might be determined on the basis of clan.

Kinship and marriage. In the Southeast, descent was almost universally reckoned in the female line, though not all societies possessed matrilineal clans. Clans were lacking among the Choctaw, and their existence among the eastern piedmont tribes has been questioned. Clans, where they existed, were apparently not restricted to nor localized within specific villages. The resulting dispersal of clan members throughout a tribe or nation thus served as a kind of social adhesive binding together the larger body politic. Certain ceremonial knowledge and privileges might also be passed down along clan lines, and clans were also important as mechanisms of social control, since vengeance for serious crimes was frequently a clan responsibility.

Marriage was often marked by a symbolic ceremonial exchange whereby the groom presented his bride with game and the bride reciprocated with vegetable food. Because residence after marriage normally found the man moving into the wife's natal household, the husband was expected to contribute to the economic maintenance of his wife's family, as a form of bride service. After a few years the couple might leave to form their own household. Most Southeastern tribes permitted and some even encouraged pre-marital sexuality. After marriage, however, adultery – especially on the part of the wife – was often severely punished. Nevertheless, divorce seems to have been a frequent and, often, almost casual event. Polygamy was permitted in most groups, although a man usually had to gain the assent of his first wife before taking on a second spouse. The levirate, a custom by which a widow was remarried to her deceased husband's brother, was fairly common, particularly as male mortality increased during the wars of the European period.

Socialization. During a woman's late pregnancy, both she and the father were often subjected to various dietary taboos and restrictions on their activities. Children were nursed until they tired of the breast or until the mother again became pregnant. Responsibility for the child's early education was vested in the mother. Later, a young boy received instruction in male skills from his father and his mother's brother; in many systems the mother's brother, as the senior male in the matrilineage, assumed considerable importance as a disciplinarian, tutor, and sponsor for his sister's son. Young girls remained at their mother's side and were trained in various duties associated with the domestic household. Behavior considered proper was reinforced with praise and encouragement, as when a boy killed his first deer or a young girl manufactured her first [220b] basket; behavior considered improper might be greeted with mild rebuke, ridicule, or shame. Children were rarely subjected to physical punishment. In those few instances in which punishment was deemed necessary, it was generally meted out by someone other than the parents. A popular method of chastisement throughout the Southeast was raking the skin with briars or a special pointed scratching instrument, but, even here, such action was regarded as strengthening or toughening the youth, rather than as delivering direct retribution for misdeeds. Young boys enjoyed much permissiveness. They spent much time with their peers in wrestling, playing games imitative of adult activities, and stalking rabbits, squirrels, and birds with blowguns and scaled-down bows and arrows. The freedom and wide behavioral space permitted the young boy contrasted markedly with the restricted sphere, close surveillance, and early responsibility training that characterized the daily routine of his sister.

Puberty rituals were either absent or only weakly developed in the Southeast. Girls were secluded during their first menstruation, but this event occasioned no public celebration. (Menstrual blood, though, was regarded as a potent and polluting substance, and women either absented themselves from the household during their periods or were subjected to restrictive taboos.) Similarly, no special rituals attended the transition from boyhood to manhood. A boy might receive instructions from tribal elders in esoteric lore or in preparation for special ritual offices, but graduation from such training seldom was marked by a formal commencement. A young man's first participation in a war party and the achievement of military honors were, however, given public recognition. Probably the clearest marker of the passage from adolescence to adulthood was marriage.

Economic systems. As already implied, the primary division of labor was by sex. Women were responsible for cultivating the fields, gathering wild-plant food, cooking and preserving food, rearing the young children, and manufacturing such basic domestic items as cordage, baskets, pottery, and clothing. Men assumed the primary roles of warriors and hunters, occupations that often took them away from the village for extended periods of time. Men also cleared the fields by girdling trees, assisted in the harvest, constructed houses and public buildings, and manufactured ceremonial objects and implements for personal use.

Except for the marginal groups on the western Gulf Coast, villages were semipermanent and located near rich alluvial soil or, in the Lower Mississippi region, near natural levees. Such land was easily tilled, possessed adequate drainage, and enjoyed enduring productivity. Fertility was enhanced by the custom of annually burning off the brush. The length of the growing season in most regions of the Southeast allowed multiple crops. Planting was done in spring, and some produce was available by midsummer. The major harvest time, however, was late summer and early fall, a time of plenty when most of the major ceremonies were celebrated. Many villages became deserted, except for older people, during the winter months, when families took to the woods in search of game. Men also departed for a shorter hunt in late spring and early summer, after the crops had been planted.

Principal foods and goods. The economic mainstay of the Southeast was maize, the cultivation of which was well established in most areas by the time of first European contact in the mid-16th century. Several varieties of maize were grown, including "little corn" (related to popcorn); flint, or hominy, corn; and flour, or dent, corn. Early corn was baked as roasting ears; later corn was pounded into hominy or cornmeal in wooden mortars made of large, upright, partly hollowed logs. Associated in the maize complex were varieties of beans and squash. Fields were prepared with mattocks and hoes and planted by punching holes in the ground with dibbles (digging sticks), inserting seed, and covering the holes with earth to form a small mound. Cornfields belonged to individual households, but among some tribes communal fields were also cultivated, with the produce going to the chiefs for [221a] support of the civil-religious hierarchy or for redistribution to the needy.

The importance of maize cultivation to the way of life of the southern Indians cannot be overemphasized. Not only did maize provide a high yield of nutritious food with a minimal expenditure of labor, but maize, beans, and squash could be easily dried and stored for later consumption. This reliable food base enabled men to spend much time away from their villages on hunting, trading, and war expeditions. It was not fortuitous that the standard war ration was parched corn.

Secondary cultivated plants included the sunflower (processed for its oil), chenopodium or orache (spinach-like greens), and tobacco. Many additional plants, such as species of wild grapes, plums, and perhaps walnut and pecan trees, can be regarded as being in a condition of incipient domestication, since there is evidence to suggest that Indians exerted some effect on selection. Important wild-plant foods were various types of berries, nuts and acorns, wild potatoes and amaranths, smilax, zamia root, and maple sugar or honey locust sap. The economic botany of the Southeastern Indians can be expanded to encompass the vast array of plants utilized for cordage, clothing, dyes, fish poisons, medicines, building materials, and various tools and utensils. Perhaps mention should be made of the distinctive Southeastern use of two species of holly (*Ilex cassine* and *Ilex vomitoria*) as ingredients in a special decoction, the "black- drink," to induce sweating and vomiting in ceremonial and medical contexts.

The only native domesticated animal in the Southeast was the dog, which was used to a minor extent in hunting and was probably more important as a sentinel to warn of the approach of strangers. In accounts of the Hernando De Soto expedition (1539-1543), there are several references to small, fat, barkless dogs that were served to the Spanish visitors by their Indian hosts. Spanish trail hogs, brought by De Soto to feed his troops, became wild and were ancestral to the modem mongrel razorback hog. Horses were introduced later, mostly through the intermediacy of tribes to the west.

The aboriginal Southeast also teemed with wild game: deer, black bears, bison, elks, beavers, squirrels, rabbit, otters, and raccoon – some of which were used for their hides, bone, or fat as well as for food. In Florida, turtles and alligators played an important part in subsistence. Among birds, wild turkeys were the principal quarry, but partridges, quails, and seasonal flights of pigeons, ducks, and geese also contributed to the larder. The feathers of eagles, hawks, swans, and cranes were highly valued for ornamentation, and in some tribes a special status was reserved for an eagle hunter.

Both on the coast and on inland rivers, streams, and lakes, a wide variety of fish were taken in weirs, fish traps, and dip nets and dragnets and by hooks and lines, bows and arrows, and spears. In the interior, poison was administered in ponds and sluggish or dammed streams to gather a rich harvest of stunned fish. Coastal groups gathered oysters, clams, mussels, cockles, and crabs. Interior groups found freshwater mussels and crawfish.

Economic organization and ecology. In the well-endowed Southeastern area, each household group was fairly self-sufficient. The economic specializations and trade networks that did develop tended to centre on subsidiary and luxury items. Salt deposits were unequally distributed and formed one basis for trade. There also was regular trade between the coast and interior, with shells, which were used for beads, pendants, and horns, exchanged for soapstone, flint, furs, and other inland resources. The presence in the Southeast of artifacts made of imported copper and certain types of red clay suggests important trade connections with the western Great Lakes tribes. Indians are popularly viewed as living in a primeval or virginal territory. Such was not the case in the Southeast. Indians maintained a delicate balance with their environment, and their presence was a vital link in a complex ecological chain. By tillage, controlled use of fire, and hunting, they altered the landscape significantly. Large areas of secondary re-growth favored certain types of berry bushes and groundnuts. The presence of this [221b] secondary-growth flora was, in turn, essential for supporting large populations of browsing deer, squirrels, rabbit, and wild turkeys on which man depended for a large measure of his sustenance. In this process and in combination with hunting, the decline of other animals, such as the wood bison, was probably accelerated. In areas where intensive maize cultivation had already taken hold, such as in the Lower Mississippi, game animals had become scarce in historical time. In the central Southeast, however, the very diversity of plant and animal resources and the highly generalized adaptation of the Indian in exploiting these resources seems to have resulted in maintenance of an equilibrated balance between man and nature.

Belief systems. World views. The delicate man-nature relationship is well expressed in what is known of Southeastern religion and world view. The world was perceived as animated by a proliferation of ghosts, witches, and spiritual essences of animals, plants, and natural objects or phenomena. As can be inferred from the frequent death elaboration of funerary practices, most groups professed and belief in an afterlife. The location of the resting place for afterlife deceased souls was either in the direction of the western setting sun or up above in a celestial firmament. It was generally thought that the souls of the recently deceased would hover around the community and try to induce close friends and relatives to join them in their journey to eternity. The elaborate funerary rites and the extensive taboos associated with death were as much a protection ' for the living as a commemoration of the dead. Death was nowhere considered a natural event but always the result of malevolent animal spirits or witches or the deadly machinations of sorcerers. If death was thought to be caused by human agents, the soul of the deceased would never rest until vengeance had been secured by living relatives.

It was also believed that animals possessed souls. Slain animals sought vengeance against man through the agency of their species "chief," a mythological animal with great supernatural power. Hunting thus became a sacred act, much imbued with taboos, ritual, and sacrifice. Most disease was attributed to failure to placate the souls of slain animals.

The plant world was considered friendly to mankind, and the Cherokees thought that every animal-sent disease could be cured by a plant antidote. The economic significance of maize was memorialized by the near universality of the Green Corn, or Busk, ceremonies throughout the Southeast. This major ceremonial was suffused with an ethos of annual renewal in which the sacred fire was rekindled; old debts and grudges were forgotten; and a sense of community was regenerated.

Spiritual power might also reside in physical objects. Medicine men possessed sacred stones, quartz crystals, and other mystically endowed paraphernalia. Other objects were consecrated to symbolize the collective solidarity of the group. The Cherokees made use of a palanquin or litter within which were placed revered objects; the Tukabahchee Creeks possessed sacred embossed copper plates; the temples of several Lower Mississippi tribes contained an assortment of idols and icons. Natural objects could be infused with sacred power in a variety of ways: contact with thunder, as in lightning-struck wood; immersion in a rapidly flowing stream; exposure to the smoke of the sacred fire or of ritually prepared tobacco.

Mythology. Remnants of a formal theology can be reconstructed from early accounts of some of the stratified societies and of tribes who survived the immediate ravages of European contact. Most groups possessed origin myths, often involving a primal deluge into which prototypical beings from on high plunged to secure a portion of mud that magically expanded to create the Earth island. The subsequent course of mythological history is frequently related in terms of a cosmic struggle between good and bad culture heroes, one of whom bestows boons on mankind, the other serving as the source of the fatality and misfortune inherent in the human condition. Southeastern myths and folktales are populated by an incredible host of nature spirits, monsters, tricksters, giants, and little people. [222a]

Among many tribes, evidence survives that suggests belief in a supreme being, or master of breath. This ultimate divinity was frequently associated with the sun and its earthly aspect, fire. In addition, the world was viewed as divided into four quarters defined by the cardinal directions; each section had a presiding deity and appropriate color symbolism. Concern with the remote supreme being seems to have rested more with the priesthood than with the everyday activities of the average man. The life of the latter was more intimately tied up with more proximal spiritual beings who were felt to intervene more directly into human affairs.

Priests and diviners. In some of the wealthier stratified societies, priests were given specialized training and became full-time religious practitioners responsible for the spiritual health of the community and assuming responsibilities for conducting the major collective religious rituals that punctuated the annual cycle.

Complementary to the priesthood were various individual magico-medical practitioners, such as sorcerers, conjurors, diviners, and medicine men, who were generally only part-time specialists and catered to individual needs and crises, especially the treatment of illness. Medical therapy was intricately enmeshed in the magical view of the world but might include such practical procedures as isolation, sweating, bathing, bloodletting, sucking, vomiting, and the internal and external application of herbal medicines.

EVOLUTION OF THE CULTURES TODAY

The complex history of the Southeastern Indians after contact with Europeans can be outlined here only briefly. The 16th century witnessed European exploration of tile Southeast, though without permanent settlement. During the 17th century, white settlement was established on the coastal fringes, and the deerskin trade made the Indians increasingly dependent on whites for firearms, metal tools, and luxury items. By the 18th century the Southeastern Indians became counters in the power struggle between France, Spain, England, and the nascent United States for control of North America. With the ascendance of the United States, the military threat of the Indians became gradually neutralized, and Indians ceded large tracts of their land in an attempt to placate the insatiable appetite of land-hungry frontiersmen and the ensuing waves of white settlers.

Removal. A short-lived Indian renaissance occurred during the first third of the 19th century, when the major surviving Southeastern groups became known as the Five Civilized Tribes. Unabated pressure for Indian land continued, however, and federal policy eventually culminated in the 1830s in the removal of the Cherokees, Choctaws, Creeks, Chickasaws, and Seminoles to the Indian Territory west of the Mississippi. In the 1890s the tribal governments of the Five Civilized Tribes were dissolved and their lands were allotted, thus paving the way for Oklahoma statehood.

Most of the surviving Southeastern Indian population currently resides in Oklahoma. Although this population reflects a full spectrum of assimilation – from oil company executives to culturally conservative "full bloods"– the increasingly numerous segment of people occupying the culturally conservative end of the continuum live in poverty. Small contingents of Cherokee, Seminole, and Choctaw who managed to escape the general removal of the 1830s presently live on small reservations in their traditional homelands. In addition, several remnant groups, such as the Catawba, Lumbee, and Houma, remain in the Southeast, though much of their cultural distinctiveness has disappeared.

Bibliography

John R Swanton, The Indians of the Southeastern United States (1946), Is the standard starting point For information on the traditional cultures of the Southeast. Other indispensable works by Swanton are *Indian Tribes of the Lower Mississippi Valley and Adjacent Coast of the Gulf Of Mexico* (1911), Early *History of the Creek Indians and Their Neighbors* (1922, Reprinted 1970), *Social Organization and Social Usages of the Indians of the Creek Confederacy* (1928), *Religious Beliefs and Medical Practices of the Creek Indians* (1928), *Social and Religious Beliefs and Usages of the Chickasaw Indians* (1928). *Myths and Tales of the Southeastern Indians* (1929), *Source Material for the Social and Ceremonial Life of the Choctaw Indians* (1931), and *Source Material on the History and Ethnology of the Caddo Indians* (1942). Also valuable are various works by Frank G Speck, including, *The Creek Indians of Taskigi Town* (1907), *Ethnology of the Yuchi Indians* (1909), and, with Leonard Broom, *Cherokee Dance and Drama* (1951). James Mooney, *Myths of the Cherokee* (1900), remains the basic source on the Cherokee and may be usefully supplemented by William H Gilbert, *The Eastern Cherokees* (1943). For the Seminoles, Clay Maccauley, *The Seminole Indians of Florida* (1887); Alexander Spoehr, *Camp, Clan and Kin among the Cow Creek Seminole of Florida* (1941), and *The Florida Seminole Camp* (1944); and various articles by William C. Sturtevant, referred to in his essay "Creek into Seminole" In EB Leacock and NO Lurie, eds., *North American Indians In Historical Perspective* (1971), provide basic background. For the Piedmont Tribes, See James Mooney, *The Siouan Tribes of the East* (1894); and recent works by Douglas S Brown, *The Catawba Indians* (1966); and Charles M Hudson, *The Catawba Nation* (1970).

On more specialized topics, Mary R Haas, "Southeastern Indian Linguistics," In CM Hudson, ed, *Red, White, and Black* (1971), is the most reliable and up-to-date published review of linguistic relations; William C Sturtevant, The Significance of Ethnological Similarities between Southeastern North America and the Antilles (1960), clears up some difficult issues; Emma L Fundaburk and Mary D F Foreman, *Sun Circles and Human Hands* (1957), provides fine illustrations and commentary on prehistoric and historic Southeastern Art; John Witthoft, *Green Corn Ceremonialism in the Eastern Woodlands* (1949), is an important contribution to southeastern religion; as is James H Howard, *The Southeastern Ceremonial*

Complex and Its Interpretation (1968). Many detailed scholarly works on the post-contact history of the Southeastern Indians include Grant Foreman, *The Five Civilized Tribes* (1934, reprinted 1971), and *Indian Removal* (1932); Angie Debo, *And Still The Waters Run* (1940, reprinted 1966), ad *The Rise And Fall Of The Choctaw Republic* (1934); Robert S Cotterill, *The Southern Indians* (1954); Verner Crane, *The Southern Frontier, 1670-1732* (1929); David H Corkran, *The Cherokee Frontier* (1962) and *The Creek Frontier* (1967); and Thurman Wilkins, *Cherokee Tragedy* (1970).

(RDFogelson)

Gadugi

CHEROKEE ECONOMIC COOPERATIVES: THE GADUGI
With Paul Kutsche, The Colorado College

INTRODUCTION[6]

The Gadugi is an economic institution of considerable age that still persists in Big Cove, one of the more culturally conservative communities of the Eastern Cherokee. For present purposes, the Gadugi may be denned as a group of men who join together to form a company, with rules and officers, for continued economic and social reciprocity. Although James Mooney, the first full-fledged field ethnographer among the Cherokee, omits mention of the Gadugi as an important economic institution, other anthropologists (Starr 1898; Bloom MS.; Gilbert 1943; Speck and Schaeffer 1945; Witthoft 1947; and Gulick 1958) have noted the existence of the Gadugi and devoted various amounts of discussion to it.

Gilbert (1943: 306) and others have characterized the Gadugi as a surviving remnant of the aboriginal Cherokee town organization. Gilbert utilized material on Cherokee town organization contained in the Payne-Buttrick manuscripts to support this contention. This material was collected in the decades prior to the Removal in 1838 but, for the most part, represents an earlier phase of Cherokee culture as remembered by a few older informants. Speck and Schaeffer learned from the late Will West Long, a noted Cherokee informant, that the office of town chief or "light" chief survived in Big Cove until about 1875 (Speck and Schaeffer, 1945: 173). There is also some linguistic evidence for the connection between [88] the Gadugi and the older town organization. Mooney notes in his glossary the term "Gatugi," alternately "sgatugi," which he translates as "town settlement." One specific place name he lists as Gatutiyi (located near Robbinsville, N.C), and translates as "town building place" or "settlement place" (Mooney 1900: 519). When we checked Mooney's lead with a Cherokee informant in 1959, the evidence was confirmed: Gaduhui, he said, is a town, like Asheville or Bryson City, the county seat. Skadugi means township; for example, Big Cove.[7]2

---

6 This paper was presented in condensed form at the 58th annual meeting of the American Anthropological Association in Mexico City, 1959. The authors do not regard the present version as final. Many questions await further elucidation through additional field observation, and some important bibliographic sources have not yet been consulted (the Payne-Buttrick manuscripts on deposit at the Newberry Library in Chicago, J Haywood's" Natural and Aboriginal History of Tennessee," and some of the papers of Benjamin Hawkins). We wish to thank the Cross-Cultural Laboratory of the Institute for Research in Social Science of the University of North Carolina, John Gulck, director, under whose auspices our fieldwork was carried out; and the Department of Anthropology, University of Pennsylvania, for financial assistance. We should also like to acknowledge the advice and criticism offered us by Mr John Atkins, Dr Robbins Burling, Mrs Josephine Dixon, Dr William N Fenton, Dr A.I Hallowell, Mr Charles H Holzinger, Mr John G Sawyer, Miss Marianne L Stoller, Mr Robert K Thomas, Dr Anthony F C Wallace, and Mr John Witthoft. A special note of acknowledgment must go to our chief informant, Mr Lloyd Runningwolf Sequoyah of Big Cove.

7 Big Cove is a social and legal political entity, but its settlement pattern is similar to that of an American rural township. There is no real central cluster of dwellings or other buildings.

Another linguistic note suggests that the word for "bread" – *gadu* – may be related to the word for "town" or "company." *Gadu anigi*, said one informant, means "to eat bread." According to the same informant Gadugi means not only the cooperative work organization, but also, "Where all the group meets and eats bread together." A better-than-average dinner is an important part of every joint work party. No one would dare seek the aid of the Gadugi without serving them fried chicken and other choice food. Our informant told us. "If a Cherokee asks, When are we going to have Gadugi?, he

The purposes of the present paper are fourfold: (1) to document further the origin of the Gadugi in the aboriginal town organization; (2) to trace historically the forces responsible for the dissolution of the older town organization; (3) to present some background to and a description of the present state of the Gadugi in Big Cove; and (4) to append some brief comparative notes and, perhaps, leads for further research.

18th-Century Cherokee Towns

The territory occupied by the Cherokee at the beginning of the 18th century may be divided conveniently into four major areas, three of which possessed distinctive, though mutually intelligible dialects (Gilbert, 1943: 178-182). The Lower Cherokee occupied comparatively flat lands on the banks of the Tugaloo and Keeowee Rivers and their branches in what is now northwestern South Carolina. The Middle Settlement or Kituhwa district was situated in the mountainous region of western North Carolina with settlements along the Little Tennessee, Tuckaseegee, and their branches. The Overhill and Valley Settlements shared a similar dialect and were located, respectively, in eastern Tennessee and the extreme western tip of North Carolina. These regions were not as mountainous as the Middle Settlements and were well watered by the Little Tennessee, Hiwassee, French Broad, and Holston Rivers, and their tributaries. These four areas formed the settlement core of the nation, but, in addition, the Cherokee claimed dominion over a much wider area extending into parts of Virginia, West Virginia, Kentucky, Alabama, and Georgia. These wider extensions were used primarily as hunting lands and [89] served as neutral buffer areas separating the Cherokee from other tribes.

Throughout the 18th century there was a great acceleration of population movement among the Cherokee attributable to the advancing white frontier. In the first half of the century, the presence of the colonists was felt indirectly through intertribal strife and boundary rearrangements precipitated by the dislocation of tribes east of the Cherokee. This phase was followed by direct contact with whites eventuating in war and the destruction of numerous Cherokee villages. Increased pressure on the frontier resulted in land cessions by the Indians, further boundary encroachments by the white settlers, and further Indian cessions. Warfare and disease were important demographic factors during the 18th century. Smallpox epidemics in 1734 and 1783 were reported to have killed half of the Cherokee population.[8]3 Costly wars severely depleted the available number of adult males. Near the end of the 18th century, all the Cherokee settlements in South Carolina were ceded, and the center of population shifted southward, with heavy settlement in northern Georgia and northeastern Alabama.

The physical and spiritual center of 18th-century Cherokee life was the town. In reviewing the older sources, we have attempted to get estimates of the number of towns and their approximate populations. While there is much discrepancy in these early population estimates, some broad limits as to town size can be obtained. The Cherokee were the most numerous tribe in the Southeast, and Kroeber (1939: 141) gives an aboriginal population estimate of 22,000. In 1709, Governor Johnson of the Carolina Colony reported that the "Chereky Indians" had 5,000 (fighting) men settled in 60 towns (Williams 1937: 67, footnote). A population estimate in 1715 has a total of 60 towns distributed as follows (Crane, 1928: 131, footnote):

---

    means, 'When are we going to have the bread eating and the working?'"

8 Since the Cherokee were in the habit of burning houses where smallpox had struck, it is likely that many whole villages wore also deserted as a result of the disease. Other factors that swelled the mortality rate from smallpox were the traditional treatment of "going to water" (sweat baths followed by plunges into a nearby stream) and an outbreak of suicide that occurred when victims beheld their disease-scarred faces. (For further detail see the eye-witness account of Adair 1776: 244-246.)

Towns:	Number	Population	Mean
Upper (Overhill)	19	2,760	145
Middle (Middle and Valley)	30	6,350	212
Lower ----------	11	2,100	191
	60	11,210	187

These figures seem rather low, since disease and warfare had not yet greatly affected population size. Also, the criteria used for determining what constituted a town seem to be in doubt, since 6 years later [90] (1721), an estimate of the Overhill population revealed only 11 towns, while the population was held relatively constant at 2,725. In the latter estimate, the population per town ranged from 95 to 543 and yields a mean of 248 people (Williams 1937: 85-86).

Another census in 1721 reports a total population of 10,376 distributed in 53 towns which would average out to 196 per town (Mooney 1900: 34). Swanton (1946: 114) cites a 1729 estimate of 64 towns and a total population of 20,000 for an average of 313. In 1735 just prior to the first smallpox epidemic, Adair says, "they had 64 towns and villages and full of women and children," and later, "they amounted to upward of six thousand fighting men" (Adair 1775: 238). On this basis Mooney (1900: 34) believes that the total population was between 16,000 and 17,000; this would result in an average town population of 258.

For the next 40 years Cherokee census data arc poor. While references to fighting strength in terms of the number of warriors appeal-frequently, fighting strength is no longer a reliable index to total population because of an imbalance in the normal age-sex ratio. In the early 1770's Bartram compiled a list of 43 Cherokee towns, but gave no overall population estimates (Bartram 1791: 401). A distribution of annuities in 1799 included reference to 51 towns (Royce 1887: 144, footnote). In 1808-9, a town-by-town census gave a population of 12,395, but many Cherokee had by this time emigrated west to the Indian Territory (Swanton 1946: 114).

From these figures, it seems safe to say that the typical (18th-century) Cherokee town numbered between 200 and 325 persons. We realize that arithmetic moans may not give a true index of central tendency, and that many of the important and sacred mother towns were much larger with perhaps 600 people as an upper limit; the smallest town reported had a population of 95.

The settlement pattern was frequently determined by the contour of the land. In many cases, houses were located at the base of hills to take maximum advantage of tillable land and also to be near sources of fresh water. Where arable land was abundant, houses were sometimes clustered in the center of fields. The typical house was square or rectangular in shape.[9],4 It was constructed of a framework of upright poles, sunk in the ground, and covered by a bark, wood, or woven siding made weather tight by earth and clay. Each household usually included a small semisubterranean "âsi" or sweat-house for ritual purification, winter sleeping, and food storage. By 1775, typical frontier-type log cabins, made possible by the [91] introduction of European woodworking tools, had replaced the earlier type of dwelling (Malone 1956: 12).

The heart of the 18th-century Cherokee town was the centrally located council house. The earliest council houses were large earth lodges, circular or heptagonal in shape. They sometimes could accommodate as many as 500 people and were usually situated on a slight manmade elevation or ancient mound, often containing the remains of previous populations. Other features frequently associated in the council house complex were outdoor pavilions serving as a summer men's house, houses for important town officials and priests, and a cleared level field for ball play (Witthoft, this volume: 70). Later council

---

9 The Cherokee had summer dwellings which were reminiscent of the Iroquois longhouse in overall dimensions – "rarely exceeds sixteen feet in breadth ... but often extends to sixty or seventy feet in length ..." (Timberlake 1765: 87) – but, as Swanton notes, this was probably a single-family dwelling unit and, unlike the Iroquois longhouse, constructed of wattle and plaster (Swanton 1946: 404).

houses were constructed of logs and built above the ground.

The Cherokee had seven exogamous sibs with sib segments of each represented in varying proportions in each town.[10] Descent was reckoned matrilineally, and the kinship type conformed to a basic Crow system. Residence tended to be matrilocal, but residence rules were not rigid. Polygyny was the preferred form of marriage but had a low incidence. Sib membership was recognized in the seating arrangement in the council house and in the composition of certain bodies of the tribal government. There is some hint that, certain sibs had special functions and prerogatives, but the evidence is not clear. The sib was a major mechanism in social control through the exaction of blood revenge (Gilbert 1943: 216-253).

The political structure of the 18th-century Cherokee town was fairly elaborate and warrants some description. Two complementary political hierarchies, the Red and the White organizations, executed political control during times of war and peace, respectively. The White organization can be best considered a form of gerontocracy. It was headed by a White Chief (*Uku*), whom early travelers and Colonial administrators often erroneously equated with the European notion of king. This position was said to have been nonhereditary, but certain lineages appeared to have produced more chiefs than might be expected on the basis of chance alone (Gilbert 1957: 552-553). The White Chief had the power to call and preside over council meetings and served as an overseer in important communal activities, including agriculture. Under the *Uku* were a deputy chief, and a chief speaker selected for his oratorical abilities. Two councils wielded considerable influence in political decision making and policy formation: a body of counselors representing the seven sibs and a council of ciders that included all men over 55 years of age (or whose [92] hair had turned gray). In addition, the White organization included important religious officials, messengers, and various minor governmental and religious assistants (Gilbert 1943: 319-325).

The rule of the White organization can be characterized as benevolent paternalism. Decisions were generally unanimous, and direct coercion or overactive leadership were strongly devalued (Gearing MS., 1956). The officials tended to gain their authority through love and respect. The power of the old men can be vividly seen in an anecdote reported by Bartram about a Creek chief from Mucclesse:

> One morning after his attendants had led him to the council fire, before seating himself, he addressed himself to the people after this manner – "You yet love me; what can I do now to merit your regard? nothing; I am good for nothing; I cannot see to shoot the buck or hunt up the sturdy bear; I know I am but a burthen to you; I have lived long enough; now let my spirit go; I want to see the warriors of my youth in the country of spirits; (bareing his breast) here is the hatchet, take it and strike." They answered with one united voice, "We will not; we cannot; we want you here." [Bartram 1791: 392].

The Red or War organization assumed leadership of the town in times of military emergency. It also administered offensive war outside the town and served as a liaison in relations between the town and foreign powers.[11] This organization was headed by the "Raven" or great Red War Chief. This was an

---

10 Ethnographic literature to date has consistently employed the term "'clan" to denote the Cherokee unit of descent. There is no evidence, however, that the aboriginal in-marrying male was considered to have joined his wife's kin group, and he certainly does not do so at present. Therefore, following Murdock's usage, we apply the term "sib" to the Cherokee descent group (Murdoch, 1949: Chs 3, 4: 247).

11 It is our impression from reviewing early sources that the war chiefs were also the major trade contacts. Names of war chiefs frequently turn up leading trailing expeditions to Charlestown, and they often entered into ceremonial "brotherships" with white traders (see Rothrock 1929). During times of peace the war chief was probably seen as a dangerous man to have permanently in the village, so the society seems to have developed a pattern of keeping him away from the village as much as possible when, the threat of war was absent.

elected office that was earned by notable exploits as a warrior. The "Raven" was considerably younger than the White Chief, and he took an active part in war parties, traditionally being the first to engage in combat with the enemy and never retreating except when his men carried him away from the fray by force. Thus, in addition to being chief strategist and decision maker in war, he was also an inspirational leader and rallying point in the heat of battle. There is also some evidence that he took a paternalistic attitude toward the safety of his men and was morally charged with the responsibility of not exposing them to unnecessary danger. Like the White Chief, the Raven had an assistant or deputy chief. There were also seven counselors of war representing the seven sibs.

Exceptional women also had a role in the War organization. These women, variously called "Pretty Women," "War Women," or "Beloved Women," usually attained their rank by past heroic actions. They had a voice in council and decided the fate of prisoners. Other war officials included a speaker, a standard bearer, a surgeon with [93] three assistants, and war priests whose influence was such that they could recall war parties from the field when omens were unfavorable. Also within the warrior class, there was a system of grading. Three special scouts, the "Wolf," "Owl," and "Fox," scouted to the right, left, and rear, respectively. Warriors who had killed an enemy were given a special title. Boys under 25 were not admitted to warrior status.[12]7

The articulation between the Red and the White organizations was marked by ritual. Before leaving for the field, warriors fasted, observed sex taboos, and participated in an all-night dance to get them into a "war-like disposition." On their return to the village, they had to undergo many days of ceremonial purification before they were able to resume peaceful civil life (Gearing MS, 1956: 70).[13]8

This dual organization would not, technically, be classified as a political moiety system by Murdock (1956). While the local town Red-White dichotomy was replicated on a national level, unlike the Creeks, the Cherokee did not divide the towns of their nation into Red and White towns.[14]9

The seasonal cycle gave a clear-cut rhythm to the 18th-century Cherokee village structure. Small hunting parties went out from late October to early spring, and shorter hunts took place during the summer months (Gearing 1958: 1150). War parties generally left the village during the late fall and winter. The yearly calendar was regularly punctuated by religious ceremonies, the most important of which were the second Green Corn Feast in mid-September and the Now Fire or New Year ceremonies which took place near the end of October. The major religious ceremonies can be viewed as rites of intensification in which old grudges were forgiven, debts canceled, offenders pardoned, and unity of the town revitalized (Bartram 1791: 399).

The Cherokee subsistence pattern was one of mixed hunting, fishing, gathering, and agriculture. Larger game included the buffalo, deer, bear, beaver, opossum, wild turkey, and "pheasant" (ruffed grouse, See Bent 1932: 310). These were hunted with the bow and later with guns, first introduced about 1700. Deer pelts became an increasingly valuable item in trade with the English Colonies. With the development of a regulated fur trade, [94] about 1720, the Indian hunter became more and more dependent on European manufactures. In the second half of the 18th century, the fur trade diminished in intensity owing to reduced game resources and the loss of hunting territories. Large-game hunting was an exclusive male activity. Hunting parties consisted of only a few individuals who allied themselves more

---

12 Most of this material dealing with the dual political system of the Cherokee has been drawn from Gearing (ms, 1956: 1958) whom the interested reader should consult for further detail.
13 It is interesting to note that one of the Cherokee names for the ball game is translated as "little war," and many elements of war ritual can still be seen in ball game ceremonialism. The senior author hopes to make the ball game the subject of a later paper.
14 Some Cherokee towns were labeled White towns and considered towns of refuge, a fact seized upon by early writers attempting to make the Hebrew equation. However, we have encountered no evidence for the existence of contrasting Red towns. Thus there is no precise parallel to the elaborate Creek political moieties described by Swanton (1928a, Haas 1940).

for companionship and protection than for necessary coordination in seeking out and killing their prey.

Smaller game, such as rabbits, squirrels, small rodents, and birds, were hunted with the blowgun or caught in various traps and snares. Hunting with the blowgun tended, in the late 18th century, to be a sport and children's amusement (Timberlake 1765: 44-45). It is probable that women assisted in animal drives that were associated with the annual burning of the brush in the local village.

Fish were an important part of the Cherokee diet. Fish were caught in weirs, by hook and line, by drives into shallow areas, by spears, and by fish poisons. Timberlake (1765: 69) says that nets were not aboriginal, but Swanton (1946: 336) feels that this is "incredible."

Animal domestication seems to have been limited to dogs in aboriginal times. The horse was introduced about 1740 and rapidly became widespread. In times of dire need, horses were killed for food. The pig was received enthusiastically and flourished on a diet of mountain greens and chestnuts. For a long time, the Cherokee rejected cattle, probably because of the large expenditure of effort in maintaining them (Timberlake 1765: 72). Nevertheless, some more acculturated Cherokee began to engage in limited stock-raising near the end of the century.

Gathering was an important part of the native economy. Responsibility for gathering was invested mainly in the women, with some assistance from children. Important gathered foodstuffs included wild fruits, berries, and nuts.

The central pillar of Cherokee domestic economy was agriculture. Land was cleared by slash-and-burn techniques – girdling the bark and subsequent burning – an early description of which is given by Adair (1775: 435). The fertility of the Overhill Cherokee land was noted in glowing terms by the military architect, De Brahm, who in 1756 called the area, "the American Canaan," with soil "equal to manure itself, impossible in, appearance ever to wear out ..." (Williams 1928: 193).

Adair alludes to a dual system of private household gardens and larger community fields. The private gardens were located close to the dwelling houses and were fenced to keep off the horses. On these small plots were grown various beans, peas, and "the smaller sort of [95] Indian corn which usually ripens in two months" (Adair 1930: 435-436). These private household gardens were in contrast to the larger "out fields," which were not fenced and were worked communally. In Adair's words:

> The chief part of the Indians begin to plant their out-fields, when the wild fruit is so ripe, as to draw off the birds from picking up the grain. This is their general rule, which is in the beginning of May, about the time the traders set off for the English settlements. Among several nations of Indians, each town usually works together. Previous thereto, an old beloved man warns the inhabitants to be ready to plant on a prefixed day. At the dawn of it, one by order goes aloft, and whoops to them with shrill calls, "that the new year is far advanced, – that he who expects to eat must work, – and that he who will not work, must expect to pay the fine according to old custom, or leave the town, as they will not sweat themselves for an healthy idle waster." At such times, may be seen many war-chieftains working in common with the people.... About an hour after sun-rise, they enter the field agreed on by lot, and fail to work with great cheerfulness; sometimes one of their orators cheers them with jests and humorous old tales, and sings several of their most agreeable wild tunes, beating also with a stick in his right hand, on the top of an earthen pot covered with a wet and well-stretched deerskin: thus they proceed from field to field, till their seed is sown [Adair 1775: 436-437].

As to the details of planting, Adair reports,

> They plant their corn in straight rows, putting five or six grains into one hole, about two inches distant – They cover them with clay in the form of a small hill. Each row is a yard asunder, and in the vacant ground they plant pumpkins, water-melons, marsh-mallows, sun-flowers, and sundry sorts of beans and peas, the last two of which yield a large increase [Ibid: 439].

The women seem to have had some special agricultural duties, for Adair also says that, "The women plant also pompions, and different sorts of melons, in separate fields, at a considerable distance from the town" (ibid: 438).

Bartram, who visited the Southern Indians in the 1770's, maintains that the reputed communism of the Indians has been "too vague and general." His description of Indian agriculture stresses communal work activity as superimposed over a system of individual ownership or land rights. Bartram's detailed observations follow:

> An Indian town is generally so situated, as to be convenient for procuring game, secure from sudden invasion, having a large district of excellent arable land adjoining, or in its vicinity, if possible on an isthmus betwixt two waters, or where the doubling of a river forms a peninsula. Such a situation generally comprises a sufficient body of excellent land for planting Corn, Potatoes, Beans, Squash, Pumpkins, Citruls, Melons, &c., and is taken in with a small expence and trouble of fencing, to secure the crops from the invasion of predatory animals. At other times however they choose such a convenient fertile spot at some distance from their town, when circumstances will not admit of having both together.
>
> This is their common plantation, and the whole town plant in one vast field together; but yet the part or share of every individual family or habitation, is [96] separated from the next adjoining, by a narrow strip, or verge of grass, or any other natural or artificial boundary.
>
> In the spring, the ground being already prepared on one and the same day, early in the morning, the whole town is summoned, by the sound of a conch shell, from the mouth of the overseer, to meet at the public square, whither the people repair with their hoes and axes; and from thence proceed to their plantation, where they begin to plant, not every one in his own little district, assigned and laid out, but the whole community united begins on one certain part of the field, where they plant on until finished; and when their rising crops are ready for dressing and cleansing they proceed after the same order, and so on day after day, until the crop is laid by for ripening. After the feast of the busk is over, and all the grain is ripe, the whole town again assemble, and every man carries off the fruits of his labor, from the part first allotted to him, which he deposits in his own granary; which is individually his own. But previous to their carrying off their crops from the field, there is a large crib or granary, erected in the plantation, which is called the king's crib; and to this each family carries and deposits a certain quantity, according to his ability or inclination, or none at all if he so chooses: this in appearance seems a tribute or revenue to the mico; but in fact is designed for another purpose, i.e. that of a public treasury, supplied by a few and voluntary contributions, and to which every citizen has the right of free and equal access, when his own private stores are consumed; to serve as a surplus to fly to for succour; to assist neighboring towns, whose crops may have failed; accommodate strangers, or travellers; afford provisions or supplies, when they go forth on hostile expeditions; and for all other exigencies of the state: and this treasure is at the disposal of the king or mico; which is surely a royal attribute, to have an exclusive right and ability in a community to distribute comfort and blessings to the necessitous. [Bartram 1791: 400-401.]

Bartram's and Adair's observations were given corroboration by Brother Martin Schneider, a Moravian missionary who journeyed into the Cherokee area in 1783-84. He writes:

> In the Midst of every Town is, as it were, a round Tower of Earth about 20 Feet high almost like a Heap where Coals are burnt, on which is a little House, but which have been mostly burnt down in the last War. Here the first Chief climbs up every Morning at the Time of the Work in

the Field, & calls the People with a loud voice together; these must come with their Indian-Corn Hoes, & go together in proper Order to Work. And tho' every Family has its own Field, yet they begin fellowshiply on one End, & continue so one after the other till they have finished all. As every one must come & hoe (he may have planted or not) it seems they prevent thereby that not easily a Family can come to Want by Carelessness. They dare not go from their Work till in the Evening, but the Women must bring them their Victuals into the Field [Williams 1928: 261].

This same communal organization of men which tilled the fields, also rapidly erected both private and public buildings in the town, and the men of one town or neighborhood frequently helped those of the next (Adair 1775: 444).

From the above-cited eyewitness accounts of 18th-century Cherokee agriculture, we may conclude that men played a more active role than has generally boon assumed. It is fairly certain that men engaged in the heavier labor of clearing the land, planting, and reaping [97] the harvest. In times of war, this arrangement was probably upset, but it is interesting to note that whenever they had any choice, as when Colonial authorities sought their aid in fighting French Indians, the Cherokee usually delayed going on the warpath until the late fall. Summer hunting parties seem to have departed after the corn was in the ground and returned before harvest time. Thus it appears that sufficient male labor was available during the most arduous phases of agriculture. We can assume that weeding and other lighter maintenance tasks in the communal fields were performed by women, older children, older men, and a few of the younger men who had chosen to stay home.[15]10

In this organization of agricultural activity, we can also see elements that persist today in the Gadugi. These elements include overseers, warners and advance notification of work days, women as cooks, a communal treasury, aid to the poor, aged, and misfortunate, and the working of each other's fields in concert.

Looked at from a broader context, the 18th-century Cherokee town can be seen as a predominantly autonomous self-sufficient unit with a highly developed sense of identity. This sense of identity can be inferred from an account by Col. George Chicken who visited the Cherokee country in 1725. He describes the town of Tellico as –

... very Compact and thick Settled ... Here are two town Housses in this Town by reason they are the people of Two towns settled together ... both Enforted and their houses which they live in all Muskett proof [Williams 1928: 98-99].

This separate identity continued to be recognized, for in 1741, Antoine Bonnefoy, a French captive, reports being taken to an Overhill settlement called "Chateauké and Talekoa [Tellico], which are two different councils, though the cabins are mingled together indistinguishably" (ibid, 1928: 152-153). Town identity was fostered by intertown rivalry, as in the ball game, a symbolic substitute for war. The separateness of the town is also underscored by the fact that, as Bartram noted, each town celebrated the busk or second Green Corn Ceremony individually, when its own harvest was ready (Bartram 1791: 399).

Although the officers of the local Red and White organizations were reduplicated on a national level, the power of the Great White Chief and chief warrior of the nation was nominal throughout all but the last phases of the 18th century. This lack of adequate centralized [98] authority was a continued source of vexation to early Colonial administrations who desired to treat with the Cherokee but were frus-

---

15 We have tried to establish a case for male participation in agriculture for the Cherokee. However, our present sources are not sufficient to determine whether the male assisted his mother and the sibmates of his matrilineal kin group in agricultural pursuits, or whether he worked in the contest of his family of procreation with his wife's group. Witthoft (pc), on the basis of sources not yet consulted by the authors, feels that males participated in farming as members of their mothers' households.

trated in securing agreements that would be binding to the whole nation. In the latter portion of the century, the Cherokee achieved increased political unification in response to the advancing white frontier. A national spirit began to emerge that gradually stripped the local town of much of its previous autonomy and independence.

The Effects of Acculturation, 1790-1838

The rhythm of Cherokee economic life was shattered after the American Revolution, which unleashed a flood of emigration toward the Cherokee borders. Cherokee strength was so sapped by constant bloodshed and the razing of their villages, that the main body of the nation sued for peace in 1782. A group of dissident Cherokee warriors, led by Dragging Canoe, refused to bury the red-stained tomahawk and removed themselves to the Chicamauga district, near present-day Chattanooga, where they were decisively defeated in 1792. This separate settlement of the Red organization can be viewed as the death blow of the older tribal political structure.

After the war, the Cherokee embarked on a path of conscious acculturation. Agriculture was given added importance in the new-scheme of things, since the former patterns of warfare and hunting were now effectively blocked through careful maintenance of peace, the ceding of hunting territories, and the thinning out of game. President Washington obligingly wrote into the Treaty of 1791 stipulations for agricultural implements and instruction. It was hoped that if the Cherokee became a nation of farmers, they would require less land and be more amenable to further land cessions to appease the growing demands of Georgia and other States. A minority of Cherokee did not want to give up the hunting life, and the Federal Government encouraged them to emigrate to the West, where they might continue to follow the older way of life with no interference. Small bands began to set out for the West about 1785, and in 1835, the "Cherokee West" numbered several thousand.

By about 1815, there were privately owned Cherokee farmsteads in north Georgia and other fertile bottom lands in the nation which rivaled any white American plantations of the area in appointments and number of Negro slaves. Commercial cropping began to replace the subsistence agriculture-plus-hunting-and-gathering of the earlier decades. Contemporary reports citing figures on livestock and produce attest to the sudden new prosperity. The owners of these plantations were wealthy mixbloods, the progeny of previous traders and coureurs de bois. This new landed gentry, many of whom were [99] educated in American schools, began to assume the role of a nascent aristocracy and rapidly gained ascendancy in Cherokee political affairs. Aboriginal patterns of kinship and religion were breaking down under the onslaught of missionaries who were successful in converting the nation to Christianity and bringing schools to the Cherokee.

However, most of these developments were taking place in the southern portion of the nation where rich bottom land abounded and communication with white population centers and markets was easy. The less richly endowed and less accessible Middle Settlements contained a greater percentage of fullbloods who tended to remain culturally conservative and marginal to the efflorescence occurring farther south. These people could not afford large numbers of slaves, and their mountain ecology would not permit a plantation system. Small-scale subsistence farming and hunting, where possible, continued to prevail.

Change in Cherokee political structure took place rapidly. A traditional type of White Chief together with a body of representative elders ruled the nation until 1820; soon thereafter, the mixbloods rose to political power and the nation was remodeled into a republic along the lines of the United States Government. A constitution ratified in 1827 provided for an elected chief and vice chief to serve as law-enforcement officers. The nation was divided into eight election districts. With these sweeping changes, the days of local town autonomy were officially over. Only as a unified national state could the Cherokee engage in their gallant, but futile, struggle to retain ancestral rights to their lands in the face of ever-increasing pressure for their removal by the young, bicep-flexing United States, bent on fulfilling its "manifest destiny."

Despite the modifications in the formal Cherokee political structure, some echo of the older form of town organization seemed to persist in some areas. As Malone notes,

> Although the villages were shown as individual spots on various maps, many were actually areas of some distance in length, containing scattered houses and farms. One of the most lasting institutions of Cherokee local government was the office of Town Chief, whose authority extended well into the period of the republic. Judging by appearance in Cherokee geography of such names as Going Snake's Town, Thomas Foreman's Town, and Vann's Old Town, the Town Chief must indeed have controlled not merely a cluster of houses, but an area more nearly like a township or a city-state [Malone 1956: 119].

We have tried to establish a case for male participation In agriculture for the Cherokee. However, our present sources are not sufficient to determine whether the male assisted his mother and the sibmates of his matrilineal kin group in agricultural pursuits, or whether he worked in the contest of his family of procreation with his wife's group. Witthoft (p. c.), on the basis of sources not yet consulted by the authors, feels that males participated in farming as members of their mothers' households.

We lack documentary evidence pertaining to the degree that communal agriculture was practiced, but it seems reasonable to assume older agricultural forms persisted in the less acculturated regions. [100]

The period of American-style agricultural prosperity, a golden few years which is unique among American Indians, exploded in catastrophe in 1835 when the fraudulent Treaty of New Echota was ratified by Congress, and 3 years later the Cherokee were forcibly removed to the Indian Territory west of the Mississippi. One sidelight of the Removal suggests the endurance of the older town organization. The United States troops experienced initial difficulty in organizing groups for Removal. After the first emigrants had departed, Chief John robs succeeded in winning a temporary postponement to avoid traveling in the sickly summer season. It was agreed that the remaining Cherokee would remove themselves in their own fashion. The subsequent emigration seems to have been organized along town lines, led by the local chief (personal conversation with Robert K Thomas).[16]11

The Gadugi in Eastern Cherokee
Community Organization, 1838-1959

Several hundred Cherokee escaped Removal by hiding in the wilderness of the Great Smoky Mountains. Realizing the impossibility of tracking down these people, Gen. Winfield Scott, charged with the responsibility of carrying out the terms of the Removal, struck a face-saving compromise. If the Indians would surrender Tsali and his brothers, who were involved in the killing of some soldiers, Scott agreed to let the others remain. This was done and Tsali and his brothers were duly executed.[17]12

The survivors of the Removal still faced the problem of being landless aliens in their own country. This problem was soon solved by Will Thomas, an enterprising white trader and lifelong friend of the Cherokee. With money donated by the estranged Indians supplemented by his own personal funds, Thomas purchased most of the tract that presently constitutes the Qualla Reservation. This land is located in Swain and Jackson Counties, one of the most rugged portions of western North Carolina. Although

---

16 It would be a worthwhile investigation to follow the fate of the local town organization in Oklahoma. A promising lead might be an examination of the reflections of the older town organization in the structure of the Kee-too-wah societies, but this Is beyond the writers' present knowledge and the scope of this paper. For the persistence of the Creek town organization in Oklahoma, see Opler 1952.

17 Accounts of Tsali's martyrdom vary in details (see Mooney 1900: 131, 157-158; Lanman 1849: 112-114; and Arthur 1914).

well watered by the Oconaluftee, a rapid mountain stream, and its various branches, good bottom land is not plentiful. At the time of purchase, the area was rich in natural timber resources and wild game. Where bottom land is not available, hillside slopes are cultivated, and 45-degree cornfields are not uncommon. During the 19th century, the reservation [101] was fairly well isolated from the rest of the world. Some idea of the relative isolation can be inferred from the fact that in 1875, a government official required 2 days to reach the reservation from Asheville, N.C, a distance of 50 miles that can now be traveled in slightly over an hour by automobile (Bloom ms: 70).

Thomas assumed a paternal role toward the Eastern Cherokee, serving as agent, adviser, and effective political leader until his health failed after the Civil War. Shortly after the Removal, the population of the Eastern Cherokee was about 1,000, a figure swelled somewhat by persons who escaped en route to Oklahoma and found their way back. Although this population was not entirely homogeneous, the vast majority were Middle Cherokee, who had long been residents of the area.

The land was divided somewhat arbitrarily into five contiguous townships that still remain today; these are called Birdtown, Yellow Hill, Painttown, Wolftown, and Big Cove. The manner in which people were assigned to these districts is not known, but it is probable that kinship, sib membership, and former local affiliation were important determinants. For our purposes, it is important to note that the new settlement arrangement was artificial in comparison with the natural unity of older town structure. On the one hand, the reservation as a whole tried to function as a single town but failed for reasons which we will go into shortly. On the other hand, the five townships, while achieving some individual integration, lacked sufficient size and diversity of membership to attain the status of towns as defined in the older sense. Nevertheless, there was a conscious attempt to graft the traditional Cherokee social organization onto the new circumstances.

Under the leadership of Yonaguska (Drowning Bear), a former peace chief, an old-style council house was erected in Wolftown to serve the needs of the whole band for a central meeting place (Mooney 1900: 161, 163). This edifice was described by Lanman in 1849 as, "... built of hewn logs, very large and circular, without any floor but that of solid earth, and without any scats but one short bench intended for the great men of the nation" (Lanman 1849: 101). We learn from the same author that a sacred fire burned continually in the center of the building and that a large ball field was located just outside (ibid: 104). Soon after Lanman's visit the building fell into disrepair and tumbled down. Gulick lists three factors responsible for the failure of the old-style council town to endure: (1) prior widespread adoption of white-type farmstead; (2) Christian influences in undermining the old ceremonial center's symbolic power; (3) the composite local origin of the people which made them resistant to becoming members of a single, highly integrated community [102] (Gulick 1958: 248). In addition, the location was not really central nor was it equally accessible to all parts of the reservation.

During the same period, the organization of the local settlements also showed considerable nativistic retention. Speck and Schaeffer obtained valuable information about the former structure of the local community from Will West Long. Each village settlement community had a "lead chief" or "light chief" (noted also in Lanman 1849: 94). Speck and Schaeffer write:

> Each settlement handled its own public, legislative, and social affairs as a small independent unit. The community chief or "lead chief" was the social factor in organizing the group's activities and formulating policies. He administered control through a body of 12 men, known as *ani tawis kagu* (smooth men)[18]13 whom he appointed. They served as police or sheriffs, having official authority to arrest and punish, according to tribal mores, men and women guilty of misdemeanor. They reserved the right to decide the degree of punishment for minor offense by whipping with sticks (4 to 12 lashes), or they could even pronounce acquittal. The mutual aid cooperative was a branch of this arm of community organization; its affairs were appointed by

---

18 One of our informants feels this term is better translated as "honest men."

the company itself, and authorized by the community lead chief.

The last "lead chief" of Big Cove was a man by the name of Chiltoski ("Tailing Corn-Tassel"), and the office fell into disuse after 1875 (Speck and Schaeffer 1945: 175).[19][14]

Lanman gives a picture of relative cultural stability and prosperity for the Qualla Cherokee during his 1848 visit:

> About three-fourths of the entire population can read in their own language, and though the majority of them understand English, a very few can speak the language. They practice, to a considerable extent, the science of agriculture, and have acquired such a knowledge of the mechanic arts as answers them for all ordinary purposes, for they manufacture their own clothing, their own ploughs, and other farming utensils, their own axes, and even their own guns .... They keep the same domestic animals that are kept by their white neighbors and cultivate all the common grains of the country. They are probably as temperate as any other class of people on the face of the earth .... They are chiefly Methodists and Baptists, and have regularly ordained ministers, who preach to them on every Sabbath, and they have also abandoned many of their more senseless superstitions .... Except on festive days, they dress after the manner of the white man, but far more picturesquely. They live in small log houses of their own construction, and have everything they need or desire in the way of food. They are, in fact, the happiest community that I have yet met within this Southern country .... [Lanman 1849: 94-95.]

Lanman (1849: 93, 100, 104) also mentions that ball games and dancing were popular activities and that about 100 Catawba were living on the reservation.[20][15] [103]

Very little information is available for the Eastern Cherokee from 1848 until the outbreak of the Civil War. When the war erupted, Thomas was made a colonel in the Confederate Army, and 400 Cherokee were recruited to serve in his Legion. The Cherokee were assigned the task of acting as a home guard and engaged in only a few minor skirmishes with Federal troops. Nevertheless, the war had some disastrous aftermaths for the Cherokee. Some of the soldiers who had joined the Union forces contracted smallpox, and on their return, an epidemic burst loose on the reservation killing about 100 persons, a sizable percentage of the population. In addition, Colonel Thomas went bankrupt and suffered a mental collapse from which he never recovered. Now, not only was leadership uncertain, but Thomas' bankruptcy threatened confiscation of the tribal lands, the deeds to which were in Thomas' name. This legal problem was not settled until 1876, when the Federal Government assumed trusteeship of the reservation.

It is not entirely clear how the Cherokee governed themselves during the slender times following the Civil War, since few travelers visited them to leave records. We are inclined to assume that they reverted to a town organization under individual "lead chiefs," with each of the five townships attaining some degree of autonomy from the others. Such an arrangement at least makes the best logical sense, in view of their previous history and in view of the economic arrangements found by later observers.

In 1870, the Eastern Cherokee revamped their government along white lines. Elections were held and a chief, vice chief, and a tribal council consisting of two representatives from each township were put into office. Five years later a written constitution was adopted (Mooney 1900: 173). The near synchronism of the new tribal government and the passing of the traditional office of "lead chief" was probably not coincidental. Leadership of the community seems to have passed into the hands of the

---

19 A man by the name of Chiltoski was reported to have still been living in a commodious house on a prosperous farmstead in Big Cove as late as 1892 (Donaldson 1892: 12).

20 Relations with these surviving Catawba soon became strained, and they left to resettle in their former homes in South Carolina before the Civil War. During their stay, there was some intermarriage, and the Catawba served to reintroduce pottery, a lost art among the Eastern Cherokee.

council representatives whose glance was now directed outward to the reservation as a whole, rather than focusing exclusively inward to the internal affairs of the local community.

The fortunes of the Eastern Cherokee seemed to vacillate during the three decades prior to 1900. One reason for this was a population decrease occasioned by the partially successful efforts of the Western Cherokee to reunify the Nation by luring Eastern Cherokee to Oklahoma. Also, the scars left by the Civil War were a long time healing. Reports in 1875 and 1880 describe the Eastern Band as "destitute and discouraged, almost without stock or farming tools" (Mooney 1900: 174), and "in a most deplorable condition," landless, "scarcely able to live," and without schools (Wardell 1938: 245). Quakers [104] remedied the lack of education by establishing the first school in 1881. The next year, travelers Zeigler and Grosscup, who stopped a few days in the Qualla Reservation, reported that the chief lived like a comfortable Victorian gentleman. But "The fields, originally of average fertility, are worn out by bad farming. There is an abundance of fruit – apples, peaches, and plums. The predominant crop is corn, which is reduced to meal by the simple little mills common to the mountain country" (Zeigler and Grosscup 1883: 36). The sale of ponies and cattle provided the small amount of cash needed for taxes and purchases.

There are descriptions of the Gadugi in essentially its present form from the early 1890's. Frederick Starr, the early physical anthropologist of the University of Chicago, visited the reservation about this time, and afterward in a grammar school text about Indians, says this of the Eastern Cherokee:

Their fields are fenced and well cultivated. They work them in companies of ten to twelve persons: such companies are formed to work the fields of each member in order [Starr 1898: 144].

In 1892, Carrington, while collecting statistics for the Interior Department, observed a similar company at work in Wolf town, and notes:

. . . upon the hillsides, so steep that it seemed as if wings or ladders would be needed for tillage, several patches of from 5 to 10 acres were green with well-developed wheat, and on one of the slopes a "working bee" of 30 men, women and children were uniting their forces to help a neighbor put in his corn. In places where even a single steer could not hold footing with the lightest plow, a long line of willing workers hoed successive parallel seed trenches [Donaldson 1892: 12].

Near the turn of the century, the Gadugis began to hire out their services to white farmers in the vicinity. Whereas formerly the Gadugi seems to have been based on a simple exchange of services between neighbors, the addition of money brought about certain changes in its organization. When the Gadugi was hired out, the funds received were placed in a common treasury which was annually divided up among the members. Members had the privilege of borrowing money from the treasury provided that they put up sufficient collateral in the form of a mortgage on items of personal property, as stock, house, etc. (Gilbert 1943: 212). Although the Gadugi felt it had the right to claim mortgaged property for failure to repay loans, we have yet to hear of any instance where such action was ever taken. Rather, it seems that until recently the threat of physical coercion or ostracism from the group was sufficient to bring recalcitrant members back into line.

Seen from historical perspective, the introduction of money and the notion of a communal treasury did not constitute an entirely new [105] dimension to the agricultural organization. The town organization of the 18th century included a communal granary, where grain was stored for assistance to needy people, special events, and the support of town officials. In one sense then, money can be seen as a functional substitute for grain. However, the analogy is far from neat, for as Gilbert mentions, the hiring out of the Gadugi –

... led to a dependence on white people for wages and subsistence instead of a reliance on their own unaided cultivation of the soil by mutual aid. Consequently the gadugi came under the North Carolina regulations as to corporations and became subject to taxation. Unable to meet the taxes from their earnings, the gadugi soon declined and mostly disappeared in the opening years of the twentieth century. To this decline the Cherokee attribute the reason for the disappearance of the once prosperous farms that used to dot the hillsides of their country. [Gilbert 1943: 362.]

These legal actions may have been the death blow to the Gadugi in many townships, but the organization still managed to survive in Big Cove.

Another significant development seems to have taken place probably about the turn of the century. The Gadugi and the poor-aid society apparently split into separate organizations. Whereas formerly these two groups were fused together as two arms of the local town organization (Speck and Schaeffer 1945: 175), they now became differentiated and possessed separate rosters of officers. These two organizations differed in that the Gadugi was a smaller, more tightly knit cooperative with regularly scheduled activities usually focusing on agriculture, while the poor-aid society tended to be a looser, more communitywide organization which was mobilized only in times of crisis or need, as the management of funerals for deceased townsmen, the rebuilding and furnishing of someone's house after fire, or the donation of material aid and labor to the aged, handicapped, or infirm. These were not entirely exclusive organizations since membership and function often overlapped. For example, if a townsman took ill, the poor-aid society might donate its services to the upkeep of his fields until he regained health (Mooney and Olbrechts 1932: 80).

The weakening of the poor-aid society in Yellow Hill as the result of white influence has been described by Gilbert (1943: 362-363). The opening of a manual training course in the Government school in which, among other things, the students built coffins, soon deposed the coffinmaker, a previously important position in the poor-aid hierarchy. In addition, the opening of an Agency hospital and the distribution of Government relief checks gradually stripped the poor-aid society of its most important functions. Today in many of the reservation communities the existence of these organizations is [106] given mere lipservice. Since World War II, Community Clubs, introduced and sponsored by the State of North Carolina, have tended to replace the poor-aid societies as organizational frameworks for communitywide action. In Big Cove some previous functions of the poor-aid society, such as grave digging, have been reabsorbed by the Gadugis.

In the 1920's, a lumber company obtained rights to cut trees on the reservation and adjoining areas. Railroad spurs and temporary sawmills were quickly constructed, and a brief period of prosperity ensued. Indians were hired singly and in Gadugi groups to assist in the lumbering operations. A few short years later the company left, having denuded the area of much, of its best timber. Many Cherokee who had come to depend on the lumber company's wages were suddenly jobless.

Following closely on the heels of the lumber company's departure was the chestnut blight. The loss of the chestnut tree had important repercussions on the local economy. Besides losing an excellent fuel and building material, the Cherokee also lost the chestnut itself, one of the delicacies in their diet. More important, the chestnut had helped maintain the local game supply, besides serving as fodder for domestic animals who in the past had been left free to forage for themselves in the forests.

Two governmental regulations also played a role in disturbing the local economy. The age-old Cherokee practice of burning the brush every autumn was deemed a threat to the forest and forbidden by the Interior Department.[21]16 The annual burning had helped to restore fertility to the soil and also helped to control secondary regrowth. The Cherokee feel that this regulation is causally linked to the chestnut blight. The enforcement of the State fencing law had a more direct effect on the economy. This law,

---

21 This makes no sense to the Cherokee. They feel that the dead brush that accumulates on the forest floor increases the possibility of serious forest fire.

which required that all domestic animals be enclosed by fences, succeeded in killing practically all stockraising in the region and was directly responsible for the declining prosperity of local farmsteads.

The national depression, although it affected the subsistence agriculture of the Cherokee less than it did industrial areas, was a severe blow. Government relief funds eased some of the economic pressure. After World War II came a tourist boom that was stimulated partly by the new Great Smoky Mountains National Park, which has a long common border with the Qualla Reservation. Economic conditions have now improved somewhat, but the relative prosperity and self-sufficiency of the independent farmer, depicted during the period from 1890-1920, which is remembered by informants as a sort of golden [107] age, has never been completely regained. At present, the tribal council is endeavoring with fair success to attract small industry to the reservation.

There are three Gadugis operating in Big Cove today. About one-fourth of the adult population belongs to these organizations. Two of these have long been separate, the division having been noted by Gilbert in 1932 (1943: 212) and probably extending further back in time. This division seems to be based on geography, one group serving "Stony" or "Calico," the lower section of Big Cove, and the other serving the "Upper Cove" and "Bunches Creek." Although Big Cove is segmented into many subdistricts or wards, the principal division between Upper and Lower Big Cove seems to have been of long standing. In the past the two sections engaged each other in stickball, and today each has its own softball team. In addition, churches are situated in each district and tend to recruit membership locally. If not impeded by external factors, this process of increasing differentiation might have led to the formation of two separate communities. A common grammar school, a community club, and common representation in the tribal council tend to unite the larger community, but the underlying sectionalism is still present. The Lower Big Cove Gadugi has deteriorated of late and only numbers about five or six active members, most of whom are "White Indians." In the past, membership was larger, and the group was more active. This Gadugi seems to have declined since the death of its former chief many years ago.

The Gadugi in Upper Big Cove split into two groups about 5 years ago because of internal dissension. The newer group blames the split on the dishonesty of the former treasurer[22]17 and the general laziness of the members, while the parent group feels the split was caused by gossiping wives. It is interesting to note that the break seems to have been along matrilineal lines, since the nucleus of the new group is formed by three sisters and their families. Although the Gadugi is supposedly a male organization, this split left two sets of brothers in different Gadugis, suggesting that while the overt structure of the Gadugi is male dominated, females possess much power in the latent structure of the organization. The newer group has about 15 active members, while the older has about 25. Although this split cannot be accounted for by geographic considerations, probably the size of the organization and the increased possibility of interpersonal clashes were important determinants. It appears that a membership of about 30 is the optimum for a smooth-running Gadugi. Beyond this size the organization seems to become unwieldy. [108]

In 1958, the larger Gadugi elected a full roster of officers.[23]18 The organization is headed by a chief and an assistant chief who decide what work shall be done and where, and serve as overseers during the work.[24]19 The secretary keeps a record of attendance at work parties, of the election of officers, and of changes in the rules. The treasurer records the amount of money collected at social meetings, and its disbursement. Theoretically speaking, women are not supposed to hold office in the Gadugi, except as cooks, but in this instance a woman was elected treasurer. Two warners or messengers, young men

---

22 This man has since been accused of squandering funds by the older Gadugi and has joined the newer group, where, we arc told, he will never be entrusted with the office of treasurer.

23 See translation of the Gadugi's minutes in Appendix 2.

24 While the data of Speck and Schaeffer (1945) suggest that the office of poor-aid leader was a survival of the older office of peace chief, Gearing (1958: 1157, footnote) states that the word for a Gadugi foreman means war chief. Our field data support Gearing's statement.

chosen from different neighborhoods, notify the members of approaching work parties. Other positions include a grave-digger's foreman, a carpenter's foreman,[25]20 and four female cooks.[26]21 This Gadugi boasts a distinctive and, we think, rather informal office – the "chairman" or adviser – filled by an elderly man who is one of the few men in Big Cove still fluent in Sequoyah's syllabary and able to keep records in Cherokee for the group.

Whenever the Gadugi works someone's fields or chops wood for a needy person, the recipient of the labor is obligated to serve the group a meal. This is no ordinary repast but a minor feast, usually including fried chicken and many other delicacies. While the elected cooks handle the cooking chores, the food must be supplied by the host. This frequently results in a seeming contradiction, of goals. A needy person requiring the help of the Gadugi often has to borrow money in order to food the group in proper fashion.

In the summer, the Gadugi can be summoned on 1 day's notice, but during the winter 3 days' notification is necessary. When the corn is planted, the Gadugi may meet to work two or three times during 1 week, and then may not meet for another 2 or 3 weeks. During the winter, the chief function of the Gadugi is to cut wood for old or incapacitated members. The Gadugi also contributes labor to the building of houses and foot bridges.

Most informants agree that in the past the Gadugi was a very efficient work team. Not only were clearing, planting, and harvesting the fields considered group endeavors, but also weeding and "topping" the corn during the growing season. White men in the community often were members of the organization and worked side by side with the Indians. In the old days, a work party was looked upon as a very happy occasion. Fifty or more people would gather at the appointed field; each person would be responsible for one or more rows of corn [109] and go along it to the end. There were so many workers that the Job was always finished quickly. Old men hated to be left out and would be given small plots to hoe along with the rest. The old people would also sit around and tell stories and contribute in general to the group morale. Children, who were also part of the scene, would play games or make themselves useful by fetching water for the workers or performing other light tasks. While the group toiled, the cooks prepared enormous feasts which are still remembered with reminiscent appetite. Those who were unable to join in the work on the announced day would often donate food or money to compensate for their absence.

Recent observations of the Gadugis in action stand in marked contrast to the sunny chunks of memory culture reported above. Work parties of the 1950's do not attract such numbers, and one hears frequent complaints about people who turn up just before dinner and disappear shortly after.

Perhaps some of the most significant recent developments in the Gadugi are pic socials and box suppers, institutions that were first introduced about 1918 by mission churches and adopted by the Gadugis within the past 10 years. One night a week at the home of one of the members, boxes of fried chicken or fish with bean bread, and other local delicacies, or cakes and pies are donated and auctioned off to the highest bidder. Hot dogs and soda pop are also sold at these social gatherings, and total proceeds are placed in the Gadugi treasury. On good nights as much as $30 is raised. Careful accounting is made of each purchase, so that the total amount put into the treasury by each member can be easily reckoned. The amount listed under a member's name helps determine how much he may borrow and facilitates settlement if the member should decide to quit the organization. Thus it can be seen that the buying of a cake or pie at a pie social represents an investment rather than a mere purchase.

As was mentioned previously, the Gadugis used to divide up their earnings once a year. Membership therefore constituted something of a 1-year contract. This notion is strengthened by the fact that the annual election of now officers is, in Cherokee, phrased as "renewing" the Gadugi. Money is no

---

25 Positions newly incorporated into the Gadugi from the poor-aid society.

26 To cook night and day – day cooks prepare food while the group is working in the fields, while night cooks handle kitchen responsibility during "setups" or all-night wakes that precede burial.

longer given back directly, except in the case of loans, but is used for sponsoring Christmas parties or purchasing equipment, as when one of the groups purchased a $180 power saw last winter. Nowadays some money remains in the treasury to tide the group over from year to year, giving the organization more continuity than it previously possessed. Also, when an expensive piece of equipment is purchased, as a power saw, members feel they own a share of it as long as it lasts. [110]

The future of the Gadugi is uncertain. Many informants feel that interest in the Gadugi is declining, with attendance not so loyal as in the past, and increased internal dissension. The fact that the Gadugi has survived as long as it has is remarkable in view of all the external factors that have jeopardized its existence. Looking into the future, the most imminent threat to the organization would seem to be an increased number of salaried jobs on the reservation and an accompanying change in the conservative value system toward greater emphasis on individual achievement. Until these changes start taking place at a more rapid rate than at present, the Gadugi should continue to persist as a viable, though atrophied institution.

Comparative Evidence

Agricultural cooperatives and mutual-aid organizations have a worldwide distribution. In his review of cooperative labor, Herskovits cites references to agricultural cooperatives in East and West Africa (with Haitian "survivals"), in North America among the Hidatsa and several Southwestern tribes, in the Pacific and in Indonesia among the Dyaks of Borneo (Herskovits 1952: 99-108). It is beyond the scope of this paper to digest and interpret these diverse data. However, some relevant comparisons can be made between the Cherokee cooperatives and those found among other Southeastern tribes and the Northern Iroquois.

Swanton has given us a concise and informative summary of the sexual division of labor for agriculture in the aboriginal Southeast.

> The greater part of the cultivation was by the women, but the cultivation of the soil in preparation for planting and some of the early cultivation was performed communally, men and women working together. Gatherings for this purpose were also made the occasion for social diversion, work ceasing at noon or soon after, a sumptuous feast following, the afternoon being devoted to a ball game and the evening to dancing. In Florida the men cultivated the ground and the women followed them, planting the seed. In Carolina Lawson says that, unlike the Iroquois, the women never planted corn, while among the Powhatan Indians, according to Smith, women did all of the work. The missionary Gravier declares that among the Tunica all of this work was done by the men. Some confusion on this point may have been due to the fact that, in addition to the communal fields, there were small garden patches about most Indian towns which were maintained entirely by women [Swanton 1928b: 691].

In another essay, Swanton, relying on Bartram, goes into greater detail for the Creek:

The smaller garden plots were cared for almost exclusively by women, but the town fields were tended by individuals of both sexes, and Bartram says that "there are not one-third as many females as males seen at work in their plantations; for, at this season of the year, by a law of the people, they do not hunt, the game not being in season till after their crops or harvest is gathered in, so the [111] males have little else with which to employ themselves." Later on in the season the same writer tells us that the labor falling upon women was harder [Swanton 1928a: 385].

The aboriginal Creek agricultural system paralleled that of the Cherokee quite closely. Townsmen were summoned by an overseer and worked fields communally in rotation. Much sociability took place during and following the work. In addition, there were communal as well as individual granaries.

Although one early source says of Chickasaw warriors "... rather than condescend to cultivate the earth (which they think beneath them) they sit and toy with their women ... lolling thus their time away with great indifference ...." Swanton notes that as the observer "entertained no love for this particular tribe, it is probable that he has not presented their usages in the most favorable light." Swanton (1928c: 228-229) believes that the Chickasaw pattern was similar to that described for the Creek. Le Page du Pratz (1758: 309) reports that among the 18th-century Natchez the men cleared the fields and hoed the corn, although he says in general, "the girls and women work more than the men and the boys."

A painting by Jacques le Moyne (1564 or 1565, engraved by Theodore de Bry) illustrates the division of labor of the Timucua of the east coast of Florida. The picture shows men and women working together in a field. The men arc breaking up the ground with "a kind of hoe made from fish bones fitted to wooden handles," while "the planting is done by the women, some making [regularly spaced] holes with sticks, into which the others drop the seeds of beans or maize" which they take from shallow baskets (Lorant 1946: 77; also reproduced, on smaller scale, in Fundaburk and Foreman 1957: 26). Laudonniere, commander of the Huguenot expedition which Le Moyne accompanied, adds these details:

> They sow their maize twice a year – to wit in March and in June – and all in one and the same soil. The said maize, from the time that it is sowed until the time that it be ready to be gathered, is but six months on the ground; the other six months, they let the earth rest. They have also fine pumpkins, and very good beans. They never dung their land, only when they would sow they set weeds on fire, which grow up the six months, and burn them all. They dig their ground with an instrument of wood, which is fastened like a broad mattock, wherewith they dig their vines in France; they put two grains of maize together. When the land is to be sowed, the king commandeth one of his men to assemble his subjects every day to labor, during which labor the king causeth store of that drink [cassine] to be made for them whereof we have spoken. At the time when the maize is gathered, it is all carried into a common house, where it is distributed to every man, according to his quality. They sow no more but that which they think will serve their turn for six months, and that very scarcely. [Quoted in Swanton 1922: 369, italics supplied. Illustrated in Lorant 1946: 79.] [112]

This account, since it predates the observations of Bartram and Adair by almost two hundred years, is of great value for assigning considerable age to male participation in communal agriculture in the Southeast. The dispensation of the drink hints at the festive or perhaps religious atmosphere surrounding the work.

Before passing to the Iroquois, we quote Lawson's description of an interesting custom practiced in the early 18th century by one of the small Eastern Siouan tribes or perhaps the Tuscarora (not specified) which seems to have certain parallels to Cherokee poor-aid practices.

> They are very kind and charitable to one another, but more especially to those of their own Nation [town or sib?]; for if any one of them has suffered any Loss, by Fire, or otherwise, they order the grieved Person to make a Feast, and invite them all thereto, which, on the day appointed, they come to, and after every Man's Meals of Victuals is deait to him, one of their Speakers, or grave old Men, makes an Harrangue, and acquaints the Company, That that Man's House has been burnt, wherein all his Goods were destroyed; That he and his Family very narrowly escaped; That he is every Man's Friend in that Company; and, That it is all their Duties to help him, as he would do to any of them had the like Misfortune befallen them. After this Oration is over, every Man, according to his Quality, throws him down upon the Ground some Present, which is commonly Beads, Roanoke, Peak, Skins, or Furs, and which very often amounts to treble the Loss he has suffered. The same Assistance they give to any Man that

wants to build a Cabin, or make a Canoe. They say it is our Duty thus to do; for there are several Works that one Man cannot effect, therefore we must give him our Help, otherwise our Society will fall, and we shall be deprived of those urgent Necessities which Life requires [Lawson 1714: 188-189].

In this example, and others which could be cited, the use of a feast as a lever for group effort can be clearly seen. This may explain the seemingly paradoxical findings for the contemporary Eastern Cherokee in which needy people feel obligated to give a meal, even on borrowed money, when the Gadugi comes to help them. Also, the use of communal male labor for difficult tasks, as house building, seems to be general throughout the Southeast.

It appears from this cursory review of the aboriginal Southeast that men, as well as women, generally played an important part in agriculture, and that organized communal labor in the fields and in assistance to the poor were fairly universal in the, area. Also, this system of cooperation was closely linked to the local town organization, which in many ways transcended the household as a basic unit in social organization.

Mutual aid and cooperative agricultural organizations among the Iroquoia have been mentioned in a number of places.[27]22 Before [113] attempting to draw some comparisons between the Cherokee cooperative institutions and those of the Iroquois, as they appeared historically and as they persist today, it might be well to consider first some relevant basic structural features in which Cherokee and Iroquois society differed.

Geographical features of the two areas seem to have encouraged differences in settlement pattern. The Iroquois area afforded an abundance of arable land in contrast to the mountainous topography that characterized much of the Cherokee homeland. As a result, Cherokee settlements tended to be more spatially diffuse, often following tillable land along meandering river valleys and irregular mountain hollows. Iroquois settlements, on the other hand, were generally more compact and able to support a more concentrated population. In addition, the openness of the Iroquois territory and the propinquity of hostile Algonkin bands and other Iroquoian groups necessitated protective measures not required in the more isolated Cherokee heartland. For defensive purposes, the Iroquois tended to locate their villages on elevated bluffs away from watercourses, and they also surrounded their villages with palisades, a practice that lasted until the end of the 17th century (Houghton 1916: 513; Stites 1905: 64, citing Lafitau). Palisaded villages were rare among the Cherokee except in those towns lying on the exposed flanks of their territory (Lewis and Kneberg 1958: 158).

In the 17th century, Iroquois villages appeared to be more populous than those of the Cherokee and fewer in number. Fenton (1940: 203) lists a total of only 10 to 13 towns for all of the Five Nations. He estimates a total Mohawk population of 2,700 in 1634 distributed in 3 towns, the largest numbering 1,035, the smallest 810 (ibid: 206). These per-town figures are almost twice as large as those reported for the largest Cherokee towns. In another place, Fenton (1951: 41) says, "Before 1687, the League Iroquois were 12 or 13 villages, ranging between 300 and 600 persons per town." This more conservative estimate would still make the average Iroquois village twice as populous as the average Cherokee village.

One of the mechanisms by which the Iroquois were able to concentrate their population was, of

---

27 The authors' grasp on Iroquois ethnography is at best tenuous. Neither of us has had first-hand field experience in Canada or New York State, nor do we pretend to adequate command of the rich documentary source material available to the Iroquois scholar. We hope merely to draw comparison and help stimulate research in the important, but too often neglected area of joint work groups. In writing this section we have rolled primarily on secondary sources. The sources consulted which mentioned mutual-aid societies or cooperative agricultural groups were: Stites 1905; Waugh 1910; Goldenweiser 1922; Fenton 1936, 1961; Quain 1937; Lyford 1945; Speck and Schaeffer 1045; Noon 1949; and Brown 1950.

course, the longhouse, a multifamily dwelling accommodating as many as one hundred or more individuals (Goldenweiser 1922: 70). Whereas the town, or symbolically the townhouse, was the principal focus of Cherokee culture, the longhouse tended to be the basic conceptual unit of Iroquois life. Iroquois residence rules seem to have been more strictly matrilocal than those [114] of the Cherokee, and the spiritual, as well as authoritarian, core of the longhouse was a group of matrilineally related kinswomen headed by an elder matron. Some of the implications of this fundamental difference in town size and house type will be dealt with shortly.

The Iroquois also seemed to have shared with the Cherokee a system of private-family gardens and larger cornfields which, while individually owned, were worked communally (Waugh 1916: 7). While the Cherokee utilized a communal granary, supplied by donations from the fields of all townsmen, for religious and civil functions and emergencies, the Iroquois are reported to have reserved special fields to provide for such purposes (ibid: 6). The Iroquois fields were closely grouped outside the walls of the village. The fields of the Cherokee were normally located within the confines of the town, interspersed amongst the houses, and sometimes were planted up to the edge of the council house.

There is much literature concerning the sexual division of labor, especially the role of women, among the aboriginal Iroquois. Male participation in agriculture was strongly devalued in Iroquois society. However, it is known that the men did participate to the extent of clearing the land by girdling trees and burning over the fields. There is also some evidence that men assumed the tasks of fencing the gardens and preparing bundles of corn for drying (Stites 190: 29, citing La Potherie and Lafitau). Moreover, certain classes of males did take part in cultivation. These included old men, children, cripples, captives who were not formally adopted into the tribe, and effeminate men. Ely S. Parker was quite explicit about the degraded status of an able-bodied man who pursued agriculture. He says,

"... when any man, excepting the cripples, old men, and those disabled in war or hunting, chose to till the earth, he was at once ostracized from the men's society, classed as a woman or squaw, and disqualified from sitting or speaking in the councils of his people until he had redeemed himself by becoming a skillful warrior or a successful hunter" [Quoted in Stites 1905: 42].

A C Parker remarks about the persistence of this attitude by noting, "Some of the old warriors whom the writer interviewed told laughable stories of grim old 'warriors' who had been caught with a hoe and how they excused themselves" (Parker 1910: 22).

This stigma attached to males who engaged in agriculture was not as strong in some Iroquoian groups. Carr says of the Hurons,

... The men not only habitually cleared the land ... but they frequently took part in what is technically known as working the crop, and also aided in the labors of the harvest field. This may not have been part of their duty ... but when asked to aid in the gathering of the crop, they did not scorn to lend a helping hand [Quoted in Stites 1905: 28].

With the Cherokee also, as we have attempted to show in the first [115] section, male participation in agriculture was frequent, despite the fact that it was chiefly a woman's activity.

One of the most tantalizing, and at the same time crucial, questions in understanding Cherokee-Iroquois local organization is the extent to which sibs or clans tended toward common residence within the local community (see footnote 5: 91). The evidence is suggestive, but unfortunately inconclusive, in the case of both the Cherokee and the Iroquois, and, because of the failure of older rules of residence to survive to the present, current fieldwork in reservation communities will not give us the answer.

With respect to the Iroquois, Goldenweiser states,

The clans, in ancient times, were associated with localities and longhouses, not in the sense of a clan claiming exclusive occupation of a village or a longhouse ... but in the sense of a clan being regarded as preeminently associated, as being in "control," in a village or a longhouse. [Goldenweiser 1913: 368.]

In a similar vein, Fenton (1951: 50) cites Asher Wright and statements by informants that, "each clan had its own chief, that formerly the different clans tended to reside together, if not in composite households, in adjacent districts of a settlement with which the name of the dominant clan was associated."

There is similar suggestive evidence for Cherokee "clan" localization. Charles Hicks, a prominent Cherokee chief, had this to say in 1818:

The national council is composed of chiefs from each clan, some sending more some less, regard being had to the population of each – though the number is not very definitely fixed. *Each clan has its separate portion of land, which it holds in common right* – the poorest man having the same right as the greatest [Quoted in Swanton 1946: 654 – italics supplied.]

Another hint of possible "clan" localization derives from the fact that after the Removal, when the present five Eastern Cherokee townships were set up, throe of the five towns were given, "clan" names (Paint-town, Wolftown, and Birdtown). This latter clue should not be taken too seriously, because of the artificial conditions under which these townships were set up. However, a close examination of local named neighborhoods within the townships, before the rules of residence had completely broken down, might have revealed positive signs of "clan" localization.

If we assume, for speculative purposes, that Iroquois clans were localized in Goldenweiser's sense of "predominant" within a subarea of a town or village, or within a longhouse, it seems reasonable to assume that the communal agriculture carried on by women, described by Mary Jemison and others, was a clan-oriented (or clan-controlled) organization. This would seem especially likely where [116], in longhouses, finding sufficient number of women of the same clan was high.

For the Cherokee, in contrast, the absence of the longhouse, the less secure evidence of clan localization, the greater participation of men in agriculture, together with evidence of a more diffuse settlement pattern and considerably smaller town size, would all be factors unfavorable to the formation of sib-dominated work groups. It is probable that cooperative work groups were locally recruited, and in towns of smaller size may have included the whole town, and thus had a community or neighborhood orientation, with sib considerations being secondary.

Let us now look briefly at some of the historical factors that helped shape the structure of the present-day Iroquois mutual aid groups. The older palisaded villages had disappeared and longhouse living patterns were fairly well broken down by the beginning of the 18th century. From this point on, Iroquois villages began to lose their former quality of compactness and came to approximate more and more their present pattern of scattered rural homesteads.

During the 18th century the Iroquois were key figures in the power struggle between Britain and France for control of the New World. Their strategic position and striking power played a significant role in the eventual British victory. Besides warfare, hunting for food and furs continued to be the major occupation of Iroquois men during this period. The Iroquois again allied themselves with the British during the American Revolution. The war left the Iroquois defeated, demoralized, and disenfranchised. They retired to reservations in the United States and Canada where a condition of general anomie prevailed.

The blocking of the traditional spheres of male activity, warfare and hunting (the latter now less profitable because of diminished game resources), dictated a social reorientation toward white-style farming. The Cherokee were faced with a similar crisis following the Revolution but were successful in rapidly assimilating white agricultural patterns, perhaps because of earlier male preadaptation to farming.

For the Iroquois, however, the transition was more difficult owing to the deep-rooted male abhorrence toward working in the fields. Also, it was believed that the connection between women and crops was such that only women could make them grow (Deardorff 1951: 94). Although the Iroquois were traditionally agriculturalists, the newer agriculture called for the use of the plow and manpower to supplant the previous female hoe agriculture (ibid.). Deardorff quotes from Jackson's observations in 1801 among Cornplanter's Seneca in reference to the cautious acceptance of the plow, only after experimentation: [117]

> "Several parts of a large field were ploughed, and the intermediate spaces prepared by women with the hoe, according to the former custom. It was all planted with corn; and the parts ploughed ... produced much the heaviest crop" [Deardorff 1951: 94].

A year or so before (1799), also in the Cornplanter area, the prophet Handsome Lake's revelations included pronouncements for men to take up the plow, thus giving supernatural sanction for the acceptance of the newer pattern.

It is difficult to trace the exact route of male entry into the female cooperative agricultural units which had already been existing for a considerable time. In one sense, the composite male-female cooperatives can be viewed as extensions of the organization of work surrounding the clearing of the land in which men had formerly participated. Fenton feels that the current mutual-aid society "apparently had its beginnings as a society of males who banded together to assist the women of a clan to whom they were married and their own sisters. They were coresidents in a composite household, or at least of the settlement" (Fenton 1951: 50). It seems as if one can take a long view and see the present organizations as continuations of the aboriginal female cooperative groups, or take a shorter view that looks at these institutions as relatively recent, appearing only with the advent of male participation in agriculture during the beginning of the 19th century.

The present-day Iroquois mutual-aid societies fall into two types: singing societies and bees (Fenton 1936: 5). Among the conservative Iroquois still practicing the Handsome Lake religion are found the singing societies, which take their name from the group singing that accompanies the "feast" after the day's labors. The ideology governing these groups is deeply rooted in the teachings of Handsome Lake. In addition to working in the fields, these groups also assist one another in chopping wood, clearing the tribal cemetery, building and repairing houses, and giving aid to needy individuals (ibid: 5); all these functions can be found in similar Cherokee groups. Fenton also mentions a field which all the people cultivate for the benefit of the poor and needy (ibid: 5), a trait that seems like an aboriginal survival. The officers of the singing society include a leader and an assistant leader from each group of four clans, a first and second drummer, and a messenger or poormaster to whom needy persons apply for aid and who notifies the other members where and when the group will work (ibid:5). Although clan considerations still obtain in the selection of a chief, locality seems to be the principal factor determining membership, and anyone can join who shows a willingness to work. [118]

Cooperative work groups are also found among the Christian Iroquois. These organizations are usually called bees, and while they function in a similar fashion to the singing societies, they are usually arms of other larger organizations inspired by the church or sponsored by civic groups (ibid: 6).[28]23

---

28 'Bee's' also occur among the modern Longhouse people at Allegany (especially) and Cattaraugua Reservations. I have attended several very pleasant quilting bees at Allegany, to raise money for the Longhouse and for mutual aid in quilting; these are women's affairs, include a meal, and are very loosely organized without formal officers, etc. Informal 'socials' held in the Longhouse resemble bees, generally to raise money for Longhouse affairs by selling food contributed by members of the community; they normally also involve singing and dancing for recreation; men participate, but women seem to be the main organizers; they also are very informally structured. These strike me as conservative rural traits, rather than aboriginal survivals" (WC Sturtevant pc).

These Iroquois cooperatives do not seem to approach the comparable Cherokee groups in complexity of formal structural features, such as elaborate roster of offices, rules, minutes, etc. Speck and Schaeffer (1945: 176), while noting these differences, feel that the Cherokee and Iroquois institutions have a similar base if stripped of their modern trapping. According to them the reconstructed prototype may be defined as, "a voluntary association of individuals, probably community-wide, organized under the supervision of a leader and several assistants to carry on mutual aid or relief within the locality on a reciprocal basis" (ibid: 178). The Iroquois and Cherokee are said to share a common pattern of "institutionalization," which differentiates them sharply from the Algonkian, and strengthens the evidence for cultural linkage in the past between these two divergent members of the same linguistic family.

It is possible the Cherokee and Iroquois joint-work groups may be modern manifestations of a genius for "institutionalization," and highly developed patterns of generosity and group effort stemming from roots genetically related in the remote prehistoric past. However, it is our impression, after reviewing the data, that the aboriginal Cherokee organization, which is ancestral to the contemporary joint-work groups, is most closely allied to similar organizations among other Southeastern Indians, notably the Creek. The more recent similarity between contemporary Cherokee and Iroquois cooperative work groups is better explained, we feel, as an example of modern convergence in response to similar historical factors, such as the overt disappearance of hunting and warrior patterns, reservation culture, and acculturation to rural American patterns of farming.

Bibliography

Adair, James 1775 *The history of the American Indians*. London. [Edition used: Samuel Cole Williams, ed., Johnson City, Tenn., 1930.]

Arthur, J.P 1914 *Western North Carolina, a history, 1730-1913*. Raleigh, N.C. [119]

Bartram, William   1791   *Travels through North & South Carolina, Georgia, east & west Florida*. Philadelphia. [Edition used: Mark Van Doren, ed., New York, 1928.]

Beauchamp,W.M 1900 Iroquois women. *Journal of American Folklore* vol. 13: 81-91.

Bent, Arthur Cleveland 1932 *Life histories of North American gallinaceous birds*. U.S. Nat. Mus. Bull. 162.

Bloom, Leonard   1937   The acculturation of the Eastern Cherokee. MS., PhD. dissertation, Duke University.

Brown, A.F 1950 On Onondaga fieldwork. Bull. Philadelphia Anthrop. Soc., vol. 3 (5): 2-4.

Crane, Verner W 1928 *The southern frontier: 1670-1752*. (Rev. ed., 1956.) Ann Arbor, Mich.

Deardorff, Merle H 1951 The religion of Handsome Lake: Its origin and development. In *Symposium on local diversity in Iroquois culture*, ed. by William N. Fenton, Bur, Amer. Ethnol. Bull. 149: 77-108.

Donaldson, Thomas   1892   The eastern band of Cherokees of North Carolina. Extra Census Bull., 11th Census U.S.

Fenton, William N 1936 Some social customs of the modern Seneca. Social Welfare Bull. vol. 7 (1-2); 4-7. New York State Dept. Social Welfare, Albany.

   1940   Problems arising from the historic northeastern position of the Iroquois. In *Essays in historical anthropology of North America*, ed. by JH Steward. Smithsonian Misc. Coll., vol.100: 159-252.

   1951 Locality as a basic factor in the development of Iroquois social structure. In *Symposium on local diversity in Iroquois culture*, ed. by William N. Fenton, Bur. Amer. Ethnol, Bull. 149: 35-54.

Fundabank, E.L., and Foreman, M.U.F, editors. 1957 *Sun circles and human hands*. Luverne, Ala.

Gearing, Frederick O   1956   Cherokee political organizations, 1730-1775. MS., PhD dissertation, University of Chicago.

   1958 The structural poses of 18th-century Cherokee villages. Amer. Anthrop., vol. 60: 1148-1157.

Gilbert, William H 1943 The Eastern Cherokee. Bur. Amer. Ethnol. Bul. 133, Anthrop. Paper No. 23: 169-413.

    1957 The Cherokee of North Carolina: Living memorials of the past. In Ann. Rep. Smithsonian Inst. for 1956: 529-555.

Goldenweiser, Alexander A 1913. On Iroquois work. Canada Dept. of Mines, Summary Report of the Geological Survey of Canada: 365-372. Ottawa.

    1922. Early Civilization. New York. [120]

Gulick, John 1958 The acculturation of Eastern Cherokee community organization. *Social Forces*, vol. 36: 246-250.

Haas, Mary R 1940 Creek intertown relations. Amer. Anthrop., vol. 43: 479-489.

Herskovits, Melville 1952 Economic anthropology. New York.

Houghton, F 1916 The characteristics of Iroquoian village sites of western New York. *Amer. Anthrop.*, n.s., vol. 18: 507-520.

Kroeber, Alfred L 1939 *Cultural and natural areas of native North America.* Univ. California Publ. in Amer. Archael. and EthnoL, vol. 38.

Lanman, Charles 1849 Letters from the Alleghany Mountains. New York.

Lawson, John 1714 *History of North Carolina.* London. [Edition used: 2d ed., 1951 (i.e., 1952), ed. by FL Harries, Richmond, Va.]

LePage du Pratz, Antoine S 1758 *Histoire de la Louisiana.* Paris. [Edition used: History of Louisiana, ed. by S.C Arthur, New Orleans, 1947]

Lewis, Thomas M.N, and Madeline Kneberg 1958 *Tribes that slumber.* Knoxville.

Lorant, Stefan 1946 *The New World: The first pictures of America.* New York.

Lyford, Carrie A 1945 Iroquois crafts. Publ, U.S. Indian Service, Indian Handcraft Pamphlets, No. 6. Haskell Institute, Lawrence, Kans.

Malone, Henry T 1956 *Cherokee of the Old South.* Athens, GA.

Mooney, James 1900 Myths of the Cherokee. 19th Ann. Rep. Bur. Amer. Ethnol 1897-98, pt. 1: 3-576.

Mooney, James, and Olbrechts, Frans 1932 The Swimmer manuscript. Bur. Amer. Ethnol Bull. 99.

Murdoch, George Peter 1949 Social structure. New York.

    1956. Political moieties: 133-147. In *The state of the social sciences*, ed. by L.D White. Chicago.

Noon, John A 1949 Law and government of the Grand River Iroquois. Viking Fund Publ. Anthrop., No, 12. New York.

Opler, Morris Edward 1952 The Creek town and the problem of Creek Indian political reorganization: 165-180. In *Human problems in technological change*, a casebook, ed. by Edward H. Spicer. Russell Sage Foundation, New York.

Parker, Arthur C 1910 Iroquois uses of maize and other food plants. New York State Educational Dept. Bull. 482 (Mus. Bull. 144).

Quain, Buell 1937 The Iroquois: 240-281. In *Cooperation and competition among primitive peoples*, ed. by M. Mead. New York. [121]

Rothrock, Mary 1929 *Carolina traders among the Overhill Cherokees, 1690-1760.* East Tennessee Hist. Soc. Publ., No. 1.

Royce, Charles C 1887 The Cherokee Nation of Indians. 5th Ann. Rep. Bur. Amer. Ethnol. 1883-84: 121-378.

Speck, Frank G, and Schaeffer, Claude E 1945 The mutual-aid volunteer company of the Eastern Cherokee. Journ. Washington Acad. Sci vol 35: 169-179.

Starr, Frederick 1898 American Indian; Ethnogeographic Reader. Vol. 2. Boston.

Stites, Sarah H. 1905 *Economics of the Iroquois.* Lancaster, Pa.

Swanton, John R 1922 Early history of the Creek Indians and their neighbors. Bur. Amer. Ethnol. Bull. 73.

    1928a Social organization and social usages of the Indiana of the Creek Confederacy. 42d Ann.

Rep. Bur. Amer. Ethnol., 1924-25: 23-472.
   1928b Aboriginal culture of the Southeast. 42d Ann. Rep. Bur. Amer. Ethnol., 1924-25: 673-726.
   1928c Social and religious beliefs and usages of the Chickasaw Indians. 44th Ann. Rep. Bur. Amer. Ethnol., 1926-27: 169-274.
   1946 The Indians of the Southeastern United States. Bur. Amer. Ethnol. Bull. 137.

Timberlake, Henry 1765 *The memoirs of Lieutenant Henry Timberlake.* London. [Edition used: Samuel Cole Williams, ed. Johnson City, Tenn., 1927).

Wardell, Morris L 1938 *A political history of the Cherokee Nation, 1838-1907.* Norman, Okla.

Wauch, F W 1916. Iroquois foods and food preparation. Canada. Dept of Mines. Geolog. Surv. Mem. 86, No. 12, Anthrop. Ser. Ottawa.

Williams, Samuel C 1937 *Dawn of Tennessee Valley and Tennessee history.* Johnson City, Tenn.

Williams, Samuel C, ed. 1928 *Early travels in the Tennessee Country, 1540-1800.* Johnson City, Tenn.

Witthoft, John 1947 Notes on a Cherokee migration story. Journ. Washington Acad. Sci., vol. 37: 304-305.
   1948 Will West Long, Cherokee informant. Amer. Anthrop., vol. 60: 355-359.

Zeigler, Wilbur G, and Grosscup, Ben S 1883 *The heart of the Alleghanies*: Or western North Carolina. Raleigh, N.C.

CHANGE, PERSISTENCE, AND ACCOMMODATION IN CHEROKEE MEDICO-MAGICAL BELIEFS[1]

The acculturation of the Eastern Cherokee must be considered atypical when compared to the general model of acculturation for most North American Indian groups. Continuous first-hand contact with Euro-American culture increased in intensity, except for brief periods of war, during the century prior to the forced removal to the Indian Territory in 1838. During this period, a loose confederation of scattered villages adhering to an aboriginal culture was rapidly transformed into a cohesive nation which was viewed by others, and viewed itself, as civilized. A few hundred Cherokee of conservative background, who had been marginal to the efflorescence that had taken place in the southern part of their nation, escaped the general removal and remained behind in the wilderness of the Great Smoky Mountains. This group, ancestral to the present Eastern Cherokee, was left to reassemble the pieces of a broken culture. The Eastern Band remained fairly isolated from the main currents of white civilization until the early years of the 20th century, when their encapsulation began to be penetrated by modern communication. This geographic isolation allowed the stabilization of a new cultural Gestalt comprised of remnants of the older Cherokee culture now blended into a general mountain-white pattern. Thus, while acculturation is taking place at a rapid pace today among the Eastern Cherokee, for the most part, the most realistic baseline from which to plot current culture change is the period of cultural resynthesis that occurred during the mid-19th century.[2]

One of the aspects of Cherokee culture that has been most resistant to change is the medico-magical practices of the conjuror. While it is generally assumed that the more covert aspects of culture embedded in a people's belief system are less likely to change than overt items are, such as material culture, the survival of Cherokee medico-magical beliefs and practices has been aided by a special mechanism – the Sequoyah syllabary. Although Sequoyah's invention (1821) was popularly hailed as a tool of "progress" enabling the Cherokee to publish their own newspaper, laws, and constitution, as well as to translate the Bible, hymns, and other religious tracts, the syllabary was also a powerful instrument for cultural retention. The conjuror was now able to transcribe into his notebook sacred formulas and other lore that had formerly been dependent on oral transmission (Mooney 1891: 308).

In aboriginal times, Cherokee medico-magical beliefs were mediated through a stratified priestly organization. With the nearly complete conversion of the Nation to Christianity, nominally at least, during the first third of the 19th century, conjurors became the repositories of the remaining fragments of what was once a quite complex aboriginal religious system. In response to the passing of the older religion and the breakup of the priestly societies, individual practitioners tended to focus their attention on more secular matters, such as curing, sorcery, and hunting-fishing and agricultural magic.

Cherokee medical and magical practices were probably rather pragmatic and flexible prior to the Removal. If a new herbal remedy was discovered or a new ceremony devised, it was probably easily incorporated into the conjuror's repertory. While many American Indian groups had definite notions of supernatural power in their ritual and vision quests, a clearly defined power concept was not so conspicuous among the Cherokee. Throughout their history, there was a decided disinclination to set

---

1 Fieldwork was carried out during the summers of 1957 and 1958 under the auspices of the Cross-Cultural Laboratory of The Institute for Research In Social Science, University of North Carolina: John Gulick, director. The writer wishes to offer grateful acknowledgment to the Department of Anthropology, Univ. of Pennsylvania, for financial assistance. The writer also wishes to express his indebtedness to John Atkins, Dr Al Hallowell, Charles Holzinger, Paul Kutsche, Robert Thomas, Dr AFC Wallace, and John Witthoft for helpful advice and criticism.

2 This period would seem to correspond to the onset of what Witthoft (this volume: 74-78) has termed 'Reservation culture'. [216]

oneself above one's fellows, and the presence of prophets was a rare phenomenon.[3] Ceremonialism and, in fact, much of Cherokee personality, seems oriented toward harmony with nature through knowledge and control, rather than through blind supplication (Thomas MS 1958).

This pragmatic outlook can be clearly seen in a myth accounting for the origin of disease and medicine. According to the myth, man once lived in harmony with the rest of creation, and disease was unknown. Because of man's inhumanity to the other living creatures through both design and carelessness, each animal group held a separate council and decided to inflict on mankind a different disease. [217] The plant kingdom took pity on man and promised assistance in counteracting the animal-sent evils (Mooney 1900: 250-252). The myth implies that there is a plant antidote for every disease; through knowledge one is able to select the appropriate remedy. Most native medical practitioners are able to identify as many as two hundred different plant species and varieties. However, if the emergency is sufficiently grave, one need not be a specialist, for it is said that any man can walk into a field and the appropriate plant will reveal itself by nodding.

Medico-magical beliefs and practices seem to have assumed a more rigid, doctrinaire quality among the surviving Eastern Cherokee. The Removal separated the remaining Cherokee from most of the creative and spiritual leadership of the Nation. Among the 18,000 or so who emigrated West were most of the highly esteemed medicine men, as well as other guardians and interpreters of traditional belief. The shock of removal and the separation from the main body of their Nation, eventuated in some culture loss, but also resulted in a more compulsive adherence to those items of medico-magical belief which remained.

The syllabary enabled the Eastern Cherokee to set down and retain much esoteric knowledge, but this new device seems to have affected medical and magical practices by discouraging some of the flexible empiricism hypothesized for the earlier conjuring. Writing down prayers, incantations, and formulas gave these items a certain tangibility that grew into reverence. The conjuror's notebook became imbued with some of the same sacredness surrounding the Christian Bible, The antiquity and conservative nature of the formulas are well verified by the many now unintelligible archaic expressions, many of which were encountered by Mooney as early as 1887 (1891: 309). Also, conjurors feel that a formula must be recited perfectly or the ceremony will be ineffective; slips of the tongue are thought to be caused by the machinations of a rival. Formulas are jealously guarded, and often the titles of more important ones are disguised or transcribed in an idiosyncratic shorthand, lest the books fall into the wrong hands. These factors, plus the relative isolation and absence of acculturative stimuli during most of the 19th century, tended to make conjuring practices tradition bound and highly stylized. Only with the intensive culture contact of the past 25 years have Cherokee medico-magical practices begun to undergo major accommodative modifications necessary for limited survival in a changing society.

The lines of medico-magical specialization are not tightly drawn, but some general distinctions can be made. Conjuring has become almost a male specialty, although women specialists have been known in the past, and even today a few of the older women know many herbal [218] remedies and a few ceremonies. None of the current practitioners are full-time specialists, and all derive their principal incomes from other sources. It is important to distinguish herbalists from conjurors. The herbalist may prescribe, dispense, or administer simples, but his treatment is rarely accompanied by a ceremony. Since knowledge of herbal remedies diffused widely throughout the population, the distinction between the laity and a herbalist rests mainly on a quantitative basis. A conjuror, in contrast, relies on a combination of simples and ceremony in his curing procedures.

To become a conjuror, one must possess a thorough knowledge of plants and competence in the Sequoyah syllabary. At present, with less than 10 percent of the population literate in their own language,

---

3 The Redbird Smith movement differs from the typical prophet-led revitalization movement, as Thomas (this volume: 165-166) has pointed out. The disinclination to set oneself above ones's fellows has been noted by Gearing (MS 1956) in 18th-century Cherokee political behavior.

this latter prerequisite assumes increased importance in the selection of conjurors. In addition, one must gain the confidence of an older practitioner and persuade him to give instruction. Conjurors are not eager to part with their knowledge, so that the disciple must possess special personal qualifications and aptitude. Information is imparted in Socratic fashion, and no tuition is expected. Instruction usually begins with the recognition of plants and their properties, soon proceeds to the commoner formulas, and ends with ceremonies for sorcery, provided the candidate shows promise of not abusing such knowledge (Mooney and Olbrechts 1932: 100). The stock-in-trade of a conjuror is his body of formulas, which are gradually obtained throughout his lifetime by inheritance, borrowing, trading, or purchase.

Some hint of a previous age-grading among practitioners still persists. Although one may receive some instruction as a young adult and practice on a modest scale, such activities are generally kept secret. If you become boastful and arrogant, another older and more knowing conjuror may "spoil" your work. After about 55 years of age, "when your hair gets gray," a conjuror is less afraid of censure and can declare himself more openly. It is reasoned that when your hair has turned gray, you have "proved yourself and followed what they said, and nobody can walk over you or tear up your ceremonies and ruin things." Even when one has passed this crisis, boastfulness is still devalued. One should not set himself above others and should never promise that he can do more than try to "lift up" his patient.

Within the general area of conjuring, there are many sub-specializations. For instance, some practitioners are noted for their ability to cure gastric illnesses, while others are known to specialize in "Dalâni" ("yellowness," usually manifested around the eyes) diseases. Other nonmedical specialties include such things as ball game conjuring, love magic, divination for lost objects, and many others. The late Will West Long, despite his profound philosophic knowledge [219] of conjuring, had little success in curing illnesses (Witthoft 1948: 358). One of my informants explains Will's failure as an example of knowing too much and not concentrating enough on any one specialty.

Today's conjurors are not organized into any sort of society. Each plies his craft secretly and alone. Relations between conjurors tend to be very circumspect and abrupt. Very seldom does one conjuror re a good word to say about another. While no practitioner will openly admit to practicing sorcery, he is quick to attribute such skills to a rival.

Occasionally conjurors will trade formulas, but only after each has felt the other out, and an equitable exchange has been negotiated. Rivalry becomes most intense during the Indian ball games which are felt to be primarily contests between, rival conjurors with the players as mere pawns.

The conjuror's clientele are drawn for the most part from the conservative segment of the population. Since the building of a modern agency hospital a number of years ago, the conjuror's curing services are less in demand than previously. Many Cherokee still have faith in native medicine and hire a practitioner while, at the same time, going to the hospital to insure receiving help from one quarter or the other. The opening of the Great Smoky National Park brought many tourists to the reservation. Among some of these tourists, a belief in the efficacy of Indian medicine persists from frontier days, when Indian medicine was not very inferior to that practiced by whites. A few of these tourists seek out conjurors for medical advice. More often than not their problems concern cases considered incurable by white medicine, as spastic children, sterility, and congenital defects. A few conjurors have traveled far from the reservation at the invitation of white clients. One man has a regular circuit of white clients whom he visits, sometimes for a few months at a time.

Mooney states that formerly conjurors received a deerskin or a pair of moccasins for their services, but that in 1887, a quantity of cloth, a garment, or a handkerchief became media of exchange (Mooney 1891: 337). Cloth was regarded not as pay, but rather as a necessary instrument in extracting the disease spirit. Today the donation of cloth for use in ceremonies still continues but is slowly giving way to monetary remuneration. It was formerly thought that receiving money would dissipate the conjuror's skills. The conjurors make a slight concession to tradition by not demanding payment or setting any fixed fee. Instead, the conjuror accepts whatever sum the client feels his work is worth and considers the payment as a gratuity.

As far as can be ascertained, all of today's conjurors consider themselves to be good Christians and feel that their work is completely consistent with Christian doctrine. The importance of faith and the [220] power of prayer are fully recognized by the conjuror. According to one informant:

When I conjure, I go by the word of God ... In ceremonies, I use the name of the Lord. When somebody's sick, you take him to the creek, wash his face by dipping with your hand, and wet his breast by the heart. It's like the spirit gives strength, like Baptism. He can feel it. If somebody's lost, it's up to the Creator to point the way. Sort of like in prayer. If it wasn't in the power of the Creator, you couldn't make anything move ...

Here, the ancient Cherokee rite of "going to the water" is neatly reconciled with Christianity. Another statement by a different informant emphasizes the conjuror's belief in a heavenly power superior to his own:

You can't overpower the Lord. If I fail, it means [the patient is] too far gone – already on that receiving line that's ready to be called away. If a grass ain't meant to help somebody, it will wither like frost before your eyes.

The close rapport between Christianity and conjuring does not seem to be a recent event, since much of Mooney's best material came from persons who combined the profession of native doctor with Sunday school preacher, as "Anâli" (the Rev Black Fox, Esq.). The local brand of Christianity in which faith healing plays a prominent part has also helped to strengthen the bond between the two systems of thought.

To recapitulate, the written formulas are the core of Cherokee medico-magical beliefs and help maintain continuity with the past. It is interesting to note that while a great many written prayers and instructions survive verbatim, the interpretation of these formulas and some of the underlying assumptions of the Cherokee theory of disease have undergone some modification. The writer, in 1958, collected a formula identical in translation to one published by Mooney (1891: 353-355). Mooney's informant said that the formula was used for frightened children, "when something is causing something to eat them." In the 1958 version, the formula is employed when "anyone takes faint or when his heart stops," without specific reference to children. The formula successively mentions and banishes a screech, owl, a hoot owl, a rabbit, and a mountain sprite (one of the "Little People"). Mooney explains that the disease is caused by these four disease spirits literally gnawing the vitals of the patient. The interpretation of a present-day conjuror differs markedly; the cause of the disease is a weak heart or "high pressure blood." The specific spirits are chosen because they are frightening – especially the rabbit who, when touched, "jumps up and scares you." Nowhere in the later interpretation is there any notion of evil disease [221] spirits gnawing at the patient's vitals, but the disease cause is given a western-sounding explanation.

The incomplete assimilation of white medical beliefs into the Cherokee system can be illustrated by many other examples. The diseases mentioned in some formulas are now simply believed to be colds caught after getting wet. Sore throats are said to be caused by an excess of "frame" (phlegm). The "*dalâni*" diseases are now attributed to the actions of the "goldstones" (gallstones). In some instances, the older Cherokee belief and modern white disease theory show some accidental correspondence and provide reinforcement for the Cherokee belief. The Cherokee anticipated the microbe theory in their notion that swellings were caused by minute microorganisms, "voluntary worms" ("*tsgâya*"), which decided to hold a subcutaneous council (Mooney 1891: 361).

Among conservative Cherokee, some opposition to white medicine still persists. In the historic past, the Cherokee felt that epidemics were special diseases invented by Europeans to exterminate the Indian. Cherokee medicine was ineffective and, in some cases, as with smallpox, detrimental in treating these diseases. Possibly as a result, the Cherokee developed a belief in the ethnospecificity of disease and treatment. White medicine might work for whites but was no good for Indians. This notion seems to have been generalized along tribal lines also, for one of the current practitioners is accused of having learned his medicine from some Dakota Indians during World War II, and it is thought that Dakota medicine was not meant for Cherokee. Some of this provincialism has broken down recently, and most conjurors grudgingly admit the hospital has superior techniques for treating some diseases. However, the native practitioners are quick to find fault with the hospital and can cite numerous instances in which the hospital "gave up" on illnesses which were later successfully treated by native doctors.

The conflict between Cherokee and white medical theory can be illustrated by a specific example. In the words of one informant:

Kidney trouble hurts Indians. Something juicy on the vine like a peach or a watermelon, the Indian doctor says no [i.e. forbids a person with a kidney disorder to eat such fruit]. Doctors here in the hospital give orange juice and grapefruit, and it makes you worse – hurts.... Anything that swells up, you shouldn't take juice, only something dry or heavy ....

The taboo on juicy foods is also invoked in cases of slow-healing sores. Implicit in this and most other Cherokee medico-magical beliefs is an underlying principle of natural analogy, in this case the idea of dehydration and absorption, with no appreciation for the healthful effects of vitamin C. [222]

In general, the impact of Western medicine on Cherokee theory and practice can be seen to involve partial assimilation, the accentuation of differences where the two theories are irreconcilable, and an overall feeling that the two systems are complementary, rather than fundamentally contradictory.

The remainder of this report will survey briefly current change, persistence, and accommodation in the nonmedical functions of the conjuror.

Hunting and fishing magic were formerly of considerable importance to the Cherokee, but now, with the disappearance of many game animals, much hunting and fishing lore has been forgotten. In the past, elaborate ritual and dancing frequently preceded and followed the hunt. Formulas were recited and imitative masks of the pursued animals were employed for the prehunt ceremonies, as well as for the actual stalking (Speck and Broom 1951: 84-96). Mooney was able to collect only four hunting formulas and one fishing formula during his stay among the Eastern Cherokee in 1887 (Mooney 1891: 369-375). Olbrechts has noted that in the past bear-hunting songs sometimes were purchased for as much as $5 (Mooney and Olbrechts 1932: 153), but during the stay of Speck and Broom (circa 1937) owners of hunting formulas did not consider them "worth holding as personal, secret property" (Speck and Broom, 1951: 95). Today no hunting or fishing formulas remain, and all that can be recovered are odd bits of hunting and fishing lore that are not necessarily of Cherokee derivation.

Agricultural magic, once an important part of the major religious ceremonies, has also largely disappeared. Some small vestiges still remain. In one field of corn, ax blades were placed on short poles facing the cardinal directions, as I was told, "to break up the thunder-heads" of an approaching storm. Once at the dinner table, a conjuror refused to eat sweet corn, because it was too early in the season, and if he ate some, he would be unable to break up dangerous thunderstorms.

Many forms of divination still persist. In the past, the "*ulŭnsata*," a quartz crystal used to predict the future, was one of the most sacred Cherokee religious objects. These objects have disappeared, but many informants reverently recall the fulfilled predictions of airplanes, automobiles, and railroad trains envisioned by the "old men" of bygone days while looking into the stone. Dreams were formerly considered disease agents, the actual mechanisms for transmitting the illness, but are now considered as omens. Nevertheless, a man who dreams of being bitten by a snake should be treated as if he actually had been bitten. There is a belief that the manifest dream content will be inevitably fulfilled, but the intervention of a conjuror may [223] succeed in delaying the prophecy or "moving it over." Thus, in the case of a person who dreams of a death in his family, the conjuror may be able to forestall such an event by "moving it" down the river to another settlement-Rolling the beads is still a widely practiced form of divination. The beads, formerly small seeds – now largely replaced by glass beads – are of three colors: red and white, symbolic of victory or success, and black, indicative of defeat or death. The red or white bead is held between the thumb and forefinger of the right hand and the black bead held similarly in the left hand. In diagnosing a person's illness, it is felt that the patient will recover if the right-hand bead shows more activity, while greater activity by the black bead is a bad omen. If the answer is unfavorable, the beads can be rolled again, but the procedure can be repeated only a fixed number of times. The beads can also be used to answer direct "yes or no" questions and are important in ball game divination.[4] Other surviving forms of divination include the use of an arrowhead suspended on a crossbar to point out the direction of lost objects and a variety of interpretations of natural phenomena to predict certain events.

Various forms of sorcery are known and practiced. Witchcraft is greatly feared and elaborate ceremonies are undertaken to counteract the malicious efforts of a witch. A witch can get to his victim directly through metamorphosis or, more often, indirectly by dispatching disease spirits. A knowledgeable conjuror can dispel these spirits and return them to the sender by recourse to the proper ceremony. One type of witch is particularly fond of attacking people in a weakened condition, so that the slightest illness is considered a serious affair. No one will confess to being a witch or to practicing sorcery, but it is said that a witch can be recognized because he (or she) will never look anyone in the eye. Also dogs are felt to be particularly keen in detecting witches. The actual amount of sorcery practiced on the reservation today is probably slight, but its presence as a psychological reality accounts for a great deal of interpersonal hostility and a means for channeling aggression.

Cherokee love magic has not received the attention it deserves in published sources (e.g., Mooney 1891: 375-384, and Mooney and Olbrechts 1932: 154-155). One informant gave a vivid description of the process. According to his account –

A man would fast alone in the woods for seven days. His only nourishment came from herbal teas, and hunger pangs were pacified by swallowed saliva. A conjuror took the man for daily baths in a "branch" and "put water over his head," while reciting love conjurations. When the man returned to the "road" (i.e. back [224] to civilization), the desired woman against whom the ceremonies were directed would seek him out, wander after him, and "crave him." She wouldn't eat anything. If she got hungry, "she'd just bend over and eat dirt and think it was bread – she'd really crave that man."

Besides the oral symbolism which also abounds in Cherokee love formulas,[5] this account points up another prevalent motif in love attraction formulas. Before the desired end – the love of a particular woman – is achieved, the woman must be degraded. Although it is not always necessary to make her stoop to geophagy, the incantation should at least "render the woman blue [symbolic of trouble or distress], let her be completely veiled in loneliness ... and bring her down," as one of Mooney's formulas implores (Mooney 1891: 376). Before it is possible to gain a woman's love, she must be made unattractive to other suitors. Thus, love attraction rites may be viewed as a type of sorcery in which one of the objects is to bring misfortune upon another person.

In the case of a spurned suitor, he may lose any positive feeling for the woman and only wish to "bring her down" out of motives for revenge. She can be made unattractive to all others and be smitten with irrational love toward the spurned suitor, in which case he can have the satisfaction of unsympathetically observing her plight and repulsing her uncontrolled advances. Other forms of love magic include formulas for breaking up a match by a jealous third party, bringing back a straying husband or wife, and preventive magic against disruption of marital bliss.

---

4 * Much ball game ceremonialism persists today. The writer hopes to treat this subject in detail at a later time.

5

Many other forms of sorcery, closely related to love magic, are conceptualized by the phrase "twisting their minds." Although this can include making a person insane, it does not always have an evil connotation. Such magic can be used to transform a former enemy into a friend. More often, such formulas are used to produce temporary confusion or compliance from another to gain a specific end. This notion is implied in many of the ball game formulas which strive to keep the opposing players from seeing the ball, or to turn the enemies' minds from the anticipated joy of victory ("making them loose their grasp on the stakes").

This type of magic serves a new function on the reservation today. Conjurors are frequently employed by Cherokee involved in legal difficulties. It is felt that certain ceremonies have the power to influence a judge's decision and lighten the sentence. One particular case will illustrate:

A man was killed in Big Cove about 20 years ago by two young Cherokee. A conjuror took a personal interest in the case, because one of the defendants had been raised in his household. Bail was raised, and the conjuror assured his client [225] that he would be cleared of charges, if he followed instructions. The boy was taken to the creek daily and the conjuror performed many ceremonies to place the entire guilt on the other boy. On the day of the trial, the conjuror was certain his ceremonies were working and even predicted that the other boy would never return to Big Cove alive. The court met several days before the conjuror's client turned state's witness and was released. The other boy drew a sentence of 15 years in the penitentiary. Ironically, he died 9 days before his scheduled release from prison, thus fulfilling the conjuror's prophecy.

It has been argued here that the largo amount of Cherokee medico-magical knowledge that persists today can be accounted for by the presence of a written language and historical events which left the Eastern Cherokee isolated for the greater part of the 19th century. Some bodies of lore, as hunting and fishing magic, have disappeared because of shifting economic patterns and changes in the local ecology. More recently, increased contact with white culture has brought about changes and accommodation in the medico-magical belief system. Since the formulas survive verbatim these changes have occurred in interpretation, emphasis, and application. Although conjuring seems to be a declining art, it would be rash to predict its immediate demise, since the evidence presented indicates that the underlying belief system is able to absorb many shocks and reintegrate successfully.

BIBLIOGRAPHY

Gearing, Frederick – Cherokee political organizations, 1730-1775. MS., Ph.D. dissertation, University of Chicago, 1956.

Mooney, James 1890 Cherokee theory and practice of medicine. *Journ. Amer. Folklore* vol. 3: 44-50.
    1891 *Sacred formulas of the Cherokee*: 302-397. 7th Ann. Rep. Bur. Amer. Ethnology.
    1900 *Myths of the Cherokee*. 19th Ann. Rep. Bur. Amer. Ethnol. 1: 3-576.

Mooney, James, and Frans Olbrechts 1932 *The Swimmer manuscript.* Bur. Amer. Ethnol. Bull. 99.

Olbrechts, Frans 1930 Some Cherokee methods of divination. 23rd Intern. Congr. Americanists Proc. 1928: 547-552.

Speck, Frank G, and Broom, Leonard 1951 *Cherokee dance and drama.* Berkeley, Calif.

Thomas, Robert K – Cherokee values and world view. MS. on deposit Cross-Cultural Laboratory, University of North Carolina, 1958.

Witthoft, John 1948 Will West Long, Cherokee informant. *American Anthropologist* 50: 355-59.

Ray Playing Stickball

THE CHEROKEE BALLGAME CYCLE: AN ETHNOGRAPHER'S VIEW[1]

This paper [327] represents an interim report on some ideas being developed in the course of collaborating on a monograph dealing with the Cherokee ballgame with Marcia Herndon, a trained ethnomusicologist. My contribution to this joint venture will involve ethnological and ethnographic data gleaned from documentary sources and from field material collected mostly in 1959/60; her contribution will embody more recent field data plus ethno-musicological information and analysis. While we have devised a rudimentary division of labor, we are discovering that our respective working areas are not sealed off in splendid isolation. Rather, I think she has found that her recent field data take on added meaning when viewed from a longer time perspective and that her rich ethnomusicological materials require contextualization within the total ballgame cycle and, ultimately, within the dynamic interaction of Cherokee personality, social, and cultural systems. For my part, Miss Herndon's later field material not only enriches and amplifies my earlier data, but also serves as a critical check on the reliability and validity of my information. We both relied heavily on the same informant, but the information that we derived from him shades off in different directions owing to our different areas of concern, differing theoretical presuppositions, and probably for other less obvious reasons. Despite these divergences, we view the ethnomusicological analysis of the pre- and post-game dances as an integral part of our larger investigation and interpretation of the Cherokee ballgame; the ethnomusicological materials are not regarded as mere appendages of interesting data included to satisfy some unsatisfiable goal of ethnographic completeness.

Before proceeding to a description of the ballgame cycle, it seems desirable to present in brief form the basic model of traditional Cherokee social structure that informs our general interpretation of the ballgame. As with all such models, this one gains elegance in direct proportion to the amount of specific detail omitted. Nevertheless, the model does hopefully direct attention to what we consider to be critical features in understanding the elaborate ritual performances surrounding the ballgame.

The basic unit of Cherokee political and religious organization was the local village or town. Cherokee settlement pattern tended toward dispersion along streams and arable bottomland. A social and ceremonial center served as [328] the locus of collective religious ritual and the focus of local level government. This nucleus constitutes the major defining attribute of a Cherokee town. Families living in an area marginal to two or more towns would, presumably, face a choice of affiliating with one or another town. When town size grew beyond a critical threshold, based on ecological adjustment and institutional interpersonal efficiency, groups would hive off to form satellite settlements (Fogelson and Kutsche 1961).

These satellite settlements might maintain, at least for a while political and religious ties to the mother town before achieving an autonomous status. Direct and indirect white contact accelerated these processes of village fission and fusion during the eighteenth century. During this time, Cherokee population was distributed among some forty-five to sixty different towns. Early demographic information is faulty, but, roughly speaking, town size ranged from a high of about 650 people to a low of 98 persons, recorded for one settlement possessing its own council house. A modal Cherokee town probably numbered between 325 and 350 people.

As Fred Gearing has documented (1962), each town was politically autonomous and characterized by a dual system of political organization. Responsibility for regulating domestic affairs was entrusted to

---

[1] This article is a slightly edited version of a paper presented for the Symposium on Ethnomusicology in Anthropology at the Southern Anthropological Society Meetings in Dallas, Texas, April 1, 1971. My thanks go to Dr Norma McLeod, the convener of the symposium, and to the American Philosophical Society, which provided research funds for the collection of data on which the present paper is based.

a hierarchy of White or Peace officials and a council of town elders and clan heads. A Red or War organization took precedence in matters external to the town. In addition to its primary association with warfare, the Red organization was responsible for long-distance hunting expeditions and for commerce with other villages, tribes, and with Europeans. The chiefs of the Red organization were active warriors and tended to be younger, by about a generation, than the corresponding officials in the White organization. Contrasting styles of leadership characterized these political divisions. Peace chiefs ruled by consensus and quiet diplomacy, while War leaders tended to be more assertive and to gain followers through their inspirational qualities.

In addition to possessing a common culture and language, the major mechanism binding the Cherokee together as a single people was the existence of seven (perhaps more at an earlier period) non-localized, exogamous, matrilineal clans. Although the percentage of people per clan could vary considerably from town to town, it was considered necessary to have local representatives of all seven clans in each town in order to conduct major civic and religious activities. Given the generally small population per town, the prohibitions of marriage into one's own or one's father's clan, and a definite tendency toward matrilocality, a large number, if not the vast majority, of young men were forced to marry out of their natal towns and take up residence in their wives' villages. It is hypothesized that in the subsequent male bonding and identification of these similarly structurally situated, young, in-married men, or "son-in-laws" as the Cherokee sometimes refer to them, [329] one can see the processes that lead to the genesis of the Red or War organization.

The White and Red dualism can, perhaps, be summarized by the following series of related fundamental oppositions operant in traditional Cherokee culture:

Peace:	War
Passive:	Active
Old:	Young
Internal:	External
Plants:	Animals
Cultivated: / Tame	Wild
Female:	Male

The fundamental opposition between peace and war led Gearing to postulate the existence of two separate "structural poses" in traditional Cherokee society (1958: 1148-57). The articulation between these Red and White structural poses has both temporal and spatial aspects, as well as repetitive and non-repetitive features.

The conceptual opposition between old and young can best be discerned in certain interlocking aspects of the traditional Cherokee life cycle and domestic cycle. As has already been implied, marriage by a young man into another town served to attenuate his ties with his natal town and his own matrilineage. Marriage, with its attendant residential relocation, thus represented one of the most significant junctures in the life cycle of a Cherokee male. A young man's position within his wife's household was clearly marginal. Land and household were controlled by senior members of the wife's matrilineage; authority over his sons was vested in the wife's brothers or other adult men of her matrilineage. Functionally related to his peripheral position within his wife's household was the sexual division of labor. A man was expected to spend a good deal of his time and energy outside the village, pursuing wild game or taking-to the warpath. The woman's domain consisted of the household and nearby corn fields. It is estimated that a young adult Cherokee man might have spent as much as five months of the year away from his procreative family. Cherokee marriages in their early years were understandably quite fragile.

However, when a Cherokee man reached his late forties or early fifties, subtle changes occurred in his life style. As his prowess as a hunter and warrior began to decline, he started to "settle down" and achieve a greater degree of parity in the domestic household. Cherokee often mark this juncture in the life cycle as taking place when a man's hair starts to turn gray. Gray hair connotes accumulated wisdom, knowledge, and power. The active, assertive, and impulsive strength of the warrior is transmuted into the passive, [330] self-constrained, measured moral force of the tribal elder. Generally his position within the family becomes increasingly solidified, particularly with the departure of his wife's brothers upon their own marriages, with the death or decline of the wife's father, the departure of a man's own sons after their marriages, and the respect and support accorded him by his daughter's husbands.[2] In other situations where tins process of progressive integration is impeded, a man might separate from his wife and return to his natal village to reside with members of his own matrilineage, where lie might enjoy the status of a "beloved old man." In sum, this critical juncture along the life cycle, involving the structural transition from the status of young man to old man, can be conceptualized as a non-repetitive transformation from Red to White.

More directly germane to consideration of the ballgame were repetitive transformations between Red and White structural poses that involved spatial conceptions. These types of transformation can, perhaps, most clearly be viewed in early accounts of Cherokee warfare. Unless a town was under threat of imminent attack from outside enemies – in which case the White organization would abdicate authority for defense to the War Chiefs – the appropriate domain of the Red organization remained outside the village. Areas beyond the settled village were regarded by the Cherokee as wild, dangerous, and populated by unpredictable animal, human, and other-than-natural spiritual beings and forces. The younger married men, exogenous to the town in terms of origin and kinship, can be conceptualized as suitable mediators between these wild and tame domains. As in terrestrial rites of passage, first brilliantly delineated by Van Gennep (1960), passage from one culturally-constituted zone to another frequently necessitated or was marked by ritual. Before departing for the field, Cherokee warriors were segregated from the rest of society, placed under a restrictive set of taboos, and subjected to collective and individual rituals. On its return, the war party submitted to various purification rites, sometimes lasting a week or more, that were held outside the town. Only after completion of these rituals of re-entry, could they resume normal interaction with their families and fellow townsmen. The important thing to remember is, as Gearing has emphasized, that all young Cherokee men alternately adjusted to White and Red structural poses. We suggest that the transformation between these structural poses was effected by ritual and that analysis of critical juncture points in the ballgame cycle helps illuminate this process of transformation.

The close connection between ball play and warfare has been noted by many observers. In fact one of the names for the ball game, *danawa usdi'* translates as "little war." While the game is unquestionably aboriginal, and while several accounts of ballgames survive from the colonial period, it seems probable that ballgames assumed greater importance and, perhaps, greater ritual elaboration in post-Revolutionary times as a symbolic surrogate for [331] actual warfare. The units of opposition were towns or, less commonly, groups of allied towns or districts. Ballgames normally took place in midsummer through late fall. A team might play ball several times over the course of a season. The regular men's game was accompanied by heavy wagering between backers of the competing teams. Games between young boys also occasionally occurred, and we have historical notes on games between women, as well. The North Carolina Cherokee continue to play the game, although it has been denuded of much of its ritual and survives ostensibly as a tourist attraction. The game is no longer regularly played among the Oklahoma Cherokee, although it persists among the neighboring Creek.

The ballgame cycle was formally initiated by conversations between respected elders representing the players of the contending towns. After agreeing to a game and working out such details as the number of players per team, which players would be eligible,[3] where and when the game would be played, and

---

2 I am indebted to Gregory Urban for this insight.
3 This could be a point of serious contention if the conflict involved choices between a man's natal town

similar matters, the negotiator returned to his town and informed the players of the decisions made. The players then sought the services of a conjuror to direct the rituals and exercise his mystical powers to promote victory for their team. In the eyes of many Cherokee, the outcome of the game was less a function of the athletic abilities of the players as it was a power struggle between opposing conjurors. The players practiced daily for two weeks or more under the careful surveillance of the conjuror and his assistants. It is interesting to note that in choosing up sides for intra-town practice games, the married men played against the single men, or, put another way, the sons against the son-in-laws. A set of taboos was imposed that prohibited sexual intercourse, the eating of certain foods, and various other specific behavioral injunctions. The players underwent a series of individual and collective rituals that involved divination, blood-letting with a native surgical instrument, and rites by the side of a river during the liminal periods of dawn and dusk. The high point of the pre-game preparation was an all-night dance on the eve of the game; some of the details of this cultural performance will be presented shortly. After the all-night dance, the players marched in military fashion to the site of the game. This march was interrupted at four resting places where additional rituals were performed. The team usually took a devious route to the ball field in order to avoid the "trail magic" of the enemy conjuror. Immediately prior to the game, last minute rituals were held, bets were negotiated, and there was a formal march, accompanied by unison war whoops, to the center of the field, where the players paired off against specific opponents.

Ball play has been described by the popular press as "the world's roughest game" and "legalized homocide". No holds were barred; players dressed only in breachclouts (more recently swimming trunks or cut-away jeans) and had no protection to cushion the frequent spills or ward off blows [332] from enemy ball sticks; there were no time-outs or substitutions. The game continued until one team scored a designated number of goals, usually twelve, and a game might last thirty minutes or be played for seven or eight hours to no conclusion, with only one or two members of the original teams surviving. Serious injuries were frequent, and ballgame deaths were not unknown. Although nominally a team sport, ball play action more often resembled twelve or so separate wrestling matches. The action in a Creek ballgame is much faster, often resembling a group tennis match. Cherokee ball play resembles old-fashioned single-wing football with the progress of the ball toward the goal measured only in inches, as a ball carrier struggles to free himself from his adversary.

After the game the players were still considered to be in a ritually dangerous condition. Taboos continued in force for days or weeks after the game, dependent on the amount and type of ritual performed for the individual player. During this post-game period, players underwent gradual purification rituals to transform themselves back from a Red to a White condition. The ballgame cycle was officially terminated by the celebration of a Victory Dance at which the conjuror was rewarded, visitors from the defeated town were welcomed, and efforts were made to restore harmony. The Victory Dance bears close similarity to the ancient Scalp Dance.

While the entire ballgame cycle can be seen to involve successive transformation, that phase of the cycle of most heightened intensity (outside of the game, itself) would seem to be the all-night dance. Although some early accounts, such as Bartram's, state that the dance was held in the "Great Rotunda" or council house, within the last century the dance was normally held outdoors at a secluded dance ground proximal to a river or stream. At the center of the ground was a fire around which the players danced in counterclockwise direction, following the lead of a male singer who kept time with a gourd rattle.

On one side of the dance ground stood an upright crossbar or "hanger," symbolizing the "home sticks" or goal posts, on which were hung the players' ball sticks when not in use. In front of this "hanger" a line of seven women danced to the accompaniment of songs sung by a specially commissioned male drummer. These seven female dancers are said by some to represent the menstruating virgins from the seven clans who were instrumental in causing the downfall of the legendary cannibalistic ogre,

---

and town of post-marital residence.

Stoneclad (cf. Mooney 1900: 319-320). They might also represent the female complement of the War organization, which sometimes accompanied the warriors into the field to take care of domestic chores around the temporary camp sites.

The less well developed female replicate Red and White organizations consisted of both War Women and older, beloved or "Pretty" women who were permitted to speak in council.[4] In addition to the specific performers, [333] the dance was attended by other members of the home community and occasional visitors from other towns. Constant vigilance was maintained to insure that no spies working for the enemy town were lurking about. Such spies might try to steal some of the fire or secure spittle from the players in devious ways in order to facilitate the contagious magic of the rival conjuror.

The transformative nature of this cultural performance is attested to by the Cherokee names for the ballgame dance as recorded by Speck and Broom (1951: 55): *Dātselia nuni'*, "things transformed" and *dane ksi notani'* "they are going to put things on their buttocks." The latter expression refers specifically to the ornamental "tail" assemblages, usually made of feathers, that were once worn by ballplayers throughout the Southeast and are accurately depicted in many of Catlin's drawings.

To explicate the transformative character of the all-night dance, three interrelated levels of analysis will be suggested. On the first level attention is drawn to the social organization of the dance. Second, an analysis of some key ritual symbols and their manipulation will be attempted. Finally, a psychological interpretation of the transformation, as it affects the focal actors, the ballplayers, will be offered.

The most striking feature about the social arrangement of the all-night dance is the alternation and strict separation between the men's and women's parts of the dance. During the course of the night, the men dance seven times for about twenty minutes. As a prelude to each male dance sequence, the players form two parallel lines facing the enemy town. A man designated as the *Talala* or redheaded woodpecker sprints between the two lines and utters sharp, tremulous war cries. The players then dance around the fire brandishing ball sticks in imitative ball play action. They antiphonally respond to the singing of their dance leader, who walks outside the circle of players and keeps time with a gourd rattle often adorned with a rattlesnake rattle.

Periodically the players shout taunts and emit war whoops in the direction of the enemy town. While the ball players retire to the riverbanks to undergo additional private ritual, the line of women dancers waves back and forth in front of the "hanger" to the rhythm and extemporaneous verses of the male drummer. Tile women sometimes chant verses along with the drummer but with subdued almost solemn voices, in sharp contrast to the vigorous singing and spontaneous shouting of the male dancers. Speck and Broom report that "The figure of speech applying to their (the women's) dance action is that they are 'stepping on the players of the opposite town'" (1951: 60). Our information reveals that this is more than a "figure of speech," since on the right side of the hanger is a rock under which are placed black beads that have been conjured to represent specific players on the enemy team. A woman dancer at the end of the line periodically steps on the rock to weaken the enemy. Enough has been said to see the operation of the [334] male-female opposition as reflected in the dance. The ballplayers exude an aura of strength and confidence as they go through their dance actions. The more passive and restrained women's sequence is directed almost exclusively at weakening and debilitating the enemy.

Among the more prominent ritual symbols employed in the dance are birds, the fire, and snakes. The prominence of bird symbolism harks back to the myth accounting for the origin of ball play in which the flying creatures defeated the quadrupedal animals (Mooney 1900: 286-287). Traditionally, a specialist from the Bird clan was in charge of collecting, dyeing, and ritually treating feathers to be worn by warriors and ballplayers. Each player identified with a different species of bird on the basis of his particular playing skills or position on the field. Thus the center fighter, who was usually the strongest

---

4 This aspect of Cherokee social structure has been scarcely recognized in the literature, let alone systematically studied.

player on the team, wore eagle feathers, after the legendary captain of the bird team. Other players might choose a specific bird known for its swiftness, its agility, or its ability to pick up objects. The wearing of tails in the dance or in the game has long since faded from memory, but players still attach feathers to their hair or to their ball sticks.

It should also be noted that birds appear to have played an important role in traditional war symbolism. One Cherokee war title is Raven, so selected for its ability to scout at night. Eagles and woodpeckers are frequently found engraved on shell gorgets associated with major prehistoric Southeastern ceremonial centers. Birds operate as multiplex symbols. On the one hand they serve as a collective representation or cognitive category binding the players together, as well as associating the team with the victors in the myth about the ballgame between the birds and the four-legged creatures. On the other hand, given the great diversity of bird species, they serve an individuating function that enables each player to have a separate identity within the collective whole.

Fire is a very complex symbol that admits of many interpretations. As Levi-Strauss well appreciates, fire is a transforming symbol par excellence, if not par boiled. In early accounts of Cherokee warfare, a war fire was sometimes carried into battle in an earthenware pot suspended by two horizontal poles. This portable fire was referred to as a sacred ark by many early observers eager to link the Indians genealogically to the Lost tribes of Israel. Conjurors are known to have brought portions of the ball dance fire in their pipes or in a lantern carried in a gunny sack to the ball field for magical purposes.

Fire was referred to by the Cherokee as father or grandfather and was regarded as an earthy aspect of astral divinities. Sacrifices of old tobacco (*nicotiana rustica*), deer tongue, first fruits, and other offerings were borne aloft to spiritual agents on high or in the earth's four quarters through the agency of smoke. During the dance, begger lice, which are forked and [335] resemble human beings, were sometimes named for particular opponents and roasted in the fire. This was intended to have the homopathic effect of causing the rival players to become feverish and short of breath during the game. I have already mentioned precautions taken to protect the fire from enemy spies.

Some other comments related to the symbolic role of fire in the ballgame dance deserve mention here. Near dawn, at the conclusion of the dance, the seven female dancers threw pine boughs into the fire to make it blaze up and create a thick smoke to envelop the players. Pine and other evergreens are considered important purifying agents by the Cherokee. Pine smoke was believed to immunize the ball players from the sorcery of their opponents. Also the dense smoke was thought to so shroud the players that their enemies would have difficulty seeing them during the game. At a signal given by the drummer, the women threw blazing pine knots at the hanger in imitative ball play action. After the fire died down, the player's backs and legs were switched with charred pine branches to impart still more magical potency.

The potency of fire as a natural symbol for warfare is further enhanced by its association with the color, red. Its transformative properties stand out in the residues of the volatility – black (charring), symbolic of death and destruction to the Cherokee, and white (ashes), symbolic of peace and the power of the elders.

Snakes, particularly rattlesnakes, occupy an important status as transformation symbols in Cherokee world view. Much of my information on Cherokee "snakelore" derives directly from an excellent unpublished undergraduate honors' thesis written by Mr Gregory Urban at the University of Chicago (Urban 1971). Many of the natural attributes of snakes contribute to their role as transformation symbols. Edmund Leach (1964: 42) has discussed certain anomalous features of snakes that make them interstitial in most native zoological classifications: the fact that snakes lay eggs, but do not fly-although Leach overlooks the fact that some snakes bring forth live offspring; the assumption that snakes are land creatures, but have no legs-again Leach conveniently dismisses the existence of water snakes. Nonetheless, snakes do possess certain attributes that contribute to their status as suitable transformation symbols. Snakes are sufficiently similar in their basic morphology, and distinctive from other animals, to be classified together as a taxonomic category. Yet within tills taxonomic unity, snakes manifest extreme behavioral variability. Snakes can be terrestrial, aquatic, or arboreal. Some species change color with the season. Snakes also can shed their skins. Their degree of potency can range from the harmlessness of the insect-eating garter snake to the venom of the rattlesnake that can prove lethal to a cow or to a human being. [336]

In common with many native peoples around the world, the Cherokee apperceive an identity between snakes and lightning. The powerful Sons of Thunder, the Little Red Men, are frequently associated with snakes in Cherokee myths and ritual formulae, particularly those dealing with war and the ballgame. One of the most powerful substances available to Cherokee warriors and ball players was lightning-struck wood. Warriors and ball players would mark their bodies with charred pieces of lightning-struck wood before confronting their enemies.

A mask with a carved rattlesnake on top was sometimes used in dances to recruit warriors for war parties. Although not a regular item of diet, rattlesnake flesh was given to ballplayers to chew in order "to make them terrible to their opponents" (Mooney 1900: 296). The cutting edge of one of the surgical instruments for the scratching ordeal consisted of rattlesnake fangs.

Snake symbolism is much in evidence at the ballgame dance. Rattlesnake rattles are often affixed to a player's hair and to the gourd rattle of the players' dance leader. Rattlesnake or lightning designs were often engraved on the player's ball sticks to give them added potency. Rattlesnake skin belts were formerly used to suspend the feathered "tails." One informant explained to me that the counterclockwise direction men's ball dance was imitative of the coiling pattern of snakes.[5]

Rattlesnakes then symbolize wildness, danger, and fierceness, both in the deadly striking power of their fangs and in the explosive kinetic energy of the lightning bolt. What more appropriate symbol could be used to dramatize the change of state from a White to a Red condition or structural pose?

This discussion of birds, fire, and snakes is meant to be illustrative and suggestive rather than definitive. Obviously much remains to be done by way of a deeper and fuller analysis to clarify their use as ritual symbols, particularly in terms of their manipulation and articulation. It should also be stressed that birds, fire, and snakes far from exhaust the repertoire of ritual symbols invoked in the ballgame.

We now come to the third level of analysis of this transformative process, the psychological affects of the events on these individual ballplayers. It seems probable that the psychological concomitant to the sociocultural transformation from White to Red was an altered state of consciousness. Many of the stimuli that psychologists and neurophysiologists posit as giving rise to altered states of consciousness seem amply represented at the ballgame dance: metabolic changes in response to fasting; mortification of the flesh in the scratching ritual; a state of near exhaustion brought on by lack of sleep and strenuous dancing; the pulsations engendered by the flickering light of the fire and the rhythmic beat of the drum and rattle, which might be sufficient to induce states of photic or sonic driving; the periods of restricted, stimulation [337] and intense concentration while the conjuror performs his rituals in the darkness of the riverbank; and the generalized atmosphere of highly charged emotion that pervades the whole night's proceedings (cf. Ludwig 1968). Under the right conditions, any one of these triggering mechanisms would be sufficient to induce an altered state of consciousness in an individual; the combination of such a wide array of potential triggering mechanisms at the ballgame dance would seem to increase the probability of such mental metamorphosis.

Reports of older men who played ball when the ritual cycle was still intact lend support to this hypothesis. One man reported feeling "light as feather during the ballgame"; another remembers being oblivious to the crowd and to events taking place on and off the field; others recall playing the game in a dream-or trance-like state. Short of replicating the entire ball game cycle, reenacting the dance, and placing electrodes on the participants to measure changes in brain wave pattern, the hypothesis that the ballgame dance induced altered states of consciousness cannot be verified directly. However, its

---

5 However, it should be noted that all circular Cherokee dances around a fire go in a counterclockwise direction.

likelihood might be enhanced by a more systematic collection of recollections by former ballplayers and by a closer analysis of the rhythms, durations, and energy expenditure in the ballplayers' dance.

In conclusion, this paper has attempted to provide a preliminary interpretation of the Cherokee ballgame cycle. The general notion of transformation has been utilized as a unifying theme linking together social structural, cultural, and psychological levels of analysis. The data and mode of interpretation offered here hopefully provide a framework within which ethno-musicological data and analysis can be more meaningfully fitted. Fuller analysis and documentation await monographic treatment.

References [338]

Fogelson, Raymond D. and Paul Kutsche 1961 Cherokee economic cooperatives: the *Gadugi*. In *Symposium on Cherokee and Iroquois culture*. WN Fenton and J Gulick, eds. Washington, DC: Smithsonian Institution, Bureau of American Ethnology, Bulletin 180.

Gearing, Fred 1958 The structural poses of 18th century Cherokee villages. American Anthropologist 60: 1148-57.

  1962 *Priests and warriors*. American Anthropological Association Memoir 93.

Leach, Edmund R 1964 Anthropological aspects of language: animal categories and verbal abuse. In E.H Lenneberg, ed. *New directions in the study of language*. Cambridge, Mass: The MIT Press.

Ludwig, Arnold M 1968 Altered states of consciousness. In R Prince, ed., *Trance and possession states*. Montreal, RM Bucke Memorial Society.

Mooney, James 1900 *Myths of the Cherokee*. Bureau of American Ethnology 19th Annual Report, Part 1. Washington, DC: Government Printing Office.

Speck, Frank G, and Leonard Bloom 1951 *Cherokee dance and drama*. (in collaboration with Will West Long) Berkeley and Los Angeles, University of California Press.

Urban, Gregory 1971 Domestic groups, myth, and the study of an animal category: eighteenth century Cherokee. Unpublished BA honors paper. University of Chicago.

Van Gennep, Arnold 1960 *The rites of passage*. Trans. by MB Vizedom and GL Caffee. London: Routledge and Kegan Paul.

AN ANALYSIS OF CHEROKEE SORCERY AND WITCHCRAFT[1]

The aboriginality of Cherokee sorcery and witchcraft beliefs and practices seems assured from comparative ethnological data, linguistic evidence, and the degree of elaboration encountered in the period when reliable ethnographic material becomes available. Several early colonial documents contain occasional allusive references to conjurers and witches. One of the earliest concise descriptions of Cherokee beliefs in this area is found in Judge John Haywood's *Natural and Aboriginal History of Tennessee*, published in 1823. Haywood notes:

> In ancient times the Cherokees had no conception of any one's dying a natural death. They universally ascribed the death of those who perished by disease to the intervention or agency of evil spirits, and witches, and conjurers, who had connexion with the Shina [Hebraic evil being], or evil spirits. They ascribe to their witches and conjurers the power to put on any shape they please, either of bird, or beast, but they are supposed generally to prefer the form of a cat or of an owl. They ascribe to them the power of passing from one place to another in as short a time as they please.... Their witches and conjurers are supposed to receive their faculties from evil spirits, and are punished to this day with death. Suspicion affixes to them the imputation of this crime. A person dying by disease, and charging his death to have been procured by means of witchcraft, or spirits, by any other person, consigns that person to inevitable death. They profess to believe that their conjurations have no effect on white men.[2][114]

That Cherokee witchcraft was a living reality rather than empty superstition is attested to by the fact that in 1824 the Arkansas Cherokees enacted legislation making it a capital offense to murder a suspected witch. In addition merely accusing someone of practicing witchcraft was punishable by whipping.[3]

Cherokee sorcery and witchcraft beliefs and practices have been studied and restudied for over eighty years by anthropologists. Despite this continuous effort, there is still no comprehensive picture of this complex subject.

James Mooney initiated modern anthropological studies of Cherokee medicomagical knowledge through his discovery of the existence of native texts, written in the Sequoyah syllabary.[4] These texts, called "sacred formulas" by Mooney, were owned by native practitioners and formed the basis of Cherokee medicomagical philosophy and practice. The writing down of this material imbued it with tangibility and an aura of sanctity that insured a fairly literal transmission of the knowledge contained

---

1 I wish to thank the American Philosophical Society for providing funds for the fieldwork on which this paper is based and the Division of Social Sciences of the University of Chicago for travel money that enabled me to present this paper. This paper was originally envisioned as part of a collaborative effort between Charles Holzinger and myself. I wish to credit him for stimulation during the early phases of preparation and I also want to acknowledge the criticism and encouragement of the following people: Carlos Dabezies, Charles Hudson, Paul Kutsche, William Sturtevant, and Albert Wahrhaftig.

2 John Haywood, *The Natural and Aboriginal History of Tennessee, up to the First Settlements Therein by the White People, in the Year 1768* (Nashville: George Wilson 1823): 267-268.

3 James Mooney, *Myths of the Cherokee*, Nineteenth Annual Report of the Bureau of American Ethnology, 1897-1898 (Washington, DC 1900): 138, citing Cephus Washburn 1869.

4 James Mooney, *Sacred Formulas of the Cherokee*, Seventh Annual Report of the Bureau of American Ethnology (Washington, DC 1891).

within these texts. It is known that Sequoyah created his syllabary in the 1820s and that his invention diffused rapidly throughout the Cherokee Nation, penetrating even culturally conservative pockets of the preremoval population where English was scarcely known and the inroads of acculturation had not yet seriously undermined the traditional belief structure. Much of the ritual knowledge contained in these texts appears to have been set down in the decades immediately preceding and following the Cherokee removal in 1838. Indirect evidence for this assumption lies in the frequent "archaisms" that bedevil anyone, even a fluent contemporary Cherokee speaker, who attempts to translate these texts. If we assume that these texts were originally recorded by tribal elders, with whom such knowledge traditionally resides, then the provenience of this material can, perhaps, be extended back to the end of the eighteenth century. These "sacred formulas" contain instructions and rituals for curing, preventing, or transmitting a multitude of culturally recognized disease entities. In addition a large number of texts deal with love magic, with various forms of divination, with special [115] rituals for the ballgame and warfare, and with a whole host of additional subjects."[5]

In *The Sacred Formulas of the Cherokee* (1891) Mooney presented a brief synopsis of beliefs and practice with regard to medicine and disease, as well as translations of twenty-eight specimen texts, including six dealing with love magic, two to prevent sorcery and witchcraft, and one "to destroy life." Mooney collected several hundred additional sacred formulas – or *idi:gawé:sdi* ("things said") to use the more appropriate Cherokee name.[6] These were deposited and remain in the Smithsonian Institution archives.

Mooney's pioneering work was extended and elaborated after his death by the Belgian anthropologist Frans Olbrechts. Olbrechts spent a year with the North Carolina Cherokees where he recollected, reedited, and retranslated a collection of medical *idi:gawé:sdi* once belonging to A.yûn.i ("Swimmer"), one of Mooney's major informants. The product of Olbrechts's dedicated labors was *The Swimmer Manuscript*,[7] which, besides containing translations of ninety-eight medical *idi:gawé:sdi*, includes a detailed introduction to Cherokee medico-magical beliefs. With the passing of so many knowledgeable curing specialists in recent decades, the information contained in The Swimmer Manuscript can be obtained from no other source today. The richness and uniqueness of the material plus the ethnographic and linguistic skills of Mooney and Olbrechts combine to make The Swimmer Manuscript probably the best study of ethnomedicine available for any North American Indian society. It is surprising with the present levels of interest in medical anthropology and native belief systems at an all-time high that the value of this monograph has scarcely been appreciated by other than Cherokee specialists.

During the 1940s Frank Speck and John Witthoft collected important information on Cherokee ceremonialism and beliefs.[8] Much of their material dealing with medicine and magic, including a considerable number of *idi:gawé:sdi* once belonging to Will West Long, has not seen the light of published day but is available for study in the library of the [116] American Philosophical Society. In the

---

5 Cf. Jack F Kilpatrick and Anna G Kilpatrick, *Run toward the Night-land: Magic of the Oklahoma Cherokees* (Dallas, Texas: Southern Methodist University Press, 1967).

6 Jack F Kilpatrick and Anna G Kilpatrick, *Walk in Your Soul: Love Incantations of the Oklahoma Cherokees* (Dallas, Tex: Southern Methodist University Press, 1965): 4-8.

7 James Mooney and Frans M Olbrechts, *The Swimmer Manuscript*, Smithsonian Institution, Bureau of American Ethnology Bulletin no. 99 (Washington, DC, 1932).

8 Frank G Speck and Leonard Broom, *Cherokee Dance and Drama* (Berkeley and Los Angeles: University of California Press, 1951); John Witthoft, *Green Corn Ceremonialism in the Eastern Woodlands*, Occasional Contributions from the Museum of Anthropology of the University of Michigan, no. 13 (Ann Arbor: University of Michigan Press, 1949); John Witthoft and Wendell S Hadlock, "Cherokee-Iroquois Little People," Journal of American Folklore 59 (1946): 413-422.

late 1950s I collected information on changing medicomagical beliefs and ballgame ritualism.[9] While I did not focus directly on the subjects of sorcery and witchcraft, a certain amount of data on these topics was obtained during the course of fieldwork.

More recently Jack and Anna Kilpatrick, two gifted Cherokee scholars with a remarkable grasp of the subtleties of written and spoken Cherokee, undertook long overdue work among the Oklahoma Cherokees, as well as translating and editing some of the manuscripts collected by Mooney and Olbrechts in North Carolina. The Kilpatricks succeeded in collecting, translating, and publishing a number of *idi:gawe:-sdi* in numerous papers[10] and in three important monographs: *Walk in Your Soul*, devoted to the topic of Cherokee love magic; *Run toward the Nightland*, a general treatment of the wide range of Cherokee magic; and a recently published monograph *Notebook of a Cherokee Shaman*,[11] a collection of fifty *idi:gawe:sdi*. The Oklahoma material is especially crucial in revealing continuities and changes in belief structure as the Western Cherokees adapted to a new ecological and social situation.

The present analysis is a preliminary attempt to comprehend some aspects of the larger structure of Cherokee witchcraft and sorcery beliefs by examining culturally recognized categories of witches and sorcerers. This study is synthetic in combining documentary sources with information gathered from informants, in considering both North Carolina and Oklahoma Cherokees, and in not adhering to a specific synchronic level. The treatment is qualitative and inferential, rather than quantitative and firmly documented as is the case, for example, in Kluckhohn's study of *Navaho Witchcraft*.[12] The arguments and generalizations offered here are not buttressed by a substantial collection of case histories. Rather, this work is an attempt to put in order some facts and speculations about Cherokee sorcery and witchcraft, to place the Cherokee data in perspective relative to comparable beliefs and practices in other societies, and to advance some generalizations about that data which can hopefully direct more specific investigations in [117] the field and in the library, especially through analysis of the rich treasure of translated and untranslated *idi:gawe:sdi*.

For purposes of this essay, sorcery and witchcraft may collectively be defined as the presumed ability of one human being to effect, directly or indirectly, undesirable transformations of state in another human being. The ability to induce adverse changes of state in another person directly through innate capacities, as acts of an inherently evil or maleficent disposition, is generally ascribed to the realm of witchcraft. Witches in many societies are thought to derive their powers through some form of putative biological inheritance. Sorcery, in contrast, usually refers to acquired knowledge of specific incantations and ritual acts that enable a practitioner to invoke spiritual agents or occult forces for the purpose of causing misfortune, illfare, or even death to a designated victim.

Another way of conceptualizing traditional distinctions between witchcraft and sorcery is to

---

9 Raymond D Fogelson, A Study of the Conjuror in Eastern Cherokee Society (MA University of Pennsylvania, 1958); Change, Persistence, and Accommodation in Cherokee Medico-magical Beliefs, in *Symposium on Cherokee and Iroquois Culture*, William N Fenton and John Gulick, Bureau of American Ethnology, Bulletin 180 (Washington DC 1961); The Cherokee Ball-game: Study in Southeastern Indian Ethnology (PhD University of Pennsylvania 1962); The Cherokee Ballgame Cycle: An Ethnographer's View, *Ethnomusicology* 15 (1971): 327-333. [129]

10 Jack F Kilpatrick, The *Siqusnid' Dil'tidegi* Collection, Southern Methodist University, Bridewell Library (Dallas, Tex: Bridewell Library, 1962); Folk Formulas of the Oklahoma Cherokees, *Journal of the Folklore Institute* 1 (1964): 214-219; Jack F Kilpatrick and Anna G Kilpatrick, Cherokee Burn Conjurations, *Journal Graduate Research Center* (SMU) 33 (1964): 17-21; A Cherokee Conjuration to Cure a Horse, *Southern Folklore Quarterly* 28 (1964); 216-218; The Foundation of Life: The Cherokee National Ritual, *American Anthropologist* 66 (1964): 1386-1389.

11 Jack F Kilpatrick and Anna G Kilpatrick, Notebook of a Cherokee Shaman, Smithsonian Contributions to Anthropology 2 (1970): 83-125.

12 Clyde Kluckhohn, *Navaho Witchcraft* (Boston: Beacon Press 1944).

employ the familiar philosophic antithesis between nature and culture, a mode of analysis that dates back at least to the pre-Socratic philosophers and is enjoying renewed vogue through the stimulating logical exercises of Claude Levi-Strauss. Witchcraft, though perhaps conceived of as unnatural or abnormal from a psychosocial point of view, nevertheless can be thought of as natural in being genetically or ontogenetically grounded and as a fact of nature in the sense of being uncontrolled and relatively uncontrollable by available human cultural resources. Sorcery, as an acquired or learned technique, is clearly a product of human cultural evolution. As such, sorcery is subject to various socio-cultural control systems. A sorcerer can decide whether, when, and in what way to employ his magical procedures. Also, as is well known, he can decide to terminate these procedures under certain circumstances. Witchcraft, as an avowedly contracultural and antisocial activity, lacks most of these control features. Other distinctions seem to follow from the nature-culture opposition. Witchcraft tends to have a quality of directness in that the witch generally works to achieve his or her ends without the use of intermediate instrumental spiritual beings or without mechanical or technological devices. Sometimes a witch [118] can influence events by mystical teleportation; more often a witch must make direct contact with the victim, usually in metamorphosed form. This latter requirement can prove to be something of a liability, since it may make the witch vulnerable to the elaborate antiwitchcraft procedures capable of being mobilized in many cultures. The directness-indirectness dimension can also be seen in the fact that witchcraft typically involves a simple two-party interaction between witch and victim, while sorcery usually involves three- and four-party interactions composed of sorcerer or sorcerers, client or clients, and victim.

While the intended effects of witchcraft and sorcery practices are often indistinguishable (i.e., both can cause identical undesirable transformations of state in a person), the two phenomena can usually be distinguished in terms of process. It is generally held that one can study witchcraft *beliefs*, but not witchcraft *procedures*. Witchcraft is regarded as eventuating from mental acts of will involving immanent powers not amenable to empirical observation. The process of sorcery, on the other hand, may be studied more directly, since the utilization of spells, curses, incantations, and ritual action generally takes the form of externalized observable magical procedures. Sorcery techniques follow a definite system of logic that can often be approached through native exegesis. To put the matter simply, it is possible to become a sorcerer's apprentice, but tutelage from a witch is, at least, pedagogically problematic.

The now traditional anthropological distinction between sorcery and witchcraft was, of course, originally formulated by E.E Evans-Pritchard to accommodate his Zande data.[13]13 The distinction rapidly became generalized to a near universal by enshrinement in most introductory anthropology textbooks. Its influence was profoundly felt as anthropologists consciously or unconsciously forced their data to fit this dichotomous mold. Such recent work as the volume edited by Middleton and Winter on *Witchcraft and Sorcery in East Africa*,[14]14 Victor Turner's critical review of this work,[15]15 the volume on witchcraft confessions and accusations edited by Mary Douglas,[16]16 and the collection of papers edited by Deward Walker entitled *Systems of North American Witchcraft and Sorcery*[17]17 all point [119] to the analytic limitations of the sorcery-witchcraft dichotomy and implicitly argue for more careful descriptions of such belief and action systems in the particular society's own terms before attempting premature cross-

---

13 EE Evans-Pritchard, *Witchcraft, Oracles, and Magic among the Azande* (Oxford: Clarendon Press, 1937).

14 John F Middleton and Edward Winter, eds., *Witchcraft and Sorcery in East Africa* (London: Routledge and Kegan Paul, 1963).

15 Victor W Turner, "Witchcraft and Sorcery: Taxonomy versus Dynamics," Africa 34 (1964): 319-324.

16 Mary Douglas, ed., *Witchcraft Confessions and Accusations*, Association of Social Anthropologists Monograph 9 (London: Tavistock Publications, 1970).

17 Deward Walker, ed., *Systems of North American Witchcraft and Sorcery*. Anthropological Monographs of the University of Idaho 1 (Moscow: University of Idaho 1970).

cultural comparison and generalization. As this study demonstrates, the sorcerer-witch distinction has only partial applicability in interpreting the Cherokee data.

Understanding of the various categories of persons who the Cherokees believe are capable of effecting adverse transformations of state in other individuals is made difficult by the coexistence, but frequent nonidentity, of native and English terms of reference. Many of the native terms today defy precise definition, and informants often disagree about the amount of semantic space occupied by analogous English terms.

We will begin by discussing those types of individuals whom contemporary Cherokees refer to by the English term witch. The two principal defining criteria of Cherokee "witches" appear to be a capacity for metamorphosis and an inherently evil disposition. Although witches are believed to possess powers of clairvoyance and can effect their wicked ends by omnipotence of thought (eg, they can read people's minds and make someone sick merely by wishing him so), the evidence suggests that Cherokee witches more commonly accomplish their nefarious designs by changing their form and making direct physical contact with their victims. The most frequently reported forms of metamorphosis include ravens, owls, cats, balls of fire, shafts of purplish light, and other human beings, including those of the opposite sex. Witches can also make themselves invisible to normal sight, although special herbal decoctions can be taken by men and dogs to detect their presence.

With respect to inherent evil, the second defining attribute of a witch, the Cherokees feel that witches are irredeemable beings whose true existence falls outside the realm of humanity. Whereas a basically humane person (*u:dáno:ti*, "a man of soul, heart, feeling") may commit an unjust act out of weakness, understandable provocation, or error, his actions may be [120] forgiven, and in the past the Cherokees had many institutionalized forms of redemption and reconciliation. However, a wrong committed by an acknowledged or suspected witch can never be condoned, since such behavior represents unmitigated malice. Witches are believed to prey on human communities by adding the unexpired normal life expectancies of their victims to their own. As a result older people are increasingly suspected of practicing witchcraft with advancing age. Old age in Cherokee society is associated with power, and the implied power commands deference by others. The traditional Cherokee tendency to defer to older persons is sometimes regarded in terms of honor or love, as exemplified in the Cherokee political category of "beloved old men." However, this usage may be a euphemistic secondary rationalization, with the underlying psychodynamic root of this deferential behavior being fear of the power of elders- Relief from the depredations of a witch is only accomplished through his or her – or perhaps more appropriately its – death.

The Cherokees employ at least three nonmutually exclusive terms that correspond roughly to the general conception of a witch. One term, *tsi:kilí*, literally means "hoot owl," a bird of ill omen who supposedly performs its maleficent activities at night.[18] A second appellation given to witches, *suna:yi aneda'i*, can be translated "they walk about during the night" or, more simply, "night walkers." Both of these terms reflect the widespread belief that witches have an affinity for darkness and that most of their activities take place under nocturnal cover.

A third term that nudges into a portion of the semantic space occupied by the Cherokee notion of witch is *ada:wé:hi*, a word defying precise translation but sometimes rendered as "wizard," suggesting a composite witch-sorcerer category. This term is very frequently used to flatter a wide variety of spiritual beings in the written *idi:gawé:sdi*, but can also be applied to a human magical practitioner who has, to use Olbrechts's apt phrase "got the utmost."[19] The Kilpatricks despairingly note that this term has indiscriminately been equated with "medicine man" by non-Cherokee writers; they comment that "the chances of the average Roman Catholic for achieving canonization are far greater than those of a

---

18 Mooney and Olbrechts, *Swimmer Manuscript*, p. 29.
19 *ibid*, p. 29.

Cherokee medicine man [121] for ever being considered an *ada:we:hi*.[20] Most contemporary Eastern Cherokees would readily agree that there are no *ani:-da:wé:hi* (plural form) among them today, although there is a hesternalgic tendency to confer such exalted status on bygone practitioners whose reputed feats become more fantastically exaggerated with the passage of time.[21]

Unlike traditional Western European belief, a Cherokee witch may be either male or female and given the mechanism of metamorphosis can be both at different times. Field data and the small amount of available literature indicate no proclivity for male or female predominance in supposed witchcraft activity. Theoretically, the status of witch is not considered to be limited to a specific age. However, as discussed previously, older people are more likely to be suspected of witchcraft than younger adults or children.

Additional insight into Cherokee conceptions of witches can be derived by examining the processes by which an individual is thought to become a witch. Although witches are described as having an inherent propensity for evil, the Cherokees do not believe such characteristics to be prenatally determined as part of a genetic or "blood" inheritance.

Olbrechts reports a procedure thought to produce witches that involves a special twenty-four day regimen imposed on infants, particularly on twins. During this period the infant is denied the mother's or any other woman's breast, subsists on liquid from fermented hominy given him only at night, and is kept strictly concealed from any visitors.[22] Data obtained by Charles Holzinger in 1957[23] provide basic confirmation of Olbrechts's information, although many details vary. Holzinger was told that with parental consent an infant could be made into a witch with the aid of a conjurer. The infant is isolated from the mother's breast for seven days and nourished on a specially decocted herbal tea. According to informant testimony:

The first born child is fed on tea for seven days before it sucks tittles. Just the mother, daddy, and conjurer are allowed to see the baby. It's got too much power, like the ravens it can go over everything's head. It can look right through a house or a woman's dress. It can tell just by [122] looking what you're going to say. If they do only part of it [i.e., terminate the ritual before the full seven days], it can crawl like a possum, but if it's the seven days, it can fly.

Olbrechts notes precocity in youngsters subjected to such treatment.[24] Besides being able to metamorphose themselves into various human and animal forms, they gratify their needs through omnipotence of thought and also can communicate and play with the "Little People," a class of mischievous, childlike spiritual beings who are normally invisible to ordinary human eyes. If other members of the community discover that someone is planning to raise a witch child, they can abort the process by slipping some food prepared by a menstruating woman into the diet of the secluded infant. If indeed these beliefs bear any relationship to actual practice, it is difficult to understand possible reasons why any Cherokee parent would voluntarily choose to have his child raised as a witch. While it is believed that children so reared are self-sufficient, with boys able to become unfailing hunters and girls able to accomplish domestic tasks through powers of thought, nevertheless such individuals become disturbing elements in the ongoing functioning of society. As Olbrechts notes, "When they are grown up they are most annoying individuals; they always know what you think, and you could not possibly mislead them. And what is worse, they can make you ill, dejected, lovesick, dying, merely by thinking

---

20 Kilpatrick and Kilpatrick, *Walk in Your Soul*, p. 9.
21 Mooney and Olbrechts, *Swimmer Manuscript*, p. 88.
22 *ibid*, p. 130.
23 Charles H Holzinger, unpublished field notes, 1957.
24 Mooney and Olbrechts, *Swimmer Manuscript*, p. 130.

you in such a condition,"[25] Moreover, a suspected witch's life is in chronic jeopardy, since an elaborate array of counterwitchcraft measures may be deployed by an outraged community.

Another method by which an individual can be made into a witch at a later age is recognized by the Cherokees, This involves a fast and the drinking of a decoction of a rare plant, which Olbrechts tentatively identifies as *Saggittaria latifollia Willd.*, said to resemble a beetlelike insect, with the stem of the plant growing through its mouth. If the infusion is drunk and the fast maintained for four consecutive days, the individual is believed to attain the capacity for metamorphosis [123] into creatures living on the surface of the ground. However, if the ritual is continued for seven days, the individual is thought to be capable of transformation into various kinds of flying creatures and to be able to travel underground in the manner of a mole or an earthworm.[26] One of the more common forms of metamorphosis for those undergoing the seven-day treatment was transformation into a raven; such a witch was designated *ká:lo:na a:yéli:ski* or "Raven Mocker." This type of witch probably bears relationship to the ancient Cherokee war title of "Raven," a position whose duties entailed scouting the enemy at night. My informant recognized the procedures just described but was unable to shed further light on the identification of the mysterious plant mentioned by Olbrechts.

We now come to the Cherokee category most closely approximating the anthropological usage of the term *sorcerer*. The Cherokees do not use the English term *sorcerer*[27] but instead use the term *conjurer*, which survives from colonial days, as a gloss for what we would consider a practitioner of sorcery. The word *conjuring* for some Cherokees encompasses the whole range of positive and negative magic and varieties of divination. For others, conjuring connotes only or primarily harmful forms of coercive magic. In point of fact it is often difficult to classify a given instance as positive or negative magic or more popularly as "white" or "black magic." For instance, in cases of love magic in which a deserted wife and mother solicits the services of a conjurer to get back her absent husband, the rituals may have a happy or positive result in reuniting the family, but the errant husband has nonetheless been a victim of sorcery.

At least three terms occur that may or may not designate different types of sorcery practitioners. The first term *didá.hnese:sgi* is the generic reference for sorcerer, occurring both in Oklahoma[28] and in North Carolina.[29] Olbrechts despairs of analyzing the etymology of the term, except to suggest that it may have some connection with the verb to droop', he translates the word as "man-killer." The Kilpatricks provide the literal meaning of the term as "putter-in and drawer-out of them, he," [124] which doubtless refers to the sorcerer's magical introjection of objects or minute animate beings into the victim, as well as the removal of vital substances or organs from the victim's body.

The Kilpatricks recognize the belief in a specific class of malevolent practitioner called *ané:li:sgi*, translated as "those who think purposefully"[30] or, more simply, "thinkers,"[31] euphemisms for "anti-social human beings who, through the power of mind, project evil upon other human beings." The Kilpatricks further remark that, "an animal or bird spirit may be the actual missile, but it was loosed by, and the guilt of its destructive effects belong to, the evil human intellect."[32] This type of sorcerer then

---

25 *ibid*, p. 131.
26 *ibid*, p. 30.
27 The English term *witch* has been almost universally adopted among North American Indian groups and in other areas where there has been significant Anglo-American influence. However I have yet to encounter any native group that has adopted the English term *sorcerer*, and the term seems of infrequent usage in popular parlance in the English-speaking world.
28 Kilpatrick and Kilpatrick, *Walk in Your Soul*, p. 9.
29 Mooney and Olbrechts, *Swimmer Manuscript*, p. 87.
30 Kilpatrick and Kilpatrick, *Notebook of a Cherokee Shaman*, p. 97.
31 Kilpatrick and Kilpatrick, *Run toward the Nightland*, p. 170.
32 Kilpatrick and Kilpatrick, *Notebook of a Cherokee Shaman*, p. 97.

would seem to possess powers of mental projection equivalent to those of a witch, though seemingly lacking the capacity for physical metamorphosis.

The named category of thinkers seems restricted to the Western Cherokee, since it is not encountered in any known Eastern Cherokee texts. However, in the latter body of materials, another term is found that may be a functional equivalent to Oklahoma Cherokee thinkers. This term *uya i:gawé:ski gewa* is rendered by Mooney[33] as "imprecator" and can be literally translated as "evil, speaker of it, he."[34] My informant in 1959 confirmed the usage of this term as "bad talker," "bad conjurer," or "curser." This native term for "imprecator" apparently does not occur in Oklahoma, although the prefix *uya* or *u.'yaga* was interpreted by one of the Kilpatricks's informants as "an evil earth-spirit."[35] I suspect that these two terms, *thinkers* and *imprecators* are functionally equivalent, though obviously differing etymologically, since Cherokee practitioners recognize a continuity between thinking, uttering, and singing *idi:gawé:sdi*;[36] the continuity emerges through a focusing of mental concentration believed to be essential to the effective performance of the ritual:

Knowledge of sorcery is generally acquired gradually, usually over the course of a lifetime. While perhaps not always the case, sorcerers tend to be men in contemporary Cherokee society and also in the time of Mooney's and Olbrechts's [125] investigations. In the normal process a young man places himself under the tutelage of an accomplished medicine man (*dida:hnvw:sgi*, "curer of them, he"). The medicine man assesses the student's aptitude, motivation, and general character, often utilizing divinatory procedures. If the applicant is judged suitable, instruction proceeds gradually through a knowledge of medicinal plants, curing rituals, procedures, and techniques, including transmission of written *idi:gawé:sdi*. The most dangerous rituals, those intended to cause misfortune to others, are only imparted after the instructor is convinced that such knowledge will not be abused by the fledgling medicine man. Olbrechts describes a kind of "postgraduate" ordeal in which the supplicant repairs to a secluded place in the woods or mountains where he subsists on a decoction made from the inner bark of sweet birch (*Betale lenta L.*) and the root of Golden Alexander (*Zizia aurea [L.]*).[37] If he maintains this vigil for four days, he will become a gifted medicine man; if he extends the ordeal for a full seven days, he becomes a powerful wizard capable of flying through the air or of burrowing through the ground. This procedure is practically identical to that described for becoming a witch, except for the different plants used and the fact that the individual undergoing the latter ritual has been carefully selected and trained in the principles of Cherokee medicine and, presumably, will utilize his exceptional powers only for positive ends.

Other individuals may acquire a more limited knowledge of sorcery by inheriting or acquiring relevant *idi:gawé:sdi* and being instructed in their use by a consenting practitioner. However, such partial knowledge is considered as dangerous to possess, especially since sorcery, when ineffectively controlled, may be returned in harmful fashion to the sender.

Several general conclusions emerge from this brief survey of named Cherokee categories within the recognizable domain of sorcery and witchcraft. First, witches are not genetically endowed with mystical powers, although special rituals might be performed at birth to make the infant into a witch. [126] Individuals also might undergo rituals later in life to enable them to attain the powers of a witch. Second, witches are regarded as essentially evil creatures who cause misfortune directly through acts of will or through metamorphosis. Third, various Other medicomagical practitioners might acquire specific knowledge of techniques to do harm to, or even kill, another human being; however, such knowledge was

---

33 James Mooney, *Sacred Formulas of the Cherokee*, p. 384.
34 Cf. Mooney and Olbrechts, *Swimmer Manuscript*, p. 256; Kilpatrick and Kilpatrick, *Notebook of a Cherokee Shaman*, p. 100.
35 Kilpatrick and Kilpatrick, *Notebook of a Cherokee Shaman*, p. 100.
36 Cf. Marcia Herndon, The Cherokee Ballgame Cycle: An Ethnomusicologist's View, *Ethnomusicology* 15 (1971): 349-350.
37 Mooney and Olbrechts, *Swimmer Manuscript*, p. 102. [130]

thought of as subject to cultural control and only invoked with just cause. Fourth, some exceptional medicomagical practitioners could acquire powers equivalent to those of witches, including the capacity for metamorphosis, such that at this level the implicit; functional contrast between witches and sorcerers disappears, except perhaps for motivations in exercising this mystical power and the manner in which it was attained. It was also suggested that Cherokee beliefs in witches is grounded in their system of ethics and ideas about the nature of persons. It is to this point that I return in concluding this essay.

Robert Thomas, in a brilliant unpublished paper on values and world view, sees the core of the traditional value system as the effort of the culturally conservative Cherokee "to maintain harmonious interpersonal relationships with his fellow Cherokee by avoiding giving offense on the negative side, and by giving of himself to his fellow Cherokee in regard to his time and material goods on the positive side."[38] I have been unable to discover a Cherokee term directly corresponding to Thomas's postulation of the undoubted Cherokee value on maintaining interpersonal harmony. However, Jack Kilpatrick has pointed out to me the overriding Cherokee commitment to a sense of justice in human relations.[39] This sense of justice, supported by human warmth and good will, is embodied in the Cherokee notion of *duyu:gh(o):dv*, a term defying precise translation, but connoting the adjectives "just," "right," "straight," "honest," "true," and "upright."[40] It is considered a positive life force, and the Cherokees manifest an extreme sensitivity to violations of *duyu:gh(o):dv*, or to what they regard as injustice. Feuds and factionalism, which have been endemic and transgenerational features of Cherokee history, [127] have their roots in perceived violations of this implicit sense of justice.

Underlying this ethical belief in *duyu:gh(o):dv* is a classification of people into two diametrically opposed moral types. A person is either *u:da:nv:ti*, which refers to a man of "soul," "heart," or "feeling" and whose behavior can be summarized as being essentially "kind," or an individual is regarded as *u:ne:go:tso:dv*, or unmitigatingly evil. It is important to emphasize that the contrast is not between "good," in the righteous sense, and "evil," but between "kind" and "evil." The classification is absolute, and a person does not shift categories according to the situation or over the course of a lifetime. A Cherokee may know a man for years before consigning him to one category or the other, but once made the classification is irrevocable. A kind man can commit errors, or in the Christian sense be guilty of sin, even to the extent of murder, but a man so classified possesses an essential humanity and can be forgiven. He shares an almost Durkheimian mechanical solidarity with his fellow Cherokee. If his breach of ethical conduct is so severe as to endanger the physical or moral well-being of the group, he willingly surrenders himself to that group and suffers the consequences of his actions. Cherokee history contains several examples of such martyrs.

In contrast, an individual who is regarded as *u:ne:go:tso'dv* is viewed as a personification of human evil, one who operates unjustly from the "blackness" of his soul. Such an individual may be excluded from the human community and be written off as dead – and given the proper time and place, he will be. So-called political homicide is also not an infrequent phenomenon to anyone with even a casual acquaintance with Cherokee history.[41]

From this perspective of ethnopersonality theory, evil individuals, whether or not they possess the extraordinary powers attributed to witches, may be considered the moral equivalent of witches. It can be argued further that evil individuals and witches fall outside the realm of humanity. Witches must be regarded as counterfeit or pseudohuman beings since humanity [128] is but one among many guises that

---

38 Robert K Thomas, "Cherokee Values and World View," MS, 1958, p. 1.

39 Jack F Kilpatrick, personal communication, 30 July 1966.

40 Jack F Kilpatrick and Anna G Kilpatrick, *The Shadow of Sequayah: Social Documents of the Cherokees, 1862-1964*, Civilization of the American Indian Series 81, (Norman: University of Oklahoma Press 1965), p. 9.

41 The well-known political assassinations of Elias Boudinot, Major Ridge, and John Ridge in the Indian Territory in 1839, and the long trail of blood ensuing from these events, serve as cases in point.

they assume in their incessant metamorphoses and in their parasitic relationship to the Cherokee community.

Sources

Douglas, Mary, ed. 1970 *Witchcraft Confessions and Accusations.* Association of Social Anthropologists Monograph 9. London: Tavistock Publications.

Evans-Pritchard, E.E 1937 *Witchcraft, Oracles, and Magic among the Azande.* Oxford: Clarendon Press.

Fogelson, Raymond D 1961 Change, Persistence, and Accommodation in Cherokee Medico-Magical Beliefs. In *Symposium on Cherokee and Iroquois Culture*, edited by W N Fenton and John Gulick. Smithsonian Institution. Bureau of American Ethnology Bulletin 180: 215-225. Washington. D.C.
   1962 The Cherokee Ballgame: A Study in Southeastern Indian Ethnology. PhD. dissertation, University of Pennsylvania.
   1971 The Cherokee Ballgame Cycle: An Ethnographer's View. *Ethnomusicology* 15: 337-338.
   1958 A Study of the Conjuror in Eastern Cherokee Society. MA thesis, University of Pennsylvania.

Haywood, John 1823 The Natural and Aboriginal History of Tennessee, up to the First Settlements Therein by the White People, in the Year 1768. Nashville, 1823.

Herndon, Marcia 1971 The Cherokee Ballgame Cycle: An Ethnomusicologist's View. *Ethnomusicology* 15; 339-352.

Holzinger, Charles H 1957 Unpublished field notes.

Kilpatrick, Jack F 1964 Folk Formulas of the Oklahoma Cherokees. *Journal Folklore Institute* 1: 214-219.
   1966 Personal communication, 30 July.
   1962 *The Siqusnid' Dil'tidegi Collection.* Southern Methodist University. Bridewell Library. Dallas, Tex.: Bridewell Library.
   1964 and Kilpatrick, Anna G Cherokee Burn Conjurations. *Journal Graduate Research Center* (Southern Methodist University) 33: 17-21.
   1964 A Cherokee Conjuration to Cure a Horse. *Southern Folklore Quarterly* 28: 216-218.
   1964 The Foundation of Life: The Cherokee National Ritual. *American Anthropologist* 66: 1386-1389.
   1970 *Notebook of a Cherokee Shaman.* Smithsonian Contributions to Anthropology 2: 83-123. [129]
   1967 *Run toward the Nightland*: *Magic of the Oklahoma Cherokees.* Dallas, Tex: Southern Methodist University Press.
   1965 *The Shadow* of Sequoyah: Social Documents of the Cherokees, 1862-1964. University of Oklahoma Civilization of the American Indian Series 81. Norman: University of Oklahoma Press.
   1965 *Walk in your Soul: Love Incantations of the Oklahoma Cherokees.* Dallas, Tex.: Southern Methodist University Press.

Kluckhohn, Clyde 1944 Navaho Witchcraft. Boston: Beacon Press.

Middleton, John F, and Winter, Edward, eds. 1963 *Witchcraft and Sorcery in East Africa.* London: Routledge and Kegan Paul.

Mooney, James 1900 *Myths of the Cherokee.* Smithsonian Institution. Nineteenth Annual Report of the Bureau of American Ethnology, 1897-1898. Washington, DC.
   1891 *Sacred Formulas of the Cherokee.* Smithsonian Institution. Seventh Annual Report of the Bureau of American Ethnology. Washington, DC.

——, and Olbrecht, Frans M 1932 *The Swimmer Manuscript.* Smithsonian Institution. Bureau of American Ethnology Bulletin no. 99. Washington, DC.

Speck, Frank G, and Broom, Leonard 1951 *Cherokee Dance and Drama.* Berkeley and Los Angeles: University of California Press.

Thomas, Robert K 1958 Cherokee Values and World View. MS.

Turner, Victor W 1964 Witchcraft and Sorcery: Taxonomy versus Dynamics." *Africa* 34: 319-334.

Walker, Deward, ed. 1970 Systems of North American Witchcraft and Sorcery. Anthropological Monographs of the University of Idaho no. 1. Moscow: University of Idaho.

Witthoft, John 1949 Green Corn Ceremonialism in the Eastern Woodlands. University of Michigan, Museum of Anthropology 13. Ann Arbor: University of Michigan Press.

Witthoft, John, and Hadlock, Wendell S 1946 Cherokee-Iroquois Little People." *Journal of American Folklore* 59: 413-422.

#14 CHEROKEE NOTIONS OF POWER

Anthropological considerations of power generally gravitate toward one of two areas of investigation. The first is oriented toward native notions of personal or impersonal mystical energy, or mana-like forces, believed to imbue phenomena, persons, places, times, and things located in various culturally constituted behavioral environments. The second area of concern involves political processes generally and decision-making specifically. In this chapter, I will first discuss traditional Cherokee ideas of power in the sense of mystical energy and then relate some aspects of these ideas to traditional Cherokee political processes.

Since Cherokee is a divergent branch of the Iroquoian linguistic family (Lounsbury 1961), and also since JNB Hewitt, in a celebrated article entitled "Orenda and a Definition of Religion" (1902: 32-46), had delineated a complex and pervasive idea of power among the Northern Iroquois, my attention was naturally drawn to the search for cognate terms and analogous concepts of power during my Cherokee fieldwork.[1] Although I failed to discover any terms even remotely cognate with *orenda*, I did find that the generic Cherokee term for "power," *'ulanigvgv'* (var.) (Alexander 1971: 121) bears resemblance to the Iroquois term *ot'gun* or *ut'gon*, a subspecies of *orenda* corresponding to 'malevolent mana'. Hewitt defines *ot'gun* as any object or being which performs its functions and exercises its assumed magic power or *orenda* in such manner as to be not only inimical to human welfare, but hostile to and destructive of human life; it is the name in common use for all ferocious and monstrous beings, animals, and persons, especially such as are not normal in size, power, and cunning, and such things in which there is marked incongruity between these properties of beings [1906: 164].

My Cherokee informant defined *ulanigvgv* as energy deriving from such phenomena as lightning and running water (both of which are personified in Cherokee world view), and from spiritual beings, including animals, ghosts, personified deities, other human beings, and from certain plants and material objects. In the western dialect, spoken by Oklahoma Cherokees, the term also encompasses electric power, ethnic power (as in "black power" or "Indian power"), and is used for most references to power in the Cherokee translation of the Christian Bible (as in St Luke 21: 27: "and then shall they see the Son of man coming in a cloud with *power* and great glory"). The main semantic difference, then, between the Iroquois concept of *ot'gun* and the Cherokee lexeme *ulanigvgv* is that the Cherokee term does not refer exclusively to evil qualities or maleficent power.

In contrast with the rich connotative and philosophic meanings of the Iroquois concepts of *orenda* and *ot'gon* elaborated by Hewitt, the analogous Cherokee concepts appear weakly developed and somewhat amorphous. The absence of a highly elaborated concept of power seems consistent, at least on a surface level, with dominant features of traditional Cherokee social structure, institutional framework, ideology, and ethos. However, in working through certain problems in medical-magical beliefs and "rituals, it soon became apparent that Cherokee beliefs and ritual practices were clearly premised on implicit notions of power and its differential distribution in the universe. Power could be acquired; it could be lost; and persons and objects could possess varying degrees of power. Moreover, in social interaction, power seemed to operate somewhat like an unmarked category in linguistics. Public display, boasting, and external symbols denoting possession of power are deemphasized or sharply circumscribed in traditional Cherokee culture. This theme is reflected in the vast majority of Cherokee myths and folktales that center on animal or human protagonists who set themselves above their fellows through arrogance, overweening pride, or assumed powers and then are brought down through retributive reaction.

---

1 Fieldwork was carried out in different intervals between 1958-1961. Most of the work was conducted among the Eastern Cherokees of North Carolina, although several brief visits were made to the Oklahoma Cherokees.

Thus, power, thought often muted, unlabeled, or unspoken, appears to operate at an implicit level in structuring much of Cherokee belief and behavior.

I now turn to a closer look at the idea of power as it manifests itself in the magical - religious sphere. First, personal power will be discussed; later, an example will be provided of power resident in certain physical objects regarded by the Cherokee as sacred.

Unlike the notion of *mana* in Polynesia, the Cherokees do not believe in genetic inheritance of power. Certain infants, often twins, were sometimes [187] given special ritual treatment involving isolation, herbal decoctions, and avoidance of the mother's breast. Such a regimen was felt to imprint infants with lifetime powers as witches. However, witches were not regarded as real persons among the Cherokees, but as pseudopersons, on the basis of their capacity for metamorphosis and exclusion from the human moral community (Fogelson 1975). Other youths might be selected to receive tutorial instruction in ritual matters from older magical – religious practitioners. However, it was generally believed that acquisition of *ulanigvgv* was open to anyone who diligently applied himself over the course of a lifetime to patient accumulation of knowledge, conscientious attention to ritual detail, and maintenance of a moral relationship to fellow Cherokees. This point needs emphasis, since the Cherokees, unlike many other American Indians, did not possess a clearly developed guardian spirit complex, wherein a youth might establish a lifetime partnership with a powerful spiritual being. In fact, the whole idea of dramatic individual religious experience and altered states of consciousness as a route to personal power seems foreign to the controlled and pragmatic Cherokee orientation toward life; we will return to this point later.

In traditional Cherokee culture, the power inhering in an individual was not regarded as a permanent attribute, since power might be dissipated through misuse, overuse, or unsuccessful conflict with individuals possessing superior *ulanigvgv*. Furthermore, retention of power often required periodic renewal. For example, a witch maintained its power and vitality by snatching the unfulfilled life expectancies of its victims; a curing specialist was supposed to rejuvenate his powers via autumnal baths in a flowing river whose waters contained medicinal properties imparted by falling leaves. Attainment of old age constituted partial confirmation of possession of *ulanigvgv*, even if the aged person might be suspected of acquiring longevity through witchcraft or malevolent sorcery. Thus there is a notable tendency in traditional Cherokee culture to defer to elders. Fred Gearing has summarized a prevailing set of associations in Cherokee thought by the equation: Old equals good equals honor (1962: 60). Perhaps in the sense of the present discussion, the equation should be rewritten to read; Old equals power equals fear (Fogelson 1963: 727-728).

Individuals who were thought to possess *ulanigvgv* or those occupying positions of legitimate authority, were regarded ambivalently by the general populace: Depending on their application of this real or assumed power, they could be perceived as public servants or public enemies. The same individual could be alternatively revered or reviled contingent on the status and viewpoint of the person making the judgement. It seems that the greater the publicly claimed or acknowledged power of the individual, the greater the degree of social distance of that individual. Thus Cherokees are understandably restrained in public flouting of personal power. For instance, on certain ceremonial occasions, such as the scalp or victory dance, warriors were permitted to [188] boast of their exploits, but this was done in a highly structured situation in which warriors were required to pay for the privilege by donating goods and spoils of war to the needy. Even a recognized specialist – one to whom community consensus attributes certain powers and skills – will usually underplay his abilities. To illustrate, a recognized curer customarily promises only to try to help his client; he never promises definite results. This defensive posture is understandable in that claims to special powers might alter his relationships within the community for the worse, even if his treatment were successful; there is also an omnipresent fear that jealous rivals might contrive to "spoil" his rituals.

This distrust of individuals claiming special power and a corresponding de-emphasis on altered states of consciousness or dramatic religious experiences as sources of spiritual or secular power are clearly reflected in Cherokee attitudes and reactions to religious prophets and revitalization movements.

Mooney (1900: 399-400) presented an instructive Cherokee "myth" or "legend," apparently based upon historical tradition, in which a wandering warrior visited some distant white settlements in which he beheld a peacock, a bird of Old World origin previously unknown to the Cherokees. He was much impressed by the star pattern of the peacock feathers and negotiated a trade for them. Upon returning to his village, he set the unusual feathers in a headdress and announced at a public gathering that he had journeyed up to the Sky and had messages to deliver from the Star Spirits. He was given a respectful audience by the townspeople and became revered as a great prophet until another Cherokee visited the white settlements, saw a peacock, and exposed the false prophet as a fraud.

In 1812 or 1813, excitement and hope for a pan-Indian alliance against the whites were generated by Tecumtha and the Shawnee Prophet and penetrated into the Southeast. From the Creeks, word spread to neighboring Cherokees in northern Georgia that on a certain day "there would be a terrible storm, with a mighty wind and hailstones as large as hominy mortars, which would destroy from the face of the earth all but the true believers who had previously taken refuge on the highest summits of the Great Smoky mountains" [Mooney 1896: 676-677]. Many Cherokees, unmindful of remonstrances of friends who placed no faith in the prophecy, heeded the word and trekked off to the Smokies with all their portable worldly effects. When the appointed time came and passed without incident, they descended from the mountain and were forced to bear the ridicule of their bemused countrymen.

Subsequent sporadic prophet-inspired movements found barren ground among the Cherokees. Perhaps the closest to a full-fledged revitalization movement among the Cherokees occurred in the Indian Territory in the late 1890s and the first decade of the twentieth century in response to the Dawes [189] Commission, the subsequent Allotment Act, and the enabling provisions set forth in the Curtis Act. A group of concerned cultural conservatives despaired over the dissolution of the tribal government and the legitimization of past, and anticipation of future, encroachment of white settlers in their midst. The movement, variously known as the Keetoowah Society, the Nighthawks, or the Red Bird Smith Movement, was politically committed to passive resistance to allotment, and its membership even considered withdrawal to Mexico or Colombia, where they might be left alone. A syncretized spiritual basis for the movement was gradually crystallized by its appointed leader, Red Bird Smith, who was charged with the responsibility of "getting back what the Keetoowahs [a term for 'real' or traditional Cherokees] had lost." After allotment became a *fait accompli*, the movement contracted, but it persists today as a traditional religion. For our purposes, the important things to note about this movement, which has been richly described by Robert K Thomas (1954, 1961), is that Red Bird Smith was an appointed leader who approximated the Cherokee ideal of moral and sagacious elder rather than a divinely inspired prophet. All major decisions, doctrinal innovations, and even the authenticity of decoded dream messages had to be approved by a committee. If Red Bird Smith possessed charisma or "power," it was a fully domesticated and socialized type of power that bound him closely to his constituency, rather than differentiating him from it.

To support further the contentions being argued here, it should be noted that distribution maps showing the modern diffusion of the Peyote Religion indicates that it stops short at the borders of the Cherokee area of Oklahoma and that peyote is unknown in North Carolina. While the Peyote Religion is particularly strong among the Delawares occupying the northern portion of the former Cherokee Nation, and while a few mixed Cherokee – Delawares and a few Cherokees in that region are Peyotists, it is no doubt culturally significant that, despite easy access, the overwhelming majority of Oklahoma Cherokees have rejected the Peyote Religion.

Finally, the Cherokees seem to have assumed a relatively low profile with respect to modem Indian militancy. Although North Carolina Cherokees have duly protested the flooding of ancestral sites and the excavation of burial grounds, and while Okalahoma Cherokees have fought for elected tribal officials, hunting rights, and have protested commercialized projects initiated by white and mixed blood entrepreneurs seeking to capitalize on Cherokee "heritage," Cherokee activism lacks the flamboyance and headline-grabbing attention characteristic of AIM and other tribal and pan-Indian movements.

For all intents and purposes, then, *ulanigvgv* remained a latent force within Cherokee social life. Power was unevenly distributed and transient within the Cherokee universe of persons. Since no one knew how much power another person commanded, overt deference and respect afforded the safest [190] course to follow in interpersonal relations. Such behavior minimized the chance of giving offense and, perhaps, suffering hostile repercussions.

Besides the universe of human persons, the Cherokees also personified animal spirits, such elemental forces as fire, water, and lightning, and certain objects that we would classify as inanimate. One such physical object was a sacred quartz crystal, referred to in Cherokee as "*ulunsata*," which was used for divination. According to myth, the crystal represents the heart of the cannibalistic ogre Stoneclad, a widespread mythic monster prototype who also is known among the Iroquois and is ultimately related to the Algonquian Windigo, whose heart of ice shares the same properties of translucence and fracturability as quartz crystal. When Stoneclad was finally brought down through the direct agency of seven menstruating maidens, he sang medicine songs before finally expiring. After his body was burned, all that remained was the crystal heart. This divining crystal was entrusted to specially consecrated priests and was wrapped in buckskin and stored in a rock shelter when not in use. In addition, the crystal had to be periodically fed drops of animal or human blood, as befits its origin, or it would cause great misfortune to its caretaker. This powerful object is also regarded as a person, since it is the immortal remains of a mythic being who continues to perform divinatory services for mankind in return for periodic blood sacrifice.

I will now examine how power was exercised in traditional Cherokee political behavior. Cherokee political life was framed in a dualistic conception of White (or peace) and Red (or war) divisions, or what Gearing has analyzed as "structural poses." The White political division was dominant in the domestic affairs of autonomous towns or villages, the essential polity in traditional Cherokee society. The White organization was headed by a peace chief, generally a man well past middle age, and also encompassed a roster of subordinate officials and a council of elders. The Red organization was led by a war chief, normally an active warrior who was younger by about a generation than the peace chief; the Red organization also had a hierarchy of lesser officials and was influenced by a War Council. The arena of the White organization was the council house, a semisubterranean structure that also served as a temple housing the sacred fire. During council meetings, decisions were arrived at by consensus, and the peace chief played a moderating role by exercising considerable diplomatic tact in subtly steering discussion but never appearing self-assertive. The Red organization was ascendant in martial affairs, and its sphere of action was primarily outside the local village. According to Gearing, qualities embodied in war chiefs included commanding demeanor, fearlessness, egocentricity, meanness, and coercive behavior. From my own reading of early Cherokee documentary sources, the war chief emerges as less of a commanding or coercive figure and more of an inspirational type of leader who attracted followers by enthusiastic personal example. Warriors were free to join a war [191] party, and once in the field, they could return home at the slightest provocation. Furthermore, the war chief operated under certain structural constraints. Usually his tenure of office was restricted to a particular engagement, and he was held accountable for the safety of his men. An unsuccessful war chief was easily deposed.

Peace and war, or inside and outside spheres of action, and collective versus more individuated authority are certainly major diagnostic features affecting styles of leadership and decision-making in the White and Red organizations. However, I see the critical distinction between the two systems as centered on differences in relative age. I think the two systems of organization can usefully be considered as male age grades. The implications of interpreting Cherokee political divisions as age grades can be seen more clearly through a brief consideration of the traditional social structure and domestic cycle.

Cherokee descent was reckoned matrilineally through seven (or perhaps more at earlier periods) exogamous clans. The kinship terminology conformed to a Crow system, and residence tended toward matrilocality. Given the small size of most Cherokee villages, perhaps averaging around 350 inhabitants, the majority of men were forced to seek wives in other-than-natal villages. Thus, marriage, with its attendant residential relocation, was a critical juncture in the male life cycle. Upon marriage, a young man's position was quite marginal in his wife's household. He had to avoid his wife's mother; he displayed deference toward her father; and he was often the painful butt of needling from his wife's brothers through the mechanism of a formalized joking relationship. From all accounts, Cherokee marriages were extremely fragile; as Alexander Longe, one 1715 observer noted, "the women rules the rost and weres [wears] the britches and sometimes will beat thire husband within an inch of thire life" [sic, quoted in Corkran 1969: 31]. In such an inhospitable setting, it is not surprising that the young man's primary identification became merged with the Red organization, whose glance was directed outward and whose membership was largely composed of young men whose domestic situations were structurally similar to his own. There is some evidence that the council house had sleeping accommodations and could serve as a kind of men's house, a welcome refuge from the matri-centered household. It is also known that young men might spend upwards of a third of the year away from the local village on extended hunting trips, in visits to distant kin, on trading expeditions, and on foreign embassies, as well as on the warpath. The relative absence of cross-cutting sodalities and ceremonial societies, in contrast to such matrilineal, matrilocal North American groups as the Northern Iroquois and Southwestern Pueblo Indians, seems to have intensified the significance of the Red organization in Cherokee social structure.

A later critical juncture in the male Cherokee life cycle was the transition from the status of young man to old man, a gradual event that was sometimes [192] culturally denoted by the appearance of grey hair at around 50 years of age. By this time, a man's active participation on war parties had slackened and his economic contributions to the household had begun to wane. In the normal course of the domestic cycle, his position within the household became more solidified. The wife's brothers presumably had departed long ago upon their own marriages. With the death of the wife's parents, he ascended to the senior generation in the household. The birth and maturation of sons and, more particularly, daughters who would eventually bring in husbands, further strengthened his position. In cases where this normal process was somehow impeded, or where the man maintained a continuing peripheral relationship to the wife's household and never became firmly incorporated into it, the transition between young man and old man might have been effected by shifting residence back to the natal town and his own matrilineage, where he might more easily assume the role of an honored elder.

Two structural features emerge from this cursory analysis of the internal dynamics of Cherokee social structure. The first is contrast between old men and young men as conceptually different categories of political persons. The second feature, of course, is the abiding antithesis between male and female.

The significance of residential relocation and profound lifestyle changes on attainment of old age has led to a recognition of something resembling age grades for Cherokee men. The careers of Cherokee women, in contrast, show considerably less discontinuity over the life cycle. The structural reasons for the absence of visible adult female age-grading would seem to rest on residential continuity and a more restricted life space. With advancing age, women, of course, did attain greater status in the household and matrilineage, but, with the exception of a few senior matrons who were given the honorific title of "beloved women," no woman was permitted to speak in council. Thus, women did not possess a replicate structure corresponding to the Red and White political divisions of the men; for purposes of structural analysis, women must be regarded as a unitary group.

However, while lacking a voice in council and being denied active participation in decision-making, women, nonetheless, exercised considerable indirect political power through their influence on brothers and sons. I think women's political roles can best be conceptualized as mediating between the Red and White organizations. If one were forced to generate appropriate symbolism from a sociological palette to designate the collective structural position of women, they would be colored pink. Perhaps women's political power in traditional Cherokee society can best be illustrated with reference to decisions concerning war.

Cherokees believed war to be a normal and expected part of the human, condition; it was regarded as the natural focus for discharge of youthful male [193] energies. As has previously been noted, responsibility for planning and executing war activities was vested in the Red organization. The White organization might dampen the martial enthusiasms of the warriors by condemning unnecessary bloodshed and urging restraint or by channeling military impulses in such a manner that different enemies were made appropriate targets of attack. But the rein of the White organization in stemming or redirecting the warriors was held loosely. Women mediated this tension between me Red and White organizations. By wailing over the unavenged deaths of sons and brothers, women could shame the warriors into action. Like many other Eastern Woodlands' tribes, the Cherokees left the fate of captives in the hands of the women. If the captive's life were spared, he might be adopted into a particular matrilineage as a replacement for a slain kinsman. Scalp ceremonies also involved symbolic adoption. On the other hand, if the women felt that too much blood had been spilt, or if they were worried about the safety of their warrior kinsmen, they could become strong advocates of peace.

Several historical instances recorded for the Colonial period indicate the pivotal and independent role of Cherokee women in war-related activities-During the Cherokee siege of Fort London, women shipped food to the beleaguered English garrison. Beloved Woman Nancy Ward frequently gave advanced warning of Cherokee attack to endangered white settlements. In 1761, William Fyffe noted "The women (as among the whites know how to persuade by praise or ridicule) employ their art to make them warlike" [quoted in Woodward 1963: 33]. Finally, the astute Scottish-Irish trader, James Adair, observed that "they [Cherokees] have been a considerable while under petticoat government [1775: 145]."

The structural implications and the limited historical clues strongly suggest that the political power of Cherokee women was not inconsequential. From a Levi-Straussian perspective (1963: 132-163), the Red and White dualism in Cherokee political life is a kind of cultural fiction masking a more fundamental triadic structure composed of young men, old men, and women.

In this chapter, I have argued that much of traditional Cherokee belief and behavior is premised on implicit notions of power. However, I have also maintained that an explicit concept of power was weakly formulated and that overt manifestations of power were de-emphasized, devalued, and circumscribed. Finally, I have indicated some correlations between notions of power and certain aspects of Cherokee ethos, institutions, and social structure.

I say correlations, because I do not feel that any simplistic causal relations can be adduced. I neither see Cherokee institutions, social structure, and their egalitarian ethos as culturally constituted defense mechanisms erected in response to implicit beliefs about the nature of power, nor do I see power beliefs as simple effects or reflections of institutional, social structural, or ethological determinants. [194]

ACKNOWLEDMENTS

I wish to acknowledge the help of R Paul Kutsche for gathering some later information on Eastern Cherokee power concepts and also the assistance of Charlotte Heth, who more recently collected, at my request, some linguistic data on Oklahoma Cherokee usage of the term "power."

Adair, James 1775 *History of the American Indians*. London: Charles Dilly.
Alexander, J T, comp. 1971 *A Dictionary of the Cherokee Indian Language*.
Corkran, David H, ed. 1969 Alexander Longe's "A Small Postcript of the Ways and Manners of the Indians Called Charikees." *Southern Indian Studies* 21: 1-49.
Fogelson, Raymond D 1963 Review of Priests and Warriors, by Fred Gearing. *American Anthropologist* 65: 726-730.
   1975 Analysis of Cherokee Witchcraft and Sorcery Beliefs and Practices. In *Four Centuries of Southern Indians*. C M Hudson, ed. Athens, Georgia: University of Georgia Press.
Gearing, Fred 1962 *Priests and Warriors: Social Structures for Cherokee Politics in the 18th Century*. Memoir 93, American Anthropological Association. 64 (5), Pt. 2.

Hewitt, JNB 1902 *Orenda* and a Definition of Religion. *American Anthropologist* 4: 33-46.

    1906 *Otkon* Handbook of American Indians North of Mexico, II. FW Hodge, ed. Bureau of American Ethnology, Bulletin 30. Washington, DC: Smithsonian Institution.

Levi-Strauss, Claude 1963 Do Dual Organizations Exist? *Structural Anthropology*: 132-163. C Levi-Strauss, ed., and C. Jacobson, trans. New York: Basic Books.

Lounsbury, Floyd 1961 Iroquois-Cherokee Linguistic Relationships. In *Symposium on Cherokee and Iroquois Culture*. W N Fenton and J. Gulick, eds. Bureau of American Ethnology, Bulletin 180. Washington, D.C.: Smithsonian Institution.

Mooney, James 1896 The *Ghost Dance Religion* and the Sioux Outbreak of 1890. 14th Annual Report, Bureau of American Ethnology, 1892-93, Part 2. Washington, D.C.: Smithsonian Institution.

    1900 *Myths of the Cherokees*. 19th Annual Report, Bureau of American Ethnology. 1897-1898, Part 1. Washington, DC: Smithsonian Institution.

Thomas, Robert K 1954 The Origin and Development of the Redbird Smith Movement. MA Thesis, Department of Anthropology, University of Arizona.

    1961 The Redbird Smith Movement. In Symposium on Cherokee and Iroquois Culture. W N Fenton and J Gulick, eds. Bureau of American Ethnology, Bulletin 180. Washington, DC: Smithsonian Institution.

Woodward, Grace S 1963 *The Cherokees*. Norman, Oklahoma: University of Oklahoma Press.

Priests and Warriors: *Social Structures/or Cherokee Politics in the 18th Century.* Fred Gearing. (American Anthropological Association Memoir 93.) Menasha, Wisconsin: The American Anthropological Association, 1962. vii, 124 pp., 7 figures, index, notes, references. $2.00.[1]

Reviewed by Raymond D. Fogelson
University of Washington

This brilliantly conceived and executed monograph may very well come to be regarded as a landmark in American structural studies. Gearing has attempted to do several things: 1) offer a situational approach to the study of social structure and political systems; 2) provide a synchronic model of early 18th century Cherokee political organization; 3) create theoretical linkages between social structure and behavior, as mediated through ethos and personality; 4) present an analytic interpretation of historical changes in Cherokee political organization from the early 1700's to the American Revolution; and 5) suggest a general developmental sequence describing the process by which sovereign villages become voluntary states. As can be seen from this approximate listing of topics, *Priests and Warriors* is ambitious in scope and, as Gearing himself anticipates, there is much with which to disagree (pp. 8-9). My stance throughout this review will be critical, hopefully constructively so, since the over-all excellence of the work demands reaction.

Gearing sees social structures not as monolithic entities but as shifting configurations of patterned role relationships adjusted to specific tasks occurring through the yearly cycle. Thus, for a given society, there may not be one social structure but several. These situationally determined patterned relationships are conceptualized as structural poses, A structural pose is defined as "the way a simple human society sees itself to be appropriately organized at a particular moment for a particular purpose" (p. 15). This notion of structural pose underlies alt else that follows in this work.

Four structural poses are felt to provide the interpersonal context for 18th century Cherokee male behavior. The first pose has to do with relationships within the local household. Gearing assumes, with some justification, that the typical Cherokee household was a matrilocal extended family. (This assumption may need some qualification, since limited archeological evidence suggests small, probably single-family, dwellings.) The activities singled out as representative of this pose are the economic pursuits of the male householders, particularly hunting. A second structural pose focuses on relations within the clan or clan section (fellow clansmen resident within the local village). Here, emphasis is placed on the functions of the clan in marriage regulation and in social control through the exaction of blood revenge.

In both these structural poses, real as they are, Gearing tends to underestimate the importance of the matrilineage in ordering Cherokee domestic affairs. I question whether a man's economic productivity was channeled exclusively into his wife's household. There are several indications that Cherokee men, even after marriage, contributed substantial economic support in the form of game, raw materials, trade goods, and clearing of fields to their mothers and sisters. With respect to blood revenge, I see the matrilineage as more influential than the clan section. Responsibility for avenging slain kinsmen seems to have fallen principally on consanguineal brothers, mother's brothers, and sisters' sons (and there are some recorded instances of fathers and sons [727] assuming this duty). Quite often, if I interpret the probabilities of relative village endogamy and exogamy correctly (cf. p. 21), these responsible persons resided in different villages and, thus, could not be members of the clan section of the slain man. (Intuitively, it seems to make good structural sense to bring in an outsider to be "hatchet man.") At any rate, the degree of town endogamy/exogamy seems to be a crucial factor in understanding Cherokee social structure. Even today Eastern Cherokee make distinctions between "sons" and "son-in-laws" (with respect to community affiliation) in organizing for ball plays. Presumably this distinction has some historical depth, and it may not be too far-fetched to suggest that the military organization may have

---

[1] *American Anthropologist* 65 (3), June 1963.

evolved out of an association of in-married "son-in-laws."

The two major structural poses involving the alternate organizations for war ("red") and internal civic-religious affairs ("white") are more directly political than the first two poses which have been described. The bulk of the monograph is devoted to exploring the various implications of this bicephalous political system. Gearing finds the domestic "white" organization, subtly steered by the tactful priest chief assisted by advisors and a body of "beloved old men," to be structurally integrated and eufunctional. The war organization, on the other hand, is viewed as so encumbered by a proliferation of status relationships that it is structurally unstable. Gearing goes so far as to consider the war organization to be acultural in the sense that strength of individual personalities filled the void of structural inadequacy. The activity spheres differentiating the "red" and "white" organizations can be seen, basically, as operant on an internal-external dimension. The "white" organization was dominant within the village, handling such tasks as council meetings, religious ceremonies, arbitration of domestic dispute, and (probably) curing. The glance of the "red" organization was directed outward not only in the management of offensive war, but also in such external relationships as diplomatic embassies and trade. In general, the officials of the "white" organization were older than their corresponding members in the "red" organization; it also seems evident that the "white" organization was ascendant over the "red" organization in terms of relative status. We shall return to some of these considerations after following Gearing's train of thought about Cherokee ethos and personality.

Gearing delimits the concept of ethos to include only role expectations (p. 30). The dominant Cherokee ethos as inferred from observation of contemporary conservative Eastern Cherokee and checked against limited clues available in the historical record, centers about a harmony ethic which emphasizes avoidance of direct face-to-face conflict, circumspection, and withdrawal as a means of escaping irresolvable disagreement or threatened disharmony. This general ethological pattern stood as an ideal construct to be approached, particularly by older men, but never fully attained. According to Gearing, younger men when outside the local village were expected to forsake the harmony ethic, and be "bad," when liberated from the restraining moral example of the "beloved old men." Cherokee ethos, then, seen in terms of role expectations, was oriented toward becoming; there was "an overriding lifetime moral purpose" (p. 46) in which discontinuity between approximation of the ideal by older and younger men was expected, if not sanctioned. On the basis of age-graded role expectations, Gearing further elaborates his ideas about Cherokee ethos. We are told that to the Cherokee way of thinking, "old equals good equals honor"; this assessment is manifested in a consistent tendency to defer to age.

While the chain of thought leading to this conception of Cherokee ethos seems logically consistent, some important links have been omitted. These missing links seem partially forged from certain Cherokee notions of supernatural power and respect for individual autonomy. Many students of the Cherokee, myself included, have deemphasized [728] the significance of power conceptions in governing Cherokee behavior. Cherokee are felt to manifest a high degree of pragmatism, rationality, and a genius for institutionalization. These conclusions are not unfounded, but they fail to appreciate the latent force exerted in Cherokee interpersonal relations by belief in an unequal distribution of power resident in different individuals. Acquisition of power through attention to ritual detail and "gaining knowledge," as the Cherokee put it, was for the most part equally available to all individuals. The characteristic circumspection and deference in Cherokee interpersonal behavior noted by Gearing seems clearly related to feelings of uncertainty about the potency of other individuals. The attainment of old age constituted a confirmation of power. Wisdom was symbolized by grey hair, the immediately perceptible evidence of successful adjustment to omnipresent dangers lurking in the natural and supernatural environment. Wisdom (or "knowledge"), as has been suggested, was equivalent to power. On the surface level, older persons were "beloved"; on a deeper level they were feared. These considerations may make Cherokee deference to age more intelligible. If I were to re-write Gearing's equation, it might come out "old equals wisdom equals power."

Respect for the autonomy of the individual also seems a relevant aspect of Cherokee ethos. The key point to be stressed here is that deferential patterns tended to be reciprocal. Not only did the young defer to the old, but the old were expected to respect the autonomy of their juniors. The genesis of these reciprocal deference patterns appears rooted in Cherokee child rearing patterns. Judge John Haywood insightfully noted,

> They are rarely aided even in infancy and never chastised with blows. Reason, they say, will guide their children, when they come to the use of it, and before that time they cannot commit fault. To chastise them would be to debase the mind and blunt the sense of honor, by the habit of slavish motive to action. (*Natural and aboriginal history of Tennessee*, Nashville, 1823, p. 272.)

Children seem to have been regarded as miniature or scaled-down adults possessing a sense of personal identity and developing adult sensitivities.

This amplification of Cherokee ethos may prove helpful in evaluating Gearing's analysis of the role played by personality in coordinating certain spheres of activity. Gearing hypothesizes a differential selection of personality types for leadership in the "red" and "white" organizations. As mentioned previously, he feels that the inefficient structuralization of the war organization placed a premium on a kind of assertive leadership that would be completely alien to the "white" organization.

While substantially agreeing with his characterization of personality attributes desirable in the priest chief, I don't follow, all the way, Gearing's portrayal of war leaders. Qualities of assertiveness, courage, and capacity to inspire others do seem requisite for successful war chiefs. However, I do not concur with the insistence that war leaders typically manifested commanding behavior and employed coercion to achieve compliance from their followers. Gearing apparently senses a problem here, for he devotes ample space to reviewing the data that imply that war chiefs were non-coercive (pp. 49-51). He also cites evidence in support of his own contention that coercion and threat of punishment were the principal devices that bound the war party together.

Perhaps, some clarification concerning the coerciveness or non-coerciveness of the war chief can be gained by examining the limiting conditions under which he operated. In comparison to the relative security adhering to the status of priest chief, the war chief occupied a rather equivocal position. He was elected by his fellow warriors, and it seems improbable (though possible) that a "mean" coercive personality would receive the voting support of his peers. His term of office was unspecified, and he might be deposed by the warriors or an indignant citizenry (perhaps maneuvered by the backstage [729] machinations of the priest chief). He was responsible for the safety of his men. If warriors were killed, he had to shoulder the blame heaped upon him by bereaved wives and mothers. It is significant to note here that the war chief was given the fictive kinship designation of "mother's brother." Gearing emphasizes the disciplinarian aspects of this kinship category, while I prefer to interpret its meaning as "male mother." Finally, as has been mentioned, war leaders were also involved in foreign relations and trade, activities that required capacity for cool deliberation and other traits reminiscent of virtues desired in a priest chief. This role may have been filled by the speaker of the war organization or the right hand man of the priest chief. Gearing is right in assuming that as the Cherokee became acculturated to European patterns of warfare, especially with the required coordination of larger bodies of men, coercion became more prominent. However in the war patterns of the typical small raiding party, individual effort and autonomy seem to have reigned supreme. The problem of war leader coercion will not be settled here.

I detect a modicum of continuity in Cherokee ethos cross-cutting both the "red" and "white" structural poses. Circumspection, coolness, patience and tact and many other qualities associated with intra-village behavior would also have value on the warpath. I also feel that the warriors, no matter how far afield, never completely escaped the influence of the elders. War priests, associated with the "red" organization, were elders who may not have been differentiated from the "beloved old men" in the apperception of the average warrior. These men were felt to influence magically the destinies of warriors through performance of ceremonies. In addition, warriors were placed under taboos which were in many ways more constraining than restrictions in the home village. Perhaps, most important of all, I suspect partial internalization of the authority of the old men prevented complete suspension of ethological commitments.

Three chapters are given over to the description and analysis of changes in Cherokee political organization during the 18th century. External pressure generated by the ever increasing involvement of English settlers in Cherokee affairs led to a transformation from a jural community into a voluntary state. This process begins in 1730 with the appointment by the English of a local war chief to the position of "Emperor" of the whole tribe. This appointment did not receive recognition by the majority of Cherokee. In the 1750's, the (probably hereditary) priestly officials of Chota, an important Over-hill town, gained ascendancy and a tribal-priest state was established following the expanded model of the local village organization. This organizational form was viable for almost a decade owing in no small measure to the political astuteness of its leaders. However, the tribal-priest state proved incapable of avoiding the seemingly inevitable conflict with the English colonists. From 1759 to 1761, the costly war wreaked considerable havoc on the Cherokee. The post-war period was marked by an increasing prominence of war leaders in political affairs. This development was capped by the emergence of Oconastota, the Great Warrior, as supreme Tribal Chief. Gearing interprets the political ascendancy of war chiefs as correlated with the need for coercive sanctions in welding together the nascent Cherokee state. Coercion had certainly become a political reality by this time.

The delineation of the various stages along the path to statehood seem essentially sound. There are some errors in interpretation of particular details and assessment of particular personalities, but Gearing is well aware of his limitations as an historian (pp. 8-9). A valuable piece of historical scholarship that can be read with profit in connection with these three chapters is David Corkran's *The Cherokee Frontier* (Norman 1962). One further bit of interpretive difference is that I see Oconastota as possessing many of the attributes typical of a priest chief. Oconastota and probably all subsequent [730] Cherokee chiefs appear to represent a coalescence of certain behavioral tendencies found in both "red" and "white" leaders.

A final chapter suggests a general process in the formation of states which Gearing labels the "Mesopotamian career to statehood." Analogies between the historical development of states are drawn between the Cherokee and the Mesopotamians. This general process is thought to be a recurrent phenomenon throughout world history and the notion of structural pose facilitates its discovery. The "Mesopotamian career to statehood" might become a useful analytic model, but additional more carefully documented instances are needed.

Before concluding, perhaps it would be worthwhile to say a few words about the usefulness of the concept of structural pose. I view this concept as a potentially valuable instrument for the analysis of social systems and their relation to personality and ethos. However, I feel that certain refinements are needed before this notion can achieve maximum utility. Gearing appears to envisage the four structural poses that he has isolated for the Cherokee as possessing relatively equal status. I see them as hierarchically integrated with the "white" pose as dominant, the "red" pose as a systematic variant or alternate form of organization. The household and clan structural poses seem much less pervasive, and one might even question whether or not they qualify as legitimate structural poses. There has to be a cut-off point somewhere or every activity that binds together a partially unique group of people would have to be considered a distinct structural pose. To carry my argument to absurdity, it might be possible to think of a public story-telling pose or even a "woman-gathering-wood" pose.

Taken as a whole, this is a remarkable book. I received considerable stimulation from it, and I am sure others will share my enthusiasm.

Histories

SYMPOSIUM ON THE AMERICAN INDIAN
On the Varieties of Indian History:
Sequoyah and Traveller Bird

Tell Them They Lie: The Sequoyah Myth. By Traveller Bird.
(Los Angeles: Westernlore Publishers, 1971. 143 pp. $7.95)

When I was a young boy growing up on the sandy outer fringes of the New Jersey Coastal Plain, I remember exploring the kitchen cupboard one day and making an astounding discovery. I seized a cylinder of Diamond Crystal Shaker Salt on which was printed a portrait of a friendly-looking Shaker lady holding an identical cylinder of salt. Turning the container from side to side, I successively discovered – as deeply as my vision could penetrate – additional Shaker ladles bearing cylinders of salt. In my own naive and independent fashion, I had stumbled upon the principle of infinite regress.

That early incident doubtless exercised a formative influence on my subsequent world view and, thus, should not be discussed lightly, *cum grano sails*. The memory recurs when I try to think about problems Implicit in the logical structure of ethnohistorical studies. As I have mentioned elsewhere,[1] ethno-history occupies an- anomalous position vis á vis the multitude of other compounded or hyphenated ethnosciences or ethno-disciplines. Most studies conducted under an ethno-prefix purposefully endeavor to examine a particular domain within another culture by utilizing the categories employed by and reflecting the outlook of participants in that other cultural system. The native categories and viewpoint may be derived from formal eliciting procedures or, as is perhaps more common, through inferences synthesized from informal native testimony, correlated ranges of observed behavior, and native exegeses of cultural productions. Some ethnohistorians assert a positive desire to reflect a native point of view in their work. Thus John Murra,[2] three years ago in his stirring presidential address to the Society for Ethnohistory, specifically charged ethnohistorians with the moral responsibility for writing what he called the "Versions of the Vanquished."

Despite such challenges, and the obvious fact that many American Indian groups do not regard themselves as vanquished, I think it fair to say that the vast majority of ethnohistorical works produced by historians or anthropologists either neglect or consciously eschew the native point of view. This is not to deny that such works often strive to adopt a morally neutral stance in that [105] elusive quest for "value-free" objectivity, or even that they frequently betray bias sympathetic to the native peoples whose history they describe. I merely mean to emphasize that the native interpretation of critical events and significant historical personages are un- or underrepresented in ethnohistorical research. This statement should evoke no surprise, since most ethnohistorian; regard documents as their primary data, and documents are still conventions if not pragmatically, defined as printed or manuscript materials, almost all produced by non-native recorders. William Sturtevant's admonitions to broaden our conception of documents to include not only maps and pictorial evidence, but also cultural artifacts and fresh field notes, have gone unheeded and unnoticed.

Thus, ethnohistory has come to denote in practice, if not in theory, the historical study of particular non-Western peoples, sometimes also including distinctive ethnic or religious groups within

---

1 Anthropology Department, The University of Chicago. An earlier version of the present paper was delivered at the annual meeting of the American Anthropological Association held In Toronto, November 1972.

Raymond D Fogelson, review of *The Shadow of Sequoyah*, by John F and Anna G Kilpatrick, *Ethnohistory*, 17 (1971): 169-70.

2 Anthropology, History, and Ethnohistory, *Ethnohistory* 13 (1966): 2-51.

Western society; for such studied a native perspective may be deemed desirable but Is not considered essential, Taken seriously, such an operational definition tends to blur possible distinctions between history and ethnohistory. At the most inoffensive level of contrast, history becomes the macro-discipline of which ethnohistory would constitute a legitimate subdiscipline. At a more invidious level, history emerges as the diachronic study of aspects of Western society as viewed, presumably, by Western scholarship, whereas ethnohistory becomes the history of non-Western peoples written from a Western perspective. If my intentionally tortuous logic be followed, an interesting possibility presents itself here: namely, that the, study of Western history by non-Westerners from a non-Western perspective could conceivably be regarded as a variety of ethnohistory. However, not wishing to strain credulity at this stage of the argument, let me express more directly the point that I've been deviously trying to develop. Blatantly stated, the point is that most ethnohistory as presently pursued is congenitally, if not unavoidably, ethnocentric.

It was with these mental reverberations bouncing around in my head that I once suggested the term ethno-ethnohistory to designate ethnohistory written from a native point of view. What I envisioned was a kind of anthropological ethnohistory in which a central role would be given to intensive fieldwork, control of the native language, use of a native time perspective, and work with native documents. These native documents would either be those already extant, as in the case of Cherokee, or even purposefully collected, as Paul Radin[3] so strenuously advocated when, in comparing his Winnebago work with the research of other members of the so-called "American Historical School of Ethnology," he came away convinced that he was the only one doing "real" history.

However, I now find that my neologism of ethno-ethnohistory, or anthropological ethnohistory, is inadequate to encompass still another variety of ethnohistory that now appears to be becoming increasingly frequent. Accompanying heightened native self-awareness and the quest for a positive historical identity, we find native peoples increasingly assuming responsibility for writing, clarifying, and in some cases inventing, if that is possible, their own collective historical experience. What we are witnessing is not an entirely new phenomenon in American Indian studies – one recalls the efforts of Jesse [107] Cornplanter to Improve on various White attempts to record Iroquois myths, or the large number of Indian autobiographies that turn out to be less life histories than eye-witness accounts of historical events.

At least four factors seem to have contributed to the current upsurge of Interest in the Indian writing of Indian history: (1) the heightened level of Indian consciousness that has resulted in movements toward general and specific retribalization,[4] (2) an increased awareness of the deficient and frequently

---

3 The Method and Theory of Ethnology (1933; reprint New York: Basic Books, (1965).

4 The term retribalization is intended here as an antithesis to the more commonly recognized and described process of detribalization. Retribalization refers to deliberate efforts by members of distinctive ethnic or cultural groups to revive or recreate, through selected symbols, aspects of their cultural heritage and to reassert their ethnic distinctive ness. The essential component in the retribalization process appears to be "blood" or the ability to trace and legitimize genealogical descent. Other seemingly secondary components of ethnic identity, such as language, music, art, dress, values, and particular customs, can be lost and later regained in either "pure" or modified form. By specific retribalization I mean the ability to trace descent to a single known and documented historical group; generalized retribalization is a higher order concept that refers to the establishment of identity from a more composite or inclusive group, as the Tribes of All Nations, which occupied Alcatraz, or the pan-Indianism reflected in such nascent institutions as urban Indian centers where generalized Identification as an Indian is tending to supersede specific tribal affiliation.

I submit that retribalization has been a recurrent phenomenon in human history, but one that is becoming more visible in the Western-influenced world with the denunciation of colonialism, melting pot ideologies, and fantasied fear of a homogeneous "global village."

racist treatment of Indian history by Whites, (3) the evident commercial and scholarly allure of Indian history as an "in" subject, and (4) an appreciation of the social functions of history in fusing an ethnic identity. Indians have reclaimed their history for their own. Indian history is becoming a private preserve and White trespassers are being warned off, or at least urged to proceed with due caution. We, thus, circuitously arrive at the third level of my saline optical illusion; one can contemplate, if the prefixal perseveration be pardoned, a possible ethno-ethno-ethnohistory, which would simply be defined as native writing of native history from a native perspective.

The major stimulus propelling me into this third level of ethnohistorical consciousness was the publication in 1971 of a book entitled *Tell Them They Lie: The Sequoyah Myth*,[5] written by Traveller Bird, a Cherokee author and direct descendent of Sequoyah. This provocative book attempts to expose as fraudulent the published interpretations of Sequoyah's biography, but in the very process of exposure a new myth of Sequoyah has been created. Without Traveller Bird's help, Sequoyah has truly emerged as a sacred symbol for contemporary Cherokees, both in North Carolina and Oklahoma. While the exploits of such other heroes of the Cherokee past as Oconostota, Dragging Canoe, John Watts, Whitepath, and Junaluska live on only in dog-eared history books and faded colonial documents, the shining genius of Sequoyah burns with undiminished intensity in the Cherokee mind.

The reasons for Sequoyah's elevation to the status of a sacred symbol cannot be fully analyzed here. However, such an analysis, I feel, would minimally have to consider the following four dimensions. First and foremost, the magnitude of Sequoyah's achievement in inventing a written language for his people requires proper recognition. This singular feat is probably unsurpassed in human history, except perhaps for the legendary accomplishments of Panini who is reputed to have singlehandedly discovered principles of phonology and syntax in ancient India.

A second factor to reckon with would be the personality traits generally attributed to Sequoyah. He was reputed to be a kind and patient man who approached the Cherokee ideal of a man of "soul, heart, and feeling." While he seems to have been self-effacing and to have shunned positions of leadership, Sequoyah did become a moral force in the Cherokee community and was "beloved" in his lifetime.

A third important factor in understanding Sequoyah's preeminence in the Cherokee pantheon of culture heroes are the uncertainties surrounding critical events in his life, lacunae that easily lend themselves to mythmaking. Three such events stand out. First, there is the matter of Sequoyah's paternity. His [108] father is generally conceded to have been an Itinerant White man, though Sequoyah was completely enculturated as a Cherokee and spoke no English.[6] Grant Foreman spends several pages in his otherwise useful biography of Sequoyah trying to prove that Sequoyah's genitor was the distinguished Nathaniel Gist, a close colleague of George Washington.[7] The implicit racist assumption here is that only White genes of superior stock could have produced an Indian genius. We will probably never know the true facts about Sequoyah's parentage, but on the face of the evidence Nathaniel Gist seems an unlikely candidate. The process of discovery in inventing the syllabary is also wrapped in mystery. Sequoyah supposedly derived the Idea of Cherokee writing from the example of Whites in what A L Kroeber regarded as a classic case of stimulus diffusion.[8] According to tradition, Sequoyah's first efforts were directed toward making idiographic signs for individual Cherokee words, but after this became too cumbersome, he hit upon the idea of a syllabary. Although part of the stimulus may have derived from ancient Indian mnemonic systems, as reflected in pictographs and beadwork, the evidence seems clear that many of the specific symbols in the final syllabary were modeled after English letters and numerals, with no equivalence in meaning. Traveller Bird's reproduction of what he considers the original 92 symbol Cherokee syllabary does depart from the standard printed form, but the relations to

---

5 *Tell Them They Lie: The Sequoyah Myth* (Los Angeles: Westernlore Publishers 1971).
6 John White, review of *Tell Them They Lie*, *Indian History* (Spring 1972).
7 *Sequoyah* (Norman: University of Oklahoma 1938).
8 Stimulus Diffusion, *American Anthropologist*, 42 (1940): 2-3.

English symbols can still be detected; the variations are no greater than those to be found in collections of "sacred formulae" handwritten by different magico-religious practitioners. The last days of Sequoyah are also subject to much speculation. In the summer of 1842, he set out with several companions to visit a detached band of Cherokee thought to be settled in Northern Mexico. The party got lost, and the old man was left behind while the others went for help. Sequoyah's mortal remains have never been recovered. Like Lao-tze and other great semi-mythic heroes, Sequoyah disappeared into the wilderness. The scarcity of reliable documentary evidence, thus, makes the task of piecing together the facts of Sequoyah's life reminiscent of the quest for the historical Jesus.

A fourth factor, which would have to be considered in assessing Sequoyah) status as a sacred symbol, was the rapid recognition of Sequoyah's genius by the White world. The issues here are quite complex and deserving of a fuller analysis. However, to understand White reaction to Sequoyah's accomplishment, one has to appreciate the significance of literacy as a marker for civilization in the implicit White view of progressive sociocultural development. From the White perspective, Sequoyah's invention served to transform the Cherokee from Illiterate savages into a Civilized Tribe. Besides being one of the most famous of American Indians, Sequoyah's statue is enshrined in the Hall of Congress, and his name has been bestowed on the world's largest organic species, the towering California redwood. The White glorification of Sequoyah undoubtedly enhanced his postmortem standing among fellow Cherokee and their descendants. Here was an Indian that even the Whites could respect and honor, and his reflected eminence brought distinction to all Cherokees, real and fictive descendants alike.

In Traveller Bird's version of Sequoyah's life, certain aspects are [109] "demythologlzed" and other aspects of his life are "remythologized." First and most importantly, Sequoyah's cadmean achievement is denied. Rather than inventing the syllabary, Sequoyah is the last scribe of the Seven Clan Society, a secret group whose origin goes back to the Taliwa, an unidentifiable southern Plains group, who are said to have invented writing in 1483 A.D. After suffering severe depopulation, the remnant Taliwa, replete with engraved golden plates, joined up with their Cherokee brethren in the East, where they introduced writing and initiated the training of clan scribes. Rather than being an innovator, Sequoyah was the last link to traditional knowledge and autochthonous wisdom. Moreover, the ancient scribe society combined literary skills with a fierce warrior ethic. We are treated to several exciting chapters detailing Sequoyah's heroic military exploits during the American Revolution and the later protracted guerilla campaigns led by Dragging Canoe. Sequoyah emerges as a fiery Cherokee nationalist who will brook no compromise or accommodation with treacherous White men and their Indian running dogs. He embodies the ethos of the strident warrior and not that of a beloved old man.

Traveller Bird conveniently fills the gaps in our knowledge of Sequoyah's life through oral tradition and over six hundred surviving documents alleged to have been written by none other than Sequoyah himself. These documents, if they really exist, would prove an unparalleled boon to Cherokee scholarship, but it is unlikely that Traveller Bird will expose them to profane eyes.[9] Sequoyah's parentage is unequivocably asserted to be full-blood. The familiar arabesque portrait of Sequoyah is alleged to be that of Thomas Maw, who is said to have replaced Sequoyah on a diplomatic embassy to Washington City, where the portrait was painted. Finally, contemporary eyewitness descriptions of Sequoyah as a slight-statured man, afflicted with lameness, are discredited. According to Traveller Bird's sources, Sequoyah was over six feet fall and was stigmatized by having his fingers cut off at the joints,

---

9   In a rebuttal to John White's negative review of his book (see note 6 above), Traveller Bird reiterates his sources as being; (1) oral testimony from "my mother's mother, mother who died in 1943 at the age of 89. She, in turn, got her information from her mother, the youngest daughter of the Cherokee man known as Sequoyah and George Guess," and (2) documents in the syllabary, though he fails this time to specify they are the actual products of Sequoyah's hand, and he continues his reluctance to make the documents available. Traveller Bird, "Correspondence," *Akwesasne Notes* (Early Winter, 1973): 40. [112]

being branded on the forehead, and having his ears cropped by pro-assimilationist Cherokees after a rigged trial for witchcraft and treason.[10] This recasting of the Sequoyah myth makes him into an appropriate culture hero for modern Indian militancy. He has been purged of any taint of Whiteness, either in terms of his parentage or the source of his invention. In Paul Radin's terms,[11] Sequoyah has been transformed from a native philosopher and thinker to a man of action, from a creative but passive Intellectual to a fighting warrior scribe.

One could, without difficulty, go carefully through Traveller Bird's account and list additional distortions and outright inaccuracies; for Instance, he makes Attakullakulla, who was born around the turn of the eighteenth century, into an Uncle Tomahawk born from a White father and a Cherokee/Lumbee mother; he claims that Cherokees were using wooden plows and oxen before the arrival of Europeans. But why go on?

John White, in a critical review, concluded that the book is an "elaborate fabrication,"[12] and certainly the book must be adjudged so by orthodox canons of historiography. But can we dismiss the book that easily? I think not.

Traveller Bird has produced a cultural document of considerable interest. Not only has he fashioned an intricate myth suitable for present consumption, [109] but he demonstrates considerable insight into the dynamics of Cherokee factionalism resulting from White contact. The picture usually presented is that of a mixed-blood elite selling out a coalition of progressive and conservative Cherokee nationalists who are futilely trying to forestall westward removal and retain ancestral homelands. What Traveller Bird has illuminated is a powerful third force in this conflict, a position that favored emigration west or to Mexico in order to preserve Cherokee culture from the despoiling influences of the Whites. Such a sentiment is poignantly expressed in Traveller Bird's re-creation of Sequoyah's reaction to missionary pronouncements about the benefits that would accrue from conversion to a civilized, Christian way of life.

> The speech of the missionaries tore into Sequoyah's soul like a winging arrow. These white people, whose armies had shattered the Cherokee Tribe and had taken their lands, were saying to the Indians, give up your culture – your life-ways which we don't like, nor understand – and do as I do. Destroy every living thing that stands in your way to accomplish this purpose in life, like the white people did. It was like telling birds to become like snakes.[13]"

The book abounds with other resonant samples of Cherokee Imagery. For example, we read, "Like kernals of corn shelled one by one from a large cob, the Cherokee Nation broke into bits.[14] Or, in describing the White frontiersmen, "These invaders were like wild hogs, with snouts in good acorn ground, rooting and pushing."[15] This is certainly not the way the descendants of these White pioneers prefer to remember their noble forebearers when they sit in the monthly meetings of the local county historical society to trace and comparer genealogy.

Again we confront the questions of what ethnohistory is, and whose history is it? What are its

---

10 Traveller Bird's assertion that Sequoyah was accused of witchcraft may be a distortion of traditional lore. According to some accounts, when Sequoyah first publicly demonstrated his Invention by communicating at some distance with his daughter by means of the syllabary, several naive spectators felt he was employing witchcraft. It seems unlikely that he was punished for political treason, and it is surprising that no other observers have commented on his supposed physical disfigurement.
11 *Primitive Man as Philosopher* (1927, rpt. New York: Dover 1957).
12 See note 6 above.
13 Traveller Bird, *Tell Them They Lie*: 83.
14 *ibid*: 22.
15 *ibid*: 23.

social functions? I have argued that these are difficult problems that admit no simple solution, but they are, nonetheless, worthy of serious consideration. I will conclude with a quotation from a wise historian of ideas, Don Cameron Allen:

Man is an incorrigible genealogist who spends his whole lifetime in search of a father. He longs for a chain of gold or blood to fasten himself to the universe in which he is committed to live.... It is the tragicomedy of the mortal dwelling with immortality, and man is aware of both the punishment and the boon. Hence, he, the finite one, seeks ever for infinity. It has been said that this obsession demonstrates the deity within man, but it seems that the contrary is proved by this madness. Man would make a miserable god.[16]

By squinting, I can dimly perceive a fourth friendly-looking Shaker Lady beckoning me with her container of salt, but, for the present, I'll resist the involutionary temptation to pursue her. [110]

---

16 *The Legend of Noah* (1949; rpt. Urbana: Univ. of Illinois, 1963): 11.

CHEROKEE BOOGER MASK TRADITON
With Amelia Bell Walker

> Nothing short of a full treatise on this primitive philosophy of analogy, and the relation thereto of maskology or disguise by costuming, painting, tattooing, bodily distortion or mutilation and the like, as a means of becoming actually incarnated with the spirits of ancestors, mythic beings, and animals, or totem gods, would fully explain the significance of the bunched animal figureheads and animistically painted human masks that we found.
>
> Frank Hamilton Cushing
>
> A Preliminary Report on the Exploration of Ancient Key-Dweller Remains on the Gulf Coast of Florida. Proceedings of the American Philosophical Society 35 (153) 1897:

The arresting account of the Cherokee Booger Dance presented, by Frank G Speck and Leonard Broom (in collaboration with Will West Long), in Cherokee Dance and Drama (1951: 25-39) has become the standard source for and the prevailing interpretation of this multiplex masked burlesque. Indeed, two recent popular anthologies of Native American dance, Reginald and Gladys Laubin's *Indian Dances of North America* (1977: 224-46) and Jamake Highwater's *Ritual of the Wind* (1977: 76-79) rely heavily on Speck and Broom.

Several scholars have attempted to relate the details of the Cherokee Booger Dance to masked dances and related phenomena found elsewhere in the Eastern Woodlands and in adjacent areas (e.g. Witthoft 1949; Speck 1950; Fenton 1961: 263 and 1978: 241-2; Kurath 1961; and Sturtevant 1961). Despite some tantalizing suggestions and demonstratable parallels, certain problems remain that obscure our understanding of the Booger Dance and its external relations. In this paper we utilize several previously uncited ethnohistorical sources,[1] comparative ethnological materials, linguistic data, and certain structural modes of analysis in an effort to achieve a broader and deeper understanding of the Cherokee Booger Dance.

Before proceeding, we present an abbreviated summary of the Booger Dance as presented by Speck and Broom (1951: 25-39), and supplemented by he neglected description written by Bernard S. Mason (1944: 194-202).[2]

The Booger Dance was traditionally performed in the late fall or winter, after the first frost, so as not to have a harmful affect upon growth and vegetation.[3] Anciently, winter dances took place within the semi-subterranean town house in which participants danced counter-clockwise around a central fire. From the beginning of the nineteenth century when sacred ceremonial centers began to disappear,[4] and

---

1. Of major [28] significance here are David H Corkran, ed. "Alexander Longe: a Small Postscipt ... 1969); the J P Evans "Sketches of Cherokee Character, Customs, and Manners (1836) unpublished manuscript in Payne-Butrick Papers, Vol. 6, Ayer Collection, Newberry Library, Chicago; and C C Trowbridge, unpublished manuscript (ca. 1825), Shea Collection, Georgetown University Library. The senior author is indebted to John Aubery for giving him access to the Evans manuscript, to Ives Goddard for originally leading him to the Trowbridge account, and to Leigh Coen for securing a copy of the latter source.

2. Mason, it is true, belongs to a hobbyist tradition and plays down the sexual and scatological features of the Booger Dance. Yet he does provide valuable choreographic detail.

3. The Cherokee year was divided into two separate segments, *gogi* (winter) and *gola* (summer). Closely associated with the Booger Dance was the Eagle Dance. Eagles could only be hunted and their capture celebrated in the winter when their chief cosmological antagonists, the snakes, were safely asleep in their dens.

4. A central council house~dance house remained in use in the Eastern Cherokee community of Wolftown

when missionaries inveighed against what they considered promiscuous pagan dancing.[5] Eastern [2] Cherokee winter dances were held at night in domestic dwellings, around an over-turned corn mortar that served as a central axis.

In the midst of a general sequence of social and animal dances. a group of from four to ten masked dancers[6] barge into the house. They wear various types of masks. Most of the masks are carved out of buckeye, or secondarily out of basswood. They are daubed with reddish-brown coloring, accentuated by black-painted eyebrows, expression lines, and black-painted hair, and sometimes augmented with animal fur that serves as hair, eyebrows, moustaches, and beards. The second most frequent masks are constructed from gourds. These masks have painted features, an attached down-pointing gourd neck nose that resembles a phallus, and applications of fur or hair. Other types of masks sometimes encountered include wooden carved buffalo or bear masks, wooden masks depicting females, carved warrior masks featuring coiled rattlesnakes on the crown of the head, masks made of wasp nests, and homemade or purchased cardboard masks. Most masks seem Intended to represent Indians but some clearly are caricatures of whites and blacks. As Mason notes, the masks "vary widely in type – some have a fierce, hideous, war-like expression, others are pleasant, and still others have a witless, imbecilic look" (1944: l95). Each mask is distinctive and the dance actions of its wearer are similarly individuated, Boogers usually wear baggy suits, old rags, tattered blankets or sheets (Mason 1944: 195); they often stuff their abdomen, buttocks, or lower legs. They sometimes wear only burlap breechcloths and moccasins (Mason 1944: l95).

Each booger has a personal name which usually is obscene – e.g. Big Testicles, Sooty Anus, Rusty Anus, Black Buttocks, Burster (Penis), Making Pudenda Swell, Sweet Phallus. They are usually associated with "people far away or across the water" – e.g. Germans, French, Spaniards, Chinese, Blacks, [3] Northerners, Southerners, and alien Indians. The intruders imitate foreign languages in a low whisper spoken only to their leader, and they may cough, growl, clear their throats, and emit resonant farts. Under their clothing they sometimes conceal gourd neck penises that discharge water at opportune moments. Sometimes boogers carry guns, bows, or clubs.[7] Many boogers hobble about with the aid of walking sticks. The general impression that the boogers present, through the facial wrinkles, occasional grey hair,

---

    until after the Civil War.

5 The following quotation from the missionary Daniel S Butrick in the 1830s helps explain the ethnographic opportunities that were unrealized:

"With regard to the all night dances, as kept up among the loose Cherokees at the present day, they are polluted and polluting. They are evidently not of Indian origin, because, although the Indians preformed the same dances, yet wives anciently followed their own husbands, and single females, their own brothers, or near relatives, with whom it would be death to have unlawful intercourse. Husbands were not separated from their wives as at the present day. The Cherokees were once, certainly, as modest and reserved in their dances as the Creeks, but they have been corrupted by the infidel sentiments, and shameful practices of abandoned white men. Therefore, as a full description of the present all night dances would do nothing towards elucidating the Indian character, an attempt to give that description would be useless" (Payne nd: 65).

6 The figures four to ten come from Speck and Broom (l951: 28). Evans (1836) reports three or four; Trowbridge (ca. 1825), fifteen to twenty; and Mason (1944: 196-7) specifically mentions eight boogermen. Will West Long told William Fenton in 1946 that he made twelve types of masks and listed eleven of them (1978: 24l).

7 In the [29] early Trowbridge account the party of masked figures fire off guns to announce their arrival. Firing of guns or making percussive noises was also integral to the Green Corn Dance (cf. Speck and Broom 1951: 47).

canes, and a stiff-legged, creaking gait, is of old people.

Upon entering the house, the boogers rudely push the spectators about, chase the women, and generally act like madmen. Soon they quiet down and sit on the benches provided for them.[8] The host, or master of ceremonies, formally announces the arrival of the visitors and converses in whispers with the booger chief to find out who they are, where they cone from, and where they are going. The answers are communicated to the audience through the host. Then the booger chief is asked what they want. The unequivocal reply is "girls!" A second request is "to fight". Neither request is granted. After the host assures the boogers that the Cherokees are peaceable folk, their final request is to dance, to which the host agrees. Next, the name of each booger is announced. Upon hearing his name the booger performs a solo dance. He lurches about in a grotesque manner and occasionally rushes toward the women.[9] After the Individual boogers complete their solos, the host asks the booger chief if they would like to choose another dance. The choice is either the Eagle (or Pigeon) Dance or the Bear Dance. Before the dancing resumes there is an intermission in which either ritual payment is made to a successful eagle hunter or a pipe is lit and passed around to the singers and musicians.[10] [4]

The climax of the Booger Dance is reached with the performance of the Eagle or Bear Dance. The boogers dance side by aide with female partners, and there ensues a Rabelaisian burlesque of sexual pantomime. Their initial wish for women being symbolically fulfilled, the boogers, with much commotion, finally disappear into the night to continue their journey. After their departure, dancing resumes with the Friendship or Mixed Dance or other dances in which the two sexes mingle.[11] The positional function of the Booger Dance in the sequence of night dances, thus, seems to effect or mark a transition from sexually segregated to mixed dancing – not unlike an "ice breaker" in a 1950's New England college "mixer".

The general interpretation of the Booger Dance advanced by Speck and Broom is that the boogers represent "the harmful powers of alien tribes and races, who, as living beings or ghosts, may be responsible for sickness or misfortune" (1951: 37) Moreover, boogers are said primarily to represent Europeans, and their sequence of demands is taken to be a condensation of the acculturational process as seen from the Cherokee perspective: first the white man tried to steal women; second he wanted to fight, and finally he was satisfied by making a fool of himself. For Speck and Broom (1951), the Booger Dance not only is a symbolic enactment of historical mistreatment and an attempt to redress grievances through parody, but it also represents a collective communal effort to exorcise disease brought into the local

---

8 Mason (1944: 196-7) describes a formal seating arrangement with two symmetrically placed benches and alternate seating by differently numbered boogermen. If valid, this may be vestigial to some form of moiety or dual organization similar to the seating arrangements of Iroquois masked, dancers (cf. Fenton 1941: 400). In the photographs in Speck and Broom (1951: plates XII-XIIa), there are two rows of chairs, one occupied by boogers, the other by musicians and a dance leader.

9 This segment of the Booger Dance bears resemblance to the portion of the Eagle, Scalp Dance, or Victory Dance in which individual warriors dance and recount their exploits. Except for the long extinct *Uku* ~ Priest Chief's Dance, which was only performed every seven years, these are the only Cherokee dances that encourage solo virtuosity.

10 Speck and Broom (1951: 33) note that the smoking rite is & diffused, form of the Calumet ritual. The paying of the Eagle Hunter is also related to the Calumet ritual, as eagle feathers were necessary for the eagle wands (formerly pipe stems) used in the Eagle Dance. Witthoft notes a possible connection between the smoking rite and the bear dance in that bear effigies were common motifs on Cherokee stone pipes (1949: 58).

11 Speck and Broom report that the Woman's Dance, Horse Dance, Beginning Dance, and Friendship Dance follow the departure of the boogers (1951: 36). Evans (1836) notes a resumption of common dancing, and Trowbridge (ca. 1825) reports a mixed dance or Raccoon Dance as the sequel to the Booger Dance.

community by foreigners.[12]

The data and interpretations of Speck and Broom (1951) are certainly compelling and have been influential in putting Cherokee masking on the ethnographic map. However, certain additional data can be adduced and existing data can be differently emphasized to produce alternate interpretations of the Booger Dance.

First, the very name, Booger Dance, is problematic, perhaps even a misnomer, [5] and may have lead Speck and. Broom astray. According to the *Compact Edition of the Oxford English Dictionary* (l97l) and to Elizabeth Mary Wright's *Rustic Speech and Folk-Lore* (l913: 192-3), the noun 'boggard' (or "boggart') refers to a spectre, a goblin, a bugbear, an apparition or ghost; the related term 'bogy' ('bogey') can refer to the devil, the evil one, a much dreaded person, or an object of terror, such as a human effigy. Also cognate is the verb 'to boggle' – as used to refer to the 'spooked' action of a startled horse, or more contemporaneously as in the expression 'the mind boggles'. Cherokee today, and at least back to the early 1930s, employ the term booger as embodied in masked dancers, in the sense of ghost of spectre. On the basis of his 1932 fieldwork, William H. Gilbert uses the term "Bugah Dance" and refers to the performers as "Bogeys or sometimes Buggers" (l943: 26l). Booger, to refer to the dance and the masked figures, was firmly established in reservation English by the tine of Speck's and Broom's fieldwork in the mid-1930s and in Mason's work (published in 1944). Grotesque masked figures certainly seem to fit our popular image of bogeymen. However, the Cherokee word for mask, '*a du tlv to di*' (Alexander 197l: 98) is similar to the word for beggar, '*a du la di s gi*' (Alexander 1971: 16).[13] It is interesting to note that the generic Cherokee word for ghost or spirit is '*a s gi li*' (Alexander 1971: 67)[14] and not similar to the word for booger~beggar. The earliest descriptions of Cherokee burlesques by C.C. Trowbridge (ca. 1825) and by J.P Evans (1836) do not mention the masked figures as being ghosts or "boogers". In his catalogue

---

12 Perhaps it is relevant to comment upon the theoretical perspectives that may have influenced Speck and Broom's interpretation. Leonard Broom (Bloom) couched all of his published Cherokee research in an acculturational framework (1939, 1942, 1943). Speck was also sensitive to culture change brought about by acculturation. Perhaps specific identification of the masked dancers with Europeans and evil was influenced by a similar statement made by {Tom} Half Moon, an Oklahoma Delaware first cited by Speck in his study of the Delaware Big House Ceremony (1931: 39), and repeated in Speck's posthumous *Concerning Iconography and the Masking Complex in Eastern North America* (1950: 36). Speck was also well aware of the close ties between disease causation and prevention among the Iroquois.

13 The semantics of beggar, in turn, seem assured, since the words for need and want are also related. We suggest that the argument for the loanshift of mask and beggar is strengthened by the similarities between the words for mask, want, beg and wish:

    a du la di   'want'   (Alexander 1971: 71)
    a du la di s di   'beg'   (Alexander 1971; 16)
    a du la di s gi   'beggar'   (Alexander 1971: l6)
    a du la di sgvf   'begging'   (Alexander 1971: l6)
    a du la da   'wished'   (Alexander 1971: 175)

14 Other [30] spellings for ghost, devil, witch and. spirit include:

    eskili   'ghost'   (De Braham 1971: 26)
    eskina   'devil'   (De Braham 1971: 125)
    s gi li   'witch'   (Alexander 1971: 175)
    a da nv to   'spirit'   (Alexander 1971: 149)
    a s gi le   'ghost'   (Alexander 1971: 67)

Note also Fogelson's discussion of Cherokee witches and the term *tsi:kili* = 'hoot owl', a bird of ill omen who supposedly performs its maleficent activities at night (1975: 120).

description of two carved wooden masks collected from the Eastern Cherokees in the late 1800s for the United States National Museum, James Mooney writes [6] "

> Masks (*agu'tulu'*): worn by certain performers in the Feather or Eagle dance, the wearers personating strangers from another tribe. The men put them on in the early evening, and the women wear them toward the close of the dance in the morning. They represent the human face and are well carved, from buckeye wood, trimmed with rabbit fur and squirrel tails for hair and beard, and painted with red and black ink procured from the whites" (quoted in Witthoft 1949: 58; photographs of these two masks appear In Fundaburk and Foreman 1957: 196).

Here again there is no reference to the masks as "boogers" or ghosts.[15]

Following the thrust of the evidence, the essential understanding of the masked figures seems to be that these figures represent mendicants, travelers from afar, seeking hospitality and sociability from the assembled Cherokees [cf. J P Evans (1836), Mooney quoted in Witthoft (1949), and Speck and Broom's statement, apparently quoted from an informant, that the masked intruders represent " 'people from far away or across the water' " (1951: 28)].

It seems possible, then, that the term 'booger' may result from a mispronunciation of the English term 'beggar'. Our effort to derive the Cherokee use of the word booger from relatively modern phonological and semantic convergence is not intended as an idle exercise in etymology. Rather, the equation of booger with beggar would bring the Cherokee data closer in line with information reported for other Iroquoians. Many of the Huron references to masked figures from the first half of the seventeenth century, collected by Elisabeth Tooker (1964 passim), regard masked figures as beggars. Also, as is well known, a large class of Iroquois False Face figures, usually impersonated by young boys, are termed 'beggars' because of their frequent solicitations for corn mush and tobacco.

The close association between the Masked or Booger Dance and the Eagle Dance and/or Bear Dance also strengthens our contention that the masked figures represent mendicants rather than ghosts. The metonymic, or part-whole, relation between the Eagle Dance and the Masked Dance is noted by [7] Evans (1836), Witthoft (1949), and Speck and Broom (l951). This imperfectly described Cherokee Eagle Dance had several seemingly disparate features. These included a scalp or victory dance portion in which warriors or ball players would individually recount their exploits, and often pay for the privilege of doing so; the celebration of the successful capture of an eagle and the "curing" of its feathers by a specially designated Eagle Hunter (cf. Mooney 1900: 281-3, 293, 453, 492-3 for additional details); and the Eagle Dance's connection with rain-making.[16] The Eagle Dance also comprised a local variant of the widely diffused, calumet ritual and featured ceremonial smoking of a pipe, the stem of which was draped with eagle feathers (Witthoft 1949). Finally, and of primary relevance to this paper, was the elaborate greeting of important visitors by dancers bearing sourwood wands with attached eagle feathers. This highly formalized greeting is mentioned by many eighteenth century white travelers to the Cherokee country [e.g. Timberlake (1750-1765) In Williams 1948: 63; Chicken (1725) in Williams 1928: 99; Cuming (1730) in Williams 1928: l35; Adair 1930: 176]. This welcome dance appears to have served a purifying function, with the power of the white eagle feathers, which derived, from their association with the higher celestial regions, neutralizing any maleficent powers brought by the strangers from the four comers of the

---

15   It is, indeed, curious that Mooney makes no other reference to masked dancing. Surely its flamboyance would have made an impression on him had he witnessed such performances, and he would have undoubtedly been sympathetic with its ritual symbolism and antisocial actions (cf. Speck 1950: 29, ftn # 10).

16   See also Harriet Holman's amusing account of the deluge precipitated by the last full-scale Eagle Dance performed by the Eastern Cherokee before the turn of the century (1976: 101-6).

earth surface.[17]

Speck and Broom (1951) not only associate Cherokee masks figures with disease, but they also identify the masks with European and Americans who carried catastrophic epidemics. The relation of masks and disease seems undeniable. However, the identification of whites as the exclusive or primary agents of disease seems unduly restrictive. Pollution, dangerous power, illness, and death are regarded as emanating from outside the narrowly circumscribed Cherokee world. The non-Cherokee world, is [8] the world of nature, the wilderness beyond the Cherokee settlements where dwelt unpredictable monsters, wild animals,[18] and feared aliens. The whites were merely the latest, albeit the most virulent, in a long succession of outside disease bearers. Portrayed as masked dancers, whites display their animal appetites and, barbaric crudity. The drama of the Booger Dance in part derives from a tension in which the Cherokee, on the one hand, try to domesticate the unruly intruders by the purifying actions of the Eagle Dance and by smoking the peace pipe, and, on the other hand, attempt to get rid of the maskers.

After the Cherokees finally accede to the dancers' original wish by giving their women in dance, the masked dancers and their diseases disappear into the darkness of the night.[19]

Although we cannot prove it, we suspect that mask dances are quite old among the Cherokees, perhaps extending back to pre-Columbian times.[20] Despite the generous applications of facial hair, very few of the wooden booger masks bear a physiognomical similarity to Caucasoids, and fewer still are painted white or left unfinished.[21] The vast majority of these masks resemble older Indians.

---

17 Eagles are a central symbol in Cherokee cosmology and are invested with polysemic values as mentioned in footnote three. Eagles can be structurally opposed to creatures like snakes and serpentine water monsters who reside below the earth's surface. In another context, as in the myth of the ball game between the birds and the four-legged creatures (Mooney 1900: 286-8), the eagle is the captain of the bird team and is opposed by the bear who serves in a complementary capacity for the land animals.

18 It is important to recognize here the deep-seated Cherokee belief that most diseases spring from the spirits of unavenged slain animals (cf Mooney 1900: 250-2).

19 The meaning of this crisis in the Booger Dance drama is unclear. It could be argued that only women have sufficient power to neutralize the negative power of the boogers. Another interpretation might maintain that by this stage in the dance the boogers had been sufficiently tamed or domesticated that they could now safely interact with women. Speck and Broom (1951) seem to feel that "the episode represents a surrender to the irresistible force of the white invaders. From a social structural viewpoint, the whole performance may be seen as a dramatization of courtship and marriage among the matrilineal Cherokee and the need to choose husbands from outside the local town. The ultimate dispersal of the boogers into the night rings true to general Cherokee theory of therapy in which the forces of disease are never really destroyed but are displaced or "moved over".

20 Part [31] of the difficulty in attributing great antiquity to the masking complex among the Cherokees is the lack of documented early specimens. The wooden masks collected "by Mooney for the National Museum of Natural History are, to the best of our knowledge, the oldest Cherokee masks on record. A mask photographed in Fundabank and Foreman (1957: 197) belonging to the North Carolina Department of Archives and History looks to be old and should be checked out. Trowbridge's account (ca. 1825) mentions but does not describe the masks; Evans' (1830 report specifies gourd masks. The late prehistoric Calusa sites in the Key Marco area, originally excavated by Cushing, have yielded carved and painted wooden masks. A similar shortage of documented early masks is true for the Iroquois. Fenton admits, "None of the masks that I have seen are older than the early 19th century" (1972: 44). Yet masks are clearly indicated in the written Huron sources dating back to the early seventeenth century.

21 Admittedly, these statements are based on impressions and do not substitute for the kind of systematic typological survey undertaken by Fenton (1941) in classifying Iroquois masks. However, the senior

We will now try to come to a deeper understanding of Cherokee masked dancing by making some comparisons with certain aspects of the masking complex among the linguistically related Five Nation Iroquois. Speck and Broom (1951: 30), and William Fenton (1978: 241-2) have been quick to point out dissimilarities between the masking traditions of the Cherokee and those of the Iroquois. Basically, Iroquois masks and masked performances are imbued with sacred religious qualities, while Cherokee masks are secular objects and the masked dances are profane, if not profaning. Cherokee masks are not carved out of a living tree, they are not surrounded by taboos, they do not require periodic "feeding" and offerings of tobacco, [9] and the wearer of the mask does not become transmogrified into assuming the living qualities inherent in the mask. Cherokee maskers do not pick up burning coals, nor do they directly attempt to cure. At best, Cherokee boogers are a voluntary group loosely organized for the specific occasion; their Iroquois counterparts comprise a formal, enduring secret society requiring initiation for membership. In this regard, the False Face Society of the Iroquois resembles such Plains dancing societies as the Dakota Heyoka, the Plains Ojibwa Windigokan, and the Iruska of the Pawnees. The ceremonial buffonary, the parodying of outsiders, and the blatant sexual and scatological aspects of these latter societies, in turn, produce distant echoes that may extend to the elaborated ritual clown traditions of the Pueblos. However, these last traits would also seem to link the performances of these Plains societies back to the Cherokee Booger Dance ... and diffusionary threads are spun into ever more complex webs.

Yet the profound differences between Iroquois and Cherokee masking complexes obscure certain basic similarities: the begging function discussed earlier; the relation to disease; the fact that masked figures in both cultures speak in whispers or in exotic languages; the idea that the masks visit from afar; the bearing of guns, clubs, or bows and arrows; and the facial qualities, bent-over gait, and use of canes that identify most maskers as old people. Fenton, on the basis of his career-long study of Iroquois masking traditions plus Cherokee knowledge gained from the literature and a brief 1946 field trip to North Carolina, magisterially concludes that "Masks and masking behavior, though present in both cultures, retain few fundamental traits common to both areas, although the analogies are strong" (1961: 263). [10]

Here we take up one such analogy that has seemingly been ignored by scholars making Cherokee-Iroquois comparisons. Iroquois specialists have been fairly clear in maintaining the differences in form, meaning, and function between carved wooden False Faces and woven corn husk masks. Students of the Cherokee, it seems, have been remiss in failing to take into account a comparable kind of distinction that may obtain between the carved wooden masks and those constructed from gourds. To express this in terms of a formal analogy, we will argue that:

False Faces	:	Husk Faces (~ "Bushy-Heads")
	as	
Wooden Booger Masks	:	Gourd Masks

In setting up the analysis in this fashion, several possible structural oppositions immediately come to mind. The most obvious of these oppositions Is the familiar Levi-Straussian dialectic between nature and culture. This opposition will be our starting point.

The principal False Face spirit is the Great World-Rim Dweller or the Great Defender. After his defeat in a power struggle with his older brother Sapling, or He-grasps-the-Sky, he is banished to the outer periphery of the earth. His twisted mouth and crooked nose are reminders of his unsuccessful combat with Sapling. As reparation for his defeat, he offers his services to man as a curer of certain diseases. Because of his remote residence, he is rarely encountered directly by human beings. However,

---

author has viewed the booger mask collection at the University Museum of the University of Pennsylvania, The National Museum of Natural History, The Museum of the American Indian, The Museum of the Cherokee Indian, as well as several from private collections.

the incarnate spirit of the Great World-Rim Dweller attends many Iroquois ceremonies as the leader of the False Face Society. This primal 'man-being' is closely associated with wild animals and serves as a kind of Controller or Master of the Game[22] who releases a sufficient quota of game for the hunter who observes the proper hunting taboos, apologizes to the spirits [11] of the slain animals, and who kills only out of need» for the disrespectful hunter, he will remove the game, make the hunter lose his way in the woods, and cause stuttering or insanity. The seemingly deeply grounded Iroquoian association between wild animals and disease is mediated by the Great Earth-Rim Dweller; he not only cures illness, but he can cause it. In this regard it is interesting to note that in order to become a member of the False Face Society, the prospective member must first violate a taboo or give some of tense that will cause the Faces to afflict the person with illness. That illness, in turn, can only be cured by a performance of the Faces. Having been cured by the Faces makes one eligible for membership in the Society.

Lesser members of the False Pace society are known as the Common Faces of the forest (*hadu'i'*) and are the underlings of the False Face leader, In their stylized gestures and physical form, they personify elderly deformed cripples and hunchbacks (Tooker 1970: 54). They are addressed as 'grandfathers' by the Iroquois. Their faces, at least in modem descriptions of the Midwinter Rites, exhibit a wide range of types, and some share the twisted mouth and crooked nose of the False Face leader. These beings are often encountered by hunters in the forest. Upon meeting, they offer safe passage through the woods and valuable hunting advice in return for donations of tobacco and corn mush from the hunter. These figures are often impersonated by younger men in the Longhouse rituals. Finally a diverse class of mask types are referred to as beggars. These masks are worn by boys who go from house to house to beg for tobacco and other offerings.

In summary, one can say that the Iroquois False Faces personify the realm of nature. They are denizens of the forest, their visages are carved from living basswood trees,[23] they have symbolic associations with animals and disease. Yet these creatures of the forest enjoy a kind of symbiotic relationship with the Iroquois by exchanging wild game, relief from disease, [12] and safe passage through the woods, for such products of human society and culture as feasts of sunflower oil and corn mush, gifts of tobacco (*Nicotiana rustica*), and respectful treatment at the Longhouse dances. One final point requires mention: False Faces are clearly masculine. They are carved by men, represent men, and are worn by men. However, the Common Faces and Beggars, while representing older men, are impersonated by younger men or boys; the leader of the False Faces is a mature male adult.

Husk Faces, or Bushy-Heads, are manufactured by women from sewn strips of plaited corn husks. Fenton offers the following description:

> The husk faces look like door mats, the only difference being that the masks have holes for eyes and mouth and the pile is cut off on the inside, but they too have a ragged fringe of hair. Thus a person awakening with his hair standing awry, like a pile of a foot mat, is said. to look like *ga dji'•sa'* – a bushy-head (1941: 411).

Certain embellishments can be made to create different types of Husk Faces,[24] but the medium is essentially more limited in its possibilities than wooden masks. The Husk Society is less formalized than the False Face Society. Its membership includes men, women, and small children. Although in the more important Longhouse rituals, some Husk Faces are meant to represent women in skirts, these roles are

---

22 In this function the Great World-Rim Dweller bears an apparent similarity to the Cherokee mythic figure *Kanati,* Lucky Hunter, who kept the game locked up inside a mountain (Mooney 1900: 242-9).
23 Speck (1949: 72) also mentions the use of maple, white pine, and poplar as suitable wood for False Faces.
24 Speck (1949: 95) mentions and photographs a Husk Face with a single-piece stuffed nose, which bears a striking similarity to the secondarily applied phallic nose of Cherokee gourd masks.

usually played by males (Speck 1949: 48). These beings carry with them mush-stirrers and staves to bang against the walls and floors.

The Husk Faces are prominent in two ritual contexts. Among the Upper Cayuga of Six Nations Reserve, they serve as auxiliaries to the False Face Society in curing rituals conducted in private homes. The Husk Faces act as messengers – literally forerunners – who announce the arrival of [13] the False Faces (Speck 1949: 86). Their curing procedures involve humorous antics in imitation of the stylized, motions of the False Faces, and their actions have been interpreted by some as obscenely profane (Speck 1949: 88). The major public performance of the Husk Face Society takes place during the Midwinter Ceremony. The Husk Face rite is usually performed only once, generally at nigh, during the latter part of the Midwinter festivities.[25] A schematic outline of the rite follows, mostly based on the data from the Tonawanda Seneca. On the sixth night of the Midwinter ceremony, two Husk Faces race in opposite directions through the Longhouse and "officially" close it. Husk Faces guard the doorways and demand tobacco from people passing in and out. Meanwhile social dancing continues until the Husk Faces again bust into the Longhouse and break up the dance by aggressively taking the instruments out of the hands of the musicians and by scattering the dancers. Accomplishing their tasks, they depart. A short while later, one of the Husk Faces re-enters the Longhouse and kidnaps a man who will serve as their interpreter. They teach him a speech to repeat to the audience inside the Longhouse.[26] The message is that the Husk Faces have come from the east and are heading west. They live on the other side of the earth, in a ravine where, between tall stumps, they grow unusually large ears of corn, giant squashes, and beans whose vines extend high into the sky. As the seasons are reversed on the other side, they are hurrying home to hoe their gardens and to take care of their crying babies. They request to dance in the Longhouse, which they do, mixing with their companions and with the audience. Shortly thereafter tobacco is given to the visitors who then depart for their home on "the other side".

The visit of the Husk Face dancers is interpreted by Fenton as a prophecy of future fertility (1941: 416). The Husk Dance seems to symbolize [14] a planting of the seeds of summer into the dead ground of winter. The mixed dancing and the mention of crying babies suggests that human fertility is also implicated.

It seems evident that Husk Faces contrast with the wooden False Faces in several significant ways. The Husk Face masks do not seem to be particularly sacred; they do not embody a living substance, nor are they surrounded by taboos. Their public performances are profane, sometimes bordering on the obscene, and they often invoke parody and burlesque. The Husk Faces have a weak connection with disease and are thought to be able to cure those few Illnesses caused by someone dreaming of them or encountering them in hallucinations (Speck 1949: 60). Rather, primary emphasis seems to focus on fertility. Although men participate actively as Husk Mask dancers, the Husk Face persona is essentially female. The Husk Faces belong to another world, which is, paradoxically, ancestral to, anticipatory of, and contemporaneous with this world. In sum, the Husk Faces can clearly be assigned to the cultural pole in the nature : culture opposition, not only is their substance a product of culture, but the manipulations of that substance – i.e. weaving – is a cultural symbol par excellence.

Carved wooden Booger masks and Iroquois False Faces share such essential features as association with disease, wildness, masculinity, and an arboreal origin. Gourd masks and Corn Husk masks also seem to operate on an equivalent plane, as both are formed from the external residue of a domesticated food plant.[27] However, neither the modem Cherokee nor their ethnological analysts seem to

---

25 Elisabeth Tooker's *Iroquois Ceremonial of Midwinter* (1970) provides an excellent outline of the structure of Midwinter Rites at six major Longhouses for which adequate information exists, and this source has been relied upon here.

26 At Coldsprings Longhouse, the speech is given to the interpreter by a <u>woman</u> leader of the Husk Faces (Tooker 1970: 72) (our emphasis).

27 It may be of interest that the Iroquois saw Corn, Beans, and Squash as coordinate and referred to them

make a conceptual or pragmatic distinction between carved wooden masks and gourd masks. This fusion of meaning and function may represent a modern confusion, and it seems probable that the two [15] types of masks, their functions, and their mythological charters were once separate.

The Cherokee company of Boogers seems much less organized and more spontaneous than their Iroquois counterparts. While the False Face Society is hierarchically organized into three levels and the Husk Face Society is divided into men, women (or men disguised as women), and children, the Cherokee Boogers are an ill-sorted, motley crew loosely coordinated by an ill-defined leader-spokesman. Among the Iroquois, only the Husk Face Society barges into the Longhouse and disrupts the ongoing dance program; with the Cherokees both wooden and gourd masked figures collaborate in this kind of boisterous intrusion. The behavior of the Boogers is more overtly sexual and scatological than the comic antics of the Husk Face performers. Most importantly, for the Iroquois, the roles of disease bringer and mendicant are clearly separated, though in some regards complementary, and neither figure has a connection with invading whitemen. For the Cherokees, these two figures are merged and, if we follow Speck and Broom's Interpretation, the resulting composite figure is identified with the white man and other exotics.

The representation of the Iroquois Husk Faces as symbols of fertility and visitors from the other side of the world has definite connections with certain traditional Cherokee beliefs. Before presenting this material, it may prove useful to provide a simplified model of Iroquoian cosmology.

Both the Cherokees and Iroquois believe that the earth is an Island floating in a primal sea. This earth-island and surrounding waters are contained by an overhanging inverted bowl-shaped firmament. Beyond this firmament reside primal and eternal spiritual beings. Entry Into this ethereal world is located in the extreme easterly and westerly directions, [16] where the sun rises and sets in its diurnal cycle. According to some cosmological Interpretations, the inverted bowl tilts in the morning to allow the sun to begin its daily circuit on the inside of the firmament and tilts again to allow the sun to exit and begin its nighttime circuit of the underside of the world. One Cherokee philosopher envisions the east and west entry-ways to the primal world as a place where the sky, the world, and the sun come together in temporary juxtaposition and then separate. He offered the image of the closing and opening of a window. The underworld is continuous with the primal world beyond the sky. This realm also can be reached by following the east-west axis to its extremities. A more direct route is to follow the underwater trails of rivers and streams.[28] The other world on the other side is a systematic inversion of this world. Thus, when it is daytime in this world, it is nighttime in the other world; when it is winter in this world, it is summer in the other world. Cherokees offer empirical evidence for seasonal reversal by maintaining that the water from underground, springs tastes cool in summer and warm in winter. In short, this is a world of vertical and horizontal *axes mundi*; it is an Einsteinian world of relative and recurved space-time.

The piece of evidence that seems to link traditional Iroquois ideas about the Husk Masks with Cherokee beliefs is contained, in the earliest extended account of Cherokee social and religious customs, Alexander Longe's "A Small Postcript of the ways and manners of the Indians called Charikees" (Corkran 1969). Longe was an English trader who lived among the Cherokees from 1714 to 1724; his account was written in 1725. In a section that he entitles "Their Notion of Enchantments", Longe presents interesting testimony from a native priest concerning the disappearance, about 1690, of a former town called Agustoghe (Corkran 1969: 40-4). [17]

Augustoghe was reputed to have 400 Inhabitants. A wise man of the town fasted four days and

---

    as the Three Sisters. Cherokees do not see such a close association. Paleobotanical studies indicate that squash probably preceded maize by almost 1,000 years in some parts of the Southeast. The broad significance of gourds to the Southeast has been given monographic treatment by Speck (1941).

28 Mooney's [32] collection of Cherokee myths provides several examples of human visits to the other world, cf The journey to the sunrise (1900: 225-36), The man who married the thunder's sister (1900: 345-7).

then disappeared for an additional four days. On his return he reported to his assembled townsmen that he had journeyed to a wonderful place where people never aged or died, where all sorts of merry making prevailed, and where green corn was available in the midst of winter. He urged all who wished to emigrate into that wondrous place to fast for four days. Invisible people from the enchanted country would then emerge from a whirlpool in the river and bring with them a sumptuous feast. All but 16 to 20 people followed the fast, and on the evening of the fourth day, a troop of women filled the temple and empty cabins with earthen pans piled high with green corn, pumpkins, watermelons, muskmelons, turkey, deer, bear, and buffalo meat. The fresh green foods were produced even though it was mid-winter. The troop of women from the enchanted country remained invisible, even though their voices were audible, and they spoke Cherokee.[29] A great feast was held, after which the wise man, to the accompaniment of a drum, led the people who had faithfully fasted for four days through the whirlpool to the land of enchantment. Sometimes their whooping, hollering, and drum beating can be heard near the river's edge.

This early material indicates that the Cherokees share with the Iroquois a belief in the possibility of visits by spiritual beings from the other world. Under special conditions human beings can travel to the other world, but their's is usually a one-way trip. If they happen to return to this world they sometimes become deranged and often die. Longe's account also illustrates the pluralistic Cherokee notion of time. Biological time is halted in the other world. Winter and summer can be [18] contemporaneous in this world, and the other. The other world is fertile and generative and can revitalize this world. Life and death, dynamism and stasis, can be enjoined.

From what has been said, it should by now be evident that the Cherokee Booger Dance and mask dancing among the Iroquois are genetically related. Similarities between the two traditions are more than mere analogies and convergences, and differences may be attributed to historical drift and diffusion, as well as to adaptation to different physical and behavioral environments. It is time to leave the persisting problem ac of Cherokee-Iroquois parallels and to consider possible relationships of the Cherokee Booger Dance to other comparable phenomena in the Southeast.

The Cherokees, though Iroquoian in language, clearly participated in the general Southeastern culture patterns (cf Lounsbury 1961; Hudson 1976; Dickens 1979). A considerable variety of archeological evidence attests to the antiquity of masking traditions in the Southeast. Shell masks of various shapes and sizes have been excavated in widely dispersed sites; distinctive miniature masks of the so-called 'long-nosed god' (Williams and Goggin 1956) turn up sporadically in the prehistoric horizons;[30] depictions of masked eagle or hawk dancers are found on shell gorgets, conch drinking cups, repoussé copper plates (cf. various illustrations in Fundaburk and Foreman 1957). Finally, there is also the remarkable recovery of carved and painted wooden face masks from the muck of Key Marco in southern Florida that were originally reported by Frank Hamilton Gushing (Gilliland 1975: 80, 85-105).

Early European observers noted the use of free standing posts with carved human heads around which Virginia and Carolina Algonkians [19] occasionally danced. This practice may or may not "be related to the carved faces on the posts of the Delaware Big House. William Sturtevant (1964: 95-99) has painstakingly surveyed, these data in his commentary on the John White drawings. William Bartram's mention of painted and sculptured, caricatures on the pillars and walls of the arbors surrounding the Creek square ground (1958: 288 and 1853: 18) may also be distantly related, to this complex, as may similar carved posts in the houses of Tunica priests.

---

29 The notion of invisible spiritual beings attending and. participating in human feasts and ceremonies is common among the Iroquois.

30 Maskettes are reported for the post-historic Iroquois and Delaware and probably other groups, but they are unknown among the Cherokees. The Seneca have a long-nosed, life-size, wooden mask whose main function is to scare children into behaving (Fenton 1941: 418 and Plate 9), but this creature appears to be a late Algonkian import.

John Lawson's 1714 description of a masked dance witnessed among the Waxhaw, an Eastern Siouan group, bears more than passing resemblance to the Cherokee Booger Dance (Lefler 1967: 44-45). Lawson's account is worth paraphrasing.[31] The faces of the intruding, feather bedecked, dancers were "covered with Vizards of Gourds"; they engaged in mock combat; they danced in a contorted manner. At the conclusion of the dance, "every Youth that was so disposed, catch'd hold of the Girl he liked best, and took her that Night for his Bed-Fellow making as short Courtship and expeditious Wedding, as the Foot Guards us'd to do with the Trulls in Salisbury-Court."

Among the Muskogian-speaking peoples to the south and west of the Cherokee, masks were once used. In connection with the Old Man's Dance. According to John R. Swanton, the Creek annual ceremonial cycle, or what might be called summer dances, began in April or May, climaxed with the Green Corn Ceremony in August, and concluded in late September or mid-October (1928a: 505-6). The Old Man's Dance, sometimes associated with the Raccoon or Wolf Dance, was the sixth and final celebration in the Creek ceremonial calendar.[32] One of Swanton's informants regarded, these "last dances" as [20] the most sacred of all (1928a: 506).

In the Old Man's Dance of the Creeks, young men impersonated, old men. They donned pumpkin, melon, or gourd masks that were sometimes stained red with the juice of recently ripened pokeweed berries (Swanton 1928: 534).[33] Sometimes the masks represented animals – e.g. bears, wolves [raccoons?], panthers, or even such domesticated animals as cattle, bulls, etc. – the masks might also portray Indians of an alien tribe (Swanton, 1928: 556). The Old Man's Dance involved a certain amount of buffoonery. Some of the male masked dancers provoked laughter by wearing women's turtle-shell leg rattles. Other dancers carried bows and arrows and engaged in a pantomimic hunt that called upon the skill and experience of the old men in order to be successful. One of Sturtevant's informants recalled a Mikasuki Old Man's Dance that conformed to the details summarized above. Sturtevant adds that the masks were probably made of bark[34] and that the dance had been moribund for fifty years or more (Sturtevant 1954:59). Frances Densmore contributes a cane to the image of the old man impersonation (1956: 144).

James Adair provides an instance of mask dancing among the eighteenth century Choctaw in conjunction with a solemn spring feast of friendship and love (1930: 119-20). During the night of this four day ceremony, young men dance till dawn and wear differently shaped gourd masks embellished with "hieroglyphic paintings". Sometimes buffalo horns are affixed to the head, and some dancers wore tails reminiscent of Catlin's drawings of Choctaw ballplayers. After the conclusion of the dance, the young men were expected to go hunting.

The masking complex in the Southeast is no longer viable, so that it is difficult to obtain the same degree of richness and complexity of meaning and usage that one sees in the Iroquois data. Nevertheless,

---

31 Speck and Broom (1951: 39) cite this account, but they misquote it and don't carry it to its sexual conclusion.

32 There appears to be a close correlation between the six major Creek celebrations, as outlined by Swanton and the six regularly scheduled Cherokee Festivals described in detail in the Payne-Butrick manuscripts and summarized by Gilbert (1943: 325-335). A systematic comparison of the Creek and Cherokee major ceremonies might produce unforeseen insights.

33 In his monograph on the use of gourds in the Southeast, Speck (1941) fails to note their use as masks by the Creeks and other Muskogean-speakers. This is most surprising since Speck did early fieldwork among the Creeks and later directed specific inquiries to Mary Haas while she was engaged in Creek field work. Even more surprising is his failure to take note of specific references to gourd masks in the writings of his contemporary, John Swanton.

34 Since this is the only reference to bark masks that we have encountered, it probably needs to be re-checked, if possible. There is some likelihood that 'bark' [or 'skin'] may only be one of the lexemes for mask.

it is [21] still possible to reconstruct the dominant themes associated with Southeastern masking from the available material, fragmentary as it may be. These themes can provide another dimension for viewing Cherokee masked, dancing.

All our historical and ethnographic sources mention the use of gourd (or domesticated plant) masks, but they are silent with respect to wooden masks until recent times. One would be tempted to argue that gourd or vegetative masks were a Southeastern trait and that carved wooden masks were a Northern trait. However, the presence of the late prehistoric wooden masks from the Calusa of south Florida cautions us against premature generalizations. One might expect that the predominance of gourd masks in the Southeast would be associated with an emphasis on agricultural fertility themes in the masked dancing. Such is not the case, since the Old Man's Dance is much concerned with animals and hunting. Some of the emphasis may reflect the position of the Old Man's Dance in the larger sequence of Creek ceremonialism. It occurs at the end of the agricultural year and immediately before the late Fall hunting season when the men take to the woods before winter sets in. Indeed, the Creek Old Man's Dance seems to be roughly coordinate with the final fall Cherokee celebration, the Festival of the Bounding Bush (or Pigeon Dance). Unfortunately, this festival is the least understood of the six major Cherokee ceremonies. It was performed to renew friendships when the community re-united after the late fall hunt.

A profane attitude pervades much Southeastern masked dancing. Joking, parody, and burlesque seem to be its lifeblood. Overt and thinly disguised [22] expressions of sexuality are a characteristic part of the dance performance. The dances seem to follow a natural progression starting with initial modesty and sexual segregation. The abrupt intrusion of libidinous masked dancers changes the tone, and mixed dancing follows their appearance. Ultimately, if we can believe Lawson and the outraged missionaries, the sequence leads to promiscuous intercourse.

Perhaps the main theme present in Southeastern masked dancing is the impersonation of older persons by younger persons. This pattern seems to hold for the Cherokee Booger Dance and also for the False Face performances of the Iroquois. Indeed, our primary early source for the Cherokees, Alexander Longe, includes an old [ould.] dance in his listing of Cherokee dances, although the use of masks is not mentioned (Corkran 1969: 24-5).

What kinds of explanations can be offered to account for this profane imitation of the old by the young? Many possibilities spring to mind. Can we consider these masked burlesques as rituals of rebellion in which young men, from behind the safe protection of a mask, act out against the authority and constraining power of the elders and, by so doing, reduce social tension? Maybe. Or can these performances be seen as attempts by the young to acquire some of the wisdom and power of the old? Something of this sort seems to be going on in the hunting aspects of the Old Man's Dance. However, we prefer to emphasize a different direction of energy flow or power investiture. It seems possible that some of the phenomena encountered in Southeastern mask dancing can be viewed as the old men gaining strength and power from the young men. In more abstract terms, rather than the mask wearer assuming and becoming one with the spirit of the mask, we are suggesting that the person being represented, by the mask, In this case an old man, absorbs life qualities from the mask wearer, [23] in this case a youth. Symbolically, at least, old men enjoy a temporary respite from the infirmities of age, feel a rejuvenation of resurgent sexual power, and "believe, at least momentarily, that the inexorable movement of biological time can be halted or reversed.

Similar ideas of reversible or suspended biological time and notions of restoration of physical power can also be found among the Iroquois. In JNB Hewitt's Onondaga version of Iroquois cosmology (1903: 218-220), Sapling, all the other primal beings ('man beings'), and all things of the earth that sprout and grow, have the capacity to retransform their bodies in such a way that they recover their youth to the age of puberty. In this way their force and potency can exist fully and undiminished. Youth and old age are not separate, temporally isolated, and irreversible stages of life, but exist simultaneously. As summer is accessible to those in the winter through transmigration to the other world, so youth is accessible to aged men through an exchange of bodies. This positional exchange is affected through a journey or ritualized pilgrimage.

We suggest that the Cherokee Booger Dance is one such performance in which young men masked as old men symbolically journey from a distant land, intrude upon, frighten, and entertain the audience of kinsmen and potential affines, achieve social solidarity by dancing with the women of the local group, and then abruptly take their leave.

Lest our paper seem too narrowly focused and restricted to parochial interests, we will, by way of conclusion, try to draw out points that may have relevance to more general theories of masks and masking.

Our culture's socialization practices and repertoire of metaphors leads us to believe that masks are disguises, false fronts behind which our [24] real selves remain hidden and inviolate. Masks deceive, mislead, and falsify. Masks are untrue.

With historical appreciation of masking in Western Civilization, with exposure to beliefs and practices regarding masks and masking In non-Western cultures, and with increased knowledge about such sub-cultural traces of vestigial masking practices as circus clowns, female impersonators, Christmas mummers, and Mardi Gras, our understanding of masks is significantly enlarged. Almost as a reaction-formation to our prior beliefs, we begin to view masks as embodiments of truth, as valid representations, as loci for a transcendent reality. Accompanying these altered connotations about masks, our formerly sacred notions of self become unreal, untrue, and falsely deceptive. As the old cigarette commercial tells us, "It's what's up front that counts". In short, there is a continuing dialogue and transaction between the mask and the self, between outside and inside, surface and core. Sometimes the self becomes absorbed into the mask to the point of obliteration. At other times the mask becomes the efficient vehicle for self-expression.

Part of the problem with many social scientific theories of masks and masking is that they are unilateral. They emphasize one side of the self-mask dialogue and ignore the other. With these considerations in mind, let us once more review some of the essential features of Eastern woodlands' masks and masked dancing.[35]

Among the Iroquois, the False Face masks are thought to be extremely powerful. The mask itself, is believed to be alive, and, as a partly autonomous, partly dependent, living being, the mask demands respect, periodic attention, and gifts of food and tobacco. If the caretakers of the mask fall in their duties, the mask can take revenge by causing [25] illness or even death. The False Faces, thus, exercise certain powers over man. Local tradition maintains, and we have no reason to doubt it, that people putting on False Face masks under the proper ritual conditions become False Faces; people cured by the False Face Society gain membership into that body. In sum, the False Face absorbs and becomes the self.

The Iroquois Husk Masks lack the inherent power of False Faces. What power they do control derives from external sources. Although connected to agriculture, fertility, and vital support systems. Husk Faces command little respect or attention, and these are fought for by snatching the instruments from Longhouse musicians and by affiliating with the more powerful False Faces. They have a minimal society devoted to their care and ceremonial performances. Since they inflict few diseases on man, their role in curing is correspondingly slight. In fact, their curing procedures are a farcical parody of those of the False Faces.

The principal function of the Husk Faces seems to be as mediators between this world and "the world on the other side." Their home base is in the ravines, amid the stumps, of the fertile other world. They travel back and forth and help maintain communication between this world and the other side. Indeed, much of their time in this world is spent as heralds. In terms of the mode of analysis being pursued here, the Husk Faces do not overwhelm and absorb the self, but they extend, it by providing

---

35 Our areal survey, it should be recognized, is incomplete, since we do not consider the Delawares and other Algonkian-speaking peoples for whom there exists considerable data on masking.

connections to the past (the primordial "world on the other side"), the present (the dark gloom of midwinter in this world), and the future (the renewal of the world next spring).

Returning to the Booger Masks of the Cherokees, we find a unique persona, differing from, but related to the Husk and False Faces of the [26] Iroquois. The Booger Dance is framed in a tragicomic drama that serves to synthesize the disparate parts of the self. Perhaps most importantly, it brings together old men and young men so that each participates simultaneously in certain qualities of the other – wisdom, maturity, and authority for the young man; vigor and virility for the old man. The self, by way of the mask, can directly experience the properties of its most significant other. The Booger Dance acts out a basic tension between old men and young men in which each fears and desires the power of the other, yet neither can exist alone.

A second important feature of this performance is that it provides the audience with a dramatization of their own primal and unenculturated qualities. The audience vicariously participates in a non-Cherokee world, that which exists outside the margins of Cherokee society. The performance sequence and style is a parody of what is basically foreign to Cherokee ethics – one does not burst into another's house uninvited, demand women, and perform hostile and sexual acts.

The masks themselves focus on these tensions. Some gourd masks poke fun at youths in their excessive preoccupation with sexuality by featuring an extended phallus surrounded by rabbit fur pubic hair directly in the middle of an unwrinkled, smooth face. Other masks satirize old age by exaggerating wrinkles and grey hats – complemented by a stooped posture and creaky gait. Other masks parody the non-Cherokee by comically impersonating Blacks, Whites, Germans, Chinese, and other exotics.

This masked drama highlights certain problematics of Cherokee life: the uncontrolled excessiveness of young men, the nagging moral authority of the elders, and the inappropriate behavior of non-Cherokees. The categories of time and space, old age and-youth, and Cherokee and non-Cherokee are extended to the limits of their cosmological, life-cyclic and sociocultural potential. [27]

In conclusion, we have tried, to show that the meaning of masks and masked, performances can best be approached by analyzing the dialectical interplay between mask and masker. Some have sought to understand masks and masked dances through detailed description of these cultural productions. The assumption is that there is an isomorphic fit between these objects and patterned behaviors and the culture that produced them. Others view the self as crucial, such that masks and masked dancing are analyzed as defense mechanisms set in motion to preserve or restore ego-identity; the content of the dances and the formal properties of the masks are regarded as direct projections of intra-psychic conflict. We advocate an approach that avoids these extremes of exclusive cultural or psychological determinism. By focusing on the interaction of mask and self we hope to restore an appreciation for the richness of intuited meaning and qualities of direct experience that are too often felt to be expendable in modem social science.

References [33]

Adair, James 1930 *Adair's History of the American Indians*. Samuel Cole Williams, ed. Johnson City, Tennessee: The Watauga Press, [First published in 1775].

Alexander, J.T 1971 *A Dictionary of the Cherokee Indian Language*. Published by J.T Alexander.

Bartram, William 1853 Observations on the Creek and Cherokee Indians. *American Ethnological Society Transactions* 3: 1-81.

  1958 *Travels*. Francis Harper, ed. New Haven: Yale University Press. (First published in 1791].

Bloom, Leonard 1939 The Cherokee Clan, A Study of Acculturation. *American Anthropologist* 41: 266-8.

  1942 The Acculturation of the Eastern Cherokee: Historical Aspects. *North Carolina Historical Review* 19: 323-58.

  1945 A Measure of Conservatism. *American Anthropologist* 47: 630-5.

Corkran, David H, ed. 1969 Alexander Longe: 'A Small Postscript on the ways and manners of the Indians called Charikees'. *Southern Indian Studies* 21: 1-49.

Cushing, Frank Hamilton 1897 The Pepper-Hearst Expedition: A Preliminary Report on the Exploration of Ancient Key-Dweller Remains on the Gulf Coast of Florida. *Proceedings of the American Philosophical Society* 25 (153).

De Brahm, Gerald William 1971 *Report of the General Survey in the Southern District of North America*. Louis De Vorsey, Jr., ed. Columbia, SC: University of South Carolina Press. [Original manuscript, 1773].

Densmore, Frances 1956 *Seminole Music*. Smithsonian Institution, Bureau of America Ethnology Bulletin 161. Washington, DC, United States Government Printing Office. [34]

Dickens, Roy S 1979 The Origins and Development of Cherokee Culture: 3-32. In *The Cherokee Indian Nation*. Duane H King, ed. Knoxville: The University of Tennessee Press.

Evans, J P 1836 Sketches of Cherokee Character, Customs, and. Manners. In The Payne-Buttrick Papers. Chicago, Ayer Collection, Newberry Library.

Fenton. William N 1941 Masked Medicine Societies of the Iroquois: 397-430. In Annual Report of the Board of Regents of the Smithsonian Institution, 1940, Washington, DC: United States Government Printing Office.

    1961 Iroquoian Culture History: A General Evaluation. In *Symposium on Cherokee and Iroquois Culture*. William N. Fenton and John Gulick, eds. Smithsonian Institution, Bureau of American Ethnology, Bulletin 180: 257-77. Washington, DC: United States Government Printing Office.

    1972 Iroquois Masks: A Living Tradition in the Northeast: 43-48. In *American Indian Art: Form and Tradition*. New York: E.P Dutton.

    1978 Cherokee-Iroquois Connections Revisited. *Journal of Cherokee Studies* 3 (4): 239-49.

Fogelson, Raymond D 1975 An Analysis of Cherokee Sorcery and Witchcraft: 113-31. In *Four Centuries of Southern Indians*, Charles M. Hudson, ed. Athens: The University of Georgia Press.

Fundaburk, Emma Lila and Mary Douglass Fundaburk Foreman, eds, 1957 *Sun Circles and Human Hands: The Southeastern Indians – Art and Industries*. Luverne, Ala; Emma Lila Fundaburk,

Gilbert, William H 1943 The Eastern Cherokees. Smithsonian Institution, Bureau of American Ethnology Bulletin 133, Paper 23: 169-413. Washington, DC: United States Government Printing Office. [35]

Gilliland, Marion Spjut 1975 *The Material Culture of Key Marco, Florida*. Gainesville: The University Presses of Florida.

Hewitt, J N B 1903 *Iroquoian Cosmology*. In Twenty-First Annual Report of the Bureau of American Ethnology, 1899-1900. Washington, DC: United States Government Printing Office.

Highwater, Jamake 1977 *Ritual of the Wind*. New York: The Viking Press.

Holman, Harriet B 1976 Cherokee Dancing Remembered: Why the Eastern Band Abjured the Old Eagle Dance. *North Carolina Folklore Journal* 26: 101-6.

Hudson, Charles 1976 The Southeastern Indians. Knoxville: University of Tennessee Press.

Kurath, Gertrude P 1961 Effects of Environment on Cherokee-Iroquois Ceremonialism. Music, and Dance. In *Symposium on Cherokee and Iroquois Culture*. William N Fenton and John Gulick, eds. Smithsonian Institution, Bureau of American Ethnology Bulletin 180: 173-95. Washington, DC: United States Government Printing Office.

Laubin, Reginald and Gladys Laubin 1977 *Indian Dances of North America*. Norman: University of Oklahoma Press.

Lefler, Hugh Talmage, ed. 1967 *A New Voyage to Carolina, by John Lawson*. Chapel Hill: The University of North Carolina Press.

Lounsbury, Floyd G 1961 Iroquois-Cherokee Linguistic Relations. In *Symposium on Cherokee and. Iroquois Culture*. William N Fenton and John Gulick, eds. Smithsonian Institution, Bureau of American Ethnology Bulletin 180: 11-8. Washington, DC.: United States Government Printing

Office. [36]

Mason, Bernard S 1944 *Dances and Stories of the American Indian.* New York: A S Barnes and Co.

Mooney, James 1900 *Myths of the Cherokees.* Smithsonian Institution, Bureau of American Ethnology, Nineteenth Annual Report, 1897-98, Pt. 1: 3-576. Washington, DC: United States Government Printing Office.

Payne, John Howard nd The Payne-Buttrick Papers, Vol IV. Chicago: Ayer Collection, Newberry Library.

Speck, Frank G 1931 *A Study of the Delaware Big House Ceremony.* Publications of the Pennsylvania Historical Commission II: 5-192.

    1941 *Gourds of the Southeastern Indians.* Boston: The New England Gourd Society.

    1949 *MidWinter Rites of the Cayuga Long House.* (in collaboration with Alexander General) Philadelphia: University of Pennsylvania Press.

    1950 Concerning Iconology and the Masking Complex in Eastern North America. *University Museum Bulletin* 15: 6-57.

Speck, Frank G. and Leonard Broom 1951 *Cherokee Dance and Drama.* (in collaboration with Will West Long) Berkeley: University of California Press.

Sturtevant, William C 1954 The Medicine Bundles and Busks of the Florida Seminole. *The Florida Anthropologist* 7 (2): 31-70.

    1961 Comment on Gertrude P. Kurath's 'Effects of Environment on Cherokee-Iroquois Ceremonialism, Music, and Dance', In *Symposium on Cherokee and Iroquois Culture.* William N Fenton and John Gulick, eds. Smithsonian Institute, Bureau of American Ethnology Bulletin 180: 199-204. Washington, DC: United States Government Printing Office.

    1964 John White's Contributions to Ethnology. In *The American Drawings of John White*, 1577-1590. Paul Hutton and. David Beers Quinn, ed. Chapel Hill: The University of North Carolina Press.

Swanton, John R 1928 *Religious Beliefs and Medical Practices of the Creek Indians.* Forty-Second Annual Report of the Bureau of American Ethnology, 1924-1925: 473-672. Washington, DC: United States Government Printing Office.

    1928a The Interpretation of Aboriginal Mounds by Means of Creek Indian Customs. Annual Report Smithsonian Institution for 1927: 495-506. Washington, DC: United States Government Printing Office.

Tooker, Elisabeth 1964 *An Ethnography of the Huron Indians, 1615-1649.* Smithsonian Institution, Bureau of American Ethnology Bulletin 190. Washington, DC: United States Government Printing Office.

    1970 The Iroquois Ceremonial of Midwinter. Syracuse, N.Y: Syracuse University Press.

Trowbridge, C C Unpublished manuscript in the Shea Collection, Georgetown University Library, D.C. [ca. 1825]

Witthoft, John 1949 Stone Pipes of the Historic Cherokees. *Southern Indian Studies* 1: 43-62.

Williams, Samuel Cole, ed. 1928 *Early Travels in the Tennessee Country, 1540-1800.* Johnson City, Tennessee: The Watauga Press.

    1948 Lieut. Henry Timberlake's Memories, 1756-1765. Marietta. Ga: Continental Book Co. [First published in 1765].

Williams, Stephen, and John M. Goggin 1956 The Long Nosed God Mask in Eastern United States. *The Missouri Archaeologist* l8 (3): 3-72. [38]

Wright, Elizabeth Mary 1913 *Rustic Speech and Folk-Lore.* New York: Oxford University Press.

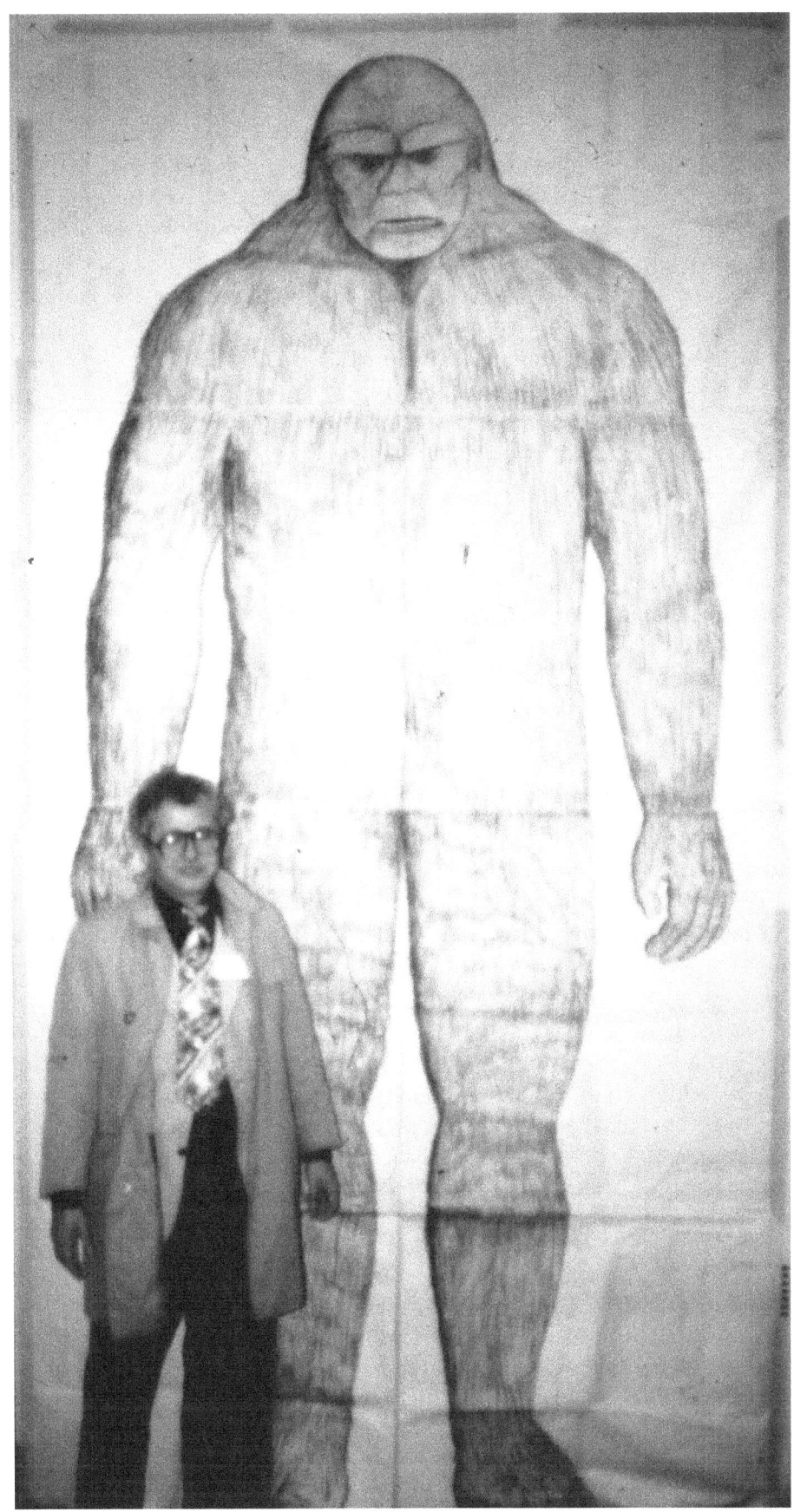

Ray & Sasquatch

WINDIGO GOES SOUTH: STONECLAD AMONG THE CHEROKEES[1]

This article examines the tradition amongst several Woodland Indian tribes of a race of manlike stone giants, with an origin predating that of mankind, who embody qualities abhorrent to native society and who act aggressively to obstruct, mislead, or destroy humans. The Stoneclad are thought to possess magical, superhuman powers, and shamans or heroes who vanquish these monsters are thereafter endowed with their powers, which they can then use to benefit their own society. The author presents two possible interpretations: that the Stoneclad represent the existence of evil in nature and define by negation evil in man; and that the Stoneclad embody specifically the forces of winter and their severe impact upon a primitive society.

Stone-covered anthropomorphic beings are well represented in the mythology of the Iroquoian-speaking peoples; seemingly related beings appear in the myths and beliefs of their Algonkian neighbors in the Eastern Woodlands and Subarctic. Sporadic reports of stone beings also occur elsewhere in North America, although a systematic search of the wider literature has not been attempted. Other defining attributes of these beings, besides their stonecovered bodies, often include such features as gigantic stature, cannibalistic appetite, and a heart of ice or quartz crystal. Secondary features sometimes associated with these mythic figures are a capacity for metamorphosis into human form (frequently transformation into a child or an old hag), the presence of a spear-shaped finger by which the livers of victims are extracted, a detached finger that indicates the direction of human game, and a magical cane that can be used as a weapon, sensing device, or be transformed into other useful objects. Stone beings are usually thought to come from the north and to have some affinity for caves and mountains. They are believed by the Indians and by themselves to be an autochthonous race predating the advent of human beings and to be independent of, and in opposition to, the spiritual beings who created mankind and who maintain responsibility for man's welfare.

Any analysis of myths from the Eastern Woodlands poses difficult problems. Much material was collected only after these narratives had lost their [133] sacred qualities and had passed into more public realms of folklore. There seem to be several strata of mythic themes and ideas represented. Some strata, doubtless, hark back to archaic times and perhaps ultimately to Asia. Other strata clearly relate to horticultural horizons and an evolved ceremonial cycle directed by sacred technicians. Dynamic processes of mythic formulation and reformulation continued and probably intensified with the European invasion of the New World that commenced in the sixteenth century. Besides the enormous time range with which we are dealing, we must also recognize that the Eastern Woodlands was a relatively open area. Migrations of people and ideas, both within and without the area, encountered few natural or cultural barriers. Such social factors as political alliances, trade relations, the adoption of captives, intermarriage, and even incorporation of alien tribal segments have greatly stimulated the diffusion of mythic motifs. I

---

1 * In the spelling of the native words in this paper, accent marks (') indicate stressed vowels. Other marks on vowels have the following values: ă as in "all"; û as in "cut"; ûñ nasalizes the u. The ' is a diacritic aspiration of the previous vowel, accented.

Grateful acknowledgement is hereby given to the Museum of Anthropology and the Centre for Continuing Education, University of British Columbia (with the assistance of the Canada Council and the University of British Columbia Press), plus the Litchstern Fund of the Department of Anthropology, University of Chicago, for travel expenses to the Conference on the Anthropology of the Unknown – Sasquatch and Similar Phenomena, for which this paper was written. I would also like to thank Jay Miller, Robert Brightman, Paul Friedrich, Thomas Buckley. Amelia Walker, and Susan Fogelson for useful comments and help, and Jennifer Rike for typing.

have reason to believe that the themes associated with Stoneclad reflect some of the deepest mythic strata in the Eastern Woodlands.[2] However, I see little hope of reconstructing a "pure" proto-myth, even if such a narrative ever existed. Yet I do feel that connections can be established between what now appear to be disparate myths, motifs, and beliefs and that through these connections the roots and meanings of Stoneclad can be approached.

I will first examine Stoneclad myths and associated beliefs among the Cherokees. Here I rely on published material as well as on data personally collected in the field. After this, the discussion will be expanded to encompass the linguistically related Huron-Wyandot and Northern Iroquois; this will be based on a fairly comprehensive but not exhaustive survey of the published literature referring to Stone Giants and related phenomena.[3] Next, specific features that seem to relate the Iroquoian material to certain Eastern and Northern Algonkian themes will be examined. Finally, some broader interpretative suggestions will be offered that may have implications for understanding the Sasquatch phenomena in the Northwest.

Brief variants of the Cherokee Stoneclad myth from Oklahoma and from North Carolina were published before the turn of the century by Herman ten Kate and James W. Terrell.[4] However, the first extended version of the myth was published in 1900 by James Mooney in his "Myths of the Cherokee."[5] Mooney collected this myth from his major informant, a medicine man named Swimmer, about 1888. I will present this version and use it as a basis for discussion of subsequent versions.

NON' YUNU' WI, THE STONE MAN

This is what the old men told me when I was a boy. Once when all the people of the settlement were out in the mountains on a great hunt. [134] one man who had gone on ahead climbed to the top of a high ridge and found a large river on the other side. While he was looking across he saw an old man walking about on the opposite ridge, with a cane that seemed to be made of some bright, shining rock. The hunter watched and saw that every little while the old man would point his cane in a certain direction, then draw it back and smell the end of it. At last he pointed it in the direction of the hunting camp on the other side of the mountain, and this time

---

2 It has been suggested that the impenetrable stone bodies of these beings may be an indirect reference to European armour. I hope to show, however, that petrous symbolism is deeply imbedded in Eastern Woodland mythology.

3 The Huron and Iroquois sources consulted include: David Cusick, "Sketches of the Ancient History of the Six Nations," in Information Respecting the History, Conditions, and Prospect of the Indian Tribes of the United State's, vol. 5, ed. H R Schoolcraft (1825; reprint ed., Philadelphia; J.B. Lippincott 1855); Erminnie A Smith. "Myths of the Iroquois," in Bureau of Ethnology, Annual Report 2 (1880-81) (Washington, DC: Government Printing Office 1883), pp. 51-115; JNB Hewitt, *Tawiskaron* in Handbook of American Indian North of Mexico, pt. 2, ed. FW Hodge (Washington, DC.: Government Printing Office 1910) and Seneca Fiction, Legends, and Myths; collected by Jeremiah Curtain and JNB Hewitt, ed, JNB Hewitt, Bureau of American Ethnology, Annual Report 32 (1910-11) Washington, 1911; C M Barbeau, Huron and Wyandot Mythology, Department of Mines, Geological Survey, Memoir 80, Anthropological series, no 11 (Ottawa 1915); Frederick Waugh, manuscript (1915-18), Waugh Collection of Iroquois Folktales, American Philosophical Society; Arthur C Parker, Seneca Myths and Folktales, Buffalo Historical Society Publications, vol. 27 ([nd]); and Jesse Cornplanter, Legends of the Longhouse (Philadelphia: JB Lippincott 1938).

4 Ten Kate, Legends of the Cherokees, *Journal of American Folklore* 2 (1889): 53-55 and Terrell, The Demon of Consumption, *Journal of American Folklore* 5 (1892): 125-26.

5 *Myths of the Cherokee*, in Bureau of American Ethnology, Nineteenth Annual Report, 1897-98, pt. 2 (Washington, DC: Government Printing Office 1900), pp. 319-20.

when he drew back the staff he sniffed it several times as if it smelled very good, and then started along the ridge straight for the camp. He moved very slowly, with the help of the cane, until he reached the end of the ridge, when he threw the cane out into the air and it became a bridge of shining rock stretching across the river. After he had crossed over upon the bridge it became a cane again, and the old man picked it up and started over the mountain toward the camp,

The hunter was frightened, and felt sure that it meant mischief, so he hurried on down the mountain and took the shortest trail back to the camp to get there before the old man. When he got there and told his story the medicine-man said the old man was a wicked cannibal monster called *Nun' yunu' wi*, "Dressed in Stone," who lived in that part of the country, and was always going about the mountains looking for some hunter to kill and eat. It was very hard to escape from him, because his stick guided him like a dog, and it was nearly as hard to kill him, because his whole body was covered with a skin of solid rock. If he came he would kill and eat them all, and there was only one way to save themselves. He could not bear to look upon a menstrual woman, and if they could find seven menstrual women to stand in the path as he came along the sight would kill him.

So they asked among all the women, and found seven who were sick in that way, and with one of them it had just begun. By the order of the medicine-man they stripped themselves and stood along the path where the old man would come. Soon they heard Nun' yunu' wi coming through the woods, feeling his way with his stone cane. He came along the trail to where the first woman was standing, and as soon as he saw her he started and cried out: "Yu! my grandchild; you are in a very bad state!" He hurried past her, but in a moment he met the next woman, and cried out again: "Yu! my child; you are in a terrible way," and hurried past her, but now he was vomiting blood. He hurried on and met the third and the fourth and the fifth woman, but with each one that he saw his step grew weaker until when he came to the last one, with whom the sickness had just begun, the blood poured from his mouth and he fell down on the trail. [135]

Then the medicine-man drove seven sourwood stakes through his body and pinned him to the ground, and when night came they piled great logs over him and set fire to them, and all the people gathered around to see. *Nun' yunu' wi* was a great *ada' wehi* and knew many secrets, and now as the fire came close to him he began to talk, and told them the medicine for all kinds of sickness. At midnight he began to sing, and sang the hunting songs for calling up the bear and the deer and all the animals of the woods and mountains. As the blaze grew hotter his voice sank low and lower, until at last when daylight came, the logs were a heap of white ashes and the voice was still.

Then the medicine-man told them to rake off the ashes, and where the body had lain they found only a large lump of red *wa'di* paint and a magic *u'lunsu'ti* stone. He kept the stone for himself, and calling the people around him he painted them, on face and breast, with the red *wa'di*, and whatever each person prayed for while the painting was being done – whether for hunting success, for working skill, or for a long life – that gift was his.

Also in Mooney's collection is a myth about an *Utlûnta*, or Spear-Finger, an old hag who menaces the Cherokee community by spearing and devouring the livers of children.[6] This ogress is finally identified and captured in a pit trap. All the arrows of the hunters fail to penetrate her stone-covered body. Finally, a chickadee directs the bowmen to aim at her right hand, where her spear finger and palm conjoin and where her heart is located. The *Utlûnta* is then killed. Mooney implies in his notes[7] that the *Utlûnta* is the female form of Stoneclad; some of his informants believe that they are husband and wife, the former slaying hunters in the woods and the latter murdering young children near their homes. There

---

6 *ibid*, pp. 316-19.
7 *ibid*, p. 467.

does seem to be some significant difference between these two monsters: the location of the heart,[8] the failure to cremate the remains of the *Utlûnta*, and the absence of any ceremonial gifts from the dying Utlûnta.[9] Another valuable version of the Spear-Finger myth was collected in Oklahoma by John B. Davis.[10] Here Spear-Finger is a female witch with a stone body who derives her power from sleeping with the chief of the underwater monsters. When she is finally killed with an arrow to the hand, her corpse is burned for seven days, after which all that remains is a scale and tip of the horn of the water monster.

A second major rendering of the Stoneclad myth was collected in the late 1930's from Will West Long, an Eastern Cherokee traditionalist, and is recorded by Frank Speck and Leonard Broom in their *Cherokee Dance and Drama*[11]. This version conforms closely to the one collected by Mooney, [136] although it is imbued with a more sacred and primordial quality. Here Stoneclad transforms himself into an orphan, is adopted into a family, and devours the livers of young children. These are the first deaths to occur in the world. Finally the monster is brought down by the seven menstruating women, and in his fiery death ordeal he sings different medicine and dance songs to offset the death and disease that he has let loose in the world. Stones from his body become specialized divining crystals. Speck and Broom remark that Stoneclad can transform himself into the old woman with the sharp forefinger, thereby suggesting that Stoneclad and *Utlûnta* are but different aspects of the same being.[12]

The Stoneclad myth still has some circulation among conservative Eastern Cherokees. Recent Cherokee informants of Jack and Anna Kilpatrick in Oklahoma knew about Stoneclad but could not, or would not, narrate the myth.[13] I had the good fortune to tape record a long version of the myth in 1960 from Elodi, a knowledgeable Eastern Cherokee medicine man. In this version Stoneclad resides in the mountains in a rock shelter and would kill deer hunters who ventured into his domain. He bludgeoned his victims to death with his stone cane, then used his awl finger to make an incision in the backs of their necks, and proceeded to suck out their blood. A medicine man sent three young men out to discover the fate of the missing hunters. Two of the boys were killed by Stoneclad, but the third managed to escape and inform the medicine man about their monstrous enemy. A plan of action utilizing women was formulated – but in this instance only four, instead of seven, young girls were employed.[14] Stoneclad grew sick when he encountered the exposed thighs of the young girls. He began vomiting the blood of the hunters he had slain, stumbled around drunkenly, and finally collapsed. He was tied to a pole, roasted to a slow night-long death,[15] meanwhile singing specialized medicine songs. All that remained in the morning ashes was his crystal heart. This was broken up and distributed to different medicine men to serve as powerful divining instruments. By scrying and interpreting revealed signs in the crystal, the

---

8 In the apparently derivative Creek version of the tale, the Big Rock Man proves vulnerable to an arrow shot in the ear (John R Swanton, Myths and Tales of the Southeastern Indians, Bureau of American Ethnology, Bulletin 88. [Washington, DC: Government Printing Office 1929), p. 38).

9 In the ten Kate version the *Utlûnta*'s stone exterior breaks apart and individual stones are preserved as amulets; the male counterpart retreats to the north (ten Kate, "Legends of the Cherokees," p. 54).

10 The Liver Eater: A Cherokee Story, in *Annals of Archeology and Anthropology* 2 (Liverpool: The University Press 1909), pp. 134-38.

11 (Berkeley and Los Angeles: University of California Press 1951.)

12 *ibid*, p. 16.

13 See their *Friends of Thunder: Folktales of the Oklahoma Cherokees* (Dallas: Southern Methodist University Press, 1964), pp. 51-61.

14 Both seven and four are sacred numbers in Cherokee numerology. [150]

15 According to the notes of Frans Olbrechts the fuel used to burn Stoneclad was basswood (*Tilia americana* L.) (quoted in Jack F Kilpatrick and Anna G Kilpatrick, Eastern Cherokee Folktales: Reconstructed from the Fieldnotes of Frans M Olbrechts, Bureau of American Ethnology, Bulletin 196, Anthropological Paper 80. Washington, DC: Government Printing Office, 1966, p. 397).

future could be foretold and answers to critical questions obtained. My friend, Elodi, compared divining crystals to the telescopes and microscopes of the Western scientist.

Additional information was elicited concerning the *ulûnsû'ti*, or Stone-dad's heart. Faithful to its origin, the crystal required as a weekly sacrifice a drop of blood.[16] Preferably this would be human blood obtained by pricking the finger with a pin or sharp instrument; animal blood might be substituted in certain circumstances. If these regular blood offerings were neglected, the spirit of Stoneclad, which was still felt to inhere in the crystal, would become uneasy. It would travel around, bother people, and try other means to slake its thirst for blood. When not being consulted the crystal was carefully [137] wrapped in deerskin and stored in a special stone niche within a dry rock shelter. One of the reasons for secreting the crystal was to protect it against the baleful influence of menstruating women. The rock shelter in which the crystal was stored could only be approached by laying down a path of seven rocks; these rocks were picked up on the return trip out of the hiding place. It seems as if human beings had to be properly insulated or "grounded" when coming near so powerful an object.

I was also told that the crystal was wrapped up with other ritual objects including the tusks, claws, or whiskers of seven or eight different animals, perhaps having totemic significance; also included were four divinatory beads colored red, white, black, and blue, representing the four cardinal directions, and ceremonially treated old tobacco (*Nicotiuna rustica*). The wrapping of these objects in deerskin is consistent with several Cherokee ideas. Deerskins were the prime trade commodity and became a standard of exchange during the Colonial period. Later, cloth was substituted for deerskin as the medium of exchange. On another level Cherokees feel that objects containing intrinsic power, including medicinal plants, must not be kept "naked" lest their powers become dissipated.

The preceding data clearly indicate the survival of medicine bundles among the Eastern Cherokees until quite recent times. The general existence of medicine bundles in the Southeast has been under-reported, although in recent years Louis Capron and William Sturtevant have independently discovered their use among the Florida Seminoles.[17]

According to oral testimony personally gathered in Oklahoma, late nineteenth-century Cherokee outlaws in the Indian Territory sometimes used small personal crystals to elude pursuing lawmen. The last divining crystal among the Eastern Cherokees reputedly was cared for by John Axe, a traditionalist who died about 1900. Statements in the Payne-Butrick manuscripts[18] indicate that it was customary for a medicine man or priest to bequeath his crystal and instructions for its use to a favorite disciple. In a very real sense the death of John Axe marked the end of a tradition, for he was unable to find a suitable successor. Before his death, he is said to have hid his crystal in a nearby mountain cave and placed seven rattlesnakes near the entry to discourage would-be fortune hunters.

Three other Cherokee myths recorded by Mooney, myself, and others Invite brief discussion here because of their connections to the Stoneclad saga and to broader comparative issues that will be considered later. On first examination the Cherokee story of Flint and the Rabbit[19] seems an innocent folktale integrated into a larger cycle of Rabbit-trickster tales. These tales were told for amusement or moral instruction and lacked sacred qualities. In this folktale Rabbit is delegated by the other animals to

---

16 The relationship between blood and crystal was probably strengthened by the fact that rutile quartz (crystal with a red mineral flaw) was common in the Southeast.

17 Capron, The Medicine Bundles of the Florida Seminole and the Green Corn Dance, in Bureau of American Ethnology, Bulletin 151 (Washington, DC: Government Printing Office, 1953), pp. 155-210 and Sturtevant, The Medicine Bundles and Busks of the Florida Seminole, *Florida Anthropologist* 7 (1954): 31-72.

18 The John Howard Payne ~ Daniel Sabin Butrick manuscripts are on deposit in the Ayer Collection at the Newberry Library, Chicago.

19 Mooney, *Myths of the Cherokee*, pp. 274-75.

visit [138] Flint, a being who lives in the mountains and has been killing animals in great numbers.[20] When Flint denies Rabbit the hospitality of his home, Rabbit invites Flint to his house for dinner. They eat picnic-style outside the Rabbit's dwelling. After dinner, Rabbit carves a wooden wedge and mallet. When Flint finally falls into a deep sleep, Rabbit drives the wedge into his flint-covered body and scurries away to his hole. There is a tremendous explosion of flint shrapnel. Rabbit is hit seven times in his anus, an event that some Cherokee narrators feel accounts for the Rabbit's peculiar pattern of pellet-like defecation: in turning around to see what hit him. Rabbit is struck in the face by a stray piece of flying flint, thus resulting in his split upper lip.

In his notes Mooney realizes that this tale involves more than an explanation of peculiarities of rabbit anatomy.[21] The Cherokee name for flint (and Flint), *tawiskala*, is directly cognate with the Iroquois term, *tawiskaron*. Tawiskaron refers to flint, ice, and to the devious mythical twin brother of the primal Iroquois culture hero, *Tarachiawagon*, also referred to as Sapling, Of Good Mind, Holder of the Heavens, and a host of other names. As is well known, the Algonkian culture hero/trickster, *Nanabozho*, often takes the form of a giant hare. Moreover, the same basic antithetical myth structure is found in many Algonkian cosmogonic myths wherein the good brother may be associated with east, sunrise, light, and life and his fraternal antagonist with west, sunset, darkness, and death. This, at least, was the early symbolic interpretation advanced by Daniel Garrison Brinton in 1868.[22] JNB Hewitt sees a similar structural opposition but rotates the axis clockwise ninety degrees, so that the good brother represents south, warmth, sun, and summer, while the bad or contrary brother signifies north, cold, ice, and winter.[23] The Iroquois and many Algonkian groups personify Winter as an ice-covered or exposed skeletal figure. A slight Cherokee story involving Winter Man was collected by Mooney.[24] A Cherokee village was engaged in the annual fall burning of the brush, when the fire got out of control and began to burn an ever-widening hole in the ground that threatened to engulf the entire world. They summoned the Winter Man from his home in the north, and he responded with snow, hail storms, and heavy rain that finally extinguished the fire.

Thus the Cherokee tale of Flint and the Rabbit seems to be a vestigial remnant of a more deeply grounded and widely spread oscillating cosmogonic struggle between the forces of good and evil (or not good), creation and destruction, life and death, and summer and winter. But even in its attenuated form, the figure of Flint bears obvious similarities to Stoneclad. Both are primarily identified with a petrous material, both are man-killers, and both can bestow magico-medical and other practical boons upon mankind after they are overcome. [139]

The Cherokees also have a profusion of myths about a monstrous, dragon-like, anthropophagous, aquatic serpent called the *Uktena*.[25] This type of creature has a widespread distribution in the belief systems of native North America. It is reported for the Iroquois, Creeks, the Shawnee (where interestingly the monster is vanquished with the aid of a menstruating woman), the Eastern Algonkians, Central Algonkians, the Yuroks, various Siouan-speaking groups, and elsewhere, including the Northwest Coast. Among the Dakota the underwater monster is called *Unkehi*, probably ultimately cognate with the Cherokee Uktena, and this term can be extended by Dakota to refer to large extinct animals in general

---

20 The condensed symbolism here doubtless relates to the use of flint for spear points and arrowheads.
21 Mooney, *Myths of the Cherokee*, p. 451.
22 *The Myths of the New World*: A Treatise on the Symbolism and Mythology of the Red Race of America (New York: Leypoldt and Holt, 1868), pp. 161-72.
23 Hewitt, *Tawiskaron*, p. 708.
24 Mooney, *Myths of the Cherokee*, pp. 322-23.
25 Charles Hudson has recently completed a richly textured analysis of the *Uktena* in a paper presented to the Cherokee-Iroquois Symposium held in Cherokee, North Carolina, in April, 1978, which is expected to appear in a forthcoming issue of the Journal of Cherokee Studies.

whose buried bones are sometimes uncovered on the Plains.[26] Obviously, the notion of underwater monsters is not restricted to native North America. Besides similarities to Chinese and European dragon-lore, and even the ripples of excitement generated by the possible existence of the Loch Ness monster, similar kinds of beings seem represented by the Melanesian *Marsalai* and the Australian Rainbow Serpent.

However, returning to Cherokee beliefs about the Uktena, several features of this mythic water monster show resemblances to Stoneclad. First, the scaly epidermis of the Uktena was also impervious to the spears and arrows of human hunters. Nevertheless, like Spear-Finger and Flint, there was a vulnerable locus on the seventh scale of the head or body. Like Stoneclad, the Uktena represents a primeval being, a survivor from the pre-human era of world creation. Finally and most importantly, the Uktena possessed a shining crystal jewel, an *ulûnsû'ti* or crystal, on the top of his head.

In several myths this carbuncle is liberated from the slain monster and serves as a major sacred tribal talisman. Its existence and mythic origin is attested to by Lieutenant Henry Timberlake and by James Adair in their descriptions of eighteenth-century Cherokee life.[27]

A great amount of information about the use of sacred crystals in Cherokee ritual is contained in the Payne-Butrick manuscripts. This material was collected from older informants in the 1830's by the celebrated playwright, actor, and adventurer John Howard Payne and by missionary Daniel S Butrick. They describe five different-sized quartz crystals that were employed for different purposes. The largest crystals were used for war. These were sometimes carried into battle along with sacred war fire in a portable box, or "ark." These crystals might also be enclosed in a weasel-skin bag and worn on the breast of the war chief. There are indirect indications that the war crystal might have been associated with Stoneclad's heart, since it is addressed as "Man eater," and it was customary to rub blood from the scalp of a slain enemy on the stone. In divining the outcome of war or in determining the duration of peace, the crystal was placed on the fleshy side of a fresh deerskin that was laid on the west floor of the council house with the head oriented to [140] the central fire and eastern door. A line of animal blood was brushed on the deerskin before the *ulûnsû'ti* was placed down, and various omens were interpreted.

Slightly smaller than the war crystals were the divining stones of the civic priests. These were primarily used to determine the future presence or absence of disease in the community. The *ulunsati* could be placed on a deerskin-covered post, on a pile of seven folded deerskins, or in the crevice of a building to catch the light of the rising sun. These stones were also sometimes worn as a pendant around the neck of the priest.

The nest smallest crystal was used to trace lost or stolen objects. The location of the missing object, often accompanied by the face of the thief, would appear in the stone. Still smaller crystals were consulted by hunters to predict if, and how much, game would be killed. The smallest crystals were used by individual conjurors to predict an individual's longevity and to answer questions involved with love magic. The three smallest crystals would be hidden on the body in no fixed place, somewhat analogous to the mobile or misplaced heart of Spear-finger.[28]

I have not dwelt on the highly elaborated usage of magical stones among the traditional Cherokee as a sterile exercise in ethnominerology, but rather to establish a parallelism between ritual usage and differentiated origin as revealed in surviving myths. Some divining crystals originated in whole or as fragments from the heart of Stoneclad. Other talismans seem to have come from Stoneclad's outer

---

26 See Albert S. Gatschet, Water Monsters of American Aborigines, *Journal of American Folklore* 12 (1899): 255-60.

27 Lieutenant Henry Timberlake, *Memoirs, 1756-1765*, ed. S C Williams (Johnson City, Tenn: [n.p] 1927), pp. 74-75; Adair, *History of the American Indians* (London: E and C Dilly 1775), pp 86-87, 237-38.

28 James Adair also mentions the use of a crystal to bring rain, which he sarcastically considers a neat feat given the heavy annual precipitation in the Cherokee area (Adair, *American Indian*, p 86).

covering. Still other divining stones derive from the crown or scales of the serpentine Uktena.

Important for later consideration is the generic Cherokee name for quartz crystal, *ulûnsû'ti*. This same word in modern Cherokee is used for glass, as in drinking glass. Although its etymology cannot be traced, the term embraces connotations of transparency, translucence, a substance through which light can penetrate. As was mentioned previously, the term for flint or chert, both as a mineral and as a mythic being, is tawiskala. The Cherokee language also preserves a related and perhaps more fundamental term, *tawiska* or *tawiskaga*, meaning 'smooth' or 'slick'.[29]

We will now examine some related myths and beliefs from the Huron-Wyandots and Northern Iroquois. In his extensive volume on *Huron and Wyandot Mythology*, the Canadian anthropologist and folklorist, C Marius Barbeau, provides several accounts of *strendu*, or Flinty Giants. Many of these narratives are virtually identical with recorded Seneca myths and doubtless reflect the long association of the Huron and Wyandot with the western Iroquois. In general, these Flinty Giants possessed a flint or stone exterior, were cannibalistic, utilized a detached finger to locate human victims, and were rather naive and easily tricked. A *strendu* could be [141] temporarily tamed by human kindness and assistance. In one myth a bucket of lard is kept for the strendu to drink and thereby forget his hunger for human meat. It should be noted here that boiling lard or grease was frequently used by Algonkians as a remedy to melt the icy heart of a Windigo cannibal or human being suspected of being in the initial stages of undergoing such a transformation. The Flinty Giants had vulnerable places on their bodies, such as their eyes, mouths, armpits, or soles of the feet. They could also be beaten to death with blocks (or pillows) of basswood.

Barbeau cites interesting material on the origin of the Wyandot Stone Giants from a previously published work by W.F Connelley.[30] According lo this source, the Stone Giants, or *Hooh-strah-dooh'*, were created by Tawiskaron, or Flint, to aid him in his battle for supremacy against his twin brother, Tarachiawagon, the culture hero. The stone coats of these giants were formed by smearing crude pine turpentine over their bodies and rolling around on dry beach sand. This process was repeated until the desired thickness was achieved. To offset this new menace, Tarachiawagon, with a fine instinct for structural complementarity, created a race of dwarfs, or Little People, who eventually succeeded in divesting the giants of their protective armor. The Stone Giants were so reduced in number that the few survivors fled to the woods where they live a solitary life, killing occasional travelers who stray into their domain.

The material on Stone Giants and related beings is quite rich amongst the Iroquois. However, the amount of material, along with its past and ongoing re interpretation, makes the information difficult to disentangle. Besides the familiar attributes of gigantic size, stone covering, and cannibalism, the Iroquois believed these monsters to possess a detached direction-finding finger, an acute sense of hearing, powerful spittle, an ability to walk under water, and a northern origin. In many myths blundering Stone Giants are outwitted by their human adversaries. According to the early account of David Cusick,[31] the Stone Giants were once ordinary humans who wandered into the wilderness, became addicted to raw fish, and wallowed in the sand until their bodies grew to gigantic proportions and their skin became so encrusted that they became immune to arrows. Arthur Parker collected a Seneca text that accords well with Cusick's.[32] The children of a boney northern race of raw-meat-eating giants rub their skin with dry sand until it becomes so calloused with scabs and sand that it takes on the consistency of stone. Other native Iroquois mythologists claimed that Stone Men were born that way.[33] These northern giants began to tire of their diet of animal flesh and raw fish, and they began to move south in search of human

---

29 Hewitt, *Tawiskaron*, p. 408.
30 Barbeau, *Huron and Wyandot Mythology*, pp. 314-15.
31 Cusick, *Sketches*, p. 637.
32 Parker, *Seneca Myths*, p. 394.
33 *Ibid.*

game. They succeeded in devouring many Indians by attacking at night and hiding out in caves during daylight. With their success the Stone Giants grew arrogant and [142] chided the creator god, Tarachiawagon, by claiming to be as great as he and to have created themselves. The terrorized Indians were helpless against the Stone Giants. They deserted their villages and prayed to Tarachiawagon, but the toll of human life continued to mount. At last, fearing that his creation, mankind, would be exterminated unless he intervened, Tarachiawagon sent an agent, sometimes identified as the West Wind, sometimes as Thunder, to destroy the Stone Giants. In one version of the myth the advancing army of Stone Giants is entrapped in a narrow defile and is crushed by boulders blown down upon them by the West Wind. In another version the Holder of Heaven causes such a mighty earthquake that the caves in which the Stone Giants are hiding collapse, and they are buried forever under the rubble.[34]

However, one of the Stone Giants, *Genonsgwa*, managed to survive the disaster and escaped to a cave in the Allegheny mountains. He continued his defiance of Tarachiawagon and the latter's allies, the Thunder spirits. In time, however, Genonsgwa became more human as his anger began to subside. Yet he was still powerful and merciless against those who trespassed against him.[35] A corner of his cave was filled with their bones.

One day a hunter was caught in a fearsome hailstorm and unknowingly sought refuge in *Genonsgwa*'s cave. The terrifying monster confronted the hunter, but decided to spare him, since he realized the hunter intended no harm. Genonsgwa identified himself as the last of his race – a powerful race that had witnessed the creation of the world long before the coming of human beings. He claimed that the spirits of his brothers continued to live in the trees of the forest and that they had much wisdom which they wished to impart to mankind: "how disease is healed"; "how man and beast and plant have the same great kind of life"; and "how man and beast and plant may talk together and learn each other's mission." He urged the hunter to dream, and he would see the faces of these dead kinsmen. He was instructed to carve their images in the living basswood trees. The hunter did as he was instructed and spent a score of years in the forest, carving masks and gaining knowledge. Finally, his apprenticeship was over, and Genonsgwa ordered the hunter to return to his people in order to establish the False Face Society.[36]

There are, of course, many other Iroquois myths in which other beings are defeated in power contests with Tarachiawagon and become the founders of the False Face Society. However, this version bears some striking similarities with the Cherokee myth of Stoneclad. Both Genonsgwa and Stoneclad are associated with stone and caves, and both reverse their roles from devourers to benefactors of mankind. In his book on Handsome Lake, Anthony Wallace has constructed a credible synthesis of different versions of the origin of the False Face Society.[37] The giant World Rim Dweller, sometimes associated with the Whirlwind, and a whole host of other spiritual beings who undo the creative acts of Tarachiawagon are interpreted by Wallace to be but symbols [143] or aspects of Tawiskaron, Flint, or the Devious One. It is Tawiskaron who creates bats, frogs, owls, worms, snakes, and monsters. When Tarachiawagon makes the rivers flow freely in opposite currents, Tawiskaron makes them flow in only one direction, and he also creates waterfalls, rapids, whirlpools, and underwater serpents. The good brother cultivates the corn bequeathed him by his dead mother, but his opposite twin introduces corn blight, hailstones, and ice. Tawiskaron, with help from his grandmother, manages to steal the sun for a brief time, before it is recaptured and returned to its present course. To Tawiskaron is attributed the invention of disease and death.

In the end, the power of Tawiskaron is neutralized by Tarachiawagon. However, to conceptualize Tawiskaron as simply an evil and entropic force is to miss his significance in Iroquois cosmology.

---

34 *ibid*, pp. 394-96.
35 *ibid*, pp. 396-97.
36 *ibid*, pp. 397-400.
37 Anthony FC Wallace, *The Death and Rebirth of Seneca* (New York: Alfred A Knopf 1970): 89-93.

Tawiskaron is a necessary complement in creating the world as we now know it. Without evil there can be no sense of good, life must be counterposed by death, happiness by sorrow, health by illness, light by darkness, summer by winter, and human beings by monstrous beings.

In contrast to the available Cherokee material, the Huron, Wyandot, and Iroquois mythic data reveal a close relationship between the Stone Giants and Tawiskaron. The Stone Giants appear as creations, transformations, or allies of Tawiskaron. This close relationship is documented even more convincingly by JNB Hewitt's etymological analysis of the word *Tawiskaron*. The nominal stem *-wiskar-* occurs in the terms for 'ice', 'hail', and 'sleet'. These latter derive from the noun *owis ă*, which has the meaning of 'ice', 'hail', 'sleet', 'frozen snow', 'glare ice', and, in modern usage, 'glass goblet'. Combining the nominal stem with the prefix and suffixes, Hewitt renders the literal meaning of Tawiskaron as 'He is arrayed in ice in a double degree'. This expression connotes an anthropomorphic figure covered with ice, or more metaphorically, the power of winter transformed into a man-being. Hewitt goes on to derive the original meaning of the nominal stem *-wiskar-* as 'crystal', 'smooth', 'slippery', and 'slick'. Thus the original stem came to designate ice, on the one hand, and flint or chert on the other.

These linguistic connections seem to unite ice, flint, crystal, and glass as objects of a single class. Presumably the qualities linking these objects together would include smoothness, hardness, translucence, and, perhaps, similar patterns of fracturability. However, stone and flint, as exterior body coverings, seem an insufficient criterion to establish an equivalence between the Cherokee Stoneclad, the Iroquoian Flint and Stone Giants, Tawiskaron (or Tawiskala), or the postulated prototype of the Winter man-being covered with ice. Flint and stone seem like surface features in more ways than one. Another dimension based on interior features of these beings would make the equivalence more convincing [144]

Once again JNB Hewitt comes to our rescue by presenting a variant mythic encounter between Tawiskaron and Tarachiawagon. Tawiskaron desires some of the corn that was entrusted to Tarachiawagon. Quoting Hewitt:

> On hearing this request Tarachiawagon replied that he would consent on the condition that Tawiskaron surrender to him "the flint whereby thou livest." To this Flint replied, "What doest thou mean? Dost thou mean my arrow with the point of flint?" To which the reply came, "No; I mean, indeed, that flint which is in thy body." To this Flint answered, "So be it as thou dost wish it." Then opening his mouth, he thrust out the flint thing in question. His brother seized it and gently pulled it; he would not break it off, although Flint asked him to do so. "Verily," his brother answered, "thy life belongs to thee, so thou thyself must break it off and give it to me, for on no other condition can our compact be fulfilled." So, reluctantly, Flint performed his part of the agreement whereupon his brother gave him two grains of the corn, one for the grandmother and one for himself. By this act Tawiskaron lost his birthright of co-equal orenda, or magic power.[38]

Hewitt goes on to liken the extruded inner flint to an icicle and suggests an analogy with the inner essence of the Winter God. For purposes of the present argument, this vital internal flint substance can be considered to be the structural equivalent of Stoneclad's quartz crystal heart.

The mythology of the Algonkian-speaking peoples of the Eastern Woodlands and Subarctic is exceedingly complex and displays a high degree of internal differentiation. Nonetheless, some salient continuities can be traced with mythic themes already outlined for the Iroquoian-speaking peoples.

In the northeastern Algonkian area we find beliefs about such related cannibalistic giants as the Montagnais *Atcen*, the Passamaquoddy and Penobscot *Ki wakwe*, and the Micmac *Chenoo* or *Djenu*.[39]

---

38 Hewitt, *Tawiskaron*, p. 709.
39 The four terms are found in, respectively: Frank G Speck, "Some Naskapi Myths from Little Whale River," *Journal of American Folklore* 28 (1915): 77; Speck, "Penobscot Tales and Religious Beliefs,"

These beings can be of cither sex and generally lack stone coverings, although the Penobscot giant is sometimes described as having a three-inch hard outer shell built up from layers of balsam pitch.[40] Rather than being considered as a separate primordial species, the existence of these monsters is usually explained in terms of human metamorphosis. This transformation is often symbolized by prolonged exposure to cold, which eventuates in a frozen heart or a piece of ice in the stomach; the effective cause of the transformation is frequently thought to be possession by an evil spirit or sorcerer and/or the eating of the heart or liver of one of these monsters. Such cannibal giants have an affinity [145] for the north, to which direction they repair in summer. The principal means of conquering these monsters is to have special shamanistic powers to enable one to become equally monstrous. Battles between "good" and "bad" monsters were fought to the death with uprooted tree trunks or magical stakes (often of sumac)[41] and resembled shamanistic medicine fights of the Western Subarctic and Siberia. When the monster was killed, the body had to be thoroughly cremated and the inner ice melted to forestall regeneration. The victorious monster could be restored to "normal" human form and feeling by swallowing hot grease or tallow to melt his icy innards. Also, several myths in the northeastern area indicate that these monsters can sometimes be temporarily domesticated by human kindness and become valuable allies.

This general type of monster seems closely related to the Iroquoian Stone Giants and can, of course, be readily identified with the more anthropologically celebrated Windigo or Weetigo of the Central Algonkian Chippewa, Ojibwa, and Cree. However, since Windigo among the latter peoples most often refers to abnormal changes of state, in either a pathological or non-pathological sense, the hypothesized connections between these varieties of monstrosity will be supported by further examination of Central Algonkian mythology and religious beliefs.

The twin deities of the Iroquois find analogues in Central Algonkian cosmogony. Among the Peoria and related groups the original brothers were said to be quadruplets. Two of the brothers either perish, are banished, or are amalgamated with the two remaining brothers. We are left with the culture hero cum trickster, *Nanabozho* – or *Glookap, Wisakedjah, Wenebojo*, or any one of the other names he bears in different groups, contexts, and transformations – and with *Chakekenapok* (in some versions the younger, in others the older, brother) who is identified with stone, white flint, or ice.[42] In the Lac Du Flambeau Chippewa version of the Wenebojo origin myth, as recited by Tom Badger and collected by Victor Barnouw,[43] Wenebojo is the eldest of triplets, the second brother becomes the spiritual guide to the land of the dead, and the third brother, Stone (*Maskdsaswabik*), instructs Wenebojo as to how to kill him: he is heated under an intense fire and doused with water. Barnouw here speculates that this form of fratricide may have some connection to the traditional sweat bath, but I think it may be related to the implicit association of stone with ice. Other variants of this myth from the Court Oreilles Chippewa bring out additional familiar elements. In one, *Wenebojo's* protagonist is clearly identified as Flint.[44] In

---

Journal of American Folklore 48 (1935): 13-14; 81-82 Charles C Leland, *The Algonquian Legends of New England* (Boston: Houghton, Mifflin, 1884), pp. 233-54; and Wilson D Wallis and Ruth S Wallis, *The Micmac Indians of Eastern Canada* (Minneapolis: University of Minnesota Press, 1953), pp. 343-45.

40 Speck, Penobscot Tales, p. 81.

41 Robert L Hall, cited in Victor Barnouw, *Wisconsin Chippewa Myths and Tales and Their Relation to Chippewa Life* (Madison; University of Wisconsin Press 1977), pp. 122-33, suggests a symbolic association of fire with sumac, in that the germination of sumac is [151] aided by fire, a fact that may or may not have been recognized by the Indians. Thus sumac as a symbol of fire and heat might serve as a natural opposition to the ice associated with the cannibal giants.

42 See JNB Hewitt, "Nanabozho," *in* Handbook of American Indians North of Mexico, pt 2, ed. F.W. Hodge (Washington, DC: Government Printing Office 1910), pp. 19-23.

43 Barnouw, *Wisconsin Chippewa Myths*, pp. 13-45.

44 *ibid*, p. 74.

another variant the opposing brother lives on an island of solid rock surrounded by pitch, which can only be neutralized by whale oil, and chops shells from his shins; he proves impervious to Wenebojo's arrows, until a chickadee indicates a braid of hair where the brother is mortally vulnerable.[45]

The Algonkian Nanabozho or Wenebojo clearly relates to the Iroquois [146] culture hero, Tarachiawagon, although there are some interesting differences between the two. Tarachiawagon is beneficent, generative, and moral; in some sense his humanity edges toward such perfection that he becomes non-human, almost a "goody two-shoes." Nanabozho is more the amoral trickster, childish and impulsive, destructive as well as creative; he eventually assumes the form of the Great Hare. The previously discussed Cherokee folktale about Flint and the Rabbit probably has direct Algonkian ancestry, perhaps coming into the Southeast through the agency of the Shawnees-

The Algonkian Chakekenapok, 'Man of Flint' or Fire Stone', occupies a parallel position with Tawiskaron in Iroquois mythology, even down to the detail of matricide through unnatural birth. Again, however, differences can be noted. The Algonkian figure tends to be less destructive and more passive than his Iroquoian counterpart. When defeated by his brother, he assumes no particular role towards mankind. Nevertheless, the identification of the two figures is secure. In some Algonkian languages, such as Chippewa, the words for flint and ice are cognate. Finally, one of the cognomens of Chakekenapok is Windigo.[46]

Thus it seems as if the human condition or transformation labeled Windigo is deeply embedded in a widely ramifying folkloristic and mythic substratum. Whether the similarities between Iroquoian and Algonkian monsters are the results of recent diffusion or descent from a common prototypical ancestor, such as the personification of Winter, cannot be satisfactorily resolved on the basis of the available material. Indeed, such questions seem anachronistic in contemporary anthropology. However, I think the material presented here does make it possible to establish kinship between the southeastern Stoneclad, with his heart of quartz crystal, and the northern Windigo, with his heart of ice.

In conclusion, I will attempt to draw out some of the wider implications of the material discussed in this paper. At first glance the material presented would seem to lend itself to a structural analysis. Certainly the data abound in oppositions, mediations, and transformations. One could envision an interlocking nest of mediated paradigmatic oppositions in order to analyze structural relations obtaining between, for example, ordinary blood and menstrual blood, between blood and pitch, between pitch and stone, between stone and fire, between fire and ice, between ice and crystal, between crystal and blood, between blood and stone, and so forth, in ever-oscillating spirals. What is the significance of basswood, sumac, grease, and chickadees? Do the connecting myth cycles symbolize the alternation of summer and winter, or life and death? Can the gross constituent elements in the plot structures of the myths be broken down and rearranged to reveal hidden messages? Such an effort seems premature without firmer ethnographic control and historical anchoring. Like the exploded body of Tawiskala, the material seems too [147] fragmented to reconstruct in any convincing fashion. Moreover, the results of such formal analysis might prove to be rather mechanical and probably would obscure what I take to be some of the evident meanings inherent in Stoneclad and related monsters. Rather than mine deep structural depths for buried riches, I prefer to pan for surface gold.

A useful beginning might be to rethink what we mean by the term monster. Monsters can be thought about from both semantic and pragmatic perspectives.

By semantics I mean those attributes that define what a monster is. Social scientists have of late

---

45 *ibid*, pp. 73-74.
46 See Hewitt, *Tawiskaron*, p. 709. Further earlier material lending to confirm the relation of Windigo (Vitico) to a primal being standing in opposition to or apposition to a benevolent deity can be found in the accounts of eighteenth-century traders, Drage, Ellis, and Umfreville, cited by Father John M Cooper, "The Northern Algonkian Supreme Being," *Primitive Man* 7, 3-4 (1933): 52, 56, 90-93.

rediscovered what perceptive humanistic scholars have long recognized – that monsters represent ambiguous or confabulated beings. The German art historian Heinz Mode has offered a nearly exhaustive typology for classifying monsters: "Animal-men" – essentially human forms with certain animal features or animal forms with human posture (such as angels, satyrs, or Lewis Caroll's March Hare); "Man-animals" – essentially animal forms with certain human features or an unmistakable animal posture (such as the sphinx, centaur); "Animal-monsters" – composite animal beings incorporating features from different animals (such as dragons, *Uktenas*, Pegasus); "Reduplicated or simplified shapes and combinations" (such as double-headed figures, cyclops) – also included here are expanded or reduced figures, such as dwarfs and giants; and man-made objects and natural phenomena in the shape of living beings (such as personified automobiles, Flint, the Winter Spirit).[47] As elegant as this schema appears, it doesn't easily accommodate many of the North American monsters considered here. Even Sasquatch experts would debate whether that being should be classified as a man-animal or animal-man.

The distinguishing physical aspects of the monsters discussed here are their enlarged size, frequent association with inanimate minerals (stone, crystal, flint), and displaced or transferred internal organs (moveable heart or heart of ice).

Other semantic dimensions that could be used to classify monsters might include moral and characterological attributes and origins. The monsters treated in this paper display exceptional power, lack of moral restraint, gluttony, egoism, and frequent stupidity. They originate either from a primordial being or group, or they can acquire their distinctive attributes through deliberate action or metamorphosis.

In attempting to define monsters pragmatically we focus on what they do, as manifested in behavior. All the monsters discussed here are anthropophagous and prey on human communities. They are also at odds with spiritual beings supportive of mankind. Monsters behave anti-culturally in trying to upset or invert the good works of the primary creative deities and culture heroes. They embody the realm of nature rather than culture. [148]

All these semantic and pragmatic features that contribute to defining particular types of monsters must be viewed contrastively. On a more general level, it should be pointed out that monsters cannot exist classificatorily, except in opposition to others. Thus a universal function of monsters is to define what is human through contrast and opposition. This marking function shows up clearly in the types of monsters reviewed in this paper. They serve to mark off different "races," different eras, different creations, and different propensities.

However, the body of myths presented here transcends the simple boundary problem of separating man from monster. Once certain differences have been established, they are subsequently dissolved. Differences between the human race and the monster race become blurred; different eras are united through transmission of significant information; separate creations are shown to be continuous; monstrous propensities become more humanized. Monsters must have victims, but in this process of blurring and dissolution there is a role reversal and the victim vanquishes the victimizer. With Stoneclad, the devourer of men is finally consumed by man's culture, which the former monster then enriches by bequeathing medicine songs and his crystal heart. Genonsgwa becomes humanized and leaves as a legacy the mysteries of the False Face Society. Chippewa shamans must themselves attain the powers of the Windigo to overcome this dreaded adversary.

Perhaps something of this same general pattern can be discerned for Sasquatch. According to Wayne Suttles' presentation at this symposium, the native image of Sasquatch has undergone dramatic change over the years. In the native bestiary he was perceived as a fearsome monster who stole women and devoured children. Doubtless as a result of the white man's interest in Sasquatch as a possible hominid ancestor or cousin, plus the economic value of Sasquatch as a commercial totem, the frightful beast is now seen as benign, gentle, and timid. In brief, Sasquatch has become demonsterized: the hunter has become the hunted, and Sasquatch's skin has become a veritable Golden Fleece.

---

47 Heinz Mode, *Fabulous Beasts and Demons* (London: Phaidon Press 1975).

Finally, I think these related myths and monstrous beings concern universal human problems. They involve rationalizing the inevitable existence of evil in this world, particularly in the form of fear, suffering, disease, and death. These myths constitute a Native American theodicy adapted to a finite and transitory world. The Stone Giants are Titans living in the margins of an Olympian universe; Stoneclad singing the medicine songs from his funeral pyre is a Prometheus ever hopeful of easing man's misery and making mankind more human; and the ancient creators and diminishing number of narrators of these myths are still trying to establish contact and communicate their wisdom.

Aní-Kutânî

WHO WERE THE ANÍ-KUTÁNÎ?
AN EXCURSION INTO CHEROKEE HISTORICAL THOUGHT

Abstract

Evidence assembled and examined in this article reviews a prehistoric revolt by the Cherokees against a priestly class or hereditary clan, the *Aní-Kutânî*, whose members, according to legend, were massacred in a public uprising in response to their corruption and sexual improprieties. Some evidence relates the *Aní-Kutânî* to the historic Cherokee clan, the *Aní- gilohí*; and some, to the historic Cherokee Fire priests. The author interprets the legend as a dramatic epitomization of Cherokee cultural processes by which tendencies towards hierarchy conflicted with tendencies towards egalitarianism.

> The relation between tradition and history has been the subject of endless controversy .... Fred Eggan, From History to Myth

The course of Southeastern prehistory and protohistory does not reflect an orthogenic development from simple social structures to complex structures. Rather, the pattern appears to be more cyclic: a build-up of energy, a concentration of wealth, more differentiated social stratification, and increased population nucleation, followed by a seemingly entropic decline, a movement toward egalitarianism, population dispersal, and abandonment of ceremonial centers. Many explanations on many different levels have been advanced to account for this cyclicity: for instance, various ecological factors and constraints on the carrying capacity of the land; changes in modes of production, distribution, and consumption; the influence of disease; the effects of migration and warfare; Kroeberian "cultural fatigue"; the rapid diffusion of religious movements; and periodic endogenous overthrow of civil-religious authority.

The last form of internal conversion or transformation – a revolt against authority – possesses great romantic appeal. Such prehistoric or protohistoric revolts are difficult to document however, especially since one person's revolution becomes another person's evolution, involution, or devolution. Nevertheless, the Cherokees possessed a persistent and fairly widespread historical legend about a priestly class or hereditary clan whose members were massacred in a public uprising in response to their corruption and sexual impropriety.

The priesthood was called the *Aní-Kutânî*. The prefix *Aní* indicates a group of individuals; the etymology of the root term *Kutânî* or *Kwatáni* is unknown. According to James Mooney (1900: 342), knowledge of the *Kutânî* was rapidly perishing when he did his Cherokee fieldwork in the late 19th century. He reports two native theories as to the origins of the *Kutânî*. One theory held that they were vestiges of a previous population of mound builders who inhabited the territory prior to Cherokee incursion into their historic homeland. This theory is consonant with the widely shared belief that indigenous peoples retain a special mystical connection with the land and its autochthonous spirits; it also helps reconcile the perception that religious language in the [256] Southeast frequently has a sacerdotal quality sometimes attributable to alien speech. Weighing against this theory, however, is the difficulty in relating Cherokee ancestors to mound building peoples,[1] as well as the unlikelihood that a minority or a conquered people would assume religious dominance.

The second theory claims that the *Aní-Kutânî* "were a clan or society in the tribe and were destroyed long ago by pestilence or other calamity" (Mooney 1900: 392). This argument is slightly more plausible, since several accounts stress that the *Ani-Kutani* were a hereditary group. Also, as is well

---

1 For a general historical review of controversies relating Cherokees to Mound Builders see Robert Silverberg (1968); more up-to-date information on Cherokee prehistory can be found in Dickens (1976) and Keel (1976).

known, special medicine societies with religious functions are a well-developed feature in many Iroquoian cultures.

Mooney cites Judge John Haywood's 1823 book, *The Natural and Aboriginal History of Tennessee*, as a primary source for the former existence of the *Aní-Kutánî*. Haywood writes,

> Tradition states that such persons lived among their ancestors and were deemed superior to others, and were extirpated long ago, in consequence of the misconduct of one of the priests, who attempted to take the wife of a man who was the brother of the leading chief of the nation (1959: 249).

Haywood's statement about the destruction of the priesthood is sandwiched between ethnographic information supplied by Charles R. Hicks, an important mixed-blooded Cherokee and Moravian convert, who was elected Principal Chief in 1827. Haywood's word choice, as well as the content, bear a close relation to a nearly contemporaneous account written by Hicks. There thus seems little doubt about the source of Haywood's information.

Mooney (1900: 393) also quotes a fuller report of the prior existence of a priesthood among the Cherokees. This account comes from an article published by Dr D J MacGowan based on a paper, "Indian Secret Societies," which he presented to the American Ethnological Society in March, 1866. MacGowan obtained his information from Chief John Ross, then resident in Philadelphia, and from Dr J B Evans, who had experience among the Cherokees and left a valuable manuscript, "Sketch of the Cherokees," now included in the Payne-Buttrick papers at the Newberry Library.[2] I reproduce the relevant passages from MacGowan's article:

The order was hereditary; in this respect peculiar, for among Indians seldom, and among the Cherokees never, does power pertain to any family as a matter of right. Yet the family of the *Nicotani* – for it seems to have been a family or clan – enjoyed this privilege. The power that they exercised was not, however, political, nor does it appear that chiefs were elected from among them.

The Nicotani were a mystical religious body, of whom the people stood in great awe, and seem to have been somewhat like the Brahmins of India. By what means they attained their ascendancy, or how long it was maintained, can never be ascertained. Their extinction by massacre is nearly all that can be discovered concerning them. They became haughty, insolent, over-bearing and licentious to an intolerable degree. Relying on their hereditary privileges and the strange awe which they inspired, they did not hesitate by fraud or violence to rend asunder the tender relations of husband and wife when a beautiful woman excited their passions. The people long brooded in silence over the oppressions and outrages of this high caste, whom they deeply hated, but greatly feared. At length a daring young man, a member of an influential family, organized a conspiracy among the people for the massacre of the priesthood. The immediate provocation was the abduction of the wife of the young leader of the conspiracy. His wife was remarkable for her beauty, and was forcibly abducted and violated by one of the *Nicolani* while he was absent [257] on the chase. On his return he found no difficulty in exciting in others the resentment which he himself experienced. So many had suffered in the same way – so many feared that they might be made to suffer – that nothing was wanted but a leader. A leader appearing in the person of the young brave whom we have named, the people rose under his direction and killed every Nicotani, young and old. Thus perished a hereditary secret society, since which time no hereditary privileges have been tolerated among the Cherokees (MacGowan 1866: 139-40).

Two additional accounts, unknown to Mooney, provide additional dimensions to the mystery of the *Aní-Kutánî*. Major John Norton, an adopted Mohawk who claimed Cherokee descent, visited the Cherokee country in 1809. He was warmly received and left a valuable journal Filled with important

---

2 Evans's manuscript has been published as "Sketches of Cherokee Characteristics" in *Journal of Cherokee Studies* 4 (1979). [262]

ethnographic and ethnological material (cf. Fogelson 1978). A day after attending a ball game near Chicamauga, Norton observed to his forty-year old Cherokee traveling companion that the Cherokees didn't seem to display the same degree of seriousness as did the Iroquois in their ceremonial speeches at the Green Corn Dance. His companion replied:

> It now appears only a matter of mutual congratulation and rejoicing that the crops have so far ripened, as to become fit for food; but it is also certain that it has originated from a religious institution. I remember when I was a boy, that a venerable person presided at these feasts, who preached in a kind of poetic strain, and in a dialect of which only a few words were intelligible to the younger part of the people:
>
> All that ever I could clearly comprehend was a few words in which they expressed; – "We are emigrating into a strange country, and now move our encampments." In the completion of the ceremony, the fires were all extinguished, and lighted again after the ancient method of kindling fire by rubbing two pieces of wood together (Klinck and Talman 1970: 79-80).

Norton provides further commentary of his own:

> This system of religion appears to have been introduced at a very distant period. At a time when the people were assembled in the Council House, a man having entered there and extinguished the fire; began to sing; repeating these words; "I have been to the Country above, and have now returned from thence; with the commands of the Great Spirit whose abode is there." He then appointed several ceremonies, dances and purifications to be observed, to obtain His favour, or avert His anger. This person was joined by many others in his office; their numbers greatly increased; their persons became sacred in the opinion of the people. They called themselves Anikanos.
>
> But whatever might have been their doctrine, it does not appear to have been strict morality; or if it were, they must have exempted themselves from the observance of the doctrine which they taught. They indulged their evil passions, without the least regard to the rights of others, or the restraints of modesty and decorum: and the superstition and reverence in which they were held, exacted the strictest compliance to their will. They however carried their wickedness to such a height that the indignation of the people was roused, and hatred and detestation of their vices succeeding to the superstitious reverence they had formerly claimed, they were finally all put to death where ever they were found (Klinck and Talman 1970: 80).

Norton's account contains several interesting details. Cherokee priests at Green Corn ceremonies spoke in an unintelligible language that seemed, in part, to recapitulate the tribal migration legend. Extinguishing the sacred fire was an audacious act that could be punished by death. Putting out the fire symbolized death and was reserved for critical junctures in world renewal ceremonies, such as the annual Green Corn Ceremony, during which the world was plunged into the temporary chaos of darkness, a condition that was [258] terminated by reviving the fire. The prophet, inspired by his visit to the Other World, introduced a new doctrine and new ritual practices. The movement attracted adherents and gained spiritual ascendancy. What we seem to perceive, however faintly, is recollection of an ancient religious revitalization movement preserved in memory through legend (cf. Wallace 1958). The continuing moral outrages perpetrated by its priesthood, however, brought upon a popular revolt and the priests were slain, but the religious forms, if not the absolute authority of a priestly hierarchy, persisted.

The final primary data on the Ani-Kutani to be presented here come from the second of a series of five letters written by the aforementioned Charles R. Hicks to John Ross, then President of the National

Aní-Kutánî

Committee. The letter, dated March 1, 1826, is contained in Volume 7 of the Payne-Buttrick Papers. Hicks notes that traditionally the Cherokees recognized three distinct orders of men: "*First*: The Head man of a town. *Second*, the *Auh, ne coo tauh, nies* (which name I have been informed means the Proud); – and [Third] the Common people – ..,"

Hicks goes on to describe the priesthood in more detail:

These Auh ne coo tauh me, or Proud. – profess themselves, as is stated by tradition to be teachers of Heavenly knowledge from the Creation; and the manner of their introduction to the assembled people is represented to have been usually at night times and when he approached near them the light of their fires were extinguished. as it was well known to them when he came near, by frequently repeating the words *Cul, lungh, lut, tee Tauh, che, lo, eh.* (I am come from above); and after been (being) seated on (a seat) which had previously been prepared for him or them, then their fires were rekindled again; but there is no account given in what kind of a discourse was given to the people at such meetings; and that this order of men had exercised their offices to an extent that it became disagreeable and oppressive to the people: for that their demands were to be complied with. be their nature what they may; who were dreaded (beings) been considered to be bearer[s of] the heavenly message; that at last their power was [annihilated] *enhalienenated* by the nation; altho' traditions differs in their statement: as some others state that they were extirpated, perhaps both statement is true in part, as it is related that [a] very respectable headman had went to hunt a few days; and a younger brother, and his wife, who is said to be very handsome, had accompanied him, and met with two of the *auh, ne coo, tauh, nies*, who had demanded the surrender of this young woman; upon which her husband hesitated, and would not give a direct reply to the demand of his wife; and that demand was repeated; but the young man continued silent; at which this Elder brother enquired if he loved his wife, – who then had replied in the affirmative: upon which the elder brother & himself had drawn their bows and arrows & killed them both: and by this circumstance the power of the *Auh ne coo tauh nies* had been ever after annihilated(?) through the nation...,

Hicks continues by pointing to similarities between traditional Cherokee religious practice and that of the ancient Hebrews, suggesting that the ancestors of the Cherokees and the children of Israel may have once been neighbors. He also believes it likely that after the priesthood was stripped of its offices, "they might have shifted their profession to that of the Jugglers and Doctors, for it is found in our days that the Jugglers and Doctors possess more knowledge of the Traditions of this nation than any others among the present race."

With Hicks's provocative account, we come full circle. As mentioned before, Hicks seems to have been the source of Haywood's statements about the priesthood, and Hicks also passed his knowledge on directly to John Ross, the [259] addressee of the letter, who in turn supplied material for MacGowan's article on "Indian Secret Societies."

Hicks's rendering of the meaning of the term *Aní-Kutánî* as "The Proud" appears to relate the discredited priesthood to a specific Cherokee clan, the *Aní-gilohí*. The *Aní-gilohí* and *Aní-Kutánî* are surely not cognate terms, but they share some similar connotations. *Aní-gilohí* is usually translated as the Long Hair, Loose Hair, Twister, or Pretty Face clan. The idea of long or loose flowing hair is usually associated with women (Mooney 1900: 508). According to William H Gilbert:

The Anigilohi clan are supposed to have derived their name in two ways. One way would be through [he word gagiloha "one who twists" changed to ugiloha, "one born twisted," and Anigilohi, "those who are born twisted": referring to the fact that they used to be a *proud* [my emphasis] people who strutted when they walked and twisted their shoulders in a very haughty manner. According to another version the name is derived from *ugilohi*, "long hair," referring to the love of adornment and display of their elaborate coiffures which was once characteristic of this people (1943: 204).

The late Lloyd Sequoyah, who was himself a member of the Ani-*ugilohi* clan, plausibly explained (personal communication) that the meaning of 'twister' referred to the braiding of long hair.

At any rate, this overlap of meaning, plus the mention of several accounts that membership in the *Aní-Kutânî* was hereditary, strongly suggest that the priesthood was a clan function, or perhaps more precisely a property of a particular lineage or family within the *Ani-gilohi* clan. Such a conclusion is supported by information attributed to Johnson Pridget and Isaac Short Arrow, which is found in a letter from Daniel S. Butrick to John Howard Payne, dated December 15, 1835:

> The ancient government of the Cherokees was a Theocracy. It is said that God at first, or at the commencement of their government, appointed a certain man to be at the head of their civil and religious affairs, instructed him in all things relative to his duty, and declared that the office should be hereditary in his family.
>
> The Chief priest, or supreme ruler, had seven Counsellors, who were also priests. The first of these was his right hand man and next to him in authority. He had also a messenger always at his call.

Buttrick goes on to mention lower order priests and counsellors in the local towns. It is also asserted that a priest's wife must be a virgin of unblemished character who could temporarily replace her husband when he died.

Another feature found in the Hicks account that deserves attention is the strong association of the *Aní-Kutânî* with night, darkness, and fire. Night of course, is associated with magic and danger, with darkness and the moon, and with death and chaos, whereas daytime is related to religious propitiation, to light and the sun, and to life-giving functions and structural order. Fire was considered an earthly equivalent of the sun and was worshipped as a potent deity (cf. Swanton 1928).

David Corkran, interpolating from Hicks's letter, assumes that the *Aní-Kutânî*, or the Proud, are identical to the Fire priests (1955: 37). The Cherokees, indeed, did recognize a special group of fire keepers who were responsible for protecting, feeding, and offering sacrifices to the perpetual fire that was kept smoldering in the central fire-pit in the semi-subterranean council house. [261]

According to C C Trowbridge, in a manuscript probably dating back to the 1820s, the fire was guarded by seven men. They enjoyed lifetime tenure and were supported by the nation. They were expected to live in the council house and were prohibited from marrying. Since none of the accounts specifically mention female members of the *Aní-Kutânî*, perhaps this was an exclusive brotherhood. A further supposition might consider the injunction against marriage as inversely related to the sexual offenses attributed to the *Aní-Kutânî*. Cherokee cultural logic would probably dictate that the seven fire keepers be recruited from the seven different clans in harmony with the fact that logs of seven different species of tree were used in the sacred fire. Also Mooney (1889: 170) retrieved some secondary recollections from his major informant, Swimmer, to the effect that the remains of seven prominent men from the seven clans were supposedly buried around the fire that would serve as the central axis of the council house. Quite possibly the men presumed to be buried in such fashion were deceased fire keepers. Unfortunately, no known excavations of Cherokee council houses have revealed such a burial configuration.

But enough idle speculation. Barring the chance discovery of new manuscript material, accidental archeological confirmation of aspects of the legend, or a linguistic breakthrough in translating some of the key terms, all the known materials pertaining to the *Aní-Kutânî* have been assembled here. The rhetorical problem of Who were the *Aní-Kutânî*? has not be resolved. Who, one might ask, besides dilettantes in Cherokee studies would even concern themselves with such a seemingly trivial non-problem?

Yet there are some larger issues involved in the legend of the *Aní-Kutânî*. For one, the conflicting tension between tendencies toward hierarchy and movements toward egalitarianism is clearly reflected in the arrogant social distancing and subsequent massacre of the offending priests. It is unimportant whether the events recounted in the legend actually occurred; what does seem important, however, is that the narrative neatly captures, summarizes, and symbolizes significant processes of culture change.

In the heuristically restricted domain of religion, Cherokee beliefs and practices underwent drastic change during the course of the 18th century. Indeed by all accounts Cherokee religious life was regulated by an elaborated priesthood during the early part of the century. By the end of the century this highly organized religious system was greatly diminished and mostly a memory. Instead of an organized priesthood, the end of the 18th century witnessed the fragmentation of traditional Cherokee religion and its partial underground survival in the form of widely dispersed and fiercely independent conjurors or medicine men (Fogelson 1961). This transformation, though doubtless gradual in processual terms, could be effectively comprehended by dramatizing the process, by encapsulating it in specific, epitomizing events, such as the massacre of the *Aní-Kutânî*.

The Cherokees seem to have generated a whole series of indexical events to refer to the decline of their traditional religious system. During the smallpox epidemic of 1738 James Adair reports "all the magic and prophetic tribe [diviners] broke their old consecrated physic-pots and threw away all the other pretended holy things they had for physical use, imagining they had lost their divine power by being polluted..." (1930: 245). Again, this is a fine, [261] condensed, dramatic image, but the use of medicine bundles persisted in some quarters well into the 19th century, and memory of their use had not completely disappeared among Eastern Cherokee during my fieldwork in the late 1950s and early 1960s. Herbal decoctions remain the mainstay of traditional Cherokee medical care in both Oklahoma and North Carolina.

Similarly, many Cherokees feel that the decline of their native religion was signaled when the sacred fire was extinguished in some of the holy mother towns and in areas ceded to whites before Removal. Yet many Cherokee traditionalists persist in the belief that the perpetual fire still smolders in mound sites as yet spared the spade of the archeologists, or unextinguished by waters stemmed by TVA dams. Others hold to the faith that sacred fire was carried west during the Removal and continues to burn uninterruptedly at Oklahoma Cherokee stomp dance grounds.³3

Stilt other Cherokees attribute the demise of traditional Cherokee religion to the capture of a portable ark, or "religious deposit," which contained sacred tribal paraphernalia, and possibly sacred fire, by a Delaware raiding party in the mid-18th century (Washburn 1869: 191-92).

These accounts all appear to be efforts to encompass and make intelligible seemingly impersonal, inevitable, and insidious processes of change through the invocation of a real or fanciful, dramatic, epitomizing event. It is also important to emphasize that these epitomizing events involve human motivation and causation: Cherokees voluntarily accepted and then rejected the power of the *Aní-Kutânî*; they felt personally responsible for the smallpox plague by immorally fornicating in the fields; the extinguishing of the sacred fire was caused by the corruption of their political leaders in ceding their ancestral homelands to whites; and surely the sacred ark deserved greater protection from Delaware marauders. The Cherokees, in common with most peoples of the world, do not view history in terms of abstract, disembodied, invisible, immutable laws and forces. History is generated by human action and, since the Cherokees believe that they are not only distinctive people, but the only "real people" in the world, their past and their destiny is self-determined.

The question, Who were the *Aní-Kutânî*? thus becomes an important clue to understanding the workings of Cherokee historical thought and world view.

---

3 About thirty years ago a delegation of Eastern Cherokees representing the Cherokee Historical Association traveled to Oklahoma to secure sacred fire. They returned with a flame burning perpetually, via a gas jet, at the outdoor theater where "Unto These Hills" is performed in summer.

Acknowledgements

I dedicate this paper to my friend and colleague, Helen H Tanner, in recognition of her election to the presidency of the American Society for Ethnohistory. A version of this paper was read at the 1982 Convention of the Society in Nashville, Tennessee. I'd like to thank Charles Hudson, who chaired the session, and Robert Brightman, George Stocking, and the anonymous referees for helpful commentary.

References

Adair, James 1930 *Adair's History of the American Indian.* Samuel Cole Williams, ed. Johnson City. Tennessee: Watauga (original, 1775).

Buttrick, Daniel S. 1835 Letter to John Howard Payne, December 15, 1835. Ayer Collection. Newberry Library, Chicago.

Corkran, David H. 1955 Cherokee Sun and Fire Observances. *Southern Indian Studies* 7:33-38.

Dickens, Roy S, Jr. 1976 *Cherokee Prehistory; The Pisgah Phase in the Appalachian Summit Region.* Knoxville: Univ. of Tennessee Press.

Eggan, Fred 1967 From History to Myth: A Hopi Example. In *Studies in Southwestern Ethnolinguistics.* Dell Hymes and William F Bittle, eds., 33-53- The Hague: Mouton.

Evans, JP 1979 Sketches of Cherokee Characteristics. *Journal of Cherokee Studies* 4(1): 5-12 <1836>.

Fogelson, Raymond D 1961 Change, Persistence, and Accommodation in Cherokee Medico-Magical Beliefs. In *Symposium on Cherokee and Iroquois Culture.* William N Fenton and John Gulick, eds. Bureau of American Ethnology Bulletin 180: 213-25. Washington, D.C: GPO.

   1978 Major John Norton as Ethno-Ethnologist. *Journal of Cherokee Studies* 3 (4): 250-55.

Gilbert, William H 1943 *The Eastern Cherokees.* Bureau of American Ethnology Bulletin 133, Paper 23. Washington, D.C.: GPO.

Haywood, John 1959 *Natural and Aboriginal History of Tennessee.* Mary U Rothrock, ed. Jackson, Tenn: McCowat-Mercer (original. 1823).

Hicks, Charles R 1826 Letter to John Ross, March 1, 1826. Ayer Collection, Newberry Library, Chicago.

Keel, Bonnie C 1976 *Cherokee Archaeology: A Study of the Appalachian Summit.* Knoxville: Univ. of Tennessee Press.

Klinck, Carl F., and James J. Talman, eds. 1970 *The Journal of Major John Norton, 1816.* Publications of the Champlain Society 46. Toronto: The Champlain Society.

MacGowan, D J 1866 Indian Secret Societies. *The Historical Magazine* 10 (5): 139-41.

Mooney, James 1900 *Myths of the Cherok*ees. Bureau of American Ethnology, 19th Annual Report, 1897-98, Part 1. Washington D.C-: GPO.

   1889 Cherokee Mound Building. *American Anthr*opologist, os 2: 167-71.

Silverberg, Robert 1968 *Mound Builders of Ancient America ~ The Archaeology of a Myth.* Greenwich, Conn: New York Graphic Society.

Swanton, John R 1928 Sun Worship in the Southeast. *American Anthropologist* 30: 206-13. [263]

Trowbridge CC [ca. 1825] Unpublished manuscript. Shea Collection, Georgetown University Library.

Wallace, AFC 1958 The Dekanawideh Myth Analyzed as the Record of a Revitalization Movement. *Ethnohistory* 5 (2): 118-30.

Washburn, Cephas 1869 *Reminiscences of the Indians.* Richmond, Va.: Presbyterian Committee of Publication.

THE ETHNOHISTORY OF EVENTS AND NONEVENTS

My original title was perverse. However, I have never regarded myself as one to flee in the face of perversity. I chronically suffer from a pathological form of premature entitlement. When asked or required to present a paper, I usually invent a clever title and then expend much worrisome effort trying to justify it. My original title, "The Ethnohistory of Nonevents," was too clever by half-thus the revised title. Andre Gidé remarked in one of his remarkable aphorisms from his 1899 La Prométhée mal enchainé (translated as Prometheus Misbound, 1953) that a man writes a book not so much because he has an idea to express but to excuse himself for having had it. So with this paper.

I also feel compelled to confess that my original choice of title was a defensive maneuver. I figured that if I failed to generate a suitable text to back up my title, I might emulate composer John Cage, whose most famous work was entitled "Silence," first performed in 1961. By following Cage's lead, I could transform this occasion into a true nonevent. But herein lies the burden of this paper: What is an event? and conversely, What is a nonevent?

Events are crucial elements in the foundations of modern physics. In simplest terms, an event can be defined as that which occurs at a given time and place, ignoring for now the uncertainties of Heisenberg. Events are also considered to have properties and relationships. With the advent of relativity physics, the concept of events assumed primary significance. For Bertrand Russell events replaced vaguer notions of body and substance, while Alfred North Whitehead saw events as formed by the nexus of actual occasions. Implicit in these conceptions is the idea that events involve processes, changes, happenings, acts, transformations, and other features that are essentially different from physical objects or concrete things. More speculative, perhaps, is the view that objects may only be congeries of associated events, with the consequence that events would be the only object in our ontology.

Philosophic debate over the theoretical possibility of admitting the existence of null events is also relevant to our present concerns. Do null events possess no properties, physical or otherwise? Do they lack physical properties but contain certain properties required in the calculus of events? Or, on a positive note, can null events be assigned definite physical magnitudes? As R M Martin (1978: 95) inquires, "If one objects to so ghostly an entity, it may be asked why admitting such [a null event] should be any worse than admitting a null class or set or relation."

Events, of course, have traditionally been considered as the primary elements in the study of history. As minimal units in historical discourse, events must be described, analyzed, ordered, and interpreted. Herbert Butterfield (1981) and others have demonstrated that the recording of events is even fundamental to the history of history. Often a distinction is made between natural and historical events. Both may be subsumed as involving chance-a unique encounter or an accident. Natural events may impinge upon, or determine, historical events, but historical events must be considered preeminently as cultural facts. The French social philosopher Raymond Aron cogently argues that "man has a history because he comes to be across time, because he builds works that survive him, because he erects monuments of the past" (quoted in Ricoeur 1980: 3). Recovery, reconstruction, and revivification of the past requires particular forms of consciousness.

The particular form of historical consciousness in the West normally entails written documents, and such entailment poses special epistemological dilemmas for ethnohistorians. How do we account for the histories of so-called "peoples without history," those who lack accustomed libraries and archives of documents? Do we simply dismiss them as cultures lacking historical consciousness? In my unhumbling estimation, all peoples possess a sense of the past, however strange and exceptional that past may seem from our own literately conditioned perspectives. An understanding of non-Western histories requires not only the generation of documents and an expanded conception of what constitutes documentation but also a determined effort to try to comprehend alien forms of historical consciousness and discourse. It was in this spirit that I once, in exasperation, suggested the necessity for what I termed an ethno-ethnohistorical approach (Fogelson 1974). Such an approach insists on taking seriously native theories of history as embedded in cosmology, in narratives, in rituals and ceremonies, and more generally in native philosophies and worldviews. Implicit here is the assumption that events may be recognized, defined, evaluated, and endowed with meaning differentially in different cultural traditions.

The centrality of events to historiography was severely challenged by French scholars associated with *l'Ecole des annales*. This ongoing revolution in historical thinking was initiated in 1929 by Lucien Febvre and Marc Bloch in opposition to so-called positivist history.[1] Positivist history should not be confused with logical positivism nor with the nineteenth-century positivistic philosophy of August Comte; Comte actually anticipates many of the tenets of the Annales school. Teggart (1941: 108) succinctly summarizes Comte's position:

> History, in order to be scientific, must be abstract; in order to pass from the concrete to the abstract state it must be cleared of all particular circumstances, and ideally, even of the names of men and of peoples. For Comte, the "events" upon which academic history lays stress are to be regarded as "essentially insignificant" comparable to "monstrosities" in biology.

I discern in the kind of positivist history that Comte and later the Annales school so vigorously attacked certain uncomfortable similarities to the explicit and implicit assumptions of ethnohistory as conventionally practiced in America. Paul Ricoeur (1980: 8) isolates five major characteristics of so-called positivist history: (1) an attitude of neutral objectivity, comparable to the physical scientist who is independent of the phenomenon he studies; (2) a reduction in focus to the collection and critical analysis of documents (including such things as their origin, provenience, date, or validity); (3) the assumption that historical fact exists preformed in the documents and merely has to be extracted or excavated (this idea might be likened to the attitudes of an Iroquois carver who envisions the visage of a false face already prefigured in a block of basswood or in a living tree); (4) explanation consists of relating particular events, or "accidents," to each other along a linear time line imposed by the documents; and (5) the individual is taken to be the ultimate locus and transmitter of historical change.

In presenting the Annalistes' critique and their deconstruction, if not dismemberment, of these basic assumptions, I will suggest some implications for ethnohistory. Value-free, empirical, objective history – what Peter Novick (1988) called *That Noble Dream* in his recently published critical retrospection of the American historical profession – may be for some an ideal in historical research, but it is an ideal that is impossible to realize simply because historians are never free from history. There is continual interaction between past and present. Scholars in the Annales tradition do not deny [136] the relevance of current events as clues for discovery of previously overlooked connections in past history (Ricoeur 1980: 9). This affirmation of the value of the present for understanding the past confronts us directly with the epistemological and methodological problem involved in the eternal opposition between "presentism" and "historicism." The dangers of presentism in distorting and falsifying the past have been well publicized, at least since Butterfield's explication of *The Whig Interpretation of History* (1976 [1931]). Yet well-intentioned American historians and textbook writers still search for a usable and relevant past. Historicism, the antithesis of presentism, attempts to contextualize historical knowledge to allow proper interpretation of past events. Historicism deliberately distances the phenomena under

---

1 Febvre and Bloch founded the influential journal *Annales d'histoire economique et sociale*, but Henri Berr's emphasis on synthetic decompartmentalized history (1900) and Francois Simiand's arguments for repeatable, quantifiable historical data (1903) anticipated major aspects of what came to be the Annales approach (Wallerstein 1979: 70). For the Annalistes, "positive history" was associated with official, establishment history that stressed a narrative ideographic form, or what might be referred to in French as *l'histoire historisante* or *l'histoire evenementielle* (ibid.).

This paper was delivered as the presidential address at the 1988 annual meeting of the American Society for Ethnohistory, Williamsburg, VA, November 12. *Ethnohistory* 36 (2): 133-147 (Sp 1989).

investigation. It also suffers from the absence of an adequate theory of context either to embed events in a particular setting or to establish a suitable framework for comparing different contexts. Too often context is taken to be explanatory, when context itself is problematic and must be explained. Recourse to exclusive context determinism has the same logical flaws as extreme environmental determinism. Every historical event and era entails a past such that history may be read stratigraphically as a series of contiguous past presentisms. The awareness of the interface between the past and present has theoretical and practical significance for ethnohistorians. If one is interested in, say, eighteenth-century Indian politics, some insights may be gleaned through observations of informal political processes still at work today in many reservation communities. Oral commentary on past events, despite partial memory loss and inevitable reinventions, can nevertheless aid in the interpretation of manuscript materials. Even events in our own contemporary culture can spark the ethnohistorical imagination. Several recent books on the Patty Hearst case, including her own account, have recently been published. Surely there is a wealth of material here that might stimulate new interpretations of Indian captivity narratives. Robert Drinnon's *Facing West* (1980), an underappreciated work, views our misadventures in Vietnam as the latest link in a continuous chain extending back to the initial European invasion of America. And our recent conquest of Grenada invites us to reread in a new light John Dryden's 1672 epic play, *The Conquest of Grenada by the Spaniards*:

> No man has more contempt, than I, of breath,
> But whence hast thou the right to give me death?
> Obey'd as Sovereign by thy subjects be,
> But know, that I alone am King of me.
> I am free as Nature first made man
> 'Ere the base Laws of Servitude began
> When wild in the woods the noble Savage ran.

I doubt that this was required reading in the Pentagon or State Department. At any rate the first usage of the term noble savage in English literature was not in reference to an American Indian, but to a defiant Moor, Almanzor.

Against the slavish subservience of the French positivists to documents, Lucien Febvre proclaimed that "there is no history; there are only historians" (quoted in Ricoeur 1980: 9). This liberating declaration calls for new creativity on the part of historians in framing new hypotheses and asking new questions of the documentary record. Mere description or reproduction of the documents, however faithful, does not fulfill the historian's task. His or her own voice must be added to those of the documents to enhance and transform our knowledge of the past.

In place of the positivist notion that historical determination could be ascertained from the orderly stringing of events along unidirectional, chronological lines, the Annales school adopted broader, more complex conceptions of time derived from sociology, economics, and demography (Ricoeur 1980: 9). Ideas of structure, trends, cycles, and growth permeate their histories. Functional and processual interdependencies that transcend short-term temporal contingencies work themselves out over long time spans. Multiple systems of time provide the interwoven threads that result in rich tapestries of human history. In such a program events are downplayed as minor disturbances on an otherwise placid surface structure. Encompassing the *Islands of History* (Sahlins 1985) is a vast ocean of regular tides, hidden undercurrents, and a self-regulating ecology. *Cum grano* Sahlins, my metaphor may not be overdetermined. Indeed, the hero of Fernand Braudel's magnum opus is the Mediterranean Sea; other French historians have focused on the Atlantic Ocean as a bridge between the New World and Spain (Ricoeur 1980: 10).

In his historiographic writings, Braudel introduced his now familiar, yet still problematic, notion of *la longue duree*, which further downplayed the significance of an event-centered history. Underlying the short-term, upbeat fluctuations marked by events was a history of slow rhythms extending over a long time span.[2] I sense in Braudel's conceptions an implicit analogy with the history of geology. Before the Darwinian theory of evolution was possible, a vastly expanded temporal vision was necessary. Earlier geological theories of catastrophism had to be replaced with the theory of uniformitarianism as championed by Charles Lyell, in which the history of the earth could be read through slow, natural, inexorable processes operating over immense time ranges and continuing into the present.

Coordinate with the Annalistes' deemphasis of events is their shift away from the individual as the primary agent of history. Rather, there is a partial assimilation of Durkheimian and Maussian sociology which stresses the determinate reality of social structure and the evocative power of collective representations that reach their fullest representations as total social facts. Just as the movement away from events leads to a dismissal of "battle histories," so the denial of the individual marks a retreat from political history in which the decisions of individual political leaders loom large (Ricoeur 1980: 10). The interest shifts to groups-to categories or classes of people-or to regions, in what may more generally be regarded as depersonalized social history.

The substantive works of scholars in the Annales tradition has centered on European history. Their ideas have been influential on more recent conceptions of historical anthropology and an anthropology of history, particularly as articulated by Marshall Sahlins (1981, 1985). Sahlins's area of interest is Polynesia, for which a rich literature of European contact exists and over which he demonstrates a masterful control. However, Sahlins is also a gifted ethnographer with a sensitive feel for particularistic detail. His long-term research has become increasingly concerned with native conceptions of history. Fusion of these approaches has produced some specifically Polynesian histories in which such Western heuristic dualities as those between structure and events, infrastructure and superstructure, presentism and historicism, individual and group, pattern and process, and the West and the rest are obliterated. Historic and mythic events are both "real" for Polynesians; their narrative traditions are densely populated with individual gods, chiefs, and heroes. Polynesian histories are seen to possess their own culturally constituted logic, validities, and internal dynamics. By an anthropology of history Sahlins intends a relativistic, pluralistic approach in which Western history is also considered as a cultural production-one among many-with no privileged claims to universal truth. I offer no critiques here of Sahlins's work. Critical reaction will undoubtedly be forthcoming as the slowly grinding jaws of academic discourse begin their digestive process.

What I am more concerned with here is the applicability of the Annales approach and developments in historical anthropology to a possibly refashioned ethnohistory of the American Indian.

Certain convergences of interest seem evident. The environmental, geohistorical, and climatic attention of Europeanists is paralleled by the surgent ethnohistorical interests in ecological and geographical factors influencing the course of pre- and postcontact New World history. Everything from plant sociology to game fluctuations, mosquitoes to rabbits, forest fires to flash floods, volcanic eruptions to earthquakes, and hyperthermal periods to little ice ages have been invoked as influential factors [139] in history. This dehumanized perspective has been slightly modified by ethnoecological and ethnogeographical efforts to consider cultural meanings attributed to these natural events.

Another apparent parallel with Europeanists' projects is the vigorous Americanist concern with demography, disease, and death, particularly but not exclusively after the introduction of European pathogens. Drastically reduced populations are obviously decisive influences on the course of American Indian history, dramatically affecting social organization, the perpetuation of traditions, religious conversion, revitalization movements, and a host of other domains. However, in the wake of numbing

---

2 In his essay "History and the Social Sciences" (1972 [1958]) Braudel delineates the multiple temporalities that he employs in his magisterial Mediterranean and the Mediterranean World in the Age of Philip II (1972-73 [1949]): structural time (or *la longue duree*), conjuncture, and event. Short-term events possess less analytic significance for Braudel than longer-term events.

number counts, we have too few accounts of the native affective reactions and cognitive rationalizations of these catastrophic die-offs.

In certain ways the culture history of the New World lends itself to ideas inherent in *la longue duree*, and in other ways it does not. The archaeological record reveals long-term processes at work, and abundant postcontact documentation can also be analyzed to reveal long-term trends, tendencies, and cycles. The dimly understood, highly specialized paleo-Indian cultures and the monotonous sameness of archaic and desert cultural adaptations give way to increasing regional specialization by Woodland times and accelerate to large differences in scale and volitility when some areas enter Mississippian and proto-Pueblo periods. Differences in cultural complexity reflect differential ecological adaptations, situations, and histories. Yet this cultural differentiation was tempered by rapid diffusions of technology, trade goods, and ideas along well-established communication networks. One can also discern some general regularities in the contact situation from the prematurely discredited and abandoned literature on acculturation.

Native North America belies the image of "cold," ahistorical, repetitive societies conceived by Claude Levi-Strauss (1966 [1962]: 233). If not exactly "hot" in his terms, North American societies certainly defrosted rapidly in late prehistoric times and continued the meltdown in response to European contact. The miraculous survival of distinctive Native American cultures to the present day despite intended and unintended policies of genocide, sociocide, and forced acculturation is usually attributed to racism, marginalization, benign neglect, and periodic waves of benevolent protectionism in the face of national and international disgrace. Less apparent to the general public are the internal strengths of Indian societies as expressed through the idiom of kinship, in the abiding sense of community, in the adaptive significance of what we derogatively view as factionalism, and in the political and legal effectiveness of native advocates. However, the factor that may prove most decisive for Indian persistence is a highly developed level of historical consciousness, a continuing sense of identity as separate peoples for whom power resides in maintaining their distinctness. History, so viewed, is not something that happens to Indians; it might better be conceived as a potent force that they actively utilize, refashion, and manipulate as a survival mechanism.

The importance of the individual in the rendering of Indian history is again highly problematic. We must be careful to distinguish individualism as an ideology from the more psychological conception of individuality, or a sense of self.[3] Certainly the ethos of many Indian societies downplays individualism in favor of more collectivist values. However, this overarching ethos also embraces a profound respect for the individual and the privacy of the person. Indian history reveals a reasonable quotient of leaders, distinctive status personalities, and gifted individuals who emerge in times of crisis. Available biographies or autobiographies of such people have increased exponentially in recent decades.[4] Indian oral traditions also highlight the miraculous feats of a wide variety of culture heroes who shaped the world and humankind in concert with their own developing individuation and achievement of selfhood. However, a proper assessment of the role of the individual in Indian history awaits fuller and more refined ethnopsychological study of culturally constituted theories of self and person, an area of research that is presently booming but is still in its babyhood.

Resistance to event-centered history by French historiographers seems to be eroding in the face of a rising tide of interest in narrativity; these tidal waves are washing ashore on both sides of the Atlantic. The idea that history should tell a story is, of course, nothing new. The quality of historical scholarship has traditionally been evaluated largely on the basis of the narrative skills of the historian. However,

---

3 See Lukes 1973 for a review of varied meanings of this ambiguous concept.

4 Two recent critical studies of Native American personal narratives survey the literature well: Arnold Krupat's *For Those Who Come After* (1985) and H David Brumble III's *American Indian Autobiography* (1988). A useful contribution to life histories of marginal frontier figures is *Being and Becoming Indian*, edited by James A Clifton (1989).

when historians started to shop around in such other social science emporiums as psychology, sociology, economics, and anthropology for new concepts and methods to make the discipline of history more rigorous and theoretical, the market value of good old-fashioned narrative history plummeted (Stone 1987). Narrative history was often demeaningly prefaced by the adjective "mere." The resurgent interest in narrativity has emerged from a confluence of several streams of thought: continental hermaneutical studies, semiotics, discourse analysis, literary criticism, and performative folklore studies, among others. Narratives are seen as fundamental means of communication, as devices for information processing and retrieval.

Human beings make and utilize narrative forms for both intra- and interpersonal communication. The fleeting sensory images of dreams may be transformed into indexical texts for personal consumption or for sharing with others. Conversely, stories can be employed to arouse emotions in others, as well as to facilitate information recall in interpersonal discourse. The components of narratives are connected series of events. Constructed narratives need not arrange events in a strict linear chronological [141] sequence. Events can be drawn from many levels, go in divergent directions, recognize different time scales, and crisscross one another. Events do not generate the narrative, but events are selected to cohere to story lines, frameworks, or plots that result in intelligible narratives. Selection is crucial here, because events may either be restricted in number or almost infinite. The criterion for selection is how the events fit the plot. Thus history cannot be considered a universal, singular absolute written with a capital H. Rather what we confront in narrative history are "histories of" – written from a particular perspective. The historian no longer needs to be a slavish servant to the available so-called facts but becomes a creative synthesizer who constructs texts from available "facts" and events. The historian makes histories. Histories do not exist as preformed narratives awaiting discovery.

The demands of narrative theory in writing ethnohistory are complicated enormously by the bi- or multicultural frames of reference within which most ethnohistorians operate, by different modes of discourse, by documentation that cannot always be limited to written manuscripts, and by recognition of different conceptions of reality. The task of constructing ethnohistories is formidable, but the potential rewards are great.

I have evaded until now my original topic of nonevents by trying to clarify the positive meanings and usages of events in historiography. I will now consider nonevents in brief schematic fashion and try to provide some suggestive illustrations of ethnohistorical relevance.

At the broadest level, we must take seriously the contention of the French Annalistes in recognizing the possibility that most history is noneventful. However, plot-generated "events" may be constructed for purposes of narrativity, for "telling the story." Yet, surrounding the "real" or constructed event is a residuum of cultural data critical for historians and ethnohistorians. These include values, meanings, symbolism, worldviews, social structural principles, and other variables of cultural analysis without which any event, real or imagined, cannot be adequately interpreted.

The reality and practical significance of uneventful history was forcibly brought home to me when I took temporary leave from the leisure of the theory class to testify before Congress on procedures for federal Indian recognition. A group petitioning for recognition must document, mainly through written records, that it is descended from historically known Indian tribes, has kept its Indian identity over time, and "has maintained tribal political influence or other authority over its members as an autonomous entity through history to the present." Documented information fulfilling these requirements is often difficult to obtain, and the minimal data available are frequently hard to interpret. Many of these groups did not get inscribed in the documentary record, and thus for purposes of federal recognition they have no history. One possible reason that the documents are silent on the existence of these groups is a deliberate adoption of a low-profile invisibility as a defensive strategy to avoid possible discrimination persecution, conscription, and perceived threats to their autonomy. They might avoid census takers, distance themselves from federal, state, or local authorities, refuse to send their children to schools, and not engage in events that were likely to be reported by newspapers. Thus the lack of an authenticated history for many of these groups begs fundamental questions about the authority of history: Who determines it? Who sets the criteria? or, in a literal sense, Who *possesses* history?

Another form of nonevent concerns differential recognition of what is considered eventful. This is a persistent problem for ethnohistorians, who normally study bi- or multicultural situations. To recycle one of my favorite examples, we may ask whether the American Revolution was a real event for American Indians or an unmarked interval in a continuing series of struggles that had begun long before 1776 and would continue after the British surrender at Yorktown. Or more cryptically, did the Revolution for Indians only represent the paternal substitution of George the First for George the Third?

Related to differential recognition of events is the variable valorization of events. This corresponds closely to what Daniel Boorstin (1962) labels "pseudo-events." Essentially there is agreement that an event had transpired, that something happened, but there is disagreement as to the significance of and consequences following from that event. Much of the ethnohistorical work on treaties illustrates this differential valorization. For Indians, the treaty-making process was highly ritualized, involved with gift exchange followed by regular alternations of joviality and solemnity. After the negotiations were completed, the treaty took on a sacred quality with expectations of eternity continued reciprocity, and enduring mutual respect. The treaty event constituted a total social fact, in Mauss's terms. For the whites, however, treaty-making represented a secular, instrumental act, to be concluded as expeditiously as possible. The provisions of the treaty were not always seen as binding and were subject to continual revision, if not outright violation.

Another type of nonevent may be labeled the imagined event: one that never happened but could have occurred or, according to the ethnologic involved, should have happened. The notion of null events derived from theoretical physics is applicable here. Possible but unrealized events, alternative scenarios, and "what if ...?" propositions can have important significance for historical analysis and interpretation. Divination and prophesy partake of imagined events. As a more mundane illustration, we can review the siege of Detroit by Pontiac and his forces during another differentially valorized event, Pontiac's so-called conspiracy. Surely Pontiac could envision the fall of Detroit and subsequent retreat of the British [143] to the eastern slope of the Alleghenies. Greg Dowd (1988) has brilliantly argued that the possible return of the French was envisioned by both sides and must figure prominently in any interpretation of these events. Another subtype of imagined event is what I have elsewhere called the epitomizing event (Fogelson 1984: 260; 1985: 84). Epitomizing events are narratives that condense, encapsulate, and dramatize longer-term historical processes. Such events are inventions but have such compelling qualities and explanatory power that they spread rapidly through the group and soon take on an ethnohistorical reality of their own. The Cherokee story of the *Aní-kutáni* is my type case. According to the abstracted narrative, the *Aní-kutáni* constituted an overbearing priesthood who abused their power by taking sexual liberties with the women of the community. An outraged warrior led a revolt, members of the priesthood were slain, and theocratic rule came to an abrupt end. Such an event probably never occurred, but I interpret the narrative, which is reported in several independent sources, as summarizing longer-range changes and the ultimate demise of indigenous, formal Cherokee religious institutions.

Another form of nonevent can be labeled the latent event. Fernand Braudel, champion of noneventful history, says that "the non-eventful ... refers to events not yet considered as such: history of the soil, of attitudes, of madness or the search for security over the ages. What will be called non-eventful is therefore the historicality we are not aware of" (quoted in Ricoeur 1980: 56).

Thus it would seem that Braudel's long time spans are ultimately eventful, if only the right questions are posed and suitable narratives are produced to reveal these undiscovered events.

My final type of nonevent involves events that actually occur, and can be documented, but are so traumatic they are denied. In my fieldwork with and ethnohistoric research on the Cherokees, I have found surprisingly few Cherokee accounts of the painful events that accompanied the actual Removal exodus. In contrast there is an abundance of documentation from the diaries of white soldiers who supervised the thousand-mile journey, from local white observers whose vivid impressions are preserved in the records of towns through which the emigrants passed, and some coverage even reached the national press. Yet there are practically no contemporaneous Cherokee materials, very few post-Removal memoirs, and only fragmentary oral traditions about this sad event.[5] It would seem that the Removal experience was so degrading, so incredible, so brutally real that it became unreal to the Cherokee mind.

By now there can be little doubt that epidemic diseases were decisive events in shaping postcontact American Indian history. However, as mentioned previously, we possess precious few native descriptions of epidemics, despite the enormous impact wrought by these events and their far-reaching consequences. As ethnohistorians, we should ask new questions, arrange new narrative plots, to try to explain the native silence, if not total amnesia, surrounding these horrendous events.

It is one thing to try to classify nonevents; it is another to go beyond mere typology and attempt to demonstrate analytic and interpretive possibilities opened up by considerations of nonevents. Let me try to suggest such a possibility by some brief and schematic remarks about a subject that has commanded the attention of historians, ethnologists, and ethnohistorians for almost a century: the Ghost Dance. Narrative accounts of these events, based primarily on nonnative sources, are now being supplemented by systematic efforts to deal with native testimony and its embedded cultural meanings.

Exemplary here is Raymond DeMallie's ethnohistorical account of the Lakota Ghost Dance (1982) and his continuing effort to make primary native texts accessible. DeMallie presents critical Lakota ethnoecological and metaphysical understandings. The disappearance of the buffalo represented a migration back to their origins within the earth. By proper ritual it was hoped that this migration might be reversed. The underworld was also the point of origination of human souls, although their ultimate destination was to the upper world. The reunion of the spirits of the dead with their living kin could be entertained as a metaphysical possibility in the Lakota belief system. Abstracting from these observations, time can be seen as circular rather than lineal, and events can be considered reversible rather than irreversible.

Russell Thornton's recent book on the Ghost Dance (1986) considers the demographic history leading up to the Ghost Dance and tries to interpret its context. Experts more competent than I may debate Thornton's figures, his assumptions, and the persuasiveness of his interpretations, but I believe he is asking significant questions.

What we seem to have neglected in our efforts to understand the Ghost Dance are native conceptions of ghosts and spirits, of the various living essences that we often too simplistically gloss as "souls," of death and eschatology, and of the meaning of mortuary practices as necessary junctures in the sequential spiritual passages from one world to another. In my general understanding of native North American spiritual beliefs, death was usually regarded less as an event and more as a process. Mortuary practices marked and facilitated this passage. One of the consequences of massive die-offs from epidemic disease and war was a practical inability to observe proper funerary rites. Collective pit burials seem to have replaced scaffold burials among the Lakota and other individuated forms of inhumation occurring elsewhere. Postburial rites were also probably ignored or severely foreshortened. Given the premises of native metaphysics and the paralyzing horror of the situation, it is perhaps conceivable that for many Indians the victims did not really or fully die. [145] In other words, there may have been a denial of death. The catastrophic die-offs might have been apperceived as incomplete or partial events, if not total nonevents, the courses of which could be reversed (cf Fogelson 1985: 80-82). Not only would the Lakota dance back the buffalo, but the dead might return from their aborted journeys to the other world. I defer to those more knowledgeable than I to judge whether my hypothesis has any validity or any value in opening up new lines of inquiry. My speculations here are intended only to suggest the explanatory possibilities of considering nonevents in the writing of ethnohistory.

I come to the end of my own personal *longue duree*, and I appreciate the patience with which it

---

5 For instance, in the special issue of the *Journal of Cherokee Studies* (1978) on primary documents of the Cherokee Removal, of the thirteen accounts only three are from native Cherokees.

was endured. Along the way, I have touched upon matters about which many will doubtless take exception. At least I hope I have provoked such disagreements and that further discussion can proceed. The development of our important field of study has for too long been stymied by the avoidance of theoretical issues and been impeded by naive epistemology. If history will not absolve me, I hope that someday ethnohistorians will.

References

Boorstin, Daniel J. 1962 *The Image or, What Happened to the American Dream.* New York: Atheneum.

Braudel, Fernand 1972-73 [1949] *The Mediterranean and the Mediterranean World in the Age of Philip II.* 2 vols. Sian Reynolds, trans. New York: Harper and Row.

    1972 [1958] History and the Social Sciences. In *Economy and Society in Early Modern Europe: Essays from An*nales. Peter Burke, ed. London: Routledge and Kegan Paul.

Brumble, H. David, III 1988 *American Indian Autobiography.* Berkeley and Los Angeles: University of California Press.

Butterfield, Herbert 1976 [1931] *The Whig Interpretation of Hist*ory. New York: AMS Press.

    1981 *The Origins of History.* Adam Watson, ed. London: Eyre Methuen.

Clifton, James A, ed. 1989 *Being and Becoming Indian: Biographical Studies of North American Frontiers.* Chicago: Dorsey Press.

DeMallie, Raymond J. 1982 The Lakota Ghost Dance: An Ethnohistorical Account. *Pacific Historical Review* 51: 385-405.

Dowd, Gregory Evans 1988 Pontiac and France. Paper delivered at the annual meeting of the American Society for Ethnohistory, Williamsburg, VA.

Drinnon, Richard 1980 *Facing West: The Metaphysics of Indian-Hating and Empire-Building.* New York: New American Library.

Fogelson, Raymond D. 1974 On the Varieties of Indian History: Sequoyah and Traveller Bird. *Journal of Ethnic Studies* 2: 105-12.

    1984 Who Were the Aní-Kutáni? An Excursion into Cherokee Historical Thought. *Ethnohistory* 31: 255-63.

    1985 Night Thoughts on Native American Social History. In The Impact of Indian History on the Teaching of United States History. Chicago: D'Arcy McNickle Center for the History of the American Indian, The Newberry Library, Occasional Papers in Curriculum, No. 3: 67-89.

Gidé, Andre 1953 [1899] *Marshlands, and Prometheus Misbound: Two Satires.* George D. Painter, trans. New York: New Directions.

King, Duane H, and E Raymond Evans 1978 The Trail of Tears: Primary Documents of the Cherokee Removal. *Journal of Cherokee Studies* 3 (3): 130-87.

Krupat, Arnold 1985 *For Those Who Come After: A Study of Native American Autobiography.* Berkeley and Los Angeles: University of California Press.

Levi-Strauss, Claude 1966 [1962] *The Savage Mind.* Chicago: University of Chicago Press.

Lukes, Steven 1973 *Individualism.* New York: Harper Torchbooks.

Martin, R M 1978 *Events, Reference, and Logical For*m. Washington: Catholic University of America Press.

Novick, Peter 1988 *That Noble Dream: The "Objectivity Question" and the American Historical Profession.* Cambridge: Cambridge University Press. [147]

Ricoeur, Paul 1980 *The Contribution of French Historiography to the Theory of History.* Zaharoff Lectures. New York: Oxford University Press.

Sahlins, Marshall 1981 *Historical Metaphors and Mythical Realities: Structure in the Early History of the Sandwich Islands Kingdom.* Association for Social Anthropology in Oceania Special Publications, No. 1. Ann Arbor: University of Michigan Press.

  1985 Islands of History. Chicago: University of Chicago Press.

Stone, Lawrence 1987 *The Past and the Present Revisited.* London: Routledge and Kegan Paul.

Teggart, Frederick J 1941 *Theory and Process of History.* Berkeley and Los Angeles: University of California Press.

Thornton, Russell 1986 *We Shall Live Again: The 1870 and 1890 Ghost Dance Movement as Demographic Revitalization.* Cambridge: Cambridge University Press.

Wallerstein, Immanuel 1979 Fernand Braudel: 69-72. In *International Encyclopedia of the Social Sciences*. Vol. 18, Biographical Supplement. David L Sills, ed. New York: The Free Press.

THE KEETOOWAH MOVEMENT IN INDIAN TERRITORY[1]

"I am happy to find that you are still alive to the subject of Cherokee History. And I fully agree with you in the opinion that the only chance of justice for us is in History" (Letter of Chief John Ross to John Howard Payne, March 5, 1836 in Moulton, Vol I, 1984: 391)

I, too, am pleased that Cherokee history continues to be a lively, if not always just, subject. When Chad Smith initially invited me to participate in this symposium, he asked for a paper topic. I offered to do something on Cherokee notions of time, space, being, and prophecy, as these related to conceptions of history. Chad discouraged such vacuous, metaphysical insubstantiality and wanted to slot me into a specific chronologic period. The later nineteenth century was then unfilled, so I suggested a paper on the Keetoowah Society. Little did I know then that several other scholars would choose a similar topic and time period. Indeed, Redbird Smith and the Keetoowahs, according to the photographs and quotations in the preliminary program, appear to be the stars of the show.

One may well ask why the Keetoowahs command so much past and present scholarly attention. How did a dissident, backwater minority of recalcitrant fullbloods become mainstream? It seems as if the romanticized lure of the forbidden and mysterious, the fact that the Keetoowahs are usually described as a <u>secret</u> society (cf. McGowan 1866) arouses curiosity. Secondly, there is a surgent, world-wide interest in resistance movements and the efforts of politically oppressed people to fend off the hegemony of the over-culture. The power of the powerless, whether in bus boycotts or booger dance burlesques, possesses intrinsic fascination.

My own interest in the Keetoowahs dates back to the late 1950s and long conversations with the late Bob Thomas, whose 1954 MA thesis remains the touchstone for Nighthawk Keetoowah [2] history. I visited Oklahoma during the summer of 1958 and again in 1960 in the company of Lloyd Runningwolf Sequoyah, a well regarded North Carolina medicine man. We attended several stomp dances and were graciously received by leaders of the United Keetoowahs, as well as by Stoke Smith and the Nighthawks.

During that period, when I wasn't doing fieldwork, I was employed as a research assistant by Anthony F C Wallace soon after he had formulated his influential theory of revitalization movements and was completing his classic account of the Handsome Lake religion, which was finally published as *The Death and Rebirth of the Senecas* (1970). While Wallace's revitalization model derives from, and most closely fits, the Handsome Lake material, it has proven to have wide applicability elsewhere. However, in considering the Nighthawk Keetoowah movement, the revitalization model did not fit comfortably.[2] Cherokee culture seemed to differ from that of the northern Iroquois in some crucial respects. Essentially, Cherokees seem to value community over individualism; they are skeptical about the reliability and validity of vision, dreams, and prophecy. Wallace's model emphasizes the role of the individual prophet and external stresses leading to a breakdown of previous mental patterns and the formation of a new

---

1. I'd like to thank Chad Smith for the invitation to the conference on which this paper is based; Chief Wilma Mankiller and other officers of the Cherokee Nation for their unstinting hospitality; Rennard Strickland for overseeing the publication.; John Aubrey at the Newberry Library for archival help; Susan Schroeder for her generous ear in listening to early drafts of this paper; and Anne Ch'ien for typing the manuscript.
2. While employed as a research assistant with Professor Wallace, I began, but did not complete, an analysis of the Nighthawk Keetoowah Movement, along with a critical review of the theoretical literature on movements. I remain indebted to Anthony Wallace for unflagging support, encouragement, and inspiration over the years, even when my interpretations ran counter to some of his theories.

apperceptive mind set that envisions a dramatically changed culture and social structure. In the Keetoowah movements, and even in the earlier movements mislabeled Ghost Dances by McLoughlin,[3] there is little evidence of dramatic mental reshuffling and the envisionment or plan of a radically altered world. Rather, like the later rebellion of Whitepath in 1823-1827, -- and note the word rebellion rather than revolution[4] – there is a general acceptance of the traditional social and cultural order, and the aim of the movement is to revive and perpetuate its major features. Thus these movements might best be classified as nativistic movements in Ralph Linton's (1943) sense. None of the Cherokee movements seem as transformative as, say, a Melanesian Cargo Cult, let alone the Handsome Lake [3] religion. This is not to deny the significance of conditions of real or relative deprivation in triggering movements, as first articulated by David Aberle (1962). In a similar vein, Russell Thornton (1993) has effectively argued that "boundary dissolution" might be an enabling condition for revitalization movements. Nor should one ignore the often decisive influence of social and political structure in shaping movements. Rather, what I am recommending is a closer examination of cultural factors as expressed in distinctive Cherokee values and patterns of behavior in relation to the Keetoowah movement.[5]

Keetoowah origins are obscure. Definite evidence from written records of a formal Keetoowah organization date back only to 1858. However, traditionalists have long insisted that the Keetoowah organization and associated religious beliefs are primordial aspects of Cherokee identity, extending far back into pre-Columbian times. One 1913 source I discovered even traces the genesis of the Keetoowahs to an extinct race of people in central Egypt. (Anon 1913: 27)

During the nineteenth century there was a widespread belief in the former existence of a priestly society, the *Ani kutani* who reputedly abused their sacred authority and were assassinated. Elsewhere (Fogelson 1984) I have collated variants of the *Ani kutani* legend and suggested that it served as an epitomizing event that condenses into comprehensive narrative form the complex processes resulting in the eighteenth-century decline of Cherokee theocratic authority. The enduring power of the *Ani kutani* legend emerges once more in Robert Conley's compelling 1992 novel, *The Way of the Priests*, and is briefly mentioned in Wilma Mankiller's recent autobiography (1993: 18).

Janey Hendrix (1983: 24, 39) reports that Cherokee scholar Anna Gritts Kilpatrick, in her unpublished papers, suggested that the *Ani kutani* may have served as the source from which the [4] Keetoowahs sprang. Such speculations should not be dismissed out-of-hand, since, according to Charles Hicks' letter of March 1, 1826, the *Auh,ne,coo,tawh,nes* ["the Proud"] professed teachings of heavenly knowledge directly from the Creator and transmitted this knowledge in the darkness of night (Moulton 1984: 115). Furthermore the roots *ku ta ni* and *kee too wah* are close enough to be confused, although probably phonemically and etymologically divergent. Frank Speck, apparently following the term

---

3 The late William McLoughlin (1984) deserves credit for having documented an outbreak of supposed Cherokee Ghost Dances during the period 1811-1813. These movements, as McLoughlin notes, "did not ... come together into a unified, coherent pattern; ... had no single prophet or leader ... [and] did not inaugurate a concerted reform program." (1984: 127-28).

4 Here I am influenced by Max Gluckman's distinction between rebellion, which challenges, but accepts the existing social order, and revolution, which seeks to overthrow and deny the legitimacy of the present social order (1963).

5 Russell Thornton (1993) sets up an antithesis between his belief that Cherokee movements of the nineteenth century can be explained by general theory and William McLoughlin's appeal to more circumstantial and historically particularistic interpretations. What seems to be invoked here is the age-old philosophical debate between induction and deduction. Obviously induction cannot produce valid explanation without some control of data, while deductive explanations are always guided by implicit or explicit theories. My appeal to consideration of distinctive Cherokee values and behavioral patterns in viewing Keetoowah movements is simultaneously inductive and deductive, if not reductive and abductive.

Cuttaws for Catawbas in Schoolcraft (III 1853: 292), mistakenly thought the term Keetoowah derived from a Catawba term (1939). I have long suspected that in regard to both sound pattern and meaning *kee too wah gi* may ultimately be related to the term *ga du gi*, the traditional Cherokee local town organization, and perhaps more distantly with the Cherokee term for bread, *gudu* (cf. Fogelson and Kutsche 1961: 88).

Less speculatively, we can definitely link the term Keetoowah with the name of a major Cherokee mother town that was abandoned in the 1760s. Located above the confluence of the Oconaluftee and Tuckaseegee, Rivers, near present-day Bryson City, North Carolina, the site of Kituwha has not to my knowledge been desecrated by the shovel of the archaeologist.

Mother towns were major ceremonial centers that spawned offspring in a manner similar to the transfer of sacred fire from one Cherokee or one Creek stomp dance ground to another. They were places of refuge where bloodshed was off-limits. However, besides their sacred character, these towns were also centers of inter- and intra-tribal trade and political exchange. Kituwha's sphere of influence spread to surrounding settlements who spoke a similar dialect and identified as *ani kee too wah gi*. As the town most accessible to northern trails and trade routes, Kituwha was in frequent contact with Iroquois, Delawares, Ottawas, and other northern visitors. Charles Hicks' letter of May 4, 1826 notes that [5]

> It has been further related that the *Nan tu wa kus* [both Mohawks and Senecas bore this name], came in considerable numbers about *Ke,tu,wauh* [Keowee (sic)] Tuckelechee [Tuckaseegee River] and came to war against the Creeks, and brought in considerable numbers of the Creek prisoners they had taken; and no doubt the Cherokees had invited them to their assistance (Moulton, I, 1984: 117).

Hicks tentatively dates this event near the beginning of Oconostota's life, which would place it in the first quarter of the eighteenth century. Hicks's account suggests that Kituwha was a cosmopolitan center open to influences from without. Among Northern Indians, the fame of Kituwha was such that it became the generic name for all Cherokees. This name generalization probably lies at the root of the usage of *Ani kee too wah gi* to refer to "real" or traditional Cherokees, a pattern that persists to the present day.

There is no definite evidence of a Keetoowah Society in pre-Removal or immediate post-Removal times. The town name was not transplanted among the Trans-Mississippi Cherokees, although in 1857 when Fort Gibson was abandoned and turned over to the Cherokee Nation, town lots were sold, and thought was given to moving the Cherokee capital from Tahlequah to this new site, which was to be called Keetoowah (Gaines 1989: 25). However, the Civil War intervened, and these plans were never realized.

It is generally acknowledged that the Keetoowah Society began in 1858 as a secret society of fullbloods to preserve Cherokee cultural traditions and defend national sovereignty. It is sometimes suggested that this was simply a missionary-inspired association intended to combat slavery. It isn't clear whether the Baptist missionaries, Evan and his son John Butrick Jones, along with Cherokee minister Budd Gritts, who wrote the Keetoowah constitution and its preamble, were manipulating the fullblood Cherokees, or whether it was the other way around. One wonders why missionaries, even liberal northern Baptists, would encourage [6] the preservation of pagan beliefs and practices. On the other hand, fullbloods and Cherokee nationalists were hardly rabid abolitionists. A few fullbloods of sufficient means were slave owners, and it must be remembered that the champion of Cherokee nationalism, Chief John Ross, owned many slaves. The major motivations of the fullbloods to band together was the recurring threat of cultural assimilation and so-called "civilization" as advanced by mixed bloods and descendants of the Treaty Party whom the fullbloods held responsible for the Removal holocaust. Transgenerational hatreds and jealousy still simmered.

Fullbloods were afraid of the growing power of the mixed bloods and feared that their interests would be sold out on the crossbars of secessionism. They worried that their very way of life was endangered.

True to their political leader, John Ross, the Keetoowahs officially advocated neutrality in the rapidly approaching War of the States. However, they secretly harbored sympathies with the North. The issues were less slavery and moral rectitude, but more the memory of past mistreatment at the hands of the Southern states and hostility toward the Southern sympathizing mixed bloods. Additionally, fullbloods were afraid of violating their treaties with the Federal Governments. They assumed that treaties were sacred and inviolable agreement vouchsafed their continued existence as a separate people.

Circumstances dictated that the Cherokees officially join the Confederacy, which they did. However, the majority of fullblood soldiers defected to Union forces at first opportunity. The more militant Keetoowahs identified themselves by crossed pins in their lapels and by certain stylized gestures and code words. The derisive term "Pin Indians" was coined by Southerners to connote terrorists and neo-savages capable of battlefield barbarities. The Cherokee Nation became a bleeding ground as Confederate and [7] Union troops alternately swept through the Indian Territory. Interestingly, it was the Confederate Cherokee battalions under General Albert Pike who were guilty of scalping slain Union soldiers (Gaines 1989: 80-81, 88-90). The death and devastation wrought by the Civil War rivaled the horror of the Removal.

Post-war adjustment was a slow and painful process as wounds continued to fester. After the war, the Keetoowah Society became, in effect, a political party. It was organized in the nine Cherokee districts through local councils and little captains, and representatives were sent to the legislative, judicial, and executive branches of the tribal government.

However, life was changing in the Cherokee Nation. Railroads completed the transformation to a market economy. Traditional religion declined or sought new venues, often in syncretized versions of Christianity: secular frolics replaced sacred dances; Christian churches attended the spiritual needs of many fullbloods; but individual medicine men still practiced. Lawlessness, alcoholism, and increased accusations of sorcery and witchcraft indexed growing social disorganization. Whites had infiltrated into the Indian Territory to such an extent that by the 1880s the fullblood Cherokees had become a minority in their own Nation.

Meanwhile up in the Catskill resort of Lake Mohonk in New York State, a group of well-intentioned "do-gooders" had been meeting regularly to address Indian problems and lobby Congress for reforms.[6] They concluded that the social disorder in the Indian Territory could be remedied and civilization could march inexorably forward by dissolving tribal governments, by allotting land to individuals, and by enfranchising the Indians as citizens of the United States. For illegally settled whites ("sooners" or "boomers") and opportunist mixed bloods, allotment promised the possibilities of commercial development and eventual statehood. [8]

For the fullbloods the loss of their tribal government and the annulment of their special treaty relations with the Federal Government left them rudderless in a floodtide they couldn't stem. The Keetoowahs, both Christian and non-Christian, registered their opposition to allotment to the Dawes Commission. However, after the allotment bill passed by a slim majority and the enabling Curtis Act was legislated in 1898, the Cherokee Nation seemed doomed and a dissident group of Keetoowahs broke away to form the Nighthawk contingent.

Redbird Smith was a staunch traditionalist with roots among the conservative Arkansas Band.[7] Less a charismatic leader and more a man who approached the Cherokee ideal of balanced judgment and

---

6 The reformers' policies and their implementation are usefully discussed in Fritz (1963), Hoxie (1984, 1988), in three works by Francis Prucha (1973, 1976, 1986), and by Washburn (1973).

7 A valuable account of the origins of the Keetoowahs, Redbird Smith, and the immediate post-Redbird Smith period is contained in the testimony of his son, John Smith, reproduced in Perdue (1980: 97-102). [14]

kindness, Redbird Smith had served in the tribal government and was well regarded in his community. He was named by the Keetoowah Council to lead the new group and was charged, in the oft repeated phrase, "to get back what the Keetoowahs had lost."

Here an important aspect of traditional Cherokee ideology comes into focus. Rather than resign themselves to despair as helpless victims of forces they cannot control, Cherokees take personal responsibility for their misfortunes. If they can maintain or return to their traditional ways, the Creator will once more look with favor upon them. But preserving a distinctive Cherokee way of life is not only the path for fullblood salvation, it is a sacred mission to save the world. The Cherokees, it is believed, were created as a separate people by divine will, and if that divine plan is shattered, the world will come to a catastrophic end.

The ideology was clear enough, but the problem of defining, redefining, and restoring tradition was something else. In carrying out his charge, Redbird Smith and company made the sacred fire and square grounds the central spiritual and physical center of their new/old religion. The initial four-sided square [9] ground arrangement was borrowed from the Creek model that Redbird had encountered through meetings of the intertribal Four Mothers Society and at traditional Creek towns. At a later time, the stomp grounds were "Cherokeeized" with the three or four Creek "beds" replaced by seven arbors to accommodate the seven Cherokee clans. This change represented more than a simple substitution of sacred numerology. During the late nineteenth century, Cherokee clan recognition had gone underground. People did not want their clans publically known, lest such information be used against them in sorcery ceremonies, which required knowledge of the clan of the intended victim (Fogelson 1975). Public acknowledgement of clan affiliation by arbor seating was a statement that the renewal of religious faith and ritual performance produced a communal solidarity that transcended fears of sorcery and bewitchment.

Seven wampum belts, originally obtained in the eighteenth century from diplomatic negotiations with the Iroquois also became central symbols in the reconstituted Keetoowah religion. These belts had become family heirlooms of the descendants of Chief John Ross. The Nighhawks arranged to "borrow" the belts from Robert B Ross, but had no intention of returning them, since they regarded themselves as the original Keetoowah Society and the only legitimate Cherokee government now that national sovereignty had been signed away. Once having acquired the wampum belts, it was another thing to ascertain their meanings, Redbird Smith and other duly appointed officers consulted with spiritual leaders from neighboring tribes, such as the Delawares, the Shawnees, the Creeks, Seneca-Cayugas, and others. Consensual meaning gradually emerged.[8]

This active seeking of knowledge by rational inquiry and mentation was supplemented by information derived from visions and dreams of Keetoowah members. Like their Creek neighbors, the Keetoowahs would seek spiritual knowledge by sleeping on the [10] dance grounds. However, before such individual, inspirational information was considered legitimate, it had to be approved and validated by committee (see again the account of John Smith in Perdue 1980: 101-02). In effect, extraordinary experience had to be socialized and domesticated.

This suspicion of charismatic individuals with "the word" cuts deeply into Cherokee collective consciousness. Recall the overthrow of the false prophets known as the *Ani Kutani* or the gullible Cherokees who heeded Tecumseh's warning about the imminent flood and climbed a mountain only to

---

8   The wampum belts fell into disuse in the late 1930s. Alice Marriott, then working for the Arts and Crafts Board of the Indian Service, reports a private viewing of the seven belts at a stomp dance ground. They were wrapped in several layers of covering: first an aged, faded, cotton cloth and a patterned silk bandana; next, dark brown cracking bark cloth; and finally, an ancient feather mantle of woodpecker top knots. The sinews on which the beads were strung were dried out and disintegrating. The Keetoowah chief, who is called "Chief Dick," allowed Marriott to re-string and mend the belts on the spot (1968: 183-84).

return shamefacedly when the prophecy failed (Mooney 1896: 676-77).[9] Most telling, perhaps, is the narrative collected by James Mooney (1900: 399-400) about a Cherokee hunter who wandered east into newly established white settlements and spied the first peacock seen in those parts. He killed the bird and made a headdress of the star-patterned feathers. Returning home, he marched into the council house and announced that he had traveled to the star country and had important messages to impart. He was accorded status as a powerful medicine man for a brief while, until another hunter traveled east, saw another peacock, and exposed the star traveler as a fraud. Cherokee ethos demanded that exceptional powers derived from visions and out-of-the-body experience had to be used for collective rather than for individual goals.

I could go on to say more about the Nighthawk Keetoowahs and how a political resistance movement transformed into a complex tribal religion, but the process has been well described in Emmet Starr's *History of the Cherokee Indians* (1921), in the unpublished MA theses of Eula E Fullerton (1931), Howard Tyner (1949), Bob Thomas (1954), and Benny Smith (1967), in Janey Hendrix's book and articles, in Janet Jordan's fulsome Ph.D dissertation (1975), in Daniel Littlefield's fine article on "Utopian Dreams among the Fullblood Cherokees (1971), in the unpublished paper of Thomas Ballenger (n.d), and in Charles [11] Wisdom's reports to the Bureau of Indian Affairs (1937, n.d). But I hope I have suggested enough about the potential of grounded cultural analysis to interpret the dynamic meanings embedded in religious movements.

Seen in another way, the Nighthawk Keetoowahs, along with the Four Mother's Society, Eli Pumpkin's break-away Seven Clan Society, and the more secular Keetoowah Incorporated and United Keetoowahs, which gained federal recognition under the Indian Reorganization Act – all these groups filled a political void attendant upon the official dissolution of the Cherokee Nation in 1906. These organizations kept alive the demand to recognize treaty rights, to negotiate land claims, and to secure other legal prerogatives. In 1938 J Bartley Milam worked hard as appointed Chief to obtain Cherokee tribal re-recognition (Meredeth 1985). Milam's successor, WW Keeler, ushered in the modern political era in 1971 by winning election as Principal Chief, and the rest is recent history. While some of the groups mentioned above were activist and confrontational, the Nighthawks employed a strategy of political avoidance and withdrawal to emphasize separatism, rejection of the Federal Government, and a coherent cultural identity as Cherokees.

To be sure, much of the Nighthawk Keetoowah religion consists in what modern social historians would regard as reinvented tradition. I often wonder who invented the reinventors. What these horse-post-modernists fail to appreciate, as they trot after the tail of the "other" only to discover themselves, is the fact that all of culture is in a constant process of invention and reinvention.[10] What is perhaps most

---

9 It is interesting to note that the great scholar of the Cherokees, James Mooney, whose classic work on the Ghost Dance religion (1896), did much to legitimize the study of Native American religious movements, did not feel the Keetoowah Society perpetuated authentic Cherokee traditions. In an office memo, concerning an offer of material from a mixed blood Cherokee, Mooney unsympathetically writes

"The Ani-Kituhwazi [sic], which he mentions, is not an ancient aboriginal organization but a secret political society dating only from the Rebellion & with its rites copied from the Masonic & other white secret orders. The red calumet, which he considers the 'Rosetta Stone of Indian mysteries' does not belong to the Cherokees at all but comes from the Sioux, as every geologist knows. The Cherokee sacred calumet was made of a white stone found near Knoxville" (quoted in Bass, 1954: 251).

10 While the notion of the reinvention of tradition has enlivened the study of social history and served post-modernist interpretations well, the political consequences for native peoples has not been fully

remarkable about Nighthawk beliefs and practices is not their diverse origins but the extent to which they had been "Cherokee-ized" into a consistent pattern. [12]

In Chicago in September 1993, the World Parliament of Religion celebrated the one hundredth anniversary of their first convention in 1893 at the World Columbian Exposition. The first Parliament was radically ecumenical for its day with almost everyone sharing the platform from Anglicans to Zoroastrians. However, Native Americans and other representatives of tribal religions were not invited. A brief paper on Indian religions was presented by the redoubtable Alice Fletcher (Mark 1988: 238-39), a pioneering anthropologist who produced much good field work, but who, ironically, was one of the Lake Mohonk architects of the allotment policy. Several hundred Indians attended the centennial of the Parliament and made their presence felt in their demands for religious freedom. I like to think that the last century has witnessed parallel attitudinal shifts in Oklahoma. One hundred years ago, and still more recently, native religions were regarded as tinder for dangerous uprisings and had to be suppressed. They were thought to embody moral backwardness, to be obstacles to social reform, and to be evolutionary deadends doomed to extinction. Indeed, many fullblooded Cherokee Christians today still regard stomp dancing as a pagan perversion, "the work of the devil." However, now, as we approach the next millennium, native religions are not only being tolerated but are celebrated as cultural assets and honored as wellsprings of ethnic pride. This new era is brightly reflected in the renewed celebrity of Redbird Smith and the movement he revived.

Bibliography [15]

Aberle, David F 1962 A Note on Relative Deprivation Theory as applied to Millenarian and Other Cult Movements. In Sylvia L. Thrupp, ed., *Millennial Dreams in Action*. The Hague: Mouton.

Anon. "History of the Keetoowahs" *The Indian School Journal* (Sept. 1913): 27-28.

Ballenger, Thomas L ms. The Keetoowahs, in the Ballenger Papers, The Newberry Library, Chicago.

Bass, Althea 1954 James Mooney in Oklahoma. *Chronicles of Oklahoma* 32: 246-62.

Clifton, James, ed. 1989 *Being and Becoming Indian: Biographical Studies of North American Frontiers*. Chicago: Dorsey Press.

Clifton, James, ed. 1994 *The Invented Indian: Cultural Fictions and Government Policies*. New Brunswick, NJ: Transactions.

Conley, Robert 1992 *The Way of the Priests*. New York: Doubleday.

Fogelson, Raymond D 1975 An Analysis of Cherokee Sorcery and Witchcraft Beliefs and Practices. In C Hudson, ed., *Four Centuries of Southern Indians*. Athens, GA: University of Georgia Press.

1984 Who Were the Ani-Kutani? An Excursion into Cherokee Historical Thought. *Ethnohistory* 31: 255-263.

Fogelson, Raymond D and Kutsche, R Paul 1961 Cherokee Economic Cooperatives: The Gadugi. In W N Fenton and J Gulick, eds., *Symposium on Cherokee and Iroquois Culture*. Bureau of American Ethnology Bulletin 180.

---

appreciated. What is at issue is the problem of ascertaining authenticity. Thus, as George Wenzel shows, animal rights groups can protest the killing of seals by Baffinland Inuits on the grounds that by using snowmobiles and rifles, instead of dog sleds and harpoons, they are no longer authentic Inuits. James Clifton, apparently is obsessed by issues of Indian authenticity. The introductions and chapter prefaces in his two recently edited books (1989, 1994) are used as an authority by protesters of Indian spear-fishing treaty rights in Wisconsin. The argument made is that modern Indians, using metal boats instead of birchbark canoes, outboard motors in place of paddles, and miners's lanterns instead of flaming torches, are not the same as the Indians who signed the treaties. Therefore, the treaties should be voided. The implicit assumption here is that white culture may be dynamic, but Indian cultures must be sealed in amber or lose their authenticity and legitimacy.

Fritz, Henry Eugene 1963 *The Movement for Indian Assimilation, 1860-1890.* Philadelphia: University of Pennsylvania Press.

Fullerton, Eula E 1931 Some Social Institutions of the Cherokees, 1820-1906. M.A Thesis, University of Oklahoma.

Gaines, W. Craig 1989 *The Confederate Cherokees: John Drew's Regiment of Mounted Rifles.* Baton Rouge: Louisiana State University Press.

Gluckman, Max 1963 Rituals of Rebellion in South-east Africa" In his *Order and Rebellion in Tribal Africa.* New York: Free Press.

Hendrix, Janey B 1983 Redbird Smith and the Nighthawk Keetoowahs. Journal of Cherokee Studies 8: 22-39, Spring; 73-86, Fall [16]

    1984 *Redbird Smith and the Nighthawk Keetoowahs.* Park Hill, OK: Cross-Cultural Educational Center.

Hoxie, Frederick E 1984 *A Final Promise: The Campaign to Assimilate the Indians, 1880-1920.* Lincoln: University of Nebraska Press.

    1988 The Curious Story of Reformers and the American Indians. In F. Hoxie, ed., *Indians in American History.* Arlington Heights, IL: Harlan Davidson.

Jordan, Janet Etheridge 1975 Politics and Religion in a Western Cherokee Community: A Century of Struggle in a White Man's World. PhD. Dissertation, University of Connecticut.

Linton, Ralph 1943 Nativistic Movements. *American Anthropologist* 45 (2): 230- .

Littlefield, Daniel F 1971 Utopian Dreams of the Cherokee Fullbloods: 1890-1930. *Journal of the West* 10: 404-27.

Mankiller, Wilma and Wallis, Michael 1993 *Mankiller: A Chief and Her People.* New York: St Martin's Press.

Mark, Joan 1988 *A Stranger in Her Native Land: Alice Fletcher and the American Indians.* Lincoln: University of Nebraska Press.

Marriott, Alice 1952 *Greener Fields.* New York: Greenwood Press [reprint 1968].

May, Katja 1990 Native Movements Among the Cherokees in the Nineteenth and Twentieth Centuries. *Journal of Cherokee Studies* 15: 27-39.

McGowan, DJ 1866 Indian Secret Societies. *History Magazine* 10: 39-41.

McLoughlin, William G 1990 Ghost Dance Movements: Some Thoughts on Definition Based on Cherokee History. *Ethnohistory* 37: 25-44.

    1990 *Champions of the Cherokees: Evan and John B. Jones.* Princeton: Princeton University Press.

    1993 *After the Trail of Tears: The Cherokees' Struggle for Sovereignty, 1830-1880.* Chapel Hill: University of North Carolina Press.

    1984 with Walter H Conser, and Virginia Duffy McLoughlin 1984 *The Cherokee Ghost Dance: Essays on Southeastern Indians, 1789-1861.* Macon GA: Mercer University Press. [17]

Meredith, Howard L 1985 *Hartley Milam: Principal Chief of the Cherokee Nation.* Muskogee, OK: Oklahoma Indian University Press.

Mooney, James 1896 The Ghost-Dance Religion and the Sioux Outbreak of 1890. Washington, DC: Fourteenth Annual Report (Part 2) of the Bureau of Ethnology, 1892-93.

    1900 Myths of the Cherokees. Nineteenth Annual Report, 1897-98 (Part 1). Washington, DC: Bureau of American Ethnology.

Moulton, Gary E, ed. 1984 *The Papers of Chief John Ross.* 2 vols. Norman: University of Oklahoma Press.

Perdue, Theda 1980 *Nations Remembered: An Oral History of the Five Civilized Tribes, 1865-1907.* Westport, Conn.: Greenwood Press.

Prucha, Francis Paul, ed. 1973 *Americanizing the American Indians: Writings by the "Friends of the Indians, 1880-1900.* Cambridge: Harvard University Press.

 1976 *American Indian Policy in Crisis: Christian Reformers and the Indian, 1865-1900.* Norman: University of Oklahoma Press.

 1986 *The Great Father: The United States Government and the American Indians.* Abridged Edition. Lincoln: University of Nebraska Press.

Schoolcraft, Henry Rowe 1853 *Historical and Statistical Information Respecting the History. Conditions, and Prospects of the Indian Tribes of the United States.* Vol 3. Philadelphia: Lippincott.

Smith, Benny 1967 The Keetoowah Society of the Cherokee Indians. MA Thesis, Northwestern Oklahoma State College.

Speck, Frank G 1939 Catawba Religious Beliefs, Mortuary Customs, and Dances. *Primitive Man* 12: 12-57.

Starr, Emmet 1921 *History of the Cherokee Indians and Their Legends and Folklore.* Oklahoma City: Warden Company.

Thomas, Robert K 1953 The Origin and Development of the Redbird Smith Movement. MA Thesis, University of Arizona.

Thomas, Robert K 1961 The Redbird Smith Movement" In W.N Fenton and J. Gulick, eds., Symposium on Cherokee and Iroquois Culture. Bureau of American Ethnology Bulletin 180. [18]

Thornton, Russell 1993 Boundary Dissolution and Revitalization Movements: The Case of the Nineteenth Century Cherokees. *Ethnohistory* ??: 339-383, Summer.

Tyner, Howard Q 1949 The Keetoowah Society in Cherokee History. MA Thesis, University of Tulsa.

Wallace, Anthony FC 1956 Revitalization Movements. *American Anthropologist* 58: 264-81.

 1970 *The Death and Rebirth of the Seneca.* New York: Knopf.

Washburn, Wilcomb E 1975 *The Assault on Indian Tribalism: The General Allotment Law (Dawes Act) of 1887.* Philadelphia: Lippincott.

Wenzel, George 1991 *Animal Rights, Human Rights: Ecology, Economy and Ideology in the Canadian Arctic.* Toronto: University of Toronto Press.

Wisdom, Charles 1937 Memorandum on the Tribal Character of the Keedoowah Society of the Cherokee. 27 May. In possession of author.

 1937? The Keetoowah Society of the Oklahoma Cherokee. In possession of author.

TRIBUTES

HISTORICISIMS, PRESENTISMS, AND THE FUTURE OF ANTHROPOLOGY IN HONOR OF
GEORGE W. STOCKING, JR.

We are gathered together today to celebrate the life and work of George Stocking.

What can I say about my friend and colleagues. Diamond George? ... I asked Ira Bashkow who, along with Matti Bunzl, has worked so hard to make this event a reality, what he wanted me to say about George. He suggested that I say something about the Stocking style. I was taken aback ... The Stocking style? Carol has style... but George? ...

Well, maybe there is a Stocking style born of buckle-headed obstinacy blended with a dash of hesitant Texas swagger. But I see by the Program that Ira plans to discern and discuss the Stocking style, so I will be spared this challenge.

George and I go back a long way. We both did our graduate work at the University of Pennsylvania and shared an uncommon mentor in the person of A. Irving Hallowell, a scholar of immense erudition and range whose reputation waxes while that of other of his generation wanes. Hallowell implanted in both of us the idea that the history of anthropology is an anthropological problem.

If the truth be told, I scarcely knew George Stocking at Pennsylvania, though we had many common friends, with uncommon names like Jim Flink, Manny Schoenhorn, and Neuro-Jack. He claims – and has embarrassing notes to support his claim – that he once attended a forgettable lecture I gave in one of Hallowell's classes. I wish he'd dispose of those notes. I do recall Hallowell later talking enthusiastically about this man. Stocking, who was doing excellent research on Boas's conceptions of race and culture.

A few years later we became casual acquaintances at various professional meetings. However, we only became close friends after he arrived at Chicago, first as a visitor and later as a regular appointment. George's work, which had already extended beyond the Boas constriction, impressed us positively. I think it was David Schneider who argued that George would be more than a house historian, that in writing the history of anthropology George was actually doing good anthropology. This was quite evident in his careful analysis of the circumstances leading to Franz Boas's expulsion from the American Anthropological Association in 1919. Surely this work was the equal of contemporary studies of Hopi factionalism, extra-processual events among the Tiv, or even Tallensi patrifiliation.

Anyway, the Department of Anthropology hired him, promoted him, and protected him from the conservative wolves of the History Department. We have never been sorry and consider George a full-fledged anthropologist, despite, or because of his consistent privileging of written documentation over observation or oral testimony.

Many of you don't realize that George and I are fictive, if not factive, kin. I am George's *Kum*, a relationship that in Serbia is likened to a best man in a wedding ceremony. But the relationship is more than that. Being a *Kum* entails reciprocal kinship obligations such that, when Serbian relatives visit America, I am responsible for entertaining them and supplying them with impressive half-gallon bottles of vodka, and I can expect similar treatment should I ever get the chance to visit them.

I recently asked some Slavic experts about the meaning of *Kum*. In its larger pan-Slavic extension, it can also mean a kind of compadre, a ritual sponsor, or a godfather, a position familiar to someone with roots in the New Jersoisie.

For now, I'd like to assume this latter status of *Kum* and offer George some godfatherly advice concerning the ordeal that is about to unfold, I can speak with some authority after having endured a similar rite of passage last year.

Some have described the experience as a kind of pre-mortem obituary, but believe me George ... it's worse than that ... It's more like a public autopsy. You'll hear things you long ago forgot, probably for good reason; you'll be outraged, illegitimately canonized, misunderstood, and be unable to recognize yourself. My advice is to keep your composure, loosen your shoe laces, smile a lot, unbuckle your headband, and be generous. The situation is a little like the detached self in a shamanic initiation where the shaman-to-be witnesses his own bodily dismemberment only to bask in the subsequent warm glow of wholeness and rememberment.

Realize, George, that this event is driven by the positive esteem and love that your friends, students, and colleagues feel toward you, so enjoy the historicisms, presentisms, and the future.

November 20, 1997
AAA, Washington, D.C.

ALFONSO ALEX ORTIZ
(1939-1997) – Anthropologist

Alfonso Ortiz was a long-term friend whose company I sorely miss.

Like the Tewa whose dualistic world he described so analytically, his own personality was complexly integrated through antitheses. He could be charmingly engaging one minute and infuriatingly remote the next. He could be demanding and insistent, yet genuinely generous with his time and resources. Alfonso was a sensitive man. a poet, a person attuned to natural beauty, but he could also be crude and insensitive in human relations. As he grew older, he became increasingly unreliable to the despair of his colleagues; he had a tendency to promise more than he could deliver. Nevertheless, I felt I could count on his wise advise and support in times of crisis. I was in close contact with him during the unpleasantness at Dickson Mounds. It is not widely known that Alfonso had acted as the personal Southwestern tour guide of one of the sponsors of this conference, Governor Jim Edgar. Alfonso was our ace-in-the-hole, fortunately a card we didn't have to play. Alfonso could be eloquent, and he could be banal. Many people do not realize that he was quite athletic when he was younger, a long-distance runner; though in later years he let himself go and became self-destructive. He had a rollicking sense of humor and we exchanged jokes at every encounter; yet one could sense an abiding sadness lurking just under the surface.

In his perceptive obituary of Alfonso, Kenneth Lincoln captures the smiling face that Al presented to his friends. He would greet Lincoln on the phone, "Yo, Ken, Alfonso here ..." followed by an elliptical chuckle. I also enjoyed a "yo-yo" relationship with Al. I came by my "Yo" legitimately, having spent much of my youth in and around Philadelphia. I almost believed they named a national park in my honor when people would greet me with "Yo-Semite." I'm not sure where Alfonso acquired his "Yo" -- perhaps from too many Sylvester Stallone movies.

However this overt jollity masked an underlying tension that could be both corrosive or creative. Alfonso was an edge person. He alternately inhabited multiple worlds: the Spanish-American world of his mother and her politically important family; the Tewa world of his father and more significantly his grandmother who served as his primary care-taker: the world of academia; the world of Native American affairs; and the world of foundation, institution-building and maintenance.

What I would like to examine in more detail today is Alfonso's career as an anthropologist. I think it is important to note his abiding loyalty to the profession and continuing identification with the discipline to the very end. While he could be critical of colleagues working in various Native American specialties, he never indulged in the "cheap-shot" sport of "anthro bashing." He was a role model who encouraged a whole generation of younger Native Americans to undertake academic studies. Although he worked [2] directly with very few students, he nevertheless, indirectly inspired and supported a large number of scholars, many of whom found their way to the Newberry and are in attendance today.

As an undergraduate at the University of New Mexico, Alfonso was a leader in Native American student activities. Although he committed the sin of majoring in sociology – it was William Auden who asserted "Thou shall not commit sociology" – he, nevertheless, was exposed to anthropology through teachers such as Florence Hawley Ellis, Harry Basehart, and Stanley Newman. As an undergraduate he engaged in brief fieldwork with the Tohono O'odam and the Navajos, as well as making informal comparative observations of different pueblos.

Alfonso went on to the University of Chicago for graduate work in anthropology. Fred Eggan, and to a lesser extent, Sol Tax, were his primary advisors; he was also influenced by David Schneider, Paul Frederich, and Clifford Geertz. When I arrived on the scene in the Fall of 1965, he had completed most of his research and was well into writing his dissertation, a manuscript that would ultimately become his major work, *The Tewa World*. From all accounts, Alfonso was popular with his fellow students, many of whom became life-long friends. Before he got involved in his dissertation his professors regarded him as a mild-mannered, competent, but somewhat bumbling student. His involvement in Indian activism was not much in evidence during his Chicago years. In writing the dissertation things came together for him. He demonstrated his intellectual virtuosity and the power of his incisive mind to illuminate profound problems in modern social anthropological theory.

It had long been known that there were fundamental differences in the social organizations of the Eastern and Western Pueblos. The Western Pueblos, as epitomized by Eggan's classical work on the Hopis, were organized into matrilineal clans, possessed a Crow-type kinship system, and had a large number of cross-cutting social and religious societies that tied the social structure together. The Eastern or Rio Grande Pueblos, in contrast, lacked clans and unilineal descent, and instead, possessed a form of dual organization in which people belonged to a Summer or Squash division or to the Winter or Turquoise division, each of which had its own chief and roster of religious and political functionaries. Political leadership of the Pueblo alternated between these two structures over the course of the year. Robin Fox had considered the Keresan Pueblos, particularly Cochiti where he had worked, as an intermediate bridge between the East and Western Pueblos. But no one had, as yet, attempted an in-depth analysis of the structure and symbolic associations of Eastern Pueblo dual organization.

Such a study would have important theoretical implications, because in several places Claude Levi-Stauss had questioned the reality of dual organizations as viable structural forms. He preferred to view such forms of society as cultural fictions disguising underlying triadic structures; he also saw so-called [3] diametric dualism as disharmonic with concentric dualism. It was time to put such reified theories co the empirical test.

Alfonso broke a long-standing anthropological taboo against studying one's own society. Such study was thought to resemble incest. In fact, one of Alfonso's alter egos, the gifted Santa Clara anthropologist Edward Dozier, first studied the Tewa-speakers of Hano amidst the Hopi at First Mesa. Later he worked in the Northern Philippines, and only near the end of his life did he attempt fieldwork in his home pueblo of Santa Clara. It is ironic that nowadays it is almost the norm for anthropologists to study their own societies.

Alfonso was well suited to take up the challenge. Not only was he a participating member of the culturally conservative Pueblo of San Juan. but he spoke the language, had at least a modicum of other fieldwork, and had access to a remarkable cohort of Tewa intellectuals whom he engaged in a continuing dialogue concerning points of meaning and interpretation. These intellectual elders included Tony Garcia (who had previously worked with Gertrude Kurath and Vera Laski), Jerry Garcia, Cipriano Garcia and his brother Peter, talented musicians who visited the Newberry on another occasion, and last but not least Alfonso's knowledgeable Uncle Steve. Stephan Trujillo (I'm grateful to Charlotte Heth for helping me recall these names). This was truly a formidable editorial board, one that was more demanding than that of Alfonso's dissertation committee or the University of Chicago Press. But as Alfonso remarks most tellingly:

"Among the Tewa, awareness of the more general considerations is restricted to only a reflective few, usually Made People, in each village, and no one of these is aware of more than a portion of the entire system of knowledge presented here." (1969: xvi)

Indeed, constructing models out of snippets from published and archival sources, from testimony of individual consultants, and from one's own well of experience and then applying these models to bygone and on-going realities is, perhaps, the crowning glory of the anthropological endeavor.

I mention all this because Alfonso has been accused by many, including the Governor of San Juan, of revealing tribal secrets, a sin for which he was compassionately forgiven at his funeral. In my experience, Alfonso always acted appropriately with respect to confidential information. His responsibilities as a member of San Juan Pueblo always took precedence over those as a member of the anthropology community. In actuality Alfonso, in *The Tewa World*, reveals nothing that was not already known. What he <u>did</u> do was to put these scattered materials together into a comprehensive schema that made the world view of the Tewa comprehensible and accessible. Alfonso's achievement and particular genius deserved not only academic acclaim but also recognition by the people of San Juan. The wisdom contained within the pages of *The Tewa World* stands as Alfonso's legacy to future generations. [4]

While I regard *The Tewa World* as Alfonso's magnum opus, he went on, as we all know, to a distinguished career as a teacher, a scholar, and as a moderate and moderating activist much in the mode of one of his later significant: mentors, our patron Saint D'Arcy McNickle.

In the summer of 1967 I visited the Southwest and spent time with Alfonso in San Juan, in First Mesa, and in Navajo country. I marveled at his store of knowledge and wide range of personal connections. Over a bottle of bourbon, I recall listening in on a long discussion of Indian affairs between Alfonso and Ed Dozier. During that trip we visited Rough Rock and witnessed the beginning of the revolution in Indian education.

I saw Alfonso a few times while he was at Princeton when I went home to visit my family in New Jersey. One time we went with my father to a serious seafood restaurant on the Jersey Shore. Alfonso, ever open to new gustatory adventures, ordered lobster.

Now, I've always wondered about the heroic first person to eat a lobster – it must have seemed like a gigantic cockroach thrown up by the sea. Alfonso stared at the lobster and the lobster stared blankly back. This courageous son of the Southwest managed to consume about half of the edible monster and had the rest boxed so that he could share it with his wife Megs, his intellectual collaborator on many anthropological projects.

In subsequent years, the Newberry became our primary meeting ground. Alfonso would come into town, contact me, set forth the agenda, and work through issues that might arise. We generally agreed about most things, but there were some rare conflicts of interest. Our yo-yo relationship would take a downward trajectory, eventually bottom out, and reverse direction and become once more ascendant. I've discovered that most of his friends at one time or another had a falling out. In my own case, the split was caused by an overestimation of the closeness of our relationship and a failure to realize that underneath the surface conviviality was a very vulnerable person who easily took offense at slight provocation. However, most of us learned that Alfonso was Alfonso, he needed space, and that prolonged rancor was not emotionally economical.

One, day last March I went to my office and was shocked to learn Alfonso had died. It was a numbing kind of shock. I didn't expect it. When I saw him last Fall, he actually looked better than he had at previous visits. He had lost some weight, was in good spirits, and was contemplating several new projects. I was asked if I wanted to go to the funeral to represent the Department. I declined, even though I knew I'd have the good company of Fred Hoxie.

I have always had mixed feelings about funeral ceremonies and eulogies to the dead – a reaction that was reinforced by the recent media-driven hysteria elicited by the dramatic deaths of [6] Princess Diana, Dodi, and their driver. I'm not sure whether my ambivalence stems from a deep-seated denial or fear of death, or, doubtless, from unresolved anger. I remember being so outraged at the vapid sentimentalities voiced at my father's funeral that I spontaneously launched into a tirade about the misrepresentations of my father's life, accomplishments, and character.

I think Alfonso shared some of my feelings about death ceremonies. He was conspicuously absent from the memorial services, held both in Santa Fe and Chicago, for his esteemed teacher and champion, Fred Eggan. A few months after Fred's death, when I was in Santa Fe assembling his papers for Regenstein Library's Special Collections, I asked Al why he didn't attend the local memorial service for Fred. He replied that he disliked such public displays of grief, that Fred was, indeed, very dear to him, and that he said good-by to him privately in Indian fashion.

Recalling Alfonso's response, the morning after learning of Alfonso's death, I retrieved some tobacco that I keep around the apartment for ceremonial purposes and retreated to my back yard. It was a raw, cold, misty, gray, March Chicago morning. I blessed the tobacco, muttered something about how sorry I was about his premature departure from this world and tossed some tobacco in the westward direction I was facing. Then I turned toward the South, offered more tobacco while saying how much I'd miss him. Next I faced the invisible rising sun and mumbled how significant and worthwhile his life had been and threw some tobacco to the east. Finally, I turned toward the blustery North. I was becoming impatient and wanted to complete this impromptu invocation lest someone spot me and wonder what the foolish old man was up to. I quickly sent some tobacco to the north, saying "so long my friend. See you soon." Almost in response to the farewell the northwestern sky suddenly brightened. I sensed somehow that Alfonso heard me and smiled down at my ceremonial message.

As Alfonso has written, death, he final rite of passage, called "releasing" by the Tewa, resolves the dualities of human life and emphasizes the unity and solidarity of the whole society and demarcates the distinction between <u>all</u> the living and the dead.

BRINGING HOME THE FIRE:
BOB THOMAS AND CHEROKEE STUDIES

Robert Knox Thomas, a.k.a. Kā.Wī, Stuart Middlestriker, GP Horsefly, and Anderson Dirtthrower, was a significant anthropologist as well as a remarkable personality.

By my count, the session at the 1996 Western Social Science Association Meetings in Reno was the fourth celebration of Bob Thomas's life since he departed this world in 1991.[1] If not in life, certainly in death, Bob is rapidly approaching the status of a cult figure, something that would bemuse him not a bit. Bob was a multiplex, as well as complex, person whose life and being touched many, both directly and obliquely. At each memorial gathering new facets of the man are revealed, new accounts about him are related, and old stories are refurbished and embellished.

Bob's sense of modern Indian issues and problems was astute and anticipatory. His first-hand knowledge of Indian cultures was astounding, ranging from Alaskan Eskimos, Niskas of northern British Columbia, the Northern Cree, to native peoples in Guatemala, the Papago (or Tohono O'odam) into whom he married, the Mesquaki, to remnant groups in the rural south and to urban Indians in Detroit and Chicago, But the Cherokees remained his first and last love. Near the end of his life he fulfilled a long held dream in bringing the Keetoowah fire from Oklahoma to North Carolina and staging a successful Green Corn Dance there. More about these events will be presented later. I'll leave it to Albert Wahrhaftig and others to comment more fully about Thomas's work in Oklahoma, particularly with regard to the Carnegie Project in Cross-cultural Education. This project was ostensibly about the renewal of Cherokee literacy but more profoundly concerned Cherokee self-determination and preparing the way for the resurgent Cherokee Nation through representative government.

Before proceeding, let me address one persistent and irrelevant question I frequently get asked: "Was Bob Thomas really a Cherokee?" I'm not sure Bob ever took the trouble to [2] become an enrolled member of the Cherokee Nation, but given the Malthusian projection, which at the present population growth rate would make half the country Cherokee in 15 generations, it doesn't much matter. Bob spoke Cherokee, thought Cherokee, embodied Cherokee values, and, most importantly, identified himself to himself and to others as a Cherokee. He claims to have grown up Cherokee.[2] He spent his youth as a wild oat sower in the Marines and elsewhere; he came into his maturity as a militant Cherokee nationalist, if not transnationalist; and later he successfully made the transition to a respected Cherokee elder. Bob Thomas can be remembered as a combination Cherokee trickster/transformer/cultural hero. Indeed, at one time or another he played all these roles with subtle aplomb.

I go back a long way with Bob. As a graduate student, I was working with the University of North Carolina project on the Eastern Cherokee, which John Gulick directed. This was a three-year study to investigate Eastern Cherokee acculturation and ultimately resulted in the monograph *Cherokee at the Crossroads* (1960), along with a narrow shelf of student theses and dissertations. Gulick's leadership of the project can best be described as reluctant,[3] and Bob was finally brought in near the end to salvage

---

1 Vine Deloria organized a memorial service for Bob at the University of Arizona shortly after his death. Sam Stanley arranged a major session at the Spring 1993 Central States Anthropological Society Meetings in Beloit, Wisconsin. And another meeting was put together by Ian McKenzie and many of Bob's Canadian admirers in British Columbia in the Fall of 1993. Future conferences are being discussed.

2 I have two unpublished autobiographical versions of Bob's Cherokee childhood. If the events didn't happen exactly as he describes them, they nevertheless have a feeling of authenticity. His accounts are certainly more convincing than Forest Tucker's *Little Tree*.

3 The first summer Gulick, a Middle Eastern specialist, lived in town looking at tourists looking at Indians; the next year he located in a small village several miles off the reservation; the third year he directed the project from Chapel Hill.

things. He spent less than a year in North Carolina from September, 1957 until June, 1958, but he was extremely productive in churning out several important papers on local Cherokee history, ethnography, and ideology, which proved decisive in Gulick's final write-up of the project. These papers were never published and remain in the project's archives at the University of North Carolina's Wilson Library.[4] The most cited of these papers, usually from second-hand sources, is entitled "Cherokee Values and World View." Here Thomas provides a highly generalized distillation of the Cherokee value system that emphasizes harmony through the avoidance of interpersonal offense and the positive attitudes toward sharing. He goes on to compare Cherokee values to nine core psychological features that George and Louise Spindler delineate in a widely circulated article [3] (1957) as generally common to American Indians. Thomas's epitomization of the Cherokee value system was transmogrified by Gulick and others into something called the "the harmony ethic" (presumably in contrast to Weber's Protestant ethic). This had the effect of overly concretizing what had been intended as a theoretical construction. Bob confided to me that he disavowed this usage, since it sounded to him too much like an oath or pledge of allegiance sworn to on a regular basis.

I first met Bob in December of 1957. He was living in a cabin in Yellow Hill. I had completed a summer in Cherokee, North Carolina and decided to spend Christmas break doing short-term fieldwork with fellow field team member Charles Holzinger of Franklin and Marshall College. My first impression of Bob Thomas is indelibly etched in my memory. He appeared almost manicuredly neat, plump, peach fuzz complected, with thinning sandy hair, uttering a nasal, teeth-clenched southern drawl that competed with a dangling pipe. With his tan Stetson hat, he struck me as resembling a Scottish Park Ranger.

We talked well into the evening, but rather than a dialogical exchange, he bombarded us with a monologue about Oklahoma Cherokees and their differences from their backwoods cousins in North Carolina. He was confident that the project might be saved by a good dose of Chicago-based social anthropological theory. His insights, as always, were acute and sophisticated. As I now realize, the major influence on his anthropological theorizing were: Edward Spicer on acculturation theory, factionalism, and enclaved communities; Robert Redfield and his conception of the "little community" and his notions of world view and ethos; and Fred Eggan's structural/functionalist synthesis and analysis of historical changes in kinship. But perhaps the most important influence was Sol Tax's insistence on listening to Indians' views of their own situation, helping them to articulate their problems, and assisting them in seeking redress for their grievances – an approach that came to be known as Action Anthropology whose implications clearly foreshadowed [4] certain contemporary theoretical concerns over agency. Holzinger and I were overwhelmed by Bob's monologic performance, and I recall that we spent much of the wee wee hours comparing notes to reconstruct what he had said.

Bob's mode of folksy discourse is playful and subtly multi-layered. As Ben Chavis noted in his presentation at Reno, Bob frequently castigated him and others in a joking manner as being "dumb as a gourd." But if others were "dumb as a gourd," Bob was "slick as a tick." Let me digress for a moment and discuss Bob's trope: "Dumb as a gourd" has a close sound correspondence to "dumb as a board," a more familiar figure of speech (and once used as a self descriptor by the Princess of Wales, Lady Di). For Cherokees, gourds were used as empty containers for a variety of purposes (viz Frank G Speck's, *The Use of Gourds among Southeastern Indians*), including phallic symbols of noses and false penises of Booger Dancers (Speck and Broom 1951: 32). So maybe Bob had other meanings in mind when he referred to people as "dumb as a gourd." Bob also once wrote to me about a "tempest in a pee pot," but I won't try to

---

4   These papers include "Report on Cherokee Social and Community Organization" (14 pp); "The Present 'Problem' of the Eastern Cherokee (35pp); "Eastern Cherokee Acculturation" (42 pp); "Cultures History of the Eastern Cherokee" (33pp); "Cherokee Values and World View" (27 pp). With the passage of time, these contemporary (1958) papers have become primary documents for a pivotal period in Eastern Cherokee history. They should be published and made accessible to a growing number of concerned scholars and to interested Cherokees.

deconstruct this tricky trope here.

Over the years, Bob and I remained in irregular contact. We had our differences that often gave rise to mild debate. Early on he accurately pegged me as a culture and personality-specialist and remained suspicious of many of that sub-field's theoretical assumptions. I, in turn, frequently questioned details of Bob's scholarship and interpretations. Nevertheless, we retained mutual respect for each other and remained fast friends until his death. I regard him as an important mentor and a continuing source of inspiration.

Some of the qualities of Bob's intellect can be discerned by some excerpts from a lengthy handwritten letter he sent me, dated August 26, 1980. I had solicited an article from him on the post-Removal Five Civilized Tribes for the presently dry-docked Southeastern volume of the Handbook of North American Indians. Bob finally came through with the help of Kenneth Fink. The [5] essay was filled with much good material, but as might be predicted, was Cherokee-centric and neglected the Creeks, Seminoles, Choctaws, and Chickasaws, I mentioned this shortcoming and made other criticisms and editorial suggestions.

I thought the paper failed to emphasize the readjustment to a new environment that the tribes underwent as they removed from the Southeast to the Indian Territory. He saw the Southern Appalachians and Western Ozarks as possessing similar ecological zones. After three pages of notes on flora, fauna, environment, and ecological history, plus two hand drawn maps. Bob felt compelled to offer credentials. Quoting from his letter (1980: 7), he modestly asserts:

As you can see, I consider myself something of an expert on ecology or human geography. It is my one talent. I had a double major on the undergraduate level, anthropology and geography. I even went with Carl Sauer one year into Sonora. But more importantly, I was early a good hunter in Oklahoma. In Arizona, I used to work with an outfit that guided hunters into the Sierra Madre of Mexico. I didn't like these urban killers of objects, but I did learn a lot about the country. In the early seventies, I lived two years, off and on, with a Cree hunting band in the Canadian Rockies. I have lived for short periods with the Dogrib out in their hunting and fishing camps in the Northwest Territories; and I even harpooned a small whale in the Arctic with the Eskimos.

With Bob it wasn't always easy to separate out what was factual from what was actual. Despite his habitual hyperbole. Bob was usually on or near the target.

Another issue of debate between us had to do with values, particularly their locus, the degree to which they were conscious, and their persistence over time. Bob writes,

I am not sure I get your point on values. It seems to me that in modern urban society it is possible to have a hiatus between "values" "taught" in the family, in a personal network of relationships and the impersonal public world of institutions and society, a structure of roles and statuses. The public world is not experiencial [sic], the self is monitored, and roles can be put on and off like a coat; then conversely, so can values from the familial world once you learn how to objectify yourself as an adult. Freud knew this only too well. So now we [6] have Ronald Reagan using what his daddy told him, in the ideal, to sock [it] to people and justify irresponsibility.

However, among tribals, since nearly all of life is personal, familial, and experiential (as Freud said about savages resembling women, children, and certain types of psychotics of his day), values are not isolatable as a "thing" from general behavior (meaning and action) and experience (the intake and change of meaning): So the questions seems to me to be – Is it true, or how true is it, that Cherokees perceive; have certain moral, philosophical premises; and a kind of being in common which is much like their ancestors of the 1700s? I suspect that most people, besides Americans, would assume that this was true and be surprised if it were not. Digression aside, am I making the point?

It is great to have a dialogue with an intellectual. There are so few left. And it is refreshing to talk in the particular with some content rather than the usual things I write (1980: 10).

I like to suppose that my critique stimulated some of this disquisition on values and other matters, but in truth it is a virtuoso performance by a gifted soloist, or as Bob might describe it, "just showin' off."

As a postscript to this remarkable letter. Bob looks ahead to future projects,

Since I have now alienated the middle class of eastern Oklahoma, Indian politicians in Canada, Lumbee Indians, and recently the Indians in the Indian education "business," I hope to expose southwest Virginia and neighboring areas of Kentucky for the frauds they are in my next article! Next I hope to do a detailed point by point comparison of the Qualla Reservation and pre-1979 Nicaragua. I think Marxist thinkers are now as conservative as their capitalist counterparts! On to the next windmill (1980: 11).

And Don Quixote rode into the sunset.

One of Bob's last major projects was an effort to restore traditional religion to the Eastern Cherokees. The Eastern Cherokee area was considered to be the holy land of Cherokee sacred geography by the culturally conservative Keetoowah followers of Red Bird Smith, and prophecy predicted a future return to the East. He felt a return of the sacred fire[5] from [7] Oklahoma would spark an increase in positive self-esteem, help combat problems associated with drug and alcohol addiction and ignite a Cherokee cultural and linguistic renewal. The manifest content of this dream goes back at least to Bob's work with the University of North Carolina project. In his 1961 article on the Redbird Smith Movement for "The Cherokee-Iroquois Symposium" (1961) Bob states that,

In North Carolina during the winter of 1957, several Cherokee became interested in reviving the old Cherokee religion. Many of them talked about this in informal groups all through the winter and spring. But the subject had not been brought up, although it was hinted at, in the formal meetings of the fullblood political organization. When I left North Carolina in June, one of the fullblood leaders said to me, "Sometime next winter we may want you to ask some of those Oklahoma chiefs to come down here and teach us all about the Fire" (1961: 165).

Bob was discussing here the deliberate and delicate mode of Cherokee decision-making.[6]

In 1960 I tape-recorded a speech to the Eastern Cherokees from Stokes Smith, youngest son of Redbird Smith and then-Chief of the Nighthawk Keetoowahs; he spoke about Cherokee religion and the

---

5 Sacred fires are central features of the Southeastern ceremonial complex. The fire can be considered an earthly incarnation of the Sun. The previous year's fire is extinguished and new fires are lit as part of the Green Corn Ceremony. The sacred fire is surrounded by powerful symbolism embedded in mythical belief and ritual practice. In a more secular context a fire represented a separate polity, or town or local grouping, The sacred fire and the accompanying socio-political structure was revived among the Western Cherokee as part of the Redbird Smith Movement or Nighthawks, a nativistic Cherokee movement that arose in reaction to the Allotment Act and the imminent dissolution of the Cherokee Nation around the beginning of the twentieth century. Bob's Arizona MA thesis (1953), which has been misappropriated by many other scholars and popularizers, remains the classic account of this movement.

6 This was traditionally true with respect to political processes operating in normal domestic, civil life under the aegis of peace chiefs. Decisions were more assertive and direct in military and other activities supervised by war chiefs.

sacred fire. I brought the tape back to Big Cove and played it to a gathering of traditionalists in Big Cove. They listened attentively, discussed the message quietly, but characteristically did nothing.

In 1979 Bob visited the Eastern Cherokee while he was doing research on the Lumbees and other unrecognized Indians in the southeast. He talked with a few elders about introducing Oklahoma-style stomp dancing; again there was cautious interest but no action. Finally in 1989, Bob returned and began to get things organized. A site was selected on Robert Blankenship's land and a ceremonial ground was laid out. The Redbird Fire was brought to Big Cove in late September of 1989 and the ground was officially inaugurated with a stomp dance. Walker Calhoun, an elder Cherokee traditionalist who still knew some Eastern Cherokee songs and dances, was appointed Chief of newly installed [8] Raven Rock Ceremonial Grounds. Walker visited Oklahoma and attended some Nighthawk stomp dances, but he soon recognized that these dances were different from those he had learned in his youth from Will West Long and others and which had been recorded by Speck and Broom in the Cherokee Dance and Drama (1951).[7]

The following year, it was decided to stage a four-day Green Corn Ceremony in Big Cove. Bob was enlisted to make the arrangements.[8] In Bob's words,

> Now, I was a little nervous about them taking on such a[n] undertaking, the first crack out of the box, but nothing would deter them, but what they wanted to have [was] that Green Corn Dance. So I offered my services and the Redbird Fire recommended that I go down to North Carolina to help them organize this big undertaking. So I went down there in June and stayed about a week with 'em. The first thing I did was to sit down with Walker Calhoun, who is the Chief there and Pat [Walker's son] who is the fire keeper, and ask them what they wanted to do. Well, to tell you the truth, they [didn't] have too much idea of what they wanted to do explicitly except to have a four-day Green Corn Dance (1990:1).

Bob set about collating various kinds of information on Green Corn, from the early accounts of Adair, Bartram, and Payne to comparative practices in Oklahoma among Cherokees and Creeks, to Will West Long's constructions as presented in Speck and Broom (1951) through recollections of some current Eastern Cherokee elders. A detailed schedule was produced, a copy of which, replete with Bob's emendations, is reproduced here [Figure I], The schedule follows the general pattern of Green Corn Ceremonies in the Eastern Woodland (cf Witthoft 1949). However, Bob established some new innovations and strategic substitutions. The significance of pipe smoking, although present in Keetoowah Green Corn Ceremonies, is less prominent among the Creeks and in traditional Eastern Cherokee practices.

Bob also instituted sweat bathing as the principal feature of the first day's activities. This apparently was intended both as a purification in place of the "going to water" ritual and as a replacement for "taking medicine," the purgative "Black Drink," which more traditionally took place, along with scratching on the [9] square ground during the third day of Green Corn.[9] An account of his travails with

---

7 Lloyd Sequoyah, an Eastern Cherokee medicine man, who accompanied me to Oklahoma in 1960, also commented on the differences between Eastern Cherokee dances, most of which focus on animals, and Oklahoma Cherokee stomp dances, which seemed to have pan-tribal, mostly Creek, derivation. Indeed, many Eastern Cherokees resent the hegemonic cultural claims of their Western kinspeople in issues of authenticity.

8 Information about the August 1990 Green Corn Dance in North Carolina comes from two reels of tape dictated by Bob Thomas to Ray Fogelson on November 22, 1990. I am deeply indebted to Jason Jackson, an advanced graduate student at Indiana University, for his careful transcription of these materials.

9 While sweat bathing was known among Southeastern Indians, it usually wasn't associated with major

establishing the sweat bath in Big Cove follows:

> So we had the sweat bath along about 4 o'clock Thursday night or early Friday morning, however you conceive of it.... And it was just as well, I thought, because you know right after that the firekeepers were going to make fire, and they were all purified before that. But anyway, before they make fire, and we started making a sweat bath about 1 o'clock and it [was difficult] getting the fire, since it was pouring down rain, and we finally got the fire started, and we then, we built the sweatlodge, and by about 3:30 or 4:00 we were in the sweatlodge, and we had a pipe smoking beforehand, and then we went into the sweatlodge. There were a couple [of] difficulties. One is the rocks weren't hot enough. Two hours of heating, in a downpour, you know, won't get your rocks too hot. Secondly, I had told those guys to get an old rug somewhere. You know, I could go buy stuff and collect stuff, but I couldn't go mooch an old rug off of somebody. I don't know most people in North Carolina that well anymore. And, of course, they hadn't got a rug, and so we had to settle for some of this plastic tent material, which lets a lot of light in. So the thing wasn't very hot and there was a lot of light come in. When you have a lot of light come in, according the theory, you know, spirits won't, aren't apt to come in and help you, as much as if you have the thing completely dark. I mean it wasn't too hot, and it wasn't too dark.
>
> Further there were a lot of ... God, that place was packed. We made a huge sweatbath. We must of had about 18 or 20 people in there, mostly young Cherokee guys, late teens and in their 20s, most of whom did not talk [Cherokee], one of the things I was really wiped out [about]. I had not realized the extent of language loss in North Carolina. And they didn't speak Cherokee and hadn't ever been in a sweatbath before.
>
> Now I have conducted sweatbaths lots of times; they asked me to conduct it, and I have some songs that were given to me just for that purpose, that is songs that I've dreamed or had come to me in vision or hallucination, however you want to think about that. And, but when you conduct it, it's hard, really emotionally draining under the best of circumstances, and difficult. The rocks weren't hot enough, and there's a lot of light in there, and these young guys felt strange. They felt strange and out of place, probably fourteen of the twenty, you know. And a boy that just ... What [10] you have to do in a sweatbath is just, is to try to build a certain kind of mood and communion among people, and [it's] very difficult to do that.

Managing the sweatbath crisis became even more tense for Bob, because

> Before that there were several girls who had come in from Oklahoma and also some North Carolina Cherokee girls, particularly about four or five of the young Calhoun women wanted to take a sweatbath for the women. So we got some. We kept the fire going, so we got some new rocks in there for them and let them go ahead. Usually when I conduct a sweatbath, I don't mix up men and women, mainly because I am not that old yet. You know, I can't keep my mind on a higher plane with naked women in the sweatlodge. But also it doesn't seem right to me either.

Clearly Bob's sense of decency was tested to the hilt in conducting mixed sweats, especially with transparent sweatlodge coverings.

---

ceremonies. Bob's activities in Canada with the Indian Ecumenical Movement, which he helped start at the Stoney Reserve, may have impressed upon him the significance of sweat baths. He certainly used sweat bathing as an adjunct to his teaching at the University of Arizona.

In Oklahoma, an arena of institutionalized gender conflict is the single pole game in which men using ball sticks and women using their hands attempt to hit a symbolic object atop a thirty foot pole with a small ball. Points are also awarded for hitting the pole above certain demarcated heights. The game is different in structure, origin, and spirit from the better-known men's two-stick ball game which involves gambling, elaborate ritual, and not-so-symbolic warfare. Bob was fearful that the ball game might get out-of-hand, so he decided to substitute a kind of soccer game in its place.[10] This event took place on the final day of the Green Corn Ceremony. In Bob's words,

> And then, I guess, long about 2 o'clock we started to play that soccer. Me and another lady, I forget her name now, were the referees. We had long switches. And boy, those kids just ate that up; they thought that was the greatest thing they had ever played. Now, but the boys were awful rough, you know. They were body blocking and tackling those girls. I finally had to stop the game and take 'em over to one side and say, "now look gentlemen, the idea of the game is just kind of symbolic of, kind of like, courting ritual. And the object of this game is to tease the girls and to devil them, not beat 'em into a pulp." So they kind of backed off a little bit, but not too much [laughs]. But anyhow the girls beat 'em. And of course, everybody wanted a second game, which is all [11] right and so we had a second game. And so they must have played for, oh, two and a half hours.

Again Bob's puritan, if not prurient, sense of decorum and sportsmanship is in evidence.

The Promethean effort to bestow the sacred fire upon the Eastern Cherokees evidently brought at least temporary enlightenment and heated excitement to the Eastern Cherokee. Only time will tell whether the fire will continue to burn and emblaze a new religious consciousness. Some final words from Bob Thomas may help clarify his intentions:

> And you know how Indians do, Ray, when ... especially Cherokees, whenever anything gets tight they turn to religion, and they want to start the fire again, thinking this is going to save their ass, the way they thought it was going to save their ass about 1900 [the period of Allotment and dissolution of the Cherokee Nation]. Now, as you know, I'm a religious man. In fact, the last time I talked to you, you called me a born-again pagan, and I guess I've always been a closet pagan. I am sure you picked that up years ago. But in 1970, when I was heavily involved in this ecumenical movement, I started to get religious. Once was because I was involved with that; the other thing was that my children were in their teens and their dad getting old. You know, as you get older, you ... most people tend to get more religious. So I guess that's what it was with me. My initial reason for getting involved in stuff with religion is that I was convinced by 1968 or so, and I am still convinced, that Indians, if we are going to get our act together, you know, it is only going to be people with religious prestige, older people, that are going to be able to do that -- develop the necessary social sanctions, set the right direction, not get sucked in by all the bullshit, that, you know, and ah, activate that community, instead of sitting there and letting all these secular programs cut the place to pieces. And after I got involved I kind of, as you know I've always had tendencies in that direction and so I was kind of looking religious. I was always a nationalist, as you probably know as well, although I never beat that drum. And so I was, guess will probably when I go back to them, get involved in helping start those fires again.

---

10 Bob claims older informants from Snowbird community near Robinsville, North Carolina had vague memories of a sacred soccer-like game. Indeed there is comparative evidence for a wide distribution of such a game. It has been recorded for Creeks; Jason Jackson has recently found evidence for its existence among the Yuchis, and it, or something like it, seems to extend to the Pueblos according to the testimony of Alfonso Ortiz (1989: 66).

Thomas

Mainly because of spiritual reasons. I do not have much hope that in Oklahoma it's going to do anything socially or culturally. We're going to have to do some other things besides just revive the fire to save our ever-loving ass. Now North Carolina is different. I think that fire can have a big impact for other reasons. One is that it will [12] be an institution not pre-empted by outsiders the way other Cherokee institutions are, either pre-empted or controlled or jacked around and used against people. And North Carolina people, except Snowbird, have a serious problem with self-confidence, as you know. This isn't true in Oklahoma, so starting those fires again are [sic] not going to give Cherokees anything more institutionally, and it's not going to make people any more self-confident, you see. And there are still social sanctions around, you know, to keep the social trouble from getting too bad. Now, you know, drinking and what-have-you, as you can see on a great many reservations ... in fact North Carolina is spectacularly free of social ills compared to most reservations, which tells you something. I'm not sure what. Well, anyhow, that's about all I'm going to say. So I'll see you next time I'm in Chicago.

I never saw my friend, Bob, in Chicago.

I last saw Bob in early June of 1991, about two weeks before his death. He was staying in a small cottage in Hulbert, Oklahoma and was attended to by his two sons, Lance and Stanley and his granddaughter. They had driven from Arizona in Bob's van. Sam Stanley had previously visited Bob in Tucson and told me what to expect. The Bob Thomas I encountered this time was suffering from the terminal stages of brain cancer. He couldn't talk; he had lost a lot of weight; his eyes had sunk back into their sockets; his thinning hair was grey. He looked to me a lot like the last photographs of Chief John Ross. He resembled a rag doll in that he couldn't sit up for long, but would slump abruptly, fast asleep. Yet there was a twinkle in his eyes, and I was pretty sure he recognized me. Communication was uncertain. Unlike the first time I met him, this time I delivered the monologue. I recalled many of the things he first introduced me to, how much of my knowledge of things Cherokee derived from him, his alerting me to the situation of the Lumbees and other unrecognized tribes, his insights into traditional native religions and the distinctiveness of Indian Christianity, his sensitivity to the excavation of Indian graves, which later led to NAGPRA and repatriation, his constant concern with problems of identity and the significance of the elders in maintaining [13] cultural continuity. He seemed to follow my living eulogy as best he could. Sustaining such an emotionally charged one-way discourse ultimately proved to be too much for me, and I took my leave into the shimmering late afternoon Oklahoma sunshine.

A few weeks later, the van headed west to Arizona, and Bob took a turn for the worst. He expired in Texas. His body was brought back to Tucson and cremated. His sons returned some of Bob's ashes to Oklahoma, where they were scattered in seven locales that he had previously selected, but the fire of Bob Thomas is not extinguished: it continues to brighten and warm the hearts of his students, friends, and colleagues. [16]

References

Carter, Forrest 1976 *The Education of Little Tree*. New York: Delacort Press/Eleanor Friede.
Gulick, John 1960 *Cherokees at the Crossroads*. Chapel Hill, NC: Institute for Research in Social Science.
Ortiz, Alfonso 1989 Some Cultural Meanings of Corn in Aboriginal North America. *Northeast Indian Quarterly*, Spring/Summer, pp. 64-73.
Speck, Frank G 1941 *Gourds of the Southeastern Indians*: A Prolegomenon on the Lagenaria Gourd in the Culture of Southeastern Indians. Boston: New England Gourd Society.
Speck, Frank G, and Leonard Broom 1951 *Cherokee Dance and Drama*. Berkeley: University of California Press,

Spindler, George D, and Louise S Spindler 1957 American Indian Personality Types and Their Sociocultural Roots. *Annals of the American Academy of Political and Social Science* 311: 147-157.

Thomas, Robert K 1953 The Origin and Development of the Redbird Smith Movement. MA Thesis, University of Arizona.

Thomas, Robert K 1961 "The Redbird Smith Movement." In *Symposium on Cherokee and Iroquois Culture*. William N Fenton and John Gulick, eds. Smithsonian Institution, Bureau of American Ethnology Bulletin 180, pp. 159-66. Washington DC: US Government Printing Office.

Thomas, Robert K 1990 Tape to Ray Fogelson on Cherokee Green Corn Dance in August of 1990 [Tape made on November 11, 1990 by Bob Thomas; transcribed by Jason Jackson, November 1994].

Witthoft, John 1949 Green Corn Ceremonials in the Eastern Woodland. *Occasional Contributions from the Museum of Anthropology* of the University of Michigan no. 13.

Figure 1 >>

Schedule for Green Corn Ceremony
August 9, 10, 11, 12, 1990

Thursday, August 9 - Gathering in day
1. eat last year's corn, beans, etc - noon
2. sweat bath medicine - 3:00 p.m.
3. pipe smoking at sweat lodge
4. sweat bath

Friday, August 10 - Getting ready day
1. make fire - before dawn
   sacrifice 7 ears of new corn given to fire keeper by old ladies from each of the seven clans –
2. fire keeper sweep grounds out from fire with new broom, then with eagle tail - late morning
3. each clan sprinkle a terrapin shell of earth on ground around fire, never ... earth on which to dance - late morning
4. each clan put new green leafy boughs on own clan arbor, select bough from a pile of boughs near grounds - early afternoon
5! Green Corn Medicine drinking at Fire 3 p.m. Peace Pipe and pipe smoking
6. Speeches - 8 or 9 p.m.
7. Stomp dance - 9 or 10 p.m.

Saturday, August 11 - Green Corn Dance day
1. go to the water - 6:00 a.m. - Gokski Smith officiating
2. Green Corn Dance - 3 or 4 p.m.   ,
3. Green Corn Feast - 6 p.m.
4. Speeches
5. Stomp dance

Sunday, August 12 - Ball play and final day
1. Cherokee soccer - 3 p.m.
2. Feast after game, eat fish soup
3. xxxxxxx
4. Speeches at Fire
5. Hand shaking in circle around Fire

MARY R HAAS AND SOUTHEASTERN ETHNOGRAPHY

Mary R Haas is justly renowned as one of America's greatest linguists. Firmly anchored in the Americanist tradition, her work emphasized field research, the collection of texts, sophisticated phonemic analysis, and the understanding of native grammars according to their own structural principles. In addition, she followed paths blazed by her mentor, Edward Sapir, in contributing to the micro- and macro-genetic classification of Native American languages and in exploring innovative facets of sociolinguistics and etymology. However, despite her singular accomplishments as a technical and theoretical linguist, Mary's small, but significant ethnographic and ethnological corpus is less well known and insufficiently appreciated. It is this body of work, in particular her South-eastern studies, that I will consider in this essay.

Before examining this work, I offer some personal reminiscences to contextualize my remarks. As a beginning student of native cultures in the Southeast, I knew of Mary's efforts to clarify the superficially simple, but actually complex, linguistic situation in the Southeast where the majority of languages were long extinct, where early word lists were scarce, and where the declining number of fluent native speakers were neglected by linguists. Mary's fieldwork during the 1930s in the wilds of Louisiana with the now prosperous, then poor, Tunicas and Koasatis, and the last Biloxi speaker, and with Natchez, Yuchi, and Muskogeans in depression-ridden Oklahoma yielded not only irreplaceable linguistic data but also valuable ethnographic observations. I recall reading with interest her classic paper "Men's and Women's Speech in Koasati" (Haas 1944), an essay that followed and went far beyond Sapir's suggestive work on gendered speech among the Yana.

However, I was most excited by Mary's paper "Creek Inter-town Relations" (Haas 1940), which is a milestone in our understanding of the dynamics of traditional Southeastern social organization. John R. Swanton's meticulous ethnohistorical work, which was reinforced by Morris E. Opler's and Alexander Spoehr's later research, established the fact that the 'town' (*i•talwa'*) or 'fire', rather than the 'tribe' or 'nation', was the effective unit of traditional Creek sociopolitical organization. These semi autonomous towns were arranged hierarchically, in terms of primary, or 'mother' towns, and satellite, or 'daughter' towns that maintained close kinship ties and usually shared the same ceremonial 'medicine'. Towns might also be connected to each other through various forms of temporary or more abiding alliances. Finally, Creek towns were [585] designated as 'White' or 'Peace' towns and 'Red' (literally, 'people of other speech') or 'War' towns. This seemed straightforward enough until one tried to assign particular towns as 'Red' or 'White', according to this political dualism. It is a testimony to Swanton's assiduousness and intellectual honesty that he recorded page after page of conflicting testimony by informants as to the 'Red' and 'White' status of particular towns: one informant might record Arbeka as a "Red" town, while another might classify it as 'White'. In short, there was little or no consensus on these matters, either from the memory of Swanton's informants or from the historical record.

Mary discovered that the dynamic determining whether a town was 'Red' or 'White' depended on the outcome of the two-stick male ball game, a ritualized form of warfare genetically related to the modem game of lacrosse (its Iroquois variant). Match games, which were a kind of total institution involving ceremonial preparations of the players, conjuring by ritual medicine men, and enthusiastic community participation through heavy wagering on the outcome, could only be contested by towns on opposite sides of the red-white duality. Most significantly, as Mary discovered, if a 'Red' town defeated a 'White' town in three or four consecutive matches, or vice versa, the defeated town was forced to change its affiliation, thereby creating an alliance and effectively putting at least a temporary end to the ritualized conflict between the two towns. Thus, the apparent contradictions in Swanton's sources became explicable.

The larger implications of Mary's discovery about Creek intertown relations continue to have relevance today in Native American Oklahoma. Separate religious communities, whether they be traditional stomp grounds, peyote groups, or Native Baptist and Methodist churches, maintain a fierce sense of their own separateness or exclusivity, but, at the same time, they are dependent on the opposition and cooperation of other such units for their viability. Alliance and antagonism stand in continuing and changing states of dialectical tension. Thus, participation of visitors is essential for a successful stomp dance, and this participation entails reciprocity. Peyote meetings are inter-tribal in scope, and visitors and converts are much desired for ego-syntonic self-justification. Similarly, Creek and Seminole Indian Baptist and Methodist churches practice a fourth Sunday rotation, whereby members of one congregation will visit another and, as they say, "help them out." While such reciprocal relations are not precisely structured in ways similar to the agonistic conflict of ball games, necessary interdependence remains constant.

I first met Mary in 1958 at the American Anthropological Association meetings in Washington, DC, where she commented on Floyd G Lounsbury's reconstruction of Iroquoian languages. She was warmly encouraging of my neophyte ethnographic work with the Eastern Cherokees. My next major interaction with her was at a planning conference in 1971 for the *Southeast* volume of the Smithsonian Institution's *Handbook of North American Indians*. The sessions were productive in shaping a basic outline for the volume and in suggesting [587] potential authors for articles. Mary agreed to write a general overview of Southeastern linguistic relationships; the unpublished draft of this article, which was one of the few to arrive promptly, was a simplified version of the classification she had published elsewhere (Haas 1971, 1973). The most memorable event during the planning conference was a late night party during which Mary, John Witthoft, Bob Thomas, Joe Caldwell, Bill Sturtevant, and myself took turns telling stories about our experiences working with Southeastern Indians. Somehow, we got fixated on ghost stories, and this group of scholars, many of whom scarcely knew each other previously, sat transfixed late into the night.

Our paths crossed again in 1975-76, when Mary was a Visiting Professor at Northwestern University. During this period, Paul Friedrich, Michael Silver-stein, and I managed to convince our colleagues in Anthropology and in Linguistics at the University of Chicago to nominate her for an honorary degree. The awarding of the honorary PhD by Chicago seemed an appropriate act of belated closure, since she had received her MA at Chicago in 1931 before deserting to Yale with Sapir. Mary was deeply impressed by the graduation ceremony and elated by the later celebration in her honor.

Our next opportunity for extended contact came in 1977, when we were both visiting professors at the University of California at San Diego. I attended a seminar that she and Margaret Langdon offered on the history of American Indian linguistics. I learned a great deal, including the fact that the primitive accents in my "pre-post-Mooney" orthographies of Cherokee probably represented tones. But, more important for my concerns was the chance to compare ethnographic notes with Mary on a frequent basis. Her memory for detail was astounding. Her stories of working with Watt Sam, the last Natchez speaker, or her description of the almost medieval social structure of Avery Island, Louisiana, where Tunicas picked peppers for the McIlhenny Tabasco empire, remain vivid.

While most of Mary's early Southeastern work was focused on salvage linguistics, the Penrose Grant that she received from the American Philosophical Society in 1938-39, with the support of Franz Boas, was directed to the history and ceremonialism of Creek towns. The aforementioned "Creek Inter-town Relations" (Haas 1940) and "Men and Women's Speech in Koasati" (Haas 1944) were the principal published works to emerge from this project, but much more data and important drafts of articles remain unpublished, Mary sent me copies of two such articles that deserve to see the light of published day.

One manuscript is an important forty-seven page paper titled "The Creek Inter-town Ball Game" that goes far beyond the published article "Creek Inter-town Relations" (Haas 1940) in supplying ritual detail pertaining to ball game ceremonialism, and its relation to war. Mary collected most of her information from elders from Cussetah, Hillabee, Eufaula, and Arbeka. She situated the major match games within the larger Creek ceremonial cycle, placing them after [588] the Green Corn Dance, which included the third annual taking of medicine and fasting, and after the midsummer annual fish fry. The intricate events preceding the game are described in careful detail: the differentiated personnel; the delicate negotiations involved in arranging a game; the roles of the medicine men, of women dancers, of various attendants, and of score keepers; the process of selecting players for designated positions; the taking of medicine; the preparation of equipment; the march to the ball field; the process of wagering; and the ritual speeches. The game itself is almost an anticlimactic footnote to these elaborate preparatory activities. Mary's rich account recognizes variation in procedure for different towns, and such data are properly cited when available. The paper takes us well beyond Swanton's useful, but somewhat mechanical, description of the Creek ball game and allows us to make closer comparisons with Choctaw and Cherokee ball games, as well as with the ball games of other, more distant tribes. Unfortunately, the account stops with the end of the game and fails to consider important postgame phenomena.

A second unpublished paper that Mary shared with me is the remarkable "Autobiography of a Creek Indian Woman." This document was collected in summer 1940 from a forty-two-year-old woman with the pseudonym of Lucy Gaines Scott. This sixty-eight-page text was recorded in English and is framed by a lengthy introduction that highlights some of the major themes and by extensive footnotes that explain and expand statements in the text. The document is divided into three major segments, each of which reveals valuable personal and ethnographic data. For instance, in the section on early childhood, we encounter Lucy's respectful fear of certain elders. Also, there is a charming account of feeding young fawns and domesticating individual deer (a phenomenon, to my knowledge, only recorded elsewhere for the Tunica, also by Haas [1950:171]). The long section on boarding school anticipates many recent, retrospective accounts by emphasizing the harshness and the regimentation, and also the development of various forms of student resistance, including "talking back."

The section on marriage and childbearing offers insight into the stresses brought about by changing balances of gender complementarity, wherein women refused to deliver their babies outside the house, as was the ancient practice, and where fathers were not supposed to touch their offspring until they were four years old (which would assure close bonding to the mother and social distance from the father, as was appropriate in a matrifocal, if no longer extended matrilocal, family). A dramatic theme that recurs throughout the account concerns illness and death. Contestation over the appropriate treatment of illness is waged between traditional medicine and white doctors and hospitalization. The account unfortunately ends abruptly, as Lucy recounts the birth of her seventh child. At that point, Mary is forced to leave the field on short notice and is unable to return (with the advent of World War II and her recruitment to the national war effort), although there is some later correspondence [589] between Lucy and Mary. In a brief epilogue, Mary appends some notes on traditional theories of disease causation, especially with regard to the power of diviners ("prophets"), sorcerers, and the elusive "little people."

Life history material for this critical period in Creek history is scarce, particularly for women. Mary was well ahead of her times in collecting such a text. Her recently deceased teacher, Sapir, would have applauded Mary's efforts.

To conclude, Mary Haas was trained as an anthropological linguist, and her research milieu was the field. Fieldwork naturally entailed close relationships with informants and careful ethnographic observation and inquiry, as well as the elicitation of linguistic material. Mary proved an astute ethnographer as well as a gifted linguist. The works discussed here encompass only a small, but significant, part of her ethnographic legacy. She was also knowledgeable about kinship systems and terminology (see Haas [1939] "Natchez and Chitimacha Clans and Kinship Terminology"; about religion (see her [1942] brief essay "The Solar Deity of the Tunica"), and about myths and folktales – and even material culture was not outside her purview (see her notes [Haas 1941] on the Creek use of gourds in Frank G. Speck's *Gourds of the Southeastern Indians*).

One wonders how much additional precious ethnographic data awaits archival excavation in Mary's extensive notes and files that have recently been deposited in the American Philosophical Society.

References

Haas, Mary R.
- 1939   Natchez and Chitimacha Clans and Kinship Terminology. *American Anthropologist* 41:597-610.
- 1940   Creek Inter-town Relations. *American Anthropologist* 42:479-89.
- 1941   Notes on the Economic Uses of Gourds among the Creeks. *In Gourds of the Southeastern Indians: A Prolegomenon on the Lagenaria Gourd in the Culture of the Southeastern Indians*, by Frank G. Speck, 89-91. Boston: The New England Gourd Society.
- 1942   The Solar Deity of the Tunica. *Papers of the Michigan Academy of Science, Arts, and Letters* 28: 531-35.
- 1944   Men's and Women's Speech in Koasati. *Language* 20: 142-49.
- 1950   *Tunica Texts*. University of California Publications in Linguistics 6: 1-174. Berkeley and Los Angeles: University of California Press.
- 1971   Southeastern Indian Linguistics. In *Red, White, and Black: Symposium on Indians in the Old South*: 44-54, edited by Charles M Hudson. Southern Anthropological Society Proceedings 5. Athens, GA: Southern Anthropological Society.
- 1973   The Southeast. *In Current Trends in Linguistics*. Vol 10, Linguistics in North America (pt. 2), edited by Thomas A Sebeok, 1210-49. The Hague: Mouton.

RAYMOND DEMALLIE

It is a pleasure to be grandfathered into this excellent assemblage of essays honoring Professor Raymond J DeMallie, a practitioner extraordinaire of the fine art of ethnohistory.

First, I sadly note that the term "Festschrift" seems to be in disrepute. Publishers may fear dismal sales for volumes put into that category, what they suspect to be collections of perfunctory, pedestrian papers that my former University of Washington colleague Melville Jacobs used to file under the category "Travel Money," referring to slight meeting presentations never destined to see the light of published day. All one had to do was smear on a dash of hagiography praising the honoree and, as the logic goes, one had a ready Festschrift article. However, as I scan my library shelves, I find that Festschriften done right are an underappreciated academic genre. Among more memorable contributions, I can recall Malinowski's piece on Melanesian material culture for the C.G Seligmann Festschrift (Evans-Pritchard 1934); Julian Steward's essay on the economic basis of bands for the Kroeber volume (Lowie 1936); A. Irving Hallowell's now classic article on Ojibwa ontology, which first appeared in a volume in honor of Paul Radin (Diamond 1960); Meyer Fortes's significant study of time and social structure among the Ashanti, which was published in a Festschrift for Radcliffe Brown (1963 [1949]); John Goggin and William Sturtevant's account of the Calusa, included in the volume honoring George Peter Murdock (Goodenough 1964); Levi-Strauss's exploration of the sex of the stars, found in the Jakobson Festschrift (1967); and many others. Festschriften often liberate untapped sources of creative energy and passionate scholarship. Such, I feel, is the case with the contributions to the present volume.

These essays have gone through several drafts and make important theoretical points. Sebastian Felix Braun deserves special credit for organizing and editing these papers in such a fashion that they form a coherent whole. Together the authors of these essays advance the field of ethnohistory in significant new directions, while duly acknowledging the positive influence of Ray DeMallie. [223]

Sebastian invited me to present an epilogue to this volume. I always imagined that an epilogue was produced by the union of two or more dialogues by intercourse or, perhaps better, by stimulating generative discourse – what New Millennium people might call sexting. But, after checking my dictionary, I find that epilogue means a closing section of a novel, play, or a speech sometimes delivered as poetry by one of the actors after the drama's conclusion. Rather than systematically commenting on each chapter, my epilogue is organized around three interrelated themes that emerge from my reading of the interdigitated individual contributions.

The first of these themes revolves around the person of Ray DeMallie. While all authors pay tribute to Ray's inspirational mentorship and his rigorous and vigorous humanism, it is David Miller who offers a detailed overview of Ray's career development and achievements. David diligently searched the documentary record and conducted direct interviews with Ray; he also makes use of his own cogent insights while a student at Indiana and his experiences as an active fieldworker in the northern plains. He presents valuable data on the early influences that led DeMallie to become a scholar of Native North America. David senses that Ray was something of a "straight arrow," if not an antiquarian, before he became an anthropologist. This coincides with my first impressions of Ray as an undergraduate when I arrived at Chicago in 1965. He seemed energetic, archivally constricted, with a clear agenda to study Lakota kinship objectively in a straightforward structural-functional fashion.

I recently discovered a delightful autobiographical fragment about John Andrew Rice, the genius behind the revolutionary education experiment, Black Mountain College:

> While he was an infant he absorbed knowledge taking it in through his tissues, without thought or care. Then in boyhood, he became a collector of birds' eggs, stamps, tobacco tags, baseball averages, dates – anything that can be arranged in series. But if he is to become a man – some do – he grows tired of counting and collecting and a terrifying thing happens: he ceases to be a

scientist; he begins to ask, "What does it mean?" and with the coming of this question comes the first step into manhood. To know is not enough [cited in Katherine C Reynolds 1998: 22].

Ray's intellectual Journey seemed to reach a similar juncture. He was well prepared for a sheltered career as a secluded ethnological scientist sifting [224] through endless documents and artifacts. The wonderful Margaret Blaker had already dusted off J. Owen Dorsey's desk should Ray seek permanent refuge at the Smithsonian. However, such was not to be.

At Chicago we readily accepted a slightly revised version of Ray's exceptional BA paper as the equivalent of a master's thesis, but we insisted that he do fieldwork for his PhD. Although he had previously made some brief excursions into the northern plains, Ray was a bit nervous about venturing into the field for an extended period. Some of his hesitation arose because of the recent condemnation of anthropologists by Vine Deloria, Jr. (1988). Among the Sioux, Ray's reticence and nonthreatening demeanor served him well, and he made a rapid and successful adjustment to fieldwork. I recall receiving a letter from him asking, "Where are the hostile Sioux? Everyone's so nice" (or words to that effect).

In his usual assiduous way, Ray collected a voluminous amount of valuable field data that supplemented and amplified his understanding of Lakota social structure from the literature. More importantly he began to view kinship relations from a Native perspective and to empathize with the Lakota's struggle to cope with the impinging modern world while attempting to preserve their traditions. Sometimes these conflicts bore bitter fruit. He was deeply depressed by the suicide of a Lakota youth whom he had befriended. Ray's objective, empirical approach to anthropology began to take a more subjective, humanistic turn as a result of his immersion in the field.

Miller also notes that the emergence of symbolic anthropology at the University of Chicago coincided with Ray's brief tenure as a graduate student. (I emphasize "brief," because Ray holds the modern record at Chicago for speed in completing his PhD, finishing in just over two years.) While not yet fully exfoliated, symbolic anthropology was already strongly represented in the department by David Schneider and Clifford Geertz, both of whom were influenced by the theoretical paradigm of Talcott Parsons. Schneider's approach, while considering culture to be "a system of symbols and meanings," seems in retrospect more closely akin to Ruth Benedict's notions of cultural configurations as abstracted summarizations of a society's values and ethos. Geertz attended more to Weberian and philosophical ideas about meaning, though couched in Native terms and bolstered by extensive field data. Later, Victor Turner and Terry Turner joined the faculty, followed soon thereafter by Nancy Munn; each offered their own versions of symbolic anthropology as ultimately derived from French sociology and British social anthropology. I remained faithful to implicit Boasian approaches to symbolism, as well as drawing inspiration from Freudian dreamwork (actually my published undergraduate paper involved an experimental study of sexual symbolism as aroused by music).

DeMallie was enthusiastic about Schneider's cultural analysis of kinship systems and hoped to combine it with Fred Eggan's more formal synthesis of [225] historical and structural-functional analysis to gain a more comprehensive understanding of Sioux kinship. Unfortunately, Ray was rebuffed by Schneider who didn't regard him as a very promising student, one, he felt, who was too tied to Eggan's and Tax's teachings. Schneider's misjudgment was dramatically exposed years later when Ray gave a sparkling presentation on the cultural dimensions of Lakota kinship at the departmental Monday seminar;
Schneider belatedly embraced him as a long-lost disciple, but it was too late.

Miller ably documents the development of Ray's close association with Vine Deloria, Jr. The 1970 American Anthropological Association meeting in San Diego was, indeed, a pivotal moment in their relationship. Ray was well prepared for the encounter by having already worked on language with Vine's father, Vine Deloria, Sr, and by having made the acquaintance of two important women relatives: Vine Jr's aunt Ella Deloria and his cousin, anthropologist Bea Medicine. Despite these personal connections and his recent fieldwork at Cheyenne River, Vine didn't see much practical value in Ray's proposed research. Nevertheless, this and subsequent encounters quickly became more cordial. Ray's work on

Sioux economic development for Sam Stanley's project at the Smithsonian may have helped change Vine's estimation of Ray's relevance; Stanley was a close confidant of Vine's. Later, Ray's archival skills made him a valuable consultant for Vine's work on treaties and federal law. However, at base, I think it was their shared interests in issues of Native spirituality that really solidified the relationship. They remained close friends until Vine's death.

Miller's accurate and informative account, nevertheless, inevitably misses some influential unwritten and unspoken factors in the unfolding of DeMallie's career. It is important to note that Ray was an only child and his relations with his parents were very close. After receiving his doctorate, I was invited to join him and his parents for a celebratory dinner at Cafe Bohemia, a wild game restaurant. His parents took extreme pride in Ray's accomplishments and the evening took on special meaning. I not only sensed mutual affection, but also a lack of generational distance. Ray was clearly a coequal member of this small, closely knit family. Ray's father died a few short years after this memorable event, and his warm, supportive mother succumbed to cancer soon thereafter. Ray was painfully distraught over the sudden disintegration of his family. A long period of private mourning and loneliness was only partially mitigated by intense work and the solace of personal friendships.

The period after Ray received his PhD in December of 1971 was particularly decisive for his subsequent career. He continued his productive postdoctoral work at the Smithsonian. If he wanted to, he might have remained there indefinitely, since he was, so to speak, "to the manor [or castle] born." He would have enjoyed a secure and successful life as a Smithsonian scientist. But the Smithsonian, for all its glorious reputation, had become an [226] increasingly stodgy, bureaucratic, and conservative research center. The abiding "natural history" approach eschewed experimentalism and cutting-edge theory. Instead, Ray accepted an assistant professorship at the University of Wyoming in 1972. Teaching and being on the other side of the academic firing lines were new challenges, since in those days, Chicago provided few opportunities for graduate students as teaching assistants.

Ray's initial teaching experience at Wyoming was positive, and he enjoyed the lifestyle of Laramie, but when the call came from Indiana University, he was ready to move on. Indiana seemed a perfect fit, with its rich tradition of Native American, linguistic, and folkloric studies, and as the original home of the fledgling subfield of ethnohistory, toward which Ray's attention was increasingly drawn. Among others at Indiana, Carl Voegelin proved a valued friend and mentor. Ray also developed close friendships with some of the younger faculty members, but he felt slightly alienated from many of his senior colleagues who provided the department with a strong Africanist orientation. During his first few years at Indiana, Ray spent much time away from campus pursuing research in Washington and at other archival sites and in the field. He once complained to me that he had trouble attracting graduate students. I responded by saying something to the effect that if he spent more time at home, they would come. The contributors to this volume and many others not included bear testimony to the accuracy of my prediction. Ray's close relationships with his students are based on mutual respect and loyalty. He treats students as colleagues and frequently accompanies them into the field, as well as coauthoring papers with them. As Paula Wagoner points out, the American Indian Studies Research Institute (AISRI) that he founded on campus became a beehive of activity and a literal community of scholars, Indiana graduate students, and visitors and others brought in for special expertise.

Ray and I engaged in an informal exchange system in which I sent to Bloomington some promising graduates of our college and MA program: Dennis Kristoferson, Kristen Alten, and Meredith Johnson come to mind. Chicago also sent some advanced graduate students for additional training. I am reminded here of the late Sharon Stephens, Tony Seeger, Jeff Anderson, and two contributors to this volume, Ray Bucko and David Dinwoodie. In return, I had the good fortune of working, however briefly, with Indiana students interested in the Southeast; these included Max White, Wyman Kirk, Matthew Bradley, and most especially another contributor, Jason Jackson. Without Jason's later crucial support, the *Southeastern Handbook of North American Indians* would never have been completed. But Ray and I also ran into discouraging delays, organizational obstacles, and editorial incompetence in completing our respective handbooks. The final, in some ways compromised products reflect the decline in the formerly high standards of the Smithsonian. [227]

The vital presence of Douglas Parks at Indiana deserves special mention. Ray and Doug continue to be a dynamic research team with complementary, yet overlapping interests in ethnology and linguistics, in both the Northern and Southern Plains, and in Siouan- and Caddoan-speaking peoples. Both are prodigious library scholars and skilled fieldworkers who are committed to giving back to the communities they study. Their interests intersect in the elicitation, collection, transcription, translation, and interpretation of Native texts. While they maintain their individual scholarly identities, they are constructive critics of each other's work. Doug's arrival in Bloomington also seemed to encourage Ray's move toward a more humanistically oriented anthropology.

Namings

STRANGERS TO RELATIVES
Commentary

Over three years ago, the dean of social sciences at the University of Chicago asked me to serve on a committee for research on human subjects. I wrote him a rhetorical letter declining the invitation. I explained that in anthropology we didn't have human subjects (or, for that matter, human objects); if anything we were the subjects, or more scientistically, the dependent variables. Field research is only conducted with the approval and forbearance of the people "subjected" to the anthropologic gaze. What had once been an expected rite of passage in the training of an anthropologist has now become more of a privilege, as anthropologists increasingly retreat to the library or the navel-gazing safety of self-reflective study of their own society or closely related Western societies. I tried to convince the dean that the notion of human subjects was an inappropriate borrowing from the medical, biological, and psychological sciences. Anthropology, despite its intermittent claims to being a positivistic science, seems less wedded to the *naturwissenschaften* and more allied to the human sciences, the *geisteswissenschaften.*

The dean said he appreciated the substance of my letter, but he insisted that I serve on the committee anyway, since federal granting agencies were requiring stricter reviews of research projects. I have learned a few things since being coerced to join this committee. The criteria for informed consent are almost as vague and slippery as the vaunted anthropological method of participant observation, a kind of Caesarian triad – *veni, vidi, velcro* (I came, I saw, I stuck around). [244]

Generally, anthropological proposals seek informant (or consultant, to be euphemistically correct) anonymity. However, a common source of contention involves the ultimate disposition of data. Do they belong to the anthropologist to whom the data were voluntarily given or acquired through purchase, or are these materials the intellectual property of tribal groups or individuals, not to be publicly disclosed without official approval?

Many of the issues regarding "human subjects" are directly and indirectly relevant to this unique collection of papers concerning the adoption and naming of anthropologists by Native Americans. As Sergei Kan points out in his introduction to this volume, adoption is a well established pattern, with many variants, that goes far back in the history of most Native American groups. Anthropologists had many predecessors as adoptees. Intra-group adoptions were common in most groups, reaching something of an apogee in the Arctic, as Ann Fienup-Riordan (chapter 10) and others document. Native adoption of captives individually or collectively was undoubtedly common long before the coming of Europeans. However, pressures occasioned by direct and indirect contact with Euro-Americans surely intensified adoption practices.

The advance guard of explorers, soldiers, traders, and missionaries were frequently given Indian names for purposes of reference as well as address. These indexical names often took the form of nicknames based on perceived peculiarities and distinctive identity markers; often these names were satirical and derisive. The idiom of kinship might also be invoked to express respect or degrees of closeness without any implication of formal or informal adoption. However, many times strangers were adopted by individuals and families for economic and political advantage or as a result of intermarriage and the birth of offspring.

Important proto-anthropologists were often adopted or intermarried into tribal societies and gained access to information denied more transitory observers. Such figures as James Adair, Mary Jemison, Louis Le Clerc Milford, John Heckewelder, John Dunn Hunter, Benjamin Arnsbard, and Henry Rowe Schoolcraft come readily to mind. As Elisabeth Tooker documents in her interesting essay, Lewis Henry Morgan requested that the Seneca formally adopt and provide names for him and three of his colleagues in their fraternal Grand [245] Order of the Iroquois. Morgan used his personal contacts with the Parker family and considered adoption almost as something owed him for services rendered. The motives of the Senecas in complying with his request are unclear. On the surface, the Senecas looked forward to the feast that Morgan and his associates promised to provide. On another level, the Senecas were facing hard times and wished to present a favorable and sympathetic image to their white neighbors. Morgan seemed a suitable person to propagate such positive publicity. Retrospectively, Morgan's grandiose belief that his fraternal order would actually replace the venerable League of the Iroquois and keep alive its traditions may have seemed plausible at that moment. However, the League endured, while Morgans Grand Order soon collapsed. Nevertheless, Morgan continued actively to support Iroquois causes throughout his life; but his adoption proved mostly honorary, as he didn't participate in ceremonies or otherwise engage in Seneca life.

William Fenton's adoption by the Seneca almost a century after Morgan was a gradual process driven by several generations of friendship between the Fenton family and the Snow family. The Snow family and relatives were his hosts, principal sources of information, and entry into the community when Fenton began fieldwork in the early 1930s. Although the Senecas already were suspicious of meddling anthropologists, Fenton's seriousness of purpose, respect for traditions, and eagerness to participate in religious "doin's" won the community over. Adoption for the Senecas seems to be based more on clanship than kinship; there was considerable discussion as to which clan or lineage would claim the young ethnographer. Part of the problem also involved the finite economy of available names. Eventually he was adopted into the Hawk clan and given the name He-lost-a-bet, the boyhood name of his sponsor, Jonas Snow.

Fenton's rich and detailed account of the adoption process is, in itself, a valuable contribution to Iroquois studies. The circulation of names among the Iroquois is epitomized in the names and titles of the hereditary chiefs of the League. These names have an existence of their own that transcends the life of a particular incumbent. Because names must be available for reassignment, the Iroquois seem chary about adopting outsiders. As Tooker notes, the adoption of Morgan and his fraternity brothers took place during a time of cultural crisis for the Iroquois; Fenton was only adopted because of transgenerational [246] family ties and after considerable exposure to the community. The Iroquois are more likely to open their society and share cultural knowledge with outsiders during these times of crisis. This appears to have been the case in Morgan's time and in the late i9th and early 20th century when John Gibson and other ritual specialists recited sacred texts to Hewitt and Goldenweiser (see Kimura 1998); Fenton's adoption took place while the effects of the Great Depression were still rampant.

Michael Harkin's analysis of Northwest Coast patterns of adoption picks up a theme implicit in many of the other essays in this volume: that is, adoption as a means of socialization and control of the alien other as a way to reduce ambiguity and reassert structure. In Maussian terms, the bestowal of a name and a place in the social structure transforms an unconnected individual into a social person or, in the assumption of a ranked title, a personage. At once the society is augmented and renewed by this incorporation, or native colonization, if you will. The new title bearer is entitled to certain privileges and bodies of knowledge adhering to the title. There is a compromise between the internal individual identity and the more enduring external one, often personified in a characteristic mask. Harkin relates naming to cycles of birth and rebirth both with regard to the individual undergoing the transformation and the reincarnation of names or titles, which "have life of their own," although they may have been dormant for many years. The assumption of important titles requires public celebration, feasting, and gift exchange.

Harkin makes an interesting comment on the associations between ethnonyms and personal names. Collective and individual names are frequently constructed by Euro-Americans on the basis of personal characteristics, much like nicknames; Native terms for Euro-Americans often are constructed in similar fashion (see Alexander Chamberlain [1911] for a compilation of Native American names for Euro-Americans).

The adoption of anthropology's totemic ancestor, Franz Boas, by the Kwakwaka'wakw brings to light some new dimensions to naming processes. Harkin notes how Boas at different times provides alternate glosses on the name he was accorded, *Heiltsakuls*. First he mistakenly renders it as "the silent one," and later he more accurately translates it as "the one who says the right thing." About the same time that Boas was engaged in his fieldwork, Sigmund Freud was demonstrating how paraplexes or "slips of the tongue" were not accidental but determined, and in most instances overdetermined by psychic processes. Perhaps "the silent one" represented Boas's idealized perception of himself as the neutral observer, the nonintervening objective scientist. Or maybe, as Harkin implies, the mistranslation was an overdetermined Native gloss intending to silence Boas and ensure that he wouldn't publicly broadcast the ceremonial secrets they were about to reveal to him. Many things are in a name.

The theme of secrecy continues in Harkin's revealing discussion of Thomas McIlwraith's exemplary ethnographic fieldwork among the Bella Coola {Nuuhaalk}. Again, adoption and naming are deployed as tribal defense mechanisms to control an investigator who was becoming privy to esoteric knowledge. Indeed, the effort at control and recognition of hierarchical status extended to Edward Sapir, McIlwraith's sponsor and superior, who also received a name, thus linking a remote Northwest Coast fishing fiord with the Canadian national seat of power in Ottawa.

These Northwest Coast adoptions presented by Harkin may represent metaphoric exocannibalism, or less atrociously reflect David Riesman's principle of refection by partial incorporation. The marginality of the anthropological stranger is only temporarily overcome by fieldwork adoption, and with few exceptions the anthropologist is ultimately "redigested" and reassimilated into the academic community.

For Mary Black-Rogers, adoption is more than a temporary form of mutual adjustment to the ambiguities of fieldwork. She adopts the reportorial mode of "who, where, when, how, and why" to explicate her adoption among the Round Lake Ojibwas ~ Crees. The adoption was unsought by Black-Rogers, unmarked by any formal ritual, and only recognized when her adoptive mother, Meme, came to greet her new son-in-law, Mary's husband, the late Ed Rogers. Memo's unilateral move to adopt Black-Rogers appeared motivated by a desire to replace a daughter, also named Mary, who had died in infancy. Black-Rogers initially failed to acknowledge her adoption, wishing to preserve her anthropological objectivity and autonomy in the community. Her avoidance and ambivalence about her adoption reflected a strenuous effort to avoid the overrated anthropological sin of "going native."

The full significance of Black-Rogers s adoptive relationship deepened over the years through ongoing correspondence, regular trips to [248] Round Lake, and visits by her Indian relatives to California and Toronto. Mary takes her kinship obligations seriously. For too many researchers, adoption becomes a manipulative field technique or a too soon forgotten romantic interlude rather than an abiding relationship of affection and trust; it's not surprising that many anthropologists are held in contempt by Native Americans for whom such relationships are far from "fictive." The death of Ed Rogers and his subsequent burial at Round Lake testify to the strength of the relationship that the Rogers have with their relatives. I know of only one other anthropologist, James GE Smith, not co-incidentally a close friend of Ed and Mary, who was also buried with his adoptive people, the Lubicon Lake Crees.

Mary Black-Rogers raises important theoretical issues in trying to distinguish adoption from fosterage. Northern Algonquians make some terminological distinctions between "raising someone" and full adoption as kin, but the sharp-edged differences get smoothed out in practice. She suggests the topic of fosterage needs more investigation.

Most anthropologists experience tension between trying to be objective scientists while at the same time recognizing the profoundly humanistic aspects of their work. For Mary Black-Rogers this entailed a partial surrender of the sharply focused "white room/black box" character of her early research in favor of a more affective tone, a move from dispassionate distance to passionate proximity. Nevertheless, through it all, Black-Rogers manages to remain a rigorous empiricist.

Bill and Maria Powers exemplify the virtues of long-term field-work, replete with its many obligations, minor vexations, and occasional conflict with anthropologic endeavors. They point up an important Lakota distinction between naming and adoption. Naming can entail the creation of a new name based on physical features or idiosyncrasies of the individual being named. Names can also be transferred from living persons or the deceased. If a living person bestows his or her name to someone else, he or she loses the use of that name; this is similar to the Iroquois practice discussed by Fenton.

Namings

Among the Lakotas, naming is not the same as adoption, although the two events often coincide. Adoption may be informally based on "selection" and unmarked by ceremony, or it may entail a highly formalized ritual ("making a relative") involving many participants and [249] much gift exchange. Not only were the Powers adopted (twice each) and given names, but their two sons were similarly incorporated into the local kin group. As the Powers and other contributors assert, naming and adoption constitute social personhood and specify the necessity for knowledge of appropriate kin term usage and proper behavior. Their long exposure to the field and plural adoptions place the Powers in a complex web of kinship that allows alternate paths to denning relationships such that they can be active players in the system. Indeed, in good Lakota fashion, Bill and Maria Powers "know who they are; know what they are; and know where they come from."

Anne Straus's cogent essay on Northern Cheyenne adoption makes several points relevant to our discussion. Adoption of non-Indian others, including anthropologists, almost never involves official enrollment in the tribe. Such a legal status would entail important citizenship prerogatives: for example, voting in tribal elections, access to special treaty rights, and other exclusive benefits vis-à-vis federal, state, and local governments. However, this does not make adoption any less meaningful or emotionally charged for the adopted anthropologist. Straus mentions that most anthropologists working with contemporary Native Americans are conflicted over their scholarly intentions and their share of collective guilt over past and present mistreatment of Indians by members of the "dominant culture," including exploitative anthropologists. Being adopted, being "selected" in the Lakota sense, binds some of this anxiety and self-doubt about moral worthiness in the eyes of others.

Straus's own adoption by Josephine Sootkis came as a surprise when she was inferentially addressed as daughter. While skeptical of those who immediately experience adoption as a life-defining moment, Straus can retrospectively appreciate the profound and abiding changes that the adoption made in her own life. She has remained a loyal and dutiful daughter and sibling in her adopted family, and her own family has been affected in varying degrees by her adoption. She notes, as do others, that the adoption opens up possibilities for acquiring cultural knowledge through adopted kin while simultaneously limiting access to perspectives from other local families and sectors of the reservation community.

Anne Straus has subsequently established self-initiated kinship relations with members of the Chicago Indian community. Rather than [250] representing a self-indulgent kind of double (or triple) dipping into the adoptive pool, these adoptions may better reflect her own bilocality and identification with multiple communities. She concludes by reminding us that adoption should not be regarded as a trophy of acceptance or a sine qua non for successful anthropological fieldwork.

Jay Miller goes Anne Straus one better by receiving four names from four very different Native American groups. One is reminded of Paul Radin's account of the overachieving Ojibwa boy who undertook multiple vision quests and obtained excessive spiritual power, which led to his self-destruction. Miller doesn't self-destruct or suffer identity diffusion; each situation he describes is distinctive and instructive. Miller's first adoption among the Delawares seems to have been carefully programmed by his benefactor, the late Nora Dean. While his adoption is publicly celebrated, his new name remains private, as is customary in Delaware tradition. His Tsimshian adoption resembles a mutually agreed upon defense pact to protect against Jay's awkwardness and orotund improprieties. As such, it represented a responsibility assumed by his newly acquired kin, and it had the effect of constraining his fieldwork. He was not formally adopted by any members of the Federated Tribes on the Colville Reservation; rather, in a manner of treatment similar to other unattached outsiders residing among them, in particular the Jesuit missionaries, the elders took general responsibility for his well-being in the absence of other family.

I witnessed Miller's acquisition of a Muskogee name and also received a name myself on the same occasion. A name legitimizes membership in the local square ground or town, but provides no legal claim to tribal membership, nor does it secure a position in the kinship or clanship system. It might best be regarded as a ceremonial name limited to participation in square ground rites. The name itself was chosen by officials at the square ground on the basis of information gleaned from a brief interview and behavioral observation, an interesting instance of ethno-ethnology.

I also was present when Jay Miller received his Tewa name during a conference at the Newberry Library. He was rewarded with a name by a Tewa musician who appreciated Jay's kindnesses. The name was more than a singular gift of thanks, since the relationship was reactivated on a subsequent visit Jay made to San Juan Pueblo.

It is interesting to note that among the Coast Salish with whom Miller had experienced some of his most intense scholarly and legal advocacy involvement, he was neither named nor adopted. The occasional use of kinship terms was more a simplified form of address than terms of reference implying inclusion within the group. Thus adoption and naming are not a necessary outcome of long-term productive fieldwork and service to the host community.

Tim Buckley's paper on Yurok "In-laws and Outlaws" challenges us to rethink adoption as a mere form of kinship extension. He presents a four-generational account beginning with the efforts of Captain Spott to improve his status by obtaining wealth and traditional spiritual knowledge. Lacking an heir to inherit this esoteric knowledge, the Captain adopted his nephew (his sister's son) as his successor. The adopted nephew, Robert Frank, became Robert Spott and referred to the Captain as his father. Robert Spott underwent rigorous training and developed into a religious virtuoso. Because of his religious calling and sexual orientation, Robert Spott never married and chose to adopt a spiritually gifted white youth named Harry Roberts. Harry absorbed much Yurok esoteric knowledge, but he left the area and spent most of his adult life in San Francisco, where he held a variety of jobs and had several marriages. As an old man, Harry returned to the Yuroks to live out his days. He was estranged from his sons, and another young white man, Tim Buckley, became his intellectual heir to Yurok knowledge through informal adoption. Harry became Tim's anthropological midwife, not his fictive father or older brother.

This provocative essay reveals an intricate skein of inside and outside adoptions, ironically like interwoven strands of DNA or the imbrication on a Porno basket. Yet Yurok transmission of sacred knowledge seems to transcend considerations of consanguineal kinship and folk genetics. Perhaps we have to think in terms of inheritance of acquired, as well as inherent, characteristics and construct models of heirship as well as kinship.

Ann Fienup-Riordan's richly embellished ethnographic paper on Yup'ik naming practices connects many points raised by the papers in this collection. Formal adoption, involving ritual announcement and official placement in the kinship system, is not highly elaborated in Eskimo society. Yet adoption is widely practiced and serves to unite communities internally and externally on many levels. Fienup-Riordan notes that most of today's adoptions take place because adults desire [252] children, rather than because children require foster parents. However, this situation may not have always prevailed in the past, given the high rates of mortality and marital instability occasioned by Euro-American contact and conduct. The large Yup'ik vocabulary for adoption implies a variety of types and motivations, but perhaps the plurality of terms indicates a movement toward a less defined, unmarked category.

The Yup'ik naming system is quite complex. Not only are there various types of calling names (or nicknames) and teasing names (for example, Anna Banana), but proper names derive primarily from deceased kindred. Proper names may be shared by two or more people. While reminiscent of Northwest Coast inheritance of titles and the immortality of names, Yup'ik naming involves a closer interactive relationship between the living and the dead. This relationship represents reembodiment through revivified breath, lifelines, and claimed personhood. Material exchange between the living and the dead manifests itself through gift giving and food offerings: clothing and food received by a living person are shared with the dead personage. The deceased name donor and the living namesake both exercise volition vis-à-vis the name sharing. Illness or death can be interpreted as rejection of the shared name by either party.

Several other aspects of Yup'ik naming deserve comment. I found it interesting that the transmission of formal names ignored criteria of age and gender, such that a young girl might acquire the name of a living or deceased male elder, or an older man might inherit a younger woman's name. Since one received several names over the course of a lifetime, one's individual identity rested more in the unique configuration of names rather than in the distinctive features of the specific names themselves- The use of fresh water in the simple naming ceremony may only be an adaptation of Christian holy water rites, or, as I suspect, it may harken back to the effort to slake the thirst of the deceased, as is common elsewhere in the northern circum-Pacific area with bear ceremonialism, whale capture, and first salmon rites, where these beings are considered to be "persons." The use of teknonomy may reflect circumspection in using proper names directly as names of address. And finally the joking relationship between opposite-sexed cross-cousins may be a vestige of the former existence of preferential cross-cousin marriage. [253]

Fienup-Riordan and her family acquired a diverse array of names that conferred personhood upon them and placed them within the Toksook community. Yet Fienup-Riordan, partly by preference, was never formally adopted. She compares her situation with that of two other female Arctic anthropologists, Barbara Bodenhorn and Jean Briggs. She notes that both women were unmarried and childless when in the field, factors that may have influenced their incorporation by making them less unconnected, vulnerable, and/or dangerous. Nevertheless, adoption or no, Ann Fienup-Riordan has clearly acquired Yup'ik personhood and has become enmeshed in the complex ties that constitute community life at Toksook. She privileges the information conveyed by her friends, who cannot be regarded as human subjects any more than Ann can assume the role of a neutral, if not neutralized, impersonal social scientist-

Sergei Kan's long-term Tlingit fieldwork is abetted by two formal adoptions that were more than honorary. Charlotte Young, a dedicated elder of the Russian Orthodox Church, befriended Kan and viewed him as a worthy replacement for a deceased male relative whose name was also kept in circulation by Charlotte's brothers son's son. The exclusive use of a name does not seem to hold for the Tlingits, unlike the situations we have seen elsewhere. Charlotte admired Sergei Kan's respect for Tlingit tradition, his Russian background and literacy, and his sense of proper behavior. Sergei's wife, Alia, was also adopted and appropriately assigned to a clan in the opposite moiety. With his newly acquired network of kith and kin afforded through Charlotte's web of affiliations, Kan was transformed from an outsider to an insider with access to privileged cultural data. He took his newly assumed obligations seriously by actively engaging in ceremonial performances, gift-giving, and maintaining regular correspondence when out of the field.

Mark Jacobs is an older Native intellectual into whose orbit Kan was increasingly drawn through shared interests in religious and cultural matters. Their friendship gradually matured into mutual respect and emotional empathy. While Sergei's relation with Charlotte tended to be more maternal and auntlike, the relationship with Mark was much closer and fraternal. In time, Mark carefully stage-managed Sergei's formal adoption into his clan and bestowed upon him the name of a deceased younger brother.

Being adopted into two different clans, albeit within the same [254] moiety, is potentially problematic but not unprecedented. Thus far Kan has managed to avoid possible sources of conflict, but one can easily envision a time or situation when he will be forced to forsake one affiliation in favor of the other.

Sergei Kan is the only contributor in this volume to address directly the pandemic phenomenon of "anthro-bashing" that has become so prevalent in Indian Country today. He shows that this growing antagonism, while watered by the crocodile tears of Vine Deloria and others, is deeply rooted and that Native Americans have always been quick to point out misunderstandings, misappropriation, and other patronizing deficiencies in anthropological descriptions of their cultures. Indeed, Mark Jacobs is sharply critical of the accounts of Tlingit culture produced by previous anthropologists. In reaction, he not only became a skilled amateur anthropologist himself by collecting and collating traditional knowledge and posing significant questions about that knowledge, but Jacobs also adopted "his own anthropologist," Kan, as an alter ego with whom he could engage in ongoing productive dialogue.

Namings

Kan feels no conflict over his regard for his Tlingit relatives and his self-declared responsibilities as a professional anthropologist. He has little use for those who naively overromanticize their adoptions and, in their own minds at least, "go native." He feels that by remaining true to their mission, anthropologists have much to contribute, both intellectually and practically, not only to their academic audience but also to the people who adopted them. Indeed, genuine adoption is a continuing reciprocal process, not a onetime adventure to provide a temporary strategic advantage in field research.

In summary, this volume is not the last word on Native North American adoptions of anthropologists but a clear first call for more investigation of this crucial area of research where so many perspectives conjoin: for example, ethno-psychological definitions of self and personhood; cross-cultural dimensions of depth psychology and emotion; constructions of kinship and constrictions of social structure; and the moral career of the anthropologist's endeavor.

These diverse essays are provocative. One wonders why, or if, the adoption of anthropologists is so widespread in Native North America and seemingly less frequent in other parts of the world where [255] anthropologists wander. Is this a legacy of the peculiar form of colonialism that has characterized historic Indian-white relations? Does shared marginality encourage adoption, or are democratic, assimilationist national policies influential?

These essays point to the need for a workable typology to capture the wide spectrum of adoptive forms and variable situations leading to adoption. But beyond classification, we need to be more sensitive to the nuanced pragmatics of adoption and to how emotions and ethics impact on both adopters and adoptees. Adoption and the attainment of a name need to be understood less as a certification of acceptance or as an instrumental fieldwork tactic by the anthropologist and less as a means of co-optation and exploitation by the adopters and more as a mutual moral commitment to honor and maintain, sometimes even beyond death. These essays eloquently emphasize the fact that adoption and naming are more than nominal acts.

References

Chamberlain, Alexander F
    1911 Race Names. In *Handbook of American Indians North of Mexico*. FW Hodge, ed. Bureau of American Ethnology, Bulletin 30, pt. 2: 348-352.

Kimura, Takeshi
    1998 The Native Chiefs' Resistance Through Myth. PhD, Divinity School, University of Chicago.

CHAPTER 9

SEX DIFFERENCES IN SEXUAL IMAGERY
AROUSED BY MUSICAL STIMULATION

With David C Beardslee

THE PURPOSE of the present research has been to investigate and measure the differences in the sexual motivation of males and females by means of content analysis of "imaginative" stories written in response to TAT pictures and to short musical selections. The experiment attempts to extend Clark's (72; 73; Clark and Sensibar Ch. 7) research in this area. Both overt or manifest sexual imagery and sexually symbolic imagery were studied.

There have been few psychologically-oriented studies concerning the effects of music on male and female sexual motivation. The experimental literature on "affective qualities of music" has depended either on preference judgments or on conscious evaluations and ratings (Sopchak: 387). In view of the important role of unconscious sexual motivation and Clark's findings as to the inhibition of sexual imagery by sexual arousal, it is difficult to interpret these studies.

Havelock Ellis (p. 115) asserts that considerable importance can be attached to the voice and to music generally as a method of sexual appeal. He feels that sexual stimulation from the voice and music has a greater effect on women than on men. It is suggested that since the change of voice at puberty is greater in the male than in the female, "a woman's voice retains childlike qualities and is therefore less specifically feminine than a man's voice is specifically masculine" (p. 52). This line of argument suggests the use of music to obtain differential sexual arousal of male and female subjects.

Procedure

Four groups of subjects were used: two groups of males and two of females. All groups were first presented with the same two pictures as stimuli for "creative" stories. Subsequently, four short musical selections [133] were played as stimuli for imaginative productions. One group of males (Group MN) and one group of females (Group FN) were presented with four "neutral" musical selections, while the remaining groups (MA and FA) were presented with "active" or "arousing" musical selections.

The stories written to the two pictures served as a control test for group differences. The first depicts a couple, arm in arm, gazing at an imaginary dream house. The second, from the standard TAT series (No- 20), portrays a vague figure of indeterminate sex standing under a streetlight.

The musical selections were chosen from within the framework of what might loosely be called "movie music." Six of the eight compositions were themes from motion pictures; the other two musical selections employed the same basic instrumentation as the "movie music." "Movie music," by virtue of the fact that it is used as a background for portrayals of human action, is quite versatile in that it must strive to represent a wide variety of human emotions and situations. Vocal music was not used in this study because male and female voices are easily recognizable and this would create a "halo effect." To eliminate specific personal associations and recollections, an effort was made to select music which had not achieved a high degree of popularity.

The assembling of "movie music" into two series, "neutral" and "arousing," was done in cooperation with a musicologist. Some of the criteria used for classifying a piece of music as active or arousing were that the music should contain a pronounced emphasis on rhythm, themes with comparatively large tonal ranges, and a gradual buildup to a climax. In contradistinction, the neutral music could be characterized as having very little rhythmic emphasis and a general evenness in melody and over-all construction.

The subjects were undergraduate elementary psychology students at two central New England liberal arts colleges. Four classes were available at the men's college, two of these constituting group MN and two group MA. The largest of the three classes available at the women's school was used as group FA, the other two comprised group FN. The two institutions are comparable in that they are both liberal arts colleges, their students are recruited from essentially similar geographic areas, and the students of the two institutions come from comparable socioeconomic backgrounds. Both collegiate groups were approximately equal in age, and neither had formally studied projective testing methods.

The subjects were given 30 seconds to observe each of the pictures, followed by four minutes to write the story suggested by the picture. The same procedure was followed for the musical selections except that each of the musical selections was approximately three minutes in duration. The subjects were permitted to write notes while the music was playing, but they were instructed not to begin the actual writing of a story until the musical selection was completed.

The subjects were given the usual instruction that "this is a test of creative imagination," etc., and were instructed to sign their names to the test booklet. The test was administered to the male subjects by one of the experimenters. It was administered to the female subjects by their regular [134] teacher, since the presence of a strange male might have influenced the result.

The sexual imagery of subjects was scored in three different ways: (a) Manifest or Overt Sex Imagery, (b) Symbolic Sex Activity, and (c) Sex Symbolism (as discussed by Freud). The first and third scoring techniques were adopted from dark, who made available his scoring criteria and stories.[11]

Dark defines Overt Sex Imagery as (a) primary – explicit or implicit evidence for sexual intercourse [score of 3]; (b) secondary – evidence for the occurrence of such secondary sex activity as kissing, dancing, or fondling [score of 2]; (c) tertiary – characters in the stories perceived as sweethearts, on a date, courting, in love, etc., but not engaged in either primary or secondary activity [score of 1]. This scoring system was used unchanged. The interscorer reliability in this study was 96 per cent agreement on categorization with "agreement on absence" ignored.

The second score, which is referred to as Symbolic Sex Activity to distinguish it from Sex Symbolism (clinically denned), is an attempt to create a public scoring definition for sexual symbolism along the lines of the definition of achievement imagery and of affiliation imagery. The basis of the definition is Freud's presentation of the fundamental characteristics of sexual activity as rhythmic self-stimulation (147, p. 585ff). Four variables[22] are scored, each for presence or absence. These are *Motion*, *Rhythm*, *Peak*, and *Penetration*.

Motion is scored if the story contains reference to gross bodily movement of an animate organism. Head, arm, or hand movement is not scored. Mere change of place is not scored. Examples: "he walked" or "he was lifting a bag" is scored; "he went" or "he was lifted in the elevator" is not scored.

Rhythm is scored if the story contains action which demonstrates a repetitive quality or character of continuous or serial nature. A single repetition is not scored. No distinction is made between animate and inanimate objects. Examples: "clapping," "swinging," and "the tree nodded" are scored. "He jumped across the brook" is not scored as rhythm.

Peak is scored whenever the story involves a general increase in tension or activity followed by a letdown. An increase without a decrease is not scored. Examples: "he climbed on up the mountain, then

---

1   We are especially indebted to David C McClelland for advice in the development of this system of scoring.
2   Detailed definitions of these categories, together with scoring definitions for the other two variables, are available from the Psychology Department, Wesleyan University.

descended" and "he became increasingly worried over the exam; when it was over he relaxed" are scored as peak.

Penetration is scored whenever the story has reference to the entrance into or movement through a resisting surface. Examples: "he dove into the water" or "he 'busted' his way through the door" is scored [135] penetration. "He went through the door" or "the arrows bounced off his armor" is not scored.

A story was scored as containing sexually symbolic activity if any two of the four variables were present in the story. The individual's score was the sum of the scores on his stories. The interscorer agreement was 95 per cent.

The scoring of Sex Symbolism was done with a clinical approach – that is, the scorer's intuition, operating with his knowledge of Freudian theory and his experience with projective materials, guides his judgment as to what is sexually symbolic. Following dark, the mere mention of a classical symbol was not scored, but the classical symbol or symbols mentioned had to be utilized or involved in some action which in and of itself could be interpreted as being symbolic. Stories were given a weight of two to indicate that symbolism was strongly present, one to indicate that some symbolism was present, and zero if no symbolism was present. An individual's score was the sum of his scores on each story. The reliability was 89 per cent agreement between dark's scoring of his own data and the scorers in this study.

All three scoring systems focus on sexual activity. Overt Sex Imagery is scored principally on the basis of occurrence of interpersonal love relations, Symbolic Sex Activity on the basis of intercourse-type activity, and Sex Symbolism (clinically denned) only when classically symbolic objects are embedded in a sexlike activity.[3]

Results

Control Pictures. Since all groups had the same two pictures, groups MN and MA are combined into a single group, as are groups FN and FA. Table I shows no significant differences between the mean scores of males and females on the two control pictures. The differences are all very small. None of the four experimental groups (MN, MA, FN, FA) differs significantly from any other on any of the three mean scores. However, if the scores for primary Overt Sex Imagery (explicit or implicit evidence for intercourse) are studied separately, it is found that 5 males wrote stories fitting this category while no females did ($p < .10$, two-tail Fisher Exact test). If the stories involving primary Overt Sex Imagery are rescored on the basis of the story exclusive of the particular phrase which led to the primary score, no major changes occur. If the stories are re-scored only on the basis of tertiary Overt Sex Imagery, the t's are almost unchanged. It may be concluded that college males and females show virtually no differences in Overt Sex Imagery to pictures except females may show less primary imagery. The male group is significantly more variable. In fact, groups MN and MA [136] individually are significantly more variable than either of the female groups.

Sex Differences in Response to Music. Table I also presents the scores of the four groups in response to musical selections. The males show significantly more Overt Sex Imagery than do females in response to neutral music, but this difference disappears when arousing music is used.

---

[3] In line with Nichol's (:319) failure to obtain differential GSR's to male and female symbols, none of these scores attempt to separate male and female symbols.

TABLE I. SEX DIFFEEENCES IN THREE KINDS OF
SEX IMAGERY IN STORIES TO PICTURES AND MUSIC

Stimulus	Group	N	Overt Sex Imagery	Symbolic Sex Activity	SexSymbolism (clinically defined)
Two Control Pictures	Females	71	1.10	.20	.46
	Males	84	1.15*	.18	.49
	Diff. (F-M)		-.05	.02	-.03
	t		.50	.07	.12
	p		NS	NS	NS
Four Neutral Music Selections	Females	43	1.65	.93	.67
	Males	38	2.50	.61	.74
	Diff.(F-M)		-.85	.32	-.09
	t		2.44	1.88	.39
	p		<.02	<.10	NS
Four Arousing Music Selections	Females	28	1.96	1.93	2.50
	Males	46	2.20	1.20	1.80
	Diff. (F-M)		-.24	.73	.70
	t		.68	2.81**	1.84
	p		NS	<.01**	<.10

* Male scores significantly more variable (p <.05).
** p corrected for significant difference in variance (Walker & Lev 423: p.157). Females more variable.

As with the pictures, primary Overt Sex Imagery, separated from the remaining overt categories, shows a strong female inhibition. Five of group MN and 6 of group MA wrote stories involving it, some writing more than one such story. One member of group FA and none of group FN yielded any primary Overt Sex Imagery. Combining the neutral and aroused groups, $X^2 = 5.82$, $d.f. = 1$, $p < .02$. A similar result was obtained in a pilot study involving a [137] comparison of male and female groups at two other colleges and using six diverse musical selections. Five of 25 males and none of 35 females wrote stories containing primary Overt Sex Imagery ($p < .02$, two-tail Fisher Exact test). It seems possible then to interpret the difference in this same direction on the control pictures as suggestive of a general tendency for women in this culture to inhibit more than men explicit or implicit reference to intercourse. That this is not wholly obvious is indicated by the fact that explicit reference to intercourse was very rare for males in these data. Most of the scores were for mention of illegitimate conception, discussion of a lecture on "the facts of life," or any mention of a mistress or prostitute. Overt-Sex-Imagery scores based on secondary and tertiary imagery only, or on tertiary imagery only, yield approximately the same results as total Overt-Sex-Imagery scores. The size of the difference between MN and FN decreases, but it remains significant at the five per cent level.

On Symbolic Sex Activity, the females score almost significantly higher than the males in response to neutral music, and very significantly higher in response to arousing music. In the neutral music groups, the female scores exceed the male scores on three of the four categories (Motion, Rhythm, Peak). In the case of Motion, the difference is statistically significant. In the aroused music groups, the females exceed the males in these same three categories and are significantly higher on Peak. The differences are insignificant for Penetration, but this category has been left because Clark's groups were significantly different on this variable. No significant difference is observed for Sex Symbolism in response to neutral music, but arousing music produces a near-significant difference between the two sexes, the females scoring higher.

In contrast to the results for the control pictures, it is clear that musical stimuli lead to different amounts of symbolic imagery in the two sexes. Females differ most from males in expressing more Symbolic Sex Activity than the males. The categories of Symbolic Sex Activity (Motion, Rhythm, Peak, and Penetration) all involve the kinesthetic aspect of sex.

Differences in Response to Types of Music. If, in Table I, the arousing and neutral music groups are compared, holding sex constant, the differences in Overt Sex Imagery are insignificant (t = .81 for males and .93 for females). The nature of the music used makes no significant difference in Overt Sex Imagery. For Symbolic Sex Activity the t is 3.47 for males and 3.83 for females (p < .01). For Sex Symbolism (clinically defined), the t is 4.33 for males and 5.44 for females (p < .01). Thus both men and women show significantly [138] more symbolic activity and symbolism to arousing music than to neutral music.

When the neutral and aroused groups are compared for Symbolic Sex Activity on each of the four records separately, the mean score for every one of the arousing records is higher than for any of the neutral records. This difference in effects of types of music is highly consistent in both sexes.

Interaction of Sex Differences and Music Differences. The data of Table I may also be analyzed for sex differences in the differential effects of the two kinds of music. The difference between neutral and aroused males may be compared with the difference between neutral and aroused females. The difference between the differences is insignificant (*t* = 1.19) for Overt Sex Imagery, but this comparison yields a *t* of 2.41 for Symbolic Sex Activity and a *t* of 2.03 for Sex Symbolism.[44] We conclude from these data that for both ways of scoring symbolism, the females show a significantly greater difference in amount of imagery to neutral and arousing music. The same trend is present for Overt Sex Imagery.

Comparison of Music and Nude Slides as Arousers of Sexual Imagery. The difference between neutral and "movie music" discussed in the preceding section may be thought of as an "arousal effect" attributable to the difference in type of music. Clark's (73) study compares the sexual imagery in stories to pictures of a control group and a group of males who were shown slides of nude females prior to writing stories to neutral pictures. His "arousal effect" is the difference between a control group and a group with prior exposure to nude slides. Figure 1 compares these "arousal effects." Scores have been reduced to a four story basis. In addition, the stories of Clark's nonalcohol groups have been scored in terms of our Symbolic Sex Activity categories. The mean of his neutral group is .37 (N = 38); the mean of his group that was aroused by prior nude slides is .023 (N = 39). The difference yields a t of 2.73, so that for prior nude slides, a significant decrease (−.347) of Symbolic Sex Activity is observed in males.

Prior exposure to nude slides under non-alcohol conditions leads to significantly less Overt Sex Imagery and Symbolic Sex Activity, and more Sex Symbolism (see bars numbered "1", Figure 1). [139]

---

4 The exact *p* levels are unavailable. The formula for *t* here assumes equal variances of all four groups (Walker and Lev (423): 158). The effect of unequal variances on the ordinary *t* tests in these data is to reduce the degrees of freedom by about 1/3. Since 151 degrees of freedom are here involved, the reduction in degrees of freedom would be unimportant; however, the true effect of unequal variances is apparently unknown.

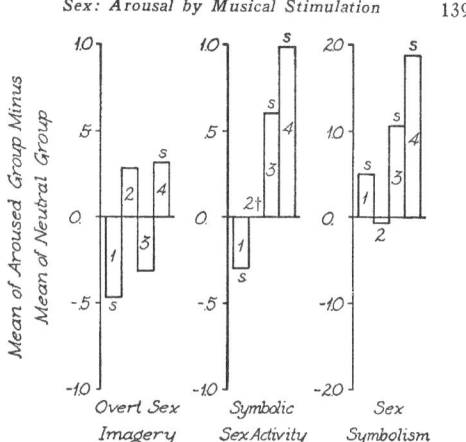

Fig. 1. Arousal effects of music and of prior exposure to nude slides.
1. Males, non-alcohol, prior exposure to nude slides.*
2. Males, alcohol, prior exposure to nude slides.*
3. Males, arousing versus neutral music.
4. Females, arousing versus neutral music.
s–These effects are significantly different from zero.

*Data from Clark (1955) multiplied by 4/5. Symbolic Sex Activity scored for this study; + data not available.

Arousing vs. neutral music for both males (bar "3") and females (bar "4") leads to insignificant change on Overt Sex Imagery, and significantly more Symbolic Sex Activity and Sex Symbolism. That is, arousing music increases Symbolic Sex Activity without increasing Overt Sex Imagery.

Relations between the Three Types of Imagery within Groups. Clark (See Table 1, 72) reports a very interesting relationship between Overt Sex Imagery and Sex Symbolism (clinically defined) in his nonalcohol groups. When the groups are divided into thirds on the basis of Overt Sex Imagery, then Clark's high and low groups both exceed the medium group in Sex Symbolism scores. The breakdown was made separately within each group, and analysis of variance showed the relationship to be significant. [140]

This relationship did not occur in any of the four groups of the present study.[5] Nor was there any consistent relationship between Overt Sex Imagery and Symbolic Sex Activity. However, Symbolic Sex

---

5 Clark's alcohol groups displayed so little sex symbolism that this relation could not be studied.

Imagery Activity and Sex Symbolism were found to be positively related in the present study. The product moment correlations calculated for each group are all positive, ranging from .20 in the MN group to .47 in the FA group.

Discussion

Since there are no indications that women produce more sexually symbolic material in response to pictures than do males, the first question these findings raise is why do women show more symbolism than men in response to music? In four comparisons involving two types of music and two scoring systems for sex symbolism, women score very significantly higher on one, almost significantly higher on two, and slightly but not significantly lower on the fourth (Table I). Furthermore, women are significantly more sensitive to the difference in type of music.

One possibility is that music as a stimulus innately arouses responses (percepts, images) in women characteristic of the sexual response. Such aspects of the musical stimulus as rhythm and dynamic changes may lead, by the nature of the female physiology and neurology, to such "pseudosexual responses." Ellis' speculations, cited earlier, as to the effect of the difference in change of voice would be consistent with this view. One might account in a similar manner for the finding of Kinsey et al. (213) that males tend to report sexual arousal by visual stimuli much more than women, while women tend to be more sexually aroused than men by motion pictures. Modern motion pictures depend on such auditory stimuli as background music, and it is from such background music that the musical selections used in the present study were drawn. This conception of an innate difference in the effectiveness of music as a "releasing" stimulus (Tinbergen 411) seems to be difficult to establish at the present time without cross cultural data.

It is also possible that the difference in sexually symbolic imagery is a function of learning. It might be argued that women listen to music more and therefore the images it arouses are higher in the habit family hierarchy and appear more readily in their stories. It has been noted that females score lower on the Penetration category than the males. Thus the Symbolic Sex Activity categories which do differentiate males and females are Motion, Rhythm, and Peak. [141]

Imagery of this type could conceivably be conditioned to music more in females than in males. The result would then be interpreted as indicating that arousing music elicits more "kinesthetic" imagery and accounts for the higher scores on Symbolic Sex Activity. The explanation would be sought in differential amounts of time spent listening to music and demonstration that the conditions under which listening occurred would, in fact, lead to the establishment of the appropriate conditioned imagery.

Razran (338) has shown that stimulus materials presented during eating come to evoke food-related verbalizations but not hunger sensations. He concludes that "what was conditioned in the study was more an unconscious cognition" (p. 282). In the case of musical stimuli, the most obvious "conditioned imagery" would be "dancing."

All stories were scored for any mention of dancing. In the neutral music groups 11 per cent of the males and 12 per cent of the females wrote one or more stories involving dancing. In the arousing music groups, 52 per cent of the males and 54 per cent of the females mentioned dancing. This does not support a "conditioned imagery to music" explanation of the sex difference. Furthermore, dark has shown that for males, at least, the Symbolic Sex Activity score is significantly altered (decreased) by nonrhythmic stimulation (nude slides). Since these pictures have quite different stimulus properties, it seems difficult to believe that imagery conditioned to music would be tripped off by them.

Finally, in the present study the females respond with almost significantly more Sex Symbolism and with a significantly larger arousal effect on this score than the males. It is hard to explain why the classical Freudian symbols (snakes, jewels, balconies, etc.) should have become conditioned to music. The nude slides of Clark's study brought about a significant increase in Sex Symbolism similar to the increase due to arousing vs. neutral music of the present study. The fact that music and pictures have equivalent effects on Sex Symbolism is strong evidence that in dealing with the effects of music, Sex Symbolism, and not happenstance conditioned imagery, is involved.

The increase in Sexual Symbolism and Symbolic Sex Activity scores produced by the arousing music might be viewed as an instance of an increase in level of activation, a construct introduced by Woodworth and Schlosberg (442) to account for changes in emotion. The Symbolic Sex Activity score is based largely on activity imagery, and the scoring of classical symbols was conditioned by Clark's restriction that these be embedded in an activity. But this sort of explanation does not account for the *decrease* in males and the lack of significant *increase* in females in Overt Sex Imagery. [142] Since secondary and tertiary Overt Sex Imagery involve activity, genera] activation would be expected to increase it.

If, then, the opposite effects of music and nude pictures on the Symbolic Sex Activity score are to be regarded as evidence that in both cases one is dealing with sex, it becomes necessary to consider the relationship between the three scores studied. Figure 1 suggests a gradient from overt to covert levels of consciousness, a gradient of indirectness of sexuality, dark hypothesized that nude slides arouse sexual motivation and also anxiety in order to explain the decrease of Overt Sex Imagery and increase of Sex Symbolism (clinically denned) in his nonalcohol group. He hypothesized lowered anxiety in the alcohol groups to explain the higher level of Overt Sex Imagery and significant increase in sexual imagery following arousal by nude slides. In our scoring of dark's data; the direct arousal of sexual motivation and anxiety by nude slides seems to suppress the intermediate category of Symbolic Sex Activity. We might hypothesize that music arouses sexual imagery but less anxiety therewith. The contrasted types of music studied would be expected to differ in the degree to which they aroused sexual motivation, but it would not be expected that arousing music would produce as widely generalized anxiety as nude slides. Hence, arousing music might produce a decrease (although not significant) of Overt Sex Imagery in males and an increase of both symbolism scores in males. The insignificant increase of Overt Sex Imagery in females is consistent with the general interpretation that music is more motivationally arousing to females but does not arouse correspondingly greater anxiety.

CULTURE AND PERSONALITY

With Anthony F. C. Wallace
University of Pennsylvania and
Eastern Pennsylvania Psychiatric Institute[1]

In this review of culture-and-personality publications, we have organized the literature between 1958 and the first half of 1960 into categories that seem to us to reflect the most significant trends of this period. These trends are: a fractionation of group character studies from studies of total personality to investigations of more limited components or aspects of personality; an increasing methodological rigor in child-development investigations; the emergence of social psychiatry as a major subject of specialization for anthropologists; a re-focusing of interests in culture change, from "slow" acculturation processes to processes of "rapid" culture change, as in revitalization movements and directed development; the beginning of a crystallization of theory in an area that may loosely be called "communication and cognition"; and the first signs of an interest in the relation of various physiological and biochemical processes to personality and culture. We have not included in the literature cited all publications relevant to the subject of culture and personality, but have tended to restrict ourselves to works by anthropologists or directed to anthropologists that undertake to extend our knowledge of the systematic interrelation of personality systems and cultural systems.

Present Status of Culture and Personality Studies

Honigmann (113) pointed out in the Biennial Review of Anthropology, 1959, that culture-and-personality studies have not been neglected by anthropologists, but still a widespread dissatisfaction with the methodological and conceptual status of this subfield persists. As Schneider (250) has noted, the subdiscipline of culture and [43] personality "is amorphous and so internally ill-differentiated that its boundaries shade off into all other fields"; one reason the boundaries are so vague is the fact that much of its conceptual apparatus, without its jargon and technique, has been gradually incorporated into the work of scholars in such fields as social organization, ethnography, area studies, community studies, applied anthropology, and the anthropology of development. Without offering elaborate discussions of national character and child-rearing practices, the writers of papers and monographs in these areas deal rather freely with such entities as values, aspirations, emotional conflicts, and life style. Much work is published that contains data or reflections relevant to culture-and-personality issues but that does not consciously attempt to contribute to the theoretical development of the field. Hence, even if the subdiscipline of culture and personality were to cease to exist tomorrow, its impact on anthropology would continue to be felt in the general "humanization" of ethnographic description, which constitutes one of the general trends in that area.

Another factor contributing to ill-defined boundaries is the intense interest on the part of nonanthropologists – particularly social psychologists, sociologists, and psychiatrists – in certain issues that anthropologists regard as culture-and-personality concerns. This interest is growing, and its results are seen in statements encouraging cross-cultural research and publication by social psychologists, sociologists, and psychiatrists, without necessarily the collaboration of anthropologists (cf. 14, 181, 201). To what extent these developments represent a diffusion from anthropology of the culture-and-personality viewpoint, and to what extent they are a line of convergent evolution, we shall leave to a future historian

---

[1] Reprinted from *Biennial Review of Anthropology*, 1961, edited by Bernard J Siegel, published by Stanford University Press, Stanford, California. [43]

of science to discover. In this review, we have not attempted to cover all of this extra-anthropological work, contenting ourselves with indicating its nature and scope and citing illustrative references.

Recent introductory texts in cultural anthropology also reveal the infusion of culture-and-personality concepts into general cultural theory. One regularly finds in these volumes discussions of personality theory, of growing up in a culture, of the relation of individual experience to societal expectations, and of various other culture-and-personality issues (see 29, 86, 94, 111, 112. 134, 287). The fulsome-ness of the welcome, or the quality of the treatment, is not the [44] question here; the fact is that no general introductory text today is considered adequate unless it not merely recognizes but incorporates culture and personality concepts.

Despite this diffuse sort of success, those interested in culture and personality as a subdiscipline are uncomfortable with its present status and uncertain about its history. One continues to find self-searching essays that attempt to make explicit its identity, history, and characteristic world-view (73, 74, 130, 147, 148, 155, 183, 184, 202, 232, 311, 312, 314, 318). Similarly, certain methodological and technical problems remain in dispute, particularly with regard to psychoanalysis and projective techniques, in whose cross-cultural use anthropologists have pioneered (5-7, 55, 65, 72, 147, 153, 158, 206, 244). Methodological problems of interdisciplinary research are discussed by Korner (144) and Lusaka (171).

The Fractionation of Group Character Studies

Theoretical Critiques

The criticism of "group character" studies (that is, studies of national character, basic personality, modal personality, ethos, and the like) has continued. Two types of criticism are found: charges of more or less gross misrepresentation of the subjects of description (119, 207), and demonstrations that the acceptable range of individual variability in temperament and style of life within society is too great to permit "exceptions" to group character formulations to be shoved to one side as deviants or misfits (66, 84). Partially in response to such criticisms, some efforts are being made to reconceptualize the whole problem of group character. These efforts generally involve redefinition or elaboration of the concept of culture in order to include phenomena that otherwise would be labeled "personality." Thus Goldschmidt (95) argues that both normative and statistical descriptions of human behavior are valid ways of characterizing a society's culture, although anthropology tends to emphasize the normative. Hsu (116) suggests that in addition to the aspects of structure, function, and process, culture has a fourth aspect of theoretical significance, namely "content." "Content" in this sense connotes such concepts as "national character," "themes," and "patterns." Honigmann (115) suggests in an interesting paper that the study of ethos [45] (the emotional style of a people) need not be dependent upon the analysis of motivational or conflict structure, and illustrates the thesis with a description of the ethos of the Great Whale River Eskimo. Lantis (157) suggests that "vernacular culture," as distinct from highly institutionalized norms, is particularly relevant to culture-and-personality research. While none of these formulations, any more than the criticisms, provides a satisfactory solution to the problem of relating the concept of national character to the concept of culture, it is evident that the issue is now widely recognized as a serious theoretical question.

Only a few empirical reports are even remotely classifiable as group character studies by anthropologists: those by Honigmann (114), Baldus (20), and Bushnell (43); Bauer and Kluckhohn's study of the Soviet system (28); Kroeber's Yurok study (46); Miner and De Vos' Casbah (194); Rohrer and Edmonson's (239) follow-up study of Davis and Dollard's earlier Children of Bondage; and reports on projective test data from Abel and Metraux's continuing study of Montserrat, B.W.I. (1, 2). Gulick's study of the Cherokee (97) contains some group character material, including a test of Spindler's hypothesized general American Indian core personality against Cherokee data. Miner and De Vos' work is perhaps the most ambitious enterprise, for in addition to providing descriptive material on culture-and-personality differences between rural and urban Algerian Arabs, they undertake to test two major culture-and-personality hypotheses: Kardiner's assumption that the forms of culture can be predicted from a knowledge of personality characteristics, and the widespread belief that basic personality is "set" in the first five years of life. Methodological difficulties render the results of these theory-testing efforts inconclusive. On a less generalized plane, two studies attempt to characterize subgroups within society: Karon's "rigorous investigation" of the effects of cultural status on Negro personality (132), and Smithson's competent study of the Havasupai woman (260). Karon's investigation supports the general opinion that the presence of severe caste sanctions makes the control of aggression a central problem in the southern American Negro personality (but the less severe sanctions in the north, surprisingly, appear to have relatively little effect, according to Karon's data). [46]

As distinct from an interest in total personality structure, a number of interesting ventures seek to explore the ways in which certain presumably universal psychological processes are handled by various cultures. The cultural patterning of sexual behavior is treated by Devereux (60), Murphy (203), Roheim (238), and Swartz (279). Devereux and Roheim provide psychoanalytic interpretations of specific sexual customs; Murphy and Swartz seek social-structural explanations of relationship patterns between the sexes. The interrelated concepts of identity, self-image, and body image are treated by several authors. Lynd (173) provides a most stimulating discussion of the nature of shame and its bearing on the search for identity, and a selection of Erikson's papers (77) on ego identity has been published as a group. Fisher and Cleveland (83) offer a review of studies relating to body image and personality, and present a polar typology of body-image concepts as a means of personality classification: the "High Barrier" and "Low Barrier" types. Kennedy and Lasswell (137) offer a new cross-cultural test of body image based on the hypothesis that perceptions of height and weight are influenced by judgments of power or value. Strauss (277), in his study of the transformations of identity, as in the processes of socialization, assimilation, and acculturation, emphasizes the importance of the long-neglected subject of "adult socialization." Stein, Vidich, and White (275) have edited a volume of readings concerning the problem of the individual's maintaining his identity in a mass society. Along more traditional lines, one paper treats the universality of typical dreams (96) and another the social functions of anxiety (256), both topics familiar to anthropologists.

Autobiographical and biographical studies have come to have a new significance in culture-and-personality writings, not so much as data for national character generalizations, but rather as windows into the experiential world of the individual in a particular culture. This interest is exemplified in one theoretical paper (75) and in several empirical presentations. Engelmann suggests that societies may be classified as more or less perceptivist or activist. The perceptivist society encourages the individual to sense fully the uniqueness of each experience; the activist society, classifying wide ranges of behavior as equivalent, encourages a monotonous uniformity in experience. [47] Casagrande (47) has edited a valuable source book containing twenty case studies (written by anthropologists) of individuals in various cultures. There are new empirical reports by Beckett (30), Biesanz, Biesanz, and Ordonez (34), Leslie (164), Lewis (166), Mintz (195), Roberts (236), Tirabutana (286), and Winter (322). Of these, Lewis's Five Families (set in Mexico) and Mintz's Worker in the Cane (set in Puerto Rico) are perhaps best known. Without self-consciously attempting to make formal structural interpretations of personalities, they describe the world of an alien culture as it is seen through the eyes of participants.

The interest in values continues to be well represented in the literature. Albert and Kluckhohn (11) have published a selected bibliography on values, ethics, and esthetics in the behavioral sciences and philosophy, and Kluckhohn has discussed scientific strategy in the cross-cultural study of values (138, 139). In two publications (70, 71), Edel deals with the responses of various cultures to the problem of ethical control of "moral" issues in behavior, and points out that there has been a revival of anthropological interest in ethics during the last decade. Dumont (67), Belshaw (32), and Kluckhohn (140) discuss certain theoretical problems related to the study of values, Belshaw urging anthropologists to emulate economists in studying values as revealed in action rather than in normative ideas and orientations, and Kluckhohn suggesting that a cultural typology based on combinations of value orientations might facilitate more formal typological endeavors. In an interesting paper Kramer (145) discusses the values of rivalry and superiority in Sumerian culture and compares the Sumerian pattern with Benedict's interpretation of the Kwakiutl. Lantis (156) reviews cultural values among the Alaskan Eskimo and presents a graphic schema to explicate on a general level the interrelations of culture, the value system, and personalities, Morrill (200) develops LaBarre's concept of "social cynosure" (the most valued role in a culture), and uses it to explain differential success in urban adaptation in two African societies. Wolfe (324) uses Florence Kluckhohn's conceptual scheme for the comparative study of values in another treatment of an African society.

Folklore and mythology continue to be of interest to students of culture and personality. The Herskovitses deal with the Oedipus [48] complex in Dahomean myths (107). In two publications (127, 128) Jacobs uses his Chinook tales as the basis for a psychological interpretation of an earlier period of Chinook history. Mead (187) points to the value of the more exact study of folklore and other "survivals" for a knowledge of the dynamics of change or conservatism. Fischer (82) experiments with the quantification of certain characteristics of folk tales in relation to the cultural context.

Before leaving the topic of group character, it is necessary to refer again to the considerable quantity of work now being done both in social psychology and in sociology. The sociological tradition is best exemplified by the work of Inkeles and his collaborators (123, 124). Social psychology has recognized the crucial methodological importance of cross-cultural control of psychological test results and questionnaire results, and the years 1958-60 have seen a spate of monographs, books, and articles by social psychologists working in Asia, Africa, South America – in virtually any place, indeed, that the field anthropologist might regard as his own "laboratory." Cross-cultural studies in the Arab Middle East are the subject of a special issue of the Journal of Social Issues (117). This attention to cultural variables is noteworthy in the study of motivation (18,169, 175), values (58, 221), preference for delayed reinforcement (196), intelligence testing (289), "personality" (56, 257), immanent justice (129), rigidity (9), sexual differentiation (226), Rorschach profiles (21, 52, 245), and other variables too numerous to include. The quantity of careful cross-cultural psychological testing produced by social psychologists now far surpasses the efforts of anthropologists, and although it is weak in its assessment of cultural background, it can usually be read profitably with an eye to the ethnographic literature. No attempt has been made here to list all relevant American or foreign social psychological studies of this kind; the titles cited are intended as a representative sample only.

Child Development and The Family

Although the traditional culture and personality interest in socialization – conceived as the mechanism for transferring both culture patterns and personality structure from generation to generation – has not abated, it would appear that the major investigative efforts are [49] now concentrated on three special problems: the cross-cultural statistical study of correlations between child-rearing practices and selected aspects of adult culture; the intensive study of child development in the Israeli kibbutz, which, by offering children a relatively afamilial milieu, constitutes a sort of general control for studies of development in the familial milieu; and (in an embryonic stage) the selection of the entire household as the unit of analysis in studies of child development and the family, rather than the mother-child relationship, which has hitherto received primary emphasis. There are, of course, strictly psychological studies of children in other cultures (for example, 69), and there has been a continuing series of publications reflecting a predominantly ethnographic interest in child development (79, 204, 231, 252, 261, 317). Reviewing earlier statements, Mead (185) discusses puberty and adolescence in their cultural contexts and urges psychoanalysis to make better use of anthropologists' cross-cultural findings on child development.

The cross-cultural "Whiting-type" studies are represented by five publications. Child, Storm, and Veroff (53) correlate the degree of emphasis on the "achievement theme" in the folk tales of 52 cultures with variables of child training related to achievement motivation. Barry, Child, and Bacon (22) evaluate the relation of child training to subsistence economy. Lambert, Triandis, and Wolf (150) correlate the degree of punitiveness in infant-training methods with the belief in the malevolence of supernatural beings. Whiting (315) discusses sorcery, the fear of ghosts, and the superego as mechanisms of social control, and in a second study (316) finds that totemism is negatively associated with cultures in which the child is separated from his parents in sleeping arrangements. Spiro and d'Andrade (269) also investigate the relation between punitiveness and quality of religious belief. In general these studies support the hypothesis that certain infant- and child-training variables do correlate significantly, cross-culturally, with various other aspects of culture, although the findings are uneven and the correlations are not necessarily high. Although not all of these studies are part of the ongoing major investigations by Whiting and Child, which have not as yet been reported in full, they have been heavily influenced by their work and contribute to its furtherance. [50]

The kibbutz studies have been conducted by both anthropologists and members of other professions (80, 92, 93, 222-27, 267, 320, 327). Since the studies form a coherent group, we shall not attempt to discriminate between anthropological and nonanthropological studies. The most ambitious and anthropologically significant publication to emerge from this body of literature is Spiro's Children of the Kibbutz (267). Based on extensive and detailed field work, and providing both statistical summaries and concrete, precise, structural descriptions, this study stands as a kind of flowering of the culture-and-personality tradition in relation to child development. But all the studies constitute significant contributions to the solution of one of the sphinx-riddles of socialization theory: what are the "good" ways of nurturing and socializing infants and children? These studies in general support Mead's contention that "adjustment is most facilitated if the child is cared for by many warm friendly people," for kibbutz children, although they do not experience the close and exclusive child-parent relationships regarded in most Western societies as normative, do not suffer from the psychological problems of "institutional" children in societies in which the centripetal family group is the norm. It may be noted that inasmuch as both the principles of "good" parent-child relations and the principles of nationalism and of the collective way of life in the Israeli kibbutz are apt to be areas of intensely emotional belief, among scientific observers as well as among the subjects, the problems of the scientist's maintaining his objectivity and of handling his own values in kibbutz studies are notable. Two studies (240, 249) discuss these difficulties, and a few others reveal their presence in the manifest sympathies of their authors.

The study of the family unit is best represented in the work of Lewis (166,167), Landy (154), Opler (211), and Birdwhistell (35). In both of Lewis's studies, careful attention is paid to the entire fabric of family living, and not merely to such traditional subjects as the mother-child relationship. Weakland, in his study of family imagery in a passage from the writings of Mao Tse-tung (308), undertakes to infer the changing structure of roles in the Chinese family since the revolution.

It should be noted that in the study of child development and [51] family life, as well as of national character, other professions, particularly psychiatry and clinical, educational, and social psychology, are showing increasing awareness of, and research interest in, the cross-cultural approach characteristic of anthropology. Thus Ackerman's treatise. The Psychodynamics of Family Life (4), discusses the influence of cultural variables; and studies such as Barry and Johnson's (23) on cultural variations in the formulation of the incest barrier and Newman's (208) and Ray's (229) on cultural differences in patterns of development demonstrate the increasing meaningful-ness of cross-cultural comparisons for the psychological profession.

The Emergence of Social Psychiatry

As the number of publications by social scientists working in the field of mental health has increased, papers have continued to appear that attempt to define the area of social psychiatry. Among such papers by anthropologists, or in journals dedicated to a cross-cultural viewpoint, may be mentioned those by Bluestone (39), Marsman (179), Mead (186), Opler (212), Strotzka (278), Wellin (313), Winokur (321), and Wittkower and Fried (323). Opler has described the methodological structure of the Midtown Study (210). Mention should also be made of three ambitious projects designed to develop a cross-cultural psychiatry: the volume entitled Culture and Mental Health, edited by Opler (215), which contains a number of papers mentioned below; Wittkower and Fried's Newsletter: Transcultural Research in Mental Health Problems, which appeared in 1958, 1959, and 1960, with valuable correspondence and abstracts of cross-cultural psychiatric materials, and their summary paper (323); and the relatively new (post-1955) International Journal of Social Psychiatry, which publishes papers in anthropology and the other social sciences as well as material by psychiatrists and psychologists. M. K. Opler is an associate editor of this publication.

Sociocultural Theories of Mental Illness

Anthropologists have begun to develop theoretical models of the schizophrenic process which, while based upon the concepts and findings of psychiatry, psychology, and sociology, are nevertheless [52] independent formulations. Bateson (25, 26), Weakland (309), Weakland and Jackson (310), and Birdwhistell (36) have been elaborating a "systems" or "communications" model of the schizophrenic family and of the schizophrenic's behavior, which in this familial context is interpreted as being in sum adjustive. Reference should be made here to the earlier paper by Bateson and others (27), in which the now widely cited "double-bind" hypothesis was first outlined (in a double-bind situation, generally speaking, one person places another in a chronic dilemma by making inconsistent demands in different logical orders and modalities of communication). Bate-son's and Weakland's papers essentially develop and extend the insights expressed in this earlier publication, while Birdwhistell discusses in detail the kind of sophisticated techniques of observation and recording necessary to provide empirical confirmation of the "disordered-communications" model of mental illness. This communications model, it should be noted, is not dependent for its value on the validation of the specific hypothesis of the schizophrenogenic nature of double-bind, but rather provides a culturally sophisticated expression of clinical assumptions about transference and counter-transference widely and inarticulately held by psychoanalysis and psychotherapists, as well as social scientists, who believe that disturbed behavior is the consequence of disturbed learning processes.

In contrast to the disordered-communications model are the formulations offered by Wallace (301) and Wallace and Ackerman (304), which suggest that many mental disorders are the culturally patterned responses of an individual to a physiologically determined decrease in the ability to assign organized meanings to experience. Generally relevant to both positions are Caudill's (48) discussion of the participation of sociocultural systems in stress reactions and Naroll's (205) effort to define an index of culture stress.

A good deal of writing on the theoretical problems of mental illness as seen from a sociocultural standpoint is of course also being done by sociologists, psychiatrists, and psychologists. Particularly worth mentioning are papers by Carothers (46), Clausen (54), Hunt (121), and Stainbrook (272). Simons (254) attacks what he regards as the "racist" theories of Tooth, Carothers, and other writers on African psychopathology. [53]

Cross-cultural and Culturally Specific Studies of Mental Disorder

The bulk of the work in social psychiatry is healthily empirical. By far the largest number of publications deal either with cross-cultural or with culturally specific analyses of particular clinical syndromes or entities, and again, much of this material is written by non-anthropologists. Limitations of space preclude listing all papers by nonanthropologists that present mental hospital statistics, symptomatic descriptions, analyses of the familial milieu of schizophrenics, geographical surveys of individual symptoms, and the like; the specialist in this field will find the growing body of literature on such matters not only in such psychiatric Journals and annuals as the International Journal of Social Psychiatry and Moreno and Masserman's Progress in Psychotherapy (181), but also in the more conventional psychiatric literature.

Empirical studies by anthropologists appear to divide into six major areas: (1) the relation of culture change to mental health (19, 85, 120, 161, 162, 165, 170); (2) the relation of sociocultural type or structure to the characteristics of mental disorder in relatively stable cultures (16, 33, 63, 81, 151, 181, 212-15, 219, 268, 284, 292); (3) the bearing of minority group status on psychopathology (131, 246, 253); (4) mental subnormality (180, 247); (5) disasters and other stress situations (48, 87, 295, 325); and (6) culturally patterned quasi-pathological states of altered mental function, such as shamanistic practice, trance, and possession (31, 168, 198, 327). Of these the publications of Leighton (161) and of Sarason and Gladwin (247) deserve special mention. Leighton and his associates have now published two volumes of a projected three-volume study of personality and mental health in a Nova Scotian community, as part of the Cornell University project in cross-cultural psychiatry, which is undertaking to obtain comparative materials on a world-wide scale. As in the earlier "Midtown" studies of a metropolitan population, Leighton and his collaborators have found emotional disorders of one sort or another to be so frequent in the observed population as to make the psychiatric "textbook normal" individual appear to be statistically rather rare. Leighton's work should also be noted for its methodological rigor and its elegance of theory construction. Sarason and [54] Gladwin endeavor to draw the attention of the social scientist to die largely untapped possibilities for research on mental subnormality, and emphasize strongly the impact of culture in defining adequate standards of performance and in determining social response to the subnormal.

Cross-Cultural and Culturally Specific Studies of Therapeutic Systems

A number of studies by anthropologists of cultural variables in the therapeutic response to overt mental disorder appeared during our survey period (50, 59, 126, 141, 143, 172, 189, 197, 216, 262, 294, 298, 299). Beyond documenting the truism that cultures will differ in therapeutic method as in other domains of behavior, these studies would seem to suggest some considerations for the theory of psychotherapy. They indicate, first, that the course of the patient's illness, independent of the effectiveness of therapeutic intervention, is affected by the culturally based conception he has of the significance of his symptoms and of their implications for treatment; and second, that the effectiveness of a psychotherapeutic procedure is markedly affected by its fit, or lack of fit, with the cultural milieu, to a degree which renders the scientific validity of its assumptions virtually a secondary consideration. It is also noteworthy that psychiatrically naive, even "primitive," societies frequently manage to evolve conceptions of psychic and psychosomatic pathology which intuitively apply psychotherapeutic principles only recently recognized in psychiatric theory.

Hospital Studies

Medical institutions – psychiatric hospitals and the like – now employ a substantial number of social scientists to appraise these pseudo-communities. The ultimate aim is to redesign these institutions, although feelings of guilt are the probable motivating factor behind the undertaking. A small group of anthropologists has participated actively in these hospital studies (49, 91, 136, 151, 214, 228, 303). Particularly noteworthy are the works of Caudill (49), Goffman (91), and Kennard (136). Caudill describes in detail from the viewpoint of a social anthropologist "the psychiatric hospital as a small society." Goffman, in an impressive article that should be read by [55] any anthropologist who undertakes hospital studies, sympathetically describes the plight of the mental patient as the public mental hospital encloses him in its inexorable and desocializing embrace. And Ken-nard, basing his work on long and intimate experience as a student of the mental hospital, outlines the major patterns of the mental hospital in the United States.

Culture Change

The interplay of change in culture and in personality during acculturation has been the aspect of culture change to which students of culture and personality have traditionally turned their attention. This aspect of culture change continues to be a major subject of research, but newer foci of interest are broadening its scope; inquiries into the problems of directed culture change, the study of revitalization movements, and the effort to develop newer models of group behavior that permit a more flexible treatment of historical process.

Acculturation and the Anthropology of Development

Africa has been the site of a large number of studies by both psychologists and anthropologists (38, 61, 62, 64, 174, 191, to list only a few). The two papers of De Vos and Miner (which are superseded, of course, by their larger report mentioned earlier in connection with group character studies) emphasize the strains placed on Arab personality in the discriminatory urban milieu of Algiers; the authors suggest, on the basis of the similarity of their Rorschach protocols to those of New York City Negroes, that there may exist certain personality tensions widely characteristic of the male members of imperfectly assimilated "minorities." The central Algonkians of the United States are also a familiar subject of personality-in-acculturation studies, and four studies in our survey period refer to this group (40, 220, 265, 266). The Spindlers' well-known studies of Menominee acculturation are extended in their joint analysis of differing male and female adaptations to culture change; they find, as have other students of the question, that females show less anxiety and disturbance. Race relations in New Zealand between Maori and white are treated by two authors (235, 285). Other acculturation [56] studies peripherally concerned with personality variables deal with the Lapp economy (12), Jamaican religious cults (255), and Japanese popular culture (133).

The trend, however, is toward a refocusing of interests in acculturation, away from the almost exclusive concern with situations of reciprocal, osmotic interchange of culture traits across a social boundary toward an interest in the intentional and aggressive efforts by a society to develop itself or its neighbor. The anthropology of development is treated elsewhere in this volume, however, and we list here only a few papers which in various ways deal with personality variables in developmental change (10, 68, 104, 119, 163, 248). In so far as these papers concern themselves with personality, they attempt to identify personal characteristics, in the developers and/or the developees, which act as barriers to the successful accomplishment of the desired social or technical changes. (The viewpoint of such studies tends, of course, to be teleological, since the context of investigation is usually one of applied anthropology. The quality of an investigation, however, need be in no wise reduced by its social engineering context, and culture and personality can find a fertile field of research and theoretical building in developmental anthropology.)

Rapid Culture Change

In some respects closely related to developmental anthropology is the burgeoning interest in processes of rapid culture change, particularly in revitalization movements of one sort or another. In addition to descriptive studies, there have been a surprisingly large number of theoretical papers on this subject.

Cargo cults in New Guinea continue to be of interest, and descriptive papers by Maher (178), Read (230), and Van der Kroef (291) have appeared. Van der Kroef's paper Ells something of a gap in the English literature by describing these movements in Dutch New Guinea. Historical and ethnographic treatments of American Indian nativistic movements are provided by Aberle (3) and Stem (276). Riley and Hobgood (234) describe a recent nativistic movement among the southern Tepehuan Indians of Mexico, and Butt outlines the development of a new religion among Carib-speaking Indians of northern South America (44). Reina (233) has treated the [57] relation between political crisis and cultural revitalization in Guatemala, European movements are touched upon by Erikson (76), Hinlde, and others (109), and Talmon (280).

Primarily theoretical papers are those of Inglis (122), Koebben (142), Mead and Schwartz (188), Smith (258, 259), Spier, Suttles, and Herskovits (264), Stanner (273), Stark (274), Voget (293), Van Baal (290), and Wallace (297, 300). The subject of rapid culture change has stimulated intense disagreements among the proponents of differing positions. For instance, Aberle's position (3) that the Prophet Dance of the Northwest Coast could have been inspired by deprivation ("a negative discrepancy between expectation and actuality") attendant upon white contact is challenged by Spier, Suttles, and Herskovits, who not only minimized the degree of culture contact in the Northwest antecedent to the Prophet Dance, but disapprove of the deprivation thesis in general. Smith, Voget, and Wallace (300) discuss from several points of view the problem of the classification of cult movements. Mead and Schwartz, in the course of a lengthy discussion of the Paliau movement among the Manus, outline a descriptive developmental model of revitalization movements, Inglis, Koebben, Stanner, and Van Baal consider revitalization movements, particularly cargo cults, from a somewhat evaluative standpoint, viewing them in the context of recent world history as more (or less) successful efforts of "primitive" non-Western peoples to enter the modem world. Stark and Wallace (294, 295) deal primarily with psychological processes in revitalization, with Wallace (295) suggesting that major stable systems – including religious beliefs, myths, and rituals – are the institutionalized legacies of half-forgotten revitalization movements whose codes have survived in distorted form.

Other Processes of Culture Change

Theoretical anthropologists are evidently beginning to chafe under the rigid, but relatively unconnected, framework of the conventional categories of culture change – innovation, diffusion, evolution, acculturation. Four recent papers can be viewed as efforts to make more flexible and integrated the theory of culture change. Bohannan (41) introduces the concept of "extra-processual events" [58] to cope with temporary institutional innovations designed to restore sociocultural equilibrium. Keesing (135) suggests that recreative behavior plays an important, if underrated, role in innovation. McFeat (176) sees in the Zuni cultural tradition the role of the "authoritative innovator," implying that, in at least one culture other than the Western industrial, there existed institutions deliberately designed to direct the course of cultural change. Mead (182) urges a more detailed analysis of the mechanisms of cultural transmission and change in order to provide a better understanding of the dynamics of cultural evolution.

Communication and Cognition

The related topics of communications and cognition theory do not, perhaps, deal with personality in the classic sense, which connotes an emphasis on the affects and on conflict structures. But it nonetheless seems appropriate to include a brief review of work in this area, for not only is much of it being done by persons who have been associated with culture and personality, but also these exploratory studies are providing a conceptual structure that will permit a more effective union of linguistics, cultural anthropology, and psychology in the study of man.

Systems and Communications Theory

If a society, together with its culture, is to be viewed as a system, it is necessary to consider that the system can function only to the extent that its component parts (whether they be groups, institutions, individuals, or even parts of individuals) are able to communicate among themselves under various circumstances of stress and relative nonstress. As we indicated in the section on social psychiatry, communications theory is proving to be of interest to a number of psychiatrically-oriented anthropologists and anthropologically-oriented psychiatrists. Ruesch (242) and Spiegel (263) discuss, respectively, the general theory and some specific problems of communications in psychiatric conditions. Bateson (24), in the Epilogue to the second edition of *Naven*, evaluates his earlier work in terms of his current interests in communications theory. Birdwhistell (37) discusses [59] kinesics and communication. And an entire issue of Etc., the journal of semantics, is devoted to an examination of the problems of inter-cultural communication (78).

Less grandly philosophical are discussions of language and its relation to cognitive process. There is still some discussion of this issue in terms of the Sapir-Whorf hypothesis or analogues of it (see 45, 57, 159, 177). The psychologist Brown (42) has written a book attempting to review the whole area of psycholinguistics, including the Whorfian metalinguistics, from the standpoint of the experimental psychologist, and Henie (105) has edited a collection of papers on language, thought, and culture. Hall (98) and Messing (192) deal with nonverbal communication. Hall's contribution being a book-length effort to survey the field, define problems, and set up a workable system of analysis.

One of the serious difficulties in communications theory is defining the role of cognitive processes in the theory. In extreme formulations, cognition is ignored; only "messages" are considered. But what is a "message"? If any meaningful stimulus (i.e., a stimulus that elicits a specific response) is a message, then indeed man communicates not only with his fellow men and a few animals, but also with sticks and stones and stars, cosmic rays and clouds, and individual onions. This can lead to a spiritually enriching, Wordsworthian pan-communication, but it makes it difficult to distinguish between processes of intentional communication and other kinds of dynamic physical systems. The analysis of intentional communication requires the study of meanings in the cognitive, semantic sense. Some of the problems in this area are examined by Wallace and Atkins (305) in a review of the technique and theory of componential analysis, as developed principally by Goodenough and Lounsbury in recent years.

Consideration of other models of cognitive process and their utility as explanatory principles in cultural analysis is provided by Gladwin (90), Hall (99), Hallowell (101), Lee (161), Rosenthal and Siegel (241), and Underhill (288). Gladwin and Hall discuss the cultural correlates of non-Western cognitive structuring of time. Rosenthal and Siegel interpret magic and witchcraft from the standpoint of dissonance theory (a psychological theory developed by Leon Festinger and his associates, which postulates certain behavioral [60] consequences of inconsistent cognitive content). Underhill offers a tentative reconstruction of the cognitive operations presumptively involved in the development of concepts of the supernatural by early man.

The Biology of Behavior

Several disciplines are already hard at work investigating the biological determinants of human social behavior. Despite the fact that anthropology includes not only cultural studies but physical studies as well, anthropologists recently have paid relatively little attention to the biology of behavior, except in the negative sense of disproving naive, racist theories of racial inferiority and superiority. But an interest in the behavioral, and therefore cultural, significance of biological variables, is beginning to increase in two areas: the evolution of "mind" and the relation of physiological variables to psychological process.

Mental Evolution

The evolution of the human mind (i.e., of human capacities for behavior) is a subject that interested Darwin and other proto-anthropologists perhaps more than recent anthropologists, who have taken these capacities for granted and studied behavior itself. The concept of capacity, however, implies significant questions of thresholds and limits. These questions are now increasingly being raised by cultural and physical anthropologists alike.

On the physical anthropologists' side, there has been a small flood of reviews and theoretical papers dealing both with the general somatic prerequisites of a human style of behavior (237, 271) and with the more particular subject of human behavior and the evolution of the brain (89, 306, 307). The interaction between primate evolution and the evolution of human culture has been ably reviewed by Tappen (283) in a paper reiterating his somewhat neglected earlier "Brief Communication" in the American Anthropologist (282). In general these views see culture and constitution as mutually dependent variables, an advance in one being associated with a correlative advance in the other.

More strictly behavioral studies divide neatly into two groups: studies of the social behavior of primates below man (103, 110, 243, 251) [61]; and theoretical considerations concerning the evolution of a distinctively "human" nature, characterized by reflection, self-identification, morality, innovation, and other features recognized by modem man in himself (100, 102, 319). In general, the problem is to relate these features of a human social mentality to some psychological capacity dependent on increase in brain size, and capacity for complex symbolic thought is usually felt to be the crucial connecting link.

Physiological Variables in Culture-relevant Behavior

Anthropological approaches to physiological studies relevant to behavior and culture are still few and must be mentioned more to mark a trend in as yet largely unpublished research than as an accomplished fact. Constitutional typology and its relation to psychological variables is evaluated by Adcock and others (8), and Tanner and Inhelder (281) review biological, psychological, and cultural variables in child development. Wallace (301) and Wallace and Acker-an (304) discuss possible physiological determinants of culturally relevant behavior in the area of psychopathology. Angel (13), reporting on his continuing studies of the relation of physical and psychological factors in culture growth, concerns himself with the relation of such matters as diet, disease, longevity, and fatigue to cultural efflorescence in Classical and Hellenic Greece. Henry (106), in a far-sighted discussion of the future of culture and personality studies, makes a plea for the more detailed consideration of such physiological and biochemical processes as are involved in the stress reaction (General Adaptation Syndrome of Selye), and foresees an inevitable reunion of physical and culture anthropology.

Literature Cited

PERSON, SELF, AND IDENTITY:
SOME ANTHROPOLOGICAL RETROSPECTS, CIRCUMSPECTS, PROSPECTS

> All clowns are masked and all personae
> Flow from choices; sad and gay, wise,
> Moody and humorous are chosen faces,
> And yet not so! For all circumstances,
> Given, like a tendency
> To colds or like blond hair and wealth
> Or war and peace or gifts from the ground,
> Stick to us in time, surround us:
> Socrates is mortal.
>
>   "All Clowns are Masked"
>   Delmore Schwartz, 1938

Anthropology has important contributions to make in extending the study of the self. An integrated and cumulative body of anthropological theory relevant to the self has yet to be realized. Nevertheless, it is possible to connect several lines of theory to suggest converging general orientations and research strategies bearing on the study of the self and related ideas. In addition, the ever-expanding comparative ethnographic record constitutes a valuable resource that can be exploited to examine the broader applicability or inapplicability of Western conceptions of the self – as well as to Investigate, In their own right, self concepts that have developed Independent of Western influence.

Anthropologists have historically displayed both an explicit and an implicit concern with the self and related concepts.[1] The late nineteenth-century British evolutionists focused primary attention on the idea of progress as it [68] was manifested .In the cumulative accretions of generic cultural growth and In the orthogenic development of supposedly universal Institutions. They anchored their theories in a conception of the human mind that operated under a self-evident, If not selfish, philosophy of utilitarianism and that adopted an appropriate logic of self-conscious "rational" choice. This self-fulfilling methodological individualism viewed the human actor as operating, to some extent, independently of social and cultural constraints. Contemporaneous reactions to aspects of British evolutionism arose In Germany and France.

Nascent German social science was strongly influenced by idealistic philosophy. <u>Vőlkerpsychologie</u> (as elaborated by Steinthal and Lazarus, Wundt, and others) stressed the existence of the group mind or collective identity, a construct based in part on biology but more decisively shaped by the cumulative effects of history and tradition. While developmentalism and transformation were parts of the overarching schemes, there was recognition of varying <u>Volkgeisten</u> (or <u>ethé</u>) – or to use Adolf Bastian's term, <u>Vőlkergedenken</u>, 'folk ideas' – produced by the different geographical situations (<u>geographicische Provincen</u>) and historical experiences of human groups.[2] Methodological

---

[1] This historical section has been informed by numerous secondary, as well as primary, sources. Among the more useful secondary sources that have influenced the present discussion are Alexander Goldenweiser (1933), Fay B Karpf (1932), A Irving Hallowell (1954a), EE Evans-Pritchard (1965), and David Bidney (1967).

[2] These German concepts defy precise translation into English. Vőlkerpsychologie can be, and has been, rendered 'group psychology', 'social psychology', and 'the psychology of peoples'. The literal translation 'folk psychology' is perhaps misleading, as it might suggest the particular people's own psychological conceptions. Therefore, it is probably wisest to retain the original German term. H Steinthal and M Lazarus, in a pragmatic article in the first issue (1860) of their Journal, *Zeitschift fur Vőlkerpsychologie und Sprachwissenshaft* (perhaps the first journal devoted to what we would now

individualism, however, continued to prevail in the sense that group psychology was conceived of as an individual psychology writ large. Various cultural Institutions were seen as differentially reflective of separate faculties of the Individual mind.[3][3]

Wilhelm Wundt rejected the simple Lockean *tabula rasa* / cause-and-effect / stimulus-response psychology of British associationism. Conation, or will, was coordinate with cognition; affects formed an important part of his system; and processes of apperception could shape and transform sensory perception. The Individual mind – and by extension, the collective mind – was capable of creative synthesis based upon particular past experiences, the momentary state of the apperceiving mind, and a whole host of other contingent factors. Cause and effect, stimulus and response, could not be understood without recourse to the Intervening mediation of the apperceptive mass. The Boasian notion of cultural integration and the particularistic resynthesis of diffused culture traits are direct analogues of the apperceiving individual mind.[4][4] [69]

In France, with the ascendancy of Durkheimian sociology (circa the turn of the century), the individual self was submerged into the collective conscience – only to surface with the dispersion of social bonds attendant on increased social density and the development of complex societies organized in terms of organic solidarity. For Durkheim and his followers, the primacy of society was taken as a (god-) given, and Individual consciousness and sense of self were products of society, rather than society being formed out of a social contract consensually created by and voluntarily entered into by autonomous Individuals.

Despite his insistence that society was a *sui generis* phenomenon, irreducible to the psychological motivations of individuals, Durkheim does discuss the position of the self or ego in his general system. These ideas are first set forth in the *Division of Labor* (1893; 1933 ed: 129-32), are reiterated *In The Elementary Forms of Religious Life* (1912; 1960 ed: 387-90), and are most fully developed in his late essay "The Duality of Human Existence" (1914; 1964 ed: 325-40). Durkheim, in essence, argues for the presence of two types of ego internalized within the individual. The first might be glossed as the psychobiological ego: that part of the self concerned with sensory processes, and given to self-interest and the satisfaction of Individual needs. The second may be rendered as the socio-cultural ego: that portion of the self that originates from outside the individual, and is involved with conceptual and moral ideas. Durkheim sees this dualism echoed In well-nigh universal notions of body and soul, to which his qualitative distinctions of profane and sacred can be affixed [and to which Levi-Strauss might apply the nature/culture antithesis (see, eg, Totemism 1963)]. These two egos coexist in a state of chronic tension

---

call Psychological Anthropology and Language and Culture), envisioned two approaches to the study of Völkerpsychologie: first, a general Völkerpsychologie that would encompass processes of generic human mental evolution; and secondly, a specific Völkerpsychologie that would be concerned with the psychology of particular peoples. [95]

The term *Völkgeist* ('folk spirit') again is difficult to translate. In the hands of nineteenth- and early twentieth-century German social philosophers, it took on varying shades of meaning ranging from a disembodied spiritual quality, to a collective sense of the French *le moral* as "mind" or "being", to the modern use of the term "ethos" as denoting the emotional tone associated with a collectivity. Gregory Bateson, in *Naven* (1936) is usually credited with establishing the modern usage of the concept of "ethos". However, it is interesting to note that John Stuart Mill uses this Greek term in its approximate modern usage, in his conception of "ethology".

[3] Thus, for example, it was argued that a people's imagination could be discovered in their literature, their moral sense in their laws and customs, their emotions in their religious rituals, etc.

[4] The implicit use of the notion of apperception can be traced back in Boas's work to his doctoral dissertation. which was a psychophysical experiment on different reports of the color of sea water. The notion of apperception was taken up and elaborated in America by William James (*Principles of Psychology* 1890), and formed an important part of his psychological system.

and opposition, a situation that becomes increasingly aggravated with the advance of civilization.

Durkheim's notion of the sociocultural ego is equivalent to the idea of a social person. The social person is, paradoxically, an Impersonal concept, almost a Kantian abstraction defined in terms of suprapersonal reason and morality. The social person refers neither to a specific Individual nor to a particular entity and can be compared, in religious terms, to the evanescent soul with its divine origin and continuous sacred connections, or can be thought of in social structural terms, as an Intersect of social [70] relations (cf. Krader 1966: 483; Krader 1967). The latter usage was Introduced into social anthropology by AR Radcliffe-Brown in the *Andaman Islanders* (1922), elaborated by him in his 1940 essay "On Social Structure" (1953 ed: 193f.), and applied by other structural-functionalists as an operational construct for the social analysis of jural, moral, economic, and religious norms and relationships.

The Durkheim image of primitive peoples emphasized their supposed lack of Individuality and consciousness of self: the strong collective consciousness and correspondingly uniform sociocultural ego overwhelmed the psychobiologlcal ego. Individual existence was inseparably tied to the group, and individual representations were consonant with collective representations. Individuation, egoism, and true self-awareness, are possible, for Durkheim, only when society begins to differentiate through increased social density and expansion of the division of labor. When the collective conscience begins to atrophy, a situation is produced in which meanings and emotions associated with collective representations rely less on principles of identity and more on equivalence (cf. Wallace 1961). Not only do individuals emerge in this social transformation; moral individualism – a cult or religion of the individual, in which the individual is imbued with dignity and sacred qualities – also arises.

The philosopher Lucien Levy-Bruhl shared many of the presuppositions of the Durkheimian school. He made much use of available ethnographic materials. Whereas Durkheim and his followers tended to use data from particular primitive cultures in intensive fashion, Levy-Bruhl's approach was more extensive and encyclopedic (although he often displayed the philosopher's uncanny knack of extracting plausible meaning from small pieces of evidence). Levy-Bruhl's primary concern was the comparative analysis of thought. His fundamental assumption – that the thought processes of primitive man were "pre-logical" (see 1910, eg) – has been much maligned and misunderstood; before his death he repudiated the term (1949; 1975 ed: 47-49). The adjective "pro-logical", as employed by Levy-Bruhl, referred less to an evolutionarily anterior or inferior mode of thought than to widely spread forms of thought that didn't recognize certain canons of logic formalized in the post-Aristotelian West. Levy-Bruhl overstated his contrast between prelogical and logical thought by failing to sufficiently appreciate [71] the enormous differences existent among primitive cultures and by neglecting the significance and incidence of prelogical thinking in modern society. Nevertheless, certain of his ideas are germane to the present discussion.

One of Levy-Bruhl's more important ideas is what he called the "Law of Participation" (In his later *Notebooks*, he ceased referring to participation as a law; op.cit: 60f.). This "Law" refers to a suprasensible mental coincidence between persons and things such that they form part of one another, almost to the point of identity. Levy-Bruhl brilliantly documents such phenomena in the mystical links connecting a man to his name, his shadow, his totem, and his clan. These participations, he maintains, must be judged from the native point-of-view as parts of the self, components of identity, and extensions of ego. Any analysis that limits consideration of self-related concepts to the boundaries of the skin must, by premature definition, be defective.

Although the connected volumes *How Natives Think* (1910; Eng. trans. 1926) and *Primitive Mentality* (1922; Eng. trans. 1923) remain the most read and most cited of Levy-Bruhl's works, his neglected volume on *The "Soul" of the Primitive* (1927; Eng. trans. 1928) is a more refined and better-illustrated statement of his position. It is also more relevant to our present concerns. The term "soul" (*l'âme*) is used, with due qualifications, as an imperfect gloss for an inner life essence and for the subjective (and sometimes objective) sense of self. Levy-Bruhl believed that notions such as self, person, or "soul" were incapable of being conceptualized and articulated by primitive peoples. Thus, such ideas could be studied only indirectly, through analysis of their collective representations.

Durkheim's lineal intellectual heir. Marcel Mauss, also provided some influential perspectives for understanding the self. Two essays are of particular interest: "*L'âme, le nom et la personne*" (1929) and "*Une Categorie de le l'esprit humain: la notion de personne celle de 'moi*" (1938). Like Durkheim and Levy-Bruhl, Mauss sees the self as a social product, which in primitive societies is relatively undifferentiated and intimately bound up with ideas of "soul", appropriation of names, and roles in ritual performance. Mauss's notion of "social person" (*personne morale*) however, differs in significant ways from Durkheim's formulation. [72]

Mauss's "social person" is an empirical entity derived directly from particular and variable cultural factors. A concretized notion of "social person" is not necessarily universally present in all societies. Mauss finds social personality existing in rudimentary form among the Zuni, Kwakiutl, and Aranda.

Although he shares with Durkheim and Levy-Bruhl the belief that a developed conception of self and person tends to emerge in more complex societies, Mauss does not view the correlation as absolute. He has difficulty in discerning a developed, objectified notion of the person in traditional China and in Buddhist and Taoist philosophy. In a brilliant excursion, Mauss accounts for the abstract, objectified category of social person in Western thought as eventuating from a transformation of meaning attributed to the Greco-Roman conception of *persona* or mask. Originally a mythic representation (*personnalité mythique*), the mask in later Roman drama comes to signify a social personality (*personne morale*). The implication is that the mythic mask Is a manifestation of a religiously based collective representation, while the later use of masks has become desacralized and represents a differentiated social status (for a more extended treatment of the concept of persona, see the discussion in Gordon Allport 1937: 24-54).

Two repetitive assumptions run through the classic French sociological interpretations of primitive man and his society. First, because primitive society is seemingly undifferentiated, it is assumed that individual personality and selfhood must be similarly undifferentiated. Indeed, Durkheim was so taken by his metaphor of mechanical society, replete with interchangeable parts, that he even briefly suggests in *The Division of Labor* (1933 ed: 133-35) that all members of a primitive society tend to look alike! The second assumption is that primitive peoples are incapable of formulating an articulate philosophy of self or individuality, since self-identity is so intimately tied to the group that the very notion of individual selfhood is an alien concept.

These assumptions were doubtless conditioned by the fact that neither Durkheim, Levy-Bruhl, nor Mauss ever had the opportunity to engage in first-hand fieldwork. It is true that all three placed a high value on the fieldwork of others and they steeped themselves in the available ethno graphic [73] literature. However, their theoretical presuppositions that primitive societies and individuals were undifferentiated and lacking in a conscious philosophy of the self led them into the logical trap of supporting their assertions by recourse to a methodology that proceeded from, and rarely went beyond, the analysis of collective representations. Had they paid more attention to Individual representations – in the form of life histories, native testimonies, and texts – their picture of primitive society, its internal variability, and the capacity of its members for self-expression might have been different. In brief, while they were able to expose the flaws of vulgar forms of methodological Individualism and simplistic psychological reductionism, their own methodology left them open to charges of sociological reification that posed problems of equal magnitude.[5](5)

The French sociological tradition continues to be influential today. Fieldwork by French scholars has made a difference. Thus, the works of Marcel Griaule and Germanie Dieterlen have revealed

---

5 It is worth emphasizing that the legitimate criticism of early culture-and-personality theory, to the effect that culture cannot be deduced from the personality of its individual members, finds an equally egregious parallel in the efforts of social-and-cultural determinists to derive the personalities from social structures or cultural systems.

sophisticated philosophical speculation among the Dogon of East Africa.[6][6] Maurice Leenhardt (a Protestant missionary anthropologist with twenty-five years of field experience in New Caledonia; and the successor to Mauss, and the predecessor of Levi-Strauss, as occupant of the chair in the History of Primitive Religions at L'Ecole Pratique des Hautes Etudes) produced a major work centrally concerned with conceptions of self and person. This book, *Do Kamo* (1947), was recently translated (1979) and is enjoying a born-again life in the English-speaking world.

Leenhardt was much influenced by Mauss, and he carried on a continuing dialogue with Levy-Bruhl (Crapanzano 1979); in fact, some of Levy-Bruhl's retractions about the nature of primitive mentality were inspired by problematic field data presented by Leenhardt. Leenhardt's description of self and person (or personage) are informed by a solid grasp of the language and its nuances, and critical ethnographic detail. His native New Caledonians are not partitive people produced from the perspective of a Parisian armchair; they are whole personages integrated into a phenomenologically real, for them, behavioral environment. As Crapanzano notes (1979: xxii-xxv), Leenhardt seems to view these native New Caledonian conceptions from two perspectives: a relational dimension and an existential one. [74]

From a relational perspective, the personage is connected to other personages – human and non-human, material and Immaterial – through a variety of affective and supra-sensible means. The distinction between self and other is blurred; and the body is only a temporary locus, and not a source of individual identity. As Levy-Bruhl and Mauss so brilliantly anticipated, a man participates in his name or names, and no simple name adequately sums up his being. Reminiscent of the Platonic dialogue between Crotylus and Hermogenes, the New Caledonians seem to feel, as does Crotylus, that names and nouns are indeed proper and are "wired into" – by a binding law of causality – the nature of the things they imitate; whereas Hermogenes would consider the connection between nouns and names and the things they nominate as arbitrary consequences of convention, treaty, contract, or covenant.

The implicit existential dimension of the New Caledonian concept of person comes out in Leenhardt's insistence that these people are not individuated – that they are, in essence, pre-persons or personages. Leenhardt's submerged evolutionism surfaces in his consideration of the New Caledonian world as cosmomorphic, which is even anterior to an anthropomorphic world-view and certainly far removed from supposed Western analytic and positivistic perspectives based ultimately on dualism and logical positivism (Crapanzano 1979: xxiv). Issues about individualism and personhood will be considered further in subsequent sections of this paper.

An interesting fusion of the Maussian approach to the person and a traditional British social anthropological perspective is represented in Meyer Fortes's insufficiently appreciated article "On the Concept of the Person Among the Tallensi" (1973). This many-layered and richly textured ethnographic account provides an exemplary analysis of self and person among this West African tribe, and resonates with ethnopsychological understanding.

Theoretical interest in the self is deeply entrenched in American social and behavioral science. A review of the notable theoretical contributions by such early figures as William James, George Horton Cooley, and James Baldwin will not be attempted here.[7][7] However, the highly germinal formulations of George Herbert Mead deserve more than passing mention, since the modern sociological and social psychological [75] symbolic-interactionist approach to the self can be traced directly to him (1913, 1934). Mead provided a philosophical and behaviorist system that accounted for the ontogenesis of the self through the emergence of symbolic capacities developed in interaction with others. The self was, then, preeminently a social product. Partly out of Mead's Influence, models of social interaction were

---

6 For major implications of Dogon philosophy, see especially Griaule (1948) and Griaule & Dieterlen (1954). These scholars also explored Dogon concepts of "soul" and "person" (e.g., Griaule 1940, 1947; Dieterlen 1941, 1973).

7 Reasonable starting points for surveying psychological understandings of the self concept can be found in Allport (1943) and Sherif (1968). [96]

constructed in dramaturgical terms. Thus sociologist Robert E. Park comments:

> It is probably no mere historical accident that the word person, in its first meaning, is a mask. It is rather a recognition of the fact that everyone is always and everywhere, more or less consciously, playing a role ... It is in these roles that we know each other; it is in these roles that we know ourselves (quoted in Goffman 1959: 19).

The view of social Interaction as drama is highly elaborated in Erving Goffman's work. Not only does social interaction consist in <u>masks</u> and <u>role-playing</u>, but we can also analyze the <u>performance</u> of <u>actors</u> in various defined <u>scenes</u> and <u>settings</u> before an <u>audience</u> located both <u>front-stage</u> and <u>backstage</u>. The gifted actor is a master at techniques of <u>impression management</u> and <u>face work</u>, and is responsive to a variety of <u>promptings</u> and <u>cues</u>. While the dramaturgical model provides a powerful tool for analyzing not only ongoing social interaction but also interaction preserved in literature and in other expressive media, it does grow out of Western dramatic conventions. Can the dramaturgical model be productively applied in non-Western contexts where different conventions and understandings, as well as different standards of dramatic performance, obtain?

As an opening wedge into this Issue, let me suggest some perspectives derived from the ethnographic study of masking and ceremonial performance among the Indians of Eastern North America.[8][8] Among some of these tribes the terms for <u>mask</u> have some interesting cognates. Whereas some experts derive the etymology of the Latin <u>persona</u> from *personare*, 'to sound through',[9][9] the Iroquois term is related to the term for "face". With other Eastern Woodlands groups we get cognates referring to "skin", "bark" – and for the Creeks, a possible etymology relating the term for "mask" to the word for "eye".[10][10] While most of the terms relate to external image or outer covering (in fact, one type of Iroquois mask was fashioned out of plaited corn-husks), I think we do not fully understand the meaning of masks in these [76] cultures If we treat their usage as analogous to our sense of masks as disguise, as distortion or caricature that covers up a true reality hidden behind the mask.

The wooden Iroquois "False Face" masks were considered to possess vital properties. They were carved from a living basswood tree (a type of wood known for its astringent and absorptive qualities), and represented a primordial mythic figure whose domain was the forest and who possessed curing powers. Custodial care of the mask involved a social relationship in that the mask required periodic "feeding". It is interesting to note that the "foods" craved by the False Face were sunflower oil, old tobacco (*Nicotlana rustica*), and corn mush – which were smeared on the protruding lips of the mask. Since these plants represent the earliest horticultural horizons in the area, it seems that the ritual feeding of the mask is an ancient practice extending back into prehistory. In symbolic terms, the relationship can be seen to represent a symbiosis whereby successful exploitation of the products of the forest (i.e., wild game) and safe passage through this dangerous domain (nature) are exchanged for the domesticated products (i.e., cultivated plants) of human labor (culture). If the terms of this traditional form of reciprocity are not honored and the masks are left unfed, nightmares, illness, and general misfortune will result.

From what has been said, Iroquois masks can be considered social persons in the Maussian sense. However, it is important to realize that the human being who dons the mask does not impersonate the

---

8 This account draws heavily on the typological work of Frank G Speck (1950) and that of William N Fenton (1940), as well as interpretative leads provided by John Witthoft (1967). An exploration into the deeply embedded meanings of Eastern Woodland masking will be found in RD Fogelson and AB Walker (1980, in press).

9 According to the Oxford English Dictionary, this popular etymology is made dubious by the long <u>o</u> in <u>persona</u>. Others have suggested other roots for the word, including an Etruscan form with a quite different meaning (Robert Elliot pc).

10 I am indebted to Amelia Bell Walker for tracing the semantics of some of this lexical material.

False Face spirit; rather he unites with and becomes that spirit in a fashion consistent with Levy-Bruhl's idea of participation. Another way of considering this phenomenon, then, is <u>not</u> to view it as role-playing or play-acting but to see it as a temporary incarnation of cosmic reality: the False Face spirit, in effect, impersonates the mask wearer.[11] To a large extent, what is real and ultimately true for the Iroquois is what is outside and "up front" in the faces and interfaces of these masked personages. Perhaps a closer approximation of the Indian reality can be gleaned from a quotation from Frank Speck (1942) regarding the "stage" upon which Indian rituals are "performed":

Ceremonial grounds, whether in the open or enclosed, represent a deeply significant allegory, a phase of the sky-world on earth within which human beings are carrying [77] on actions in ceremonial form, the counterpart of those of the spirits above, the latter being invisibly present during performances accompanying their living kinfolk.

Regretfully, I take leave of the living world of masks, but I hope enough has been said to show the relevance of this topic to studies of self and person, as well as to indicate some of the strengths and limitations of the Western dramaturgical approach to performances.

The concept of <u>identity</u>, as employed by many contemporary social scientists, shows close connections to social-interaction theories. The notion of identity first gained currency through the work of Erik Erikson (1950, 1959). Erikson's version of psychoanalytic ego psychology stressed the enduring sense of self and self-continuity that he labeled "identity". Identity was shaped by the historic unfolding of this sense of self as it passed through specific epigenetic phases. The course of movement through these phases was conditioned by the residual effects of resolution or non-resolution of phase-specific conflicts encountered at previous stages in the epigenetic cycle. Despite developmental change. Identity can be likened to, in Dylan Thomas's words, a "green fuse" that provides a sense of continuity and sameness through the individual life cycle.

Erikson boldly endeavored (1968) to use the concept of ego identity as a bridge that would connect the psychobiologlcal drives of man's Inner nature with those Influences on the self originating from society and culture. Despite his efforts to effect a psychosocial synthesis, Erikson's model is ultimately powered by the ineluctable forces of the Freudian <u>Id</u>. To his credit, Erikson did spend two brief periods doing fieldwork among the Sioux and the Yurok. He succeeded in making some acute observations regarding childhood and world-view; but in place of ethnopsychological insight, we get applied psychoanalysis. Thus, weaponless Sioux warriors skewer their externalized feminine superegos around a Sun Dance pole; and, alas, the poor Yurok find themselves drifting up the alimentary canal without a paddle.

Erikson became something of a godfather to troubled youth of the 1960s, with his popular notions of identity crises and psychological moratorium. He produced innovative work in psychobiography; *Young Man Luther* (1958), in particular, [78] must stand as a modern masterpiece of this genre. However, I think it fair to conclude that Erikson's notion of identity, with its universalist psychological grid and residual influence of sociocultural factors, has only a limited utility for comparative studies of the self.

The term identity is used generally by many theorists to denote an image of the self. Richard Robbing (l973a) has produced a survey of the use of the Identity concept within anthropology. He isolates three basic approaches or models: 1) the identity-health model, which stresses processes of adjustment and maladjustment – mostly from a clinical perspective (cf. Kenneth Soddy 1961, for a review

---

11 Many of the Iroquois False Faces have twisted visages, supposedly resulting from an unsuccessful power struggle in which the prototypical False Face was defeated by the Great Spirit or Sapling. William Sturtevant, in a paper presented to the 1979 International Congress of Americanists, related an instance in which one of these masks slipped off a dancer during a ceremony, and the face of the man behind the mask mirrored the distorted physiognomy represented by the mask.

of some of the relevant issues involved here); 2) the identity-interaction model, which has been discussed above; and 3) the identity world-view model, which emphasizes culturally constituted meanings and values, and will be treated below.

For analytic purposes, most theorists have found it necessary to divide the concept of identity into various aspects, components, or dimensions. Thus Erikson felt the need to separate ego identity from the more generic concept of identity and to distinguish positive from negative identity. Daniel R. Miller (1963: 673) differentiates public identity from self-identity. In other analytic models, the structure of identity is seen as consisting of different interacting regions or stratigraphic layers arranged hierarchically or in terms of temporal priorities. A typical example here would be Miller's tripartite scheme, which recognizes a core identity, various sub-identities, and a peripheral personal identity (pp. 674-76).

Identity can also be broken down into components that refer to evaluative or self-appraisal functions. For these purposes, Miller proposed (pp. 679-83) analytic distinctions between what he labels actual identity, potential identity, and ideal identity. A somewhat more elaborated model of this type was developed by Anthony FC Wallace and myself (1965) to examine certain encounters that we termed identity struggles. In this scheme, total identity is divided into the following four components: a real identity, indicating a self-report about where the individual "really" stands with regard to particular dimensions of identity; an ideal identity, referring to the kind of positive identity the individual would like to emulate; a feared identity, a negatively valued identity that the Individual desires to avoid; and a [79] claimed identity, a set of images that the individual presents to others in order to influence their evaluation of his identity.

Some illustrations may clarify the distinctions. Certain dimensions of identity may be ordered on a lineal scale. Stature provides an obvious example: thus I may have a real identity of being 5' 6¾", an ideal identity of 6'2", a feared identity of being a four foot midget, and a claimed identity – claimed on the basis of wearing platform shoes, hot-air-fluffed hair, and an erect posture – of 5'8". Other identity dimensions may not be ordinal. A college freshman may have an ideal image of himself as a "Big Man on Campus", a feared identity of being regarded as a "nerd", a real identity as a pedestrian B-minus student from the middle-class suburbs, and a claimed identity – proclaimed by a weather-beaten fringed leather jacket, a shoulder-length haircut, and a crimson headband – as an Apache warrior.

In general, the individual strives to move the real identity closer to the ideal identity and to maximize distance from the feared identity. This is attempted through manipulation of the claimed identity in social interaction by "identity work", a process similar to Goffman's notion of "face work" (Wallace 1967). The model has proven useful in analyzing the dynamics of family therapy sessions, as well as for charting identity struggles occurring in certain other cultural arenas (Wallace and Fogelson 1965: 387-98). Lawrence C Watson (1970) has applied this framework to study identity processes among the Guajiro Indians of Venezuela. Robbins (1973b) has employed it in his investigation of drinking behavior among the Naskapi Indians of Northeastern Canada, and John L Caughey (1980) has adopted the general model to help understand the relationship of personal identity to social identity on Truk.

The concept of identity has been extended to the level of groups. An enormously diverse literature has grown up around such notions as "national Identity" and the currently fashionable concept of "ethnic identity" (eg, DeVos & Romanucci-Ross 1975). I have no desire to review this research here and shall restrict myself to two general comments. First, I do not feel that individual identity is a microcosm of collective identity, as is too often assumed. It is the very lack of isomorphism between these two levels that seems to generate some of the most interesting problems [80] (eg, Kevin Avruch's 1981 book on American Immigrants to Israel). Secondly, I think that certain analytic frameworks developed for studying individual identity can be usefully extended to the group level. However, I also believe that data for constructing a collective identity should be sought less from individuals and more from analyses of collective cultural expressions. I have in mind here the interpretation of particular culture-heroes and their roles as group images, the analysis of themes from literature and popular media, and the study of cultural performances (at home or abroad) wherein a group encapsulates selected aspects of its identity that it wishes to present to others and to itself (see Bell 1968, Singer 1977).

Having considered social-interactionist viewpoints on the self, with special emphasis on the concept of identity, I now turn to certain cultural perspectives on the self as developed within American anthropology.

The modern pluralistic and relativistic concept of culture remains one of the hallmarks of Boasian and Boasian-derived anthropology. While Boas himself retained a healthy respect for the individual as the ultimate locus of culture, some of his followers – most notably A.L. Kroeber (1917) and Robert Lowie (1917) – conceived of culture as possessing its own ontological reality, and argued for a sharp separation between psychological and cultural levels of explanation. This extreme form of cultural determinism, particularly as manifested in Kroeber's superorganic view, precipitated a reaction among certain Boasian anthropologists that ultimately led to the Culture and Personality movement. While classic Culture and Personality studies drew heavily on psychological and psychoanalytic theory, it too remained at base a form of cultural determinism (see Aberle 1957). It was culture that determined personality and not vice versa; the individual was lost in the aggregated picture of an ideal type congruent with cultural premises: deviations from the ideal type were considered to represent maladjustment and pathology.

However, early attacks on the superorganic position, particularly those launched by Edward Sapir (1917) and Alexander Goldenweiser (1917), led to a reaffirmation of the significance of the individual – not only as a passive bearer and transmitter of culture, but also as an active creator and re-creator of culture. Sapir's (1938;1949 ed: 569ff) [81] rediscovery of missionary J Owen Dorsey's notation on an Omaha text, "But Two Crows denies this", indicated that members of the same culture could disagree about fundamental parts of their cultural belief system. Culture was not an infallible multilith machine printing identical copies. Recognition of the existence of individuals within primitive societies pointed to the theoretical Issues posed by intra-cultural variations. Some of these issues can, perhaps, best be highlighted by a brief consideration of the work of Paul Radin.

Perhaps more important to the present discussion is Radin's pioneering book, published in 1927, *Primitive Man as Philosopher*. In this work, Radin took aim on continental social philosophers and armchair anthropologists who denied the existence of elaborated philosophical systems among primitive peoples. Through a synoptic survey of native cosmologies, recorded informant testimony, and oral literature (including myths, proverbs and aphorisms) he demonstrated that primitive man does, indeed, ask questions about such ultimate epistemological concerns as the origin and meaning of life and death; about ethical concerns regarding human conduct, morality, and the good life; about logic and the nature of evidence. He also demonstrated that some members of primitive societies exercise a healthy skepticism about the supposedly prelogical beliefs and mystical participations attributed to them by Levy-Bruhl and others.

Radin is probably most remembered today for his introduction of the life history as a technique in fieldwork (1913, 1920). Such documents often offered an inside glimpse into the personal recall and experiencing of events. If nothing else, the material contained in life histories demonstrated that the individual did not always mechanically retrace the blueprints of his culture. Life histories have many limitations. Boas, in his austere search for scientific truth, distrusted the technique because he felt informants were wont to lie and exaggerate, and investigators could never control for their own bias (1938: 680-82). A more serious consideration is that life history and autobiography are alien forms of expression that have no precedent in most native cultures. Indeed, personal history as a literary genre emerges in the Western World only in Renaissance times.[12][12] [82]

---

12   Thus we read in Paul Murray Kendall's fascinating entry, "Biographical Literature", *New Encyclopaedia Britannica* (Macropaedia 11: 1010):

Speaking generally, then, it can be said that autobiography begins with the Renaissance in the 15th century; and, surprisingly enough, the first example was written not in Italy but in England

Radin argued that all societies contained two intellectual classes or personality types: the philosophic type, who is given to reflection; and the man of action, who unquestioningly follows the dictates of the culture and derives his fulfillment through doing rather than thinking. If I can abruptly transpose the antithesis to modern preferences in Scotch whiskey; the man of action would prefer Dewar's White Label, while the philosopher would settle for Teachers Highland Cream. The philosophers are always outnumbered by the man of action, but Radin maintained that both types – and certain recurring dialectical relationships between them – are necessary for a society to remain viable.

One chapter in *Primitive Man as Philosopher* is of particular concern here: "The Nature of the Ego and Human Personality" (1927: 257-74). In this chapter Radin summarizes data reported for the Maori, Oglala Sioux, and Batak that indicate the presence of sophisticated notions of the ego. The ego is regarded by these peoples as multiplex and dynamic; it is composed of a substantive body and various named insubstantive essences. Radin bewailed the fact that too few of his fellow ethnologists had attempted to obtain systematic accounts of the ego from informed natives (1927, p. 260). Unfortunately, with few exceptions (eg, Lee 1945 and Smith 1952), Radin's admonitions were not heeded for another quarter-century.[13]13

---

by a woman entirely untouched by the "new learning" or literature. In her old age Margery Kempe, the sobbing mystic, or hysteric, of Lynn in Norfolk, dictated an account of her bustling, far-faring life, which, however concerned with religious experience, racily reveals her somewhat abrasive personality and the impact she made on her fellows. This is done in a series of scenes, mainly developed by dialogue. Though calling herself, in abject humility, "the creature," Margery knew, and has effectively transmitted the proof, that she was a remarkable person. [97]

The questions of why the genre of autobiography emerges in the West only in the 15th century, in England, with an unstable woman, and why the major form is dialogic – these are indeed matters for the sociology (or anthropology) of knowledge to ponder.

13 Discussion of conceptual issues concerning "the individual" and "individualism" continue to generate much heat, but little light, in the recent literature. It seems to me that three separable issues have become hopelessly confused in these recent discussions: 1) the "reality" of the individual in society and culture; 2) the analytic utility of such a concept for comparative research; and 3) the nature of individualism as an ideological doctrine or value emphasis in different cultures.

With regard to the first issue, the "reality" of individuals seems undeniable. Culture, language, mind, and thought seem premised on the existence of a reflexive, self-monitoring, individual self. What seems at issue is culture variation and differential degrees of articulateness and elaboration of this individual self. Thus the boundaries of the individual vary enormously, as do body-image conception, and the components of the individual self – the latter frequently phrased as material entitles or immaterial essences that approximate the notion of "soul". The reality of the individual self or ego can be vouchsafed by the observation made long ago by Franz Boas in *The Mind of Primitive Man* (1911) that no known language lacked personal pronouns to indicate "I, thou, and he" (1938 ed: 165).

The utility of a concept of the individual in historical and cross-cultural work has been questioned by many. Perhaps most visible in this debate has been Louis Dumont, who considers the notion of the individual an obstacle to understanding Indian society and history (1965a, 1965b, 1967). Dumont's more encompassing concern has been to contrast basic orientations in Western and Indian civilizations. While one can concede that Hindu society is less "individualistic" than Western society in terms of value emphases and styles of thought. It would be harder to concede that Indians lack a vocabulary for expressing notions of an individual [98] self, do not have a system of names that help label and differentiate an "individual," or that Indians are incapable of internal dialogues, self-reflection, and distinctions between self and other(s), all of which imply an individual self.

Self

A major stimulus for renewed interest in the self within American anthropology was a series of brilliant papers by A Irving Hallowell. A programmatic essay, "The Self and Its Behavioral Environment", appeared in 1954; a related group of papers on behavioral evolution, which paid special attention to the evolutionary significance of the self, culminated in "Personality, Culture, and Society in Behavioral Evolution" (1963a); several other papers provided in-depth analyses of the conceptions of self and person among the Ojibwa Indians (1955, 1960, l963b, 1966).

Hallowell regarded self-awareness, with the implicit corollary assumption of subject/object distinction, as a generic prerequisite for and universal feature of all human culture. The notion of the self as an object that could be differentiated from other objects that were non-self developed ontogenetically as a product of social interaction. However, self concepts were also seen to be culturally constituted and

---

The second issue, as represented by Dumont, is obviously related to the third: individualism as ideology. Individualism has long been pointed out as an abiding value and mode of thought in Western society. Steven Lukes (1973) offers a useful survey of the history and components of the Western idea of individualism as expressed in philosophy and social science. (It is interesting to note here that Western intellectuals have so internalized the notion of individualism as dominant in Western world-view that they tend to ignore or deemphasize the presence of such competing ideas as the development of socialism as a particularly Western notion, or the wisdom of the collective voice as embodied in the idea of *vox populi* (see G Boas 1969).

Kenelm Burridge's recent book *Someone, No One* (1979) is an ambitious effort to clarify the understanding of individuality. I cannot here do justice to the subtlety of his argument, which involves cross-cultural as well as Western historical data, Burridge poses an analytic opposition between a person – defined as someone with a social and moral identity – and an individual, who lacks such an identity and therefore is capable of a conscious perception of morality and society and thus can act as an independent commentator and innovator. Burridge questions the simplistic association of individualism with greed, selfishness, and exploitation of others and discerns a positive value in individualistic moral responsibility that he traces back to the New Testament and Early Christianity. Nevertheless, his distinction seems almost a modern reiteration of classical evolutionary and French sociological theories, since individualism is viewed as a Western development historically precipitated from more general matrix of undifferentiated personalism. While Burridge's scheme bears superficial resemblance to Radin's distinction between men of thought ("individuals") and men of action ("social persons"), Radin would be more prone to recognize the existence of primitive philosophers. [99]

Another trend in recent considerations of the individual self is to see the construction (and deconstruction) of the self as a dynamic process mediated by symbols. Such a viewpoint is implicit in "The Invention of the Self" (a chapter in Roy Wagner's *The Invention of Culture* 1975), explicit in Abner Cohen's "Symbolic Action and the Structure of the Self" (1977), and in Bruce Kapferer's essay "Mind, Self, and Other In Demonic Illness; The Negation and Reconstruction of Self" (1979). While less dynamic, Milton Singer's attempt to establish a semiotic anthropology of the self (1980), based upon Peirce's theory of signs, represents a notable effort to incorporate the self into mainstream symbolic anthropology.

In partial opposition, perhaps, to symbolic studies of the individual or self, which are premised on an essential dualism between self as subject and self as object, are various recent pleas for a more holistic and phenomenologically informed understanding of the self. These would include T M S Evens' essay on "The Predication of the Individual in Anthropological Interactionism" (1977); Lawrence Watson's attempt to distinguish the study of personality from the study of individuals more or less on the basis of nomothetic versus ideographic emphases (1978); and Gelya Frank's eloquent plea for a phenomenological perspective that will emphasize the experiencing self in life-history research (1979).

thus variable In different human groups. [83] Hallowell situated the self in what he termed the behavioral environment – a culturally constituted field that is meaningful, perceptible, and phenomenologically real for participants in a particular culture. Hallowell felt that the self and the behavioral environment, so delineated, were subjects amenable to empirical research. To facilitate such study, he outlined a set of five basic orientations – provided by every culture – that function instrumentally in the individual's psychological adjustment to his world. These orientations are: a self orientation, an object-orientation, a spatio-temporal orientation, a motivational orientation, and a normative orientation.

In his related article on "The Ojibwa Self and Its Behavioral Environment" (1955), Hallowell makes an initial foray into this newly charted territory. He utilizes a synthetic first-person autobiographical statement to elucidate some dimensions of the Ojibwa self, but he doesn't formally analyze the five orientations listed above.

The article "Ojibwa Ontology, Behavior, and World View" (1960), originally published in a festschrift for Paul Radin, has probably had the greatest impact of all of Hallowell's writings on the self and related concepts. In this brilliant exploration of ethnometaphysics, Hallowell concentrates on the Ojibwa view of the person. Culturally recognized classes of beings are delineated, and the concept of "person" is shown to be not coterminous with human beings. The category of person can include certain culturally postulated other-than-human beings who play a significant role in the Ojibwa's adjustment to their behavioral environment. The notion of person serves as an important tool for bringing to the surface many deeply embedded aspects of Ojibwa world-view; seemingly inconsistent features of Algonkian grammatical categories, name usage, ideas about power, mythologic beliefs, conceptions of dreams, metamorphoses, and "souls" are unified into a coherent moral universe.

Hallowell1a richly detailed (1960) account does offer some startling insights into Ojibwa ethnometaphysics, but certain conceptual and methodological questions remain: how is the concept of the person related to the notion of the self that Hallowell discussed so cogently in previous programmatic statements? How are data relevant to notions of the self and person collected? Let us consider some of these issues in some of the work that attempts to follow Hallowell's lead. [84]

Mary Black, in her unpublished doctoral dissertation (1967) and in several Important papers (1969a, 1969b, 1976, 1977a, and 1977b), has attempted to test Hallowell's informally derived classification of Ojibwa ontology with more formal ethnosemantic eliciting procedures. She has paid particular attention to a taxonomy encompassing "persons".

In general, Black's findings tend to validate the general classification of "persons" advanced by Hallowell. Black shows that agreement as to what is included in the category of non-human persons is not altogether consistent for her Ojibwa Informants. Hallowell had anticipated some of these difficulties by recognizing that outward appearance of form – the basis of most classification – might obscure a common inner essence; he also noted that certain Ojibwa "persons" were capable of metamorphosis and thus couldn't be constrained to a single taxonomic category. Black extends the explanation of categorical ambiguity to include situational variables (1977a) and native notions of Inherent and transitory power (1977b). She also argues that a certain degree of *percept ambiguity* and categorical indeterminancy may be an Important (and necessary?) feature of Ojibwa (and all?) cognitive orientations.

One interesting feature of Black's (and Hallowell's) analysis is that by making an initial distinction between self and objects-other-than-self, the category of persons (both human and other-than-human) is subsumed under the category of living things, which in turn becomes a sub-category of objects-other-than-self. The unexamined implication of all this hierarchical taxonomy is that the self cannot be considered a person, either as a human being or as an object possessing other-than-human attributes (e.g., degrees of power). Such a conclusion seems incongruous in the face of Ojibwa ethnographic data, and calls for a more detailed and inclusive treatment of the taxonomic features defining the Ojibwa self (a topic that Hallowell leaves incompletely analyzed in his article "The Ojibwa Self and Its Behavioral Environment").

Self

Black's reanalysis of Hallowell's Northern Ojibwa data, plus her own focused fieldwork among related Minnesota Chippewa, invite consideration of appropriate methodological approaches to studying such complex matters as the _self_ and [85] _person_. Hallowell's insights into the significance of the self and person came only late in his career – after extended ethnographic field research, control of the documentary record, acquisition of linguistic proficiency, and experience derived from administering projective tests. He did not set out explicitly to study the self and person; the significance of these concepts for understanding Ojibwa phenomenological realities arose gradually. Evidence for the structure of Ojibwa ethnometaphysics was based on linguistic clues, critical anecdotes, and apparent relations between different ranges and levels of ethnographic data. Only in his later papers did he attempt to construct a taxonomic model that unintentionally resembled the paradigm of the ethnoscientists.

Black's work decisively builds on the foundation provided by Hallowell and goes directly to the problem of the Ojibwa classification of things, or ontology. Rather than a distillation of implicit emic categories derived from what Geertz (1973) would label "thick description", Black utilizes formal eliciting procedures from her informants ("teachers") to generate ethnosemantic distinctions. Ethnographic grounding and salience are clearly of secondary concern, although certain suggestive insights into matters such as Ojibwa ideas of "power-control" and medicine (1977b) do emerge from her continuing research.

However, the degree of linguistic determination inherent in Black's approach may preclude deeper understanding of the notions of self and person. Black is not so naive as to fall victim to the nominalistic fallacy: "If the natives do not have a term for something, then it doesn't exist." Like Hallowell, she recognizes that the fact that the Ojibwa do not have a term for "person" does not deny its reality as a "covert category" occupying demarcatable semantic space in the Ojibwa classification of living things. Nevertheless, Black's adherence to formal eliciting procedures conducted in artificial settings makes one wonder if perhaps she is tapping only verbal behavior (and artifical behavior, at that, since it is divorced from everyday discourse).

I do not mean to dismiss the significance of formal ethnosemantic inquiry. Obviously the preponderance of information that an anthropologist obtains in the field comes from interviews and conversations. The more structured and controlled these interactions are, the more reliable these [86] data tend to be. But I do feel that ungrounded ethnosemantics will lead us only part-way toward understanding Ideas such as self and person.[14][14]

Another approach to the study of self and person, which also utilizes Ojibwa data and builds upon some of Hallowell's ideas, is represented in the work of Thomas Hay (1968, 1973, 1977). Hay distinguishes between a conscious self-concept (which is relatively easily verbalizable) and an unconscious self-concept (usually out of awareness; when raised to consciousness, subject to vigorous

---

14 I do not mean to disparage the quality and significance of Mary Black's work, for which I have considerable respect; for her, ethnoscientific analysis is a means to an end of deeper understanding of native conceptions, rather than an end in itself. Rather, I think, the barreness of the ethnoscientific approach to ethnopersonallty study is most clearly revealed in recent work with the Melanesian A'ara by Geoffrey White (1978, 1980) and similar research in Africa among the Masai by Kirk & Burton (1977), Burton & Kirk (1979). In these methodologically sophisticated studies, formally elicited "personality descriptors" are mapped and statistically analyzed with regard to particular Individuals and situations. This meticulous work comes close to a revival of a discredited trait-psychology in exotic dress". The "personality descriptors" themselves do not [100] seem to form part of a natural system recognized or recognizable by the A'ara or Masai, and the lateral and deeper semantic associations of those decontextualized lexemes are Inadequately explored. We end up with admirably "clean" studies that possess undoubted reliability, but the validity is limited to such an artificial and restricted domain – so abstracted from real people, real behavior, and real situations – that we learn very little about A'ara or Masai ethnopersonality.

denial). These two self-concepts, thus, can be Inconsistent.

To illustrate, Hay points out that the conscious Ojibwa self-concept emphasizes a lack of "powers," either natural or magical, and denial of capacity for anger. However, according to Hay, they unconsciously attribute to themselves great magical power, especially when angry; they further assume that this anger can be easily triggered and can have dangerous consequences for the object of their anger. Hay interprets this inconsistency between the conscious and unconscious self-concepts as psychodynamically premised on repression of these powerful capacities to harm others and projection of these Impulses onto other-than-human or *pawaganak* persons. The conscious self of the Ojibwa avoids expression of anger and behavior toward others that might be considered demanding; they picture themselves as helpless and powerless, petitioning the powerful *pawaganak* for assistance in times of need. By analyzing over 600 observed adult responses to annoying behavior by children. Hay supports his hypothesis that the unconscious self-concept accounts for the observed behavior better than the conscious self-concept does. He goes on to argue that the genesis of the Ojibwa unconscious self-concept results from characteristic adult noncontrol of aggressive behavior in children.

While some of Hay's assumptions may be questioned and alternate interpretations of his data could be advanced, I think his work is important in demonstrating the salience of unconscious and non-verbalizable aspects of the self that would be missed in the type of analysis pursued by Black. Hay's approach also shows how systematic and statistical use can be made of naturally occurring observed behavior. However, it is important to recognize that the emic level of interpretation, the Ojibwa's <u>own</u> conscious theories about their self-concept and motivational dispositions, loses out [87] to Hay's psychoanalytic-based Interpretations. In short, Hay provides a sufficient but not a necessary explanation of certain aspects of the Ojibwa self.

Anne Straus's ethnopsychological research among the Northern Cheyenne (1976, 1977) also clearly grows out of the pioneering studies of Hallowell. Since Dr Straus is a contributor to this volume and is more than capable of speaking for herself, I won't presume to summarize her contributions. However, I will take the opportunity to comment briefly on some aspects of her work that strike me as relevant to the present discussion. Unlike the fragmentary description of the Ojibwa self presented by Hallowell, Black, and Hay, Straus provides a comprehensive account of the Cheyenne conception of self, including its component parts and their integration. She also offers a native model of the normal development of the self through the procreative-life-death cycle, a course marked with interlocking sets of Cheyenne symbols that sum up to an enclosed total system.

Finally, she offers an extended description and analysis of the Cheyenne concept of person. Unlike the Ojibwa case, person is a named concept among the Cheyenne. The Cheyenne notion of person also extends beyond human beings to encompass various other-than-human persons. However, not all human beings are persons. Personhood is a status that must be attained through participation in the Cheyenne moral community of persons. Children lack knowledge and responsibility for their own actions, and thus are considered only potential persons. Deaf-mutes lacking powers of Cheyenne speech are non-persona, as are the insane and the celebrated Cheyenne "contraries".

Personhood is regarded as a status that can be lost. Depersonalization can eventuate from serious transgressions against the tribal norms, such as murder or violations of sacred taboos. My own research among the Cherokees also indicates that not all human beings are persons. Witches, for example, can assume a human appearance and thereby be classified as human beings; but they are not persons, since they operate outside the constraints of the moral community. Personhood is just one of their guises; they are considered to be counterfeit persons. They subsist only by capturing the life essence of others. In fact, some Cherokees do not even consider witches to be living beings. For all intents and purposes, witches are "dead" vis-à-vis the human community, [88] and once exposed, given the right time and opportunity, they are killed (Fogelson 1975).

The Cheyenne self attains individuation through different admixtures of qualities arranged along two polar continual a good/crazy axis and a wisdom~energy axis. Differentially accented combinations are characteristic of different stages of the life cycle and appropriate to complementary sex-role patterning. Thus, while personhood embodies a minimal set of shared qualities necessary for participating and functioning within the Cheyenne moral universe, Cheyenne persons possess distinctive selves.

Straus's orientation and methodology in obtaining this extraordinary rich corpus of material deserve comment. Like Mary Black, she clearly set out to study aspects of ethno-psychology: her project was not a serendipitous spin-off of more general ethnographic concerns; from the outset, she had misgivings about the dominant thrust of psychological anthropology in which the major effort is to apply Western theories of psychological processes and Western conceptions of personality to understand, or translate, the beliefs and behaviors of non-Western peoples. While in the field, she consciously kept Western theories and models at arm's length and attempted, as much as possible, to gain an emic reading of Cheyenne psychology and personality (or conversely, to obtain the Cheyenne's own etic categories in these areas). In order to accomplish this, she acquired a working knowledge of the Cheyenne language, she engaged in intensive participant-observation, and she developed some close friendships with her Cheyenne colleagues. Much of her data derive from the close questioning and counter-questioning of her Cheyenne friends. The results from sporadic attempts to use formal testing and eliciting techniques were disappointing. As in most successful fieldwork, the ultimate instrument proved to be a sensitive and responsive Investigator.

Perhaps the next step is to relax the arm-length hold on folk and formal Western psychological theories. Maybe these theories can now be brought into closer proximity to Cheyenne formulations, in an effort to discern significant similarities and differences. Another future strategy might be to attempt a more fine-grained comparison between Cheyenne and Ojibwa concepts of self and person. The Cheyenne and Ojibwa languages both belong to the Macro-Algonkian [89] family. If I am correct in assuming that a proper understanding of concepts like the self and person involves much more than linguistic labeling and taxonomic classification, then critical differences between Cheyenne and Ojibwa ethno-psychology demand historical, sociological, and cultural explanations. In short, there are possibilities here for at least partially controlled comparisons and the raising of questions that could stimulate reanalysis of existing materials and the collection of critical new data.

I want to reemphasize here my conviction that the proper study of ethnopsychology and ethnopersonality requires more than fragmentary ethnographic observations supposedly reflective of primitive, or qualitatively different, mentalities; more than a collection of linguistic terms imprecisely translated into approximate English equivalents, without consideration of the connotative and etymological meanings of these terms or their sociolinguistic usage; more than the construction of a taxonomy (taxonomy is, after all, only a tool for understanding and should not be an end in itself). Rather, ethnopsychological and ethnopersonality data must be integrated into the larger structures of meaning inherent in any cultural system. Perhaps my plea will ring less hollow if I provide a truncated example of the kind of understanding that I am advocating.

Levy-Bruhl, in *The "Soul" of the Primitive* (1927; 1928 ed., p. 134f), cites the following quotation from the early government ethnologist James Mooney as testimony for the Cherokee belief in the existence of an "external soul":

> Some war-captains knew how to put their lives up in the tree-tops during a fight, so that even if they were struck by the enemy they could not be killed. Once in a battle with the Shawano [Shawnee], the Cherokee leader stood directly in front of the enemy and let the whole party shoot at him, but was not hurt until the Shauano captain, who knew this war medicine himself, ordered his men to shoot into the branches above the head of the other. They did this and the Cherokee leader fell dead.

Levy-Bruhl perceptively notes that the term "life", rather than the much-abused term "soul," is used in this account to refer to "vital principle". He poses the seeming paradox of how an Individual can gain security by removing "life" or "vital essence" from his corporeal body and answers that the prelogical mind sees nothing extraordinary about bi-presence in which a being can coexist in two places at once. [90]

I have collected several Cherokee sacred formulas, written in the Sequoyah syllabary, dealing with war and ballgame "medicine". In these documents, the "life essence" (which my informant did, indeed, translate as 'soul') is frequently elevated to the safety of the "tree-top trail", whereas the 'soul' of the enemy is conversely mired in the ground, where it is exposed and can be trod upon. Displacement of "vital essences", or of life-sustaining organs, within the body is also characteristic of certain Cherokee mythological figures whose "hearts" may be located in their fingers or some other unnatural locus.

Levy-Bruhl would probably be amused. If not startled, to learn that Cherokee metaphysics posits the existence of four separate vital essences or souls. The first soul, which can be glossed as the 'soul of consciousness'. Is located in the head or throat and is associated with saliva. The second soul is centered in the liver, is related to black and yellow bile, and can be termed the 'hepatic soul'. The third soul can be translated as the 'visceral soul', is located in the flesh, and is associated with blood. The fourth and final soul is the 'osseous soul' that resides in the bones and is associated with sperm.

These four souls normally coexist within the body; but one or several can depart during sleep or by means of certain ritual actions, as in the war medicine cited by Levy-Bruhl. These souls can be affected by or be captured by the machinations of a sorcerer or witch and result in illness or death. The specific bodily fluids, or humours, mentioned above contain vital properties and provide contiguous connection between the internal bodily soul and Its external manifestation. Care must be exercised in disposing of these substances.

Cherokee beliefs about death are associated with this quadripartite-soul theory. Death is less of an event and more of a process, in the Cherokee belief system. What we would regard as physical or clinical death is marked for the Cherokees by the loss and permanent departure of the soul of consciousness. One week later, often after primary burial, the hepatic soul takes its leave of the body. The visceral soul departs a month (or 28 days, to use the multiple of the two sacred Cherokee numbers: four and seven) after physical death; this timing may once have coincided with secondary interment, reburial after the flesh was freed from the bone. [91]

The osseous soul separates from the skeleton one year after physical death, and this final juncture in the life-death cycle was commemorated among some Southeastern tribes by a feast of the dead.

As implied earlier, this normal sequence of soul departure can be inverted by sorcery and witchcraft. Thus, a man whose liver soul has been stolen and destroyed is already dead – though he, and any one else, may not know it until he expires within the span of seven days.

Many Cherokee disease categories also have reference to soul disturbances. Thus one class of disease literally translates as "my saliva is spoiled"; a variety of liver malfunctions are diagnosed as the "Yellow", the "Black", or in combination as the "Black Yellowness having Spots"; blood disorders, including one that resembles our commercial syndrome of "tired blood", are recognized, as are various diseases of the bone that tend to afflict older people.

The Cherokee notion of progressive soul departure is recapitulated in reverse order in their theory of procreation. The soul of consciousness is bestowed by the ultimate creator-being on high, who probably can be identified with the Sun (the 'apportioner', in the sense of the one who divides night and day). I have been unable to derive the source of the hepatic soul, but I suspect it may originate from an underworld power who stands in opposition to the aim. Flesh and blood are contributed by the mother, while the father provides bone, which in its uncongealed state exists as sperm. The frequent metaphoric relationship between blood and descent thus takes a more substantive turn among the matrilineal Cherokee.

I could go on to document the linkage of soul concepts to Cherokee taboos, burial customs, directional symbols, calendrics, and color categories; but I hope I have said enough to convince the skeptic that these components of the Cherokee self, these life-essences or souls, are linked to other domains of Cherokee culture by a ramifying system of ethno-logic. The structure of the Cherokee self possesses a systemic coherence that demands attention in its own terms. This structure organizes, makes meaningful, and almost seems to generate superficially disparate ranges of Cherokee belief, behavior, and experience. The Cherokee self system outlined here cannot be properly understood without some [92] comprehension of the larger culture of which it is part. The life essence in the tree-tops represents more than an example of the prelogical mind violating our law of contradiction with vouchsafed impunity.

Our ultimate purpose in the comparative study of the self and related concepts should be to develop analytic frameworks, methodological procedures, and theoretical explanations that can not only accommodate diverse data from non-Western societies, but can also preserve and capitalize on the distinctive features and embedded meanings Inherent In these materials. To approach these distant and possibly unattainable goals, let me suggest some more proximal research priorities and strategies.

First, we need more systematic examination of our own folk and scientific theories of the self. In studying our folk conceptions, a possible first step might be to look at semantic usage. What are the assumptions underlying such commonplace expressions as: "It was a self-less act", "I was beside myself", "He has an inflated ego", "She attended in-person", "He has a lot of personality", "New Jersey suffers an identity crisis in being located between Philadelphia and New York", "The Russians saved face by rejecting the Salt Treaty". Examples of such statements from everyday speech are not hard to come by; but the question to be asked is how such utterances can be decoded and combined to produce coherent systems of meaning, and how these revealed systems relate to other aspects of culture. The example of New Jersey's identity crisis, attributed to former Governor Hughes, was purposely included to demonstrate that social scientific terminology (frequently scorned as jargon) is not always insulated from popular usage. And, indeed, as has been long recognized, folk cultural assumptions permeate scientific conceptions.

If this paper has demonstrated nothing else, it has shown how muddled our own scholarly and scientific conceptions about the self have become. What would a Cherokee philosopher be able to make of our overlapping – and often contradictory – conceptions of <u>self</u>, <u>ego</u>, <u>person</u>, <u>identity</u>, <u>individuality</u>, <u>persona</u>, <u>personality</u> ... ? Sometimes these conceptions are used as synonyms; at other times, to stress different dimensions or shades of meaning. A comprehensive and consistent semantic and pragmatic systematization of these concepts is probably too much to envision. [93]

More intensive and coordinated work on non-Western concepts of the self and person are needed.[15][15] The available literature, deficient as it frequently is, should be reexamined with an eye to clarifying and synthesizing what is already known and to discover problems that might yield to fresh

---

15 The focus in this text has been on the ethnopersonality of Algonkian-speaking Indians mainly because a certain continuity in research has been achieved here, and various approaches to the study of ethnopersonality can be illustrated and evaluated. Important ethnopersonality work has been reported in other parts of the world and seems to be Increasing: e.g., Read did pioneering work on the person concept among the Gahuku-Gama of New Guinea (1954/1955); Valentine produced an interesting analysis of Lakalai (New Britain) ethnopsychology (1963); Geertz's extended essay on "Person, Time and Conduct In Bali" (1966) follows an interesting perspective; Fred Myers has described the self and personhood for the Pintupi Aborigines of Australia (1979); Mary Druke has demonstrated the possibilities for deriving ethnopersonality from ethnohistoric documents concerning the Iroquois (1980); Christopher Boehm has examined the moral self among Montenegrens (1980); and J Christopher Crocker has published two papers on self concepts among the Bororo of South America (1977, 1979).

Michelle Rosaldo's monograph (1980) on the Ilongot of the Philippines contains rich ethnopersonality data (although it is not always informed by a consistent analytic or theoretical scheme). Finally, several manuscripts by McKim Marriott should soon see the light of published day and illuminate the complexities of Hindu ethnopsychology.

research. I have in mind here a review not only of published material directly dealing with the self and related concerns, but the excavation of usable data buried in ethnographic writings. My exploration into Cherokee soul concepts suggests that a reinterpretation of other theories of the soul might be a productive endeavor. The soul figured prominently in early disputes about primitive religion that were initiated by EB Tylor's *Primitive Culture* (1871) and continued by his critics and followers. Much recyclable material probably exists in monographic treatments of the soul, such as those produced by AE Crawley (1909), Sir James Frazer (1911), Levy-Bruhl (1927), and Ake Hultkrantz (1953).

More important, certainly, will be new field investigations in which systematic study of self and person concepts becomes a central rather than a peripheral concern. The primitive world was fast disappearing when anthropology first became a scholarly discipline. The situation is even more urgent today. It is important that evidence of the thought-ways of non-Western peoples be recorded before such material becomes permanently erased from the human record. All three Cherokee instructors who taught me about Cherokee notions of the self are now dead.

Prospective investigators of ethnopersonality should have a grasp of the native language and sensitivity to linguistic nuance. They should be skilled ethnographers capable of collecting behavioral and social interactional data relevant to the expression of the self. Knowledge of the general culture is also essential because, as my Cherokee example tried to indicate, pursuit of ideas about the self can lead in unforeseen directions.

The acquisition of self-conceptions through socialization and enculturation is an obviously important topic that has been neglected in this presentation. The application of Piagetian and other developmental schemes to non-Western peoples should continue to prove useful In studying processes leading to self-awareness and subsequent capacities. My only caution is that such schemes be juxtaposed with implicit [94] and explicit native models of human development, the existence of which is well illustrated by Straus (1977) and Robin and Tonia Ridington (1970).

The immediate results of following through on the kinds of research priorities and strategies proposed here will be the discovery of a plurality of theories and conceptions regarding the self. In time, however, the seemingly chaotic multiplicity may be reduced through careful comparative analysis. General principles and dimensions may be adduced that will approach universal validity.

The anthropology of the self is in its infancy, and it awaits self-awareness of its own significance.

References [101]

Aberle, D 1957 The Influence of Linguistics on Early Culture and Personality Theory. In *Essays In the Science of Culture* (ed. by G. Dole & R. Carneiro, New York; T.Y. Crowell), pp. 1-29.
Allport, G W 1937 *Personality*: A Psychological Interpretation. New York: Henry Holt.
Allport, G W 1943 The Ego In Contemporary Psychology. *Psychological Review* L: 451-78.
Avruch, K 1981 American Immigrants In Israel: Social Identities and Change. Chicago: University of Chicago Press.
Bateson, R 1965 *Naven. A Survey of the Problems Suggested by a Composite Picture of a New Guinea Tribe Drawn from Three Points of View.* 2nd ed. Stanford: Stanford University Press.
Bell, D 1968 National Character Revisited: A Proposal for Renegotiating the Concept. In *The Study of Personality: An Interdisciplinary Appraisal* (ed. by E. Norbeck, D Price-Williams, & E. McCord. New York: Holt, Reinhart and Winston), pp.103-20.
Bidney, D 1953 *Theoretical Anthropology*. 1967, augmented ed. New York: Schocken.
Black, MB 1967 An Ethnoscience Investigation of Ojibwa Ontology and World View. PhD Dissertation, Stanford University.
Black, MB 1969a Eliciting Folk Taxonomy in Ojibwa. In *Cognitive Anthropology* (ed. by SA Tyler. New York: Holt, Reinhart and Winston). pp. 165-89.

Black, MB   1969b   A Note on Gender In Eliciting Ojibwa Semantic Structures. *Anthropological Linguistics* XI: 177-86.

Black, MB 1976 Semantic Variability in a Northern Ojibwa Community. Papers in Linguistics, (special issue: Language Use in Canada, ed. by R. Darnel. Edmonton: Linguistic Research, Inc), IX: 129-57.

Black, MB 1977a Ojibwa Taxonomy and Percept Ambiguity. *Ethos* V: 90-118.

Black, MB 1977b Ojibwa Power Belief System. In *The Anthropology of Power* (ed. by R.D. Fogelson & R.N. Adams, New York: Academic Press), pp. 141-51. [102]

Boas, F 1911 *The Mind of Primitive Man*. 1938 rev. ed. New York: Macmillan.

Boas, F 1938 Methods of Research. *General Anthropology*, (Boston: DC Heath), pp. 666-86.

Boas, G 1969 *Vox Populi*: *Essays in the History of an Idea*. Baltimore: Johns Hopkins Press.

Boehm, C 1980 Exposing the Moral Self in Montenegro: The Use of Natural Definitions to Keep Ethnography Descriptive. *American Ethnologist* VII: 1-26.

Burridge, K 1979 *Someone, No One: An Essay on Individuality*. Princeton. NJ: Princeton Univ. Press.

Burton, M & L Kirk   1979   Sex Differences in Masai Cognition of Personality and Social Identity. *American Anthropologist* LXXXI: 84l-73.

Caughey, JL 1980 Personal Identity and Social Organization. Ethos, VI1I;173-203.

Cohen, A 1977 Symbolic Action and the Structure of the Self. In *Symbols and Sentiments* (ed. by I. Lewis, New York: Academic Press), pp. 117-28.

Crapanzano, V 1979 Preface to *Do Kamo* (see Leenhardt 1947).

Crawley, AE 1909 The Idea of the Soul. London: Methuen.

Crocker, JC 1977 The Mirrored Self: Identity and Ritual Inversion Among Eastern Bororo. *Ethnology* XVI: 129-45.

Crocker, JC 1979 Selves and Alters Among the Eastern Bororo. In *Dialectical Societies* (ed. by D. Maybury-Lewis, Cambridge: Harvard University Press), pp. 249-300.

DeVos, G & L Romanucci-Ross 1975 *Ethnic Identity*. *Cultural Continuities and Change*. Palo Alto: Mayfield Publishing Co.

Dieterlen, G 1941 Les Ames des Dogon. Paris; Institut d'Ethnologle (Travaux et memoires, 40).

Dieterlen, G, ed. 1973 Collogue International sur la notion de personne en Afrique. Paris: Centre National de la Recherche Scientifique.

Druke, MA   1980   The Concept of Personhood in Seventeenth and Eighteenth Century Iroquois Ethnopersonality. In *Studies on Iroquoian Culture* (ed. by N. Bonvillain, Occasional Papers in Northeastern Anthropology, No. 6), pp. 59-70. [103]

Dumont, L 1965a The 'Individual' In Two Types of Society. *Contributions to Indian Sociology* 8: 8-61.

Dumont, L 1965b The Functional Equivalents of the Individual in Caste Society. *Contributions to Indian Sociology* 8: 85-99.

Dumon, L 1967 The Individual as an Impediment to Sociological Comparison and Indian History. In *Social and Economic Change* (ed. by VB Singh & B Singh, Bombay: Allied Publishers), pp. 226-48.

Dumont, L 1977 *From Mandeville to Marx*. Chicago: University of Chicago Press.

Durkheim, E (1893) *The Division of Labor In Society*. 1933 ed. trans. by GE Simpson, New York: Macmillan.

Durkheim, E (1912) *The Elementary Forms of Religious Life*. 1915 ed., trans. by JW Swain, 1960 repr., New York: the Free Press.

Durkheim, E (1914) The Duality of Human Existence. 1964 repr. in *Essays in Sociology and Philosophy*, ed. by K Wolff, trans. by C Blend, New York: Harper and Row, pp. 325-40.

Erikson, EH 1950 Childhood and Society. New York: Norton.

Erikson, EH 1958 *Young Man Luther*. New York: Norton.

Erikson, EH 1959 *Identity and the Life Cycle: Selected Papers*. Psychological Issues, New York International Universities Press, I, 1.

Erikson, EH 1968 Identity ~ Psychosocial. In International Encyclopedia of the Social Sciences (New

York: MacMillan and Free Press), VII: 61-5.

Evans-Pritchard, EE 1965 *Theories of Primitive Religion.* London: Oxford University Press.

Evens, TMS 1977 The Predication of the Individual in Anthropological Interactionism. *American Anthropologist* LXXIX: 579-97.

Fenton, WN 1940 Masked Medicine Societies of the Iroquois. Smithsonian Annual Report, Publication 3624: 397-430.

Fogelson, RD 1975 An Analysis of Cherokee Sorcery and Witchcraft Beliefs and Practices. *In Four Centuries of Southern Indians* (ed. by C Hudson, Athens, GA: University of Georgia Press): 113-31.

Fogelson, RD & AB Walker 1980 Self and Other In Cherokee Booger Masks. *Journal of Cherokee Studies* V: 88-102. [104]

Fogelson, RD. & AB Walker In press The Cherokee Booger Mask Tradition. In *Masks and Masquerades in the Americas* (ed. by N.R. Crumrine, Vancouver, B.C: University of British Columbia Press).

Fortes, M 1973 On the Concept of the Person among the Tallensi. In *Collogue international sur le notion de personne en Afrique* (see Dieterlen 1973), pp. 283-319.

Frank, G 1979 Finding the Common Denominator: A Phenomological Critique of Life History Method. *Ethos* VII: 68-94.

Frazer, J 1911 *Taboo and the Perils of the Soul.* London: Macmillan.

Geertz, C 1966 Person, Time and Conduct In Bali: An Essay In Cultural Analysis. 1973 repr. In *The Interpretation of Culture* (see above), pp. 360-411.

Geertz, C 1973 Thick Description. *The Interpretation of Cultures.* (New York: Basic Books): 3-30.

Goffman, E 1959 *The Presentation of the Self in Everyday Life.* Garden City, N.Y.: Doubleday,

Goldenweiser, A 1917 The Autonomy of the Social. *American Anthropologist* XIX: 447-49.

Goldenweiser, A 1933 *History, Psychology, and Culture.* New York: Knopf.

Griaule, M 1940 La Personnalité chez les Dogons (Soudan Francais). Journal de Psychologie Normale et Pathologique XXXVII: 468-75.

Griaule, M 1947 Nouvelles recherches sur la notion de Personne chez les Dogon (Soudan Francais). Journal Psychologie de Normale et Pathologique XL: 425-31.

Griaule, M (1948) *Conversations with Ogotemmeli.* 1965 ed., trans. by R. Butler, A.I. Richards, & B Hooke; London: Oxford University Press.

Griaule, M 1965 *Le Renard p*âle. Paris: Institut d'Ethnologie (Travaux et memoires 72).

Griaule, M. & G Dieterlen 1954 The Dogon of the French Sudan. In *African Worlds* (ed. by D. Forde, London: Oxford University Press), pp. 83-110.

Hallowell, AI 1954a The Self and Its Behavioral Environment. 1955 repr. In *Culture and Experience* (Philadelphia: University of Pennsylvania Press), pp. 75-110. [105]

Hallowell, AI 1954b Psychology and Anthropology. 1976 repr. in Contributions to Anthropology (Chicago: University of Chicago Press), pp. 163-209.

Hallowell, AI 1955 The Ojibwa Self and Its Behavioral Environment. In *Culture and Experience* (see above), pp. 172-82.

Hallowell, AI 1960 Ojibwa Ontology, Behavior, and World View. 1976 repr. in *Contributions to Anthropology* (see above), pp. 357-90.

Hallowell, AI 1963a Personality, Culture, and Society In Behavioral Evolution. 1976 repr. in *Contributions to Anthropology* (see above), pp. 230-310.

Hallowell. AI 1963b The Ojibwa World View and Disease. 1976 repr. In *Contributions to Anthropology* (see above), pp. 381-448.

Hallowell, AI 1966 The Role of Dreams In Ojibwa Culture. 1976 repr. in *Contributions to Anthropology* (see above), pp. 449-74.

Hay, T 1968 Ojibwa Restraint and the Socialization Process. PhD, Michigan State University.

Hay, T 1973 A Technique of Formalizing and Testing Models of Behavior: Two Models of Ojibwa

Restraint. *American Anthropologist* LXXV: 708-30.
Hay, T 1977 The Development of Some Aspects of the Ojibwa Self and Its Behavioral Environment. *Ethos* V: 71-89.
Hultkrantz, A 1953 *Conceptions of the Soul Among North American Indians: A Study in Religious Ethnology*. Stockholm: The Ethnographical Museum of Sweden, Monograph Series 1.
Janes, W 1890 *Principles of Psychology*. 2 vols. New York: Henry Holt.
Kapferer, B 1979 Mind, Self, and Other In Demonic Illness: The Negation and Reconstruction of Self. *American Ethnologist* VI: 110-33.
Karpf, FB 1932 *American Social Psychology: Its Origins. Development, and European Background*. New York: McGraw-Hill.
Kendall, PM 1975 Biographical Literature. In Macro-paedia II (The New Encyclopaedia Britannica, 15th ed., Chicago: Encyclopaedia Britannica, Inc.)
Kirk, L & ML Burton 1977 Meaning and Context: A Study of Contextual Shifts In the Meaning of [106] Masai Personality Descriptors. *American Ethnologist* IV: 734-61.
Krader, L 1966 Person, Ego, Human Spirit In Marcel Mauss. *Psychoanalytic Review* LIII: 481-90.
Krader, L 1967 *Persona et Culture*. Les Etudes Philosophiques, November.
Kroeber, AL 1917. The "Superorganic". *American Anthropologist* XIX: 163-213.
Lee, D 1945 Notes on the Conception of Self Among the Wintu Indians. 1959 repr. in *Freedom and Culture* (Englewood Cliffs. N.J.: Prentice-Hall), pp. 131-40.
Leenhardt, M (1947) *Do Kamo: Person and Myth in the Melanesian World*. 1979 ed., trans. by B.M. Gulati. Chicago: University of Chicago Press.
Levi-Straus, C 1963 *Totemism*. Trans. by R Needham. Boston: Beacon Press.
Levy-Bruhl, L (1910) *How Natives Think*. 1962 trans. by LA Clare, London: George Allen and Unwin.
Levy-Bruhl, L (1922) *Primitive Mentality*. 1923 trans. by LA Clare, London: George Allen and Unwin.
Levy-Bruhl, L (1927) *The "Soul" of the Primitive*. 1928 trans. by LA Clare, London: George Allen and Unwin, Ltd.
Levy-Bruhl, L (1949) *The Notebooks on Primitive Men*tality. 1975 by P Riviere. NY: Harper and Row.
Lowie, R.H 1917 *Culture and Ethnology*. New York: Douglas C. McMurtrie.
Lukes, S 1973 *Individualism*. New York: Harper and Row.
Mauss, M 1929. L'âme, le nom, la personne. 1968 repr. in *Oeuvres*, (Paris: Les Editions de Minuit), II: 131-35.
Mauss, M 1938 Une Categorie de l'esprit humain: la notion de personne celle de 'mol'. Journal of the Royal Anthropological Institute, LVHI: 263-81. 1979 Eng. trans. by B. Brewster, in *Sociology and Psychology* (London: Routledge & Kegan Paul), pp. 57-94.
Mead, GH 1913 The Social Self. *Journal of Philosophy* X: 374-80.
Head, GH 1934 *Mind, Self and Society*. Chicago: University of Chicago Press. [107]
Miller, DR 1963 The Study of Social Relationships: Situation, Identity, and Social Interaction. In *Psychology: A Study of a Science* (ed. by S. Koch, New York; McGraw-Hill), V: 639-738.
Myers, PP 1979 Emotions and the Self: A Theory of Personhood and Political Order Among Pintupi Aborigines. *Ethos* VII: 343-70.
Radcliffe-Brown, A.R 1922 *The Andamen Islanders*. 1948 ed., Glencoe, I1l: The Free Press.
Radcliffe-Brown. AR 1940 On Social Structure. 1952 repr. In *Structure and Function In Primitive Society* (New York; The Free Press), pp. 108-204.
Radin, P 1913 Personal Reminiscences of a Winnebago Indian. *Journal of American Folklore* XXVI: 293-318.
Radin, P 1920 The Autobiography of a Winnebago Indian. University of California Publications In American Archaeology and Ethnology XVI: 381-473.
Radin, P 1927 *Primitive Man as Philosopher*. New York: Appleton and Co.
Read, KB 1954/55 Morality and the Concept of the Person Among the Gabuku Gama, Eastern Highland,

New Guinea. *Oceania* XXV: 233-82.

Ridington, R & T 1970 The Inner Eye of Shamanism and Totemism. *History of Religions* X: 49-61.

Robbins, RH 1973a Identity, Culture and Behavior. In *Handbook of Social and Cultural Anthropology* (ed. by JJ Honigmann, Chicago: Rand McNally), pp. 1199-1222.

Robbins, RH 1973b Alcohol and the Identity Struggle: Some Effects of Economic Change on Interpersonal Relations. *American Anthropologist* LXXV: 99-122.

Rosaldo, MZ 1980 *Knowledge and Passion: Ilongot Notions of Self and Social Life.* Cambridge; Cambridge University Press.

Sapir, E 1917 Do We Need a 'Superorganic'?. *American Anthropologist* XIX: 441-47.

Sapir, E 1938 Why Cultural Anthropology Needs the Psychiatrist. 1949 repr. In *Selected Writings of Edward Sapir* in *Language, Culture and Personality* (ed. by D.G. Mandelbaum, Berkeley: University of California Press), pp. 569-77.

Sherif, M 1968 Self Concept. In *International Encyclopedia of the Social Sciences* (New York: Macmillan and Free Press), XIV: l50-59. [108]

Singer, M 1977 On the Symbolic and Historic Structure of an American Identity. *Ethos* V: 431-54.

Singer, M 1980 Signs of the Self: An Exploration In Semantic Anthropology. *American Anthropologist* LXXXII: 485-507.

Smith, MW 1952 Different Cultural Concepts of Past, Present and Future: A Study of Ego Extension. *Psychiatry* XV: 395-400.

Soddy, K, ed. 1961 *Identity: Mental Health and Value Systems.* London: World Health Organization.

Speck, FG 1942 *The Tutelo Spirit Adoption Ceremony ~ Reclothing the Living In the Name of the Dead.* Harrisburg: Publication of the Pennsylvania Historical Commission.

Speck, FG 1950 Concerning Iconology and the Masking Complex In Eastern North America. Philadelphia: University of Pennsylvania) Museum Bulletin, XV: 6-57.

Straus, AS 1976 Being Human In the Cheyenne Way. Ph.D. dissertation, University of Chicago.

Straus, AS 1977 Northern Cheyenne Ethnopsychology. *Ethos* V: 326~57.

Tylor, EB 1871 *Primitive Culture* (2 vols.). London: John Murray.

Valentine, C 1963 Man of Anger and Man of Shame: Lakalai Ethnopsychology and Its Implications for Sociopsychological Theory. *Ethnology* 11: 441-77.

Wagner, R 1975 The Invention of Culture. Englewood Cliffs, N.J.: Prentice-Hall.

Wallace, AFC 1961 *Culture and Personality.* 1970 rev. ed.. New York: Random House.

Wallace, AFC 1967 Identity Processes in Personality and in Culture. In Cognition, Personality and Clinical Psychology (ed. by R. Jessor & S. Feshbach. San Francisco: Jossey Bass): 62-89.

Wallace, AFC & RD. Fogelson 1965 The Identity Struggle. In Intensive Family Therapy (ed. by I. Boszormeny-Nagy & J.L. Framo, New York: Harper and Row): 365-406.

Watson. LC 1970 Self and Ideal in a Guajiro Life History. *Acta Ethnologica et Linguistics*, Series Americana 5, Vienna.

Watson, LC 1978 The Study of Personality and the Study of Individuals: Two Approaches, Two Types of Explanation. *Ethos* VI: 3-21. [109]

White, GM 1978 Ambiguity and Ambivalence in A'ara Personality Descriptors. *American Ethnologist* V: 33A-60.

White, GM 1980 Social Images and Social Change in a Melanesian Society. *American Ethnologist* VII: 352-70.

Witthoft, J 1967 The American Indian as Hunter. Harrisburg: Pennsylvania Historical and Museum Commission.

Psyche

INTERPRETATIONS OF THE AMERICAN INDIAN PSYCHE: SOME HISTORICAL NOTES
Ideologies and Issues

Prelude

This essay approaches the "psyche" of the American Indian from two separate, yet convergent, perspectives.[1] The first perspective treats the psychology of the American Indian from the context of Western intellectual history and the history of anthropology. The second perspective considers some Native American psychological ideas and attempts to assess their historical and contemporary significance.

The first perspective, which occupies the major portion of this essay, is initially concerned with the general philosophical and theological background of Western psychological assumptions, secondarily with more specific moral and political issues in American history that affected Native Americans, and finally with the psychological substratum that influenced the nature and direction of early ethnological science in the United States. As much as possible, Western psychology is viewed not as a progressive ideological revelation of [5] self-evident truths about the nature of human nature, but as a product of a particular on-going historical and cultural tradition.

The second perspective keys into modern efforts to study ethnopsychology. Only recently have we begun to appreciate the richness and complexity of indigenous psychological systems, to study systematically native theories of personality, to take into account native-defined contexts of behavior, and to examine the culturally constituted structuring of personal and interpersonal experience. The study of ethnopsychology involves working through native languages to gain insights into world view and knowledge of the localized behavioral environment. Ethnopsychology seeks to explore such topics as cultural conceptions of self and person, ideas about procreation, naming practices, education, recognized life stages, and processes of death and eschatology. Also of significance are native dream theories and visionary realities, categories of deviance and pathology, and the ethno-logic and ethno-meta-physics embedded in symbolic features of myth and ritual. This ambitious program is far from fulfillment. Few, if any, adequate accounts of Native American ethnopsychology exist.

While there is heuristic value in treating Western psychology and Native American psychologies as separate traditions, a conjunctive approach is necessary to analyze the nearly 500-year interaction between these different traditions. It is evident that Native American psychologies have not been impervious to Western ideas, and modern Western psychology gives promise of being enriched and expanded by exposure to non-Western psychological concepts. In approaching the subject conjunctively an effort should be made to avoid the inevitable pratfalls of presentism and to adopt, as much as possible, an historicist stance. It must be recognized that Western psychology, as a separate scientific discipline, only emerges in the mid-18th century. Although the first use of the term psychology, meaning "the science of the soul," is attributed to Goclenius, an obscure 16th-century professor at Marburg (Mueller 1973: 10), the term is rarely encountered until the 18th century. According to the Oxford English

---

[1] Acknowledgements. I am grateful to George Stocking for a fast and critical reading of an early draft of this manuscript that forced revision in organization. I also thank Robert Brightman, June Helm, and Polly Strong for useful discussion on certain issues. Queen Ward typed the manuscript and displayed extraordinary power of extrasensory perception in deciphering my handwriting.

1. I am indebted to George Stocking for suggesting this extension to my hypothesis on color coding. See also Leslie Fiedler (1968: 29-36) for a similar symbolic tripartite division of the world before the post-Columbian discovery of a terrestrial West.

Dictionary (1971: 2347), the first English usage occurs in the 1693 translation of the second edition of *Blunchard's Physical Dictionary* under the following heading:

> Anthropologia, the Description of Man, or the Doctrine concerning him. Bartholine divides it into Two Parts; viz. Anatomy, which treats of the Body / Psychology, which treats of the soul.

A Irving Hallowell (1965) regarded the history of anthropology as an anthropological problem; perhaps the same can be said of the history of psychology.

With or without the term psychology, Europeans have been "psychologizing" the American Indian ever since the discovery of their New World. Much of this material has been collated and interpreted in a recent proliferation of useful volumes that survey initial European impressions of the natives of the New World (e.g., Chiapelli, Alien and Benson 1976), later Euro-American images of the Indian (eg, Baudet 1965; Saum 1965; Honour 1975; Powell 1977; Biltington 1981), and pervasive Indian *stereotypes* (eg, [6] Berkhofer 1978; Stedman 1982). However, when consulting the primary sources, one does not find such terms as first impressions, perceptions, or images, let alone stereotypes, since stereotypic printing wasn't even invented until the turn of the 19lh century. Rather, what we take to be Indian psychology is described as character, constitution, nature, trails, habits, manners, customs, and moral state or condition – terms that haul much different semantic freight than those in current use. Therefore it is important to try to understand the implicit and explicit psychological theories governing the use of these terms and informing the reported observations.

Toward the Western "Science of the Soul"

Most orthodox histories of western psychology (e.g., Peters 1962; Murphy 1949) begin with the ancient Greeks. The meaning of the term psyche undergoes considerable modification from the time of Homer to the flowering of Greek philosophy with Plato and Aristotle. In the Homeric texts the term psyche competes with several other 'soul' words and refers generally to a kind of negative residuum. According to Claus (1981: 1), the Homeric psyche "signifies both the 'life' that is lost at death and 'shade' or 'wrailh', as in the description of death in battle." Pre-socratic philosophers and dramatists elaborated the eschatological and 'life force' aspects of the soul, but it was only with Plato that these notions crystallize into a comprehensive conception of a personal 'soul' – "the immortal and divine part of man, the self as a center or microcosm of his whole being, the seat of the rational intelligence and thus of moral choice, that which is not body and which is related to body as master is to slave" (Claus 1981: 1). This conception of soul, with its essential mind-body dualism, comes to dominate much of subsequent Western thought. The notion of psyche as soul or mind is an a priori theory, one that can be sustained by following the charier of the Delphic oracle for introspection,

Another major legacy of the ancient Greeks to later Western psychological thought was the Hippocratic medical tradition. Hippocratic theory was based on the distinctive properties of humors, or internal bodily fluids. These humors not only affected physical and mental functioning but also gave rise to specific characters or temperamental types. Hippocratic theory also recognized the effects that environment could exert on individuals or human groups, Besides its enduring heritage in promoting a naturalist approach to medical diagnosis and treatment, Hippocratic theory, with its quadrapartite divisions, its use of polarities and analogies, provided a widely applicable cognitive model for classifying and structuring observations of the physical and mental nature of man. The influence of this model was still strong through the 18th century.

Introspection, which remained the basic method of psychology, at least until the advent of experimental psychology in the late 19th century, was consonant with Christian theology's emphasis on the inner life and conscience. It is interesting to note that individualism, which becomes so prominent a theme in Western thought, such that psychology is sometimes defined as the science of the individual, appears to be a late medieval development (Lukes 1973). [7]

Seventeenth-and 18th-century philosophic thought bearing on psychology can only be touched upon here. Cartesian dualism gave rise to a distinctively mechanical approach to mind-body relations that can be viewed retrospectively as paving the way for a separate science of psychology, as well as serving as an important antecedent to modern behaviorism. The widely disseminated 18th-century theories of John Locke, which played such a great role in the ideological positions of the founders of the American Republic, stressed the importance of experience in shaping mentality and gave rise to an optimism about the degree to which thinking could be modified through education. The Leibnitzian notion of preexistent intelligence necessary for meaningful experience may in certain ways be considered as ancestral to Gestalt psychology and modern phenomenology. Kant's later synthesis of these diverse strands and contrary approaches can be taken as the touchstone for modern Western philosophies of the mind.

This highly selective and grossly oversimplified survey of psychological ideas about the soul and mentality would have to be qualified, expanded, and correlated with developments in Western society and culture to constitute a serious contribution to the anthropology of knowledge. However, this truncated review perhaps suffices to indicate some of the elements in the mix of assumptions and presuppositions that Europeans brought with them when they encountered the native inhabitants of America.

Many of these ideas were further elaborated in 17th- and 18th-century American theology, moral philosophy, political theory, and economics, and their reverberations were fell on the popular level in literature, proverbs, folk religion, art, and in practical applications. Beliefs about the nature of the soul were refined by various influential theologians representing such different Protestant denominations as the Puritans, Anglicans, and Quakers. The body-soul antithesis was central to most of these theologies, and, while the soul was seen as possessing divine attributes capable of redemption and salvation, the body was considered more fallible and subject to Satanic influence and direction. Sin was not of divine origin but was a moral ill produced by mankind and, like a contagious disease, could be transmitted interpersonally. The intellect, which was thought to reside in the head, was considered a mixed blessing, since it could be diverted from its true calling as the servant of God. The easily corruptible will was the source of appetites and affections and usually located in the heart. Without attempting to include the subtle shades of difference in these systems of belief, what was constructed was a coherent theory of human nature. Moreover, with a confidence borne of faith, the attempt was made to universalize this highly valorized model of human nature.

White on Red

When Columbus landed in the West Indies, he was convinced that he had arrived at the outskirts of the prelapsarian Earthly Paradise. He regarded the native Arawaks in a positive manner. Their nakedness seemed to indicate primordial innocence. They were initially timorous, generous almost to a fault, and in their navigational knowledge displayed acute intelligence. The [8] natives appeared to lack religion, although they did possess vague beliefs in higher powers and an afterlife. They lived communally and seemingly lacked notions of private properly. Columbus learned about other peoples who were viewed less positively: he was told, or chose to believe in, the existence of various monstrous races reminiscent of the descriptions in Herodotus. Pliny, and the medieval bestiaries. The ferocious Caribs, (from whose name we derive the word cannibal) were traditional enemies of the Arawaks, and considered to be irrevocably anthropophagous.

Americus Vespucci's description inspired European engravers to produce the first widely circulated visual impressions of the New World. According to Vespucci, the natives lived without laws, according to nature; their skin color was "reddish"; the women were highly libidinous, and the whole society was promiscuous. The natives lacked religion and were avid cannibals, but they enjoyed remarkable health and long lives.

After a half-century of despoliation, degradation, and decimation of the native population of the

New World, learned debates took place about the moral status of the so-called "Indies." At issue was the question of whether these peoples were fully human. The definition of humanness rested on possession of a soul and capacity for attaining a stale of grace. In practical terms, this debate concerned whether the natives could, or should, be converted to Christianity or whether their natural inferiority provided moral justification for slavery and genocide. These issues culminated in [lie celebrated confrontations in Spain between Bartholome de Las Casas, "the apostle of the Indians," and his opponents, led by Juan Gines de Sepulveda, a versatile renaissance philosopher (Hanke 1959).

Several psychological features emerge from these early Spanish sources. Natives were evaluated in the context of an overarching theological frame. On the one hand, they represented a stale of unspoiled, childish innocence; on the other, a condition of degraded bestiality. Direct descriptions of the Indians had a redundant, formulaic quality, focusing on such physical traits as skin color, hair, and general bodily conformation. Native sexual proclivities aroused interest, as did the communalistic nature of their society, which seemed to engender generosity. The Spanish also seem obsessed with the problem of cannibalism. It is possible, as Hayden White (1976: 125) has argued that the very features the Spaniards singled out for attention were those that seemed to violate some of the strongest taboos in contemporary European society: nakedness, community of properly, lawlessness, sexual promiscuity, and cannibalism. While some of these customs undoubtedly represented unconscious wish-fulfillments of Europeans, 1 think they can be also be understood as a European apperception of the New World as both old and young. The New World was conceived as old in the sense that the inhabitants approximated presumed primordial conditions of mankind existent at the time of the Fall; it could be considered young or childlike in the sense that the natives reflected an arrested state of development or actual degeneration occasioned by ignorance of the true faith. [9]

One notes that many of the psychological traits attributed to the American natives by Europeans were anomalous, antithetical, and fluid before they later hardened into imprinted stereotypes. First, let us examine some physical characteristics that were felt to index psychological dispositions.

Skin color was of great concern to early explorers and later European settlers. However, as Alden Vaughan (1982) has shown, recognition of the Indian as a Redskin was slow to develop in Anglo-American awareness and did not receive general acceptance until the 19lh century. Early accounts report the natives as being tawny, olive, swarthy, brown, russet, or copper-colored, and their slightly darker skin pigmentation was believed to be caused by exposure to the elements or application of body paint. The essential early Anglo-American view was that Indian skin color fell within the range of that found in Europeans. Vaughan (1982: 939) plausibly argues that Indians become Redskins because of "the Anglo-Americans' anger al Indian hostility, their frustration over Indian rejection of Christianity and 'civilization,' and their adoption of 18th-century racial theories." Without denying the significance of these interactive factors, I'd like to offer an alternative hypothesis about why the American Indian became red.

Basically, what I assume is that color serves as a cognitive coding device to distinguish peoples of extreme cultural and geographic difference. The interconnected classical Mediterranean world recognized gradations in skin pigmentation ranging from black-skinned Nubians to the extremely light skins of Northern European barbarians. These differences could be encompassed on an achromatic scale ranging from degrees of darkness to lightness. However, with the discovery of Far Eastern peoples, Native North Americans, Pacific Islanders, and Australian Aborigines during the Age of Exploration, the older achromatic scale proved inadequate to make what were, at base, necessary cultural distinctions, and there was a switch to a chromatic classification. While the correlation is not perfect, the development of skin color classification roughly parallels the evolution of color lexemes postulated by Berlin and Kay (1969). Thus the designation of Indians as red – once Euro-Americans decided to claim no kinship with Indians and concluded that Indians were essentially different – does not seem fortuitous. To support my hypothesis of skin color as a cultural marker, not only were Indians initially viewed as while, or of a slightly darker hue than Europeans, yet clearly to be differentiated from Africans, but one early cosmographer, with the unlikely name John of Holywood, writes in the 1498 edition of *Sphaera Mundi* that the native inhabitants of the New World are "blue in color with square heads" (quoted in Hanke 1959: 4). A generative aspect of my cognitive hypothesis can perhaps be inferred when denizens of outer or inner space are popularly depicted as green or purple.

Another way of formulating the switch from an achromatic to a chromatic code is to apply the structural principles implicit in humoral theory to directional geography and the inhabitants of the four quarters of the world.' In diagrammatic form, the world may be quadrasected as follows: [10]

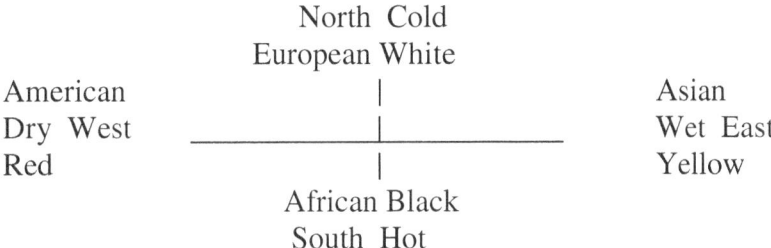

The ancient Cold-Hot, North-South, White-Black axis is bisected by a Wet-Dry, East-West axis encompassing a Yellow-Red polarity. Other symbolic connotations may be added; the north associated with snow, lack of sun, and winter; the south with torrid heat and summer; the east with sunrise, dew, and spring; the west with sunset, desiccation, and autumn. The center of this quadrasection might be temporally associated with the Garden of Eden or Mount Ararat where Noah's ark found terra firma.

Such a conceptual scheme seems to have been in the back of Linnaeus's mind when he set about to classify the peoples of the world. He also made use of the temperamental types of classical humoral theory. Europeans (*albus*) were considered sanguine, Africans (*niger*) were phlegmatic, Asiatics (*fuscus*) were melancholic, and Americans (*rubescens*) were choleric.

The redness of the American Indian was thus given scientific certification in Linnaeus's influential *Syslema Naturae*. In the 1740 edition Native Americans are binomially classified simply as *Amercanus rubescens*. In later editions Linnaeus switched to the trinominal designation *Homo sapiens Americanus*, and was more detailed with respect to defining attributes. This variety of human being was, according to the great Swedish naturalist;

> reddish, choleric, erect
> *Hair* black, straight, thick;
> *Nostrils* wide;
> *Face* freckled; Chin beardless
> *Persevering*, content, free
> *Paints*, himself with skillful red lines
> *Governed* by custom   [Quoted in Berkhofer 1978: 40]

Several psychological trails are embodied in this diffuse definition, and some contradictions are apparent. Thus a choleric temperament usually signifies a quickness to anger and lack of impulse control, yet Linnaeus here couples the choleric type with a persevering (sometimes translated from Latin to English as "obstinate") character and contentment. But not only are biological and psychological traits combined, but such cultural features as body painting and government by custom are also confabulated in Linnaeus's definition.

Another physical trail laden with psychological significance for Europeans was hair. There was general agreement that Native Americans had straight, black hair, and some observers noted that their hair did not become [11] gray until relatively advanced age, a fact that may have contributed to the myth of Indian longevity. Also gray hair, especially premature graying, was often interpreted in European folk thought as a response to frightening trauma or overly intense mental activity. Thus, the late appearance of gray hair among Indians could be taken as indirect evidence that they lived carefree lives and did not worry themselves with serious intellection. But it was the natives' relative lack of facial and bodily hair that held the greatest psychological interest for Europeans. Hair was associated with virility, with "animal passion." Too little hair signified immaturity, emasculation, and lack of sexual drive, while too much hair represented the kind of crudity, bestiality, and unrestrained lust epitomized in the abiding popular notion of the shaggy Wild Man.[2] Europeans, of course, considered themselves to occupy the desirable median on this hirsute continuum.

The supposed sexual inferiority of the Indian male reached something of an apogee in the mid-18th-century writings of the great French naturalist, Count Button. According to this authority, the male Indian's "organs of reproduction are small and feeble," which tended to make him impotent; Native Americans display no "ardour for the female"; and they were "cold and languid" (quoted in Berkhofer 1978: 42-43). The Abbé Corneille De Pauw in 1768 went so far as to suggest that beardless Indian males lactated (Pearce 1965: 78).

Yet this idea that Indian men were genitally underdeveloped or lacking in sexual passion had its antithesis. Thus we read in Shakespeare's Henry VIII:

> Or have we some strange Indian with
> the great tool come to court,
> the women so besiege us? Bless me,
> what a fray of fornication is at the door. [Act 5, Scene 4)

And a collective nightmare of the frontier unconscious was the stalking, blood-thirsty savage about to massacre a White settlement and take the women off into captivity for carnal pleasure. For the Euro-American imagination, captivity implied more than mere capture. It often involved projected fears that the oppressed While woman might prefer life, and perhaps enjoy sexual fulfillment, with her captors. She might literally become captivated by some dark mysterious power possessed by the Indians.[3] The modern morality drama of the captivity of Patty Hearst by the Symbionese Liberation Army echoes similar deep-seated fears.

Whereas European women were viewed as weak, passive, and vulnerable, Indian women were often seen as sexually aggressive, wanton, and exploitive. Yet their apparent sexual freedom was won at high cost, for Indian women were considered to be highly industrious, productive, and responsible as compared to their lazy, indolent menfolk. Yet even these positive attributes of Indian women were transformed into a negative stereotype. As Smits (1982) has well documented, the image of the "squaw drudge" was taken by Euro-Americans as an "index of savagism" rather than an acknowledgement of the power and high status that women enjoyed in many Native American societies. [12]

For Euro-Americans, Indian sex-role patterning represented an inversion of the natural order and,

---

2 Despite the observed absence of facial and body hair, the Indian preference for long head hair, often braided and adorned, was considered vain and offensive to the Puritans. Thus one of the first prerequisites for civilizing the Indian was a haircut (Axtell 1981: 59-61).

3 These fears were aspects of a larger phenomenon – what A. Irving Hallowell (1963) has labeled the process of transculturization. This process has been further analyzed and richly documented by James Axtell (1981) in Chapters Six and Ten of his collected essays, *The European and the Indian*. Axtell acutely points out that colonial New England was involved not only in a struggle for land and military conquest against the Indians but also in a moral battle for souls. The desire to neutralize the Indian threat through conversion was counterbalanced by the fear that members of their own repressive society would be attracted to the freedom of Indian life and become transculturized "White Indians."

as such, indicated an inferior, primitive, or degenerate form of society.

One psychological characteristic that Whites consistently commented upon from the time of Columbus thereafter was the generosity of the Indian. While early accounts consider this a positive virtue, later commentators begin to interpret generosity as a partial indication of moral weakness. Generosity had become linked up in the While mind with a deficient sense of private properly that was rcinforced by their view of Native American society as communistic and lacking in a .sense of individualism. A chronic source of cross-cultural misunderstanding was the White insistence in regarding the objects of Indian generosity as outright "gifts," whereas the natives considered such offerings as efforts to establish, affirm, or reaffirm social solidarity with expectations of long- or short-term reciprocity. The native expectation of equivalent return gave rise to the derogatory expression "Indian gift" or "Indian giver," which can be traced back to at least 1765 in Thomas Hutchinson's *History of Massachusetts* where the usage was already considered "proverbial" (noted in Oxford English Dictionary 1971: 1415).

The overriding Euro-American conception of the Indian as hunter, with the accompanying denial or deemphasis on horticultural activity – despite the revolution that indigenous American cultigens precipitated in the world economy – served obvious ideological and political purposes. Not only did categorization as a hunting society place Native American cultures lower than European on ethnocentric scales of universal development, but it also served as moral justification for expropriating Indian land. Consistent with these notions were psychological assumptions. Native Americans were considered highly mobile peoples characterized by a restless inability to settle down or be contained. For some writers this migratory impulse was regarded almost as instinctive, a reflexive response to follow an irresistible "call of the wild" and to escape the constraints of civilized society. Such a theme resounds as a popular literary refrain. To take but one example, Philip Freneau's late 18th-century poem, "The Indian Student" tells of a "copper-coloured boy" from the savage tribes of the upper Susquehanna who matriculates at Harvard, shows promise as a scholar, but soon departs because of "the force of nature" urging him to return

> Where Nature's ancient forests grow
> and mingled laurel never fades,
> My heart is fixed; – and I must go
> To die among my native shades.
>
> [Reprinted in Turner 1974: 448-490]

Freneau's poetry symbolically marks the emergence of another set of attitudes toward Native Americans – attitudes that help provide the context for much of 19th-century American ethnological science.

The Rise of American Ethnology[4]

Nineteenth-century American ethnology can be viewed as a national intellectual and practical movement that was directly heir to ideological issues [13] inherited from the American Revolution. In fostering a new collective American identity and envisioning the future, leaders of public opinion found problematic the place of Blacks and of Indians in the new republic. The founding fathers were virtually unanimous in consigning Blacks to a status of permanent inferiority, basing this judgement on assumed racial inadequacies of mind und body. However, there was more equivocation in assessing Indian physical, intellectual, and moral qualities and the Redman's future in the United Stales. To judge the

---

4 Before writing this section, I had occasion to read Robert Bieder's excellent manuscript, "A Fearful Responsibility," which covers the beginnings of American ethnology in comprehensive fashion. Bieder's treatment has influenced the presentation offered here.

Indian as an inherently inferior species was also, by implication, to judge the North American continent and climate as an unfit natural environment for building a new civilization. Certainly Jefferson's (1964) famous defense of the American Indian in *Note's on the State of Virginia* against charges of inferiority by European intellectuals was motivated by such concern. As aboriginal inhabitants of the continent, Indians became positive icons, if not totems, of a refashioned past.

The celebrated Dr Benjamin Rush, a prominent Philadelphia patriot, signer of the Declaration of Independence, and important figure in the early history of American psychiatry, has much of interest to say about the natives of America. In his *Medical Inquiries and Observation upon the diseases of the Mind* (1812), he fails to find "a single instance of MADNESS, MELANCHOLY, or FATUITY among the Indians" (quoted in Takaki 1979: 28). Owing to their equality of power and properly, envy was not one of their traits. However, Rush felt their principal vices were: (1) "UNCLEANNESS," especially "nastiness" exemplified in their "food – drinks – persons – and above all, in their total disregard for decency in the *time – place –* and *manner* of their natural evacuations"; (2) "IDLENESS" – Indians not only were "too lazy to work, but even to think," and their taciturn disposition resulted from a kind of mental constipation; and (3) a susceptibility to alcoholism that Rush predicted would probably lead to their extirpation (Takaki 1979: 28-29).

Thomas Jefferson's views of the Indian, while judged liberal for the times, nevertheless had a pragmatic cast that demanded a forced choice between assimilation into American society or ultimate extermination. The root problem was economic. The only hope for Indian integration was to destroy the hunting base of their societies and transform them into settled farmers. In practical political terms Jefferson thought an agrarian way of life would reduce the threat of Indian militarism and, most important, open up new land for White settlement.

Jefferson's psychology was greatly influenced by the philosophy of John Locke. While mankind possessed an innate moral sense, a basic capacity to distinguish right from wrong, mentality and customs were largely determined by experience. Jefferson believed that, while all groups were created equal in the moral sense, there were, nevertheless, inherent differences in intelligence and capacity for civilization. It was here that Jefferson drew a line between Blacks and Indians. As he wrote in a 1785 letter to the Marquis de Chastellux,

> I am safe in affirming that the proofs of genius given by the Indians of N. America, place them on a level with whites in the same uncultivated state. ... I believe the Indian then to be in body and mind [14] equal to the white man. I have supposed the black man, in his present state, might not be so. [Quoted in Takaki 1979: 581]

Jefferson found evidence for Indian intelligence in artistic ability and, above all, in the imagery and rhetorical flourishes of native oratory.

Jefferson was also encouraged by the progress toward civilization made by Southeastern tribes in adopting an agrarian democracy, even though, in retrospect, much of this seeming progress was premised on slave labor and the ascendancy of a class of in-married White or mixed-blood plantation owners. He favored Indian-White intermarriage as a means for accelerating the assimilation process. However, intermixture with Blacks, though a continuously insistent biological fact, was publicly condemned by Jefferson.

Interesting shifts may be discerned in Jefferson's direct dealing with Indian leaders. In an 1802 letter to Handsome Lake, he reciprocates the Seneca prophet's usage in addressing him as "brother." However, a more paternalistic mode is adopted in later official correspondence when Indians are addressed as "sons" or "children" (Drinnon 1980: 86-88). The "great White father" imagery, previously prevailing in relation to the English crown and its representatives, was apparently reasserted after a brief egalitarian interlude.

Jefferson serves as a direct link between the enlightenment philosophy of the 18th century and

19th-century ethnology. His political philosophy and its practical applications encouraged the scholarly study of Native American peoples. This is manifest in Jefferson's early interest in archaeology, in American languages, and in comparative study of the customs of various tribes residing within the dramatically expanding territorial boundaries of the United States. These interests and correspondence with leading authorities on these subjects continued to command Jefferson's attention until his death on July 4, 1826. Although his substantive contributions were slight, Jefferson's encouragement of such study did much to legitimize ethnological research in America.

Jefferson's guarded optimism about Indian potential for civilization was not shared by many of his contemporaries and by few of his direct intellectual descendants. Increasingly, as in the portentous poetry of Freneau or in the dire predictions of Rush, a pessimism prevailed over the possibility that Indians could attain parity with their White conquerors. Reasons for this pessimism were many. Native populations continued to decline in the face of disease, warfare, and the dispiriting effects of alcohol; tribes on the frontier continued to engage in warfare, and the threat of hostile uprisings among supposedly pacified groups had not yet been extinguished; Christianity had reaped a scant harvest of permanent converts, and among many groups missionary efforts were rejected in favor of retention of traditional beliefs; government-sponsored programs to reform Indian society through education and technical change had not proven, on balance, successful. By 1847, Francis Parkman could write about an "impassible gulf" that separated Red men from White (quoted in Pearce 1965: 164).

It was in this climate of opinion that the fledgling science of ethnology took flight in America. A coherent program for American ethnology can be [15] delineated retrospectively. While some influences from English and Continental scholarship are clearly apparent, early American ethnology can best be considered an autochthonous intellectual movement largely devoted to American concerns. As a new nation, America eagerly sought to create for herself a past, to measure herself against other peoples past and present, to rationalize apparent contradictions between American ideals and realities, and to fulfill what was taken to be a divinely ordained destiny. Ethnology, as a composite field, attracted and encouraged diverse specialists to meet these newly felt national needs.

Systematic study of the American Indian was focal to these national concerns. What, after -so much speculation, were the true origins of the Indians? How long had they resided in this hemisphere? What was the nature of traditional Indian culture and society? How could one scientifically assess Indian biology and mentality? What underlying factors could be held responsible for the contemporary "Indian problem"? And what were the future prospects of the Indian on this continent? Problems of origins and antiquity stimulated archaeological study, and the discoveries of mounds in North America and remains of ancient civilizations in Middle and South America piqued public curiosity. Philological research was enlisted in the search for origins, in tracing relations between different groups, and to make inferences about Indian mentality. The comparative study of customs and beliefs might clarify the degree of Indian cultural attainment and potentiality for improvement. Investigation of the physical anthropology of New World peoples was considered crucial for ascertaining their racial status, particularly in comparison with Caucasians, Africans, and Asians. Underlying these emergent and convergent approaches to ethnology was a shared concern with American Indian mentality.

Nineteenth-century American ethnology was intrinsically involved with issues of race that had surfaced with the application of systematic biology to man in the mid-18th century. The tricolor composition of the American population – Red, White, and Black – posed moral and practical problems for the dominant Euro-American majority. Had the native inhabitants been treated justly? Could they be assimilated into the republic and, if so, how? Or were they biologically foredoomed to extinction? Was Black slavery morally justifiable? Should Blacks be placed in separate states of the Union, allowed to exist as a permanent under-caste in American society, or should they be transported back to Africa?

One preoccupation of the era was concern over the consequences of race mixture. Opponents argued that intermarriage would produce menial and physical degeneration and infertility in the offspring; others were sensitive to the sociological and psychological problems confronted by children of mixed unions. Proponents of intermarriage felt that in the process of admixture the more desirable traits would win out and become dominant. Black-While unions were, of course, given the opprobrious label of miscegenation and officially condemned. Red-White intermarriage was considered less degrading and in some quarters encouraged as the only hope for Indian salvation. The renowned Southern literary figure, William Gilmore Simms, in a discursive 1845 review of two books by the American ethnologist Schoolcraft, actually suggests that the intermixture might benefit the White race: [16]

> Properly diluted, there was no better blood than that of Cherokee and Natchez. It would have been a good infusion into the paler fountain of Quaker and Puritan – the very infusion which would put our national vanity in subjection lo our pride, and keep us as thoroughly independent of the mother country, in intellectual, as we believe ourselves to be in political respects. [Reprinted in Chapman 1975: 178]

The racial issue in America rapidly polarized into two competing intellectual ideologies. The orthodox Biblical proposition of monogenesis – that all mankind was directly descended from Adam and Eve, via Noah and his three sons, and therefore genealogically related – was challenged, especially in American ethnology, by an upsurge of interest in the formerly heretical polygenist position, which held that different races represented separate creations. The polygenist thesis was favored by those who held that the races were inherently different in physical and menial endowment, while monogenesis was more consistent with the idea of progress and ultimate possibilities for equality. However, it is important to recognize that from the perspective of the present both polygenists and monogenists would he considered racist. Thus, the monogenist position, while admitting original unity, usually invoked progressive degeneration or permanent retardation to account for differences in cultural attainment by different branches of mankind. At least theoretically, if not in practice, advocates of polygenesis could make a positive virtue of inherent racial difference as part of a divine plan, or as a celebration of pluralism, in which each race possessed a particular genius. However, in their common efforts to rank the races of mankind into higher or tower orders, proponents of both monogenesis and polygenesis sought empirical support for the a priori assumption of White supremacy and Black inferiority, with Indians occupying an intermediate status.

The work of some of the more prominent American ethnologists will now be examined with a particular eye to their conclusions about the psychology of the American Indian.

Samuel O Morton, a Philadelphia physician and naturalist with training in Scotland, has been called the father of American physical anthropology. He assembled an impressive collection of crania, including over 300 American Indian specimens. The skulls were subjected to several sets of measurements, and cranial capacity was determined by measuring the volume of mustard seed, later lead BB shot, that the cranium could hold. In his monumental *Crania Americana* (1839), Morton compared the cranial capacities of what were thought to be, following Blumenbach, the five major races – the Caucasian, Mongolian, Malay, American (Indian), and Ethiopian (Negro). The basic assumption was that brain size correlated with intelligence. The results supported the popular prejudices of the day: Caucasians clearly had the largest brains, followed in order by Mongolians, Malays, and Americans, with Ethiopians significantly lowest in brain size. This relative ranking was subsequently confirmed with a larger sample in a brief article published by Morton in 1849. Stephen Jay Gould (1981: 50-69) has recently completed a careful restudy of Morton's data and concluded that Morton's seemingly objective procedures [17] contained several systematic unconscious biases that, when corrected for, yield no significant racial difference in brain size. Morton was somewhat cautious about inferring civilizational potential from his data, since a large component of his American sample was composed of relatively small-brained prehistoric Peruvians who participated in a complex society al or approaching a civilizational level.

More important, Morton believed his craniometry had established the American Indians, excepting the Polar peoples, as a separate and relatively homogeneous race. The aggregate statistics did not support a Eurasian origin for the American natives. Older archaeological specimens did not show differences from skulls of more recent Indians, suggesting a strong hereditary and permanent basis for racial differences. Morton fell his evidence ran counter to dominant monogenist theories that explained the physical differences of mankind as caused by environmental factors. Increasingly Morton moved toward a more openly polygenist position.

Morton was not loath to infer moral and mental attributes associated with his physical findings on the American race. The natives of America were "averse to cultivation, and slow in acquiring knowledge; restless, revengeful, fond of war, and wholly destitute of maritime adventure" (Morton 1839: 6). Indians "are not only averse to the restraints of education, but for the most part are incapable of a continued process of reasoning on abstract subjects" (quoted in Gould 1981: 57). On the positive side, Indians displayed great physical stamina and perseverance in following a determined course. In marked contrast with Blacks, the Indian was "incapable of servitude and thus his spirit sank at once in captivity, and with it his physical energy" (quoted in Stanton 1960: 34). Morton's *Crania Americana* also contained an essay on American Indian phrenology by a leading exponent of that nascent discipline. George Combe, which essentially reinforced the conclusions about mentality that Morton had reached from his general readings of travelers, missionaries, and others on Indian character. In sum, Morton's comments on the psychology of the American Indian represent no more than a distillation of popular impressions that had hardened into permanent stereotypes over the previous 350 years.

Linguistics comprised a second component in the synthesis of American ethnology. Previously collected word lists and grammatical forms were recovered and published in the early 19th century by such scholars as John Pickering and Peter Du Ponceau; efforts were mounted to standardize orthography and obtain new data through questionnaires, li was Albert Gallatin, the elderly distinguished statesman, who put these diverse materials together to construct the first modern classification of North American Indian languages east of the Rocky Mountains, first published in 1836 and revised in 1848 shortly before his death. For Gallatin classification was an important step toward unraveling the complex problem of American Indian origins and tracing subsequent migrations. Gallatin remained a steadfast believer in mono-genesis and stages of development (Bieder 1975: 93-96).

Comparative linguistics lacked much of the authority it holds today. When Gallatin questioned Morton's exclusion of Eskimos from his grand [18] American Race, Morton dismissed philology as insufficiently exact in comparison with physical measurements. He noted that, as in Madagascar, distinctive races often spoke the same language. Thus for Morton languages were subject to historical circumstances, while only physical and menial trails were enduring (Stanton 1960: 97-98).

However, Gallatin and such colleagues as Pickering, Lewis Cass, and Schoolcraft were convinced that linguistics might provide important insights not only into origins but also into thought processes of Native Americans. Through learning Ojibwa, Schoolcraft noted the paucity of terms in certain domains, heavy reliance on figurative metaphors, extremes of repetitiveness, inclusive and exclusive forms of personal pronouns, animate and inanimate noun classification, frequent use of circumlocution, and impoverished mathematical concepts. Linguistics thus could provide a key to thought, but the potentiality of this approach was scarcely realized by 19th-century American ethnologists.

The leading figure in mid-19th-century American archaeology was Ephraim G. Squier who, with Edwin H Davis, gained scholarly fame for his scientific investigations of the mounds of the Mississippi Valley. He later published additional research on antiquities and engaged in pioneering ethnographic work in Middle America. Although a confirmed believer in polygenesis, Squier assumed a position of leadership in the American Ethnological Society after Gallatin's death. Squier's lively theoretical views and speculative comparisons were held in check by the sober, scientific hand of Joseph Henry, the first Secretary of the Smithsonian Institution, who supervised Squier's publications on mounds (Tax 1975). Squier considered himself primarily an ethnologist and maintained a strong interest in religious symbolism as manifested in material remains and in the belief systems of living peoples. Through the interpretation of such subjects as serpent worship and solar beliefs, Squier felt he could penetrate to the depths of the Indian mind and educe similarities between the symbolism of Middle American civilizations and core religious beliefs of North American tribes. Such connections were intended to demonstrate the unity of the American race and its separation from other branches of humanity.

But it was Henry Rowe Schoolcraft who probably did the most both to legitimize and popularize the study of Indian myths and religious beliefs in the 19th century. As Indian agent and husband of an educated mixed-blood Ojibwa woman, he was able to achieve the kind of first-hand, continuous observations denied most other ethnologists. Possessed of a poetic, if somewhat romantic, nature, Schoolcraft was able to see through some of the popular stereotypes and discern some of the less appreciated aesthetic, humanistic, and philosophic features of Indian thought. As he writes in his memoirs,

> I had always heard the Indian spoken of as [] revengeful, bloodthirsty man, who was steeled to endurance and delight in deeds of cruelty. To find him a man capable of feelings and affections, with a heart open to the wants and responsive to the ties of social life, was amazing. But the surprise reached its acme when 1 found him whiling away a part of the [19] tedium of his long winter evenings in relating tales and legends for the amusement of the lodge circle. These fictions were sometimes employed. I observed, to convey instruction or impress examples of courage, daring, or right action. But they were, at all times replete with the wild forest of notions of spiritual agencies, necromancy, and demonology. They revealed abundantly the cause of his hopes and fears, his notions of a Deity, and his belief in a future state. [Quoted in Hallowell 1960: 41]

Schoolcraft wanted to examine the philosophy underlying the Indian mind, rather than limit himself to external customs, manners, physical traits, and historical peculiarities (1839, 1: 10). His accounts of Indian life and collections of tales (expurgated for popular consumption) earned him a deserved reputation as the leading ethnologist of his day.

However, as a result of a dramatic personal religious experience during his tenure as Indian Agent at Sault Ste. Marie, Schoolcraft's sympathy and empathy for Indians changed radically (Freeman 1965). He became increasingly impatient with their retention of pagan superstitions and failure to embrace Christianity as completely as he had; Indian obstinacy had resulted in moral degeneracy. Schoolcraft's interest in Indians thereafter took a more pragmatic and pessimistic turn. The principal value of learning about the deeper workings of the Indian mind was to facilitate conversion and to reorient their society in a more Christian direction.

Schoolcraft's damped hopes for Indian progress are clearly revealed in 1839:

> He does not seem to open his eyes on the prospect of civilization and mental exaltation held up before him, as one to whom the scene is new or attractive. These scenes have been pictured before him by teachers and philanthropists for more than two centuries; but there has been nothing in them to arouse and inspire him to press onward in the career of prospective civilization and refinement. He has rather turned away with the air of one to whom all things "new" were "old" and chose emphatically to re-embrace his woods, his wigwams, and his canoe. [Quoted in Zolla 1973: 153-154]

He soon left the frontier to pursue a career as a professional scholar of and spokesman on Indian studies.[5]

---

5 Schoolcraft's later years seem to represent a complete repudiation of his earlier life. His southern-born second wife, Mary Howard, was an ardent defender of slavery. In her thinly disguised *roman a clef*

Schoolcraft developed a plan for a comprehensive collaborative investigation of American ethnology, a project that ultimately resulted in his government-sponsored six-volume compendium, *Historical and Statistical Information Respecting the History, Condition, and Prospects of the Indian Tribes of the United States* (1851-57). Despite the quest for objectivity, some of the questionnaire inquiries used to generate data for the project betray Schoolcraft's prejudice. For example, "Do certain adepts [Conjurors] really think they are inspired by devils?" "What positive proofs exist for these hallucinations?" (quoted in Zolla 1973: 153). These ponderous volumes, or an [20] "immense scrap book" according to von Humholdt (cited in Drinnon 1972: 150), failed to have the impact Schoolcraft desired. Yet the project did signal the federal government's recognition of the value of ethnological research on American Indians and helped prepare the ground for the establishment of the Smithsonian's Bureau of Ethnology in 1879.

If this foreshortened review of the beginning of formal ethnology in America accomplishes nothing else, it should demonstrate that the common thread tying these diverse approaches together was an interest in American Indian mentality. The scholars singled out for discussion participated in a shared discourse, and all were connected with the American Ethnological Society (Bieder and Tax 1976). Part of that shared discourse can be discerned in the general agreement about the menial attributes of Native Americans. Despite efforts to make ethnology scientific, the psychology of the American Indian remained little more than a summary of continuous and prevailing popular imagery. Consensual opinion decreed that the obdurate character of the Indian would lead to racial demise. Historian Francis Parkman captures the dominant contemporary sentiment in the following passage:

> Nature has stamped the Indian with a hard and stern physiognomy. Ambition, revenge, envy, jealousy, are his ruling passions; and his cold temperament is little exposed to those effeminate vices which are the bane of milder races.... [Some races are) moulded in wax, soft and melting, at once plastic and feeble. Some races, like some metals, combine the greatest flexibility with the greatest strengths. But the Indian is hewn out of rock. You can rarely change the form without destruction of the substance. ... He will not learn the arts of civilisation, and he and his forest must perish together. (Quoted in Grossett 1963: 243-244)

It is worth noting that Parkman's metaphors for racial intractability fail to convey the fact that the praiseworthy flexible, yet strong, metals are normally alloys.

It would he desirable to continue the discussion of White conceptions of American Indian psychology through the influential work of such later scholars as Lewis Henry Morgan, John Wesley Powell and the Smithsonian ethnologists, and the neglected Daniel Garrison Brinton. Also rewarding would be a review of the psychological views of the American Indian implicit in the approach of Franz Boas and some of his followers, such as Frank Speck, Herman Haeberlin, Paul Radin, and Alexander Goldenweiser, prior to the advent of the culture-and-personality movement in the 1930s. However, such excursions must await another occasion. In the remainder of this paper I examine some selected aspects of indigenous Native American psychology.

b

---

novel, *The Black Gauntlet* (1860), she deplores Indian-White marriage as a "dangerous amalgamation of races," a "suicidal ... experiment." The hero of the turgid novel, who bears similarity to her husband, initially feels that "the union of the American aborigines with the noble Anglo-Saxon would produce the highest specimen of humanity," but after contemplating the wayward nature of his offspring, he concludes that nothing can "make them or Ham equal to Japhet, for God predestined their inequality forever" (quotations from Scheick 1979: 21).

Psyche

Cosmological Convergences and Contradictions of the Soul

Just as a formal psychology can be differentiated from popular or folk psychology in Western tradition, so too was psychological knowledge and theory differentially distributed in Native American societies. Shamans and [21] religious practitioners often possessed esoteric knowledge of a psychological nature denied less privileged fellow tribesmen. Some systems of thought gradually evolved toward greater consistency and increased complexity. Other systems were less stable and readily incorporated new elements or idea clusters from other groups through normal processes of diffusion or through the compelling messages of inspired prophets.

Whitemen were initially seen by most Native Americans as yet another alien tribe with an alternate set of beliefs and practices. However, the power of the European invaders, the devastation of native cultures, and the persistent proselytizing of missionaries and other "men of good will" precipitated both native resistance and accommodation. Some of the religious and philosophic concepts underlying indigenous psychology became entrenched in an oppositional ideology of traditionalism, while other concepts underwent syncretistic change.

Some of these processes may be illustrated by comparing certain critical psychological aspects of many Native American religions with those of Christianity. Christian monotheism contrasted sharply with the apparent plethora of spiritual beings recognized in Native American religions. While Europeans submitted to an awesome, almighty God, Indians were less enthralled by their divinities, whom they tended to placate in a matter-of-fact manner. Perhaps the greatest obstacle to Indian conversion was exclusive surrender to and dependence upon a single omnipotence. Nevertheless, in the recesses of native theology there often lurked remote beings or impersonal, diffuse powers on high. Rarely propitiated directly, such forces often served an intellectual function as a prime mover or first cause. In later Indian belief these forces became more personified and proximal in the form of a Creator, Great Spirit, Master of Life, or Master of Breath and came to resemble more closely the Christian God. A similar convergence seems to develop to a slight degree between major Indian culture heroes and the figure of Christ, although the pre-social, amoral, trickster qualities of most culture heroes often prove resistant to allegorization.

Christians viewed mankind as predisposed to sin and subject to temptations of evil. These inner weaknesses were projected outward and externalized in the figure of Satan. Most Indians did not subscribe to beliefs in the inherent sinfulness of man and weaknesses of the flesh, yet maleficent spirits, sorcerers, witches, and ghosts constituted real forces that demanded greater ritual attention than more beneficent beings. Thus, to give one early example, in a 1570 account from the South Atlantic coast the Jesuit Father Rogel reports a sympathetic hearing when he told the Yamassee [?]

> such truths of our holy religion as are manifest by the light of nature, such as the unity of God, His power and majesty, that He is the cause and creator of all things, how He loves what is good and abhors evil; and also certain truths that our Father teaches us, as rewards and punishments in another life, the immortality of the soul, and the resurrection of the dead. [22]

However, when he told them that they must become enemies of the Demon [*el Deinono*]}, "they became greatly displeased, and so bitter was the hatred that they conceived against me, that they refused to see or hear me any more" (Brinton 1861: 328). This reluctance to abandon belief in the reality of maleficent spirits was doubtless one of the principal reasons that the New England Puritans perceived the Indians as having an inviolable "pact with the devil."

Native American cosmologies often recognized the creation of an earth island in a primal sea and a multi-tiered upper world and underworld. Powerful spirits often resided on high, but the concept of a celestial heaven was only weakly, if at all, developed, and the land of the dead was frequently located toward the west or the south or beyond the sea. The underworld was usually populated by primordial beings and characterized by systematic reversal of the situation on earth in terms of the seasons and day and night. The reality of these other worlds was frequently verified by the spiritual journeys of shamans and others. The underworld is not imbued with the negative connotations that Western Civilization attributes to it; it is not the locus of hell and eternal damnation. Despite these profound differences, many Indian cosmologies in time came to approximate the Christian notions of a vertically situated heaven and hell.

The essence of both Indian and Western psychologies is contained in metaphysical notions of the soul.[6] The Christian belief in a unitary soul as a divine attribute that survives the mortal demise of the body was paralleled in some Native American cultures. However, more frequently we encounter multiple soul concepts in Indian psychology. Ake Hultkrantz's (1953) herculean labor in classifying *Conceptions of the Soul among North American Indians* displays prodigious scholarship, yet remains unsatisfying in its typological formalism. Hultkrantz attempts to force a basic dualistic distinction between an ego (mind) or body soul and a life or free soul. Such conceptualization unduly simplifies and obscures the richness and profoundity revealed in his massive collation of data. The comparative classificatory urge does not permit Hultkrantz to appreciate the centrality of soul beliefs in relation to such other ramifying aspects of culture as theories of procreation, mortuary practice, theories of illness and witchcraft, the logic of taboo systems, as well as ethnobiology and ideas of self and person.

One fundamental difference in the soul beliefs of Euro-Americans and many Native Americans has to do with species exclusivity and metempsychosis, the doctrine that the soul could migrate from body to body, from human to animal, and vice versa. The soul of the Christian, particularly one who had been saved, possessed the divine quality of reason that sharply differentiated him from infra-human forms of creation. In contrast, many Native American systems of thought considered that animals, in some cases plants, and objects and forces that we might classify as inanimate, also possessed souls. In most instances these souls were considered equivalent to those of humans. Bodily form might be variable, but inner essences and the disembodied soul entities were constant. Such a notion not only helps us understand the religious basis of Native American hunting practices, but it goes far in clarifying the nature of Indian totemic beliefs, guardian spirit concepts, and the logic of metempsychosis. [23]

The implications of this metaphysical idea of shared or exchanged soul substance are many. For one, it would seem to link Native Americans in a more intrinsically lateral fashion to creatures and forces in this world, while the assumed vertical connection of the Christian mind to a celestial God would tend to place human beings spiritually above nature as a special creation. Other implications of distinctive Native American soul conceptions remain to be worked out on both a more specific and generalized level. Unfortunately, data on these critical ethnometaphysical problems are thin or lacking, often' contradictory, and difficult to obtain. Much of this knowledge has been lost or modified beyond recognition with the absorption of Euro-American religious and philosophical psychology and with the drastically changed conditions of Native American life. However, rather than mourn what is beyond reclamation, the newest of the new ethnologies should celebrate the fact that there are still historical and ethnographic documents to interpret, additional information to be gathered, and new questions to be posed.

The distinctive features of Native American psychologies are far from moribund. In his courageous book, *God is Red*, Vine Deloria (1973) argues for the necessity of perpetuating and reviving traditional Native American religion as a viable alternative to Christianity. My main disagreement with Deloria's profound treatise is his assertion that, unlike Christianity, Native American religion is ahistorical. What is insufficiently realized, perhaps, is that Native American history has become, and perhaps always was, prophecy.

This prophetic tradition today emphasizes that the survival of Native American peoples and

---

6 The English term 'soul' is, of course, only an approximate gloss for conceptions and terms having to do with immaterial inner essence, 'ego', detachable part of the self, life force, and that part of the individual that survives death. Meanings, and cognate usage, in each particular Native American language would have to be worked out to make specific comparisons.

cultures cannot be separated from the survival of the world. If, as John Locke maintained, "in the beginning all the world was America," an America without Indians may be considered no world at all. One of the central theses of this essay has been to document the shift of White attitudes in the late 18th and 19th century from optimism to pessimism regarding the future of the Indian. Previous to this time there was the hope that the Redman, if not yet fully equal to the Whiteman, had the possibility of assimilating into American society. This pseudo-equality was symbolically expressed in the indeterminate skin color of the Indian and in the kinship convention of addressing Indian leaders as "brother." Soon thereafter Indians became indelibly Red and were called "sons" and "children." They became a separate race with an inherent incapacity to partake of the privileges of civilization. However, Indians seemed to have always viewed themselves as a separate and distinctive, if not unequal, peoples, and they transformed their attributed deficiency into a virtue. Maybe the United States is finally prepared mentally to accept moral, cultural, and psychological pluralism and to lake seriously the messages of Indian prophecy.

Postlude

This essay does not lend itself to easy conclusions. Perhaps a statement by a historian of ideas will serve as both an epitomizing epilogue and provocative prolegomenon: [24]

It becomes more and more clear that human behavior, taken as a whole, is so complex that any doctrinal idea claiming to be exclusive is only an illusion; in short it is clear that psychological sciences must guard themselves above all against dehumanizing man, and must recognize that all their hypotheses are entailed by an anthropology in perpetual process, and therefore necessarily incomplete. [Mueller 1973: 15] [25]

References

Axtell, James 1981 *The European and the Indian: Essays in the Ethnohistory of Colonial North America.* Oxford: Oxford University Press.

Baudet, Henri 1965 *Paradise on Earth: Some Thoughts on European Images of Non-European Man.* E. Wentholl, trans. New Haven: Yale University Press.

Berkhofer, Robert F, Jr. 1978 *The White Man's Indian.* New York: Alfred A. Knopf.

Berlin, Brent and Paul Kay 1969 *Basic Color Terms: Their Universality and Evolution.* Berkeley: University of California Press.

Bieder, Robert E 1975 Albert Gallatin and the Survival of Enlightenment Thought in Nineteenth-Century American Anthropology. In *Toward a Science of Man.* THH Thoresen, ed., pp. 91-98. The Hague: Mouton.

Bieder, Robert E, and Thomas G. Tax 1976 From Ethnologists to Anthropologists: A Brief History of the American Ethnological Society. In *American Anthropology: the Early Years.* John V. Murra, ed. 1974 Proceedings of the American Ethnological Society. St Paul: West.

Billington, Ray Allen 1981 *Land of Savagery, Land of Promise: The European Image of the American Frontier.* New York: W.W. Norton.

Brinton, Daniel Garrison 1861 Rogel's Account of the Florida Mission (1569-70). *Historical Magazine* 5 (11): 327-330.

Chapman, Abraham, ed. 1975 *Literature of the American Indians: Views and Interpretations.* New York: New American Library.

Chiappelli, Fredi, ed., Michael J. B. Alien and Robert I. Benson, co-eds. 1976 *First Images of America.* 2 vols. Berkeley: University of California Press.

Claus, David B. 1981 *Toward the Soul: An Inquiry into the Meaning of **** before Plato.* New Haven: Yale University Press.

Deloria, Vine, Jr 1973 *God is Red.* New York: Grossett & Dunlap.

Drinnon, Richard 1972 *White Savage: The Case of. John Dunn Hunter.* New York: Schocken Books.

— 1980 *Facing West: The Metaphysics of Indian-Haling and Empire-Building.* New York: New American Library.

Fiedler, Leslie A 1968 *The Return of the Vanishing American.* New York: Stein & Day.

Freeman, John Finley 1965 Religion and Personality in the Anthropology of Henry Schoolcraft. *Journal of the History of the Behavioral Sciences* 1 (4): 299-313.

Gould, Stephen Jay 1981 *The Mismeasure of Man.* New York: W. W. Norton. [26]

Grossett, Thomas F 1963 *Race: The History of an Idea in America.* Dallas: Southern Methodist University Press.

Hallowell, A Irving 1960 The Beginnings of Anthropology in America. In *Selected Papers from the American Anthropologist*, 1888-1920. F de Laguna, ed., pp. 1-90. Evanston, IL: Row, Peterson.

— 1963 American Indians. White and Black: The Phenomenon of Transculturation. *Current Anthropology* 4: 519-531.

— 1965 The History of Anthropology as an Anthropological Problem. *Journal of the History of the Behavioral Sciences* 1: 24-38.

Hanke, Lewis 1959 *Aristotle and the American Indians; A Study in Race Prejudice in the Modern World.* Chicago: Henry Regnery.

Honour, Hugh 1975 *The New Golden Land.* New York: Pantheon Books.

Hultkrantz, Ake 1953 *Conceptions of the Soul among North American Indians.* Stockholm: The Ethnographical Museum of Sweden.

Jefferson, Thomas 1964 *Notes on the State of Virginia.* T.P. Abernathy, ed. New York: Harper & Row.

Lukes, Steven 1973 *Individualism.* New York: Harper Torchbooks.

Morton, Samuel G 1839 *Crania Americana.* Philadelphia: John Pennington.

Mueller, Fernand-Lucien 1973 Psychological Schools in American Thought. In *Dictionary of the History of Ideas.* PP Wiener, ed. New York: Scribners.

Murphy, Gardner 1949 *Historical Introduction to Modern Psychology.* Rev. ed. New York: Harcourt, Brace.

Pearce, Roy Harvey 1965 *The Savages of America.* Rev. ed. Baltimore: The Johns Hopkins Press.

Peters, RS, ed. 1962 *Brett's History of Psychology.* Rev. ed. Cambridge, MA: M.I.T. Press.

Powell, JM 1977 *Mirrors of the New World: Images and Image-Makers in the Settlement Process.* Kent, England: W. Dawson.

Saum, Lewis O 1965 *The Fur Trader and the Indian.* Seattle: University of Washington Press.

Scheick, William J 1979 *The Half-Blood: A Cultural Symbol in the 19th-century American Fiction.* Lexington: University Press of Kentucky.

Schoolcraft, Henry Rowe 1839 *Algic Researchers*, Comprising Inquiries Respecting the Mental Characteristics of the North American Indian. First Series. Indian Tales and Legends. 2 vols. New York: Harper.

— 1851-57 Information Regarding the History. Condition and Prospects of the Indian Tribes of the United States: Collected and Prepared under the Direction of the Bureau of Indian Affairs. 6 vols. Philadelphia: Lippincott, Grambo & Co. [27]

Smits, David D 1982 The "Squaw Drudge": A Prime Index of Savagism. *Ethnohistory* 29 (4): 281-306.

Stanton, William 1960 *The Leopard's Spots: Scientific Attitudes toward Race in America, 1815-59.* Chicago: University of Chicago Press.

Stedman, Raymond W 1982 *Shadows of the Indian: Stereotypes in American Culture.* Norman: University of Oklahoma Press.

Takaki, Ronald T 1979 *Iron Cages: Race and Culture in Nineteenth-Century America.* New York:

Alfred A Knopf.

Tax, Thomas G 1975 E George Squier and the Mounds, 1845-1850. In *Toward a Science of Man*. THH Thoresen, ed., pp. 99-124. The Hague: Mouton.

Turner, Frederick W, III 1974 *The Portable North American Indian Reader*. New York: Viking Press.

Vaughan, Alden T 1982 From White Man to Redskin: Changing Anglo-American Perceptions of the American Indian. *The American Historical Review* 87 (4): 917-953.

White, Hayden 1976 The Noble Savage Theme as Fetish. In *First Images of America*. Vol. 1. F Chiappelli, ed., MJB Alien and RL Benson, co-eds., pp. 121-135. Berkeley: University of California Press.

Zolla, Elemire 1973 *The Writer and the Shaman: A Morphology of the American Indian*. R Rosenthal, trans. New York: Harcourt, Brace, Jovanovich.

NIGHT THOUGHTS ON
NATIVE AMERICAN SOCIAL HISTORY

When Fred Hoxie invited me to participate in this conference by presenting a paper on "social history," I readily accepted. It was only afterward when I started to think through what I might say that I experienced perplexity. The assigned topic, "social history," seemed rather diffuse and open-ended. I had difficulty imagining an asocial history. The miracle that Native American cultures still survive, and in many instances flourish, despite almost five centuries of intentional and unintentional policies of genocide, ethnocide, and directed culture change, is underappreciated. This persistence certainly testifies to the strength of a continuous sense of collective identity engendered through abiding ties of kinship and community.

Yet there is a recognizable intellectual movement called social history that has self-consciously broken with previous approaches to history. Primarily centered in Europe, this movement has already influenced American scholarship profoundly and promises to exert a significant impact on future historical research concerning Native North America.

I will organize my remarks on social history under three subheadings: first, "What's Going On"; second, "Where We've Been"; and third, "Where Me Should Be Going." These rubrics at first glance correspond to our familiar tripartite temporal divisions of present, [67] past, and future. However, such a correspondence deflects my aim, since "What's Going on" has been going on for some time, at least extending into a near past, and it threatens to project into an unknowable future. Similarly, "Where We've Been" will be perceived as a cumulative and progressive past and a still prevalent now pushing into an indefinite beyond now. Finally, "Where We Should Be Going" will express some personal preferences for a conditional future premised on a putative past and a privileged present. Any tension produced by my contentious, if not pretentious, sense of tense may be reduced by considering each of the categories as imbued with eternal qualities of "everywhen".[1]

I. What's Going On

The modern movement toward "social history" derives from a confluence of several sources, but any derivation that failed to consider the *Annales* tradition would be deficient.

The publication of the *Annales* was begun by Marc Bloch and Lucien Febvre in 1929 as an effort to rescue the study of history from constriction caused by an almost exclusive focus on political history, individual personalities, and short-term events. The editorial policy of the *Annales* sought to open up historical research to previously ignored topics and encouraged closer rapprochement with the social sciences in the hope that a clearer understanding of the present might illuminate the past.

If the traditional version of the history of history be accepted as a sequential transformation from annals to chronicles to "true" [69] interpretative history, then the very title *Annales* may represent a symbolic return of the surpassed, a journey back to primary, descriptive beginnings. The *Annales* approach is avowed in the publication's subtitle: "*Economies, societés, civilisation.*" Besides reflecting diverse approaches to historical subjects, this tripartite emphasis represents an analysis in terms of levels. Economics, which includes geographic situation, demography, and material culture, provides the bedrock that supports a distinctive social structure, which in turn gives rise to the particular character of the civilisation. *Civilisation* implies a particular *mentalité* or mode of thought and can also be satisfactorily translated as "culture," in its modern anthropological sense.

---

[1] "Everyvhen" is a delightful gloss offered by WEH Stanner on the Australian Aboriginal notion of "the Dreaming" or "Dream time." This eternal composite of past, present, and future seems analogous to many Native American conceptions of a continuous primordial time.

Fernand Braudel in the preface of his magisterial study of *The Mediterranean and the Mediterranean World in the Age of Philip II*, and in his more recent trilogy on *Civilization and Capitalism, the 15th-18th Century*, clearly delineates three levels of history. The first level is geographical and concerns human relations to the environment and is characterized by imperceptible change, repetition, and recurrent cycles. This timeless history is more than background setting; it represents a chronic force. Braudel's second level is social history, which displays slow but perceptible rhythms with swelling tides of change in social groups and institutions. The third level comprises traditional or conventional history as constructed on the scale of individuals and events. Braudel sees traditional history as consisting of brief, episodic fluctuations that he likens to surface disturbances. This level offers superficial explanations that do not penetrate to the deeper, more submerged currents of history [69] which remain unsuspected by either observers or participants.

The levels of environmental and social history, with their focus upon longer-term realities, can be seen, in their horizontal aspects, to comprise structure or structural relations, while traditional history, with its shorter-term realities, has a more vertical orientation that constitutes conjuncture, or temporal contingency. The interaction of structures and conjunctures, or long-term processes versus short-term events, poses fundamental contradictions that confront any student of history; indeed, the more things change, the more they are the same and vice versa.

A somewhat similar three-tiered model is proposed by Braudel in his stimulating study of *Capitalism and Material Life, 1400-1800*, where material life, the subject of most of his book. Is regarded as the relatively passive, repetitive, "ground floor of history," while economic life represents a more active, expansive level and, finally, capitalism constitutes a third-stage super-system that encroaches on all prior forms of life, economic and material.

This general notion of levels, of surface events and deep structures, and the assumption that cultural or superstructural phenomena not only presuppose but are determined by such infrastructural levels as social organization and environment, makes this scheme congenial to Marxist theories of history, to the Parsonian theory of social action, as well as to modern varieties of structural analysis, and to other unlikely bedfellows. Yet, as we shall see, levels ultimately must be regarded as heuristic devices and not all of the assumptions of the French social historians need be accepted without question. [70]

The *Annales* approach to social history contains several other themes worthy of brief mention. The focus on social groupings and instructions has served to exclude consideration of the individual as a significant force in history. At best the individual appears only as an icon of an idea. While not excluding the upper classes or intelligentsia as factors in historical process, social historians have paid special attention to the everyday life of commoners and of diverse occupational groups and socio-economic statuses. Richly detailed descriptions of material culture, folklore, family structure, and ceremonial life have become the hallmark of such social historians as Braudel, Emanuel LaRoy Ladurie, Philippe Ariés, and others. Social historians take special delight in tracing topics off the beaten tracks of mainline historiography. The late Michel Foucault looked at punishment, clinics, and sexuality; Aries studied the life cyclical extremities of childhood and death; and LaRoy Ladurie meticulously reconstructed festivals. These embroidered ethnographic accounts often succeed in not only making the pre-modern cultures of Europe, and occasionally elsewhere, more familiar but also serve to make the superficially familiar more exotic.

The strongly positivistic bent of most social historians associated with the *Annales* tradition also becomes manifest in their seemingly obsessive concern with quantification. Almost anything that can be counted will be. Many of the simple statistical charts and tables come directly from archival material. Statistics, at least until the late nineteenth century, remained true to its etymological origin and primarily referred to social enumerations collected by the state as unfocussed information-gathering devices. In France social [71] statistics figured prominently in the formative social theories of Montesquieu, La Place, Quetelet, and continued through early Durkheimian sociology. Statistical data, as deployed by most social historians, are mainly used in an adjunctive fashion to illustrate trends and buttress arguments;

rarely are statistics used for formal hypothesis-testing. The limitations of such quantitative data in terms of reliability, validity, and sample adequacy are many; often multiple Interpretations are possible and the statistical data frequently raise more questions than they render.

Many specifics of the *Annales* approach seem distinctively French, Yet general similarities can be discovered in Anglo-American efforts at writing social history. In England the works that come readily to mind include Raymond Williams' studies of material and popular culture, E.P, Thompson's penetrating description and analysis of the rise of the English working class, Peter Laslett's reconstruction of *The World We Have Lost*, Norman Cohn's accounts of Millenarian movements, and Keith Thomases and Alan Macfarland's anthropologically informed interpretations of sixteenth and seventeenth century English witchcraft beliefs.

In the United States one work stands out as a clear and independent anticipation of the flowering of French social history, Walter Prescott Webb's *The Great Plains* (1931) not only is solidly grounded in geography, but it sees the white settlement of the Plains as contingent on the presence of three crucial items of material culture – the windmill, the six-shooter, and barbed wire. Moreover, Webb rarely mentions individuals; rather things were accomplished by people. [72]

It is beyond my range of competence to review the varieties, home-grown or otherwise, of American social history. However, even as a casual consumer, some comments seem evident. Certainly there has been a revived interest in historical geography as witnessed by the enthusiastic reception of the works of Alfred Crosby and William Cronon; in demographics as reflected in statistical census studies and in the proliferation of interest in family history; in material culture and technology as exemplified In the elegant studies of rural architecture and artifacts by Henry Glassie; in the exploding interest in popular culture, both past and present; in broad economic analyses based upon the world systems theory of Immanuel Wallerstein, particularly as epitomized by Eric Wolf's provocative book, *Europe and the People without History*; in Anthony FC Wallace's and Tamara Hareven's historical ethnographies of life in factory towns; and in the numerous social histories of various immigrant groups among which Irving Howe's *World of Our Fathers* is particularly noteworthy.

Yet, within this broad spectrum of American interest in social history, very little deals directly with Native American history. Why this seems to be so and the shape of alternative modes of treating Native American history may emerge in sharper relief when we consider "Where We've Been."

II. Where We've Been

The forthright contemporary historian Charles Tilly is reported to have argued that "history is too important to be left to the "historian" (statement of Lee Benson in Graubard 1969: 891).[2] What [73] Tilly was calling attention to is the need of historians to draw upon the models, theories, and methods of the social sciences to bring forth the significance of their documents. Historians and anthropologists claim overlapping dominion over the scholarly study of American Indian history. The approaches followed by historians and anthropologists have been both opposed and complementary.

In the mid-nineteenth century such luminaries as Parkman. Prescott, and Bancroft synthesized earlier source materials to produce their grandiose, if not grand, epic histories of Indian-White relations. These eloquent and popular writers clearly reflected the political biases of their time. They chronicled conflict, depicted the decline of the Redman, and flowed with the irresistible flood tide of White supremacy. The heroic virtues of some individual Indians might be two-dimensionally recounted, but by and large little sympathy and even less empathy were directed toward Indian society and culture.

Lewis Henry Morgan was acutely sensitive to the limits of naiveté among historians. In a footnote to *Ancient Society* he asserts,

---

[2] Tilly's statement neatly complements Curtis Hinsley's sentiment, in the preface to his *Savages and Scientists* (1981: 10), that "the history of anthropology ... should not be left to the anthropologists."

The historian of Spanish America may be trusted in whatever relates to the acts of the Spaniards, and to the acts and personal characteristics of the Indians; in whatever relates to their weapons, implements and utensils, fabrics, food and raiment, and things of a similar character. But in whatever relates to Indian society and government, their social relations, and plan of life, they are nearly worthless, because they learned nothing of either. We are at full liberty to reject them in these respects and commence anew; using any facts they might contain which harmonize with what is known of Indian society (1877:191).

As we can ascertain from our present perspective, Morgan had blinders of his own. However, in the quotation above he seems to be posing a rhetoric of ethnology against a rhetoric of history. Historians might record events, describe surface features of a culture, but with [74] respect to the deeper, more enduring social and political structures, their understanding was deficient. Morgan felt that such understanding could only come from fieldwork, such as he had experienced with the Iroquois and certain Western tribes, or from careful comparative analysis of ethnological data to generate models of social relationships that were genuinely alien to Euro-American systems. Morgan can, indeed, be considered a social historian, but one interested in general long-range historical processes. He seemed impatient with the imponderabilia of everyday life, except where such data – be they kin terms, house types, or bedclothes – might provide clues to unrecorded historical relationships.

The legacy that Morgan bequeathed to American anthropology was largely rejected during the ascendancy of Franz Boas and the advent of so-called "historical particularism." The Boasian program called for more comprehensive field ethnography, a movement away from grand evolutionary schemes, and a greater concern with cultural meaning as mediated through language. Historical reconstruction, in the absence of an adequate archaeology or written records, might be pursued by distributional studies of linguistic affiliations and culture traits. However, increasingly Boas felt that each culture possessed its own particular genius or distinctive configuration that made comparison futile.

Except in specific areas like the Southeast, where the traditional cultures had disappeared or been greatly modified, little use was made of archival materials. One case that demonstrates the consequences of deliberate ignorance of written records is Leslie Spier's methodological exercise in tracing the development and [75] diffusion of the Sun Dance (1921). After decomposing the Sun Dance into 280 discrete traits, Spier plotted the distribution of these traits on tribal maps. The largest clustering of traits occurred in the central area of the Northern Plains occupied by the historic Cheyenne and Arapaho, which suggested this as the center of Sun Dance dispersal. This hypothetical reconstruction would have deserved reconsideration had Spier consulted George Catlin's readily accessible observations in the 1830s of the *O-kee-pa* ceremony among the Mandans of the Missouri River region, where clear parallels with major features of the Sun Dance are unequivocally evident (1967). Margot Liberty's otherwise useful updated survey of Sun Dance research (1980) also strangely ignores Catlin's Mandan data.

While ethnologists stumbled blindly in their efforts to supply time depth to cultures and culture areas without the aid of historical documentation, American historians developed a new expository genre of their own – the tribal history. The prototype of this genre is equivalent to the common denominator of the majority of early volumes in the University of Oklahoma Preset insipid Civilization of the American Indian Series. Prehistory, cultural affiliation, and a timeless, highly condensed ethnographic sketch are compressed into an Introduction or initial chapter. With this backdrop we pass directly into the realm of 'real' history and are provided with a chronologically ordered dry-as-dust account of Indian-White relations sifted from primary and secondary Euro-American sources. In these narratives the Indian point of view is either omitted entirely or distorted beyond recognition. Civilization In the series title refers less to a special *mentalité*, world view, or collective representation of a [76] particular society than to an unexamined, ethnocentric belief in inevitable progress. Native cultures are confronted with a Hobson's choice of genocide or ethnocide, the gun or the book, extinction or assimilation.

When ethnohistory emerged as a distinct specialty, a middle ground was established for collaborative efforts between historians and anthropologists. Some would deny to ethnohistory the status of a separate subdiscipline but would rather see ethnohistory as an approach involving a critical investigation and evaluation of documents pertaining to an ethnic group that are subsequently subjected to an anthropological analysis to elicit cultural insights (Wedel and DeMallie 1980: 110). Others would consider ethnohistory as a synthetic approach that combines ethnology, oral history, and written documents to provide a holistic view of a people's past. Still others, including myself (Fogelson 1974), favor making ethnohistory cognate with other ethno-prefixed disciplines that emphasize a native perspective on particular bounded domains.

A great stimulus was given to ethnohistorical research by the solicitation of expert testimony before hearings of the Indian Claims Commission, which was established in 1946, and in conjunction with more recent cases of state and federal recognition of tribal groups. However, it should be recognized that such cases often Imposed certain definitional constraints as to what constituted social groups, land rights, and boundaries, which, while necessary for legal adjudication nevertheless frequently violated native realities.

In taking an overview of ethnohistorical studies over the past quarter century, one can discern certain trends. Certainly both the [77] quantity and quality of research has improved dramatically. We now possess a critical density of exemplary monographs; new problem areas have been opened up; and older subjects of concern, such as the fur trade, have been reinvigorated by new data and interpretations.

If earlier accounts suffered from implicit racism and subscribed to the fatalistic inevitability of Indian cultural disappearance, more recently we survived an era of scholarship submerged in guilt-edged tubs of liberal bathos. From this vantage point the Indian was overwhelmed by the technologically superior but morally inferior force of Western Civilization. As a powerless pawn drawn into the chess game of international conflict, the Indian, according to this view, never had a chance. Regarding Native Americans as hopeless victims may be yet a more subtle form of racism, since it strips them of certain attributes of humanity and denies then responsibility for their own actions and destiny. It has only recently become the new ethnohistorical orthodoxy to recognize that Indians were, if not kings, queens or bishops, at least active knights and castles on the colonial and post-colonial chessboard.

Perhaps as a backlash reaction against liberal apologetics, many recent studies espouse a revisionist, or re-revisionist, position whereby formerly negative Indian stereotypes are reevaluated. Thus, the public is reassured that Indians did take trophy heads and scalps before the arrival of Europeans; they did, technically speaking, worship fetishes and idols; and they did, indeed, beat their dogs, torture captives, and practice cannibalism. While the weight of evidence adduced seems convincing, these studies usually fail to probe much below a typological reality and tend to ignore relevant [79] symbolism, the native meanings of such behavior, and the ethno-metaphysics and ethno-logic intrinsically bound up with such practices.

Probably the ongoing research project that has generated the most discussion in ethnohistorical circles and beyond has been Henry Dobyns' recalculation of aboriginal population figures. Dobyns has consistently argued that early population figures have been woefully underestimated owing to a failure to recognize the devastating impact of European diseases. Most scholars disagree with the magnitude of the miscalculation, some question Dobyns' assumptions and statistical procedures, others worry about his failure to utilize archaeological and prehistoric skeletal material, and still others are bothered with other specific details, but none will deny that the European invasion of the Americas would have been much more difficult without the assistance of pathogenic allies. Moreover, indigenous social structures and cultures probably were much different than those that were observed only after diseases had taken their toll. Dobyns' approach was Inspired by the historical demographic work of Cook and Borah, mainly in Latin America. Nevertheless, Dobyns' strong empiricism and his discovery of previously unnoticed factors that had a definite effect on long-term social history should endear him to followers of the <u>Annales</u> tradition.

However, as in the European holocaust or Vietnamese body counts, it Is not easy to envision the Impact of population decimation by numbers alone. We can intellectually grasp the structural and functional implications of drastically reduced populations, but it is much more difficult to come to a symbolic and emotional understanding [80] of such events from the perspective of another culture.

Buried deeply in a footnote to his engaging book on *The Great Cat Massacre*, there is a perceptive comment in which Robert Darnton observes, "While Americans tend to ignore systems of relations, the French generally neglect systems of meaning" (1984: 283). Perhaps this exhumed footnote will serve as a suitable transition to the third and final part of this Gauling paper.

III. <u>Where We Should Be Going</u>

One day in the summer of 1965 I was searching for historic Shuswap sites along the Frazer River in British Columbia. My guide, Joe Popp of the Soda Creek Reserve, led me to a sandy bluff, open to the south but protected from the north winds, where we came upon a series of large saucer-like depressions reminiscent of a lunar landscape. The following exchange ensued:

"My grandparents used to live here," said Joe.
[I began to measure the diameters of the former pit houses and commented on how smart the Shuswaps were to have invented such ecologically efficient dwellings.
"The old people were like animals," continued Joe.
"What do you mean?" I asked.
"They used to go underground in the winter in the Keekalee houses (Chinook jargon for semi-subterranean dwellings] and come out in the spring.... And they died there.... Back when the sickness come they went to the Keekalee houses to die. At night you could hear them singing until they all died out."

Such an account, fragmentary as it is, conjures up more resonant imagery than an entry that might simply state that 62 Shuswap from a settlement north of Alkali Lake perished from an epidemic in 1884.

In Joe Popp's statement we sense the alternating cycles of the seasons, the antithesis of spring and winter, of life and death. In [80] this account death is a collective event, a social fact. The singing of songs is intended not as a death knell but as a final invocation of powerful medicine to counteract the evil sorcery afflicting them.

All that I am trying to establish is that behind recorded events and numbing number lie cultural meanings and that these meanings are not mere epiphenomena but possess primary interpretative significance.

Perhaps a hypothetical reinterpretation or a more familiar episode in Indian history will help make my point. The Ghost Dance Religion, particularly its manifestations among the Sioux, has been studied and re-studied for so long that I will consider myself blessed if I never have to read another student paper on the subject. One prominent feature of Ghost Dance ideology was the resurrection of the dead. But how can we hope to understand this feature without examining Sioux beliefs about the process of death and indigenous ideas of eschatology? Siouan mortuary practices were variable, but the dominant form involved scaffold burial with appropriate offerings of grave goods to insure safe passage to another plane of being. The wrapping of the corpse in buckskin, the construction of the scaffold, the accumulation of grave goods, and the conducting of public ritual all involved considerable expenditures of time and energy on the part of living survivors. In situations of multiple deaths the costs rose proportionately. One wonders whether proper burials were carried out in connection with the massive loss of life occasioned by disease, warfare, and famine that frequently recurred during the latter half of the nineteenth century. Perhaps, without proper burial, those who perished under such circumstances were not considered to be "officially" or completely dead. In partial support of this [81] hypothesis, there does exist a Lakota belief that If a favored child suffers an untimely death, the corpse can be denied burial and be given special ritual treatment and the child will be restored to life (information supplied by Carlo Krieger). Siouan-speaking peoples, along with many other Native American cultures, possess a rich store of Orpheus-type tales (cf. Hultkrantz 1957). Thus, certain features of the Ghost Dance among the Sioux may be less keyed to the adoption of Christian Ideas of millenarian resurrection and more to indigenous conceptions that consider death to be a potentially reversible process.

One could go on to demonstrate that interpretations of such practices as scalping and cannibalism, which have been the subject of so much revisionist attention, might also be profitably reexamined from the point of view of native notions of souls or living essences, spirit adoption, and concepts of power. However, such analysis must be postponed lest it lead us too far astray from our appointed rounds of social history.

Continental social history, as mentioned previously, de-emphsizes the role of the individual in history. In partial contrast, American scholars – anthropologists as well as historians – have tended to single out Individual Native Americans as leaders, heroes, and subjects for life histories, even though the idea of biography or autobiography is foreign Co most non-Western cultures (cf. Fogelson 1982). Americans seem almost obsessed with a cult of leadership and tend to ignore what Max Weber recognized long ago: that systems of authority, be they traditional, charismatic, or bureaucratic, must be conceived as <u>social</u> relationships. I look forward to the time when we will see [82] Institutes, training programs, and Newberry conferences devoted to the topic of followership.

<u>Contra</u> Ruth Beebee Hill and her grim fantasy, *Hanta-Yo*, the evidence seems to indicate that supposed Native American individualism can only be understood as a social phenomenon involving relationships. Perhaps greater conceptual clarity will be achieved if we dispense with the idea of individualism and substitute the notion of personhood, a concept that considers the individual as social being with a distinctive nexus of social relationships that may include other-than-human beings as well as other human beings. Thus what we might initially take to be a quintessential individuating experience, the solitary vision quest, may be seen as the development of a personal Identity through social Interaction with a culturally-constituted other-than-human person.

From a Native American perspective, persons, as defined above, can be active agents in history, and much historical causation must be considered personal. These historical persons range from personified first causes to later culture heroes, from legendary personages to great people of the recent past, and from important individual personalities of the present to figures of the future. But I've slipped Into linear chronology, and we must recognize Native American assumptions that allow first causes to continue to operate, that expect culture heroes to return, that keep legends alive, and that believe great people of the past continue to exist as long as people of the present remember and emulate them.

A native-oriented, folk history or ethno-ethnohistory must take into account the complex interaction of several concurrent systems of [84] time. A non-exhaustive list could include: cosmological time, social structural time, seasonal time, life cyclical time, prophetic time, and experiential time that can often be classed as time-out-of-time. Most of these temporal orientations are oscillating and repetitive, and non-lineal, if not curvilinear.

For most Native Americans time is marked by events, and these events are more than the temporary surface disturbances that French social historians disdainfully dismiss. Occurrences that take place in myths. In folk narratives, and in native historical traditions are often what I term epitomizing events. Epitomizing events brings several forces together in dramatic combination; they condense various subtle changes into a single transformative act. Whether such events actually took place or not is immaterial; they are explanatory mnemonics of the mind and emotional engrams of the heart and, as such, are 'real' for members of the culture.

What I have been arguing for in a re-envisioned social history is greater concern with culturally-constituted meaning. Discussion has centered around conceptions of life and death, notions of person, temporal orientations, and the nature of events. Idioms of kinship and clanship and their embracive metaphorical extensions might have been elaborated in a longer lecture. Finally, systems of time cannot be divorced from intrinsically related conceptions of space, in both the grounded or localized and relational senses. Certainly, misunderstandings between Whites and Indians about the nature of land have been a major motif in their historic and continuing confrontations.

Some day, soon I hope, social history will be written in such a manner that native cosmogenesis and ethnogenesis will be gracefully [84] incorporated as an integral part of a complexly unfolding narrative rather than as a fleeting frontispiece; such a social history will also heed native prophecy as a powerful voice In articulating that history and in maintaining a special sense of collective density; in short, what is envisioned is a social history that will ring true to native perspectives.

In conclusion, I return to Lewis Henry Morgan's questions about who shall write social history and how that history should be written. We live in an era of increased specialization characterized by even finer divisions of labor and explosive technological developments that threatens to besiege even the ivory tower and take no hostages. At the risk of sounding like an unregenerate, computer-phobic, academic Luddite, let me assert that in my experience the roost productive interdisciplinary collaboration takes place within a single cerebrum located under a single cranium. In their 1846 essay on "German Ideology" Marx and Engels anticipate my judgment. They write:

> In communist society...where nobody has an exclusive area of activity and each can train himself In any branch he wishes, society regulates the general production, making it possible for me to do one thing today and another tomorrow, to hunt in the morning, fish in the afternoon, breed cattle In the evening, criticize after dinner, just as I like without ever becoming a hunter, a fisherman, a herdsman, or a critic (Easton and Guddat 1967: 424).

This mode of existence, which ironically is not unlike that approximated by many Native Americans, might be transposed for the social historian such that he might hunt the library stacks and archives in the morning, engage in fieldwork and collect oral testimony in the afternoon, compile statistics and learn linguistics in the evening, and engage in critical philosophy in the wee wee hours when everyone else is asleep. [86]

References

Aries, Philippe *The Hour of our Death.* Trans. H. Weaver. New York: Vintage, 1982.
— *Centuries of Childhood: A Social History of Family Life.* Trans. R. Baldick. London: Jonathan Cape, 1962.
— *Western Attitudes toward Death from the Middle Ages to the Present.* Trans. P.N. Ranum. Baltimore: Johns Hopkins University Press. 1974.
Braudel, Ferdnand 1972 *The Mediterranean and the Mediterranean World in the Age of Philip II.* Trans. S Reynolds, New York: Harper.
    1975 *Capitalism and Material Life, 1400-1800.* Trans. M Kochum. New York: Harper. 1975.
Catlin, George 1967 *O-Kee-Pa: A Religious Ceremony and other Customs of the Mandan.* JC Ewers, ed. New Haven, Yale University Press.
Cohn, Norman 1957 *The Pursuit of the Millennium.* London: Seeker and Warburg.
    1975 *Europe's Inner Demons.* New York: Basic Books.
Cronon, William 1983 *Changes in the Land.* New York: Hill and Wang.
Crosby, Alfred 1972 *The Columbian Exchange.* Westport, CT. Greenwood.
Darnton, Robert 1984 *The Great Cat Massacre and Other Episodes in French Cultural History.* New York: Basic Books.
Easton. L and K Guddat, eds. 1967 *Writings of the Young Marx on Philosophy and Society.* New York.
Fogelson, Raymond D 1974 On the varieties of Indian history: Sequoyah and Traveller Bird." *Journal*

of Ethnic Studies 2 (1).
— "Person, self, and identity ~ Some anthropological retrospects, circumspects, and prospects". In B Lee, ed., *Psychosocial Theories of the Self.* New York: Plenum Press, 1982.
Foucault, Michel 1975 *The Birth of the Clinic.* Trans. A.M.S. Smith. New York: Vintage, 1975. [87]
　　　1980 *The History of Sexuality.* Vol. I: Introduction. Trans. R. Harley. New York: Vintage.
　　　1979 *Discipline and Punishment: The Birth of the Prison.* New York: Pantheon.
Glassie, Henry 1968 *Pattern in the Material Folk Culture of the Eastern United States.* Philadelphia: University of Pennsylvania Press.
Graubard, D, ed. 1969 New Trends in History. *Daedalus* 98 (4).
Hareven, Tamara K and Randolph Langenbach 1978 *Amoskeag: Life and Work in an American Factory City.* New York: Pantheon Books.
Hill, Ruth Beebe 1978 *Hante Yo.* New York: Doubleday.
Hinsley, Curtis M 1981 *Savages and Scientists: The Smithsonian Institution and the Development of American Anthropology 1846-1910.* Washington, D.C.: Smithsonian Institution Press.
Howe, Irving 1976 *World of Our Fathers.* New York: Harcourt, Brace, Jovanovich.
Hultkrantz, Ake 1953 Conceptions of the Soul among North American Indians. Statens Etnografiska Museum (Sweden), Monograph 1.
Laslett, Peter 1969 *The World We Have Lost.* New York: Scribners.
LeRoy Ladurie, Emanuel 1979 *Carnival in Romans.* Trans. by M. Feeney. New York: George Braziller.
Liberty. Margot 1980 "The Sun Dance" in WR Wood and M Liberty, eds. *Anthropology on the Great Plains.* Lincoln: University of Nebraska Press.
Macfarlane, Alan 1970 *Witchcraft in Tudor and Stuart England.* London Routledge and Kegan Paul.
Morgan, Lewis Henry 1877 *Ancient Society.* New York: Henry Holt.
Spier, Leslie 1921 The Sun Dance of the Plains Indians: Its Development and Diffusion. *Anthropological Papers, American Museum of Natural History* 16: 7. [88]
Stanner, WEH 1958 "The Dreaming" *in* W Lessa and EZ Vogt, eds, *Reader in Comparative Religion.* New York: Row, Peterson.
Thomas, Keith 1971 *Religion and the Decline of Magic.* New York: Scribners.
Thompson, EP 1963 *The Making of the English Working Class.* New York: Vintage.
Wallace. Anthony FC 1978 *Rockdale.* New York: Knopf.
Webb, Walter Prescott 1931 *The Great Plains.* Boston: Ginn.
Wedel, Mildred M and Raymond J DeMallie 1980 "The ethnohistorical approach in Plains area studies". In WR Wood and M Liberty, ed. *Anthropology on the Great Plains.* Lincoln: University of Nebraska Press.
Williams, Raymond 1980 *Problems in Materialism and Culture.* London: Verso.
　　　1981 *Culture.* Glasgow: Fontana.
Wolf, Eric 1982 *Europe and the People Without History.* Berkeley, University of California Press.

Balloons

MAN'S GASSY ESSENCE[1]

Inflatable and deflatable toys and novelties exerted a particular, if not peculiar, power over the popular imagination of early twentieth-century America. For over a century, the scientific and technologic mind had already conquered its Icarus complex by ascending into the sky in-hot air or gas balloons. Inflatable animal blatter balls had long been used for games and sports. However, by 1900 the ready availability of cheap commercial rubber soon made tires, as well as toy and decorative balloons commonplace objects. Andre Gidé remarked in *Le Prométhée Mal enchainée.* (1899) translated as *Prometheus Misbound*, that elasticity is only inertia postponed. However, during the delay, exhalation and elastic containment can conspire to produce some novel effects.

My exclusive text for this excursion into the flatable and inflatable world is the *1929 Johnson Smith and Company Catalogue* (reprinted 1970). As raconteur and social historian Jean Shepard remarks, [2]

Only America could have produced Johnson Smith. There is nothing else in the world like it. Johnson Smith is to Man's darker side what Sears Roebuck represents to the clean-limbed, soil tilling righteous aide ... The Johnson Smith catalogue is a magnificent, smudgy thumbprint of a totally lusty, vibrant, alive, crude post-frontier society, a society that was, and in some ways still remains, an exotic mixture of moralistic piety and violent, primitive humor (1970:V).

The catalogue advertises the incontinent dribble glass, points to the virtues of the menacing potato pistol that relies on vegitative ammunition, and extols the redolent aroma of anarchist stink bombs. Ethnic stereotypes abound: The Performing Coons – Sambo and Dinah, the Indian Warrior Hat, Jewish Nickels, Spanish Athletic Certificates, Irish Monkey Masks, and Nigger Make-up. The catalogue aims primarily at a younger male market. It provides a veritable arsenal for the attention-seeking, life-of-the-party, ubiquitous trickster. As a mail-order house, headquartered in Racine, Wisconsin, Johnson Smith and Company reached out to the tap roots of contemporary agrarian America. For better or for worse, Johnson Smith represents a monument to Midwestern Civilization. [3]

But back to the balloons. I've selected eleven inflatable and deflatable specimens from the 1929 catalogue. First, we will consider

ROLY POLY OR THE RUBBER COP:

Roly Poly is made of rubber and is filled with air just like an ordinary rubber balloon. You can throw him up in the air, lay him down, or stand him on his head. He will always land on his feet every time, and what is more will stay on his feet. He is well and strongly made of the best para rubber, comes complete with rubber necktie and cardboard "feet" and taking it all round will stand more abuse than any other cop we know of. 10¢, 3 for 25¢, 75¢ per doz, postpaid (1970: 461).

Nothing too tricky here; Roly Poly exemplifies the principle of weighted gravity. His treatment echoes a populist anti-authoritarian theme.

THE MAMMOTH SIZE WATERMELON BALLOON is reported to be "Strong and Durable". Reading the copy,

---

1 Paper presented in the Symposium on Tools and Toys at the Central States Anthropological Society Meeting, Columbus, Ohio, 4 April 1987.

Balloons

Here is a tremendous size WATERMELON BALLOON that, when inflated is NEARLY TWO FEET IN LENGTH. It is a wonderful imitation of a regular melon, green skin and stripes. Children will derive lots of fun playing with this MAMMOTH balloon and, on account of its large size, they are not so likely to destroy it as with small balloons. Nothing pleases them more. You should get one and make your children happy with a balloon that may be larger than themselves. For decorative purposes it is a very interesting novelty that is sure to attract attention. Each Balloon is fitted with a special valve so that it may be inflated and deflated at will, and it is made of particularly strong and durable rubber consistent with its enormous size.
Price 15¢, POSTPAID, three for 40¢, 1 doz. for $1.35 (1970: 282).

In this example, manufacture imitates agriculture. The principle feature focuses on relative size - a balloon as big as a child. As we shall soon see, the valve is a devise that will stimulate the geniuses at Johnson Smith to rise to greater creative possibilities.

My next specimen is the RUBBER SAUSAGE BALLOON.

This is a very attractive Balloon of a shape that makes it very popular with children. This is made of the very best Para Rubber and being of a select quality, it will stand blowing exceptionally high without fear of breakage. It is fitted with a long stem and whistle, and will make the most weird sound until finally collapsed.
Only 5 Cents Each or in a very much larger size 10 Cents. One of each for 13 Cents POSTPAID. Three of each for 35 Cents (1970:240).

I'm uncertain about the supposed affinity of children for sausage shaped balloons. Here is the first example in this series of the use of deflation, employed in this instance to produce a weird whistling sound.

Surprise Pipes, modeled after the venerable corncob, are a lesser-known item in the Johnson Smith inventory.

They are not only charming toys for little folks but they serve as novel favors on all sorts of occasions. A breath into the pipe stem and Br'er Rabbit or Chick-a-Biddie or Donkey pops out. Continue to blow and the pipe whistles. Or, an in-take of breath, with a finger covering the whistle in the bottom of the bowl, and the rabbit, chicken [6] or donkey disappears into the bowl again in a manner quite astonishing.
Price 15¢, 3 for 40¢, or $1.35 per dozen, postpaid (1970:285).

The surprise Pipes not only incorporate a sonic dimension, but they also employ a backdraft of inhalation to retract the astonishing creatures. If re-marketed today, these pipes might enjoy strong sales as anti-smoking devices.

The next examples involves strange facial distortion; The Balloon Nose Disguise.

Here is something new in disguises. There is a well moulded false nose made of Papier-Maché effectively colored, with spectacle frame (without glasses) and a fairly vigorous mustache. But the most astonishing feature of the disguise is the red rubber balloon at the end of the nose. This connects with a rubber tube to the mouth enabling you to blow the nose up to an enormous size. The effect is most extraordinary. You can create genuine sensation with this disguise. 75¢ (1970: 594).

The un-inflated balloon dangles from the tip of the false nose like an exteriorized post nasal drip.

Balloons

The metaphoric bulbous nose here becomes metamorphic. Its size is blown out of all proportion and gives the phrase "blowing your nose" new dimensions. [7]

The Novelty Aerial Balloon uplifts inflatable toys to new technological heights. According to the catalogue,

> This is the Very Latest. FLIES GRACEFULLY IN OR OUTDOORS. This is the VERY LATEST SENSATION IN BALLOONS. A brightly colored balloon that measures sixteen inches long is blown up in the usual way, and when released the air pressure sends the balloon SOARING UPWARD, the 3½ inch propeller SPINNING AROUND AT A LIVELY RATE. The effect is startling, It is a graceful flier that makes the youngsters WILD WITH JOY. May be used repeatedly indoors or outdoors. An immensely interesting toy. Price, 10 cents each, 3 for 25, 75¢ per dozen. Postpaid (1970: 283).

Pseudo-negentropy is featured here. The force of the deflationary air is used to drive a propeller that appears to serve more as ornament then as propulsion motion.

Technology strikes again with the Surprise Windmill.

> It is a neat little contrivance with which you can have a lot of fun. Everyone will want to blow it to see the thing work. Immediately when they start blowing the windmill, there is a very surprising development as the victim is rewarded for his efforts by the soot that blows back into his face Price 35¢ (1970: 590). [8]

Here the cybrenstic feedback loop is impelled by forced air and results in a self-inflicted blinding backlash. Don Quixote, where are you when we need you to do battle against treacherous windmills?

Next we come to one of the more popular items in the Johnson Smith catalogue. The Dying Pig is

> The most laughable novelty yet produced. It is made of rubber, and you have only to blow it up and stand the pig on his feet, when he begins to squeal as he slowly collapses and finally lies down and dies in the most natural manner. You can blow him up as often as desired and each time he will go through the same performance to the great amusement and delight of your friends. Price 15¢, 3 for 40¢, 1 Dozen for $1.35 Postpaid (1970: 313).

This is a rather existential toy, dealing as it does with ultimate concerns. It is also dissipative structure, par excellence. The humor is not completely clear. Nevertheless, the success of the Dying Pig prompted Johnson Smith and Company to introduce a barnyard companion, the Dying Rooster: A very Laughable Novelty Balloon. The advertisement reads,

> The Dying Rooster is a rubber balloon similar to the Dying Pig that is described elsewhere in their catalog and which has always been so popular [9] with our customers. The Rooster is blown up to its capacity in the customary manner and placed on the table, as it gradually deflates, the Rooster collapses and the accompanying squaks that it emits as it slowly dies, cause the greatest merriment. If you have had a Pig you will want a Rooster too. 20¢, 3 for 35¢, or $1.80 per dozen. Postpaid (1970: 264).

Agonizing animal death seems to strike the funny bone of the farmer, but the more mystical significance of this novelty eludes this city dweller.

My next-to-last specimen is praised as a "Sensational Novelty", the ""Self-Blowing Hot Dog".

> Hot Dog is one of the most surprising novelties recently brought out. This is a small rubber tube

resembling a small balloon, less than 2 inches long. It contains a very curious chemical that acts in a most remarkable way. You have merely to grasp it tightly in the hand and it suddenly becomes filled with air just as if you had blown into it. You can play all sorts of jokes with this novelty. You can lay it on a chair, or place it secretly underneath anyone and when they sit [10] down there develops from an insignificant piece of rubber a large and superbly colored balloon, filled with air. Put it in someone's pocket and then watch his astonishment when, after friction has developed, he finds the enormous thing in his pocket. Or you can place it underneath a person's pillow, in fact there is no end to the jokes that can be played with this remarkable novelty. Each Hot Dog is placed in a small tube-shaped box, and he is ready for business any time. 15¢, 3 for 40¢, or $1.35 per dozen. Postpaid (1970: 142).

The identity of the curious auto-inflating chemical is indeterminate. Human contact rather than human breath is activating trigger. From the not so subtle phallic symbolism of the expanding hot dog, it is but a small regressive step to my final and quintessential Johnson Smith novelty, the notorious Whoopie Cushion.

The Whooppie Cushion or "PooPoo" Cushion as it is sometimes called is made of rubber. When the victim unsuspectingly sits upon the cushion, it gives forth noises that can better be imagined than described.
By mail Postpaid 25¢ (1970: XIII).

The anonymous ad writer scripted a masterpiece of understatement. The Whoopie Cushion evidently was Johnson Smith's largest seller and remains infamous to this day. The company even marketed a deluxe version, which, according to another blurb, "is made of heavier material and is superior in every way". The super Whoopie Cushion was priced at $1.25 rather than a quarter - a five-fold inflation (1970: 639).

I'm not certain what to conclude from this fatuous foray. The inflatable and deflatable toys of Johnson Smith mirror reality only from an askew angle. It is difficult to see these toys and novelties as tools or as teaching devices for the young, or the perpetually young. Merdyne Anderson (1986: 12) has suggested, "the adult anticipates the child and the tool creates the toy"; this surely seems to fit the situation of Johnson Smith and company. Yet toys are us, and in good Pogo logic, us are toys. We are the ultimate balloons, if not buffoons. Inflatable and deflatable toys effect energetic transfer and comprise the temporary capture and deliberate remodeling of invisible, yet vital, energy. This invisible energy emanates from ourselves and thus may justly be regarded as an extension of the self. The invisible substance is man's gassy essence.

References

Anderson, Myrdene 1986 On the Discrimination of Discard, or What is Not a Tool-Toy. Paper in the Symposium, "Tools", "Toys" and other Dissipative Structures, 62nd Annual Meeting of the Central States Anthropological Society, Chicago, 21-23 March.
Gidé, Andre 1953 *Marshlands and Prometheus Misbound.* New York: New Directions.
Goodstone, Toney, ed. 1970 1929 *Johnson Smith and Co. Catalogue.* New York: Chelsea House.
Shepard, Jean 1970 "Mail Order America", In T. Goodstone, ed., 1929 *Johnson Smith and Co. Catalogue*, New York: Chelsea House.

PoliticoHistory

THE CONTEXT OF AMERICAN INDIAN POLITICAL HISTORY

I begin with a serious confession. I do not know at this writing what this conference is about. Political autonomy is a notion less difficult to define than to apply. The Greek etymology of the word autonomy is simple enough: <u>auto</u> equals 'self', and <u>nomos</u> refers to 'law', governing', 'managing', or 'dealing out'. Thus 'self-government' is a fairly literal meaning. It is with the qualifier 'political' that we encounter difficulties. On one level the adjective 'political' seems necessary to distinguish political autonomy from other forms of autonomy arising in later usages, such as self-regulating organisms in botany, the autonomic nervous system in physiology, and such conceptions as individual autonomy or ego autonomy in psychology. On another level the word political presupposes a clear understanding of what is meant by a polity.

In the West a polity has come to refer to an organized community or body or a system of government. Since at least the time of Aristotle contrasting types of polity have been recognized. When Europeans crossed the Atlantic, they arrived with an array of accumulated political concepts that they believed could be directly applied, with little or no loss in translation, to native understandings of governance. They recognized sovereign Indian nations ruled by indigenous kings or emperors, often with princes and princesses-in-waiting; they came equipped with various conceptions of law, such as natural rights, rights of conquest, divine rights, property rights, legal procedures concerning alienation of land, and conceptions of criminal justice. Moreover, these legal and political notions were thought to be sanctioned by and embraced within universal religious orthodoxy and orthroproxsy. Over time these European political theories and practices were modulated and modified as the combined result of internal ideological changes and of practical experiences in dealing with native populations.

In dialectical fashion, native political institutions and understandings underwent adaptive changes in response to the increasingly manifest unequal balance of power between native societies and European colonial governments and the emergent American nation state. Some of these general changes in Native American societies included active and passive resistance to external threat and encroachment; a subordination of individual initiative in an effort to strengthen collective solidarity; internal consolidation into tribal entities and confederacies; the development of new types of leadership to deal with outside authority; the increased significance of land as a basis for separate identity, along with clearer demarcation of territorial boundaries; a corresponding emphasis on descent, expressed through the metaphoric medium of blood quantum, as a primary criterion for group membership; the development of a supra-tribal ethnic and politico-legal status as Indians; the refashioning of political processes and governmental structures in the direction of closer conformity to Euro-American models; and the maintenance, manipulation, and reinvention of tradition to mark cultural distinctiveness vis á vis the dominant American culture and to maintain cultural distance from other minority populations. My major point is that European-derived political and legal conceptions and the policies following therefrom and the native reactions to these conceptions and policies combined to overwhelm and obscure aboriginal beliefs and realities and, over time, led to [9] their transformation. I paint these long-term trends with a broad brush. I expect the conference participants to fill in many of the finer details, to provide foregrounding and backgrounding perspectives, and to apply nuanced textures to my lightly limned picture.

The Native American struggle for political autonomy is an on-going process that has become increasingly visible and vocal during the past quarter century. Current Native American legal status vis á vis the Federal Government and state and local authorities is defined by statute but subject to continuous interpretation and reinterpretation. We know much about the formal organization of contemporary tribal governments but much less about their informal processes of decision-making. We have witnessed the accelerated fight for self-determination, preservation of Native rights, and cultural renewal.

An assumption underlying the structure of this conference is that Native American societies possessed political autonomy before the intrusive arrival Western Civilization. My task, as I understood it, is to suggest some of the dimensions of indigenous political organizations through which that autonomy was expressed before white contact wrought significant change. Your task as contributors to this conference is to examine the vicissitudes of Native American political autonomy in terms of historical processes underlying the transformations of how we got from there to here.

The interaction of two variables, played out through historical time, strikes me as especially crucial to our considerations. First, the nature of particular native social systems and their internal dynamics would appear to influence the subsequent direction of political change. The different political histories of, say, the Hopis and the Navajos, or the Iroquois and Chippewas, would seem to illustrate differential resistance or accommodation to change. The second variable concerns the nature and objectives of the specific sectors of white society impinging directly or indirectly upon native political systems. Initial contact situations vary considerably over space and time, as do later pressures on native social institutions. These differential circumstances must be factored into any account of political persistence and change. I stress that my two angles of approach are both variable; neither is a constant, nor can one be construed as an independent variable and the other as a dependant variable. The interaction is a dynamic one.

I turn now to a brief discussion of general theory in political anthropology to help orient some of my later remarks on traditional political systems in Native North America. The modern sub-field of political anthropology is said by some (Colson 1968: 189 and Lewellan 1983: x) to have come into being in 1940 with the publication of *African Political Systems*, edited by Meyer Fortes and EE Evans-Pritchard and containing an influential preface by A.R. Radcliffe-Brown. However, this late emergence was surely preceded by an incubation period at least as long as the history of anthropology as a formal discipline. The genre of ethnographic monographs initiated by Lewis Henry Morgan's *League of the Ho-de-no-sau-nee, or Iroquois* (1851) included at least minimal descriptions of political systems, and in Morgan's case the treatment was more maximal than minimal. Classical evolutionists from Sir Henry Maine and Herbert Spencer through Morgan, Tylor, and later scholars provided hypothetical stages of unilineal political progression. Practically all pre-1940 anthropology textbooks and anthologies contained discussions of forms of political organization found throughout the primitive world.

By my rapid reckoning at least three Americanist scholars anticipate developments in modern political anthropology. First and foremost is Robert H. [10] Lowie. His *Primitive Society* (1920) and *The Origin of the State* (1927) emphasized three criteria for statehood: "territoriality, legitimacy, and monopoly of violence" (Murphy 1972: 67). Lowie discerned continuity between the tribe and the state through the abiding importance of kinship and locality and of the significance of sodalities or associations that were not based upon kinship, and in some ways diluted or complemented the power of kinship as an organizing principle. For Lowie sodalities were perceived as seeds of the state.

Lowie's student, Julian Steward, has to be regarded as an important political anthropologist for his classic work on the social organization of bands, especially his *Basin-Plateau Sociopolitical Groups* (1938) and for his cultural ecological approach to the study of culture change. His later theory of multilineal evolution, featuring levels of socio-cultural integration, provides the basis for most later American topologies of political organization (Steward 1955).

A more or less forgotten figure who deserves remembrance for his efforts to fuse an historical approach together with a comparative study of Native American political organization is William Christie MacLeod. MacLeod's three major works – *The Origin of the State: Reconsidered in the Date of Aboriginal North America* (1924); *The American Indian Frontier* (1928); and *The Origin and History of Politics* (1931) – are all laced with interesting data, raise issues that were to lie dormant for at least another generation, and attest to a lively intellect.

The British structural-functionalists who were said to initiate modern politician anthropology played out their synchronic, equilibrium models in Sub-Saharan Africa. Centralized states possessing differentiated political institutions with well defined political offices, principles of succession, hierarchies of authority and communication, and clear control of force were contrasted with so-called acephalous or stateless societies. Though usually smaller in scale, these acephalous societies often approached centralized states in size and in technological and economic complexity. The normal modes of analysis developed in Western political science were unequal to the task of explaining how these systems operated. Political action in these superficially amorphous, stateless societies was found to be structured through corporate unilineal descent groups and through segmentary lineages.

After more than a decade of fine-grained empirical research, the limitations of static structural-functionalism were becoming apparent and more dynamic models began to surface. Max Gluckman (1960) emphasized the role of conflict in political processes, especially in his notion of "rituals of rebellion." Increased attention was also paid to the role of factionalism as a dynamic force in political processes. Edmund Leach, analyzing data from Highland Burma (1954), recognized the co-existence of alternative models of political action within the same social system. He was also one of the first to appreciate the significance of discrepancies between normative models that political actors carried in their heads and on-the-ground realities. For Leach political systems were seen less as monolithic and constraining and more as option structures that could be manipulated by political actors. The gradual shift in British political anthropology moved away from structural stability and functional equilibrium toward considerations of process and change.

These theoretical developments in Britain had very little direct impact upon the way in which Native American political systems were studied. For instance in the American *Festschrift* for Radcliffe-Brown, *The Social Anthropology of North American Tribes* (1937), only John Province's essay, "The Underlying Sanctions of Plains Culture" deals with a political subject. E. Adamson Hoebel's [11] 1940 monograph on *The Political Organization and Law Ways of the Comanche Indians*, as well as his better known work on the *Cheyennes* (1941, 1960), bears some faint traces of British structural-functional influence. Even Robert H. Lowie in his Huxley Memorial Lecture, "Some Aspects of Political Organization Among The American Indians" (1948), delivered before the Royal Anthropological Institute, avoids most of the issues in political anthropology raised by his British colleagues and audience.

One of the few Americanist studies clearly informed by British theory is Fred Gearing's *Priests and Warriors: Social Structures for Cherokee Politics in the 18th Century* (1962). Gearing not only shows how clan and lineage structures operated in traditional Cherokee political structures, but he recognizes the existence of alternate structures, what he terms "structural poses," attuned to different social tasks. Gearing also analyzes the processes by which the political model localized on the village level was extended to a tribal level and later transformed into a self-proclaimed state formation known as the Cherokee Nation. In my review of *Priests and Warriors* for the *American Anthropologist* (1962), I criticize some of the details but labeled it a landmark study. Over a quarter of a century later, I find no reason to revise my judgment. Elizabeth Colson's monograph on the modern Makah (1953) as well as several modern studies by Canadian scholars represent partial exceptions to the general lack of British influence on the study of American Indian political institutions.

Many explanations for the failure of British theories to take hold in the study of Native North American political systems may be advanced. On one level these theories developed out of the investigation of on-going African societies during a rare period of temporary stability afforded by British colonial rule. In contrast, American efforts to study Native American politics, including Gearing's, were primarily reconstructive and historical. Until recently studies of the politics of contemporary reservation communities were scorned as applied anthropology, having little or no theoretical import.

However, on another level, while the British had to shed their structural-functional strait jackets to discover change and history, American anthropologists had always maintained a primary concern with diachronic processes. At the same period that modern political anthropology matured in Britain, acculturation studies flourished in America. Moreover, post-World War II American Anthropology witnessed a resurgent interest in cultural evolutionary studies spearheaded by Leslie White and Julian Steward and enshafted by developmental theories concerning the origins of the state in archeology. With regard to political anthropology much effort went into the construction of taxonomies, the theoretical inadequacies of which we are still wrestling with today. The models of political evolution proposed by Steward (1955), by Elman Service (1962, 1975), and by Morton Fried (1967) were primarily descriptive rather than causal. Causal models, denoted by arrows and buttressed by quantitative data were more common in archeology, but they suffered from an almost inevitable materialist bias.

The basic classification of preindustrial political systems recognizes a first-order distinction between centralized and uncentralized, or so-called "egalitarian" systems. At a second level, centralized systems are usually subdivided into states, characterized by stratification into classes, and into chiefdoms based upon rank. Uncentralized systems are subdivided into tribes with a wide variety of characteristics and into smaller-scale bands. [12]

When Native North America is reviewed in terms of such topological classifications numerous problems arise. Despite the optimistic vision of the McNickle Center in sponsoring a volume about America in 1492, our knowledge of the details of Native North American political organization at that arbitrary time-marker can only be glimpsed imperfectly through the lens of archeology or through qualified interpolations from later periods. Even utilization of a moving baseline extending from the early sixteenth century to the mid-nineteenth century docs not insure that drastic changes in native political structures have not occurred before the establishment of permanent white contact. Charles Hudson perceived a "black hole" in Southeastern ethnohistory spanning the time between the elaborate chieftainships described by the Desoto chronicles and the more egalitarian eighteenth-century confederacies, tribes, tribelets, and autonomous villages observed by traders, travelers, and early settlers. Marvin Smith (1987) has tried to fill this singular lacuna through archeological research, and it seems certain that increased warfare, population dislocations, and the effects of epidemic disease contributed to the political transformations in the interior Southeast.

Eleanor Leacock (1954) has documented the early effect of the fur trade in sharpening the territorial boundaries of Montagnais-Naskapi hunting bands. While not denying the influence of the fur trade in accentuating Montagnais-Naskapi territorialism, I believe a more flexible and generalized religious basis for Northern Algonkian territorialism can be discerned. Paraphrasing informant testimony, Julius Lips surmised

> that many Indians seem to believe that not the Indians but rather the game animals were the true owners of the hunting grounds. It seemed to me that Naskapi hunters regard themselves merely as servants of the chieftains of the game animals whose ceremonial prescriptions at the hunt they have to follow to safeguard their own livelihood (1947: 388).

The family band headman often served as the primarily ritual specialist who negotiated with the ultimate landlords, the animal "bosses" (cf Tanner 1979).

My major points at this juncture are that the search for pristine, primordial political structures may be a futile effort to capture an anthropological chimera, that native political structures tended to be fluid and forever adapting to new contingencies, and that internal native understandings of "how the system worked" must be considered along with external formal features favored by political taxonomists.

Another feature that impresses one in surveying traditional political systems in Native North America is their variety and differences of scale, ranging from small hunting bands in the Arctic, Sub-Arctic, and Great Basin to political systems approaching stratified states in the Lower Mississippi and Caddoan areas. Practically every society was interactive with other societies, as we can determine from trade networks, trail systems, redistributive centers, ethno-cartography, and lists of names for other groups. Maybe the only exception to this truism were the Eskimos of Thule who were surprised to learn that there were other people in the world when they first encountered Admiral Peary and his Polar exploring party.

My impression is that Native American social groups were quite mobile in pre-contact times, despite the absence of the horse. When we think of mobility, we usually associate it with yearly cycles of hunting and gathering bands, but it was generally true that coastal peoples were bilocal, as were many [13] Mississippian farmers in the Midwest. Village sites changed frequently for a variety of reasons. The documented historical resettlement of the Tutelos and Tuscaroras among the Iroquois, the Yuchis among the Creeks, the Seminole movement into sub-tropical Florida, the Tewa enclave of Hano among the Hopis of First Mesa, the expansion of the Cherokees into the Overhills area of Tennessee and into northern Georgia, the Kickapoo exodus to Mexico – all these large-scale population movements doubtless had pre-contact precedents and analogues. Mixed ethnic settlements, a frequent post-contact phenomenon, probably also existed prehistorically, as is suggested by the totally different contemporaneous art styles reflected in the shell engraving from the Craig Mound at Spiro (Phillips and Brown 1975-1982).

I would now like to take a closer look at the major taxonomic categories of political systems and consider how well they fit the North American data. I will focus primarily on the category of tribe, since tribes are now the primary political units for Indian identification and recognition. I've already mentioned that true states – in the sense of class stratification, sovereign leadership with aristocratic bureaucracies, full-time priesthoods, the power to collect formal tribute, levy taxes, or recruit labor, and the existence of formal legal codes – were seemingly absent in Native North America, although some Mississippian chiefdoms and their historical descendants were approaching statehood.

At the other end of the political spectrum are bands. Bands arc assumed to be limited in population to 25 to 150 persons. In many areas micro-and macro-bands are recognized, their constitution usually being dependant upon fluctuation of the food supply, as in aggregations at summer fishing camps, or upon the need for additional personnel to exploit particular resources, as in Great Basin rabbit drives or winter seal hunting at breathing holes among Central Eskimos. Bands are further classified into patrilocal bands, composite bands, and more anomalous types.

Julian Steward (1936) was the first to argue for the adaptive value of patrilocal residence for hunting groups. The essential logic of the argument assumed that it was advantageous for a man to maintain residential continuity after marriage because of his knowledge of the local hunting area. Elman Service (1962) generalized patrilocality to a near universal among hunting peoples. Unfortunately, many northern hunting groups turn out to be either matrilineal or bilateral in terms of descent. Moreover, ethnohistorical information indicates the Algonkian-speaking Montagnais-Naskapi were matrilocal (Leacock 1955), as were a significant number of Northern Athabascan bands (see Krech 1980: 84-88 for a review of evidence). If the logic lying behind the supposed advantage of patrilocality for hunting efficiency is reexamined, one could just as well argue that a hunter would be doubly advantaged by knowing two hunting areas: that his natal family and that of his wife and in-laws.

Composite bands are diffuse groups that lack the requirements for band exogamy or post-marital residences rules. Service (1975) argues that composite bands are post-contact phenomena deriving from the breakdown of patrilocal bands after severe depopulation. However, I think it likely that composite bands always existed as fluid forms of organization that allowed individuals and their families the freedom to leave because of personal animosities, lack of confidence in the skills or mystical powers of hunt leaders in the band, or, perhaps, a positive desire for a change of scene. The freedom of movement in composite bands could also serve an important latent function in regulating band size.

So-called anomalous bands are usually based upon particular families and display a variety of structural forms. Such types are characteristic of much of [14] the northern Arctic and the Great Basin. Steward's (1938) meticulous analysis of the great variation in socio-political structure from valley to valley in the Great Basin stresses micro-ecological differences. Given the extremely low population density, some of the variability might also be explained in terms of reproductive randomness, such that one generation might produce a surplus of sons, another of daughters; there might be great variations in birth order; the effects of infant mortality and other premature deaths might be magnified in altering the social composition of the local group. The results of these factors can be viewed as analogous to the effects of random genetic drift in small breeding population.

Probably the principal difficulty with the taxonomic category of band is that the term has also been used to designate components of larger taxonomic entities. Thus the Pawnees were historically known to comprise at least four separate and politically autonomous bands. The Pomo consisted of at least six linguistically differentiated sub-groups. The Cheyenne Nation was composed of separate bands that assembled in the summer to form the great camp circle for the collective buffalo hunt, annual religious ceremonies, and political deliberations. The North Carolina Cherokees, whose population is now pushing 10,000, are officially designated as the Eastern Band of the Cherokees and have long severed legal or political connections with their kin in Oklahoma

If we understand the band to be an autonomous or semi-autonomous localized political segment of a larger unit that we usually consider to be a tribe or nation or people, then I submit that bands were probably the predominant form of socio-political organization in aboriginal America.

I have always found the topological distinctions between chiefdoms and tribes particularly perplexing. I have painful memories of urgent phone calls from Southeastern archaeologists describing the results of excavations at particular sites and asking me whether they were dealing with a chiefdom or a tribe. It's hard to communicate a shrug over the telephone. The distinctions between tribes and chiefdoms are usually ones of degree rather than qualitative differences. Tribes are said to be more egalitarian, while individuals and lineages are more ranked in chiefdoms; political systems are said to be uncentralized in tribes, while chiefdoms have more mechanisms of centralization. Economic exchange tends to be based on reciprocity in tribes, while chiefs frequently serve as nodes of redistribution in chiefdoms. Both tribes and chiefdoms may possess unilineal descent groups, but the clans and lineages tend to be ranked in chiefdoms. One could go on, but the ultimate test of any topology is its applicability.

In a recent introductory text on political anthropology by Ted Lewellan, the Cheyennes and the historic Iroquois are classified as tribes, while the Kwakiulth achieve the level of a chiefdom (1983: 21). As we have indicated, the Cheyennes can probably be considered a tribe, at least for the few weeks of the summer encampment, but the rest of the year they divide up into semi-autonomous bands. It is not clear whether the Iroquois are being evaluated in terms of the League or the component units of the League. Certainly the Iroquois possessed centralized political mechanisms, and chiefly titles were inherited through matrilineages. They, or at least the women, were intensive agriculturalists, and their Iroquois religious system was fairly elaborate. In contrast, the Kwakiulth, despite their strong emphasis on rank and individual rights to titles, names, privileges, and ritual artifacts, generally lacked strong political integration, unilineal descent groups, and intensive agriculture – all criteria supposedly associated with chiefdoms. I could continue and try to force-fit societies that I have personally studied, such as the Cherokees and the Creeks, into the [15] appropriate taxonomic boxes. However, when all is said and done, I am still not sure whether the Cherokees and Creeks qualify as chiefdom or tribes, and furthermore I don't much care.

Richard Sattler (1980) has published a valuable paper that employs a multi-dimensional taxonomy borrowed from Peter Lloyd's study of political structures in African kingdoms (1965). Sattler compares the Hurons, Caddos, and Muskogees. Some interesting differences arc elicited, probably owing to the sensitivity of the dimensions to processual features rather than to formal categories. These three societies are of comparable scale such that a controlled comparison does succeed in drawing out some fine-grained distinctions. However, in general I still remain skeptical of the power of topologies to make valid sense out of such ill-defined units as tribes, chiefdoms, or bands that encompass discrete societies which share so few common qualities, on the one hand, and blend into each other, on the other.

Multi-dimensional taxonomies can be diagrammed as matrices. In so doing there is a natural tendency to try to fill all the cells as a reactive kind of logical *horror vacuo*. Seen from this framework, tribes become matrix-generated residua needed to fill empty cells separating bands from chiefdoms and states. Although tribes fill a logical space in the paradigm, their definition and distinctive features remain problematic. Defining tribes is a little like trying to nail jelly to the wall. Or to quote some lines from my favorite poet, Donald Weismann,

> Jelly, he said, and no one got the word,
> Not even gooseflesh in the backdraft.
>
> Jelly was the word as surely as
> a fair bat! batted backwards
> Is foul. (1965: 13)

I should stop here, but I want to take a closer look at the concept of the tribe.

Let me begin with some assertions certain to provoke my scholarly colleagues and bound to irritate my Indian friends. Tribes are not the primordial political entities we assume them to be. There were no, or at least very few, tribes in the strict sense existing in Native North America before the permanent presence of Europeans was established in the New World. Before throwing rocks, rotten fruit, or up, please hear me out. The argument is that tribes are secondary formations produced by the interaction between complex, stratified, state societies and egalitarian, kinship-based societies. Tribal forms of political structure are the result of the process of history. I wish I could claim originality for these ideas, but they were first presented in a paper by the late Morton Fried delivered at the 1967 Meeting of the American Ethnological Society. Fried later elaborated his thesis in a short monograph entitled *The Notion of Tribe* (1975). I shall selectively summarize some of the issues raised by Fried and offer my reactions to them in the hope that they will have some relevance to this conference.

Some insight into the meaning of the concept of tribe may be gleaned by briefly examining the etymology of the term 'tribe' comes directly from the Latin *tribus*, which was originally applied to the three-fold division of the people of Rome. Criteria for membership in these three tribes is unclear. According to Fried (1975: 7), the Latin word *tribus* was used to refer to the [16] ancient "tribes" of Israel mentioned in the Bible, and it is in this context that the term enters the English language, with the approximate meaning of a group of persons forming a community and claiming descent from a common ancestor. This Biblical association may help explain the frequent early English identification of American Indians with the lost tribes of Israel. To venture a further speculation that should be checked out, the word tribus may also have been used to designate the many barbarian hordes of Europe who chronically threatened and ultimately overwhelmed Rome. *Tribus* also seems to be cognate with the term 'tribute,' which may have been exacted from and given to barbarian headmen. In the long-term process of interaction and agreements, political power would have become more centralized and consolidated in the barbarian bands, with the result that a tribal political structure would eventually develop. Negotiation could proceed "government to government," as President Reagan liked to say in reference to Federal dealings with Indian tribes.

Some investigators view tribes as separate breeding populations and attempt to see tribal endogamy as a defining attribute. However, as I tried to suggest before, incorporation of alien groups and individuals was frequent in North America as far back as our information goes. Fried (1975:21) cites data collected in 1909 by Kroeber and Waterman showing that over 13 percent of Yurok marriage were with neighboring tribes, a modest statistic that takes on added significance when it is realized that most of these marriages occurred between spouses who spoke totally unrelated languages. Similar notes of tribal out-marriage have been reported elsewhere in North America. It is doubtful then that tribal membership is, or ever was, closely correlated with biology.

Tribes have also frequently been identified as distinctive language groups. Here again the fit is far from perfect, as indicated by the aforementioned Yurok data, by the frequent presence and usefulness of bi-and multi-lingual speakers in tribal communities, and by the fact that speakers of the same language may be members of different tribes. We tend to forget that the source of much of our voluminous ethnographic information on the Kwakiutl came from Boas's principal informant and collaborator, Quesilid or George Hunt, whose mother was Tlingit.

PoliticoHistory

The possession of a collective tribal name seems to be a <u>sine qua non</u> for the identification of a group or a tribe. It is hard to imagine nameless tribes. What would we put on our maps? However, as is well known, the names by which a tribe is known may not be of their own making. The name Cherokee or *Tsalagi* most probably derives from the Muskoghean term *Tciloki*, which glosses as 'people of other speech'. While the name *Tsalagi* has been assimilated by the Cherokees over the past three hundred years, they posses alternate terms for self-reference, such as *ani'yunwi*, 'people', or *ani katuwagi*, which has reference to one of the major sacred towns in the East and to the Ketoowah Society in the West, and is used by cultural conservatives to refer to people considered to be "real" Cherokees.

Often the names by which a group is known are negative stereotypes imposed by others. As is well known, the name Eskimo is of Algonkian origin and means 'eaters of raw flesh', which bears connotations of wildness and subhuman behavior in much the same manner as *steak tartar* (incidentally a name for diffuse central Asian peoples) surrounded by slices of bread is sometimes referred to as a "cannibal sandwich." The implicit negative ethnocentrism of 'Eskimo' led to its replacement by the term Inuit, which contains a root for 'soul' plus a locative suffix. [17]

Some peoples didn't fare so badly in the origin and meaning of their tribal name. For the edification of our host, Fred Hoxie, I will summarize what is known about the tribal name Crow. The following discussion derives from Fried's distillation (1975: 31) of Robert Lowie's primary data. The Crow often referred to themselves as *biruke*, 'us' as contrasted to others. They also used the term *Apsaruke* for self-reference. Lowie reported that early French interpreters translated the term as *corbeaux*, or 'crow'. However, Lowie ascertained that *Absaruke* really referred to a "a peculiar kind of fork-tailed bird resembling the blue jay or magpie" that was no longer present in their area. Nevertheless, they seem to have accepted the eponym Crow without any difficulty.

The Lumbee people, who have been seeking Federal recognition as an acknowledged tribe for over a century, make an instructive contrast with the situation among the Crow. One of the problems that has impeded the recognition of the Lumbees has been the failure to link them with a known historical tribe (Blu 1980). Recent unpublished ethnohistorical research by Jack Campisi prepared for the Lumbee recognition case provides fairly conclusive evidence that the Lumbees can be traced back to the Cheraws, and I am hopeful that the Lumbers will soon be recognized by Congress. However, in their long struggle for recognition the Lumbees adopted a series of different names. For a brief interlude they identified themselves as Cherokees of Robeson County, NC; some current Lumbees regard themselves as Tuscaroras; they also considered themselves as Siouians in the 1930s. The name Lumbee derives from the Lumber River that flows through their territory. However, the first name that they assumed in their quest for recognition in the late 1880s was the inspiration of a sympathetic amateur local historian who identified them with the Croatians of Lost Colony fame. This was accepted until prejudiced local whites shortened the name and began to refer to them derisively as Crows. Given their black admixture and the association with Jim Crow, the Lumbees soon discarded the name.

The early ethnologist J Owen Dorsey once footnoted an Omaha text with a statement that a second Omaha informant, "Two Crows denies this." Edward Sapir (1938) recycled the footnote to indicate that two presumably reliable informants could disagree about the meanings of a particular custom, thus indicating the ultimate locus of culture in the individual. In the cases of the Montana Crows and the North Carolina Crows, one Crow denies this tribal appellation. What's in a name? Obviously a great deal.

Time, attention span, and my ebbing energy level prevent further summarization and commentary on Fried's important and neglected monograph. There is much more of value contained in it, and I encourage you to consult it. Let me conclude.

I have advocated a binocular vision of how we should view the struggle for political autonomy by Native Americans. We should keep one eye on the nature of traditional Native American political systems as they existed before significant white contact, since these structures conditioned subsequent response. The other eye should be trained on Euro-American political structures and their evolving intervention in native political affairs. When combined in stereoscopic fashion the two perspectives should produce a three-dimensional picture of the historical processes leading to the present situations of tribal political system, including opportunities for and constraints upon the expression of political autonomy. I presented some theoretical approaches derived from political anthropology and attempted to assess their utility in [18] analyzing Native American political structure. Through a dark looking glass I selectively surveyed certain aspects of aboriginal political structures. I perceived a wide variety of political systems. I then tried to narrow my focus on the tribe, but my vision became blurred. Following Morton Fried, I noted that tribes only came into view after significant native interaction with Euro-American political states.

Tribal political structures became more regularized and comparable through time, and today they constitute the vital organizations through which political action, including the call for increased autonomy, is expressed. However, the Federal Government, especially through the agency of the Bureau of Indian Affairs, continues to exercise considerable direct and indirect power over Native American political life, even to the extent of defining the essential criteria as to what constitutes an Indian tribe. Non-treaty groups petitioning for Federal recognition must prove descent from historically known tribes, must demonstrate continuous identification as Indians, must show that a substantial portion of their membership has continued to reside in a specific geographical area that formed part of its territory from historical times, and they must give evidence of tribal political influence or other forms of authority over its members as an autonomous entity from historical times to the present.

Satisfactory fulfillment of these criteria is a lengthy and expensive matter. The BIA Branch of Acknowledgment currently has a backlog of over one-hundred pending cases. With the present staff size and rate of resolution of cases, it will probably take another fifty years to process submitted petitions. A new bill has been introduced to Congress to expedite the process, but its fate is uncertain at this writing.

I find many of the current criteria used to define Indian tribes to be unduly restrictive. Indeed, many currently recognized tribes would have difficulty fulfilling the BIA criteria. One would like to see Native Americans have a greater self-determining say in ascertaining who is and who isn't an Indian. One would also welcome increased Indian autonomy in more substantive, rather than symbolic, political action. However, I suspect that in the long run the Federal Government will continue to have a decisive voice in defining and determining the type of political structure it did so much to create. [19]

REFERENCES

Blu, Karen 1980 *The Lumbee Problem*. New York: Cambridge University Press.
Colson, Elizabeth 1953 *The Makah Indians*. Minneapolis: University of Minnesota Press.
    1968 "Political Anthropology: The Field. *International Encyclopedia Of The Social Sciences*. Edited by DL Sills. New York: MacMillan and Free Press, Vol. 12: 189-193.
Fogelson, Raymond D 1963 Review of Fred Gearing, *Priests and Warriors*. *American Anthropologist* 65: 726-730.
Fortes, Meyer and E.E Evans-Pritchard, eds. 1940 *African Political Systems*. Oxford University Press.
Fried, Morton 1967 *The Evolution Of Political Society*. New York: Random House.
    1968 On The Concept Of "Tribe" and "Tribal Society." IN *Essays On The Problem Of Tribe*: Proceedings of the 1967 Annual Spring Meeting Of The American Ethnological Society. Seattle: University of Washington Press.
    1975 *The Notion of Tribe*. Menlo Park: Cummings Publishing Co.
Gearing, Fred 1962 *Priests And Warriors: Social Structures For Cherokee Politics In the 18th Century*. American Anthropological Association. Memoir 93.
Gluckman, Max 1960 *Order And Rebellion In Tribal Africa*. Glencoe: Free Press.
Hoebel, E Adamson 1940 *Political Organization and Law Ways of the Comanche Indians*. American Anthropological Association Memoir 54.
    1978 *The Cheyennes: Indians Of The Great Plains*. New York: Holt. Rinehart. Winston.

Krech, S, III 1980 Northern Athapascan Ethnology in the 1970s. IN *Annual Review Of Anthropology*. Edited by B.J. Siegel, AR Beals, and SA Tyler. Vol. 9. Palo Alto: Annual Reviews, pp. 83-100.

Leach, Edmund R 1954 *Political Systems of Highland Burma*. Cambridge: Harvard University Press.

Leacock, Eleanor 1954 The Montagnais "Hunting Territory" and the Fur Trade. American Anthropological Association Memoir 78.

   1981 Matrilocality Among The Montagnais-Naskapi. Chapter 5 IN *Myths of Male Dominance*. New York; Monthly Review Press. [Originally published in 1955 as "Matrilocality in a Simple Hunting Economy," Southwestern Journal of Anthropology 11 (1).]

Lewellen, Ted C 1983 *Political Anthropology: An Introduction*. South Hadley, MA: Bergin and Garvey. [19]

Lips, Julius E 1947 Naskapi Law. *American Philosophical Society, Transactions*, New Series 37, part 4.

Llewellyn, Karl N, and E Adamson Hoebel 1941 *The Cheyenne Way: Conflict And Case Law In Primitive Jurisprudence*. Norman: University of Oklahoma Press.

Lloyd, Peter C 1965 The Political Structure of African Kingdoms: An Exploratory Model, IN *Political Systems and the Distribution Of Power*. Edited by M. Banton. ASA Monograph 2.

Lowie, Robert H 1920 *Primitive Society*. New York: Boni and Liveright.

   1927 *The Origins Of The State*. New York: Harcourt Brace.

   1948 Some Aspects of Political Organization Among The American Indians. *Journal of the Royal Anthropological Society* 78: 11-22.

MacLeod, William Christie 1924 *The Origin Of The State: Reconsidered in the Light of the Data of Aboriginal North America*. Philadelphia: Westbrook.

   1928 *The American Frontier*. London; Kegan Paul, Trench, Trubner.

   1931 *The Origin and History of Politics*. New York: John Wiley.

Morgan, Lewis Henry 1851 *League of the Ho-de-no-sau-nee or Iroquois*. Rochester: Sage.

Murphy, Robert F 1972 *Robert H Lowie*. New York: Columbia University Press.

Phillips, Philip and James A Brown 1975-82 *Pre-Columbian Shell Engravings From The Craig Mound at Spiro, Oklahoma*. 6 Volumes. Cambridge: Peabody Museum Press.

Province, John 1937 The Underlying Sanctions Of Plains Culture. IN *The Social Anthropology Of North American Tribes*. Edited by Fred Eggan. University of Chicago Press.

Sapir, Edward 1938 Why Cultural Anthropology Needs The Psychiatrist. *Psychiatry* 1: 7-12.

Sattler, Richard A 1980 The Comparative Analysis of Native American Political Organization. *Papers in Anthropology* (University of Oklahoma) 21 (2): 163-173.

Service, Elman 1962 *Primitive Social Organization: An Evolutionary Perspective*. New York: Random House.

   1975 *Origin of the State and Civilization: The Process of Cultural Evolution*. New York: WW Norton.

Smith, Marvin T 1987 *Archaeology of Aboriginal Culture Change in the Interior Southeast*. Gainsville: University of Florida Press. [20]

Steward, Julian H 1936 The Economic ad Social Basis o Primitive Bands. IN *Essays In Anthropology Presented to AL Kroeber*. Edited by RH Lowie. Berkeley: University of California Press.

   1938 Basin-Plateau Sociopolitical Groups. *Bureau Of American Ethnology*, Bulletin 120.

   1955 *Theory of Culture Ch*ange. Urbana: University of Illinois Press.

Tanner, Adrian 1974 *Bringing Home Animals*. New York: St Martin's Press.

Weismann, Donald L 1965 *Jelly Was The Word*. Austin, TX: Pemberton Press. [21]

PoliticoHistory

SUMMARY

As those of you who know me are aware, I am quite interested in the subject of ritual, a very powerful force in social interaction. Obviously, ritual is also very much involved in politics. Although none of the papers really focused on this aspect, the power of ritual is omnipresent. Even conferences like this one are rituals. We often start off with a series of ritual excuses: "I didn't get the papers in time," "I've written it all out, but it's too long," "To save time, I'll summarize my remarks" (which usually takes longer than if one had read them). These are forms of ritual behavior.

In my view of conferences as rituals, they turn out to be what Marcel Mauss described as total social facts or, at least total academic social facts. The various kinds of presentations, offerings, counter-offerings, levels of exchange, time-out-of-time, space-out-of-space (the special Newberry milieu), exchanges in the hall, during breaks, after sessions, all these do indeed occur, but the obvious structure is provided by the papers. In good Maussian fashion, the papers can be seen as gifts, offerings, reciprocated by commentary, questions, both formally and informally.

My task is to provide an overall commentary, particularly since some of the papers were slighted by commentary that sometimes produced interesting mini-papers in their own right. I shall comment on each paper in turn. My mode of presentation will borrow from a Southeastern Middle Woodland style of pottery decoration called "stab and drag:" I will pick on a few points and try to drag something out of them by free association. Let me make it clear at the outset that most of the papers were fine and stimulated our thinking, as were the commentators.

Richard White's paper on the "middleground" provides a progress statement on how his thinking is going, but I don't think this concept is fully defined as yet. When we think of "ground," we sense a spatial notion, but the boundaries are not completely clear. Also, White's excellent paper asserts that the middleground existed in time, but when it began and ended are not fully worked out, although he does provide 1650-1812 as bracket dates. What is most striking is that White is a special kind of historian, one who attempts to make generalizations relying directly or indirectly on social science. I heartily approve of his efforts. White, himself, can be seen as a kind of middleground between history and social science.

He focuses on interactions and exchanges. One of the most evocative statements in the paper was the degree to which everyone in the middleground functioned in terms of agreed upon misunderstandings. Rather than that being exceptional, I submit that most communication, including what I am providing now, is also based upon agreed upon misunderstandings. If we all understood each other perfectly, we wouldn't have anything to talk about. I applaud this kind of approach. He extended his interpretive approach by using kinship idioms, which are so universally important. However, he did not work out their full ramifications. I'd like to suggest how to push this dimension a little further. [171]

The role of father became a metaphor for many kinds of relationships involving Indians and the French colonial government. The notion of a father/children relationship is an important one. Mothers are also important, as are other kinship relations that need to be examined. As Bill Fenton noted, a longstanding interest of his, and of Frank Speck before him, has been the use of kinship metaphors to discuss relations between groups, which change over time. Whether, for instance, Delawares are fathers, brothers, nephews, or mothers to other Eastern Woodland groups is variously expressed in early documents, treaties, and communications.

At the start of the paper, White discussed applications of the concept of "sauvage" by the French and of "manitou" by the Algonquians. There is a vast literature on the subject of the manitou, which is sometimes conceived as diffuse power, like mana in the Pacific, and which is more frequently concentrated in spiritual beings and locales where humans can interact with and form relationships with it/them. Manitous are close to the Ojibwa notions of *pawaganaks*, beings encountered in vision quests who bestow individual powers, prerogatives, the right to create bundles, and impart songs to maintain the relationship. These are personified partnerships with the spiritual world. Usually, the kinship term applied to these beings is grandfather.

What I am suggesting is that we look for a three-generational model in which Europeans start as grandfathers, shift to fathers, and, in the middleground, might achieve a temporary equivalence as brothers. For example, consider the two letters between Handsome Lake, the Seneca prophet, and Thomas Jefferson, where the President refers to the Seneca as his brother or his son, suggesting aspects of a relationship changing over time. If it started as grandfather/grandson, the implied power differential helps explicate references to the natives beseeching the French, as an appropriate appeal to perceived power. In terms of a father, the kinship relations imply guidance, advice, support, and council, depending on the overall descent system (matri-, bi-, or patri-lineality). More can be done with contextualizing these kinship metaphors.

David Weber dealt with a large area from Florida to the Southwest and California. As he noted, most of the scholarship of this region has been influenced by Herbert Bolton's work to show the human side of the Spanish in contrast to the "Black Legend". Weber did not mention that Bolton also had a close, careful interest in Indians, especially in his early work. His manuscript on the Hasinai, a Caddo group, was finally published recently, Bolton also corresponded with John Swanton, the premier ethnohistorian of the Southeast.

On a more general note, unlike White's interest in social science, Weber is a traditional historian who looks at the documents, although he is sympathetic and interested in getting the Indian side of things. But here he runs into a block. How do we get the Indian side? It is not in the documents.

Historians devote their lives to documents. These records are analyzed, dated, arranged, and probed in the expectation that, magically, an account will jump out of them. As most of you know, however, that is not the way it works in ethnohistory. Regardless of one's orientation or training, we try to tell a good story informed by some kind of script.

For a long time, the story telling ability of historians was just assumed. It was just something that was done. You were good at it or you were not. More and more, I think, we are becoming self-conscious about this ability and looking at it in terms of narrativity: What the script actually is.

Certain modern French thinkers have argued that the script is very, very important. For them, the major task of history is to make public the script, [173] perhaps even to generate it. This runs counter to most historical orthodoxy, which holds that we should not be inventing history, even though we do. There is no such thing as objective history. It is all a story of one sort or another. Some stories are close to known facts and some are more adventuresome.

Thus, when a block is encountered, such as the lack of documents from the Indians and their more general silence in Western history, the only way out of this dilemma is to write some scripts, advance some "history", and see what happens.

The construction of relations in a script can be useful, sometimes. To phrase this in more pseudo-scientific jargonese, we need to construct a narrative model to suggest alternatives and insights. This strategy might benefit Weber and others when faced with the difficulty of tapping into the native point-of-view.

A great problem in the missionization of Native American people is how missionaries were initially regarded. Missionaries came without weapons, but were often accepted and made converts to some degree. How? What was the original structure involved? What was the nature of the encounter?

We can look at what might have happened when the first Jesuits met the Hurons- (I hope that Fr. Prucha will absolve me of any sins I might commit here.)

> Imagine a day in February or March. It is cold and gray in Huronia. You are sitting in your village with hunger hovering around. The hunters are out, but there has been no fresh game in days. People are sick and dying. The world is dead. Suddenly, three black-robed Jesuits arrive. You look at them and communicate as best you can.
>
> They have wonders. A mass kit. They open it. A Jesuit pulls out a splinter. What is it?

A piece of the True Cross. He pulls out some bones. What are they? Relics of saints. You know what bones are about. What else? A porcelain statue of a man nailed to two boards. You look closely and see holes in the rib cage with blood running out. You know that splinters intruded into bodies cause illness. You know the power of bones. You know aspects of torture. Clearly, these guys have some powerful stuff.

They also have a drink. They call it the blood of their lord and savior. You think about that for a while. Finally, you ask them what they <u>really</u> want. They say "Your souls." It must have been a frightening experience.

I made all of this up, but such a tale can generate questions about the encounter. Weber talked of syncretism, but we do not have Timucua views of the mission. We know that missions provided vectors for disease and killed off the Georgia Guale and provided sitting ducks for English raiders. Missions were dangerous places to be.

What we really need also is an ethnography of the missionaries. Who were these people? What was their mind set? What were they trying to accomplish? How representative were they of the people who were to come after them?

Weber's point about chastity is well taken. In the Southwest particularly, it was admired because it showed that priests did have power. But given the missionary experience and the massive die-offs, I think something else was going on. There was a perception of the mission as inhabited by a doomed population. Missionaries knew the inhabitants would die off. Thus, their task was not to convert people in order to move them into mainstream society. The role of the mission was more a preparation for a good death and afterlife, a [174] good life leading directly to a beautiful death. Throughout mission records there are repeated expressions of joy about the deaths of faithful converts. There are hints of a death cult, a pre-Ghost Dance movement. There is a sense of sweet sadness (*triste*) in De Smet and others when they moved into the Northwest and viewed it as a virginal field for conversion.

George Phillips raised more questions than he answered. His description of the *alcalde* system was fascinating, but I have difficulty perceiving the situation, which seems to fit Erving Goffman's description of a total institution, I sensed the underlying structure of a prison with straw bosses or of a concentration camp with all of the associated behaviors that such a structure breeds. Also, there is a sense that it was a proving ground for leaders who would emerge and move in various directions, cither toward resistance or acculturation. It was something of an officers' training school with appropriate attributes. Despite these many aspects, what Phillip's did not say and what upsets so many native Californians today, is the circumstances under which the missions started. Were these coercive institutions, sweeping up whole communities and forcing this new life upon them, or was it voluntary? Surely, it changed with time and place. Jay Miller reminded me that Raymond White's study of the Luiseño mentions that shamans sent a son to the mission to learn about this new source of power, while other sons were sent into the hills for safety and others were trained at home. The strategy resembled a game theory in playing the options and hedging the bets.

Phillip's paper was strong on data and interesting in terms of devices. Imagine whips as thick as a wrist. When and how did these come in? The same sort of question can be asked in the Southeast, How and why did the Cherokees institute Jails? These were strange things: people cages. Throughout, this is a transformation toward the brutal and the grotesque about which I would like to learn more.

I have little to say about Mary Young's spirited paper because I agree with most of it. She undertook an ambitious job in comparing five tribes over forty critical years and she accomplished her task well. Bill Fenton has taught us much about the Iroquois, but we know next to nothing about the Creek confederacy. We really need a good study of the Creeks, also the Caddoans and others. Young is right to distinguish between the Cherokee as more open to innovation and change, whereas the Creeks were closed, more like Southwestern Pueblos in their tight adherence to forms and hierarchy. She needs, however, to look more closely at the Chickasaw, who were more state-like, with ranks and stratification.

This may have been a factor in their more rapid assimilation to Euro-American ways.

I would particularly like to put to rest the unfortunate term "harmony ethic" as applied to the Cherokees. Something like it did exist, but it became distorted in the literature. Robert Thomas introduced the term, and it was adopted by John Gulick who began its over elaboration. The "harmony ethic" was more a tendency and ideal than anything like a vital factor in social relations.

Sidney Barring's paper was also ambitious. He marched in where angels dared to tread, probably because of the pigs. His research contributes important evidence on the Crazy Snake Rebellion, the coexistence of two systems of law, and role of courts as mediators between towns and the nation. We need also to look at the Crazy Snake Movement in the context of emerging social classes. The Creeks were not a state, but classes were added to their society in the nineteenth century. Much of the Civil War in Oklahoma can be expressed as [175] class warfare, with elites and mixed bloods on the side of the South and conservatives and full-bloods joining the Union. The war took a terrible toll.

In its aftermath, Crazy Snake emerged as a preserver of traditions threatened by the Dawes and Curtis Acts. Simultaneously, there were similar movements in the other Southeastern tribes through the agency of the Four Mothers Society. There are strong parallels with the Cherokee Nighthawk Keetoowah or Redbird Smith movement.

Harring is particularly sensitive the idea of politics as a cultural system with meanings. But how do we get at the native system of justice? Among the Cherokees, when I looked for notions of law and justice, I asked for native terms for the "harmony ethic." Jack Kirkpatrick and I corresponded about it, but found no solution. Instead, I learned that the Cherokee sense of justice is supported by human warmth and good will embodied in a native concept that connotes justice, righteousness, straightness, honesty, truth, and uprightness. It is considered a positive life force. Traditional Cherokee are extremely sensitive to its violation, which constitutes injustice. Thus, there are stories of debts pursued to the ends of the earth. Letters ask about a 5 cent loan made 10 years ago. There was a strict keeping of account books, particularly by the cooperatives *gadugi*).

Feuds and factionalism can be traced to injustices. To push this further, underlying this sense of justice is a basic bipartite classification of people into opposed moral types: one of heart-soul-feeling exhibited in kind behavior and one of unmitigated evil. The classification is absolute. Someone does not shift categories or change morality over the course of a life time. A Cherokee may know someone for years before consigning that person to one or the other category. Once classified, however, the status is irrevocable. I also note parallels for the Creek. To become a member of a town, you are on probation for four years or so before you are fully incorporated. You have to prove that you are a good person.

A kind person (the opposition is kind/evil) can make mistakes, but he or she has an essential humanity and can be forgiven. Indeed, Cherokee had individual and institutional mechanisms for forgiveness, including crimes as serious as murder. If you entered a Green Corn ceremony and made reparations, you could be absolved of your sins. If the ethical breached endangers the physical or moral wellbeing of the group, the kind person will suffer consequences and give up his or her life if necessary.

There is a wonderful account of a murder trial where a "kind" man was sentenced to die. A week before his execution, he was released to settle his affairs. The appointed time for carrying out the sentence came and the man had not returned. Half an hour later, he stumbled in complaining that his horse died under him as he rushed back to be hanged. This shows clear solidarity with the group. Of such are martyrs made.

Those who are evil act from the darkness of their very souls. Such individuals may be excluded from humanity, regarded as socially dead, until they are actually killed. They cease to exist once they are so characterized. They are the moral equivalent of witches- In Cherokee history, political homicides arc rooted in these beliefs and actions. Native courts which let people off, such as Ned Christy and Zeke Proctor, illustrate native ideals of traditional justice, in comparison to federal courts and justice.

Fred Hoxie reminds us that reservations were oppressive structures. Some of his paper was oriented around a rejection of notions of persistence. I am one of those soft-hearted, liberal scholars who thinks that cultural persistence is [175] always, or should be, there, and who find it, perhaps, where it isn't. There is tradition, but it is consistently, constantly, chronically being refined. Hoxie has a very dramatic script whose full implications need to be worked out. I think it is a very rich script, ready for a film, of Sword Bearer and his crew shooting up the agency. Hoxie has portrayed the scenario vividly.

There was a dissatisfaction with traditional leaders like Plenty Coups. A crisis was going on, but we do not know how it fits into long term Crow patterns. What native meanings were involved. Was Sword Bearer a contrary, a warrior out to count coup. At a deeper level, Hoxie suggests a transformation in leadership based on age.

Max Weber haunts our conference, reminding us that systems of authority rely on the social relationship of leader and follower both. There have been institutes for Indian leaders, where everyone gets a crew cut and a pocket full of pens. But we also need institutes for followership. The two go together as a process. For Weber, there were three ideal types of authority: 1) - traditional, relying on longstanding normative sanctions; 2) - charismatic, which was less a personality trait and more an interactive concept involving a break with traditions and the new ways of prophets, which, if they take hold, create a new orthodoxy and tradition as they become routinized; and 3) - bureaucratic, a Western social invention in which the office not the person is obeyed. I can see a transformation among these types as Plenty Coups tried to orchestrate the situation and still remain aloof until the final outcome. Ultimately, authority fell to bureaucracy after this period of transition.

Another dimension present here is the problem of leadership thrust upon the young by suddenly raising them up to positions of power. This destroys or ignores the traditional bases of authority within society and can cause great misfortune. Let's remember Clyde Warrior, a very imposing figure, a Ponca over six feet tall with a deep voice. He was a founder of the American Indian Youth Council, and regularly traveled to Washington, DC to meet with BIA officials and various lobbying groups. At receptions, ladies with blue-tinted hair asked him what they could do for the Indians and he'd say "Give us guns!" He got a lot of attention, but he was a very disturbed person. All of the stress and strain led to alcoholism. He tried to believe that he was, indeed, the hope for the future as whiles had told him. Everyone said that the young leaders were the hope for Indian society, but this challenged the authority structure of traditional native society. Clyde knew that respect had to be given back to the fathers and grandfathers before the sons and grandsons could fulfill their own destinies. There was a lack of appreciation of the generational nature of leadership. Clyde paid for this disjuncture with his life.

Don Fixico gave us an excellent background paper on termination, a compelling threat to the trust relationship between Indian tribes and the Federal Government. For Indians, trust was assumed to be permanent, infused with a sacred quality. Ever since John Marshall referred to the relationship as like that of a guardian to a ward, the social relationship has been confused or ignored. It never involved individuals, nor was it intended to. This was not the wardship of Robin to Batman. There is a profoundly legal side to these obligations.

We need to look at the power of words: Consider the multiple connotation of the word, "ward." Getting back to Fixico's paper, what if the word "termination" had not been used and the process was called "liberation"? Would it have had more appeal to various Indians with different degrees of [177] education or to different generations? Words and their connotations are important.

At any rate, there is no unilineal process moving inevitably from tradition to an iron cage-tike bureaucracy. Charismatic aspects intrude throughout to provide processual fluidity.

Fred Ragsdale gave us a futuristic look at autonomy and a typology rich in permutations. He provided insights that may prove useful, although his distinctions arc not always comparable and can not be simplisticly lumped together. He did well to remind us of the preciousness of tradition and the need to guard it as the basis of distinctiveness. To preserve tradition is to preserve Indian culture and identity. Complete equality will probably mean an end to a native identity. While Indians have been quite successful with the law, Ragdale's question remains: How can they win so much and still ultimately lose. Ragsdale's metaphor of the casino – that if you play long enough you will loose – may be inappropriate.

We need to consider other games.

Compare the situation of the hand game (*lahal*) where people face off against each other as teams and one person hides two bones (one plain and one marked with a black band) in either hand. Everyone sings and plays drums. It is technically a game of chance, so you should be right 50 percent of the time. But the long-term results show this is not the case. Some win and others loose more than allowed for by the laws of chance. Essentially, people do not accept randomness. The guesser keeps trying to find a strategy for out-guessing the one holding the bones. They try to read each other's minds. It is a cognitive game. Staying in the game says something about being Indian, having power and influencing fate. There are long-term winners and losers.

As I began, let me remind you that games, like meetings, are rituals. They provide a kind of divination, using bones – the "seeds" of regeneration, to connect with cosmic and human forces. The players become consumed with the possibility that it is the only game in town, and indeed it may be. The game is not only a test of individual powers, but must be regarded as a mode of social reproduction as well. [178]

THE RED MAN IN THE WHITE CITY

> "Perhaps, after all, America has never been discovered.
> I myself would say that it had merely been detected."
>
> Oscar Wilde (The Picture of Dorian Gray)

On May 1, 1893 a restive crowd estimated at somewhere between 350,000 and 500,000 gathered in front of the Administration Building to witness the opening ceremonies of Chicago's long-awaited World Columbian Exposition. At 11:15 recently elected President Grover Cleveland and an entourage of Fair officials and visiting dignitaries – including the Duke of Veragas, a lineal descendant of Columbus – took their places on the podium. Amid rousing cheers a near panic ensued as the mob surged forward to get a better view of the proceedings.[1]

Meanwhile, "high up on the portico of the Administration Building several Oglala Sioux braves in full ceremonial dress watched with detached curiosity the chaos below" (Badger 1979: xii). This paper will attempt to summarize the representation of Native North Americans at the Chicago Fair and try to analyze some of the apparent moral ambiguities surrounding their participation in this international spectacular.

Hosting the World Columbian Exposition fulfilled a conscious desire by the emergent Chicago business and social elite to change their city's image from a boisterous, corrupt porkopolis to a world-class center of commerce and culture. Chicago had recovered from the disastrous fire of 1871 and had experienced dynamic growth. However, behind the facade of prosperity and [2] civic boosterism lurked serious social problems. The country as a whole was suffering a severe economic recession that had local repercussions in the form of abject poverty, chronic labor strife, high crime rates, and a repressive and corrupt city government. Winning the competition to host the World's Fair provided a great boon for troubled Chicago. Jobs for laborers and artisans and anticipated tourist dollars temporarily eased the crisis and galvanized city morale. Out of the swampy lakeside lagoons of Jackson Park emerged monumental structures of impressive impermanence – the fabulous White City, clusters of enormous Neo-classical and Renaissance buildings built of "staff", a combination of plaster of parts and concrete bound together with jute or other fibers.[2]

World's Fairs were evolving institutions with each attempting to surpass or improve upon its predecessors.[3] Most official reports and many popular accounts of particular fairs usually begin with a history of previous fairs. This historicity implied a teological theory of cultural development. While fairs

---

[1] A full account of the Dedicatory Ceremonies held on October 21, 1892 and the Opening Day Ceremonies of May 1, 1893 can be found in the official Memorial of the World's Columbian Exposition (Joint Committee on Ceremonies 1893).

[2] "Staff" materiel was invented in Paris about 1876 and was used in the Exposition Universelle de Paris of 1878. It was essentially composed of powdered gypsum, with additives of alumina and glycerine, as well as fibrous material as binder. Mixed with water, "staff" could be moulded or applied directly on wood lath. When hardened, it had an ivory cast, but could easily become discolored. As a result, to obtain a uniform, durable color for the "White City" and to make the structures more water-proof, the "staff" had to be painted. In the deadline "crunch." necessity again mothered invention, as Frank D. Millet, an artist in charge of the Decoration Department, devised a means to discharge a mist of paint using an air-pump driven by electric power (Bancroft nd: 67-68). This was the first, large-scale use of spray-painting.

[3] Burton Benedict provides a provocative and timely review of "The Anthropology of World's Fairs" in his book on the San Francisco Panama Pacific International Exposition of 1915.

of some sort may be a generic feature of historic human culture, international world's fairs are products of the Industrial Revolution, usually thought to begin with the 1851 Crystal Palace Exhibition in London.[4] Though many World's Fairs occurred between those of Hyde Park, London and Hyde Park, Chicago, two such events had special influences on the World Columbian Exposition.

The 1876 Centennial Celebration in Philadelphia was the first American fair of international scope. Government support played a large role in the Philadelphia Fair's success, even [3] though the Centennial lost money. The Smithsonian Institution was represented in many capacities, including exhibits documenting the history and present conditions of the American Indian (McCabe 1975: 205-206). Philadelphia also featured a separate Woman's Pavilion administered and financed by a national Woman's Centennial Commission. While the Philadelphia Fair was long on machinery and fine arts, including a model of Sleeping Iolanthe sculpted in butter by Caroline Brooks of Arkansas (Ingram 1876: 705-706),[5] it was short on amusement. Outside the fairgrounds arose an unofficial "Shantyville" devoted to less austere pleasures.

The immediately preceding Paris World's Fair of 1889 set new standards of excellence. With the dominating symbol of the Eiffel Tower and the unquestioned elegance of Paris, the Exposition exuded an unmistakable *joie de vivre*. One significant innovation that impressed American visitors was the native villages from far-flung French colonies. These villages provided a living ethnographic presence and complemented the usual museum-case displays of artifacts.

The ostensible theme of the Chicago Fair was, of course, Columbus's discoveries, and Columbian imagery was ubiquitous in everything from numismatics and postage stamps to heroic statuary. A replica of the monastery of La Rabida, where Columbus retreated after initial failures to secure support for his proposed voyage, was built on the fairgrounds and filled with historical manuscripts, artifacts, and other Columbian memorabilia, 890 items in all. These relics, assembled by [4] William Curtis of the State Department, were lent by the Pope, the Spanish government. West Indian sources, and by the Duke of Veragua and other descendants of Columbus [Smith and Graham 1893, 1 (4): 9]. The collection was curated by Col. J.G. Bourke, an important early anthropologist and folklorist who published extensively on Southwestern ethnology as well as authoring a notorious volume, *The Scatological Rites of All Nations* (1891).[6]

However, the fundamental ethos pervading the World Columbian exhibitions and their organization was the idea of progress, especially as manifested in the assumed triumph of civilization in

---

4 The significance of the Crystal Palace Exhibition as a collective representation for the Industrial Revolution and the emergence of sociocultural evolutionary theory is highlighted in the Prologue to George W Stocking, Jr's *Victorian Anthropology* (1987: 1-6).

5 Mrs Brooks repeated her butter performance at the Arkansas Pavilion in the Chicago Fair seventeen years later. Some of her more "serious" and enduring work was also displayed in the Woman's Building at Chicago.

6 Princess Eulalia, the Infanta of Spain, visited La Rabida on June 12, 1893 in an intoxicated state and behaved rudely. Bourke derisively comments in his diary,

the Bourbons of Spain who have not been strumpets have been lunatics back to Crazy Jane of Naples, daughter of Ferdinand and Isabella, who remained bereft of reason for 54 years, after she had given birth to Charles V in a water closet of a nunnery in Ghent. Altogether the Bourbon line, especially the Spanish branch, has been consistently contemptible... I showed my indifference to it, by walking in front of the Infanta, with my back to her (quoted in Porter 1986: 296-297).

Despite the honors bestowed on Spanish dignitaries during the Columbian celebration, Bourke's antipathies appear to anticipate the Spanish-American War that arose five years later.

the North American continent. In this self-congratulatory orgy of ethnocentrism, the world's uncivilized races and cultures were taken as markers to measure the distance that separated "them" from "us". As our predecessors on this continent. Native Americans played a special role in this evolutionary docu-drama. Indians were judged to be a disappearing species doomed either to physical extinction or cultural assimilation. Their presence at the Fair was justified for their historical, educational, and scientific value.

At Chicago the fledgling discipline of anthropology flapped its wings to support and popularize these dogmas. The significance of anthropology was greater in Chicago than at any previous or subsequent world's fair.

Ideas of civilizational progress are implicit in the spatial arrangements of world's fairs. The central core of most fairs was heavy industry, marvels of modern science, commercial [5] products, fine art and the arts of refinement. Generally outside the central core were ethnic displays and performances of popular arts by colorfully dressed peasants and national minorities. At the extreme periphery were the exotic primitives and their supposed affines, the freaks and atavistic throwbacks, who constituted not the main show but the side show.

The correlation is not perfect, but the arrangement of center and periphery, resembling a kind of pre-Wisslerian age-area hypothesis, seems to hold at the Chicago Fair. The center was the majestic White City whose architectural splendor took on an almost sacred or Utopian quality. Its mission was enlightenment and elevation of the spirit. For Chicago, as Miller (1990) suggests, the White City represented the culmination of a redemptive apocalypse set in motion by the purifying fire of 1871.

The Midway was a narrow strip of land extending almost a mile westward, away from the lake, appended to the White City. Its name derives from the fact that it originally served as landscaped passage connecting Jackson Park with Washington Park. In the early planning for the Fair consideration was given to locating some of the exhibits in Washington Park and in Grant Park in the Loop.[7] The Midway was intended to control the excesses that took place outside the fairground at Philadelphia, to accommodate native villages, to serve as a bazaar, and to be the center of popular entertainment. The exhibits on the Midway were expected to have redeeming cultural, historical, or educational value and to be displayed in a dignified and [6] decorous manner. Oversight of the Midway was entrusted to Department M, "Ethnology, Archaeology, Progress of Labor and Invention, and Collective Exhibits"[8], under the overburdened directorship of Professor Frederick Ward Putnam (Dexter 1966). Putnam's rein was loose, and entertainment soon overwhelmed education on the Midway. In contrast to the serenity of the White City, the Midway became a cacophony of barker spoils, runaway donkey carts, and jostling tourists. Although the sleaze factor on the Midway has been exaggerated – Little Egypt may never have performed there nor was there any hootchy-cootchy dancing, according to entrepreneur Sol Bloom (1948)[9] –

---

7 Miller (1990: 212-216) comments on the symbolic separation of the Fair from the City as something resembling the distinction between the sacred and profane. The discontinuity is especially marked by architectural choice with the Fair opting for Romanesque Neo-Classicism, while an ongoing architectural revolution was going on downtown with the recently completed Adler~Sullivan Auditorium Theater and the prototypical skyscrapers. Unlike the 1933 Century of Progress, which made practical use of existing cultural resources, the World Columbian Exposition did not link itself to the new Art Institute (built ironically on the previous site of the Interstate Exposition Building erected in 1873), the Auditorium Theater, the Newberry Library, the Chicago Historical Society, or other cultural centers of the "new" Chicago.

8 The classification into lettered Departments was constructed by G. Brown Goode, Assistant Secretary of the Smithsonian and a noted museum administrator and ichthyologist. Goode continually stressed that exhibitions should primarily concern [22] systematic ideas rather than objects and that visual arts were increasingly important in presenting the living thoughts of civilization (Rydell 1984: 43-46).

9 There were probably many "Little Egypts", but it is impossible to be sure that whoever bore the name at the Chicago Fair was identical to the belly-dancer who later gained fame at Coney Island.

nevertheless, the Danse du Venire, more colloquially known as "belly dancing", of Middle Eastern maidens aroused male libidos and compromised their superegos. A subtitle on a contemporary photograph of a belly-dance performance states:

> The danse du ventre, ... which was executed by girls not only in the Egyptian theater, but also in the Persian, Turkish, and with some modification, in the Moorish Theatres, on the Plaisance, is a suggestively lascivious contorting of the abdominal muscles, which is extremely ungraceful and almost shockingly disgusting. Curiosity prompted many to view the performance, but very few remained more than five minutes before this was fully satisfied [Smith and Graham 1893, Vol. 1 (16): 13].

Professor Putnam rides to a relativistic rescue of the redeeming educational value of this popular Midway attraction:

> the national dans [sic] du venire which not being understood was by many regarded as low and repulsive. What wonderful muscular movements did those dancers make, and how strange did this dance seem to us; but is it not probable that our waltz would seem equally strange to these dusky women of Egypt. What is a dance, is a question one was forced to ask after a trip through the Midway. [7]

> Every nation had its own form. With some it was rhythmic movement of the hands and arms; with others of the feet and legs; and with others of the body; some were ceremonial, others for amusement, according to the national traditions and customs (1894: 2).

Comparative choreography proved to be a lucrative enterprise.

One can perceive a primitive-civilized gradient in the locations on the Midway. Near the western gate was a Bedouin encampment, where "Wild East" shows were enacted; Sitting Bull's grounds featured daily war dances by various Indian troupes; nearby was a village of languid Lapplanders {Sami}, an ostrich farm, and a settlement of 100 recently pacified Dahomeans, popularly believed to be cannibals. Toward the center of the Midway could be found Old Vienna, Algerian and Tunisian exhibits, a Chinese Theater, Cairo Street, Persian and Turkish concessions, a German beer hall, and an extensive Javanese Village with a theater for puppet plays. Further on were large Irish concessions, a small settlement of Malays, a popular exhibit of South Sea Islanders, and a diorama of a Hawaiian Volcano. Closer to the entrance to the White City were corporate displays by such firms as the Diamond Match Company and Libby Glass. The Midway also featured ascents in a captive balloon and rides on the gigantic Ferris Wheel, which rotated to a height of 265 feet and became, for many, the Fair's central symbol.[10]

Buffalo Bill's Wild West and Congress of Rough Riders of the World reached its theatrical apex at the Columbian Exposition. Unable to be accommodated within the fairgrounds proper, the show leased over fifteen acres between 62nd and 63rd Streets outside the southwest confines of the Fair. A horseshoe-shaped [8] covered arena seating 18,000 spectators was hastily erected, surrounded by an open campground. Two hundred Indians, mostly Oglala Sioux (but falsely advertised to include large contingents of Blackfeet, Comanches, Pawnees, as well), along with spectacular equestrian groups from

---

Appelbaum (1980: 97, 102) presents evidence that "hootchy-cootchy" dancing did, indeed, take place on the Midway, probably performed by Algerian women.

10 Perhaps it is symbolic that in the shadow of the Ferns Wheel at a French concession was a miniature Eiffel Tower, the central icon of the 1889 Paris Fair. Unlike the Eiffel Tower, the Ferris Wheel did not become a permanent landmark. It was dismantled and later installed in north Chicago. The Ferris Wheel made a final appearance at the St Louis Fair in 1904 before being scrapped.

Russia, Arabia, France, Germany, and England, plus many cowboys, a troop of American soldiers, and various auxiliary personnel swelled the campground population to over 500 people. The Show opened on April 3, 1893, four weeks before the official opening of the Fair, and had two performances daily, including Sunday,[11]13 until the close of the Fair on October 29th. It is estimated that over four million people attended the Buffalo Bill Show, and the event netted more than a million dollars.

The Indians from the Wild West Show were a conspicuous presence on the Fairgrounds. Chief Rain-in-the-Face, Red Cloud, Kicking Bear, Two Strike, Young Bull, Young Man Afraid-of-Horses, Rocky Bear, and No Neck regularly made the rounds and frequently became the subjects of photographic portraits (Sell and Weybright 1955: 194-195). They spent much time on the beach observing vast Lake Michigan and occasionally riding the boats. They were also fascinated by the merry-go-round, which they would ride for hours at a time. One account tells of a night

> when fifteen painted, blanketed chiefs marched up, bought tickets and solemnly mounted the painted ponies. When the machine started and the big calliope began to play "Maggie Murphy's Home," Chief No Neck held on to the bridle with both hands as his blanket floated out behind him. Then as the horses whirled more swiftly, he let go a full-throated war cry, "Yip, yip, yi, yi, yip!" The others at once took it up and the tent walls billowed to the breeze (Yost 1979: 240).[9]

The Indians developed a taste for popcorn, peanuts, and chewing gum and also indulged their fancy by purchasing buttonhole posies, glass canes, and coconut fiber hats (Yost 1979: 240). Much has been written on Buffalo Bill as an Indian fighter and perpetrator of negative Indian stereotypes. However, no less an authority than Vine Deloria, Jr. argues that Buffalo Bill generally treated the Indians fairly, gave them an opportunity to escape reservation persecution, and allowed them to demonstrate their equestrian skills on a par with horsemen of other nationalities (1981: 52-56).

Surviving guide maps also reveal that the center-periphery hypothesis also holds up well with respect to the White City, proper. A village of Eskimos from Southern Labrador was situated in the extreme Northwest corner of the Fair near the 57th Street entrance. There was snow on the ground when the Eskimos arrived in March, 1893, but they grew increasingly uncomfortable as the summer heat arrived. Unfortunately several of the 57 people and six dogs perished. Little Prince Pommiuk gained celebrity with his dexterity in whip-snapping. The Eskimo contingent were housed in dark, bark-shingled huts with framed windows, and they brought with them stone lamps, supplies of seal oil and whale blubber, and stone carvings. Anthropologist Harlan Smith (1901) collected texts from some of the elders, as well as valuable ethnographic material on shamanism, although most of his informants professed Christianity, having been converted by the Moravians. The [10] Eskimos displayed their proverbial ingenuity by adapting their heavy sledges to wheels after the snow disappeared (Jenks 1893: 96).

The Anthropology Building was located in the extreme southwest corner of the fairgrounds. Originally Putnam planned to display the extensive collections that had been assembled for the Fair from all over the world in the centrally located Manufactures and Liberal Arts Building, but he soon discovered that he needed more space. The Anthropology Building was hastily constructed and fully operational two months after the Fair opened, although as Appelbaum notes (1980: 95), it had little architectural merit.

Putnam also reserved some land immediately south of the Anthropology Building where an artificial mountain of Cliff Dwellers[12] was built and fabricated monuments from Yucatan were installed.[13]

---

11 The Fair agreements contracted for Sunday closings to observe the Sabbath. However, after the first month the Fair stayed open seven days a week. The early Sunday closings had a positive effect in increasing attendance at the Wild West Show.

12 The imposing Cliff Dweller exhibit was a fairly accurate reproduction of an archaeological site from southern Colorado, supposedly ancestral to contemporary Moquees [Hopis]. Lieutenant Schwatka was in charge of the restoration. The exhibit failed to attract public interest and met with some

Also located in this area was a small Penobscot village with three birchbark tepees and a square dwelling occupied by four families from Old Town, Maine; an Iroquois settlement, sponsored by New York State, featured four traditional dwellings and a longhouse accompanied by 12 Tuscaroras and Senecas; the spectacular Kwakiutl exhibit was also installed here, as well as individual house structures from other tribes. Some of the themes, variations, as well as overriding progressivist ideology are captured in a misplaced caption for a Canadian Indian exhibit in the Manufactures and Liberal Arts Building:

> This is one of the most popular features of the World's Fair at the south end, and is associated with outdoor exhibits of decidedly living [11] interest ... Here they have their canoes, fishing and hunting tackle, costumes and all the appurtenances of Indian life. They carry on their industries, cook their meals, perform their songs and dances, and go through all the routine of daily life as in their own villages. Those who employ themselves in making trinkets, beaded necklaces and moccasins, pipes and other souvenirs, do a thriving business with the visitors. The tribes and their habitations are various. The Esquimaux dwell in a tent of skins. Skin and bark wigwams form the lodging of the Crees and Chippewas of Northwestern Canada. The Winnebagoes from Wisconsin live in a house of bark and mats, the Penobscots of Maine have used birch-bark, and there are skin tepees, hogans and other dwellings belonging to the various Western tribes. They are all in amazing contrast to the white palaces stretching away to the north, that evidence the skill and prosperity of their successors in this western domain (Anonymous nd).

Indeed, from the perspective of the nameless caption writer, the domestic achievements of the Red Man pale in comparison with the edifice complexes of the White City.

Putnam's staff numbered over 100 people (Dexter 1966: 315). His chief assistants were Franz Boas, who handled much of the ethnology and physical anthropology, and Joseph Jastrow, who was in charge of the psychological laboratories and exhibits and also advised on religious studies. Zelia Nuttall consulted on the Middle American displays, and George Dorsey handled South America. CC Abbot and Ernest Volk helped with the archaeological materials from New Jersey, while Midwestern archaeological exhibits were in the hands of Charles Metz, G Frederick Wright, Harlan Smith, and Warren K Moorehead, fresh from his important work at Hopewell (Collier 1969: 4). The librarian duties were assumed by the British anthropologist, C Staniland Wake, who later edited the papers of the International [12] Congress of Anthropology (1894) that convened at the Fair in late August, 1893. In addition to the huge collection of New World artifacts, a sample of materials from elsewhere, and the active laboratories, the Anthropology Building also highlighted archaeological materials from Greece, Assyria, Egypt, and Rome; collections of fossils, shells, and corals; mounted skins and skeletons of mammals, birds, reptiles, and fishes? and human anatomical and skeletal specimens. Stewart Culin's comparative exhibition of games drew much attention, as did special displays on religious symbols and folklore.

The Smithsonian's Indian Exhibits enjoyed a central location in the Government Building. Primarily the responsibility of Otis T Mason and WH Holmes, the Smithsonian exhibits did not feature living Indians. Archaeological materials were displayed in glass cases, while ethnological information was conveyed innovatively through Mason's pioneering effort to delineate culture areas. Taking JW Powell's recently published classification of linguistic families as his cue. Mason tried to depict major cultural types through photographs, drawings, representative artifacts, and life size models engaged in characteristic industries. Each major area was allotted a separate alcove fronted by a pedestal-mounted

---

scientific scorn, particularly from the illustrious Frank Hamilton Cushing of the Smithsonian.

13 The Yucatan ruins were from the Labna group and from Uxmal and included the celebrated "House of the Nuns." Papier-mâché moulds were taken from the original ruins by Mr EH Thompson, US Consul at Yucatan, under instructions from Professor Putnam, and cast in staff by artisans at the Fair. Their installation was enhanced by native flora (Anonymous 1893c: 97).

bust of a famous chief or life-size mannequin. Although incompletely realized, these exhibits, conceived by Mason and executed by Holmes,[14]14 set new museological standards.

Mason was also prevailed upon to set up an exhibit on primitive feminine industries for the Women's Building. Mary Lockwood, supported by the head of the Woman's Commission, Mrs [13] Potter Palmer, wanted to represent the role of woman as inventor of such domestic products as dressed skins, sewing, weaving, basket-making, and pottery, all of which were considered vital in human cultural development. An official statement by one of the Women Managers bears an uncanny resemblance to contemporary gender controversies: "Women, among all the primitive peoples, were the originators of most of the industrial arts, and that it was not until these became lucrative that they were appropriated by men, and women pushed aside" (quoted in Bancroft n.d: 267). A basic collection of relevant materials from the National Museum was assembled and supplemented by newer acquisitions from Colorado, New Mexico, South Dakota, and Alaska. "Woman's Work in Savagery" comprised many cases that filled a large suite of rooms and displayed embroidery, bodkins, beadwork, needle cases, work bag fasteners, baskets, pots, dishes, spoons, dolls, weaving implements, and Navajo blankets. A Navajo weaver was even imported from Arizona to demonstrate her skills (Weimann 1981: 393-404). Involvement in this project doubtless inspired Otis Mason to publish *Woman's Share in Primitive Culture* in 1897.

Native American materials also found their way into many of the State buildings. Although most of these edifices were used as clubhouses and meeting places, many housed exhibits. The Utah Building displayed mummies of Cliff Dwellers along with supporting photographs and descriptions; Minnesota was reported to have exhibited historical Indian relics; the combined Arizona, Oklahoma, New Mexico Building contained such Indian [14] handicrafts as Navajo blankets, Moqui {Hopi} water baskets, and Apache whips; the Washington State Building featured a fine collection of Northwest Coast artifacts; and the Michigan Building proudly displayed a poem, "Red Man's Rebuke," written on birchbark by the last chief of the Pottawatomies. Ambitious exhibits were mounted by the host state of Illinois: these included a comprehensive review of Illinois archaeology based upon the researches of Professor William McAdams of Alton. McAdams surveyed private collections, borrowed objects, made photographs, engaged in new mound explorations, and produced an Interesting, 77-page illustrated report for the Illinois Board of World's Fair Commissioners (Springfield 1895).

An Alaskan Exhibit, sponsored by the Bureau of the Interior, was located in the Government Building. Naval Lieutenant George T Emmons assembled a major collection of Tlingit and Alaskan Eskimo materials that ultimately was acquired by the American Museum of Natural History, where it survives today along with his valuable ethnographic notes. The collection included a war canoe, sleds, totem poles, an extensive collection of furs, ceremonial pipes, headdresses, robes, blankets, weapons, household and fishing implements, clothing, and various charms and ornaments (Bancroft nd: 123).

A model Indian school building, located just south of Putnam's outdoor villages, was a source of contention. Originally, the Indian school was to be administered by Putnam in collaboration with the Bureau of Indian Affairs. However, Putnam had come under attack from many quarters. The decision [15] to locate some Indians on the Midway was felt to be degrading by many. Richard Henry Pratt, the heavy-handed founder of the Carlisle Indian School, was particularly vocal in his criticism of the Fair's emphasis on traditional Indian culture at the expense of showcasing Indian progress. He refused an invitation to direct a proposed Indian Exhibit in the Government Building, jointly sponsored by the Bureau of Indian Affairs and the Bureau of American Ethnology. This exhibit would contrast "the red

---

14 WH Holmes, an illustrator cum geologist and archaeologist, stayed on in Chicago after the Fair to become the Director of the Field Columbian Museum, a post he relinquished in 1897 to return to the U.S National Museum in Washington. It is interesting to note the little-known fact that Holmes was listed as an original faculty member of newly established University of Chicago for 1892-93. His title was "Non-Resident Professor of Archaeologic Geology" (Goodspeed 1916: 487) and there is no record of his ever having taught classes at the University.

man as a savage wrapped in a blanket, and his child in the dress of civilization endeavoring to master benignant mysteries" (quoted in Badger 1979: 105). Pratt saw the exhibit as "contrived by two government bureaus calculated to keep the nation's attention and the Indian's energies fixed upon his valueless past, through spectacular aboriginal housing, dressing, and curio employments it instituted" (quoted in Badger 1979: 105). In Pratt's view such exhibits were detrimental to educating Indians for the modern world.

The model BIA School, located north of the living Indian villages and between the Agricultural Building and the Krupp Gun Exhibit, contained workshops, classrooms, sitting rooms, a dining room, kitchen, dormitories, and apartments for employees. The walls were decorated with pictures of famous chiefs and objects of native industry; the windows were covered with transparencies illustrating Indian culture (Bancroft n.d: 122). After the Pratt falling-out, BIA Commissioner Morgan recruited delegations of Indian students from government and religious schools to attend the Fair. Over a thousand tourists a week [16] witnessed Indian students studying, reciting, working at trades, preparing meals, and displaying products of their industry (Hoxie 1984: 88-89).[15]

Pratt relocated his Carlisle School in the East Gallery of the Manufactures and Liberal Arts Building. Displayed here in glass cases were penmanship, map-drawing, uniforms, and fancy work made by students (Bancroft nd: 256). Pratt arranged to bring ten platoons of Carlisle students to Chicago to march in the October 1892 Dedication celebrations. Each platoon paraded in sharp military precision, bearing icons of their academic and industrial training (Hoxie 1984: 89y Bancroft n.d: 87). Over the course of summer over 500 Carlisle students visited the Fair where they presented marching and musical performances and trooped under the banner "Into Civilization and Citizenship" (Badger 1979: 161).

An anonymous sub-text to a photograph of a small Canadian Indian exhibit in the Manufactures and Liberal Arts Building, showing a teepee, snowshoes, nets, and canoes, reiterates a similar refrain regarding Indian progress:

In Canada no less than in this country the aboriginal American seems doomed to extinction ... Nor has Canada been much more successful in teaching him civilization, though it is apparent that very humane and enlightened efforts are put forth in this direction ... [one] learns with interest that in older provinces of Canada the Indians have long since been gathered into settlements, under the care of proper government offices, and in some cases with industrial schools and other helps for hastening their progress to an equalty [sic] in all respects with the white settler. Missions under the care of different Christian bodies have also undertaken the work of their religious training and supervision of their schools. An interesting [17] contrast is seen in the above exhibit between the products of these settlements, both of handicraft and intelligence, and the rude appliances of war and the chase from the tribes that still roam free by the Saskatchewan and Red River (Anon nd).

The civilized-primitive dilemma of public presentation was confronted directly by Rev. John W. Sanborn who supervised the Iroquois delegation to the Fair:

The Indians are emerging from their former state of semi-barbarism and awakening to the better condition which is before them; the question, therefore, whether the New York Iroquois should represent at Chicago their ancient savagery, and go back to what they were 400 years ago, or show the progress which they have made and the civilization which they have attained, was difficult to determine; but as director-in-chief of this exhibit, my conclusion was that it would be

---

[15] Another demonstration of Indian education was presented in the Children's Building where methods of teaching native children were displayed with a class of young girls from the Ramona Indian School of Santa Fe, New Mexico (Bancroft nd: 293).

an injustice to our high-minded and self-respecting chiefs to require them to lapse into barbarism even for one summer for the sake of showing their past history. It did seem proper, however, that the most ancient bark houses should be erected, and that the people should dress in deer-skin suits of the genuine Iroquois pattern, while at the same time, they gave daily exhibition of their progress in education, religion and the arts of peace. The thousands of visitors were, for the most part, astonished to learn that our Indians were capable of such improvement as was shown (1894: 498).

The moral conflict surrounding how living Indians were to be presented at the Fair - whether to have them portray their traditional cultures as staged authenticity (cf. MacCannell 1976: 91-107) in the name of science and/or popular entertainment or to have them demonstrate the degree to which they embraced civilization and had assimilated into late nineteenth-century American life - was, to be sure, more a problem for whites than it appears to have been for Indians. What is lacking in this supposed moral drama are sufficient [18] Indian voices. The few soundings we can record reverberate positively. As Deloria maintains (1981), few, if any, Sioux felt demeaned by their participation in Buffalo Bill's Wild West Show. The hundreds of Indian students who attended the Fair probably for the most part found it an exciting adventure and enlightening experience. Many Kwakiutls who participated in the Columbian Exposition were eager for a return engagement eleven years later in St Louis, despite the fact that the media were not very kind to them. Seneca Chief Solomon O'Bail, a direct descendant of Cornplanter and an outspoken traditionalist, expressed his feelings about the Fair in the following fashion: "Had good time all summer; no mad words; good time" (Sanborn 1894: 501).

Indian feelings about the Fair notwithstanding, the person who took the most fire in this controversy was Frederick Ward Putnam, who occupied a hot seat as Director of Section M. Part of Putnam's problem was his inability to control the activities on the Midway where the educational and scientific ideals rapidly eroded into tawdry amusement and the feverish quest for a fast buck. It soon became apparent that the Midway was the money pump that would guarantee the financial fluidity of the Fair. Putnam never gave up his belief in the positive virtues of the Midway, but soon surrendered his authority to the enterprising Sol Bloom who later became a real estate tycoon and national politician who helped draft the United Nations charter (Rydell 1984: 62). In his autobiography Bloom wryly comments that "To have made this unhappy gentleman [Professor Putnam] [19] responsible for the establishment of a successful venture in the field of entertainment was about as intelligent a decision as it would be today to make Albert Einstein manager of the Ringling Brothers and Barnum and Bailey Circus" (quoted in Badger 1979: 81).

But Putnam was also threatened from within his ranks. One of his staff members, an outspoken woman named Emma Sickles objected to the degradation of Indians at the Fair, particularly those located on the Midway. Ms. Sickles was summarily fired and complained in a letter to the New York Times that the exhibits had "been used to work up sentiments against the Indian by showing that he is either savage or can be educated only by Government agencies ... Every means was used to keep the self-civilized Indians out of the Fair" (quoted in Rydell 1984: 63). Indeed, representatives from the Five Civilized Tribes in Oklahoma were scarce in Chicago. Perhaps their conservative members seemed less civilized in light of their on-going struggle against allotment of their lands and the dissolution of their tribal governments.

It is easy in retrospect to brand Putnam as a racist and as a person lacking in cultural sensitivity. However, he must be judged in the contexts of his times, and credit is due him for his efforts to promote anthropology as a scientific discipline, to popularize its research, and to leave Chicago with a permanent legacy in the form of the collections that later became the nucleus of the Field Museum. [20]

The World Columbian Exposition ended on a tragic note with the assassination of popular Mayor Carter Harrison by a deranged office-seeker. Like the city he led. Mayor Harrison experienced something of a spiritual and social rebirth during the Fair and was even anticipating a third marriage. The elaborately planned closing ceremonies were sharply curtailed. The angry crowds on the Midway grew ugly. Soon the exhibits were slowly dismantled and the buildings deserted. Economic and labor woes continued to beset Chicago in the winter of 1893/94, and the fairgrounds were vandalized by unemployed vagrants and roving street gangs. The desecration of the White City was completed on July 5, 1894, when the great structures were torched by striking railway workers. The White City was reduced to skeletal girders and burned-out rubble. Only the Palace of Art survived this holocaust because of its brick construction and marginal location and today houses the Museum of Science and Industry.[16]16 Time has obliterated even trace memories of the momentous events that took place in Hyde Park almost a century ago. The nameless Oglala Sioux warriors who witnessed the Opening Day ceremonies are long gone, but the circumstantial moral issues posed by Indian presence at the Fair remain with us today. Such is progress.

References [23]

Anonymous 1893a *Das Columbische Weltausstellungs-Album.* Rand, McNally and Company, Chicago.
    1893b *Glimpses of the World's Fair.* Laird and Lee, Chicago.
    1893c *The Columbian Exposition Album.* Rand, McNally and Company, Chicago.
    n.d *The Vanished City.* Werner Company, Chicago.
Appelbaum, Stanley 1980 *The Chicago World's Fair of 1893: A Photographic Record.* Dover Publications. New York.
Badger, R Reid 1979 *The Great American Fair.* Nelson Hall, Chicago.
Bancroft, Hubert Howe n.d *The Book of the Fair.* 1894. Reprint. Bounty Books, New York.
Benedict, Burton 1983 The Autobiography of World's Fairs. In *The Anthropology of World's Fairs: San Francisco's Panama Pacific International Exposition of 1915*: 1-65. Burton Benedict, et al. The Lowie Museum of Anthropology, Berkeley, in association with Scolar Press.
Bloom, Sol 1948 *The Autobiography of Sol Bloom.* G.P Putnam's Sons, New York.
Bourke, John G 1891 *Scatologic Rites of All Nations: A Dissertation upon the Employment of Excrementious Remedial Agents in Religion, Therapeutics, Divination, Love Philters, etc. in All Parts of the Globe.* W.H Lowdermilk, Washington, D.C.
Collier, Donald 1969 Chicago Comes of Age: The World's Columbian Exposition and the Birth of the Field Museum. *Bulletin Field Museum of Natural History* 40 (5): 2-7.
Deloria, Vine Jr 1981 The Indians. In George Weisman et al., *Buffalo Bill and the Wild West.* University of Pittsburgh Press, Pittsburgh.
Dexter. Ralph W 1966 Putnam's Problems Popularizing Anthropology. *American Scientist* 54: 315-332.
Goodspeed, Thomas Wakefield 1916 *A History of the University of Chicago: The First Quarter-Century.* University of Chicago Press, Chicago. [24]
Hoxie, Frederick E 1984 *A Final Promise: The Campaign to Assimilate the Indians, 1880-1920.* Cambridge University Press, New York.
Ingram, J.S 1876 *The Centennial Exposition Described and Illustrated.* Hubbard Bros., Philadelphia.
Jenks, Tudor 1893 *The Century World's Fair Book for Boys and Girls.* Century Co., New York.
Joint Committee on Ceremonies 1893 *Memorial of the World's Columbian Exposition.* Stone, Kastler, and Painter, Chicago.
MacCannell, Dean 1976 *The Tourist: A New Theory of the Leisure Class.* Schocken Books, New York.
Mason, Otis Tufton 1897 *Woman's Share in Primitive Culture.* D. Appleton and Company, New York.
McCabe, James D 1975 *The Illustrated History of the Centennial Exhibition.* 1876. Reprint. National

---

16 The building was refurbished and made permanent by a generous gift from philanthropist Julius Rosenwald of Sears-Roebuck before the Century of Progress in 1933-34.

Publishing Company, Philadelphia.

Miller, Ross 1990 *American Apocalypse: The Great Fire and the Myth of Chicago.* University of Chicago Press, Chicago.

Porter, Joseph C 1986 *Paper Medicine Man: John Gregory Bourke and his American West.* University of Oklahoma Press, Norman.

Putnam, FW 1894 Introduction. *Portrait Types of the Midway Plaisance.* N.D Thompson Publishing Co., St Louis.

Rydell, Robert W 1984 *All the World's a* Fair. University of Chicago Press, Chicago,

Sanborn, Rev John W 1894 Report on the New York Indian Exhibit. In *Report of the Board of General Managers of the Exhibit of the State of New York at the World's Columbian Exposition.* James B. Lyon, Albany.

Sell, Henry Blackman, and Victor Weybright 1955 *Buffalo Bill and the Wild West.* Oxford University Press. New York. [25]

Smith, Harlan I]901 Notes on Eskimo Traditions. In *Report of the Committee on Awards of the World's Columbian Commission.* House of Representatives Document No. 510, Vol. 1: 347-354. Government Printing Office, Washington.

Smith, HS, And CR Graham 1893 *The Magic City: A Portfolio of Original Photographic Views of the Great World's Fair.* Historical Publishing Co., Philadelphia.

Stocking, George W, Jr 1987 *Victorian Anthropology.* The Free Press, New York and London.

Todd, F Dundas 1893 *World's Fair through a Camera.* Woodward and Tiernan Printing, St Louis.

Wake, C Staniland 1894 *Memoirs of the International Congress of Anthropology.* The Schulte Publishing Company, Chicago.

Weimann, Jeanne Madeline 1981 *The Fair Women: The Story of the Woman's Building. World's Columbian Exposition.* Chicago 1893. Academy Chicago, Chicago.

Yost, Nellie Snyder 1979 *Buffalo Bill: His Family, Friends, Fame, Failures, and Fortunes.* The Swallow Press, Chicago.

St Louis

EXHIBITING NATIONALISM AT THE 1904 ST LOUIS WORLD'S FAIR

The Universal Exposition at St Louis in 1904 commemorated, one year late, the centenary of the Louisiana Purchase. This acquisition substantially expanded and consolidated the territorial boundaries of the new American republic. The St Louis Fair also celebrated the emergence of the United States as a world power, with its own internal and overseas colonies, following the Spanish American War. In a previous paper, "Red Man in the White City." I discussed the presentation and representation of American Indians at Chicago's World Columbian Exposition in 1893. Along with other commentators. I noted a serious conflict, or crisis of representation, vis a vis the American Indian and, to a lesser extent, other native peoples bought to the Fair for display. Should Indians embody their distinctive neo-aboriginal "otherness" or should they demonstrate the progress made along the long hard trail of civilization through education? For many in the civilizational camp, the appearance of Indians in reconstructed ethnologic villages, in wild west shows, and in other exploitative commercial ventures was demeaning and retrogressive. Others, including many Indians themselves, took a more benign or positive view of participation in such staged cultural performances. As L.G Moses (1991) has convincingly shown, the show business Indian was just beginning to be recognized as a valid social category. Commissioner of Indian Affairs, Thomas Jefferson Morgan, took a compromised position whereby displays of traditional Indian cultures might be juxtaposed against model Indian schools to illustrate the inexorable march of progress between generations of grandparents and grandchildren. As is well known, Indian population hit its nadir of about 250,000 people in the 1890s; the general sentiment was that the passing of the not-so-great race was at hand. Disappearance through extinction or assimilation seemed imminent.

Chicago in 1893 witnessed the apotheosis of Christopher Columbus and an appreciation of Spanish contributions to the discovery and conquest of the New World. Columbian memorabilia, some 890 items in all. were collected and displayed in a replica of the La Rabida monastery. Over five hundred statues of Columbus adorned the [2] landscaped grounds of the pristine White City.

In another paper that I delivered to this association in 1991,1 noted the sea change that took place between Chicago's Fair in 1893 and the 1904 St Louis Fair. With the successful conclusion of the Spanish American War, the United States took control of the Spanish colonies of Puerto Rico, Cuba, Guam, and the Philippines and assumed responsibility for new colonial "wards." Particular attention focused upon the native inhabitants of the Philippines, who ranged from "primitive pygmies" and "heathen head hunters" to Muslim pirates, and acculturated Christians.

Given the theme of the Louisiana Purchase and the recency of the Spanish American War, Columbus's stature, as well as his statuary, was greatly diminished in the 1904 St Louis Fair. Thomas Jefferson, if anyone, was the patron saint of the Louisiana Purchase Exposition.

An arrangement of strategically selected and commissioned human statues symbolized historical process. First were the early explorers of the Mississippi Valley – such figures as Cabeza de Vaca, De Soto, La Salle, and Father Marquette. Some Indian statuary of a token sort, such as a highly stylized depiction of a Buffalo Dance, was interspersed along with representations of white frontiersmen, such as the bemused image of a cowboy at rest. More laden with social commentary and allegorical pathos were two statues of downtrodden Indian chiefs. Thus we read in a picture caption of JE Eraser's statue of a Cherokee Chief: "the sculptor has followed nature closely copying the physical defects of both man and horse. The slovenly Indian with his barbaric trappings astride an ungainly pony of degenerate breed." More poignant is Cyrus Dallius's statue of a Sioux chief in a dramatic pose of resistance. Let me provide the captioned word slide:

The Protest of the Sioux – That advancing civilization in the Territory of Louisiana was not altogether by unobstructed pathway is told in sculpture. "The Protest" is mute but intense. The Indian warrior who gestures his defiance is stripped for battle. He belongs to the period before the white man's weapons found their way into the red man's hand. A single strip of leather gives his bridle control. The horse is not the Indian pony of later days on the reservation. He is well built and spirited, a reminiscence of the generations ago when droves of wild horses ranged over the western plains. The Indian leans forward and weaponless throws out his clenched fist toward the coming invasion of his country. The emotion is further expressed in the jerk which the left hand has given to the rawhide, pulling the horse backward almost to his haunches and wrenching the mouth open. Rider and horse together tell the story of the rage and the impotent antagonism to the inevitable. The nakedness of the Indian and the ragged hair of the horse add to the desperation of "The Protest" [in [3] their revelation of its usefulness [sic?]] On all sides the World's Fair presents the evidence of the white man's accomplishment in the Louisiana Territory. The spirit of development abounds. The noise of progress fills the air. One solitary attitude of defiance, one fierce note of discord is "The Protest of the Sioux."

The parade of statuary continues with important men of government and foreign affairs, ultimately culminating in heroic statues of Napoleon and Jefferson.

The St Louis Fair was literally an anthropological field day. Indeed, Professor Frederick Starr even instructed University of Chicago co-eds by using native villages at the Fair as his classroom. Fresh from his scandal-chastened departure as head of the Bureau of American Ethnology, WJ McGee was in charge of far-flung Section N, Anthropology. Efforts to popularize anthropology transcended even those of Chicago in 1893. McGee saw the mission of his Department of Anthropology to be "to show each half of the world how the other half lives, and thereby to promote not only knowledge but also peace and goodwill among the nations; for it is the lesson of experience that personal contact is the best solvent of enmity and distrust between persons and people ... this department is planned and organized in accordance with the motive of bringing together so many as may be of the world's races and peoples in harmonious assemblage, to the end that all the world may profit by mutual and sympathetic study of Man and Men's achievement." Despite these noble goals, McGee's popularization of anthropology often took jingoist and racist turns.

Nevertheless, a wide spectrum of the world's people came to St Louis. Starr brought nine mild-mannered Ainus from northern Hokkaido. There were large numbers of Zulus and Kaffirs who performed in the daily reenactment of the Boer War. Extremes of physical type included seven Tuelche Patagonian supposed giants, who turned out to be shorter than Cocopa men brought in from southeastern California, and four Batwa Pygmies from the wilds of Central Africa who were brought to the Fair. One African Pygmy, Ota Benga by name, later gained notoriety by being installed in a cage with apes in the Bronx Zoo and later ended his tragic life by suicide in a seminary in Lynchburg, Virginia.

American Indians were a prominent presence on the Pike, St Louis's answer to Chicago's Midway. There were cliff-dwelling Zuni's and Hopis displaying their traditional life-ways and performing the Snake and Antelope Dances. Cummins' Indian Congress and Wild West Show convened beside the Pike and featured scores of Plains warriors. Alaskan [4] Eskimos and Aleuts had their own area of artificial icebergs and glacial ponds to give at least an illusion of tepid coolness to the damp summer St Louis heat.

All told, there were reported to be representatives of over 70 tribes, including delegations of Sioux, Pawnees, Wichitas, Arapahos, Cheyennes, Osages, Kiowas, Kickapoos, Maricopas, Cocopas, Navajos, Apaches, Kwakiutls and Nootkas. The largest concentration of Indians was located on an intertribal reservation of 40 acres on the extreme western side of the fairgrounds. The reservation was dominated by a large Indian school, executed in mission-style architecture, which displayed within a wide range of arts and crafts, as well as educational exhibits. Elsewhere on the Indian reservation were various teepees, wigwams, and other traditional dwellings, as well as "huts and little cottages which," as one source cites, "Uncle Sam builds for his copper-colored children."

Just north of the Indian encampment could be found another forty acre area reserved for peoples of the Philippines. The Philippine reservation really constituted a fair within a fair. One crossed Arrowhead Lake by one of several bridges and entered a replica of the old walled city of Manila. Here and in the surrounding area were several substantial buildings that replicated major organizing categories of the larger exposition. There was a government building, education building, and separate buildings devoted to commerce, agriculture, mining, forestry, fish and game, women, and ethnology. Over eleven hundred Filipinos lived in native villages or in military encampments on the Philippine reserve.

The original inspiration for bringing over such a large and diverse contingent of Filipinos was former civil governor William Howard Taft. The stated goal was:

"to familiarize the American public with the various and incongruous elements of the Philippine population, differing in race, language, and religion, and representing many stages of social progress form the lowest type of head-hunting savage to the best products of Christian Civilization and culture. A polyglot assemblage of Negritos, Igorrotes, Moros, Bogobos, and Visayans – of Christians, Mohammedans, and heathens – was the best possible demonstration of the need of a common language and American common schools to efface tribal antagonisms and fit these people for local self-government and eventually transform them into a harmonious and vigorous nationality."

American officials accused the former Spanish colonial government of deliberately keeping Philippine populations separate and diverse to forestall any possible Pan-Philippine insurrection. [5]

One release by the Department of Press and Publicity captures the contrast of the Indian and Philippine exhibitions in succinct rhetorical fashion:

"The red man of America and the brown man of Oceanica, both races the wards of Uncle Sam, both including many tribes are side by side, each on a forty-acre tract. One pathetic difference between the red man and the brown is brought out at this twin exhibition, and that is the Indian is a disappearing race, while the Filipino appears to be just on the eve of a substantial and lasting development."

However, extremes within the Philippine cultural continuum are clearly recognized by the official publicist of the Fair:

"About the time the World's Fair city is waking at early morning, one hundred [sic] bare-limbed Igarot often sacrifice and eat a dog on the Philippine reservation. At the same hour scarcely two hundred yards away, a bugle sounds reveille, and four-hundred well-trained soldiers in the blue of the United States Army hustle from their tents. They are the Philippine Scouts. The yells of the dog-dance have scarcely ceased before the blue line is formed for roll calls, and the Philippine soldiers stand at attention beneath an American flag, while a Philippine band plays an American air. All of these people live on the same island in the Philippines. The Igorot represent the wildest race of savages, the Scouts stand for the results of American rule – the extremes of the social order in the islands."

The dog-eating Bantoc Igorots attracted throngs of Fair visitors, and the St Louis Department of Sanitation was hard-pressed to maintain a steady supply of stray dogs. Fair officials were slightly embarrassed by the public, if not Igorot taste, while humane societies were outraged by dog feasts. Yet even these nearly naked, head-hunting, dog-eating Igorots could be salvaged. It was declared by scientists, "that with proper training they are susceptible of a high stage of development, and unlike the

American Indians, will accept rather than defy the advance of American Civilization."

To conclude, American nationalist sentiments were clearly ascendant in St Louis in 1904. The Louisiana Purchase Exposition not only celebrated a defining event in American nationhood, but provided a nation-building and nation-demolition site with regard to the treatment of, evaluation of, and hopes for indigenous peoples. Remaining claims to distinctive nationhood status for American Indians were predicted to wither away, while Philippine national aspirations were expected to flourish under the American banner. It is ironic that Philippine national integration is still far from realized today and that relations with Uncle Sam, the former avuncular benefactor, have turned sour. American Indians, [6] contrary to prescribed wisdom, refused to vanish, either biologically, culturally, or politically. They still vigorously defend their tribal sovereignty vis á vis federal and state governments. And dreams of nationalism linger.

BAR ON RECOGNITION CRITERIA:
Myth-Making and History-Making at the
Branch of Acknowledgement and Research of
The Bureau of Indian Affairs[1]

Mainstream media manifest increased interest in problems involved with Federal recognition of Indian tribes. Many recent articles have appeared that acknowledge recognition as a serious issue. Cynthia Brown's "The Vanished Native Americans", published in the October 11th issue of *The Nation* (1993: 384-389), provides an informal survey of the economic and political factors implicated in the recognition process. Kirk Johnson's brief account on "Tribal Rights: Refining the Law of Recognition," which appeared in the New York Times (October 17, 1993), is more alarmist in reporting the dangers of gambling interest influencing tribal recognition of such groups as the Ramapough Mountain Indians of New Jersey, whose petition was subsequently turned down by the Branch of Acknowledgement and Research [BAR], and the Golden Hill Paugussetts of Bridgeport, Connecticut, whose chances of recognition appear slim. Tribal recognition of these groups, located on the periphery of greater New York City, and the subsequent establishment of gaming facilities would have doubtless not only skimmed off some of the profits at Foxwoods, but also significantly lowered the take at Atlantic City.

The financial profits of gaming cannot be underestimated as a major motivation for seeking Federal recognition. Fear of organized crime gaining control of gambling operations is not [2] fantasy. The casino on the Rincon reservation in the mountains of southern California was allegedly run by the Chicago mob, and big-time gambling interests are suspected to be responsible for some of the recent "unpleasantness" among the Mohawks at Akwasasne. Gaming serves as a short-term fix for troubled tribal economies, but it doesn't seem to be the solution to more enduring problems of poverty, unemployment, and social disorganization. However, if the gaming windfall is invested wisely, as seems to be happening among the Mashantucket Pequots, in such things as increasing the reservation land base, building up local infrastructure, encouraging education, offering human services, and promoting industrial and/or tourist development, there can be a longer-term payoff. Too many tribes think the golden goose will continue to lay golden eggs indefinitely, or to employ an analogy used by many tribes, believe the return of "the buffalo" is permanent. In many areas of the country, gaming already shows signs of reaching a saturation point of diminishing returns. However, if gaming continues to be a dramatic growth industry, the white over-culture will surely challenge the Indian monopoly. Before there is roulette in the Ramapough Mountains, or blackjack in Bridgeport, there will doubtless be high-stakes riverboat casinos plying the Hudson.

The longer-term benefits of Federal recognition seem more mundane, yet ultimately more substantial, than the immediate glitter of gaming. Yet it should be emphasized that BIA funds to Indian tribes represent only a small fraction of the income [3] garnered from gaming. With recognition comes improved health provisions, educational services, housing and programs, seed money for economic development, and self-government. Federal recognition is not, however, the unmixed blessing that many unrecognized groups imagine it to be. Dealing with the BIA can bring stressful bureaucratic frustrations. The promise of new prosperity can prove delusional. Thus even though I strongly support Lumbee recognition on ethnohistorical and legal grounds, I have encountered some Lumbees who feel that recognition would only accentuate cleavages already present in their society, such as the split between the

---

1 I offer gratitude to Jack Campisi and Bill Starna for inviting me to the Second Mashantucket Pequot History Conference, October 21-23, 1993, for which this paper was prepared. I wish to thank Chairman Richard Hayward and Terry H Bell of the Mashantucket Pequot Tribal Nation for their unstinting hospitality and for doing such a fine job in arranging the Conference. Terry Straus gave this paper a good critical reading. I would also like to acknowledge Susan Schroeder for inspiration and Anne Ch'ien for the perspiration of preparing this manuscript.

Lumbees living in cities and towns and those residing in the rural countryside.

The significance of identity is, perhaps, harder to estimate in evaluating group and individual motivations to seek Federal recognition. For people who have kept alive claims to be Indians in the face of chronic discrimination and disenfranchisement, the achievement of Federal recognition can, indeed, be very ego-syntonic and self-fulfilling, even to the point of transcending considerations of material gain. For other groups, such as the Wampanoags of Gay Head, as described by Bill Starna in this volume, attainment of Federal recognition can result in anti-climactic depression. Some groups who could mount strong cases for Federal recognition do not feel the effort is worthwhile. Thus, until recently, many Tidewater Virginia groups, such as the Pumunkeys, Chicahominies and Mattaponies, who can directly trace their descent back to the Powhattan Confederacy were satisfied in [4] asserting and maintaining their status as state recognized Indians by annually delivering a dressed deer as tribute to the Governor of Virginia. Now, however, they are actively pursuing Federal recognition. In sum, motivations to seek, or not seek, Federal recognition are highly variable both within and without different groups, and these motivations can change over time. We must check tendencies to overgeneralize, simplify and demean motives for seeking Federal recognition as Indians.

I now turn to a critical discussion of the location of recognition procedures in the Federal government. As Jack Campisi (1990: 180) has noted, and directly confronted, there are three ways for an Indian group to receive recognition from the Federal Government: first through court action to compel the United States to recognize its trust obligations; second, through direct application to Congress; and third through following the procedure established within the Department of the Interior by the Branch of Acknowledgement and Research [BAR] of the Bureau of Indian Affairs. At first glance these three paths to recognition serendipitously parallel the three macro branches of the United States government: the judiciary, the legislative, and the executive. Each division has its own domains of responsibility, distinctive organization, and primary mode of decision-making. Ideally, at least, the three branches of government serve to diffuse power by operating as a system of checks and balances. In practice, however, this ideal is rarely realized. With respect to Federal recognition of Indian tribes, [5] very few cases are decided through the courts, although those that are often become precedent-setting. The ultimate authority for recognizing Indian tribes has historically and continues to rest with Congress. Until 1871 the only mechanism defining political relations between the United States and Indian Nations were treaties: Treaties required congressional ratification. After the end of the treaty-making period in 1871, Congress continued to legislate Indian political status directly. It was only well into the present century that Congress began to delegate responsibility for Indian recognition to the Department of the Interior. There are provisions in the 1934 Indian Reorganization Act to identify and recognize Indians of one-half or more blood quantum (see Heald this volume). The efforts to ascertain scientifically the blood quantum of the Lumbees under IRA remain a classical example of mindless physical anthropology run amok. Thus at least five Lumbee individuals were identified as having the requisite one-half degree of Indian blood. However, frequently their siblings and parents failed these validating scientific tests.

The procedures for recognition became formalized in 1978 with the establishment of the BAR and with the codification of regulations setting forth necessary and sufficient criteria for recognizing groups as Indian tribes possessing government-to-government relations vis á vis the United States. As is reiterated in these papers, the BAR has been inordinately slow in processing petitions for recognition. Often in frustration and [6] despair many petitioners, including the Lumbees and the Mashantucket Pequots, have sought recognition directly through congressional action. While Congress has unequivocally retained its right to recognize Indians directly, it has frequently declined to exercise its prerogative without strong sponsorship by Senators or Members of the House of Representatives.

Already recognized Indian tribes and many non-Indian interest groups both wish to limit the number of Federally recognized Indian tribes. They have sometimes characterized direct appeals to Congress for recognition as "end runs" around the strict constructionist or constrictionist interpretations of the BAR criteria (Johnson 1993: 6). However, extending the unfortunate football carrying analogy, one would scarcely describe following the BAR regulations as "quarterback sneaks" through the center of the line, even when, as seems to be the case, the defensive line is so stacked against the petitioners. Play-action misdirection may be the better part of career ending valor.

With all due respect to historical contingency, one can ask in retrospect whether the Department of the Interior and its Bureau of Indian Affairs is or has been the most appropriate locale for processing petitions for Federal recognition. Indian affairs were originally located in the War Department. In 1871, with gradual pacification of the frontier, Indian affairs were placed in the Department of the Interior. There the Bureau of Indian Affairs ultimately co-existed with the Bureau of Land [7] Management, Bureau of Mines, Geological Survey, Fish and Wildlife Service, and the National Park Service. Eastern Indians, including the Pequots, were mostly considered to be extinct or; at best, insignificant anachronisms; living or "real" Indians were considered part of the Western environment, almost regarded as a bio-degradable, non-renewable resource. For too many unscrupulous entrepreneurs the path to financial riches was seen to run through Indian lands. The treatment of Indian affairs within the context of the Interior Department naturally lent itself to corruption and mismanagement. The Indian New Deal and other reforms have improved the situation considerably, but as long as the BIA remains in the Department of the Interior, rather than in say. Health, Education and Welfare, where its responsibilities more appropriately belong, suspicions of conflicts of interest will linger.

It should be noted that the wider location of the BIA within the executive branch of government makes it subject, directly or indirectly, to Presidential political influence. The last several administrations have not been particularly friendly to Indian concerns. At several points in recent time, the government expressed a desire to "get out of the Indian business." Encouragement of distinctively Indian life styles and values was viewed as promoting Indian dependency on the Federal government and as raising the incidence of various types of social pathology. With these kinds of voiced or unvoiced sets of assumptions, the atmosphere was not conducive to the recognition [8] of more Indian tribes and more potential government "wards." Despite the recent change of administration and the appointment of an enlightened Commissioner of Indian Affairs, the Honorable Ada Deer, these attitudes of downsizing the number of clients or minimally holding to the status quo seem to persist among the BIA rank and file.

The members of the BAR take pride in trying to be objective in their findings and being above and beyond political influence emanating from outside lobbyists, from representatives of recognized Indians, or from pressures within the agency itself and/or superior sources of authority in the Department of the Interior or the executive branch. Value-free research may be devoutly desired, but it is rarely achieved in the social and human sciences.

In saying all this, I do not intend to impugn the integrity of individual members of the BAR, two of whom fortunately or unfortunately are former Chicago students. As far as I know they are honest, hardworking, well-meaning scholars. However, they may not be immune to the subtle presuppositions and biases inherent in the agency culture in which they operate. As Stephen J Gould has argued in his brilliant book of *The Mismeasure of Man* (1981), unconscious bias and personal equations can even affect such seemingly hard-headed, objective activities as measuring crania. Dr Holly Record, present chief of the BAR is reported to have said, regarding the seven criteria set forth in the regulations that "Fairness is not our eighth criterion" [9] (Brown 1993: 387). Even out of context, this statement seems psychodynamically overdetermined!

Another anomaly arises in locating the BAR within the BIA. The basic charge of the BIA is to administer government programs and to minister to the needs of federally recognized Indians. Thus, in effect, the same public agency, the BIA, apparently has the power to choose whom they will or will not serve. The situation is a bit like that of a public restaurant in which the waiters and waitresses decide that they will serve some customers but not others.

If the BIA and, along with it, the BAR were to be relocated elsewhere in the Executive Branch, then, as I suggested before, the Department of Health, Education and Welfare might be a suitable home. If one were intent on separating the BAR from the BIA, then having recognition responsibilities return to

Congress would seem an obvious move. However, if Congress resumed these primary responsibilities, regional politics would soon become an even larger influence in deciding which tribes get recognized and which do not. Conflicts between state and federal interests would accelerate. Although I haven't thought through all the ramifications, the Department of Justice might prove an appropriate site for adjudications or for referring tribal recognition cases to appropriate agencies.

However, at present, it seems unlikely that the BAR will relocate. Rather, the thinking in Washington seems to be that more appropriations for additional staffing at the BAR will speed [10] up the processing of recognition petitions. While I am happy to see more anthropologists hired by the government, especially if they are former students, this solution doesn't seem to get at the roots of the problem that reside in the BAR regulations themselves.

These regulations were devised by former Acknowledgement Branch Chief John (Bud) Shapard in 1978. The regulations derived from many assumptions implicitly or explicitly expressed in the evolving body of Indian law. Shapard has stated that he intended the regulations to serve as guidelines to simplify rather than complicate the recognition process. However, as is painfully obvious, they have had an opposite effect; they have become the source of much contention over their meaning, interpretation, and application. Shapard, himself, publically repudiates the regulations and believes it is necessary to start anew in determining recognition criteria.

There seems to have been a discernable shift since 1978 from supple guidelines to rules engraven in stone. The notion of guidelines suggests a flexible directionality to be followed rather than a rigid set of commandments to be obeyed unswervingly. This transmogrification from guidelines to unbending regulations, the almost obsessive concern with the letter of law, rather than the spirit of the law, and the adversarial rather than cooperative conduct of inquiry, all indicate to me the pressures under which the BAR staff labors. As employees of the BIA, they are answerable to that agency in [11] one way or another; at the same time they must yield to the ultimate authority of Congress in these matters; they should also be sensitive to the interests of already recognized Indian clients trying to protect their turf and special privileges; and finally they must be able to defend their decisions against dissenting lawyers, advocacy researchers working for unsuccessful petitioners, outspoken ethnohistorians, and all other challenges. Indeed, Holly Record's statement that fairness is not an eighth criterion becomes more explicable.

It is impossible to render a comprehensive critique of the regulations here. However, the concept of a tribe is crucial to the recognition process and can be singled out for discussion. The definition of an Indian tribe has proved vexing not only to legal specialists but to generations of social scientists as well. Elsewhere (Fogelson 1989) I have critically reviewed the various and often contradictory understandings of the meaning of "tribes" in Native North America. In general, I concluded that "tribes" in the exclusive, bounded, legal sense invoked today were rare. Rather, as Morton Fried's underappreciated research (1975) indicated, tribes, as formal sociopolitical entities, emerged primarily in the interactions between native groups and Euro-Americans. In a very real sense political alliances and treaties were a cause as well as effect of tribalism.

This is not to assert that Native Americans lacked cohesive social groups, senses of social solidarity, means of social control, or particular signs and symbols of distinctive identity. [12]

These social entities can be referred to as ethnic groups, or nations, in the etymological sense of membership by birthright, as cultures, or, to employ a newer neologism that I favor, peoplehoods, as a particular collectivity of social persons. My point is that these were dynamic social units that lacked some of the typological specificities, continuities, and permanence demanded by the present BAR criteria.

Immanuel Wallerstein, in a recent book entitled *Race, Nation, Class: Ambiguous Identities* that he co-authored with Etienne Balibar, captures the kind of dynamism and historicity that I argue characterize tribes. Let me quote Wallerstein:

> the multiple communities to which all belong, whose values we hold, towards which we express

"loyalties", which define our "social identity", are all, one and all, historical constructs, and even more importantly, they are historical constructs perpetually undergoing reconstruction. This is not to say they are not solid or meaningful or that we think them ephemeral. Far from it! But these values, loyalties, identities are never primordial and, that being the case, any historical description of their structure or their development through the centuries is necessarily primarily a reflection of present-day ideology (1991: 228).

Picking up on Wallerstein's final point about the presentist bias in historical descriptions of structure and process, we can readily appreciate how our own attitudes about tribes and tribalism have changed radically over time. Charles F Wilkinson, in his book *American Indians, Time, and the Law* (1987), has cogently shown how official attitudes and policies toward Indian tribes have varied over time between ideas of permanence and impermanence. If one believed that tribalism represented a backward, atavistic, or anachronistic way of life, [13] then extermination and termination, religious conversion or relocation, allotment of lands and assimilation could all be rationalized as legitimate governmental policies. However, if tribes and tribalism are taken as permanent conditions, as a valid alternate life style, then such policies as those embedded in the Indian Reorganization Act, the Indian Claims Commission, or movements directed toward self-determination, rematriation or repatriation, retribalization, religious freedom, and an increase in the number of Federally recognized tribes are all justified. While I don't think that ideology is all-determinant, I do think it has much to do with how supposed objective facts are prioritized and interpreted.

When Bill Starna and Jack Campisi initially invited me to participate in this symposium, I asked them what I should talk about. They half seriously suggested that I might examine whether the Eastern Cherokees would be recognized today if they were compelled to satisfy BAR recognition criteria, Campisi and Starna are motivated by the fact that the Eastern Cherokees have been outspoken opponents of Federal recognition for the Lumbees. Although I refuse to be suckered into advocating anything like Eastern Cherokee detribalization, for I maintain enduring respect and affection for the Eastern Cherokee people. The Starna/Campisi challenge, nevertheless, does help make my point about how selection or interpretation of evidence can be manipulated to support ideological concerns.

If one were to make a positive case for Eastern Cherokee [14] tribal recognition, there would be no problem of identification with and descent from a historically known tribe or of their spatial separation and cultural distinctiveness from their neighbors. The Eastern Cherokees have never been without traditional or elected chiefs and tribal councils. They have never become members of another tribe.

However, if one were to decide against Eastern Cherokee recognition, one could show that most of the immediate ancestors of the Eastern Cherokees were residing on lands that had been ceded by treaty to the United States in 1819, that they struck a deal with local white authorities to remain in their isolated locale in the Great Smokies, but that they had no legal status vis á vis the state of North Carolina nor with the Federal government (King 1979: 165). The mountain Cherokees mostly managed to escape the tragic 1838 Removal of the Cherokee Nation to lands in the Indian Territory. The *Journal of Cherokee Studies* (Fall 1979) provides a fine compilation of primary accounts on the events that enabled the Eastern Cherokees to remain in North Carolina. Despite repeated efforts to reunite them with their Western tribesmen, the Eastern Cherokees steadfastly refused to leave their homeland. Such action might be interpreted by legal specialists hell bent on detribalizing the Eastern Cherokees, as voluntary termination, a conscious, unforced decision to separate from the main body of their tribe. In other words, they would fail to satisfy the seventh criterion for Federal recognition. The ambiguous legal status of the [15] Eastern Cherokees was not resolved until the 1880s when the Federal government assumed trusteeship over threatened Cherokee lands and legally established the reservation of the Eastern Band of the Cherokee Indians (Finger 1984: 101-125). Although denominated as a band, for all intents and legal purposes the Eastern Cherokees have been ever since treated as a separate tribe by the Federal government.

The case of the emigrated Western Cherokees can also be taken to demonstrate variable interpretations of recognition criteria. Like the Pequots, whose tribal rebirth we honor after the nearly successful "ethnic cleansing" of 1637, the Cherokee Nation has experienced several renaissances. The Cherokees survived several scorchings of their settlements during the Colonial period. After pacification and the rebuilding of their towns and villages, the Cherokees became the popular prototype for a progressive, civilized Indian tribe. In 1838 the Cherokee Nation was once more nearly destroyed by the dislocation and death caused by the Trail of Tears, 'the path where we wept'. Again the Cherokee Nation was reconstituted in the West only to endure another catastrophe with the Civil War in which Cherokees fought Cherokees and the land was devastated as Confederate and Union troops took turns crisscrossing the Indian Territory. In the 1890s the Cherokee Nation was legally dismembered. The opening of the Cherokee Outlet, an illegal land grab whose recent centennial was officially commemorated by U.S. postal stamps, statues, and public celebrations, was an event that shook [16] Cherokee sovereignty to the core. This is a day of mourning for Cherokees. Opening the outlet to boomers and sooners smoothed the way for the Dawes Commission, set the stage for the Allotment Act, and led to the dissolution of the Cherokee Nation through the enabling legislation of the Curtis Act in 1898. The Cherokee Nation supposedly officially expired in 1907 with Oklahoma statehood.

However, today another Cherokee renaissance is occurring. The Cherokees are the second largest tribe in the United States. Federal money is pouring into the Cherokee Nation in the form of job corps training, HUD, and various economic development programs. The Cherokees recently staged a successful conference to celebrate their own history, and soon after hosted a momentous intertribal conclave that included Indian leaders from all over the continent. Under Chief Wilma Mankiller, who has achieved national visibility, the general mood is upbeat. The manner in which the moribund Cherokee Nation was resuscitated should give pause to the recognition experts at the BAR.

After Allotment, a skeletal Cherokee government was briefly maintained to settle final affairs. In subsequent years, except for temporary appointments to attend to previous treaty obligations and claims, the Cherokee had no official government. In the late 1930s a wealthy oil man of Cherokee descent, J. Bartley Milam, assumed leadership and began to shape the most recent rebirth of the Cherokee Nation. His efforts were officially recognized by the United States in 1941 when he was [17] named Principal Chief (Meredeth 1985). Before his death in 1949, Milam presided over a national convention that restored the tribal council and provided for other tribal offices. W.W. Keeler, another wealthy oil man with some Cherokee ancestry was appointed Principal Chief by Harry Truman in 1949. Keeler remained Chief for 26 years, but it was a part-time job at best, since most of the time he spent as President and Chairman of the Board of Phillips Petroleum Company. In 1971 the Cherokees by referendum decided to hold elections for tribal officials, Keeler won easily. He was succeeded by his hand-picked successor, Ross Swimmer, who resigned in mid-term to become Assistant Secretary of the Department of the Interior. Wilma Mankiller, as Deputy Chief, filled Swimmer's unexpired term and later won a landslide election of her own.

Before Keeler retired, a new constitution was approved by referendum in 1975. It called for the election of a Principal Chief, Deputy Principal Chief, and a Council of fifteen members elected at-large (Meredith 1985: 127). The new constitution also restored the three branches of government: the legislative, executive, and judicial.

In brief, not only was the Cherokee Nation terminated in 1907 and thus would fail the Branch of Acknowledgement's seventh criterion, but it could also be reasonably argued that from 1907 to at least 1941, the Cherokees lacked a recognizable form of government and thus failed the Branch's third criterion. Nevertheless, I don't think the BAR would care to challenge the [18] legitimacy of the Cherokee Nation today.

These reviews of the two Cherokee tribes, then, reinforce the conclusions made by many others about the inconsistencies and apparent arbitrariness of the BAR criteria for recognition. I also contend that the decisions of the BAR are not value-free nor devoid of ideological influences. Indeed, if the government's policy is to "get out of the Indian business" and keep down the number of tribes it must deal with, then a logical strategy would be to complicate the interpretation of the criteria for recognition unduly as a way to discourage petitioners from exercising their legal rights and to downshift the process into low stall.

One can complain about the slowness of the recognition process, as well as the fairness of some of the decisions, especially the Miami Nation of Indiana case and the Samish case, but the majority of the rejected cases had little claim to recognized tribal status. I think most people would agree that there has to be some gate-keeping mechanism at work to prevent Federal recognition of any group of Wanabees. But it will take a massive effort to rethink and reform the present recognition procedures, as well as to undo the damage already done.

By way of conclusion, I'll try to explicate my title. By myth-making at the BIA, I refer to the setting up of criteria for recognition that are neither meaningful nor culturally sensitive to Indian realities or to the particular experiences of the groups to whom the criteria are mechanically applied. Secondly, [19] the BAR seems to believe in the primordial existence of and uniformity of historically constructed social entities called tribes. As such, the BAR procedures contribute to the myth of the tribe and in so doing help to create and perpetuate that which they are trying to define through mechanical application of questionable recognition criteria.

By history-making I mean the tons of documentation and testimony that are generated by the procedures for completing petitions. This history, however, is distorted and biased toward the limited set of issues required to answer the BAR criteria, But of even more history-making significance is the dramatic effect that BAR decisions have and will have on the careers of various social groups.

The BAR has taken on a profound and awesome responsibility – reminiscent, perhaps, of such momentous and awe-filled undertakings as the task that God bestowed on Adam, to nominalize the world and name all its beings. But does the BAR have such divine sanction?

References [21]

Balibar, Etienne, and Immanuel Wallerstein 1991 *Race, Nation, Class: Ambiguous Identities.* New York: Verso.
Brown, Cynthia 1993 The Vanished Native Americans. The Nation (October 11): 384-389.
Campisi, Jack 1990 The New England Tribes and Their Quest for Justice. *The Pequots in Southern New England.* LM Hauptman and JD Wherry, eds. Norman: University of Oklahoma Press.
Finger, John R 1984 *The Eastern Band of Cherokees, 1819-1900.* Knoxville: University of Tennessee Press.
Fogelson, Raymond D 1989 The Context of American Indian Political History: An Overview and Critique IN *The Struggle for Political Autonomy.* F Hoxie, ed. Occasional Papers in Curriculum Series No. 11: 8-21. Chicago: The Newberry Library.
Fried, Morton H 1975 *The Notion of the Tribe.* Menlo Park, CA: Cummings.
Gould, Stephen J 1981 *The Mismeasure of Man.* New York: Norton.
Johnson, Kirk 1993 Tribal Rights: Refining the Law of Recognition. New York Times (October 17).
Journal of Cherokee Studies 1979 Vol. 4, Fall.
King, Duane H 1979 The Origin of the Eastern Cherokees as a Social and Political Entity, IN Duane H. King, ed., *The Cherokee Indian Nation: A Troubled History.* Knoxville: University of Tennessee Press.
Meredeth, Howard L 1985 *Hartley Milam: Principal Chief of the Cherokee Nation.* Muskogee, OK: Indian University Press.
Wilkinson, Charles F 1987 *American Indians, Time, and the Law.* New Haven: Yale University Press.

Identity

PERSPECTIVES NATIVE AMERICAN IDENTITY

Native American identity is central to the concerns of Native American studies programs. This chapter offers some perspectives on this complex topic. Perspectives are ways of viewing or lines of vision. To gain perspective, one usually steps back in space and time. The perspectives on identity offered here are conceptual and historical. By "conceptual" I mean that the idea of identity is neither singular nor monolithic but has many dimensions that may be usefully separated for purposes of analysis. The presentation followed here is loosely historical in that I am interested in the development of external images, as well as self-reflection, of Indianness through time. However, I am not a (or an) historian, so that specific dating, contextual circumstances, and complete citations may often be lacking. One commentator on an earlier draft of this chapter noted that it needs more Indian "voices." I agree. Hopefully what I have to say wilt provoke the critical acumen of historical colleagues as well as raise Native American voices from both the living and the dead.

I begin with some general considerations of the meaning of identity. Next I survey names that have been collectively applied to the native inhabitants of the New World. A discussion of three primary attributes of Native American identity follows: blood and descent, relations to land, and sense of community. Many other attributes of identity are recognized by Indians and non-Indians, including language usage, cultural participation and performances, dress, physical features, consumption of Indian foods, and particular styles of [41] life. However, blood, land, and community remain the sine qua non for legal recognition as tribal Indians, whereas other identity markers tend to be employed more flexibly: they can be lost and regained or, if I may be excused, invented or reinvented.[1]

General Considerations on Identity

We hear and read much about identity politics, identity struggles, and ethnic identity, but rarely is identity itself clearly or consistently defined. One set of meanings refers to an image or set of images of oneself or one's group. The basic notions of identity in these usages involve communication of a sense of oneself or one's group intrapsychically to oneself or projected outwardly to others. Identity in this regard may contain several components. For instance, Anthony FC Wallace and RD Fogelson recognize that an individual, and by extension a group, may comprise an ideal identity, an image of oneself that one wishes to realize; a feared identity, which one values negatively and wishes to avoid; a "real" identity, which an individual thinks closely approximates an accurate representation of the self or reference group;[2] and a claimed identity that is presented to others for confirmation, challenge, or negotiation in an effort to move the "real" identity closer to the ideal and further from the feared identity.[3]

---

1 I would like to thank Russell Thornton for his patience and encouragement in helping me complete this chapter. When he originally suggested that I write 'something on Native American identity, I realized that the course was uncharted and would be difficult to navigate, but I never thought I would be at sea, out of sight of land, for so long. Anne Straus and Raymond DeMallie offered useful dialogue, and I also appreciate the commentary of acerbic and fitful readers who helped me keep my bearings. Paul Spruhan was an important interlocutor and bibliographic source.

    The notion of "reinvented culture" is irksome, since it not only sounds like a mechanical "clink," but suggests a lack of authenticity, a fraud perpetrated by "phony folk." Culture is always being reinvented. Who invents the reinventors? See Erik Hobsbawm and Terence Ranger, eds., *The Invention of Tradition* (Cambridge: Cambridge University Press, 1983), for discussion and examples of this approach.

2 "Real" is placed in quotation marks because all identities are real in some sense.

3 See Anthony FC Wallace and Raymond D Fogelson, The Identity Struggle, in *Intensive Family*

These identity components can be arranged in a lineal or ordinal fashion-Thus, in a particular situation a Native American's ideal identity might be that of full blood, a feared identity might be a Wannabee, a "real" identity is a person having three-eighth's blood quantum, and a claimed identity is a person with a nine-sixteenths degree of Indian blood. However, identity components are rarely so ordinal or quantifiable. A group of protesting Native Americans might see their ideal identity as that of traditional warriors, have a feared identity as self-serving "radishes, a "real" identity as a disenfranchised minority fighting for their rights, and a claimed identity, claimed by black T-shirts with a distinctive logo, as active members of the American Indian Movement (AIM). The total image may be instantaneous, although micro-shifts in the relations and content of these identity components might occur in the process of interaction. Identity in this sense is primarily synchronic, concerning the here and now.

I want to emphasize that identity struggles are more social than individual psychological phenomena. Identities are negotiated through interaction with another person or group. Let me produce an imagined scenario to make my point. There is a large discourse about the legal aspects of the Native American Graves Protection and Repatriation Act (NAGPRA), but we have few ethnographic accounts of the implementation of its provisions. One can imagine a confrontation between a Native American tribal representative and a [42] museum anthropologist that takes the form of an identity struggle. The Native American may have an ideal image of himself as an altruistic champion of his tribe, a feared identity as a publicity-seeking fraud representing only himself, a "real" identity as someone trying to reclaim tribal patrimony from the museum, and a claimed identity, marked by braids and shades, a headband, and a finger-woven sash, as a traditional leader. In contrast, the museum anthropologist has an ideal identity as a professional curator responsible for the collections in his or her care and responsive to the politico-legal situation surrounding them. The anthropologist may have a feared identity as a despised "anthro" with an anachronistic colonial mentality who assumes unwarranted expertise. The "real" identity centers on being someone who is negotiating in good faith to return artifacts and physical remains to their rightful heirs. The claimed identity, signaled by a long while coat, an identification badge, and calipers or other tools of the trade, is that of Dr Science, the dispassionate arbiter of objectivity. It is these two claimed identities that meet in the museum storeroom. The potential for misunderstanding and bitter conflict is great, but mutual understanding may be achieved by compromise and through the very process of interaction. Hopefully claims and counterclaims can be settled amicably before a painful and prolonged court case ensues in which nobody really "wins." In short, identities can change through social interaction.

The term "identity" was given a different emphasis by Erik Erikson, who introduced the concept into the social science literature.[4] For Erikson, identity was a processual or historical concept representing the cumulative effects of a series of life cyclical nuclear conflicts. Although the individual changed throughout the life course, identity was held together by threads of continuity. Indeed, in its etymological, sense "identity" means "sameness." (Thus, Erikson's conception of identity resembled William Wordsworth's dictum "the child is father to the man" or Dylan Thomas's image of a "green fuse" that predetermined the pattern of a plant's exfoliation.)

Erikson explained the ethos and ego structure of members of two Native American tribes in terms of unresolved childhood conflicts. Sioux ego identity was epitomized by the skewering of the pectoral muscles in the Sun Dance, reflecting, Erikson thought, an externalized feminine superego. Alas, the poor Yuroks found themselves up the alimentary canal without a paddle, as they worked out their anal fixations

---

Therapy: Theoretical and Practical Aspects, Ivan Boszomen-i-Nagy and James L Framo, eds. (New York: Harper and Row 1965): 365-406. [56]

4 See, for example, Erik H Erikson, *Childhood and Society*, 2d ed. (New York: Norton 1963 [1950]); Erik H Erikson, *Identity and the Life Cycle: Selected Papers*, Psychological Issues, I (1) (New York: International Universities Press 1967 [1959]; Erik H Erikson, "Identity, Psychosocial" in *International Encyclopedia of the Social Sciences* vol. 7, David L Sills, ed. (New York: Macmillan 1968): 61-63.

in adult litigiousness and other forms of mean-spiritedness.[5] [43] continuous form of political organization or community.[6] It is assumed that there exists a linkage forged by a chain of blood and continuous social interaction between historical tribes and their modern descendants, even though there may be such radical discontinuity that present-day Yuroks or Sioux would have a difficult time recognizing, let alone identifying with, the cultures of their ancestors. The "ancient ones" would seem like aliens.

The two conceptions of identity – the communication of self-images and the epigenetic or historical unfolding of identity – are not mutually exclusive. The identity dynamics of presenting self-concepts to others, be they Euro-Americans or other Native Americans, produced counterimages that might be accepted, rejected, or partially assimilated by the individual or group in question. This dialectic, working itself out over long periods of time, could give rise to a sense of historical identity in Erikson's sense of contingent continuity.

Collective Names for Native North American Peoples

The story of how the European-styled "New World" was named in honor of a self-promoting Florentine adventurer, Amerigo Vespucci, requires neither additional retelling nor retailing.[7] Columbus's geographic miscalculation, which resulted in labeling the newly found lands the Indies and its people the Indians ("Los Indies"), is equally well known. "American Indians," used to distinguish those so referred to from Asian or East Indians, became the most general term for the native inhabitants of the United States, Sometimes the term "American Indian" was contracted, a la Euro-American, into "Amerind," but this never received much acceptance from either American Indians or whites (perhaps because it sounds like the peel of an exotic fruit). In the late 1950s there was a brief effort to invert the word order by using the expression "Indian Americans." This shift apparently was an effort to deemphasize the racial, legal, and historical distinctiveness of Native Americans and allow them to achieve parity with, if not become a parody of other assimilated ethnic groups, such as Italian Americans or Japanese Americans. It is not surprising that contemporary efforts at establishing a binomial taxonomy utilizing continent of origins as genus and continent of current residence as species, such as Asian American or African American, or the agglutinatively congealed Euro-American, has avoided the redundancy of American Americans.[8]

Today, the politically correct, and in many cases official, designation is "Native Americans." However, there may be a gradual shift back toward the simpler term "Indians." indeed, the preference for "American Indians" by many tribal leaders and others may reflect the legal language of treaties and other documents securing Indian rights, which references "Indians" and not "Native Americans."[9] One rarely hears Native Americans refer to themselves as Native Americans. "Indians" (sometimes with unvoiced d)

---

5 Erikson, *Childhood and Society*, 114-86.
6 See Frank W Porter III, "Nonrecognized American Indian tribes: An historical and legal perspective," Newberry Library Center for the History of the American Indian, *Occasional Paper Series*, no. 7 (Chicago; Newberry Library 1983).
7 Soon after European colonization, the "New World" also became a new world for surviving Native Americans. See James Merrell, *The Indians' New World: The Catawbas and Their Neighbors from European Contact Through the Era of Removal* (Chapel Hill: University of North Carolina Press 1989); Richard White, *The Middle Ground: Indians, Empires, and Republics in the Great Lakes Region, 1650-1813* (Cambridge: Cambridge University Press 1991).
8 Other terms prevail in other parts of the Americas. "First People" is the preferred term in Canada, although to a badly attuned ear this sounds too grammatical, as in first person plural, or "we"; "*Indigenisia*" is widely used in Latin America; and occasionally one hears "American Aborigines" or, much more rarely (thank goodness), "American Autochthons."
9 I am indebted to one of the anonymous reviewers of an earlier draft of this chapter for this observation.

Identity

seems the term [44] of choice in local discourse. Such differences between official and vernacular terms raise the question of appropriate usage. Native Americans can call Native Americans "Indians" as well as a whole host of other terms generally regarded as derogatory (e.g., "bloods." "skins," "long hairs"), but others use such terms, especially the derogatory ones at their own peril.

"Anthros," a term popularized by Vine Deloria and Floyd Westerman, is taken as a token of derision and calculated disrespect for anthropologists, since it calls into question the moral dimensions of the profession. Anthropologists find it particularly appalling when historians get on the bandwagon and tauntingly refer to them as "anthros"; they sometimes counterattack in kind by referring to historians as "histos," with a long drawn-out sibilants. If anthropologists refer to each other as "anthros," however, it marks a kind of privileged joking relationship. The situation is not unlike the current mascot controversy, which really at base is a problem of totemism. Activists protest against the appropriation of Native American names for sports teams, such as "Indians," "Braves," "Chiefs," "Redskins," "Siwash." One can sympathize with such resentment and recognize the bitter irony in the fact that the people who coined the term "totem" (a Central Algonquian root, usually having reference to a spiritual animal) have become totemized themselves. However, activists conveniently ignore the kind of auto-totemism (not Pontiacs, Jeep Cherokees, or Sun Dances) manifested in the frequent use of terms like "Indians," "warriors," "braves," "chiefs," and more by sports teams at Native American schools and colleges. Without disparaging or belittling the mascot protest, one can observe that when it comes to using stereotypical labels for people's identity, it makes a big difference who calls whom what.

The Attributes of Native American Identity

Native American identity is minimally premised, both endogenously and exogenously on three prerequisites: blood and descent, land, and community.

Blood and Descent

While many Native Americans possessed elaborate theories about the symbolic significance of blood, including theories of procreation, taboos regarding menstrual blood, the function of blood in health and illness, its association with warfare, and its connections with death, the idea of blood quantum as a marker of identity was foreign. For Native Americans identity was primarily associated with kinship. Kinship not only included those with whom one could trace familiar common descent, but could be extended to include more ramifying groups like clans, moieties, and even nations. Moreover, besides biological reproduction, individuals and groups could be recruited into kinship [45] networks through naturalization, adoption, marriage, and alliance. Identity encompassed inner qualities that were made manifest through social action and cultural belief.

In contrast, Euro-American assessments of Native American identity tended to proceed from outside to inside. Skin color and head and body hair figured prominently in early European efforts to classify American Indians and locate their place in nature and the human family. (It will not be reviewed here how Native Americans became red, nor how long head hair and sparse body hair were interpreted as indices of inferiority.)[10] 10 External trails were soon conjoined to more determinate inner physical and psychical entities and processes. The nature of the American Indian "soul" and its relationship to character and salvation were the subject of much debate, as were considerations of menial dispositions, passions, and reason-

---

10 For some discussion of these matters see Raymond D Fogelson, "Interpretation of the American Indian psyche: Some historical notes," *Social Contexts of American Ethnology*, 1840-1984, 1984 Proceeding of the American Ethnological Society, June Helm, ed. (DC: American Anthropological Association 1985): 4-27.

Identity

For Euro-Americans, blood was thought both to symbolize ideally and to embody materially genetic or racial differences. Blood was understood as more than a metaphor for descent; it was believed to be intrinsically important in human generation and regeneration. Female blood was thought to be directly deposited in the fetus, while the male blood was distilled in the testes into semen or seed.[11] These beliefs, which are rooted in western folk biology, bestowed on blood an abiding inherency and transgenerational permanence. Modern science perpetuates these attitudes by employing blood typing as a stable measure of descent, population differences, and individual identity, but, as we learned in the OJ Simpson trial, such measures are hardly foolproof.

The "myth of blood," as Juan Comas terms it, gave rise to ideas of racial purity as a quality to be preserved and to a view of miscegenation as "unnatural," abominable, and polluting.[12] For example, fifteenth-century Spanish ecclesiastical policy considered Spanish intermixture with Moors or with Jews to be defiling to *limpieza de sangre* or "clean blood."[13] The "myth of blood" diffused to the New World along with European flora, fauna, pathogens, and the institution of slavery. Throughout Latin America there developed elaborate classification codes to distinguish degrees of racial admixture between whites and blacks. A person possessing three-quarters black blood was referred to as a "griffe" or "sambo," while seven-eighths blacks were called "sacatris" or "mangos." "Mulatto" designated persons who were one-half black and one-half white; a "quadroon" was one-quarter black; and an "octoroon" was one-eighth black. In some areas the classification went further to include terms for individuals with one-sixteenth, one-thirty-second, or one-sixty-fourth degree of black blood.[14] This complex terminology had only minor utility for Anglo-America. North of Mexico, the proverbial "one drop of black blood" was sufficient to classify a person as black. However, colonial records in Virginia report that one-eighth black blood made one legally a Negro, while in North Carolina the rule was one-sixteenth[15] (and thus the "stigma" of being black [46] might be erased in four or five generations, respectively, and one could legally pass as white provided no additional black blood was acquired).

It is tempting to see the Spanish/Portuguese conception of race mixture as directly ancestral to the development of notions of blood quantum in identifying degrees of Native American ancestry. A similar mindset may be at work, but as Frederick Lomayesva argues, blood quantum arose as a means to define Indian identity for purposes of legal jurisdiction over criminal defendants and went back to the Trade and Intercourse Act of 1834.[16] Also, as Paul Spruhan points out, blood quantification is clearly present in English common law regulating properly inheritance by upper-class heirs of different degrees of blood relationship. Finally, quantitative degrees of relationship were also well established by breeders of livestock.[17]

Intermarriage between whiles and Native Americans was generally considered by Euro-Americans to be less degrading and unnatural than miscegenation with blacks. However, at different times and places such unions were looked upon with scorn. Thus, whites with American Indian wives were

---

11 Winthrop D Jordan, *White Over Black: American Attitudes Toward the Negro* (Chapel Hill: University of North Carolina Press 1968): 166.

12 Juan Comas, *Racial Myths* (Westport: Greenwood 1976 [1951]).

13 JH Elliot, *Imperial Spain*, 1469-1716 (Baltimore: Penguin 1990), 107.

14 See Jordan, *White Over Black*; Russell Thornton, *American Indian Holocaust and Survival: A Population History Since 1492* (Norman: University of Oklahoma Press 1987): 187; and Jack D Forbes, *Africans and Native Americans: The Language of Race and the Evolution of Red-Black Peoples*. 2d ed. (Champaign: University of Illinois Press 1993 [1988]), for excellent discussions of these systems of fractionated descent.

15 Jordan, *White Over Black*: 168.

16 Frederick K Lomayesva, Indian identity and degree of Indian blood, *Red Ink* 3 (1995): 33-37.

17 Paul Spruhan, Quantum of power: Historical origins of blood identification in United States Indian policy, (thesis, Master of Arts Program in the Social Sciences, University of Chicago 1996).

sometimes called "squaw men"; whites with American Indian husbands were referred to as "buck women"; and the offspring of such unions were sometimes derisively referred to as "mixed breeds" or "white Indians." The term "mustee," derived from mestizo, is sporadically reported from colonial Virginia, the Carolinas, and New York to indicate tribally unrecognized people of mixed American Indian-white or American Indian-black descent.[18] Such people, also referred to as "remnant groups," mestizos, or "triracial isolates," have become more visible in recent years as they seek state or federal recognition as American Indian tribes.[19]

In some sections of the colonial and antebellum South (and elsewhere), marriage with American Indians was positively valued. Starting with Pocahontas and John Rolfe, such marriages were often considered, at least temporarily, as politically advantageous for Indians and whites alike. Traders found it both convenient and economically expedient to have Native American wives and mixed-blood children. Later some southern intellectuals, such as William Gilmore Simms, argued that an infusion of American Indian blood might invigorate the local white population.[20] Intermarriage with American Indians was also regarded by some as a solution to the so-called Indian problem, which was at base a white problem. Intermarriage was viewed as an irreversible step along the path to civilization and the inevitable physical incorporation and cultural assimilation of native peoples. Symbolically, intermarriage with American Indians retroactively legitimized the occupation of Indian territory and assimilated Euro-Americans to the landscape, while distancing them from their European origins.

By the nineteenth century the European "myth of blood" became transmogrified into the calculation of a blood quantum to ascertain degree of [47] "Indianness."[21] Less a deliberate "divide and

---

18 Jordan, *White Over Black*: 168-69; Forbes, *Africans and Native Americans*: 15-18, 221-33.

19 For discussions of some of these groups, see James Mooney, Indian tribes of the District of Columbia. *American Anthropologist* 2 (1889): 259-66; Roland M [57] Harper, A statistical study of the Croatans, *Rural Sociology* 1 (1937): 444-56; Brewton Berry, The Mestizos of South Carolina, *American Journal of Sociology* 51 (1945): 34-41; William H Gilbert, Jr, Memorandum concerning the characteristics of the larger mixed-blood racial islands of the eastern United Slates, *Social Forces* 24 (1946): 438-47; William H. Gilbert, Jr, Surviving Indian groups of the eastern United States, Annual Report of the Smithsonian Institution (Washington, DC: US Government Printing Office 1948); Edward T Price, A geographic analysis of White-Indian-Negro racial mixtures in the eastern United States, Annuls of the Association of American Geographers, 43 (1953): 138-55; Brewton Berry, *Almost White: A Study of Certain Racial Hybrids in the Eastern United States* (New York: Macmillan 1963); Forbes, *Africans and Native Americans*; Joel Williamson, *New People: Miscegenation and Mulattoes in the United States* (New York: New American Library 1975): 178.

20 Simms's remarks appear in an 1845 review of two works by the early American ethnologist Henry Rowe Schoolcraft, which is reprinted in Abraham Chapman, ed., *Literature of the American Indians: Views and Interpretation* (New York: New American Library 1975): 178.

21 Perhaps the best critical review of the issue of blood quantum is Terry P Wilson, "Blood quantum: Native American bloods," in *Racially Mixed People in America*, Maria PP Root, ed. (Newbury Park, Calif.: Sage, 1992): 108-25. See also Spruhan, "Quantum of power," which is a fine recent overview of the historical origins of blood quantum and its uses and abuses in U.S Indian policy. Blood quantum first appears in a legal context to determine jurisdiction over criminal defendants. The key case is United States v. Rogers (1846). William Rogers, white, moved to Indian Territory, married a Cherokee woman, and was adopted into the Cherokee Nation. He was accused of killing another white man who had been similarly adopted. The court ruled that although his adoption made him a legitimate member of the Cherokee Nation, he was still a white man and subject to federal prosecution. See Lomayesva, "Indian identity," for further details.

As is well known, blood quantum later was employed to establish tribal rolls, particularly in connection with implementing the Allotment Act in the 1890s and the later Indian Reorganization

conquer" strategy, blood quantum functioned more as an administrative mechanism for effecting policies of inclusion and exclusion, entitlement and disqualification in such issues as child custody, receipt of health benefits and scholarships, artistic license to authenticate one's work as Indian art, political and criminal jurisdiction, eligibility for health care, settlements of land claims, mining and other resource royalties, and local and federal taxation.[22] However, the long-term consequences of policies employing blood quantum created, and continue to generate, social structural strain and psychological stress, as mixed-bloods often became liminal figures, neither fully American Indian nor fully white. Some mixed-bloods were able to bridge the two culture systems, and they often rose to prominence as political leaders and cultural brokers. Nevertheless, just as frequently mixed-blooded individuals and classes became ready scapegoats for the ills of American Indian communities from the perspectives of both whites and Native Americans. They were taken as degenerate examples of the evils of miscegenation. Later schisms in Indian societies were, of course, marked by opposition between mixed-bloods and/or progressives on one hand and full bloods and/or traditionalists on the other. Yet one must always be cautious in equating blood quantum with cultural and political orientations.

The U.S government, according to Thomas Jefferson Morgan, [he Commissioner of Indian Affairs in the late nineteenth century, was advised to maintain "a liberal and not technical or restrictive construction" with regard to the recognition and rights of mixed-blooded Indians.[23] Thus, many mixed-bloods of varying degrees who were recognized as tribal members by the tribes themselves were declared eligible for property settlements and other benefits due to tribal members from the federal government. This seeming anticipation of Native American self-determination was not as liberal as it appears, for if blood quantum had been construed narrowly in properly rights and other benefits, then most, if not all, treaties that American Indian tribes had entered into with the federal government would have to be declared void and invalid, since mixed-bloods were often instrumental in negotiating treaties and were significant signatories.

Act of the 1930s. See David Beaulieu, "Curly hair and big feet: Physical anthropology and the implementation of land allotment on the While Earth Chippewa reservation," *American Indian Quarterly* 7 (1984): 281-313; Melissa L. Meyer, *The White Earth Tragedy: Ethnicity and Dispossession at a Minnesota Anishinaabe Reservation, 1889-1920* (Lincoln: University of Nebraska Press, 1994), for detailed accounts of the implementation and consequences of allotment based upon blood quantum in a northern Chippewa community.

22 The most spirited defender of the position that employment of blood quantum was a deliberate effort by the federal government to divide American Indians and ultimately bring about genocide is M. Annette Jaimes. See her "Federal Indian identification policy: A usurpation of indigenous sovereignty in North America." in *The State of Native America: Genocide, Colonization and Resistance*, M Annette Jaimes, ed. (Boston: South End Press 1992), and her article "American Indians. American racism: On race, eugenics, and 'mixed bloods,' " in *Occasional Papers in Curriculum* Series 17 (Chicago: Newberry Library 1995).

C Matthew Snipp usefully contrasts administrative definitions of race with mystical [58] and biological definitions in his *American Indians: The First of This Land* (New York: Russell Sage 1989): 28-35. Snipp favors tribal determination of who is and who is not an Indian and is rightfully suspicious of biological tests of identity. Compared with Jaimes, however, his view of governmental intentions in employing blood quantum is less conspiratorial.

The final chapter, "The problematic of American Indian ethnicity," in Joanne Nagel's *American Indian Ethnic Renewal: Red Power and the Resurgence of Identity and Culture* (New York: Oxford University Press 1996), offers a useful summary of many of the issues debated here.

23 U.S Commissioner of Indian Affairs, Annual Report of the Commissioner of Indian Affairs to the Secretary of the Interior for the Year 1890 (Washington, DC: US Government Printing Office 1890): 37.

Identity

The federal government and the courts seemed to favor, at least through the 1930s, a norm of one-half Indian blood for recognition as an American Indian; this was subject, of course, to qualification by already recognized tribes, who might choose to set blood quantum much lower.[24] In fact, the government tried mightily to transform the "myth of blood" into scientific reality by employing physical anthropologists to conduct anthropometric studies and to utilize newly developed serological tests to ascertain blood quantum with scientific precision. Fortunately or unfortunately, such government scientists as Ales Hrdlicka and Frank Setzler were not up to these challenges. After the Indian New Deal under Commissioner of Indian Affairs John Collier in the 1930s and [48] early 1940s, responsibility for setting blood quantum requirements for tribal membership was increasingly vested in individual tribal governments.

Relations to Land

A second defining attribute of Native American identity is land or, better, relations to land. For Europeans, land has always possessed a close and al times metaphysical connection to kinship and descent, as can be inferred from such notions as fatherland and motherland. Eastern European immigrants from a common town or region often felt themselves bound together by special ties as landsmen. Land and descent merge as identity indicators in such expressions as "our boys fight for the land of their fathers and often pay for that land in blood." Europeans had definite ideas of land ownership, whether that ownership was vested in the individual living upon or working the land or whether ultimate ownership rested with a lord, or literally a landlord, a sovereign, or the Lord God of Hosts.[25]

Most of these ideas about land were alien to Native Americans when Europeans first set foot on their shores. Even more strange, surely, were the curious landing rituals the invaders reenacted when they claimed the territory in the name of their country, king, and God and left an effigy or some other marker to memorialize the event.[26] Native Americans certainly had notions of land tenure, land and group boundaries, and right of usage. Moreover, many Native Americans maintained an attachment to land in which their ancestors were buried. NAGPRA is not a recent reflex of political correctness but a delayed response to longstanding Indian grievances. As early as Thomas Jefferson's *Notes on the State of Virginia*, there is reference to Indians making regular pilgrimages to burial mounds; Plains Indians frequently complained about white desecration of scaffold burial sites; and the Iroquois had a taboo

---

24 For one attempt by a Native American to consider some of these issues, see Frell M Owl, Who and what is an American Indian? *Ethnohistory* 9 (1962): 265-84. William T Hagen, Full blood, mixed blood, generic, and ersatz: The persisting problem of Indian identity, *Arizona and the West* 27 (1985): 309-26, offers useful historical understandings. Chapters 1 and 2 in Snipp, *American Indians*, provide lucid discussions of identity issues. For a recent attempt to consider the resurgence of American Indian identity, see Joanne Nagel, "Politics and the resurgence of American Indian ethnic identity," *American Sociological Review* 60 (1995): 947-65. For related issues, see Steven Pratt, "Being an Indian among Indians," (PhD diss., University of Oklahoma, 1985); D Lawrence Wieder and Steven Pratt, On being a recognizable Indian among Indians, in *Cultural Communication and Intercultural Contact*, Donal Carbaugh, ed. (Hillsdale, NJ: Lawrence Erlbaum Associates 1990): 45-64; D Lawrence Wieder and Steven Pratt, "On the occasioned and situated character of member's questions and answers: Reflections on the question, Is he or she a real Indian, ibid: 65-75.

25 See, for instance, MJ Field, *Angels and Ministers of Grace: An Ethnopsychiatrist's Contribution to Biblical Criticism* (London: Longman 1971), especially 6-19, for a provocative interpretation of early western views of land ownership.

26 See especially Patricia Seed, *Ceremonies of Possession in Europe's Conquest of the New World, 1492-1640* (Cambridge: Cambridge University Press 1995), and also LC Green and Olive P Dickason, *The Law of Nations and the New World* (Edmonton: University of Alberta Press 1989): 7-17.

against eating the meat of animals that inhabited graveyards (by the same logic they would probably have avoided eating archaeologists).[27]

The idea that land was property that could be exclusively possessed, expropriated, or alienated was foreign to native North America. The notion of real estate was as unreal as the demarcation of the seas or the sale of rights to the air. Nevertheless, Native American identity was connected to the land as a site of origination in narratives of ethnogenesis, as a home area where life was lived, and as the final resting place of mortal remains. Later, Native Americans came to accept Euro-American conceptions of land as a commodity that could be alienated through sale during treaty negotiations and be a source of re-compensation through decisions of the Indian Claims Commission. Land lost through conquest or purchase continued to have sentimental value for those who once inhabited the area and their descendants.

Regarding indigenous ideas of private property, much controversy has been [49] aroused over whether ownership of hunting territories was a pre-Columbian institution among northern Algonquian hunters or whether the practice only emerged in connection with the fur trade.[28] Obviously the issue hinges on what is understood by "ownership." The Naskapis, studied by Julius Lips in the 1930s, believed that the local animal "bosses" or masters of the game "owned" the territory;[29] specific human individuals were empowered to treat with the local animal spirits through special ceremonies, knowledge of which was usually transmitted transgenerationally through family lines and may represent in terms of both descent and locality the source of totemism. Other groups seem lo have respected the boundaries of the hunting territory, less out of deference to its human caretakers and more out of fear of giving offense to the spiritual landlords, the masters of the game. Similar ideas seem to have been present in the Northwest with regard to fishing stations, berry patches, and other resource sites.

Just as the "myth of blood" helped promote the idea that American Indians were a separate race of people, so the "myth of nomadism" played a major role in justifying Euro-American claims to lands that had previously been controlled by Indians. This "myth" appears early. Certainly it was strongly represented in the divinely ordained rhetoric of the buckle-headed Puritans, and it has proven remarkably persistent. Essentially the myth avows that Indians are habitually migratory, cannot settle down, have a restless urge to move on; they do not cultivate the soil nor make their mark on the landscape, and thus

---

27 Thomas Jefferson, Notes on the State of Virginia (New York; Harper and Row 1964 [1787]): 95-96; FW Waugh, *Iroquois Foods and Food Preparation*, Memoir 86, no. 12, Anthropological Series (Ottawa: Government Printing Bureau 1916): 131.

28 Some of the more important contributions to this controversy include Frank G Speck, The family hunting band as the basis of Algonkian social organization, *American Anthropologist* 17 (1915): 289-305; Frank G Speck and Loren C Eiseley, The significance of hunting territory systems of the Algonkian in social theory, *American Anthropologist* 41 (1939): 269-80; John M Cooper, Is the Algonquian family hunting ground system pre-Columbian? *American Anthropologist* 41 (1939): 66-90; Eleanor B Leacock, The Montagnais "Hunting Territory" and the Fur Trade, American Anthropological Association, Memoir no. 78 (Washington, DC: American Anthropological Association 1954); Charles A Bishop and Toby Morantz, eds., "Who owns the beaver? Northern Algonquian land tenure reconsidered," Special Issue of [59] *Anthropologica* 28 (1986): 1-219; Adrian Tanner, *Bringing Home Animals: Religious Ideology and Mode of Production of Misiassini Cree Hunters* (New York: St Martin's Press, 1979); Harvey A Feit, The construction of Algonquian hunting territories: Private properly as moral lesson, policy advocacy, and ethnographic error, in *Colonial Situations: Essays on the Contextualization of Ethnographic Knowledge*, GW Stocking, ed. (Madison: University of Wisconsin Press 1991): 109-34; Richard B Lee and Richard H Daley, Eleanor Leacock, Labrador, and the Politics of Gatherer-Hunters," in *From Labrador to Samoa: The Theory and Practice of Eleanor Burke Leacock*. CR Sutton, ed. (DC: American Anthropological Association, 1993): 33-46.

29 Lips is cited in Tanner, *Bringing Home Animals:* 107.

they are on the land but not of the land. The "myth of nomadism" conveniently ignores the facts that many, if not most, Indians traditionally lived a settled existence in semipermanent villages and became unsettled mainly in response to direct and indirect Euro-American pressures or in order to lake advantage of new lifestyles made possible by horses, firearms, or steel traps. Only now are we beginning to appreciate the extent to which precontact Native Americans transformed their environments and cultivated the soil to produce plants that would help revolutionize the world economy.

Around Thanksgiving Day, schoolchildren are often taught to recite a long grocery list of plants that the American Indians bestowed upon their while friends as "gifts."[30] Doubtless the most valuable "gift" of all was the land, since this was a gift that kept on giving. It is difficult lo imagine how the government of the American Republic was financed before the establishment of corporate income taxes in 1909 and personal income taxes in 1913. The sale of Indian lands was a significant source of government funding, and ironically Native Americans indirectly contributed to the endowment of an American Republic that scorned them, patronized them, impoverished them, and fully expected to bury them in the alienable ground.

The Euro-American claim to Indian land and "the myth of nomadism" are clearly articulated in Indian Commissioner Morgan's 1890 report: [50] On account of their ignorance, their savage condition, and their customs and habits, the Indians were never deemed to have the right of property in the soil of the portion of the country over which the tribe or band had established by force of strength the right to roam in search of game, etc. or which had been set apart for its use by treaties with the United States, act of Congress, or Executive order, but only to have the right to occupy said portion of country. The fee in the land of the country occupied and roamed over by the Indians was deemed to be first in the European sovereigns or countries, but now held to be in the Government of the United States.[31]

Morgan goes on to note that, despite the ultimate claim to the land by the United States, the Native American right of occupancy was recognized and had to be purchased. (It is impossible here to explicate all the assumptions, contradictions, and secondary rationalizations contained in this statement of government policy regarding land.)

The displacement of American Indians took place historically in two fashions. First, Native American populations were removed ever westward and resettled behind natural boundaries, like the Appalachian Mountains or the Mississippi River, or behind artificial lines where they were promised perpetual freedom to roam and pursue accustomed lifeways without interference. Secondly, Native American groups were encircled and placed on reservations where they could be confined, controlled, civilized, and Christianized.[32] However, even reservation lands proved not to be inalienable, as title was extinguished through usurpation, allotment, and termination.

Nevertheless, collective possession of land became an important attribute of tribal identity, in terms of both external recognition and sense of self. Reservation land, especially if located in the same general vicinity where first contact with whites occurred, assumed a primordial quality replete with sacred and historic sites. With over two-thirds of the present Native American population residing off-reservation, reservations have come to resemble holy lands, pilgrimage destinations, and retirement homes. To counteract the diaspora, many tribes have instituted annual fairs or powwows that function as homecomings to renew ties to the base community.

---

30 My late friend Alfonso Ortiz would feign befuddlement at references to these "gifts." "What gifts?" he would ask, "They stole those things." Indeed, the expression "Indian giver" goes back to mid-eighteenth-century New England and is less indicative of Native American mendacity than of the Puritan failure to comprehend the reciprocity involved in gift giving.
31 Commissioner of Indian Affairs, Annual Report for 1890: 33.
32 The first reservations date back to the first half of the seventeenth century in colonial New England, but the reservation system did not become fully institutionalized as a federal governmental responsibility until the nineteenth century.

Identity

Continuity of land occupancy is one of the criteria considered in petitions for U.S federal recognition as an American Indian tribe. For example, the decisive factor leading to the recognition of the Mashantucket Pequots was the fact that the last few acres of their original colonial reserve continued to be occupied by the elderly George sisters after all other relatives and tribes-people had left, mostly to seek gainful employment. The Mashantuckets, with their sudden casino wealth, are actively purchasing land to restore the original boundaries of their reservation, as well as buying other choice properties in the area for investment purposes. This does not please white neighbors, since lands added to the reservation are removed from local tax rolls. The reacquisition [51] of land by wealthy Indian tribes reverses long-term historical trends and looms large in future identity politics.

Sense of Community

In addition to blood and land, a sense of community constitutes a third defining attribute of Native American identity. To a large extent one is identified as a Native American because one lives in or has close connections to an Indian community. The idea of communities is preferable to the idea of tribes, since tribes are politico-legal entities rather than direct face-to-face interactive social groups. Furthermore, in aboriginal and neo-aboriginal times there were very few true tribes, in the sense of institutions with clear lines of political authority, chiefs, councils, and strict membership criteria. Rather, as Morton Fried argues,[33] tribes as discernible units mostly arose out of the contact with Europeans. Tribes were not primordial polities but institutions created to facilitate interaction with states. However, the "myth of the tribe" as an eternal and enduring entity is subscribed to by Euro-American and Native Americans alike. For the former, belief in the existence of tribes is of operational value in that it postulates a political entity with which to treat and to enter into binding agreements on a government-to-government basis.

In earlier eras, when American Indians were still regarded as possessing considerable autonomy, military power, and political might, the term "nation" was frequently applied to Native American polities. (The .term was sometimes, however, reserved for larger, more complex societies and suggested greater equivalence with European nation-states or their colonies than smaller tribes or bands.) When the balance of power shifted and Native Americans were considered as dependent nations or wards of the U.S government, the term "tribe" became more widespread. In addition, for Euro-Americans "tribe," connoted an earlier evolutionary stage of social development and cultural progress. Even when an American Indian society became highly acculturated and assimilated white values and institutions, it remained a tribe, albeit a "civilized tribe," which if not oxymoronic seems to suggest an unstable liminality in which forces for further progress contended with pressures to return to a more tribal existence. Tribalism reflected not only a state of society but an appropriate mentality. Civilization was seen as a thin patina covering a less refined tribal mentality that would burst forth under the right conditions. For example, during the U.S Civil War observers wondered whether Cherokee soldiers, fighting for the Union or for the Confederacy, would revert lo scalping in the heal of battle.

Notions of tribe and tribalism convey an inferior, primitive, or negative identity in certain areas of white discourse, but these very same terms are [52] valued positively by Native Americans. Tribal sovereignty is vigorously defended, and the federal government is held strictly accountable for the fulfillment of treaty and other legal obligations. The tribe becomes the site of one's identity and distinctiveness not only vis-à-vis whites but also with respect to other Native American tribes. Members

---

33 Morton H Fried, On the concepts of 'tribe' and 'tribal society,' in *Essays on the Problem of Tribe*, June Helm, ed. (Seattle: University of Washington Press, 1968): 3-20; Morton H Fried, *The Notion of Tribe* (Menlo Park, NJ: Cummings, 1975). See also Raymond D Fogelson, The context of American Indian political history: An overview and critique, *Occasional Papers* in Curriculum Series, no. 11 (Chicago: Newberry Library 1989): 8-21.

are felt to be united not only by blood, a common land base, and law, but also by a sense of belonging to a moral community with a shared history and destiny. Participation in this moral community entails practical and emotional costs, but, as with American Express, membership has its privileges, be they health care, tax-free status for certain items. Bureau of Indian Affairs services, or license to operate gambling facilities, and these privileges are jealously guarded and strongly defended. The upshot is that if tribes did not exist aboriginally, they most surely do exist today,

One may very well ask what forms of social organization prevailed in aboriginal America in lieu of the tribe. Certainly there were distinctive peoples speaking different languages and participating in different cultures. They belonged to what could be called peoplehood, as a pluralized form of personhood.[34] Peoplehoods comprised widely spread networks of differentially connected individuals having reciprocal rights and duties toward one another and sharing a collective sense of community.

The social structure of peoplehoods, of course, varied from area to area in aboriginal North America. The native inhabitants of the eastern seaboard whom the English settlers first encountered appear to represent loose federations of related, interdigitated local groups extending from the Carolina coast to Massachusetts, all speaking Algonquian dialects. Elite intermarriage seems to have been an important mechanism for linking these groups together. Most resided in settled villages but were often seasonally mobile. The Lenapes knew about the summer attractions of the seashore long before Philadelphians became bilocal. Small-scale chiefdoms rose and fell with a fair degree of regularity, yet Powhatan was no emperor and Philip no king. The Iroquois Confederacy probably existed before the coming of whites, but it was a loose and fragile alliance at best, and not the formidable political and military machine it became during the colonial period.

In the interior of the Southeast, individual towns or linked sets of towns, not tribes, were the autonomous political units. Complex chiefdoms emphasizing hierarchy and central control characterized societies in the Caddoan and Mississippi drainage areas, while village organization prevailed in much of the Midwest. To the north, family and composite bands were the norm, as was the case in the pedestrian Plains and the Great Basin. In the Southwest, then as now, individual Pueblos were the loci of political authority. The groups of the lower Colorado River and the Mohave may have approximated "true" tribes, but in densely populated California, the units of political organization were what Alfred L Kroeber aptly called "tribelets."[35] On the Northwest Coast and [53] into the Plateau, villages or regional districts were the main units of individual and group identity, while, within the villages, households provided the specific locus of identity.

The major mechanism holding all of these diverse peoplehoods together was kinship. Kinship truly was a model of and a model for political integration. In some instances, where there was a ruling elite, we may be dealing directly with kinship and consanguineal systems of descent. Elsewhere, kinship served as a metaphor for social and political relations that could be inwardly intensive, such that everyone was related to everyone else through direct descent, clan affiliation, or adoption, and could be outwardly extensive, such that the idiom of kinship could be used as a means to establish and structure relations with strangers and alien societies.

In expanding the world of personhood, rituals of adoption and diplomatic protocol with outside groups nearly always involved the manipulation of symbols of identity. It is doubtful whether the

---

34 The notion of personhood employed here derives from Marcel Mauss's pioneering conceptualization (1938), which has been retranslated and discussed from several angles in Michael Carrithers, Steven Collins, and Steven Lukes, eds., *The Category of the Person: Anthropology, Philosophy, History* (Cambridge: Cambridge University Press 1985). For the author's understanding of personhood and related concepts, see Raymond D Fogelson, "Self, person, and identity: Some anthropological retrospects, circumspects and prospects," in *Psychosocial Theories of the Self*, Benjamin Lee, ed. (New York: Plenum Press 1982): 67-109.

35 AL Kroeber, Nature of the land-holding group, Ethnohistory 2 (1955): 303-14.

proverbial blood brotherhood, in which actual blood was exchanged through mutual incision, was widely practiced, but intermarriage surely reflected symbolic exchanges of blood. Very often adoption rituals involved the trading of clothing. Clothing was sympathetically related to its wearer through principles of contagion and represented an exchange of skin. Animal skins, of course, became measurable wealth during the fur trade. On some more profound level, personified animal spirits bestowed their skins on human persons to reveal and reassert primordial kinship and identity relations with human beings. Diplomatic embassies were frequently concerned with adjudicated territorial boundaries and might even involve transactions of land, the second major attribute of identity discussed in this chapter. Increasingly in historical time, Indian-white diplomatic relations focused on land issues, either because whites were seeking to acquire more land through cessions or American Indians were complaining about white boundary jumpers and seeking redress.

Finally, with respect to adoption and diplomacy, cultural exchange was manifested in gift giving, feasting, and other acts of hospitality. Whites took this treatment as their due or as an instance of inherent native generosity. Native Americans, however, viewed these events as efforts to expand the community, to extend personhood by establishing or renewing relationships. They expected reciprocity on the part of whiles to sustain the relationship. When they were disappointed in this expectation and reciprocity was not forthcoming, communalism was destroyed, identity was threatened, and the speeches of whites were perceived as the deliberate deceptions of a "forked tongue." Whiles reacted by referring to their formerly generous hosts and hostesses as "Indian givers," and the identity struggle began anew. [54]

Conclusion

In this chapter, Native American identity is considered in terms of three defining attributes: blood and descent, land, and community. Some of the subjective aspects of these attributes are suggested, but more emphasis is placed on political and legal dimensions, since these have been used to offer supposedly objective criteria for determining who and what is a Native American. This is a problem that is, or should be, of central concern to Native American studies programs.

Today, the assumptions underlying the effort to employ stable and objective measures of Native American identity are under fire. Blood quantum is being questioned not only because it reduces identity to biology and race, but also because the original information on which it was based may be flawed or erroneous. Scientific measures of blood type, DNA, anthropometry, and earwax texture are often unreliable and invalid identity markers. Land holdings can be ascertained, but the subjective associations with land are harder to evaluate. Finally, measures of community integration, which may include the structure and functioning of political organizations, voting behavior, church attendance, powwow participation, visiting patterns, telephone records, and other sociological indicators of community and communication, cannot provide conclusive evidence of a "sense of community."

The Branch of Acknowledgment and Recognition of the Bureau of Indian Affairs holds implicitly that once Indian tribal identity is lost or surrendered, it can never be regained. This notion is also problematic from a worldwide perspective. Cultural revivals, ethnic renewals, and nationalistic movements are rampant today. One has only to look at the breakup of the Soviet Union, the dismemberment of the former Yugoslavia, and the less brutal division of Czechoslovakia, at efforts by the Sami, the Maori, and other Fourth World peoples to gain sovereignty, at separatist movements in Wales, Scotland, and Ireland, as well as in Hawaii, Papua New Guinea, and Guatemala. Similar phenomena recur in the Middle East, South America, South and Central Africa, and many parts of Asia. A few generations ago most colonial powers viewed detribalization as an inevitable evolutionary trend on a one-way street leading to assimilation into the modern nation-state. Now the demands for independence and the movement toward retribalization and ethnic revival have forced social scientists and philosophers of history to reconfigure their theories of social change.

The determination of Native American identity has increasingly become the responsibility of federally recognized tribes. Some have chosen to lighten blood quantum requirements, while others apply different criteria to determine tribal membership. However, given the current diaspora of Native Americans in which perhaps as much as 70 percent of the population now resides [55] off-reservation and far from tribal territories, specific tribal identity comes lo take on more of a symbolic than a pragmatic reality. Nevertheless, many Native Americans do regroup in the cities to form multitribal communities and build new institutions as connections with former "home" communities become attenuated.

The growth of the Native American population in the United States has been phenomenal in recent decades. Substantial natural increase has been greatly supplemented with ever larger numbers of individuals claiming Native American identity in the decennial censuses. Many of these people are "Wannabees"; others claim partial Native American descent; still others are members of federally nonrecognized tribes. Such claims are a cause of concern for federally recognized tribes, who feel that their own special status vis-à-vis the federal government may be threatened. Indeed, the State of Georgia, which pressed for the removal of American Indians from its borders in the 1820s and 1830s, leading to the tragic Trail of Tears, recently reversed its policy by giving stale recognition to scores of groups dubiously claiming to be Cherokees, much to the consternation of recognized Cherokee tribal officials in North Carolina and Oklahoma.

The times they are a-changing. However, it would be premature to predict the demise of tribes in the next century, as did Commissioner of Indian Affairs Thomas Jefferson Morgan in 1893 at the World's Columbian Exposition.[36] Issues of Native American identity will continue to be actively debated during the next millennium. Native American studies programs are strategically situated to monitor and interpret the ongoing identity struggle over who and what is an Indian. These will be interesting times.

---

36 Thomas J Morgan, "The Indian tribes will disappear," in *Today Then: America's Best Minds Look 100 Years Into the Future on the Occasion of the 1893 World's Columbian Exposition,* Dave Waller, compiler (Helena: American and World Geographic Publishing, 1992): 43-44. Morgan did, however, predict a Native American population of a million or so by 1993, and: "There will be here and there wandering bands of blanket beggars. These aboriginal tramps will perpetuate the absurdities and enormities of Indian life either as a profession or as a providential object lesson for students of history." (I am not certain whether Morgan here is envisioning the gypsy life of some PhDs in anthropology or history or professors in Native American Studies programs).

5 NATIONALISM AND THE AMERICANIST TRADITION

Anthropology, especially in its British mode following Evans-Pritchard, has often been referred to as 'the step-child of colonialism.' American anthropology and the development of the Americanist Tradition, I will argue, can best be considered as the ward of nationalism. The ideology of Americanism was certainly conditioned by previous colonial experiences. New nations in the Western hemisphere were created out of the wreckage of overseas European empires large and small. Such world powers and power-failures as Sweden, Portugal, Holland, Spain, France, and England all had their variable moments in the New World sun before retreating to the post-colonial shade.

The treatment of the indigenous and mestizo populations by the modem successors to the initial invaders can be regarded as a form of colonialism. Indeed, the late Robert K. Thomas coined the term 'internal colonialism' to describe the dependent condition of reservation and otherwise spatially segregated Indian populations (1966-7). Thomas's notion of 'internal colonialism' has recently been rediscovered and endorsed by Marxist theorist and outspoken American Indian Movement spokesman Ward Churchill (1993).

Despite the analytic robustness and rhetorical appeal of the colonial model, I find efforts at nation-building, international competition, and competing forms of nationalism to be more compelling stimuli in accounting for the emergence of the Americanist Tradition and ethnic nationalism within the United States and Canada. Not only did new nations usually strive mightily to separate themselves from their parental motherlands or fatherlands, but they actively attempted to create a distinctive identity of their own. This identity work included such things as the framing of constitutional law, the creation of national symbols, the establishment of traditions, the setting of annual ceremonial calendars, the maintenance of boundaries, and efforts to merge and blend into the newly enclosed landscape. I use the notion of identity here not only in [76] terms of self-image as contrasted with the alter-images of others, but also in its literal sense: identity emphasizes a sense of sameness and continuity over time. Nationhood thus involves both newness in the process of separation and the forging of a distinctive polity and national character, but it also seeks legitimacy through perpetuation of enduring values and connections with an essentialized or primordial state of being.

Nations and nationalism are difficult to define. Their meanings change radically over time and space. Ideas of nationalism can be traced back to antiquity, but modem nationalist movements are thought to have begun in pre-pre-modern Western Europe, first with England, and later spreading into North America and Central and Eastern Europe, where bitter issues of nationalism and ethnicity continue to be contested. Eventually nationalism diffuses globally to the so-called Third and Fourth Worlds, where some of them become First Nations or one of the Five Hundred Nations.

Just as nationalism spreads globally, with various changes in meaning, over time, so does nationalism change internally. European or American nationalism is not the same in 1840 as it is in 1890. In 1840 nationalism could be regarded as a democratic revolutionary movement of the people; by 1890 it had become predominantly a conservative and reactionary movement pitting the upper classes against the people, and manifesting strong opposition to internationalism. Exclusivity and self-centred closed societies became the norm (Kohn 1973: 328).

Defining nation and nationalism is a bit like trying to nail jello to the wall. However, most definitions require as a *sine qua non* the notion of a community of people, real or theoretical, occupying a common territory, or at least once occupying a common homeland or promising to do so in the future. Often the community speaks a common language, possesses distinctive customs, and, at least formerly, believes itself to be connected by common descent through a mystical chain of blood. The last feature seems anachronistic today when race and racism are taboos, politically wrong topics. Nevertheless, etymologically, we must recognize that the term *nation* derives from the Latin 'to give birth,' or 'to breed.'

Nationalism

Nationality is still considered by us to be a birthright, and the process by which an alien attains membership in the nation is called 'naturalization'; in crossing national borders one must have customs checked.

Nations are also sometimes defined in terms of scale, being larger than a tribe or a localized ethnic group and more stable and historically developed than a federation. Issues of scale confront us directly in the manner in which Europeans classified Native American polities. My impression is that, while the term tribe is used fairly commonly, and confederacy or empire occurs exceptionally, a large number of groups in the colonial records are referred to as nations. [77]

The designation is only roughly correlated with size or scale, since we read of the Huron Nation, the Catawba Nation, the Cherokee Nation, the Sioux Nation, and the Pequot Nation, and so on. What seems to be occurring here is the recognition of sovereignty, independence, and power. When a nation is defeated it either ceases to exist, its remnants are scattered, or it is reduced to the status of a tribe. Pauline Strong and Barrik Van Winkle (1993: 12) date the shift from Indian 'nations' to Indian 'tribes' to the Commerce Clause of the United States Constitution in 1787.

Pequot history is recorded in all these registers. In the early seventeenth century, the Pequots were considered a powerful nation controlling the wampum trade up and down the rivers of southern New England. After they were massacred by the Puritans in 1636 at Fort Mystic, buckle-headed Captain John Mason declared that the Pequots ceased to be a people. Indeed, they achieved some measure of literary immortality in Melville's Moby Dick by being referred to as 'extinct as the Medes.' Yet, as we know, individual Pequots survived, banded together, and became a federally recognized tribe. They now proudly refer to themselves as a nation, with an open line to Washington and with transnational connections, by virtue of their present control of another kind of wampum trade in southern New England, big-time casino gambling.

The attribution of nationhood to Indians was never a simple evolutionary correlate of civilization. The major Indian groups in the southeastern United States attained the trappings of civilization before their removal to the West in the i830s. However, they were collectively referred to as the Five Civilized Tribes, not the Five Civilized Nations, even though individually the groups were still referred to as Indian Nations – the Seminole Nation, the Creek Nation, the Cherokee Nation, the Choctaw Nation, and the Chickasaw Nation.

I want to turn now to consider the Americanist Tradition in relation to nationalism. As far as I can determine, the term Americanist first appears in 1881 in connection with the first meeting of the Congress of Americanists in Madrid in September of 1881. It is interesting to note that the Congress was international in scope and dominated by European scholars, as is the Society of Americanists today. However, the roots of the Americanist Tradition go far back into the colonial period, when interests in recording information on native customs and manners, languages, physical types, and antiquities were all pursued in hopes of ascertaining who the New World Natives were and how they related to known Old World populations. These quests for knowledge were also inspired by religious and political concerns.

After the American Revolution, the Americanist Tradition began in earnest. Perhaps no figure is more quintessentially Americanist than Thomas Jefferson. He disputed with European scholars over the thesis that America was an inferior [78] habitat for plants, animals, and human beings. His keen interest in Indian ethnology can be seen in his instructions to the explorers Lewis and Clark; he was a serious student of American Indian linguistics and was directly or indirectly responsible for many of the early word lists that found their way to the American Philosophical Society. He also is remembered for conducting the first stratigraphically controlled excavation of a burial mound located near his home of Monticello. This did not immediately inaugurate scientific archaeological excavation techniques, but it did demonstrate continuity of the past with the present; Jefferson even reports periodic visits of living Indians to the grave site. On the practical side, Jefferson's Indian policy, while superficially liberal, aimed to transform what were thought to be wild, warlike, nomadic hunting groups into tame, peaceful, settled agriculturalists. The implicit choice was acculturation and assimilation or cultural death and disappearance.

The theme of disappearance continues to haunt the nineteenth century. The issue of Indian sovereignty in the United States is addressed in the 1831 Supreme Court case of the Cherokee Nation vs. Georgia, in which Chief Justice John Marshall articulates the doctrine of 'domestic dependent nation' status in which the Federal Government's relationship to the Cherokee Nation is compared to that of a 'guardian to his ward.' The full implications of this ruling have remained open to variable legal interpretation down to the present day.

On the one hand, wardship suggests immaturity and vulnerability. On the other hand, the relationship suggests definite obligations on the part of the more powerful protector to assist and defend the interests of the ward. Domestic dependent nation status entails loyalty, such that Indian Nations coming under this ruling were no longer permitted to make independent alliances with foreign powers or take up arms against the federal government. It was implicitly expected that Indian wards would perish long before reaching full maturity or that they would grow up in such a fashion as to be unrecognizable to their ancestors.

The main thrust of emerging nineteenth-century scholarly studies of the American Indian was oriented to the past. Several learned societies and multi-faceted institutions and projects provided a support structure for research. I have already mentioned the American Philosophical Society, which took the lead in philological studies and ethnology. The American Antiquarian Society became a nerve centre for archaeological work during the second quarter of the nineteenth century. The American Ethnological Society was founded in 1842 and stimulated important research during the middle part of the century. Henry Rowe Schoolcraft's elephantine six-volume encyclopedia, *Information Regarding the History, Condition, and Prospects of the Indian Tribes of the United States*, brought together much valuable material. However, Schoolcraft's [79] compilation was long on history and past traditions, but short on prospects and current conditions.

The Smithsonian Institution made an auspicious debut in 1848 with the publication of Squier and Davis's *Ancient Monuments in the Mississippi Valley*, but it had to wait until the latter part of the century for more sustained research under the aegis of the Geological Survey, the Bureau of Ethnology, and the U.S. National Museum. The Anthropological Society of Washington and the Woman's Anthropological Society, the parents of the American Anthropological Association, were already formed in the late i88os, and the American Association for the Advancement of Science was an active arena for presenting the results of Americanist research. A comparable institutional survey could be done for nineteenth-century Canada.

Archaeology occupied centre stage in the nineteenth-century focus on the past. The mystery of the mound builders preoccupied many notable and unnotable minds. The question of the antiquity of human occupation of the New World and the .search for early skeletal material formed important arenas of inquiry and speculation. The discovery of ancient monuments and evidence of early man were legitimizing efforts to provide the New World with parity to sites and finds in the Old World. Indeed, American archaeology develops almost as a reflex to European prehistory. Neanderthal skeletons are countered with claims for specimens like the Natchez pelvis; the contemporaneity of European Palaeolithic populations with elephants and mammoths is matched in America by the fraudulent elephant pipes in Davenport, or the false depiction of mammoths on the Lenape Stone unearthed in Eastern Pennsylvania. It should be noted that Henry Chapman Mercer, who published the major report on the Lenape Stone, had already participated in extensive excavations in France and Spain. To continue: an analogue to European Palaeolithic stone industries was thought to be present in the Trenton gravels and in the Upper Delaware Valley. Soon after the mesolithic remains of the Swiss Lake dwellers ' were revealed to an interested public, Frank Hamilton Cushing brought to destructive light complex wooden artefacts from the muck of Key Marco. This kind of transatlantic ping-pong began to slow down as the twentieth century approached.

The fusion of nationalism with the Americanist Tradition is clearly revealed in the nineteenth-century history of archaeological site preservation and antiquities laws. Frederick Ward Putnam purchased the Great Serpent Mound in Southern Ohio for Harvard's Peabody Museum, which later turned the site over lo the Ohio Archaeological and Historical Society for safe keeping. The discovery of spectacular Anasazi sites in the Southwest drew visitors, pot hunters, and scholars. However, it was only when Nordenskjold started to crate up artifacts [80] for shipment to European museums that legislative action was taken to protect what was now considered a national heritage.

Later, when Yellowstone was declared a national park, part of the motivation for doing so was to keep out Shoshone and Crow visitors (Peter Nabokov pc). Antiquity laws were enacted to preserve sites for archaeological science. Only in recent years have Indians been consulted about site conservation and the possible religious significance to current Native historical consciousness. Thus, the process of assimilation and appropriation of Indian culture concerns not only the living, but the dead as well.

If any figure most fully embodied the culmination of the nineteenth-century Americanist position, it was Daniel Garrison Brinton. Regna Darnell has written definitively about this gentlemanly Philadelphia polymath (1988). He was, at once, a trained physician, a talented linguist, a critical interpreter of ethnological and archaeological data and theory, a significant student of folklore and myth, and an early specialist in comparative religion and primitive psychology. In many ways, he resembles an American EB Tylor, not only in his range of interests, in his Quaker tolerance, and in his abiding evolutionism, but also in his preference for the armchair over the field and his tenure as an early but inactive professor of anthropology of his time.

As Darnell notes, Brinton declares his divergent stance from most anthropologists in the preface of his Essays of an Americanist (1890). He believed in a considerable antiquity for humans on this continent, in a distinct American race, in genetic similarities in all American languages, in the importance of the abstract and symbolic features of myth, in the phonetic character of graphic methods, in the existence of poetic feelings in American tribes, and in an autochthony of American cultures that denied late immigration by way of the Bering Straits. Brinton also felt that the psychology of savage life was greatly underrated by most anthropologists owing to superficial observation, judging the past conditions of a tribe from modem and degenerate representatives, an inability to speak the languages, and the imposition of preconceived theories about Native thought and feeling. The anthropologists from whom Brinton distanced himself included younger scholars like Franz Boas, who emphasized fieldwork, whose outlook was more international, and who didn't subscribe to all of Brinton's parochial Americanist tenets.

The 1893 World Columbian Exposition marked a transition point in Americanist anthropology. Several Americanist crises of representation were played out at the Chicago fair. The scientists of the Smithsonian, particularly Otis Mason and William Henry Holmes, took a taxidermist turn, creating life figures of dead Indians and encasing them in simplified dioramas. Buffalo Bill and his Congress of Rough Riders employed show-business Indians, mostly Oglala [81] Sioux, to portray dramatic episodes in the losing of the West. Frederick Ward Putnam and Franz Boas favored replicas of traditional Indian habitations populated by living Indians recreating the traditional cultures of their forebears. Finally, government boarding-school children sat properly at their desks in model Indian schools displaying their penmanship and lace-making ability. Meanwhile, the Carlisle brigades of Colonel Richard Henry Pratt marched under the banner of 'civilization and citizenship.'

Archaeology figured prominently at the Chicago fair: there were state, national, and international archaeological exhibits, including a massive replica of a Cliff Dweller site, and reconstructed stelae and public buildings from Yucatan.

However, one sensed that the progress celebrated at the fair sounded the death knell of the traditional Indian. As is well known, Frederick Jackson Turner announced the closing of the frontier at a history convention held in conjunction with the Chicago World's Fair. As is probably less well known, Daniel Brinton delivered a presidential address at the International Congress of Anthropology, also convened at the fair. Significantly, Brinton's talk was entitled 'The Nation as an Element in Anthropology' (1894). The address is a curious mixture of outworn evolutionary dogma combined with some forward-looking insights into the effects of nationality on various anthropological domains. Brinton's lecture reflects the old and the new, the nineteenth century and the twentieth century.

Another set of World's Fair documents that has recently surfaced is a series of predictions by various commentators about the state of the world a century into the future, that is, 1993 (Walter 1992). One of the prognosticators was Thomas Jefferson Morgan, then Commissioner of Indian Affairs. He predicted that Indian tribes as political entities would disappear, even though the Indian population would increase four-fold. He foresaw 'wandering bands of blanket beggars ... aboriginal tramps [who] will perpetuate the absurdities and enormities of Indian life either as a profession or as a providential object lesson for students of history.' Moreover, '[t]he great body of Indians will become merged in the indistinguishable mass of our population' (Morgan, in Walter 1992: 44).

This feeling of imminent loss of Indian culture pervades the activities of the first generation of trained, professional anthropologists after the turn of the century. Americanist anthropology was assumed from the start to be a salvage operation. The dominant Boasian modus operandi favored short-term field-work, collaboration with key elder informants, and the co-production of texts, preferably in the native language. Sometimes these one-on-one interactions became so intense as to resemble *folie á deux*. The ultimate ethnological aim, however, remained the reconstruction of cultural history. [82]

By the late 1920s and 19303, new theoretical currents began to affect the Americanist Tradition from both within and without. Functionalism in its various guises placed greater emphasis on the wholeness and integration of cultures and social structures. The dynamics of social and cultural change were .sought in more complex processes than simple evolution and diffusionism. Finally, and most important, attention shifted away from an unknowable, idealized past and more toward a more accessible, realistic present. It is difficult to single out specific works that signal this transformation, but if pushed to the wall, I'd nominate Margaret Mead's study of the Omaha, *The Changing Culture of an Indian Tribe* (1932), despite its many flaws. I'd also dust off dark Wissler's seldom cited work, *Indian Cavalcade* (1938), which looked at reservation communities as apt subjects of study in and of themselves. It should be noted that Wissler sponsored Mead and Reo Fortune's Omaha work, and that he was also influential in the Lynds' study of Muncie, Indiana, better known as Middletown, which was a pace-setting American community study.

During this period, American anthropologists began to take a more active interest in the welfare and survival of the societies they observed and analyzed. Applied anthropology came to the fore as anthropologists worked closely with government agencies to enact legislation and to administer programs intended to benefit and empower Indians. The anthropological role began to shift from passive undertakers of Indian culture to active take-over policy makers in Indian affairs.

Subsequent debates have witnessed a steady decline in anthropological studies in Native North America. Although heirs to a rich and important research tradition, Americanist scholars are increasingly marginalized and made to feel irrelevant within the wider anthropological profession. This marginalization seems to have less to do with quality of work or the neglect of significant theoretical issues and more to do with conditions of work.

As Indian sovereignty has been reaffirmed, as movements for self-determination have gained momentum, and as formerly mute Indian voices become more strident, Native confrontations with anthropology and anthropologists become inevitable. For many, these developments herald the death of the Americanist Tradition. It takes almost the zeal of a missionary to convince funding agencies, skeptical colleagues, and reluctant tribal government officials about the significance of Americanist research. It is hard to persuade intelligent graduate students to forego the attractions of postcolonial studies in Africa, the Pacific, and elsewhere, or the allure of postmodern, transnational research in Eastern Europe, or the narcissism of self-reflective analyses of American society. They are dissuaded by the ordeal of negotiating research permissions with tribal councils; they are not enchanted with the pleasures of reservation life; they [83] want to avoid the great, white American guilt trip; and they are uncomfortable being the butt of 'anthro' jokes and being subjected to chronic 'anthro-bashing.'

Nationalism

If there is to be a resurrection of Americanist studies, and I think there will be, anthropologists will have to become wards to the people they purport to study. They will have to pledge allegiances to new nationalisms. They will have to face the challenges of transmitting and translating the past and continuing results of Americanist research to new audiences in new contexts.

References

Brinton, Daniel G 1890 *Essays of an Americanist*. Philadelphia: David McKay.
    1894 The "Nation" as an Element in Anthropology. In D Staniland Wake, ed.. Memoirs of the International Congress of Anthropology. 19-34. Chicago: Schulte Publishing.
Churchill, Ward 1993 *Struggle for the Land: Indigenous Resistance to Genocide, Ecocide and Expropriation in Contemporary North America.* Monroe, ME: Common Courage Press.
Darnell. Regna 1988 Daniel Garrison Brinton: The 'Fearless Critic' of Philadelphia. Philadelphia: University of Pennsylvania Publications in Anthropology.
Mead, Margaret 1932 *The Changing Culture of an Indian Tribe.* New York: Columbia University Press.
Strong, Pauline Turner, and Barrik Van Winkle 1993 'Tribe and Nation: American Indian and American Nationalism. *Social Analysis* 33: 9-20.
Thomas, Robert K 1966-7. Colonialism: Classic and Internal. *New University Thought* 4 (4).
Walter, Dave (compiler) 1992 *Today Then: America's Best Minds Look 100 Years into the Future on the Occasion of the 1893 World's Columbian Exposition.* Helena, MT: American and World Geographic Publishing.
Wissler, Clark 1938 *Indian Cavalcade or Life on the Old-Time Indian Reservations.* New York: Sheridan House.

TOTEMISM RECONSIDERED
With Robert A Brightman[1]

The work and days of William C. Sturtevant provide an important link between the final breath of the Bureau of American Ethnology and a revived Americanist anthropology in the new millennium. Sturtevant's multi faceted interests combine rigorous description and thorough scholarship with an openness to entertain, if not always embrace, contemporary international developments in anthropological method and theory. One major theme that connects much of his work is a constant concern with classification; another is his abiding interest in exploring curious comers of the hidden history of anthropology. This essay bears on both these interests.

Categorial Impositions

The use of animal categories as classificatory devices is an old, largely unconscious convention haunting much of the history if Western ideas. These categories were pushed into consciousness with the "discovery" of totemism as a recurrent feature of "primitive" societies by the late nineteenth-century evolutionary theorists. Totemism was taken as a primary diagnostic feature that distinguished the "primitive other" from "civilized us." In 1903 Durkheim and Mauss (1963) set forth an agenda or what would become their version of the sociology of knowledge by means of a comparative analysis of Aristotelian categories of thought – such concepts as space, time, number, person, and classification itself. The notion of totemism as a classificatory device was then already assumed, at least implicitly. We, as well as the "primitive others," classify our worlds by many means, for example, by number (both Roman and Arabic numerals), by letter (both upper and lower case), by color (color coding for race being a particularly pernicious example), by various measures of time (chronological, cosmological, diurnal, and life cyclical, among others), by space or location (e.g., left, right, center, or cardinal directions), and, as we have come to recognize, by animals (political groups, nations, sports earns, and automobiles being conspicuous examples.)

As a culture we are very concerned about the consequences of animal extinction. The cause of conservation attracts both Green Peace activists and segments of the religious right who see the preservation of nature as keeping faith with God's divine plan for the universe. Biological scientists worry about shrinking gene pools and diminished genetic data banks. Animal extinctions might even affect early childhood learning – mastery of the alphabet might be imperiled without books containing pictures of animals ranging from Aardvarks to Zebras.

Anthropology has long recognized native people's use of animal categories. Such peoples claimed descent from, named social groups after, arranged marriages according to, and observed taboos with respect to certain animal species, more rarely plants, still more rarely natural phenomena (stars, lightning, etc.), and most rarely manufactured cultural objects (projectile points, baskets, etc.). These categories were usually applied to classes or species of animals, but less frequently they were applied to individual members of particular species. Sometimes, as with peoples in northern North America, partnerships between specific representatives of animal species and human individuals are mutually established through vision quest or dream experiences. In parts of Latin America and elsewhere certain individual animals are believed to be sympathetically connected to particular human beings, such that what happens to the animal may literally or figuratively affect the related human individual. This kind of relationship

---

1 This paper has been in process a long time. Those we can recall who made useful comments on it include Anne Chi'en, Raymond DeMallie, Ives Goddard, Robert McKinley, Toby Morantz, Jay Miller, Frank Siebert, and George Stocking.

usually is referred to as *nagualism* rather than as totemism, although the two phenomena may possess intrinsic similarity. Sometimes, rather than an entire species or animal, subclasses of animal species or particular body parts are recognized as totems. Thus we may have the Bear Paw clan or the Falcon Wing lineage; or color qualifiers may be employed, as in Red Deer versus Brown Deer groups, White Wolf and Gray Wolf clans, or as in Black Cockatoo versus White Cockatoo moieties in Australia.

At the end of the nineteenth century and during the first two decades of the twentieth century, anthropologists and their friends confabulated, mystified, reified, transmogrified, and exoticized the notion of totemism to reflect, in Levi-Straussian terms, the deep chasm between nature and culture, between the primitive and the civilized, between "them" and "us" (Levi-Strauss 1963: 3). Totemism, or the totemic complex, was seen as a primordial form of social organization, an elementary form of religion, a primitive system of philosophy, and an essentialized manifestation of the primitive mind at work and play.

The origins of totemism, its diffusion, and its logical types were subjects of learned debate. Even Sigmund Freud (1952) took part with his still-interesting book Totem and Taboo, in which he drew analogies between the behavior of primitive peoples vis á vis their totemic rites and taboos and the obsessive, compulsive behavior of some of his patients. That Freud himself was not beyond the temptation to utilize animal categories may be recognized in his labeling of two of his classic case studies the Wolf Man and the Rat Man.

As noted by French structuralist anthropologist Claude Levi-Strauss (1963: 3-10), the anthropological obsession with totemism peaked by 1920 and soon became a moribund topic. It is widely believed that Alexander Goldenweiser, a brilliant, first-generation student of Franz Boas, refuted the validity of the concept of totemism in his analytic critique of 1910. In slightly over 100 tightly argued pages, Goldenweiser took issue with the enormous literature that regarded totemism as a unitary phenomenon. He maintained that the assumed totemic complex did not cohere, could not be essentialized, that it was an artificial anthropological construct, a snare, and an illusion. Shapiro (1991), however, noted that Goldenweiser's feat may itself have been mythologized and that Goldenweiser avowed a fundamental unity of totemism through structural and historical relations and metaphysical connections between animals and clans in his important later articles 'The Origin of Totemism" (1933a) and "Form and Content in Totemism" (1933b). Indeed, as Shapiro cogently argued, Goldenweiser's rehabilitated totemism anticipated the Levi-Straussian structural version in many crucial respects.

It is certainly the case that the subject of totemism was resurrected and given new direction by Levi-Strauss's *Totemism* (1963; the full French title of which translates as "Totemism Today") and *The Savage Mind* (1966). Levi-Strauss tried to understand the fascination with animal-human relations that so preoccupied some of the best minds of the West. As condensed in his critique of Malinowski's utilitarian theory of totemism, Levi-Strauss maintained that it isn't that animals are good for eating, but that they are good for thinking. Animal categories serve as logical operators in that they encompass naturally occurring gradational differences.

Levi-Strauss's intellectualist theory has considerable power and appeal. Yet totems are more than bloodless cognitive categories good for thinking; totems are also good to feel, to experience, to react to. The World War I soldier is expressing more than his divisional affiliation when he says "I am Rainbow" (Linton 1924: 296). The outrage felt by Chicago policemen during the 1968 Democratic Convention at being called "pigs" by Yippie protesters reflected more than categorical boundary transgression. Totemic identification has an affective dimension that is based on more than analogy or metaphoric extension. In this paper we search out and reconsider the original sources responsible for introducing the concept of totemism into scholarly discourse.

Native North American Totemism Retransformed

The original homeland of the term "totemism" is the north-central Algonquian-speaking area of

North America. Much confusion revolves around the meaning of the term "totem." In the original published reference to the phenomenon by the English trader John Long, in 1791, totemism clearly refers to an individual tutelary or personal guardian spirit (Long 1904). The more usual scholarly usage of the term denotes a relationship between descent groups – sibs, clans, phratries, moieties – and their eponymous natural species. Such units are often referred to in early documents as a tribe, family, or, more rarely, a nation; moreover, in native usage the Ojibwa stem -do•de•m and its close cognates can also refer to a local territorial group, or what may be technically classed as a <u>deme</u>. In the case of the Ojibwa, -do•de•m referred both to one's fellow patrilineal clan members and to an eponymous animal from which the clan was held to be descended or with which its ancestors were otherwise associated (Warren 1957:41-53; Jones 1970:138). Thus, for example, the trader Nicolas Perrot recorded in the seventeenth century an Ojibwa myth describing the creation by the Great Hare (presumably *Nenabozho*, the Ojibwa trickster-culture hero) of the clan ancestors from the corpses of different animals: "Accordingly some of the savages derive their origin from a bear, others from moose, and others similarly from various kinds of animals" (Blair 1996: 37). In academic practice the sociological referent of totemism has become the unmarked category, while the guardian-spirit complex, when associated with totemism, is marked or qualified as individual totemism (cf. Schoolcraft 1855: 196; Tylor 1898; Durkheim 1965; Goldenweiser 1910; Frazer 1934; and Levi-Strauss 1963).

Long's introduction of the terms "totem" and "totemism" into the literature was duly noted by Wundt, Tylor, Durkheim, Frazer, Freud, Boas, and Levi-Strauss, among others, but it appears that few of these scholars had actually read the original 1791 Long account, *Voyages and Travels of an Indian Interpreter and Trader*, despite its eventual accessibility in reprinted editions published in Reuben Gold Thwaites's *Early Western Travels* series (Long 1904) and in the later Lakeside Classics series published by RR Donnelley (Long 1922). John Long worked out of Caughnawaga and had a close familiarity with North American Indians. He spoke French and possessed a working knowledge of some variety of Northern Iroquoian and of a variety of Ojibwa used in the fur trade, and his book contains appended word lists. Long spent several winters with Indian companions in the bush; he was even adopted into an Ojibwa band and given the appropriate name *Amik*, or "Beaver." Given that Long's account of totemism remains a source of considerable misunderstanding and ignorance, it deserves to be quoted in its entirety:

> One part of the religious superstition of the Savages, consists in each of them having his *totam*, or favorite spirit, which he believes watches over him. This *totam* they conceive assumes the shape of some beast or other, and therefore they never kill, hunt, or eat the animal whose form they think this *totam* bears.
>
> The evening previous to the departure of the band, one of them, whose *totam* was a bear, dreamed that if he could go to a piece of swampy ground, at the foot of a high mountain, about five days march from my wigwam, he would see a large herd of elks, moose, and other animals; but that he must be accompanied by at least ten good hunters. When he awoke he acquainted the band with his dream, and desired them to go with him: they all refused, saying it was out their way, and that their hunting grounds were nearer. The Indian having a superstitious reverence for his dream (which ignorance, and the prevalence of example among the Savages, carries to a great height), thinking himself obliged to do so, as his companions had refused to go with him, went alone, and coming near the spot, saw the animals he dreamed of; he instantly fired, and killed a bear. Shocked at the transaction, and dreading the displeasure of Master of Life, whom he conceived he had highly offended, he fell down, and lay senseless for some lime: recovering from his state of insensibility, he got up, and was making the best of his way to my house, when he was met in road by another large bear, who pulled him down, and scratched his face. The Indian relating this event at his return added, in the simplicity of his nature, that the bear asked him what could induce him to kill his *totam*; to which he replied, that he did not know he was among the animals when he fired at the herd; that he was very sorry for the misfortune, and

hoped he would have pity him: that the bear suffered him to depart, told him to be more cautious in future, and acquaint all the Indians with the circumstance, that their *totam* might be safe, and the Master of Life not be angry with them. As he entered my house, he looked at [me and said] "*Amik, hunjey ta Kitchee Anniscartissey nin, O Totam, cawwicka nee wee geossay sannegat debwoye*: – or, "Beaver, my faith is lost, my *totam* is angry. I shall never be able to hunt anymore" (Long 1904: 123-125).

Long (1904: 125) then explained:

This idea of destiny, or, if I may be allowed the phrase, "totamism" however strange, is not confined to the Savages; many instances might be adduced from history, to prove how strong these impressions have been on minds above the vulgar and unlearned. To instance one, in the history of the private life of Louis XV, translated by Justamond, among some particulars of the life of the famous Samuel Bernard, the Jew banker, of the court of France, he says, that he was superstitious as the people of his nation are, and had a black hen, to which he thought his destiny was attached; he had the greatest care taken of her, and the loss of this fowl was, in fact, the period of his own existence, in January, 1739.

Long's account prompts several comments. First, as is generally agreed, Long's description seems to refer to the guardian-spirit complex rather than to sociological or clan totemism, a point emphasized by Schoolcraft (1855: 196) and Tylor (1898), neither of whom seems to have read Long directly. They believed that sociological totemism and individual totemism were different phenomena, with different origins, that should not be conflated. Apparently, Long confused the two leas by subsuming them under a single term.

It should be mentioned, however, that Long's presumed error linking the term *totem* with "guardian spirit" was independently repeated by the famous Jesuit missionary, Pierre de Smet. In an article dating to 1838-1839 (and reprinted in his collected *Life, Letters and Trips* (1905)), de Smet mentioned a Potawatomi naming ceremony in which a 17-year-old male's name, obtained from previous dream experience, is publicly proclaimed. To quote de Smet (1905: 1093), "The animal which presents itself to him will become his manitou or totem dodeme), and all his life long he will carry about him a badge it, whether a claw, a tail, a feather, it matters not." Further, the image of the animal, or dodeme, the guardian spirit, was [307] painted in red on the top of the grave post of the deceased person (de Smet 1905: 1091-1092).

Linguistic evidence is crucial in demonstrating that in native usage the root from which Long constructed his terms totam and totamism refers to kinship. In Algonquian languages, the nouns corresponding to English *totem* are dependent stems, which occur only in possessed nouns: thus "my totem" or "our totem" but not "[a] totem," According to Ives Goddard (p.c. cited in Callender 1978: 621), the Proto-Algonquian (PA) verb stem *o•te•- can be translated as 'to dwell together as a group, village'. Through regular derivation, *o•te•- would have formed a noun * o•te•-wa 'dweller', the possessed form of which would be (here with third-person possessor) *wet-o•te•-m-ali, with third-person prefix *wet- (incorporating the intervocalic connective *t), possessive ending *-m, and animate obviative singular ending *-ali. Ojibwa -do•de•m and its cognates in other Algonquian languages are reflexes of this form. PA *weto•te•mali can then be glossed as 'his or her co- or fellow dweller'. It is also interesting to consider that the reflexes of *o•te•- together with the final abstract noun-forming suffix *-naw formed such Algonquian words for "village, town, or settlement" as Ojibwa o•de•na and Woods Cree o•ti•naw. We observe, then, two lexical affinities of *o•te•-, one with coresidential kinship groups and the other with residential localities.

The semantics of the reflexes of PA *weto•te•mali refer to diverse kinds of consanguineal, affinal, and coresidential relationships. In Ojibwa, -do•de•m clearly exhibits the dual meanings of 'patrilineal clan' (or 'member of patrilineal clan') and 'eponymous clan animal'. For Algonquin at Lake of the Two Mountains, Jean-Baptiste Thavenet (in Cuoq 1886: 312-313) glossed the first-person possessed form *nindo•de•m* ("*nind otem*") as "*ma tribu*" (possibly the patrilineal clan), or an individual member of the same. Thavenet correctly identified the stem as *o•te•-* and glossed it as 'family', but he erred in seeking to derive it from *-te•ʔ* 'heart'. He also remarked on the use of such constructions as *makwa nindo•de•m* 'the bear is my clan', which clearly exemplify the association of kin groups with eponymous animals. For the same dialect (historically the Nipissing variety of Eastern Ojibwa), Cuoq (1886: 312) gave *o•te•* both as the stem of *nindo•de•m* 'my totem' and as having the meaning 'village'; he also gave *o•de•naw* 'village' but did not connect the two forms. JNB Hewitt (1910: 787-788), who relied heavily on Cuoq, rendered *o•de•-* in Ojibwa "and other cognate Algonquian dialects" as referring to kinship between siblings and, by extension, to all members of the exogamic kinship group; he thus glossed *odo•de•man* (with third person affixes) as "his brother-sister kin." Hewitt also glossed the Ojibwa abstract noun-forming final *-na(w)* (which he gave with incorrect vowel length) as "dwelling place" and thus glossed Ojibwa *o•-de•-na* or *o•-de•-naw* 'village' as "dwelling place of the clan." Note that not all Algonquian societies possessed patrilineal descent groups – the probable referent of [308] Hewitt's "clan" – and that this institution, therefore, cannot be assumed to have been a feature of Proto-Algonquian social structure or to have been a meaning of PA **welo•le•mali*. We can infer that Ojibwa *-do•de•m* (singular) meant 'clan relative' (and, by abstraction, the membership of the clan as a collectivity) and that *-do•de•mag* (plural) meant 'clan relatives'. In a unilinear system, it would make little sense to gloss the plural of the dependent noun *-do•de•m* as 'clans', although rhetorical contexts for such a meaning are imaginable. The usage of two nineteenth-century Ojibwa historians of their own people, William Warren and Peter Jones, makes clear that *-do•de•m* referred both to the patrilineal clan and to its eponymous animal emblem (Warren 1957: 42; Jones 1970: 138; see also Nichols and Nyholm 1995: 66, *indo•de•m* 'my totem, my clan')..

Fox exhibits a similar range of meanings. Goddard (1973 pc, 1997) gave *o•te•-* as the stem of *o•te•-weni* 'town'. For *neto•te•ma*, the meanings 'my sibling' and 'my same-sex sibling' are attested and can possibly be extended to 'my fellow clansperson'. The Fox noun for patrilineal clan, however, is not *-to•te•m* but *mi•so•ni* 'name'. For Fox *oto•te•mani*, Jones (1911: 810) gave the meanings "his eldest brother" (specificity dubious), "his master" (incorrect), "his clan tutelary," and "his giver of supernatural power." The last gloss shows affinities with Long's Ojibwa usage, although no textual exemplifications exist; however, *neto•te•ma* does occur in texts as a term of reciprocal address between clan members and their totemic animals.

For Menominee, Bloomfield (1962: 260-261, 397, 1975: 6) gave the medial *-o•tɛ•* – as 'household, family', and glossed *-(t)o•tɛ•m* as 'my totem animal, my totemic ancestor'. In Woods Cree, singular *nito•ti•m* is 'my relative or friend', and plural *nito•ti•mak* is 'all my relatives and friends'; Crees lack patrilineal descent groups, and *-to•ti•m* has no reference to eponymous animals.

The form is also present in the eastern branch of the Algonquian language family, where, however, the social denotata are commonly friends or affines. Western Abenaki *-dodam* is 'animal ancestor, totem' (Day 1994), i.e., the eponymous animals of patrilineal clans. Penobscot *-totem* is 'friend' and, more specifically, 'affine' (Frank Siebert pc, Aug 1997). Micmac *-tuttem* is glossed as "totem" (somewhat anomalously given the absence of Micmac descent groups) and also possesses the meanings "friend of another nation," "gentleman friend," and (as *-tuttemisqw*) "lady friend" (Rand 1888; De Blois and Metallic 1984).

Individual totems, guardian spirits, or personal tutelaries are often regarded as an extended type of kin. The vision quest experience can be likened to an initiation adoption ritual in which a new kinship relationship is established. Many Algonquian-speaking peoples refer to the individual totem as a specific manitou, a term that has historically defied precise translation but can be loosely associated with power, medicine, or a divine being. The Ojibwa *bawa-gan* – an other-than-human [308b] person encountered in dreams or visions (Hallowell 1976: 369) – could function as a guardian spirit, as could *a•dizo•ka•nag*, ancestral spirits or primordial myth beings called grandfathers (Hallowell 1976: 365). Adrian Tanner

(1979: 95, 103) described Mistassini Cree beliefs about winds associated with the cardinal directions and with seasonality. These winds are personified as spiritual beings who control weather and can be propitiated or magically manipulated to insure successful hunting. In particular, the spirit connected with the north and winter, *Ciiwetinsuu* (and secondarily the spirit of the west wind), can affect the hunting of nonhibernating, non-migratory game upon which humans depend for their winter survival. This being is honorifically referred to as "your grandfather," suggesting not only esteem and kinship but also descent. These directional and seasonal spiritual beings thus function as masters of generalized classes of game animals. In effect, they mediate between the souls of humans and those of animal spirits. As such, these beings represent a more general and inclusive power than that obtained through the species-specific guardian spirit or individual totem. "Grandfather" is also a common term of address or reference for spirit entities among the Saulteaux Ojibwa and Woods Cree of Manitoba (Hallowell 1976: 369; Brightman 1993: 109) and perhaps among other Algonquian groups.

Seldom mentioned in connection with Long's celebrated discovery of totemism is the fact that he clearly recognized the existence of descent-group or sociological totemism. In the beginning of his book, Long (1904: 10) cited Cadwallader Colden in reference to the Five Nations Iroquois: "each of these nations is again divided into three tribes or families, who are distinguished by the names of the Tortoise, Bear, and Wolf." These three family totems are recognized among the Mohawk-Oneida and some Eastern Algonquian groups. Visual evidence of totemic affiliation is afforded in the famous full-length portraits painted by John Verelst during the visit to London of one Mahican and three Mohawk chiefs (or "kings") in 1710. At the foot of the Mahican is a turtle, two of the Mohawks are accompanied by wolves, and the third Mohawk, the grandfather of the late eighteenth-century political leader Joseph Brant, sports a small bear (Editors of Time-Life Books 1992: 74-75). Clearly, Long knew of descent group or sociological totemism as well as individual totemism, and he presumably recognized the presence of both among the Ojibwa..

Returning to Long's narrative, in the recorded Ojibwa speech of the accidental bear slayer is the form "nin, O Totam" for 'my totem'. The expected form would be *nindo•de•m*. Recent research indicates that Long possessed, as he claimed, a certain Ojibwa fluency, but it was in the grammatically simplified trade language known locally as broken Ojibwa rather than in *Ojibwe•mowin* or "Ojibwa proper" (Nichols 1992; Bakker 1994). The lexical forms (and presumably the semantics) of broken Ojibwa, however, were clearly Algonquian, and Long's "nin, O Totam" is recognizable as a pidgin rendering of Ojibwa [309a] *nindo•de•m*. The supposition that Long's interlocutor used the word *-do•de•m* as a pidgin improvisation for *manido•* or *bawa•gan* 'individual spirit guardian', although possible, is not especially probable. Long's reputed error may be less the result of faulty diction (Hewitt 1910: 789) and more the lack of a native appreciation of the subtle analytic and conceptual distinctions posited by late-nineteenth- and twentieth-century armchair anthropologists and social theorists.

We find it especially difficult to believe that Levi-Strauss, who, along with most everyone else, dutifully cited Long as the first to enter the term totemism into our discourse (thus becoming our totemic ancestor), would fail to mention the French Jewish banker's black hen as an anticipation of his thesis about he universal manifestations of totemic thought. Samuel Bernard was, indeed, an important personage, and his portrait hangs in the French chateau Chenonceau. Without trying to advance a Jewish theory of totemism, we do think that had Levi-Strauss directly consulted Long's account we might have been spared the tortuous genealogy of metaphoric totemism from Rousseau out of Bergson through Linton's AEF Rainbow Division and Radcliffe-Brown's second theory of totemism (Levi-Strauss 1963: 7-8, 83-104).

The question of the relationship between so-called individual totems and hereditary clan totems is interestingly posed by the classicist and religious anthropologist James Frazer (1934) in the third volume of his massive, if not magnum, opus *Totemism and Exogamy*, originally published in 1910. Although he accepted Tylor's objection that individual totemism and clan totemism are different phenomena that should not be classed together under the same rubric, Frazer sensed a similarity in attitudes of respect and affection toward the totemic being. He suggested that American ethnologists with direct field experience – most notably the Canadian Charles Hill-Tout, who worked primarily with the Coast Salish – tended to derive clan totems from guardian spirits. The essential argument is the belief that the guardian spirit of the ancestor of the clan is transmitted by social inheritance to his or her descendants, either in the male or the female line. While Frazer granted a certain plausibility to this position, he noted that other scholars, with equal plausibility, inverted the argument by maintaining the priority of clan totemism. For these theorists, guardian-spirit beliefs emerged "at a time when the totemism of clans was falling into decay, and when consequently individuals, deprived of the protection of the clan totem, looked about for a personal guardian of their own to supply its place" (Frazer 1934 (3): 371). Frazer attributed the latter position to ES Hartland, AC Haddon, Henri Hubert, Marcel Mauss, and to personal communication with a young Cambridge colleague named AR Brown. It is tempting to see Frazer's counter-positions American individualism matched against European social apriorists, but we won't pursue this here.[2] [309b]

Frazer was skilled at posing dilemmas in studying problems of origins, but he was less successful in resolving them. By tracing the distributions of guardian spirit complexes and clan totemism over Native North America, he found an expectable overlap; yet some areas clearly possessed totemic clans without guardian spirits, and in other areas the situation was reversed. Temporal priority cannot be established on the basis of distribution. Although the question of origins is probably moot, if not mute, in modem anthropology, it is possible to examine the relationships of clan totems to guardian spirits from other angles besides the kind of distributional analyses favored by Frazer and others, or, at another extreme, the elegant types of analogical exercises championed by structuralists. The diverse semantics of Algonquian words for totem allowed us to reexamine the late ethnohistorian Harold Hickerson's (1970: 42-50) argument that the basic social structure of the Chippewas at first contact comprised localized clan groups possessing animal eponyms. He employed an etymology identical to that followed above to interpret the term o•de•na as signifying "clan village" (he cited Landes 1937: 33-35, who in turn credited Truman Michelson). Hickerson amassed impressive data to demonstrate the equivalence between Chippewa clan names and their names for local groups. One key quotation from Nicolas Perrot appears to clinch Hickerson's argument for original clan settlements: "You will hear [the Indians] say that their villages bear the name of the animal which has given its people their being – as that of the crane, or the bear, or of other animals" (quoted in Hickerson 1970: 47).

We find difficulties with the notion of exclusive clan villages. It was desirable, if not necessary, to have lineal relatives residing in other settlements.[32] As Tylor (1888: 266) speculated long ago, "Again and again in the world's history, savage tribes must have had plainly before their minds the simple practical alternative between marrying out and being killed-out." Such localized kin groups would seem to be extremely fragile, volatile, and vulnerable to processes of segmentation or amalgamation, or both. Yet there is less difficulty in recognizing clan villages as a kind of cultural fiction, a positive ideology stressing the dominance or ascendancy of a particular clan or lineage in a particular locale. Here the Stewardian patrilineal bands imagined by Hickerson converged with the Ojibwas' own representations. Such a group might provide political or religious leadership in the local community, serve as the bearers of collective sacred bundles or traditions, or possess special rights or relations to a particular territory and

---

2 The American, or better, Canadian, evidence for deriving sociological totemism from group totemism was partly dismissed by Frazer in noting that Northwest Coast cultures were already highly developed and could not be placed on a comparable evolutionary plane as the Australian Aborigines, who were regarded by most contemporary scholars as embodying a pristine form of totems. Paradoxically, totemism, a Native American phenomenon, came to be measured and evaluated against Australian Aboriginal standards and was found to be anomalous.

3 Indeed, Landes (1937: 33) pointed out that the *dodems* at Eno and Manitou Reserve "are not localized, whether as villages or within the village," although she noted that Radin reported clan localization for the Winnebago, and Michelson believed in its former existence among the Fox.

its resources.

We agree with Hickerson that, going back in time, distinctions between clan and local group become blurred. We part company in interpreting the nature of the relationship between the totemic group and the local territory. Here, spatial coordinates defining locality and generational time inherent in descent intersect. Ideological factors, especially notions of guardian spirits or masters or mistresses of the game, or both, become relevant. [310a]

Hickerson's neglect of ideological factors is understandable given his strong ecological and cultural-materialist orientation, Moreover, he seemed to accept unquestionably Eleanor Leacock's (1954) seemingly persuasive evidence, generalized from the Montagnais, that family hunting territories came into existence only after the establishment of the fur trade (1954). The advent of a fur-trading economy, along with devastating epidemic disease, certainly brought profound changes to traditional systems of territorialism, but many recent fieldworkers and ethnohistorians, such as Robert Brightman (1993), Harvey Feit (1973, 1991), Charles Bishop and Toby Morantz (1986), Adrian Tanner (1979), and David Turner (1978), view this transformation as less abrupt and absolute. They have also detected certain continuities in ethnoecology and in deeply ingrained cultural belief structures about relations between animals and humans and between each of these and the land – a kind of symbolic ecology, as it were.

Leacock (1954) and her followers tend to emphasize the establishment of sharp boundaries, rules against trespass, and strict notions of ownership in the sense of private property as defining features characterizing the appearance of family hunting territories with commercial commodification of animals. Boundaries, although marked and ethnocartographically mapped, probably were always somewhat fluid, and few legal sanctions other than threats to mutual understanding and fears of divine punishment protected them against trespass.

Ownership and private property seem to be the sources of contention. The overriding principle is not so much that land is owned by individuals or by a local group, but that these persons have rights to the resources, particularly fur-bearing animals, present in that area. In a more than casual remark, the German emigré ethnologist Julius Lips once stated that among the Mistassini Cree, animals, not humans, were the true owners of the territory (cited in Tanner 1979: 107).

Adrian Tanner's (1979) study of modern Mistassini modes of production and religious ideology, Bringing Home Animals, took the comment of Lips seriously and described in detail the cultural constitution of Cree spatial orientations, the complexities of divinatory communication with animal spirits and forces of nature, the rituals regulating relations between hunters and their quarry, and the ritualized respect owed to slain animals. Successful hunting, from the native perspective, depends as much upon these ritual relations as upon technical proficiency in hunting. It is thought that certain individuals, usually elder males and nominal heads of the local group, have established special enduring relations of friendship with local spirits who control the numbers of animals and access to them. It is further believed that these spiritual connections can be inherited by a successor, normally a son or an adoptive member of the group who has resided in the territory for an extended period of time.

We suggest that the beliefs and practices that Tanner has so cogently described for the Mistassini Cree may formerly have [310b] been much more widespread and that clan totemism, locality, and individual totemism were more integrally connected than has generally been supposed. Two independent attestations exist – Long's and de Smet's – of Ojibwa-Potawatomi *-do•de•m* with the meaning 'individual totem or spirit guardian' (see above). Thus, for these groups at least, the noun possessed multiple meanings. In Long's time, Ojibwa *nindo•de•m* 'my totem' could mean 'my clan relative' and 'my individual spirit guardian' and 'my clan animal'; pluralized, it meant 'my clan relatives' or 'my clan'. Thus, eponymous group totems and individual guardian spirits need not succeed one another in lock-step evolutionary succession but could coexist in the same societies (Goldenweiser 1910). An Ojibwa might have Wolf as clan totem and Beaver as an individual spirit guardian, or the reverse, or might imaginably possess as guardian spirit a being of the same type as the clan totem.

Consider, for example, Speck's (1917) reflections on "totemism" among the Penobscots of Maine.

Lacking the unilineal-descent groups of the Ojibwas and other Great Lakes Algonquians (and of other Atlantic Coast Algonquians to the south), the Penobscots nonetheless were "totemically" organized: 13 out of 22 residential bands present in the late nineteenth century were named for an individual animal species (beaver, otter, moose, eel, etc.) deemed to be distinctively and exceptionally populous on their traditional winter foraging territories. The individual guardian spirit, which Speck gave as "baohigan" (*páwəhikan* 'token, talisman, fetish object used for magic purposes by shamans' (Frank Siebert pc, Aug 1997; Ives Goddard p.c. 27 Aug 1997)) was not commonly an animal of the type of the group totem. In contrast to Ojibwa, the Penobscot word -totem lacks known reference to spirit or animal beings, and neither does it refer lo a primary kin group; the sociological reference excludes "consanguines" and seems rather to refer to such "solidary nonkin" as friends, acquaintances, and relatives by marriage (Frank Siebert p.c., Aug 1997). Speck compared the group totemism of the Penobscot with the individual spirit-guardian practices of the Quebec Mistassini Cree to the north.[4] Mistassini bands lacked zoonymic band totems, and Penobscot group totems were distinct from individual spirit guardians, Speck, nevertheless, identified a significant parallel between the Penobscot totems and the individual dream spirits of the Mistassini: both involved animal species that were dietary staples and were commonly hunted on the winter foraging territory. In hindsight, we can say that it is a question of Penobscot attentiveness to la difference. Although the same project of dream-inspired foraging confronted both groups, the Penobscot improvised upon regional disparities in particular game species to develop a genuinely totemic system in which otherwise homogeneous winter bands were differentiated on the basis of statistical heterogeneity in the densities of particular species [311a] on otherwise homogeneous foraging tracts. Thus, with apologies to Levi-Strauss:

$$\begin{aligned} \text{species}_1 &\neq \text{species}_2 \neq \text{species}_3 \\ \text{tract}_1 &\neq \text{tract}_2 \neq \text{tract}_3 \\ \text{band}_1 &\neq \text{band}_2 \neq \text{band}_3 \end{aligned}$$

Here also are parallels between the dietary regulation of human-animal relationships in the clan totemic and guardian-spirit relationships. Nowhere in the literature on the Ojibwa or other Great Lakes Algonquians is there evidence that individuals practiced a classically Australian Aborigine dietary renunciation of their clan totem animal. Indeed, such renunciation would entail impracticable hardship for groups whose eponymous clan totems were dietary staples; consider, for example, the winter prospects of bands exclusively composed of male hunters of the *Mo•z* 'moose' or *Amik* 'beaver' clans. Thus, for example, the testimony of an Ojibwa member of the *Awa•zisi* 'Bullhead' (*Aspidophorus cataphractes*) clan: "We have great respect of our *do'dam*, but we eat them; I have often eaten bullhead" (Hilger 1992: 155; see also Landes 1937: 33). Speck (1917: 30) long ago observed that Subarctic Algonquian "band totemism" of the Penobscot type formed a dietary inversion of Australian totemism: the Australians "reproduced" the eponymous species by renouncing it as food, whereas the Algonquians accomplished the same end by ritual consumption (see Brightman 1993: 213-243). The same could perhaps be said of the dietary relation between the patrilineal clans of the Great Lakes Algonquians and their eponymous animals.

The dietary relation to the individual spirit guardian is more variable. Speck (1917) emphasized the dietary parallels between Penobscot bands and their animal totems and between Mistassini hunters and individual guardian-spirit animals (both were eaten), but there is evidence that guardian-spirit animals sometimes imposed dietary taboos on animals of the same species. Thus the individual renunciation of the animal-spirit guardian attested in Long's eighteenth-century text is paralleled in the contemporary

---

4 The spirit-guardian experiences of the Quebec Algonquians differ substantially from those of the Crees and Ojibwas to the west. The being was not acquired at puberty during a formal protracted fast but through involuntary dreams during early adulthood.

practices of some Woods Cree hunters of Manitoba. Among the latter, the logistical difficulties are sometimes adjusted by exempting from the taboo the meat of animals of one or the other sex or of those killed by others. In cases known to us, for example, a man whose *pawa•kan*, or guardian spirit, is a female beaver abstains from eating them, and a man who survived drowning by dreaming of a sturgeon thereafter renounced sturgeon meat.

The semantics of totemism in Algonquian languages and cultures thus exhibits a rich and geographically variable network of associations that reaches from the Atlantic Coast to the Great Lakes and north into the boreal forest: coresidential kin groups (patrilineal or bilateral), winter foraging tracts, eponymous animals, and individual animal spirit guardians. Even though the distribution of the cultural forms in question does not permit us to reconstruct a Proto-Algonquian totemic system, if such ever existed, we observe in them associations [311b] counter to the rigid typological separation of group from individual totemism and counter to the assumption that Long got it all wrong at the beginning. In Penobscot totemism we observe clear parallels to Tanner's (1979) Mistassini themes of animal ownership of the foraging tracts and of enduring transgenerational relations between the humans and animals habitually subsisting in the same landscapes. Groups, even nomadic ones, dwelt in places, and – Leacock notwithstanding – there was intergenerational continuity between groups and places before the fur trade and thus possible relationships with theriomorphic spirits-of-place that could be both individual guardians and group totems. Curiously, but perhaps not coincidentally, it is with the meaning of individual spirit guardian rather than group eponym that "totem" has been assimilated to the pop Indian spirituality of New Age devotees (Steiger 1997).

Conclusion

This exploration of totemism in its native homeland may not have resolved the "problem" of the origin of totemism (Jewish or otherwise) that has perplexed the minds of so many social scientific theorists. We can, however, perhaps discern in the situation of parallel existence and reciprocity obtaining between humans and animals, and their mediators, a possible solution to the classic classificatory problem of reconciling so-called individual totemism with the hereditary totemism of descent groups. The radical dissociation between individual and group totemism may be more an analytic dream, and anthropological nightmare, than a native reality.

Finally, if nothing else, we hope to have indicated the relevance of Native American data to past and continuing debates in anthropology, something Claude Levi-Strauss always appreciated and Bill Sturtevant always knew. [312 a]

Literature

Bakker, Peter 1994 Is John Long's Chippeway (1791) an Ojibwa Pidgin? In William Cowan, editor, *Actes du Vingl-Cinquieme Congres des Algonquinistes*, pages 13-31. Ottawa, Ontario: Carleton University.

Bishop, Charles A., and Toby Morantz, eds. 1986 Who Owns the Beaver? Northern Algonquian Land Tenure Reconsidered. *Anthropologica*, special issue, 28 (1-2): 219+[5] pages.

Blair, Emma H 1996 *The Indian Tribes of the Upper Mississippi Valley and the Region of the Great Lakes*. 2 volumes. Lincoln: University of Nebraska Press. [Originally published in 1911 by the Arthur H. Clark Co., Cleveland, Ohio.]

Bloomfield, Leonard 1962 *The Menomini Language*. xi+515 pages. New Haven, Connecticut: Yale University Press.

1975 *Menomini Lexicon*. C.F. Hockett, editor. Milwaukee Public Museum Publications in Anthropology and History 3: xviii+289 pages. Milwaukee, Wisconsin: Milwaukee Public Museum Press.

Brightman, Robert 1993 *Grateful Prey: Rock Cree Human-Animal Relationships*. xvi+396 pages. Berkeley: University of California Press.

Callender, Charles 1978 Great Lakes-Riverine Sociopolitical Organization. In William C. Sturtevant, general editor. Handbook of North American Indians. Bruce G Trigger, ed. *Northeast*, volume 15: 610-621. Washington, DC: Smithsonian Institution.

Cuoq, Jean-Andre 1886 *Lexique de la langue algonquine*. xii+446 pages. Montreal: J Chapleau et Fils.

Day, Gordon 1994 *Western Abenaki Dictionary*, Volume I: Abenaki-English. Paper (Canadian Ethnology Service) 128: lxxii+538 pages. Hull, Quebec: Canadian Museum of Civilization.

De Blois, Albert D, and Alphonse Metallic 1984 *Micmac Lexicon*. Paper (Canadian Ethnology Service), 91; xvii+392 pages, Ottawa, Ontario: National Museums of Canada.

de Smet, Pierre-Jean 1905 *Life, Letters and Travels of Father Pierre-Jean DeSmet, SJ*. Hiram M. Chittenden and A.T. Richardson, eds. 4 volumes. New York: Francis P. Harper.

Durkheim, Emile 1965 *The Elementary Forms of the Religious Life*. Translated from the French by Joseph W. Swain, 507 pages. New York: Free Press. [Originally published in 1915 by G. Alien and Unwin, London,]

Durkheim, Emile, and Marcel Mauss 1963 *Primitive Classification*. Translated from the French and edited with an introduction by Rodney Needham, xlviii+96 pages. London: Cohen and West. [Translation of "De quelques formes primitives de classification," published in 1903 in Annee Sociologique, 1901 1902.]

Editors of Time-Life Books 1992 *The European Challenge*. 192 pages. Alexandria, Virginia: Time-Life Books.

Feit, Harvey A 1973 The Ethno-Ecology of the Waswanipi Cree; or How Hunters Can Manage Their Resources. In Bruce Cox, editor. *Cultural Ecology*: 115-125. Toronto, Ontario: McClelland and Stewart.

  1991 The Construction of Algonquian Hunting Territories: Private Property as Moral Lesson, Policy Advocacy, and Ethnographic Error. In George W. Stocking, ed. *Colonial Situations: Essays on the Contextualization of Ethnographic Know*ledge: 109-134. Madison: University of Wisconsin Press.

Frazer, J.G 1934 *Totemism and Exogamy*. 4 volumes. Cambridge: Trinity College.

Freud, Sigmund 1952 *Totem and Taboo: some Points of Agreement between the Mental Lives of Savages and Neurotics*. x+172 pages. New York: Norton. [Originally published in 1913 by Hugo Heller, Vienna.]

Goddard, Ives 1973 A Report on Ethnographic and Philological Studies of Michelson's Fox Texts. [Paper read at the Algonquian Conference, Green Bay, Wisconsin, 6 Apr 1973]

Goldenweiser, Alexander 1910 Totemism, an Analytic Study. *Journal of American Folklore* 23: 179-293.

  1933a The Origin of Totemism. In Alexander Goldenweiser, *History, Psychology and Culture*: 335-342. New York: Alfred A Knopf.

  1933b Form and Content in Totemism. In Alexander Goldenweiser, *History, Psychology and Culture*: 343-354. New York: Alfred A Knopf.

Hallowell, A Irving 1976 Ojibwa Ontology, Behavior, and World View: 357-390. In Raymond D Fogelson, ed. *Contributions to Anthropology: Selected Papers of A. Irving Hallowell*. Chicago: University of Chicago Press.

Hewitt, JNB 1910 Totem. In F.W, Hodge, editor. *Handbook of American Indians North of Mexico*. Bulletin, Bureau of American Ethnology. 30 (2): 787-794.

Hickerson, Harold 1970 *The Chippewa and Their Neighbors: A Study in Ethnohistory*. x+133 pages. New York: Holt, Rinehart and Winston.

Hilger, M. Inez 1992 *Chippewa Child Life and Its Cultural Background*, xxxii+204 pages. St Paul: Minnesota Historical Society Press. [Originally published in 1951 by the Government Printing

Office, Washington, DC]

Jones, Peter 1970 *History of the Ojbway Indians, with Especial Reference to Their Conversion to Christianity*, vi+278 pages, Freeport, New York: Books for Libraries. [Originally published in 1861 by A.W. Bennett, London.]

Jones, William 1911 Algonquian (Fox). Revised by Truman Michelson. In Franz Boas, *Handbook of American Indian Languages*. Bulletin, Bureau of American Ethnology, 40 (1): 735-873.

Landes, Ruth 1937 *Ojibwa Sociology*. [6]+144+[2] pages. New York: Columbia University Press.

Leacock, Eleanor 1954 The Montagnais "Hunting Territory" and the Fur Trade. American Anthropological Association, *Memoirs* 78: xi+59 pages.

Levi-Strauss, Claude 1963 *Totemism*. Translated from the French by Rodney Needham. 116 pages. Boston: Beacon Press. [Translation of Totemisme anjourd'hui, published in 1962 by Presses Universitaires de France, Paris.]

  1966 *The Savage Mind*. xii+290 pages. Chicago: University of Chicago Press. [Translation of La Pensee Sauvage, published in 1962 by Plon.]

Linton, Ralph 1924 Totemism and the A.E.F. *American Anthropologist* 26: 296-300.

Long, John 1904 Voyages and Travels of an Indian Interpreter and Trader ... April 10, 1768-Spring, 1782. In Reuben Gold Thwaites, editor. *Early Western Travels, 1748-1846*, volume 2: 329+[4] pages. Cleveland, Ohio: Arthur H. Clark. [Originally published in 1791]. [313a]

  1922 *John Long's Voyages and Travels in the Years 1768-1788*. Edited with historical introduction and notes by Milo Quaife. xxx+238 pages. Chicago, Illinois: RR Donnelley and Sons. [Originally published in 1791].

Nichols, John D 1992 "Broken Oghibbeway": An Algonquian Trade Language. [Paper read at the twenty-fourth Algonquian Conference, Carleton University, Ottawa, Ontario.]

Nichols, John D, and Earl Nyholm 1995 *A Concise Dictionary of Minnesota Ojibwa*. xxviii+288 pages. Minneapolis: University of Minnesota Press.

Rand, Silas T 1888 *Dictionary of the Language of the Micmac Indians, Who Reside in Nova Scotia. New Brunswick, Prince Edward Island, Cape Breton Newfoundland*. 2 pages of leaves+[iii]-viii, 286 pages. Halifax, Nova Scotia: Nova Scotia Printing Co.

Schoolcraft, Henry R 1855 *Information Respecting the History, Condition and Prospects of the Indian Tribe of the United States*. Volume 5: [vii]-xxiv+25-712 pages. Philadelphia, Pennsylvania: JB Lippincott and Co.

Shapiro, Warren 1991 Claude Levi-Strauss Meets Alexander Goldenweiser. *American Anthropologist* 93: 599-610.

Speck, Frank G 1917 Game Totems among the Northeastern Algonquians. *American Anthropologist* 19: 9-18.

Steiger, Brad 1997 *Totems*: The Transformative Power of Your Personal Animal Totem. 218pps. San Francisco, California: Harper.

Tanner, Adrian 1979 *Bringing Home Animals: Religious Ideology and Mode of Production of the Mistassini Cree Hunters*. xx+233 pages. New York: St Martin's Press.

Turner, David H 1978 Dialectics in Tradition: Myth and Social Structure in Two Hunter-Gatherer Societies. *Occasional Paper*, Royal Anthropological Institute of Great Britain and Ireland, 36: iv+46 pages.

Tylor, E.B 1888 On a Method of Investigating the Development of Institutions. *Journal of the Royal Anthropological Institute* 18: 245-272.

  1898 Remarks on Totemism with Especial Reference to Some Modern Theories Concerning It. *Journal of the Royal Anthropological Institute* 28: 138-148.

Warren, William 1957 *History of the Ojibwa Nation*. 527 pages. Minneapolis, Minnesota: Ross and Haines. [Originally published in 1885 in volume 5 of Collections of the Minnesota Historical Society].

Class

ADVANCED SOCIAL SCIENCES
RELIGIOUS MOVEMENTS
IN NATIVE NORTH AMERICA

New Agers essentialize and romanticize Native American religions. Religious beliefs and practices are assumed to be primordial, eternal, and invariable. However a closer examination reveals that Native American religions are highly dynamic and adaptive, ever reactive to internal pressure and external circumstances. Perhaps, the most dramatic forms of religious change are the transformations that anthropologists recognize as nativistic or revitalization movements. These movements on one level represent conscious breaks with an immediate negative past and they anticipate a positive future in which present sources of oppression are overcome.

Such movements have occurred fairly regularly in the historical record and doubtless occurred prehistorically as well. Indeed the collective memory of such events may be enshrined in myths. Many contemporary Native American movements, be they political and/or religious, can be understood as sharing similar dynamics to past movements.

The Ghost Dance is often considered to be the prototypical Native American religious movement. We will read the classic account of the Ghost Dance by James Mooney. In addition we will examine Anthony Wallace's analysis of the Handsome Lake Religion among the Senecas. Also we will consider religious movements surrounding the Creeks of the Southeast during the war of 1812, as well as Prophet Movements in the Northwest, and religious movements in the Southwest.

This course will be taught by Raymond D Fogelson, Professor, Social Sciences Collegiate Division, and Professor Departments of Anthropology and Psychology (Human Development). He has devoted most of his career to the study of North American Indians and also has abiding interests in psychological anthropology, the anthropology of religion, and tourism.

www.ingramcontent.com/pod-product-compliance
Lightning Source LLC
Chambersburg PA
CBHW081343280526
45788CB00009B/2759